FACT, VALUE, POLICY

POLICY

Reading and
Writing Arguments

FACT, VALUE,
POLICY

Reading and Writing Arguments

A. Harris Fairbanks

University of Connecticut

McGraw-Hill, Inc.

New York   St. Louis   San Francisco   Auckland   Bogotá   Caracas
Lisbon   London   Madrid   Mexico City   Milan   Montreal
New Delhi   San Juan   Singapore   Sydney   Tokyo   Toronto

This book was developed by STEVEN PENSINGER, Inc.

FACT, VALUE, POLICY
Reading and Writing Arguments

Permissions Acknowledgments appear on pages 521–523, and on
this page by reference.

This book is printed on acid-free paper.

1 2 3 4 5 6 7 8 9 0 DOC DOC 9 0 9 8 7 6 5 4 3

ISBN 0-07-019872-1

This book was set in Minion by Beacon Graphics Corporation.
The editors were Steve Pensinger and Tom Holton;
the design was done by Keithley and Associates, Inc.;
the production supervisor was Elizabeth Strange.
R. R. Donnelley & Sons Company was printer and binder.

Library of Congress Cataloging-in-Publication Data

Fact, value, policy: reading and writing arguments / [edited by] A.
   Harris Fairbanks
       p.   cm.
   Includes index.
   ISBN 0-07-019872-1 (alk. paper)
   1. English language — Rhetoric.   2. Persuasion (Rhetoric)
   3. College readers.   I. Fairbanks, A. Harris.
   PE1431.F28   1994
   808'.042 — dc20   93-1665

About the Author

A. Harris Fairbanks is Associate Professor of English at the University of Connecticut at Storrs where he has taught since 1970. He received his B.A. with honors from Swarthmore College, an M.A.T. from Johns Hopkins University, and his Ph.D. in English from the University of California at Berkeley.

He has published in *PMLA, The Wordsworth Circle,* and other journals, and has organized and participated in a number of regional conferences on the teaching of writing. He has directed a Study Abroad program in London, and has served for nine years as Director of Freshman English at the University of Connecticut.

For Ruth

Contents

Preface   xiii

1. Sorting Out the Issues   1

The Nature of Argument   1
Critical Thinking   2
The Three Kinds of Issues   3
    The Fact/Value Distinction   4
    The Stock Issues of Policy Arguments   5

2. Fact   9

Factual Claims and the Observable World   9
    Deductive versus Empirical Reasoning   9
    Verifiability and Refutability   10
Categorizing and Defining in Factual Arguments   11
    Defining by Necessary and Sufficient Criteria   11
    Defining by Family Relationships Based on Common Cause   12
    Defining Operationally   14
    Avoiding a Contested Term   15
    Focusing on the Inadequacy of Other Terms   16
Causal Reasoning and Factual Arguments   18
    Types of Factual Claims   18
    Causes, Conditions, and Factors   20
    Forming Hypotheses   22
    Testing Hypotheses   26
    PHILIP GOLDBERG   Are Women Prejudiced against Women?   28
Applications   34

3. Value   38

Value Claims and the Value System   38
    The Structure of the Value System   40
    Whose Value System?   41
    Justice and Expediency   42
Categorizing and Defining in Values Arguments   43
    God Terms and Devil Terms   46

Public Statement by Eight Alabama Clergymen   **48**

Deductive Reasoning and Strategies of Evaluative
Arguments   **49**

Deduction from More General Principles   **49**

Constructive Arguments by Analogy   **53**

Counterarguments from Specific Judgments   **55**

Example of an Evaluative Argument   **56**

MARTIN LUTHER KING, JR.   Letter from Birmingham Jail   **56**

Analysis of King's Letter   **70**

4. Policy   73

Affirmative and Negative Policy Claims   **74**

The Stock Issues of Debate   **75**

1. Is There a Serious Need for Change?   **75**

2. Is the Need Inherent?   **76**

3. Does the Plan Meet the Need?   **76**

4. Is the Plan Feasible?   **76**

5. Is the Plan Free of Crippling Disadvantages?   **77**

A Checklist for Full Proposals   **78**

Sample Proposal   **79**

JONATHAN SWIFT   A Modest Proposal   **79**

Analysis of Swift's Proposal   **86**

CHARLES KRAUTHAMMER   Fetal Tissue Research:
Hostage to Abortion Politics   **87**

5. Writing with Direction   90

ISAAC ASIMOV   Time and Tide   **92**

Beginning a Writing Project   **100**

Free Writing   **101**

Organizing   **102**

Assessing the Project   **104**

In What Discussion Are You Taking Part?   **104**

What Will Your Argument Contribute?   **104**

Who Is Your Audience?   **105**

Do You Have One Paper or Several?   **106**

Does Lateral Thinking Suggest a Change in Approach
or Scope?   **107**

Research   **108**

The Citation Trail   **109**

Subject Guides   **109**

Citation Indexes   **111**

Summary   **112**

The First Draft and Sentence Outline   **113**

SHANNON STERN-SALB   Recognize Sexuality Is a
Political Issue   **114**

Sentence Outline of Stern-Salb's Article   **116**

The Revised Draft   **117**

Specialized Tasks: Writing in Response to Writing   **118**

Animal Rights   **121**

PETER SINGER   Animal Liberation   **122**

C. A. J. COADY   Defending Human Chauvinism   **136**

MARIAN DAWKINS   Do Hens Suffer in Battery Cages?   **142**

TIMOTHY NOAH   Monkey Business   **163**

ALEX PACHECO   Testimony: House Hearings on the Use of Animals in Medical Research and Testing   **170**

MICHAEL E. DEBAKEY   Holding Human Health Hostage   **176**

Business and Professional Ethics   **181**

ALBERT CARR   Is Business Bluffing Ethical?   **183**

ARTHUR KELLY   Case Study: Italian Tax Mores   **197**

LEAH MARGULIES   Bottle Babies: Death and Business Get Their Market   **201**

OSWALDO BALLARIN   Prepared Statement to the United States Subcommittee on Health and Scientific Research   **212**

ANONYMOUS   Editorials on the U.S. Vote against the WHO Code of Ethics for Companies Marketing Infant Foods   **216**

JOAN KONNER   *From* "Women in the Marketplace"   **231**

KATHERINE FULTON   *From* "Writing and Liberty in a Consumer Culture"   **234**

JOHN CORRY   TV News and the Neutrality Principle   **238**

DANIEL HALLIN   TV's Clean Little War   **245**

MORGAN STRONG   Portions of the Gulf War Were Brought to You by...the Folks at Hill and Knowlton   **251**

JACK TATUM with BILL KUSHNER   I Plead Guilty, But Only to Aggressive Play   **254**

MONROE H. FREEDMAN   Professional Responsibility of the Criminal Defense Lawyer: The Three Hardest Questions   **266**

Literature and the Arts   **280**

J. A. KOTEN   Music Hath Charms to Soothe a Savage Breast, but Can It Put Bread on the Table?   **282**

TERRY EAGLETON   What Is Literature?   **289**

LAURA BOHANNAN   Shakespeare in the Bush   **303**

EUDORA WELTY   A Worn Path   **313**

NEIL D. ISAACS   Life for Phoenix   **320**

ROLAND BARTEL   Life and Death in Eudora Welty's "A Worn Path"   **325**

EUDORA WELTY   "Is Phoenix Jackson's Grandson Really Dead?"   **328**

ROBERT PENN WARREN   *From* "Why Do We Read Fiction?"   **332**

SUSAN SONTAG   Against Interpretation   **334**

RICHARD BERNSTEIN   The Arts Catch Up with a Society
in Disarray   **344**

HOWARDENA PINDELL   Colonial Culture   **353**

KATHA POLLITT   Why We Read   **356**

SUZI GABLIK   Toward an Ecological Self   **360**

Intelligence and Aptitude   370

STEPHEN JAY GOULD   *From* "The Hereditarian Theory of IQ"   **372**

GEORGE B. CUTTEN   *From* "The Reconstruction of
Democracy"   **398**

WALTER LIPPMANN   Three Essays on Intelligence Tests   **403**
The Mental Age of Americans   **403**
The Mystery of the "A" Men   **407**
The Reliability of Intelligence Tests   **411**

HOWARD GARDNER   What Is an Intelligence?   **416**

DAVID OWEN   The Last Days of ETS   **425**

CAROL ANNE DWYER   Testimony at the House Subcommittee
Hearings on Sex and Race Differences on Standardized Tests,
April 23, 1987   **457**

PHYLLIS ROSSER   Testimony at the House Subcommittee Hearings
on Sex and Race Differences on Standardized Tests,
April 23, 1987   **468**

DANIEL SELIGMAN   The Rich Are Different   **479**

JUDY GAHAGAN   Wisdom and Wealth: The Great Education
Hoax   **481**

LUIS ALBERTO MACHADO   *From* "The Right to be Intelligent"   **487**

Appendix: More about Logic   495

Categorical Propositions: Rule, Case, and Attribute   **495**
The Three Forms of Inference   **497**
1. Deduction   **497**
2. Induction   **498**
3. Abduction   **500**
The Analysis of Deductive Arguments   **501**
The Form of Categorical Propositions   **501**
More about Distribution   **503**
Rules of Deductive Validity   **503**
Common Errors in Using Categorical Syllogisms   **504**
Diagramming Syllogisms   **507**
Hypothetical Syllogisms   **514**
Disjunctive Syllogisms   **517**
Enthymemes   **518**
Applications   **519**
Permissions Acknowledgments   **521**
Index   **524**

Preface

Although this book grew out of the nine years I served as Director of Freshman English at the University of Connecticut, it was provoked not so much by my immersion in the academic study of rhetoric as by regularly sitting on committees. Argumentation is the main business of committees, and the arguments concern real choices with real consequences. In this highly pragmatic context, I found that the best arguments were distinguished primarily by a command of fact, by an incisive partitioning of the issues, and by an understanding of the logic appropriate to different sorts of claims.

The pages that follow offer students and teachers a rhetoric of argument stressing these skills, along with a body of interesting, challenging readings and an optional appendix on logic. The rhetoric and the anthology are coordinated with each other. The readings are frequently used to illustrate the rhetorical principles, while study questions in the anthology relate the selections back to the rhetorical principles, thus enabling students to read each selection with enhanced critical judgment and with greater understanding of the writer's strategies.

The Rhetoric

The rhetoric divides argumentative discourse into three categories of claims: those of fact, value, and policy. Chapter 1 offers a brief overview of the relationships among these three categories; Chapters 2, 3, and 4 then discuss the categories of fact, value, and policy individually, offering not only a theoretical understanding of each mode of argument, but flexible heuristics (not rigid formulae) to guide students in constructing their own arguments. Following these first four chapters, which all concern primarily the logic of the three argumentative modes, Chapter 5, "Writing with Direction," addresses the writing process. It is based on the assumption that all arguments grow out of a social context, and that therefore every argument is implicitly a counterargument to factual beliefs, value positions, or policy proposals in the surrounding culture. This chapter describes strategies of research, organization, and writing that students can use as they enter this cultural debate. It makes the task of writing relatively unthreatening by allowing for considerable freedom and exploration at the outset. Yet it encourages a professional standard of achievement by stressing the concept of "direction" that marks truly distinguished writing and by showing how a sentence outline can be used to achieve that direction. The chapter includes analyses of two articles that possess this quality to a high degree, one on factual issues and one on a values issue with whose central position many readers—perhaps most—are likely to disagree prior to reading the writer's argument.

A skillful and accurate handling of facts is enormously important in argument. An empirical claim is sound insofar as it is more consistent than any rival hypotheses with *observable* evidence. The most fruitful method for analyzing and testing empirical claims is the scientific method. The chapter on factual reasoning outlines this method and traces its application in a scientific article. At the end of the chapter students are walked through a sample problem—"Is alcoholism a disease?"—which, like so many other topics student writers naturally select, includes empirical questions in an ethically charged context. This sample topic shows how, by carefully segregating the empirical aspects of the question and investigating them according to the precepts offered earlier in the chapter, students can lay a strong foundation for later ethical analysis and enhance their rhetorical effectiveness. Factual reasoning requires several abilities that college students rarely possess without training:

- to express their claims precisely, in terms denoting observable conditions
- to identify rival claims that they are ruling out
- to identify observable evidence that is consistent with their own claim but inconsistent with rival claims

Questions of value are settled by demonstrating the consistency of one's conclusion not with observable conditions, but with values already a matter of consensus between writer and audience. The question, "Is Business Bluffing Ethical?" posed by one title in this collection is syntactically similar to that posed by another, "Do Hens Suffer in Battery Cages?" But the two arguments in response to these questions are worlds apart in method. The argument about hens is empirical and enlists the strategies of empirical arguments: translation of a hypothesis into observable terms followed by testing of observed facts against those predicted. The argument that business bluffing is ethical requires the strategies of evaluative arguments: demonstrating that the conclusion is consistent with tolerance of bluffing elsewhere in our value system.

A given piece of writing that aims ultimately at evaluation may include facts. For instance, Singer's "Animal Liberation" argues empirically that certain human enterprises cause animals to suffer before it goes on to the quite distinct evaluative argument that causing animals to suffer is immoral. The point is that the two modes of argumentation within the essay are radically different, and often the best way to clarify a confused debate is to sort out the empirical issues from the issues of value.

Policy arguments, or proposals, include both factual arguments ("X is the case now; Y would become the case if my plan were implemented") and evaluative arguments ("Y would be better than X"), yet these two kinds of arguments take on special properties when combined into a proposition whose verb is "should" or its equivalent. All "should" statements, or proposals, have common features that are very usefully approached through the heuristic of the "stock issues" of debate.

The Readings

The readings in the anthology were selected with the following criteria in mind:

- The selections fall into four thematic categories that have recently generated factual questions, elicited expressions of conflicting values, and presented difficult choices about personal, institutional, or public policies. The thematic groups provide enough context for students to offer informed contributions to the cultural debate.
- Within each section, some documents offer a broad philosophical view of the theme. Others take sharply contrasting views on some particular topic within the broader theme.
- Within each section, some documents examine empirical questions, some articulate ethical or aesthetic values, and some present or oppose proposals for future action. The casebook groupings of selections also enables students to see how empirical and evaluative arguments are brought to bear on policy decisions through such means as legislative hearings, reports of government agencies, and codes of professional ethics.
- Each section includes at least one pair of selections that directly oppose each other; often one member of the pair was expressly written as a rebuttal or critique of the other. But each section also includes selections that differ from each other more subtly, forcing the student who would compare them to discover the underlying assumptions and hidden consequences of the arguments.
- While most selections are contemporary, historical context is often necessary to understand a present-day dispute. Some dated arguments are deliberately included to give historical perspective and illustrate contemporary arguments by contrast.
- Some of the arguments included are badly flawed. Finding that such arguments have been printed by reputable publishers and endorsed by the

major scientists and academic institutions of their day encourages students to think critically.

- Each section includes selections of various lengths. Most are over ten pages long, since fully developed arguments usually require a certain scope, but ample shorter selections are included as well to provide more contained subjects for discussion and illustration.

Logic

It is probably safe to say that esteem for logic as an important, valuable component of training in argumentation is the lowest it has been in 2500 years and that "traditional" logic (as opposed to informal logic and especially the Toulmin model[1]) is in the greatest disesteem of all. In an article published at the end of 1988, Richard Fulkerson offered a devastating critique of the garbled and truncated form ("comp-logic," as Fulkerson calls it) in which traditional logic is presented by many composition textbooks, and he goes on to criticize the Toulmin model as well.[2]

My own position is that the attempt to present a comprehensive view of logic in the composition course is, for most teachers and most students, a misapplication of the time available. Rightly or wrongly, students perceive such instruction as a blizzard of technical terms and frightening quasi-algebraic operations, and even those who understand the logical concepts in the abstract find it difficult to apply them to their own writing or to the analysis of others'. On the other hand, a grasp of a few elementary logical principles is essential to effective argument, and no treatise on rhetoric would be complete without some treatment of the principles that determine when the relationship between a claim and the grounds on which it is based is a sound one. With these reasons in mind, I have tried to embody the modest requisite logical principles in the text. I have also provided an appendix in which the curious student can find a fuller treatment.

The appendix includes instruction in what is normally understood as "formal logic"—namely the deductive syllogism—because categorical reasoning is an important cognitive skill that can only be fully grasped when students are held to certain rules (such as keeping the wording of the categories constant and making quantifiers explicit), rules that are often dispensed with in informal logic. The deductive syllogism is an important tool in evaluative arguments, especially when it is used to generate the missing premise in an enthymeme, a task it can accomplish with certainty only by applying the classical rules of validity. It is often

---

[1] Stephen Toulmin, *The Uses of Argument* (Cambridge: Cambridge University Press, 1958).
[2] Richard Fulkerson, "Technical Logic, Comp-Logic, and the Teaching of Writing," *CCC* 39 (1988): 436–52.

said that deductive logic is only a diagnostic or analytic tool rather than an aid to invention, but this position seems to me mistaken. Most of us invent arguments precisely because we disagree with someone else's analysis; this premise is central to the view of the writing process presented in Chapter 5. Logic is a way of putting our finger on the reasons behind our disagreements with others and therefore a potent source of material for constructing our own positions. (See Kaufer and Neuwirth for an elaboration of this view and some practical classroom exercises for implementing it.)[3]

However, it is also important to recognize that logic is not restricted to the deductive syllogism and that our understanding of logic has developed since the age of Aristotle. As Toulmin and other critics have rightly pointed out, the deductive syllogism is not well adapted to probabilistic reasoning or, indeed, to many arguments about factual issues. Toulmin and other informal logicians address this weakness by presenting a more flexible argument form that can handle a broader range of arguments, and this approach has proven useful to many composition teachers. But since this book stresses the radical difference between factual and evaluative arguments, I have chosen instead to preserve the deductive syllogism for claims of value while stressing other aspects of logic, according to our modern understanding of them, for claims of fact.

The kind of logic appropriate to factual claims is not usually described in rhetoric texts, although a number of them have misleadingly identified induction as the basic method of empirical reasoning. But in fact, those who think systematically almost never rely on induction as anything more than a way station to a more satisfying argument or as a way of confirming an argument arrived at by a more complex route. This mode of discovery was first fully described by the philosopher Charles Sanders Peirce, who called it *abduction* or *the method of hypothesis.*[4] In this process, someone first notes some surprising or anomalous fact, then creates a hypothesis to explain it. Next the researcher *deduces* what further observable phenomena would be true if the hypothesis itself were true and carries out the required observations to see whether the predicted phenomena appear. If the observations are repeatedly consistent with the predictions the hypothesis generated, the hypothesis is taken on the principles of *induction* to be provisionally true. The conclusion is not regarded as utterly certain, but becomes, as Karl Popper put it, "the science of the day."[5] Scientists who wish to be scrupulously accurate often point out that they have not so much *proved* their hypotheses as *failed to disprove* them. Training in the method of hypothesis sharpens students'

[3] David Kaufer and Christine Neuwirth, "Integrating Formal Logic and the New Rhetoric: A Four-Stage Heuristic," *CE* 45 (1983): 380–89.
[4] Charles Sanders Peirce, *Collected Papers*, Vol. II, *Elements of Logic*, ed. Charles Hartshorne and Paul Weiss (Cambridge: The Belknap Press of Harvard, 1965).
[5] Karl Popper, *The Logic of Scientific Discovery* (New York and Evanston: Harper & Row, 1968), 33, 277.

ability to handle any empirical question because it teaches them to consider alternative explanations for puzzling phenomena and to generate tests for deciding among the rival explanations.

The appendix of this book tries to improve on the normal treatment of traditional logic by placing the deductive syllogism in this larger context of systematic reasoning as well as by avoiding oversimplifications, by stressing the commonsense basis of all logical thought, and by showing students how to diagram syllogisms and thus complement abstract verbal arguments with visual aids.

Acknowledgments

I have incurred many debts of gratitude in compiling this book, and it gives me great pleasure to thank those who have shaped my thinking on the issues covered here, who have suggested selections, read the manuscript in part or in whole, and offered constructive criticism:

Michael Scriven's philosophy courses at Swarthmore in the late 1950s taught me a great deal about critical thinking and introduced me to many of the ideas that inform Chapter 2.

Kevin Riordan first suggested that I write this book and supported me along the way.

In 1982 the Connecticut Humanities Council partially funded a conference that I organized on Heuristics and Critical Thinking. It offered instructive presentations and workshops on the subjects of fact, value, and policy. At this conference Thomas Terry, Associate Professor of Molecular and Cell Biology at the University of Connecticut, ran the workshop pertaining to factual claims and contributed valuable materials, including the exercise example on p. 17; Scott Lehmann of the Philosophy Department was responsible for the component pertaining to values; Richard Katula of the University of Rhode Island presented material on policy proposals. I should add that his presentation, along with an article he coauthored with Richard W. Roth, "A Stock Issues Approach to Writing Arguments," *CCC* 31 (May 1980), 183–96, influenced the entire approach of Chapter 4 of this book.

I also wish to acknowledge the generous and professional assistance of several colleagues at the Homer Babbidge Library of the University of Connecticut: Ellen Embardo, who enlightened me about the alternative press and about indexes and other reference material bearing on it; Lucy DeLuca, who helped me to find my way around the government documents; and especially Scott Kennedy, who advised me about reference resources and generously read Chapter 5 in its entirety. His suggestions and corrections were invaluable.

Jim Scully suggested two of the selections in the anthology, but our many conversations over the seven years we shared an office have exerted a more pervasive shaping influence.

Harvey Maksvytis, M.D., and Ann Keuper offered steady encouragement as well as useful advice about causal reasoning and contemporary issues in art respectively.

I owe particular thanks also to Janie Kaufmann, who put me in contact with Steve Pensinger and is thus responsible for my consistently gratifying affiliation with McGraw-Hill.

At McGraw-Hill, Steve Pensinger has recruited intelligent and sensitive readers to review the manuscript and has himself offered trenchant but always tactful suggestions. Among those who have reviewed the manuscript, I wish to thank: Miriam Brody, Ithaca College; James Howland, Cal Poly, San Luis Obispo; Richard Larson, Lehman College; John Lyne, University of Iowa; Barry Maid, University of Arkansas, Little Rock; Deanne Milan, San Francisco City College; Donovan J. Ochs, University of Iowa; and Tom Zaniello, Northern Kentucky University.

Finally, thanks upon thanks to my wife Ruth for her patience and support, as well as for bringing her keen intelligence and feeling for words to bear on this project.

A. Harris Fairbanks

FACT, VALUE, POLICY

POLICY

Reading and
Writing Arguments

1 Sorting Out the Issues

The Nature of Argument

This is a book about writing arguments. Arguments are the kind of writing you do when your main point, or conclusion, would seem implausible to your reader if you didn't support it with evidence, or reasons. The term *argument* does not imply in the least that your discourse is acrimonious or combative. This systematic approach to reaching satisfying conclusions and presenting them to others can occur in collaborative deliberations as well as in adversary proceedings such as debates in the courtroom or legislature.

Arguments differ from *expository writing,* which passes on an already established fact to an audience that is uninformed but disposed to accept the facts offered. If you are telling someone how to prepare a raised-bed garden or reporting how many calls the fire department answered in a given month or explaining recent developments in a field in which you are expert, you are probably not required to prove your points, but only to present them intelligibly. However, if you were to present a significantly unorthodox way of preparing raised-bed gardens, you would have to present evidence that your method was superior, and your discourse would become argumentative rather than expository. A position that requires an argument in one time period will require only exposition in another. For Galileo, the claim that the earth moves around the sun was an argument because it was inconsistent with the beliefs of his day, and the task of persuading people to accept his factual arguments was made more difficult because they presented a challenge to the prevailing system of values as well.

Like Galileo's, virtually every argument has a social context. Usually when you are led to write argumentatively about any subject, you have heard it debated, or you have read or heard something about it with which you disagree or which indicates to you that your facts or values diverge from those that have some currency. The support that you are required to provide for your claim will depend not only on the nature of your subject, but on the climate of beliefs and values around you.

You will encounter arguments frequently in your academic career and later in your professional, civic, and even private life. Sometimes you will encounter them as a reader and sometimes as a writer. Usually intellectual life follows a rhythm of reading or listening to various arguments on a given topic, mulling these arguments over in your mind, and then writing something based on your sources as synthesized or modified by your own reflections and experience.

One example of this pattern occurs when scholars study the causes of the Civil War. Typically, they might read one article arguing that the main cause was Northern hostility to slavery in the South; another arguing that the cause was economic competition between the two areas; another arguing that the cause was competition for control of new states forming in the Midwest; and another arguing that the cause was one of cultural animosity between the aristocratic South and the bourgeois North. Scholars would have to ask themselves first whether these articles were truly incompatible: Could the war have been caused by some combination of these causes? Insofar as the articles were incompatible with each other, scholars would have to judge what reasons underlay the differences between the various conclusions. Did the authors of the articles rely on conflicting evidence? Did they reason differently about the same evidence? Did they differ in other underlying assumptions about human motivation generally?

Virtually the same pattern of reading, reflection, and writing takes place in areas quite apart from scholarship. Business managers must receive reports and proposals from subordinates. Almost inevitably these reports will conflict, since those reporting are likely to represent their own departments as crucial to the firm's future and in need of higher budgets. Managers must digest these reports and present a synthesis and recommendations to their own superiors and ultimately to the stockholders. Physicians must evaluate conflicting reports from researchers and pharmaceutical firms (both of whom may be motivated by self-interest) and arrive at diagnostic and therapeutic decisions that they can defend to patients, lawyers, and hospital boards of review. Military officers must process reports from intelligence sources, suppliers, and subordinates to arrive at strategies that they can present to civilian authorities for approval.

Critical Thinking

It is in the nature of things that anyone in a position of responsibility—and any college student—must contend with a welter of discourse, much of it deficient or contradictory in the information it presents, the values with which it is informed, the recommendations it makes for the future. In such situations, it is essential to be a critical thinker. (The term "critical" is derived from the Greek *krinein,* "to judge.") Critical thinkers are able to judge whether arguments are sound or not, and when confronted with conflicting arguments, they are able to judge which is stronger. Moreover, when critical thinkers read conflicting arguments, they can understand the causes of the discrepancy. (Perhaps most important of all, they are in some measure equipped to recognize situations in which not all the evidence is in, and where it is therefore prudent to withhold final judgment.)

If, when you reconcile your bank statement with your checkbook balance, your bottom line is different from the bank's, there must be at least one other discrepancy in the accounts. You cannot concede that the bank is right in its starting balance, credits, debits, and arithmetic and still claim that it is wrong at the bottom line. Eventually you will discover at least one difference in these earlier calculations that accounts for the difference in the final balance. Likewise, if you disagree with the conclusion of an argument, you will also disagree with something else in the argument that is logically prior to the conclusion. You may have good reason to believe that the argument is based on inaccurate or incomplete evidence, you may find a flaw in its reasoning, you may subscribe to different values, or you may anticipate consequences of an argument that the author failed to foresee; any or all of these may account for the difference in your conclusions. But only after you can consciously formulate these reasons are you in a position to decide whether the argument you are considering is unsound or whether you should change your own mind.

We have considered various vocational contexts in which you might be required to read and respond critically to discrepant arguments. But critical thinking is also crucial to the most personal aspects of your life. Consider people who engaged in practices such as burning witches or holding slaves or working in extermination camps. These atrocities seem to us today terrible blind spots in the cultures that tolerated them. Yet we sometimes encounter arguments holding that *we* are the victims of comparable moral blind spots. The essay by Peter Singer on page 122, implies that if you eat meat, you are guilty of a moral offense comparable in severity to holding slaves. In reading his essay, you may come to decide that he is right and choose to stop eating meat, or you may discover in his argument a premise that you do not share or an error in his reasoning. But to reject his conclusion without detecting some flaw in his argument is to indulge in the same kind of intellectual and moral laziness that we condemn in the slaveholders who disregarded abolitionist arguments.

✳ The Three Kinds of Issues

Central to critical thinking is the notion of *issues.* Typically, the resolution of a question, whether it is being debated between two or more people or within the mind of an individual, demands that a number of subsidiary questions be resolved first. These subsidiary questions are the issues. All issues fall into three categories: those of fact, value, and policy. You can do nothing more valuable for your powers of critical thinking than to understand the differences between these three kinds of issues. To help you do this is the purpose of the next three chapters. But first it will be helpful to consider how these three types of issues relate to each other and how they can combine into complex arguments.

The Fact/Value Distinction

First, consider the distinction between issues of fact and value. *Factual issues* are those which can in principle be settled by *empirical* means, that is, by observation of evidence that is unambiguously determinable or measurable. The statement "Abraham Lincoln was the tallest American President prior to 1870" is a factual claim because relative height is a quality that can be determined by yardsticks. On the other hand, the statement "Abraham Lincoln was the greatest American President prior to 1870" is a values claim. "Greatness" cannot be measured by physical observations. True, someone might try to support this claim by observable and even measurable evidence, such as a count of favorable references to Lincoln in newspapers and history books compared with such references to other Presidents; but someone else might respond that these references testify to Lincoln's popularity or reputation rather than to true greatness. Two people could agree on a list of all the facts that either one felt was relevant to this value judgment, and yet they might disagree about whether those facts added up to "greatness."

Notice that the distinction between the *factual* and the *evaluative* is not the same as the common distinction between *fact* and *opinion.* Many factual claims are at present a matter of opinion because we lack the technology or the opportunity to discover the relevant evidence. For example, "The surface of the planet Pluto contains gold in a ratio of at least three parts per million" is a factual claim because, even though it does not express a fact that we can at present establish with certainty, we know what kind of tests would confirm or refute it if only we possessed the technology to conduct them. Many statements about past history are factual in nature even though we may never be able to answer them conclusively, and predictions can be factual though their truth can be verified or refuted only in the future.

Just as there may be factual issues on which opinion is divided, there may be evaluative issues on which opinion is virtually unanimous. Few people would disagree that "Abraham Lincoln was the greatest President between 1850 and 1870." (In this comparison he is pitted against Taylor, Fillmore, Pierce, Andrew Johnson, and Grant.) But here what we have is simply a unanimous opinion about an evaluation rather than an empirical fact, because "greatness" in the context of Presidential caliber is not objectively measurable. Prevailing views of the greatness of many political leaders, writers, and artists have often changed radically, not because any new factual evidence has arisen, but because shifting values bring about a new interpretation of the existing evidence.

The distinction between factual and evaluative issues is important because their resolutions demand different strategies of gathering support, arguing logically, and defining terms, as we shall see in Chapter 2, "Fact" and Chapter 3, "Value": Factual arguments always seek to show that their conclusions match physical reality; evaluative arguments seek to show that their conclusions match the value systems of the readers addressed. Factual arguments rely on causal reasoning; evaluative arguments rely on deductive reasoning. The terms of factual arguments must be defined by their observable properties, causes, or effects; those of evaluative arguments must be defined by appeals to the value system. Some arguments are entirely factual, especially those presented in scientific studies. Essays may be purely evaluative as well, though more commonly those that argue for some revision of a prevailing value judgment will also present new factual evidence by way of support.

The Stock Issues of Policy Arguments

Chapter 4 deals with policy arguments, which propose that some agent undertake a specified course of action. Such an argument might be a proposal for a town to buy a parcel of land for recreational use, for a state or national legislature to pass a law, for a firm to adopt a new marketing strategy, or for voters to support a political candidate. Policy arguments do not require a third kind of logic beyond those of fact and value that we have just surveyed. Policy proposals always contain factual issues, for they must demonstrate that the plan they propose will bring about the conditions they envision. They always confront value issues as well in showing that these changed conditions, including any side effects of their plan, are more desirable, in the aggregate, than the status quo. In fact all the issues of a policy argument are either factual or evaluative. We might think of the three kinds of argument as the confluence of two streams of thought, facts and values, that together form the larger stream of a policy argument:

However, the operative word in any proposal is "should," and that makes policy arguments a rather special blend of fact and value that lends itself to a special mode of analysis. To see the confusions that arise from failing to sort out the issues, imagine the following dialogue in a city where there is known to be considerable intravenous drug use and where several cases of AIDS have appeared at the local hospital:

1. X: Perhaps the city ought to start a needle-exchange program, like the one in Zurich.

2. Y: Drug users wouldn't reveal themselves to a city agency. Anyhow, by your plan you are condoning an illegal activity.

3. X: No, I'm not condoning it. I'm trying to save lives. And not just the lives of the users. Everyone is threatened if you encourage the growth of a population that is going to incubate AIDS, which can be spread to anyone by sexual contact.

4. Y: Look, if the users want to save their lives, they can stop using drugs. Anyway, a program like that is going to be expensive.

5. X: It's a lot more expensive to care for a patient with AIDS.

6. Y: The public shouldn't have to pay for patients who contract diseases from life-styles they know are risky.

7. X: Do you think it's an accident that so many drug users are poor and belong disproportionately to minority groups? Don't you think that society has some responsibility to care for people whose problems are clearly products of social inequities? Isn't it only humane?

8. Y: Well, I can't see that it is either responsible or humane to adopt a policy that is going to encourage further drug use…

This chaotic conversation is a microcosmic version of debates on social issues that take place at various levels of our culture. Conversations like these— whether they are discussions in which you are actually involved or debates conducted in the media, in institutions, in legislatures, or in street rallies—often make up that social context out of which your own written arguments will grow.

As a first step, we might sort the specific issues raised by X and Y into two categories, issues of fact and issues of value (the numbers in parentheses refer to the numbers in the margin of the dialogue above; NEP = needle exchange program):

Fact
- How many drug users will contract AIDS if there is no NEP? (1)
- How many lives will be saved if there is a NEP? (1)
- Will the lives of nonusers be saved? (3)

Value
- Would implementation of a NEP constitute moral approval of drug use? (2)
- Is the public morally obliged to care for patients whose risky behavior has contributed to their illness? (6)

- Would users accept clean needles from a city agency? (2)
- Can drug users stop using drugs? (4)
- How much will the NEP cost? (4)
- How much does care for an AIDS patient cost? (5)
- Have social practices contributed to drug use? (7)
- Would a NEP encourage drug use? (8)

- If the NEP would contribute to further drug use but also prevent some HIV infection, would it be responsible and humane? (8)
- Can social practices that contribute to drug use be described as "inequities"? (7)
- If social inequities have contributed to drug use, is the public morally obliged to pay for the care of users? (7)

While the division into issues of fact and value offers some guidance as to how the individual issues might be argued, we also need guidance on how the issues should be grouped and in what sequence they should be considered. Chapter 4 offers a decision procedure for cutting through the confusion of policy debates. It offers a set of "stock issues"—issues, that is, that are pertinent to any claim that someone should take some action:

- Does a serious need exist?
- Does the need require action or will it take care of itself?
- Will the proposed plan meet this need?
- Is the plan feasible?
- Does the plan have disadvantages, and if so, do they outweigh the plan's advantages?
- Is the proposed plan the best way of meeting the need?

The stock issues perform two functions: first, they can consolidate groups of the specific issues above into categories such as "need" and "feasibility," categories that reflect the issues' position in the structure of a policy argument. For instance in the category of "Need," (or a need for the public to take action against HIV contagion among IV drug users), several points raised by X and Y are relevant:

- X implicitly claims that drug users (1) and others—their sexual contacts, babies born to infected mothers, etc., (3)—will die of AIDS if there is no such program.
- Y's claim (4), that users can simply stop using drugs, implies that a NEP is not needed because the use of needles themselves can be stopped.
- Y's claim (6), that the public is not obliged to care for those who knowingly risk their health, implies that while the health problem exists, there is no need for public action.
- X responds (7) that if social inequities have been responsible for this drug use, then the public is morally obliged to take action.

By isolating these issues pertinent to need, we can see more readily how they relate to each other and, where they conflict, what kind of evidence and reasoning are required to judge which are stronger.

The second function of the stock issues is to establish a sequence and priorities for the different clusters of issues. After X claims that the plan would save lives, Y immediately makes two counterclaims, one factual—that the plan wouldn't work because the users would refuse to participate (feasibility)—and one moral—that it would condone drug use (disadvantage). These two objections have very different logical bearings on the argument. If Y is right that the plan would not work, then X's proposal must be abandoned. But if the evidence showed that the plan would indeed save many lives (including perhaps the lives of some who did not knowingly indulge in risky behavior), the moral objection, while not trivial, might strike even Y as insufficient to outweigh the benefits. Clearly the disadvantages of any plan cannot be intelligently weighed against the advantages until causal reasoning has established what those benefits are likely to be.

Let's begin, then, by considering the logic of factual claims (Chapter 2), then move on to the logic of values claims (Chapter 3), and finally take up the way both kinds of issues are combined and brought to bear in the distinctive structure of policy proposals (Chapter 4).

2 *Fact*

Factual Claims and the Observable World

Deductive Versus Empirical Reasoning

It was once hoped by philosophers that truths about the world could be arrived at by pure reasoning, like the truths of mathematics. The theorem of Euclidean geometry, that "the sum of the angles of any triangle equals a straight angle," is not intuitively obvious, but it can be proven by pure deduction from the definitions, axioms, and postulates of the Euclidean system. This demonstration does not prove anything about the physical world, however. Contemporary physicists contend that if we consider triangles on an interstellar scale, the angles of a triangle made up of lines as "straight" as we can conceive—the lines taken by a beam of light—might well total more than 180 degrees. This is not to say that Euclidean geometry is wrong, but only that it may not describe physical space empirically as well as some other geometric system might.

Early scientists tried to apply the methods of geometry to studies of the physical world, hoping to be able to attain certain truth in this area as well. We now understand that knowledge of the physical world (including knowledge about human behavior) can never be reliably ascertained by pure reasoning. Deduction can make predictions, and in fields where theory is far advanced, those predictions carry a high level of probability. Archimedes gives an elegant, purely deductive proof of the principle that a floating object displaces its own weight of the fluid in which it floats, but even this apparently "proven" principle could not be accepted as fact until it was tested experimentally because, for one thing, it rested on certain assumptions about the nature of fluids that could not be known to be true until the tests were performed. In Archimedes' case, an educated guess about the behavior of nature proved accurate, but in other cases, it might not. Prescientific philosophers reasoned that planetary orbits must be circular because a circle is the perfect shape and because God would not have created orbits in a less than perfect shape; but planetary orbits are not perfectly circular. Nor is the problem simply that the philosophers selected the wrong premises. *Any* premises used to predict the shape of a planet's orbit would have to be based ultimately on observation, not on pure reasoning. Consider what would appear to be an even simpler conclusion based on pure deduction. It "makes sense" that a quart of water added to a quart of alcohol should produce two quarts of liquid, but it doesn't (because the water absorbs some of the alcohol).

If deductions as simple and basic as this can be overthrown by empirical tests, it is obvious that "deductions" about human behavior are very dangerous. Inexperienced writers frequently make the mistake of generalizing about human behavior on the basis of what "makes sense" or what "logic" seems to dictate, for example, "If alcohol is made illegal, people won't drink any more," or, "If the government institutes a 'squeal law' in birth-control clinics, minors who don't want their parents to be told of their visit will simply decide to stop all sexual activity."

Verifiability and Refutability

A factual statement about the physical world must be *verifiable:* We must be able to specify what conditions we would be able to observe for the statement to be true. For example, "Oil is lighter than water" is a factual statement. It is clear what kinds of observations we might make to verify its truth. We might measure out equal volumes of the two substances and weigh them; we might pour the oil into the water to see which floated on the other; we might float a piece of wood in each substance and observe whether it sank more deeply into one than the other. The answers to these tests will tell us whether the claim is *true,* but simply knowing what observable occurrences would verify the statement is to understand what the claim *means.*

A factual claim must also be in principle refutable. That is, there must be some conceivable kind of evidence that would prove it wrong. Predictions and promises often avoid any chance of being refuted by describing the future in terms that could apply to virtually any outcome. As a New York weather forecaster might say in July, "We should see some sun tomorrow, but there's a chance of some clouds and perhaps even showers as well. Temperatures will be within a seasonable range." Nothing short of a snowstorm could falsify this forecast. Or leaders of political parties, when asked whether their legislative representatives will pass a bill or reject it, may say, "They will do what is best for the country." The informational content of a claim is directly proportional to the range of outcomes that could refute it.

Some factual claims avoid refutability not by vagueness, but by building into the thesis some principle that will explain away contrary evidence. This style of reasoning is often found in discussions of conspiracies of any sort:

> JUAN: The Portuguese discovered the New World before Columbus, thinking that they had found a route to the Indies, but they were required by government decree to keep their discovery a secret in order to conceal a potentially valuable trade route from commercial rivals.
>
> PABLO: That's not true. There is no evidence that the Portuguese found a route to the New World before Columbus.
>
> JUAN: Ah, you see? Just what my theory would predict. The Portuguese were entirely successful in maintaining their secret.[1]

Even if Pablo discovered a letter from a Portuguese explorer or government official stating that his country's explorations were confined to the coast of Africa and insisting that it would be madness to sail far west into the Atlantic, Juan could dismiss it as a further attempt to mislead potential trade rivals and conceal Portuguese successes in reaching the Indies. Obviously, however, Juan cannot claim success for his hypothesis on the grounds that all the evidence favors it; there is no evidence favoring it. Rather, it appears to succeed because no evidence could conceivably count against it. Such an argument is said to be a *circular argument* because it presupposes the conclusion and uses that conclusion to explain away counterevidence.

Categorizing and Defining in Factual Arguments

Categorizing and defining are complementary activities. To categorize things is to say that they make up a class or belong to some recognized class; to define that class is to state the *criteria* that an individual member must meet to be included in the class. Since factual claims must be verifiable and refutable, their words must be definable in observable terms. Let us consider some ways of confronting problems in establishing the boundaries of categories or in defining them empirically:

Defining by Necessary and Sufficient Criteria

The classic, most satisfying kind of definition defines the term by first placing it in a genus (or broader category), then listing its "differentiae," a set of necessary and sufficient properties that distinguish it from other members of its genus. Thus a "triangle" is "a plane geometrical figure" (its genus) "that is bounded and has three straight sides" (its differentiae). These differentiae present the criteria

---

[1] This imaginary dialogue is based on an analysis by Samuel Eliot Morison as quoted by Daniel J. Boorstin, *The Discoverers* (New York: Random House, 1983), 269.

that are *necessary* (for every triangle must have them) and *sufficient* (for if a figure has both of them, it is bound to be a triangle.) Triangles can have other properties such as being equilateral, obtuse, right, or the side of a pyramid, but these are all *accidental* properties.

Sometimes people think that unless such a definition can be given, especially in an argument that pretends to be scientific or otherwise intellectually rigorous, the writer cannot be said to have a firm grasp of the subject. In a great many cases, though, this kind of definition is impossible, and in such a case you should not feel intimidated because you cannot formulate one.

Definitions by necessary and sufficient criteria are easiest to apply to classes that are defined into existence. This is the case with triangles, in fact, for although we speak loosely of timbers in a wall or marks on paper forming a "triangle," the triangles described in geometry are abstract and perceptible only to the intellect, not to the eye (since the lines that form the sides have no breadth). All triangles have their necessary and sufficient characteristics because we define them that way. If in the timbers of a building we discover a "triangle" with a crooked side, or one whose sides don't quite meet at the top, we don't announce that we have experimentally disproved the traditional definition of the triangle by discovering a counterexample.

The process of defining categories into existence also happens in legal or regulatory contexts with terms like "full-time student," "veteran," "grand larceny," or "insolvent." If a college says that only full-time students are eligible to play on varsity teams, it must offer some definition of "full-time student," such as "one who is enrolled for at least twelve credits." Such a definition is arbitrary. The college could have set the credit limit at nine or fifteen, or might have invoked other criteria instead of or in addition to course enrollment. Certainly in this case the definition creates the class rather than the other way around, as it would have done had the authorities first rounded up all the students they considered full-time and then tried to figure out what they had in common.

Defining by Family Relationships Based on Common Cause

When we leave the contexts of legal and geometrical definitions, the relationship of the definition to the category defined is reversed. Nature seems to provide what we might call "natural classes," such as "mammals," whose defining characteristics and membership are to be *discovered* by man rather than arbitrarily *stipulated*. Not every class of natural objects or creatures is necessarily a "natural class." For example, we could create a class of "flying creatures" that would include blue jays, bumblebees, and bats, but the members of such a class would have almost nothing in common beyond the one characteristic of flight that was the basis for their selection in the first place. A natural class such as mammals, on the other hand, has great predictive value. If we see that an animal has the distinguishing features of a mammal, such as fur or hair, mammary glands, and warm-bloodedness, then whether its forelimb is a leg, an arm, a wing, or a flipper, we will find some homologue of our humerus, radius, and ulna. Early scientists believed that if they could identify natural classes by necessary and sufficient criteria like a triangle's, they could then confidently identify members of the class and make generalizations about them based on studies of selected samples.

But this view posed problems whenever a specimen turned up that matched most but not all of the supposed defining criteria of the class. Prior to the 1790s, it was thought that one necessary criterion of a mammal was reproduction by live birth, but then the existence of the platypus, an egg-laying animal that in other respects is similar to mammals, came to the attention of Europeans and suggested that the definition of "mammal" needed adjustment. This need posed a dilemma: How could scientists discover what properties all mammals had in common unless they collected all the specimens and inspected them? But on the other hand, how could they decide what specimens should go into the collection to be inspected unless they previously possessed a set of defining features against which to match them?

We understand today as scientists did not two hundred years ago that mammals form a natural class because they share a common ancestor, some of whose characteristics happen to have remained stable in all her descendants despite the varied evolutionary development of other characteristics. This common hereditary endowment is also, of course, the causal explanation of why mammals should share traits above and beyond those that we regard as the defining traits of the class.

This understanding of the causal basis of natural categorization frees us from rigid reliance on necessary and sufficient criteria. Instead, we might think of "family relationships" as determining membership in a class. This term was coined by the philosopher Ludwig Wittgenstein, who pointed out that a word like "game," even though it does not seem an especially vague term, has no set of necessary and sufficient criteria. Most games involve two or more people; solitaire does not. Many games are competitive; "catch" is not. Many games are played for fun; professional football is played as an occupation. Many games require a board or other equipment; "twenty questions" does not. There seems to be no single property that all games have in common, but instead, says Wittgenstein, a set of "family relationships," of which any game is likely to have a few.[2]

You may see this general strategy of definition at work in Howard Gardner's essay, "What Is an Intelligence?" on page 416. Though Gardner is aware that "intelligence" is a value-laden term, and although he even acknowledges that he will consider extending this term only to culturally valued intellectual capacities, he states that the ones he is trying to identify are "sets of intelligences

---

[2] Ludwig Wittgenstein, *Philosophical Investigations,* trans. G. E. M. Anscombe (Oxford: Basil Blackwell, 1958) secs. 66–77.

which meet certain biological and physiological specifications," in other words, "an empirically grounded set of faculties." He then lists eight criteria, or "signs," of an intelligence, the first being "potential isolation by brain damage." "Linguistic intelligence" meets this criterion because brain damage from a blow or a stroke can selectively destroy linguistic competence through aphasia. He can call this first criterion "empirically grounded" because observation will tell us whether candidate intelligences can or cannot be isolated by brain damage.

Definitions specifying family relationships are not limited to literal families in the sense of biological descendents, but may be used to define any class whose members show similarities based on similar causes. Cumulus and cirrus clouds, sedimentary and igneous rocks, and inner-city schools all form classes based on similarities in their formative causes. Definitions by family relationships have also been applied with great success to categories of cultural objects by critics who treat them as though they were biological species. This strategy works because when artists form movements or schools, publish manifestos, and generally learn from one another, there are sound causal reasons why their works take on similar characteristics. Here is Meyer Abrams' definition of a class of poems that he was the first to recognize and describe, the "greater Romantic lyric":

> They present a determinate speaker in a particularized, and usually a localized, outdoor setting, whom we overhear as he carries on, in a fluent vernacular which rises easily to a more formal speech, a sustained colloquy, sometimes with himself or with the outer scene, but more frequently with a silent human auditor, present or absent. The speaker begins with a description of the landscape; an aspect or change of aspect in the landscape evokes a varied but integral process of memory, thought, anticipation, and feeling which remains closely intervolved with the outer scene. In the course of this meditation the lyric speaker achieves an insight, faces up to a tragic loss, comes to a moral decision, or resolves an emotional problem. Often the poem rounds on itself to end where it began, at the outer scene, but with an altered mood and deepened understanding which is the result of the intervening meditation.[3]

Having defined this class in terms of criteria that are observably either present or absent in given poems, Abrams is then able to make empirical claims about the class.

Defining Operationally

Sometimes the nature of a phenomenon to be studied is such that it is impossible to observe its properties directly. For example, although "self-awareness" seems to most of us an intelligible concept, it received little scientific attention until

---

[3] Meyer H. Abrams, "Structure and Style in the Greater Romantic Lyric," *From Sensibility to Romanticism: Essays Presented to Frederick A. Pottle,* ed. Frederick W. Hilles and Harold Bloom (New York: Oxford University Press, 1965), 527–28.

recently, even in humans, because it did not seem accessible to observation. Obviously this obstacle is even greater if we consider self-awareness in other animals. A definition in observable terms seems out of the question, for whatever defining properties we assigned to self-awareness in an animal, we would be unable by inspection to tell whether they were present.

In such a situation, an operational definition may be possible, that is, a definition in terms of some observable behavior by which the hidden phenomenon may be measured. In one set of experiments, a researcher accustomed four chimpanzees to mirrors. At first the chimpanzees responded to the image as though it were another animal, but after a few days this sort of behavior abated. At this point, the researcher anesthetized the chimpanzees and painted a spot of red dye above one eye and on one ear. After the chimpanzees recovered from the anesthesia, he observed that they touched the spots of color only infrequently and were apparently unaware of them. When he showed them the mirror, however, they immediately and repeatedly touched the spots, tried to remove them, and smelled their fingers to try to identify the substance. Two other chimpanzees who underwent the same procedure but had no prior experience with mirrors did not touch the spots any more frequently after seeing their reflection than before. The researcher concluded that the subject chimpanzees would not have become aware of the spots if they had not recognized the image in the mirror as their own, and to do this, he reasoned, they must have had a mental self-image to match with the image in the mirror.[4]

One problem with operational definitions is that readers may not be convinced that the operational procedure truly reflects the hidden phenomenon supposedly being measured. For years researchers in the field of intelligence took performance on standard intelligence tests to be an operational definition of intelligence. But then if the question arises, "How do we know that it is intelligence that the test is really measuring?" no satisfying answer is possible. It was this quandary that led one social scientist to offer a famous wry definition: "Intelligence is what intelligence tests measure." Howard Gardner's essay, "What Is an Intelligence?" is, as we have just seen, an attempt to avoid this weakness of operational definitions and define intelligence more satisfactorily in terms of empirical criteria.

Avoiding a Contested Term

Some disputes that appear to be factual are really *semantic* disputes. For instance, scientists have debated for some time whether apes can learn to use language. All parties to the debate are able to agree that some chimpanzees have been taught to use American Sign Language or symbols on a computer console to indicate

---

[4] Gordon G. Gallup, Jr., "Towards an Operational Definition of Self-Awareness," *Socioecology and Psychology of Primates,* ed. Russell H. Tuttle (The Hague: Mouton, 1975), 309–41.

objects and actions and to make some of their wishes known to their keepers. The chimpanzee Washoe could sign "open" when she wanted a door to be opened. Still, though, some linguists reserve the word "language" for symbolic systems that display more complex structure. They deny that Washoe's request exhibits any ability different in principle from the conditioned response of the cat who scratches at the screen door and looks around at her owner when she wants to be let out.

Semantic deadlocks of this kind often occur because the empirical proposition has important moral or political implications. Thus, if apes can really use language, an accomplishment that we have customarily considered unique to our own species, then perhaps they possess a level of intelligence, awareness, sensitivity, and self-consciousness that would entitle them not merely to kind treatment, but to something approaching civil rights. One would like to be able to isolate a purely empirical, or scientific, definition of "language," but scientists are still divided on the question of whether human language is a qualitatively different phenomenon from anything lower animals possess or whether it is simply a more advanced point on a continuum that would include the signing of trained apes, birdsong, and the dances of honeybees.

One way of avoiding a semantic argument is to fall back on words that will express your point without seeming to claim more than your evidence supports. For instance, it has sometimes been claimed that the utterances of animals lack the flexibility of human words, which can be adapted to a variety of circumstances. Yet you might argue that Washoe's communications sometimes demonstrated this flexibility, as when she applied the word "open" to briefcases and refrigerators when she had learned it only in connection with a door.[5] Thus, instead of arguing that apes can learn language, you might argue that their communication shows a flexibility that was previously considered unique to human language.

The advantage of thus restricting your claim is that your claim is fully supported; the disadvantage is that if your factual claim was a prelude to an ethical comment about the relationships between people and animals, you may lose some dramatic impact.

Focusing on the Inadequacy of Other Terms

This strategy in effect asks of an ape's communication, "If it isn't language, what is it?" This approach is attractive if skeptics have applied some rival description that seems to you inadequate. For instance, Washoe's request to open a briefcase, besides demonstrating an attribute of human language, is difficult to categorize

---

[5] R. Allen Gardner and Beatrix T. Gardner, "A Cross-Fostering Laboratory," *Teaching Sign Language to Chimpanzees*, ed. R. Allen Gardner, Beatrix T. Gardner, and Thomas E. Van Cantfort (Albany: State University of New York Press, 1989), 17.

in any other way. At least it cannot as readily be explained away as a conditioned response. The gorilla Koko, when asked whether she was a person or an animal, signed, "Fine animal gorilla."[6] This highly pertinent response is even more difficult to account for except as linguistic behavior.

EXERCISE 1

"The worst famine in history is going on right now" is basically an empirical claim. Despite the inclusion of the term "worst," which is often a value term, it clearly refers in context to measurable effects of food deprivation on human beings. However, we need to stipulate which of these effects are to be considered and how they are to be weighted in establishing the seriousness of a famine. Should we compare numbers of deaths only, or should we measure other effects of food shortage, such as rickets, scurvy, mental retardation, and increased susceptibility to nonnutritional diseases? In measuring the effects of food shortages, should we include hunger victims for whom food is nearby but who are prevented by political obstacles from having the food distributed to them? Is the "worst famine" to be determined by raw numbers of people affected in a given time unit or by a percentage of the world population?

Once these questions are decided, the sort of evidence that would confirm or refute is fairly clear. Various international organizations supply current figures on death and illness caused by hunger, and such figures from the past can be found in histories, chronicles, town records, and the like or reconstructed by correlating death rates with other evidence about crop failures such as may be gained from a study of tree rings. The fact that such evidence may be inaccurate (in the case of histories) or conjectural may make the question difficult to answer with certainty, but it does not make it any the less empirical.

Below are a number of statements to discuss in similar fashion. Which of these statements are empirical claims? In doubtful cases, stipulate definitions of key terms that in your view would make the statement an empirical claim. For all statements you eventually consider to be empirical, describe what kind of evidence would serve to confirm it and what kind would serve to refute it.

a. Some computers can actually think.
b. Human consciousness did not evolve until about 1000 B.C.
c. Women are more intuitive than men.
d. Near-death experiences prove that there is an afterlife.
e. Every human being on earth bears a blood relationship to every other human being that is never more distant than fiftieth cousin.
f. Between 1970 and 1990 the Supreme Court grew more conservative.

---

[6] Francine Patterson, "Conversations with a Gorilla," *National Geographic*, October 1978: 465.

g. Psychoanalysis is effective in alleviating some kinds of mental illness.
h. It is bad for young children to be left in day-care centers.
i. It is not illegal to disobey an unconstitutional law.
j. In Shakespeare's play, Hamlet's revenge is delayed not because of procrastination but for entirely sound, sensible reasons.
k. Although Robert Frost's poem "Stopping by Woods on a Snowy Evening" makes no explicit mention of death, its real subject is a death wish.
l. A dolphin resembles a field mouse more nearly than it resembles a shark.
m. Some people possess extrasensory perception.

EXERCISE 2

Consider this brief argument:

> *The Beatles were Communist agents. The beat of their songs was precisely timed to the teenager's pulse beat, exercising a hypnotic effect on his mind and thus rendering him susceptible to the immoral message of the lyrics.*

How many distinct factual claims appear in this argument? What evaluative claim is made? What kind of evidence would tend to confirm or refute the factual claims?

Causal Reasoning and Factual Arguments

Types of Factual Claims

Everyone is aware that some factual questions are concerned with causes and effects:

> What *caused* seven people in Miami to contract botulism Friday night?
> *Why* did technology develop in Europe so much sooner than in China?
> What *effect* will a tax reduction have on the economy?

These are all marked as causal questions by words like "cause," "effect," and "why."

What is not so often recognized is that *any question calling for a factual argument is a causal question, and any factual argument is a causal argument.* To see why this is so, let us consider various kinds of factual arguments:

Claims That Something Exists

Arguments do not concern the existence of things that can be seen directly or held up for inspection, but rather things whose existence is controversial and has to be argued for—the abominable snowman, intelligent life elsewhere in the universe, a new disease, a subatomic particle, a hidden meaning encoded within a poem. Claims that such things exist are based on *evidence,* that is, the "evident" signs of a hidden cause. We have not seen the abominable snowman directly, but we have seen footprints in the snow shaped like those of a grown man but twice as large. The issue is whether the footprints were *caused* by a huge humanlike animal or by something else. They may, for instance, be normal human footprints that grew larger as the sun melted the snow around their edges.

Besides interpreting the supposed evidence for the existence of the abominable snowman, causal reasoning also inquires about the effects the abominable snowman might be expected to produce if it existed. One might expect to find skeletal remains of such a creature, and if no such remains are found, the case for its existence is weakened.

Claims That Something Happened

Often such arguments are disguised causal claims. For example, "Zachary Taylor was poisoned" can be rephrased, "Poison was the cause of Zachary Taylor's death." In other cases, such as, "Norsemen reached the North American continent before Columbus," an argument must present evidence such as stone markers, inscriptions, chronicles, and maps. As in the case of the abominable snowman, the issues will be whether the presence and properties of these bits of evidence were caused by Norse explorers before Columbus or by some other agents.

General Claims

"Left-handed persons have a shorter life expectancy than right-handed persons." Claims of this form are sometimes not so much arguments as expository reports, especially if someone notes an unexpected correlation but has no idea how to account for it. Our example here, which was published in 1991, happened to include the causal speculation that in a world designed primarily for right-handed persons, lefties might suffer more accidents, especially in driving, where emergencies sometimes cause drivers to pull sharply downward with their dominant hand, a maneuver that steers right-handed drivers off the road but left-handed drivers into oncoming traffic.

But even if this causal explanation is omitted from the claim, the reasoning still depends on proper regard for causal influences. For instance, if the subjects on which this claim was based were all hospital patients at the time of their death, one might expect that they would include a higher proportion of accident victims than if the sample had included people who died at home in bed or in nursing homes, and it may be that, for reasons suggested above, left-handed people are slightly more vulnerable to accidents than right-handed people.

Predictions

Predictions are always based on the assumption that a causal mechanism that has operated in the past or is operating in the present will operate in the future as well. Some factual claims predict what will happen if nothing is done (e.g., that global warming will take place if destruction of the rain forests is not stopped); others (and this includes all policy proposals) predict that if a certain action is taken, certain results will appear.

Interpretive Claims

Any claim that a law, a document, a poem, a painting, an action, a particular production or performance of an artistic work, or the like *means* something argues either from a *cause* (the intention of the author, painter, director, or other agent) or from an *effect* (the way the perceiver has reacted to it). Interpretation may sometimes dwell on meanings that an author supposedly embedded in the work deliberately, as when commentators try to reconstruct Milton's doctrine of free will from *Paradise Lost,* but at other times they may point out aspects of the work that betray a subconscious meaning or one that the author might wish to disavow (e.g., Milton's secret admiration for Satan or antifeminist tendencies.) In any case, elements of the work itself are taken as evidence of beliefs, values, attitudes, or prejudices thought to underlie the work.

Causes, Conditions, and Factors

Invariably a number of conditions must be simultaneously present for a given effect to take place. Suppose that you see a light go on at the other end of a long living room, and you ask your companion, "What made the light go on?" The answer might point to any one of a number of events and conditions that all contribute to the answer:

- "It's operated by a motion sensor whenever anyone enters the room." (This would be an appropriate response if your question were prompted by your surprise at seeing a light go on without visible human agency.)
- "When the switch was closed, it created an electrical circuit that included the filament of the bulb." (Appropriate in response to a child who doesn't know how lamps produce light.)
- "We have a gasoline generator." (Appropriate if the question is prompted by surprise that the lamp should work during a power blackout.)

In terms of empirical reasoning, all of these answers are equally correct in assigning a cause to the illumination of the bulb. The light would indeed not have gone on without the copresence of all the indicated factors—a human or mechanical agent to turn it on, a switch to allow alterations from off to on, and a source of power. In practical terms, we usually call those aspects of the situation that we take for granted *conditions* and reserve the term *cause* for those aspects of the situation that we bring about by deliberate action, that depart from a norm, or that we can control, but there is no logical basis for this distinction.

Often, in fact, people are blocked from creative solutions to problems because, by focusing on a single cause, they fail to see that other conditions might be manipulable. Consider the following case:

> SUPERVISOR: You can't go on vacation in July, because Fred's taking his vacation then, and one of you has to be here when we assemble the widget.
>
> EMPLOYEE: We can assemble the widget in June.

In this case, the supervisor saw the presence of at least one of two key employees as a necessary cause of the assembly of the widget but failed to see the timing of this assembly as a manipulable condition.

Sometimes an effect depends on a variety of causal conditions. In this case we are likely to speak of *causal factors* rather than a single "cause." Even though a number of conditions are required for an electric light to operate, a failure of the light is almost always due to the failure of one component, such as filament, switch, fuse, or power source, and so we don't usually speak of factors. But how an eight-year-old scores on an I.Q. test appears to be influenced both by genetic factors and by such factors as his mother's prenatal care, his diet, his early exposure to sensory stimuli, and his early education. To say that diet is a factor means that by intervening to give young children nourishing food, we can improve their performance on certain kinds of tasks. To say that genetics is a factor (that at present we cannot manipulate) is to say that at least part of the child's test performance is beyond our present power to control.

Statistical methods can identify causal factors which, though genuine, actually account for a miniscule portion of the total pattern of causation that brings about a given event. A proponent of nuclear energy once claimed that "The burning of coal was a factor in 8000 deaths in New York City last year." When pressed to elucidate, it turned out that he was including all cases of death from respiratory failure, even when the patients were over ninety-five years old, on the grounds that the burning of coal in New York City was bound to hasten the death, if only by minutes, of anyone with a respiratory ailment.

Errors can intrude into causal reasoning if, in considering a change in one of the causal factors, we forget the role of surrounding conditions. Suppose a state that relies on a 4 percent sales tax for most of its revenue faces a deficit one year and discovers that for the next year it must raise exactly twice as much revenue. Some legislator is bound to propose what superficially seems an obvious solution: raise the sales tax to 8 percent. But suppose the conditions include the facts that the state in question is very small and is surrounded by four other states with 6 percent sales taxes. Under these conditions the proposed change might well fall short for three reasons:

> Citizens may be deterred by the higher tax from buying items such as cars and refrigerators that they would have bought at the lower rate.

Citizens may now go to neighboring states to make their more expensive purchases.

Consumers who had previously come in from other states to take advantage of the 4 percent sales tax will now shift their business to their home states.

This principle—that predictions of the effects of any proposed change must be made in the light of surrounding conditions—is a crucial one that must be considered in any policy proposal.

Causal reasoning is also vulnerable to what is known as the *post hoc, ergo propter hoc* fallacy. This Latin term means, "after this, therefore because of this." It refers to cases in which, because Y occurs after X, it is assumed to have occurred because of X. For example, malaria was at one time thought to have been caused by "bad air" (hence the name of the disease). When people in countries plagued by malaria walk in damp areas at night, they are very likely to contract malaria—but only because such conditions favor propagation of the mosquito that carries the disease.

Whether a writer has committed the *post hoc* fallacy often becomes an issue in discussion of social questions. For instance, it is sometimes argued that men convicted of rape and other sexual crimes have been avid readers of pornography. Can we safely conclude that reading pornography has led to their sexual deviency? Not necessarily; it may be that they suffer from psychological abnormalities that cause both their fondness for pornography and their criminal behavior. Sometimes opponents of censorship even advance evidence that pornography reduces the rate of sexual crime by offering an outlet to men with antisocial sexual tendencies.

Forming Hypotheses

Let us consider a classic case of causal investigation, one that includes the crucial stages of observing evidence, forming a hypothesis, making a prediction based on the hypothesis, and testing the hypothesis. We shall focus on *hypothesis formation* and on the concept of *evidence*.

Sherlock Holmes investigates a case in which a thirty-year-old woman undergoes some terrible fright in the room where she sleeps alone, unlocks the door of the room, staggers out into the corridor, shrieks, "It was the speckled band!" and dies in convulsions. The victim's twin sister, who has enlisted Holmes's aid, is being forced by building repairs to move out of her room into the room where her sister died, and she suspects that she is being set up for a similar fate. She offers Holmes the following additional facts:

- The victim's shutters were barred and the door locked when she went to bed.
- The deceased mother of the twins had left her money in their stepfather's control, but with the stipulation that each daughter should receive a substantial portion of it at the time of her marriage.

- The victim's hair was prematurely gray.
- She was wearing her nightdress.
- When she staggered out of her room, she held a burnt match in one hand and a matchbox in the other.
- This stepfather was a doctor and had spent years in India.
- He kept a baboon and cheetah as pets.
- A band of gypsies who wore spotted handkerchiefs on their heads were camped nearby.
- At the time of her death, the victim was to have been married within two weeks.
- The coroner found no marks of violence on the victim's body and no residue of poison (though forensic techniques of the day could not identify all poisons).
- At the time of the victim's death, her sister heard a low whistle and a metallic clank.

Holmes's associate, Watson, says in this story that he admires "the rapid deductions, as swift as intuitions, and yet always founded on a rational basis," with which Holmes solved his cases. It is true that Holmes employs deductions as a *part* of his rational process. For instance, from the facts above Holmes deduced that the stepfather would have had a motive to murder the victim:

A substantial portion of the money in the stepfather's control was to have been transferred to the daughter at the time of her marriage.

If she had lived, she was to have been married in two weeks.

Therefore, if she had lived, a substantial portion of money in the stepfather's control was to have been transferred to the daughter in two weeks.

But surely it is not this sort of routine reasoning that so impressed Watson and has made Sherlock Holmes a stock example of brilliant detection.

Nor is Holmes's principal method induction, which is only the logic whereby, as Charles Sanders Peirce says, "we generalize from a number of cases of which something is true, and infer that the same thing is true of the whole class." To be sure, Holmes's vast fund of knowledge owes a great deal to inductive methods. For instance, when his client first arrives, he amazes her by telling her in detail what vehicles she used to get to his chambers: "There is no mystery, my dear madam," he says, "The left arm of your jacket is spattered with mud in no less than seven places. The marks are perfectly fresh. There is no vehicle save a dog-cart which throws up mud in that way, and then only when you sit on the left-hand side of the driver." The overall train of reasoning here is not inductive, but one portion of it is: The premise that "there is no vehicle save a dog-cart" which throws up mud on passengers in the manner shown on the client's sleeve is founded on repeated observations of dog-carts and other vehicles. Holmes gains inductive knowledge very often when he is doing his homework, e.g., learning that a certain poison always has a certain kind of effect. But inductive logic is not what amazes Watson any more than deductive logic was. It provides some premises that help him solve his cases, but it can never provide the conclusions themselves.

Rather, Holmes's principal method is *abduction* or the method of *hypothesis*. We form a hypothesis when confronted with some curious fact or combination of facts. The hypothesis is the tentative supposition of a fact which, if true, would make these curious facts no longer surprising or puzzling or anomalous. In other words, it would *explain* the facts.

Indeed, Holmes's dramatic observation that his client had travelled by dog-cart is abductive. Faced with the "curious fact" of mud on her sleeve, he hypothesizes a cause by combining premises from his store of information:

> The marks were fresh and must have been made after she began her journey.
> She probably used some vehicle to get to the London train.
> A dog-cart splashes the sleeve in the way her sleeve is splashed.
> No other vehicle splashes a sleeve that way.

Holmes's conclusion is a guess, though an astute and, as it turns out, accurate one; but it is a guess nonetheless, and he might have been wrong. Certainly his conclusion is not a deduction. The conclusion of a deductive argument is strictly controlled by the premises and in effect is simply a reorganization of the facts contained in them. Holmes's hypothesis goes beyond the premises listed above. And while Holmes's reasoning about the mud stains uses information gained through induction to generate two of the four premises above, his conclusion is much more than a generalization from observed samples.

Holmes's method of solving the mystery of the sister's death is also abductive. The principal curious fact to be explained is the death of the sister, but there was no direct evidence of the cause, since the coroner found no indication of poisoning or other injury. Does the list of facts contained in the client's account include evidence, then? In a sense, no. The list contains only facts, and they can become evidence only for or against a hypothesis. They must be facts that might be effects of the causal train that also eventuated in the sister's death. Therefore some of the facts on the list are unlikely to be evidence (for instance, it is entirely normal that the sister should have been wearing a nightdress). However, the list also includes some "curious facts" whose explanation might also explain the death of the sister.

One curious fact in the list above is that the victim in her dying words said, "It was the speckled band!" Her sister hypothesizes that these words refer to the band of gypsies, and that the sister called the band "speckled" because of the distinctive spotted handkerchiefs they wore on their heads. Prior to visiting the scene, Holmes extends this hypothesis: He tentatively suggests that the dying words did refer to the gypsies, who did something that frightened the victim; that the stepfather, who had an interest in preventing the victim's marriage, signaled to the gypsies by a whistle; and that the metallic clang was caused by the metal bars on the shutters falling into place as the gypsies left. This hypothesis has the merit of *accounting for,* or removing the mystery from, several items on our list of facts, but it is deficient in that it does not explain the central curious fact, namely how the victim died. This is not to say that it is necessarily wrong, only that it is incomplete.

One thing that Holmes's hypothesis would predict is that the shutters, when closed for the night, would be able to be opened from the outside by the gypsies. However, when Holmes visits the scene to test his prediction, he discovers that when the shutters are secured by the metal bars, they cannot be opened from the outside. "Hum," he says, "my theory certainly presents some difficulties."

He now must construct a new hypothesis, but to do so he must collect further evidence, that is, more anomalous facts that might be the effects of the hypothetical cause of the sister's death. A visit to the scene of the death reveals the following:

- A saucer of milk was on the metal safe in the stepfather's room.
- A small whip formed into a loop at the end hung from his bed.
- His room was connected with the victim's by a small ventilator.
- The chimney was impassible to a human being, and the ventilator "was so small that a rat could hardly pass through."
- A bell rope was attached to a hook beside the ventilator, but it was not connected to any bell system.
- The bed was clamped to the floor beneath the bell rope.

Again, there is no way of knowing by inspection which if any of these facts may be evidence. On the basis of these further facts, Holmes is able to deduce that since the door and shutters were locked and all other potential entry points impassible, no person other than the victim could have been in her room on the night of her death.

From these additional facts Holmes is able to construct a new hypothesis. If he is right, the stepfather will soon make an attempt on the life of Holmes's client by the same means he used against her sister. The repairs being made to her own room are a pretext to force her to sleep in the room where her sister died. Holmes can test whether his hypothesis is right by seeing whether the attack that it predicts takes place.

EXERCISE

From the facts about the case listed above, what hypotheses can you suggest that would explain the victim's death? If you want to know the hypothesis that

Holmes actually constructs and proves to be true, read "The Speckled Band" by Arthur Conan Doyle.

Testing Hypotheses

The natural and social sciences are the fields par excellence for the systematic study of empirical questions. Scientists call their procedure the *hypothetico-deductive method* because it involves first constructing a *hypothesis* (or tentative answer) to the question, *deducing* the consequences that ought to be observable if the hypothesis is true, then conducting an experiment to *observe* whether the predicted consequences are present.

We employ the hypothetico-deductive method frequently in everyday life. For instance, if your kitchen light fails to go on when you flick the switch, you might first glance quickly at a clock on the same circuit to see if it is stopped as well. Why would you do this? Because, perhaps unconsciously, you have run quickly through the steps of scientific reasoning by

1 Noticing an anomaly—that is, a phenomenon that requires explanation (the light doesn't work)
2 Creating a hypothesis—the statement of conditions which, if true, would explain the anomaly (the fuse is blown)
3 Deducing what observable evidence would be present if the hypothesis were true (the clock wouldn't work either)
4 Observing whether the predicted fact were true

If your inspection reveals that the clock is running, then you have disproved your hypothesis. The steps of your reasoning and observations correspond with the parts of a *hypothetical syllogism* (for a discussion of hypothetical syllogisms, see Appendix, pp. 495–520):

> If the fuse is blown (hypothesis), then the clock will be stopped
> (deduced observable fact).
> The clock is not stopped (observed fact).
> _____
> The fuse is not blown (conclusion).

This is an example of deductive reasoning: If the premises are true, the form of the reasoning guarantees that the conclusion will be true as well. (Obviously, if the clock is battery operated or on a different circuit from the light, the first premise will be false and the truth of the conclusion is not guaranteed.)

Suppose, however, that the result of your observation is different and the clock is stopped. Now your hypothetical syllogism will look like this:

> If the fuse is blown, the clock will be stopped.
> The clock is stopped.
> _____
> Therefore the fuse is blown???

Here the conclusion *may* be right, but even if the premises are true, the reasoning does not guarantee that the conclusion will be true as well. Although the clock is on the same circuit as the light, it may be that there has been a general power failure in the neighborhood or that a wire has broken within the circuit while the fuse is perfectly intact. As of now, however, the conclusion has the status of a live hypothesis rather than a proven fact.

This example illustrates a crucial point about empirical arguments: The fact that the evidence is consistent with a hypothesis does not mean that the hypothesis is necessarily true. Many philosophers of science, following the lead of Karl Popper, maintain that the main business of science is to disprove its hypotheses, and that hypotheses that withstand this attempt are not thereby certain knowledge, but simply the science of the day, which must always be considered theoretically subject to disproof.

For scientists, an "experiment" sometimes means only looking in the right place or the right time. When the archaeologist Heinrich Schliemann hypothesized that the hill of Hissarlik in Asia Minor was the site of ancient Troy, he deduced that since the ruins of abandoned cities become buried in time, he should, if his hypothesis about the location of Troy were true, encounter the remains of buildings if he dug on the site. He dug, found several strata of buildings, and, when he reached the bottom stratum, announced that he had discovered the ruins of Troy.

Interestingly, Schliemann's excavations also illustrate two points made above. First, before seeking positive evidence consistent with his own hypothesis, he saw fit to disprove the principal alternative hypothesis of his day—that the site of Homeric Troy was a different hill near Hissarlik. By digging with a shovel, Schliemann demonstrated that at the alternative site only bedrock underlay the soil. Second, though the evidence Schliemann unearthed at Hissarlik supported his hypothesis, he was probably wrong about the particular ruins that he identified as Homeric Troy. He assumed that the deepest buildings he encountered were the ruins of Priam's city. In fact, these were probably older buildings, and Schliemann had probably passed through the ruins he was seeking at an earlier stage of his excavations.[7]

Sometimes scientists cannot test a hypothesis simply by examining existing evidence as Schliemann did, but instead have to create controlled conditions for their observations. For instance, consider the hypothesis that women are prejudiced against women. To confirm this hypothesis, we would have to observe evidence of two distinct propositions:

   1 That women hold men in higher regard than they hold other women
   2 That their preference is based on prejudice rather than on other factors

---

[7] William M. Calder, III, and David A. Traill, *Myth, Scandal, and History* (Detroit: Wayne State University Press, 1986), 102–03. The authors note that Schliemann's dig at the alternate site was "intended to furnish a negative proof."

It is difficult to think of a situation in which evidence of this sort could be found without experimental manipulation of the conditions. We might try to conduct such a study by selecting a location in which women had equal access to both male and female physicians. If they showed a preference for male practitioners, we might be led to believe that prejudice was a factor, and yet we could hardly be sure. It might be that the male doctors simply had the most convenient offices. An antifeminist witness to the study might even say, "That doesn't show that women are prejudiced against women; men make better doctors than women, and the patients are only making an informed, rational choice." Indeed, how could we ever find a situation in which two absolutely identical performances or products, one by a male and one by a female, could be presented to women to see which they would prefer?

What follows is a report on a classic experiment where ingeniously controlled conditions produce just this situation, one in which all variables apart from the sex of the person being judged are canceled:

PHILIP GOLDBERG

Are Women Prejudiced Against Women?

1   "Woman," advised Aristotle, "may be said to be an inferior man."

2   Because he was a man, Aristotle was probably biased. But what do women themselves think? Do they, consciously or unconsciously, consider their own sex inferior? And if so, does this belief prejudice them against other women — that is, make them view women, simply because they *are* women, as less competent than men?

3   According to a study conducted by myself and my associates, the answer to both questions is Yes. Women *do* consider their own sex inferior. And even when the facts give no support to this belief, they will persist in downgrading the competence — in particular, the intellectual and professional competence — of their fellow females.

4   Over the years, psychologists and psychiatrists have shown that both sexes consistently value men more highly than women. Characteristics considered male are usually praised; those considered female are usually criticized. In 1957 A. C. Sheriffs and J. P. McKee noted that "women are regarded as guilty of snobbery and irrational and unpleasant emotionality." Consistent with this report, E. G. French and G. S. Lesser found in 1964 that "women who value intellectual attainment feel they must reject the woman's role" — intellectual accomplishment apparently being considered, even among intellectual women, a masculine preserve. In addition, ardent

feminists like Simone de Beauvoir and Betty Friedan believe that men, in important ways, are superior to women.

5   Now, is this belief simply prejudice, or are the characteristics and achievements of women really inferior to those of men? In answering this question, we need to draw some careful distinctions.

Different or Inferior?

6   Most important, we need to recognize that there are two distinct dimensions to the issue of sex differences. The first question is whether sex differences exist at all, apart from the obvious physical ones. The answer to this question seems to be a unanimous Yes — men, women, and social scientists agree that, psychologically and emotionally as well as physically, women *are* different from men.

7   But is being different the same as being inferior? It is quite possible to perceive a difference accurately but to value it inaccurately. Do women automatically view their differences from men as *deficiencies?* The evidence is that they do, and that this value judgment opens the door to anti-female prejudice. For if someone (male or female) concludes that women are inferior, his perceptions of women — their personalities, behavior, abilities, and accomplishments — will tend to be colored by his low expectations of women.

8   As Gordon W. Allport has pointed out in *The Nature of Prejudice,* whatever the facts about sex differences, anti-feminism — like any other prejudice — *distorts perception and experience.* What defines anti-feminism is not so much believing that women are inferior, as allowing that belief to distort one's perceptions of women. More generally, it is not the partiality itself, but the distortion born of that partiality, that defines prejudice.

9   Thus, an anti-Semite watching a Jew may see devious or sneaky behavior. But, in a Christian, he would regard such behavior only as quiet, reserved, or perhaps even shy. Prejudice is self-sustaining: It continually distorts the "evidence" on which the prejudiced person claims to base his beliefs. Allport makes it clear that anti-feminism, like anti-Semitism or any other prejudice, consistently twists the "evidence" of experience. We see not what is there, but what we *expect* to see.

10   The purpose of our study was to investigate whether there is real prejudice by women against women — whether perception itself is distorted unfavorably. Specifically, will women evaluate a professional article with a jaundiced eye when they think it is the work of a woman, but praise the same article when they think its author is a man? Our hypotheses were:

- Even when the work is identical, women value the professional work of men more highly than that of women.

- But when the professional field happens to be one traditionally reserved for women (nursing, dietetics), this tendency will be reversed, or at least greatly diminished.

11   Some 140 college girls selected at random, were our subjects. One hundred were used for the preliminary work; 40 participated in the experiment proper.

12   To test the second hypothesis, we gave the 100 girls a list of 50 occupations and asked them to rate "the degree to which you associate the field with men or with women." We found that law and city planning were fields strongly associated with men, elementary-school teaching and dietetics were fields strongly associated with women, and two fields — linguistics and art history — were chosen as neutrals, not strongly associated with either sex.

13   Now we were ready for the main experiment. From the professional literature of each of these six fields, we took one article. The articles were edited and abridged to about 1500 words, then combined into two equal sets of booklets. The crucial manipulation had to do with the authors' names — the same article bore a male name in one set of booklets, a female name in the other set. An example: If, in set one, the first article bore the name John T. McKay, in set two the same article would appear under the name Joan T. McKay. Each booklet contained three articles by "men" and three articles by "women."

14   The girls, seated together in a large lecture hall, were told to read the articles in their booklets and given these instructions:

> *In this booklet you will find excerpts of six articles, written by six different authors in six different professional fields. At the end of each article you will find several questions.... You are not presumed to be sophisticated or knowledgeable in all the fields. We are interested in the ability of college students to make critical evaluations....*

Note that no mention at all was made of the authors' sexes. That information was contained — apparently only by coincidence — in the authors' names. The girls could not know, therefore, what we were really looking for.

15   At the end of each article were nine questions asking the girls to rate the articles for value, persuasiveness, and profundity — and to rate the authors for writing style, professional competence, professional status, and ability to sway the reader. On each item, the girls gave a rating of from 1 (highly favorable) to 5 (highly unfavorable).

16   Generally, the results were in line with our expectations — but not completely. In analyzing these results, we used three different methods: We compared the amount of anti-female bias in the different occupational fields (would men be rated as better city planners, but women as better

dieticians?); we compared the amount of bias shown on the nine questions that followed each article (would men be rated as more competent, but women as more persuasive?); and we ran an overall comparison, including both fields and rating questions.

17   Starting with the analysis of bias by occupational field, we immediately ran into a major surprise. (See box below.) That there is a general bias by women against women, and that it is strongest in traditionally masculine

---

LAW: A STRONG MASCULINE PRESERVE

These are the total scores the college girls gave to the six pairs of articles they read. The lowest possible score—9—would be the most favorable; the highest possible score—45—the most critical. While male authors received more favorable ratings in all occupational fields, the differences were statistically significant only in city planning, linguistics, and—especially—law.

	MEAN	
FIELD OF ARTICLE	MALE	FEMALE
Art History	23.35	23.10
Dietetics	22.05	23.45
Education	20.20	21.75
City Planning	23.10	27.30
Linguistics	26.95	30.70
Law	21.20	25.60

---

fields, was clearly borne out. But in other fields the situation seemed rather confused. We had expected the anti-female trend to be reversed in traditionally feminine fields. But it appears that, even here, women consider themselves inferior to men. Women seem to think that men are better at *everything*—including elementary-school teaching and dietetics!

18   Scrutiny of the nine rating questions yielded similar results. On all nine questions, regardless of the author's occupational field, the girls consistently found an article more valuable—and its author more competent—when the article bore a male name. Though the articles themselves were exactly the same, the girls felt that those written by the John T. McKays were definitely more impressive, and reflected more glory on their authors, than did the mediocre offerings of the Joan T. McKays. Perhaps because the world has accepted female authors for a long time, the girls were willing to concede that the female professionals' writing styles were not *far* inferior to those of the men. But such a concession to female competence was rare indeed.

19   Statistical analysis confirms these impressions and makes them more definite. With a total of six articles, and with nine questions after each one,

there were 54 points at which comparisons could be drawn between the male authors and the female authors. Out of these 54 comparisons, three were tied, seven favored the female authors—and the number favoring the male authors was 44!

20   Clearly, there is a tendency among women to downgrade the work of professionals of their own sex. But the hypothesis that this tendency would decrease as the "femaleness" of the professional field increased was not supported. Even in traditionally female fields, anti-feminism holds sway.

21   Since the articles supposedly written by men were exactly the same as those supposedly written by women, the perception that the men's articles were superior was obviously a distortion. For reasons of their own, the female subjects were sensitive to the sex of the author, and this apparently irrelevant information biased their judgments. Both the distortion and the sensitivity that precedes it are characteristic of prejudice. Women—at least these young college women—are prejudiced against female professionals and, regardless of the actual accomplishments of these professionals, will firmly refuse to recognize them as the equals of their male colleagues.

22   Is the intellectual double-standard really dead? Not at all—and if the college girls in this study are typical of the educated and presumably progressive segments of the population, it may not even be dying. Whatever lip service these girls pay to modern ideas of equality between men and women, their beliefs are staunchly traditional. Their real coach in the battle of the sexes is not Simone de Beauvoir or Betty Friedan. Their coach is Aristotle.

STUDY QUESTIONS

1. What is the hypothesis of this study?
2. How does the author define "prejudice"? Is it defined in such a way that the results of the experiment constitute empirical evidence that prejudice, as defined, has occurred?
3. The hypothesis includes the concept that women value the work of men more highly than that of women. How does the experiment make the mental act of valuing observable?
4. Why did the experimenters manipulate the names of the authors of the articles used in the experiments rather than simply telling the subjects whether an article had been written by a man or a woman?

5. Do the results of the study show that all forty subjects were prejudiced against women?

6. A possible counterargument to this study is as follows: One of the categories on which the fictional authors of the articles were to be judged was "professional status." The subjects of the experiment might very well have guessed that a female author's "professional status" would have been lower than a male's because the subjects knew that professions often discriminated against women, not because the subject felt that the author was undeserving of professional status. Thus the subject's answer in this category would have reflected not her prejudice against women, but her awareness of prejudice in the society around her. Conceivably the questions about "persuasiveness" and "ability to sway the audience" (what is the difference between these two?) might also have been affected by the subjects' belief that a reader's judgment would not be as readily swayed by a woman as a man because of social prejudice.

   Is this a valid objection? What aspects of the raw data would help you to decide whether the experiment truly measured prejudice?

7. The text of the article states that "Women seem to think that men are better at *everything*" than men. Do the mean scores in the box support this statement?

Goldberg's study purports to show that women are prejudiced against women, but immediately several questions arise. Does it show that all or only some women are prejudiced against other women? Even among the forty subjects who rated the articles, we learn from the study only that the mean scores in various categories of evaluation totaled higher for articles when they were attributed to men than when they were attributed to women. We do not know from the report whether the discrepancies in means were created by a general tendency of most subjects to rate the "men's" essays higher or by violent antifeminist prejudice on the part of a few subjects counterbalanced by nonprejudiced subjects or even some subjects biased in favor of women.

Presumably Goldberg intended to claim only that *in the aggregate* women are prejudiced against women, allowing for the possibility of widespread counterexamples. Yet how can we be confident that his findings support even this restricted claim about women in general? Goldberg is inferring inductively that what is true of the women in his sample is true of women generally. Obviously the likelihood that the inference is true depends on the sample's being truly representative. Suppose you see a large bag of beans and want to know what color they are. If you open the bag, scoop a handful off the top, and find that they are all white, you have some basis to infer that all the beans in the bag are white, but your inference would have a much stronger base if you plunged your arm into the bag, stirred the beans around for two hours, and then took a handful made up of beans from different parts of the bag. If at this trial you find that two-thirds of the beans are white and one-third are red, you could make a probable (but not certain) inference that the same proportions would occur in the bag as a whole.

Now, were Goldberg's subjects representative of women in general? Suppose Goldberg had asked only a single pair of subjects to evaluate the articles in his study (the putative sex of the authors being reversed in the two versions of the tests). Clearly we would have virtually no confidence in any generalization about prejudice in women from so narrow a sample. Simply increasing the number of subjects, as Goldberg did, allows for greater confidence, but still we need to feel that the sample on which the inference is based is representative of the entire class to which the conclusion is being extended. It might be argued that students at a highly ranked women's college are not a fair sample of women, but on the other hand, it is precisely college educated women whom we would have expected in 1968 to have had, among the general class of women, the greatest belief that women can attain professional excellence. Thus we might reasonably accept that insofar as his sample was not representative, it probably understated rather than overstated the magnitude of antifeminist prejudice among women in the population as a whole.

Science progresses by experiments that try to refine the findings of prior experiments. One follow-up study to Goldberg's assigned a similar article-evaluation task to women who were less well educated to see whether they would be so impressed by the accomplishments of the supposedly female authors that the margin of preference for the supposedly male authors would be diminished or eliminated. Other follow-up studies sought to find whether similar prejudice would be found in the evaluation of paintings or of résumés.

Often controlled experiments like Goldberg's are impossible: Clearly it would be unethical to raise randomly selected children in an environment of deliberately impoverished sensory and intellectual stimulation to see whether their IQs would thereby be lowered. In such cases, though, the world itself may have arranged (in effect) a controlled experiment. Questions of nature versus nurture often rely on studies of identical twins raised in different environments, for in such cases the genetic factor is held constant while environmental factors are varied.

Applications

Of course, you cannot achieve scientific precision in every factual claim you make; often you will be assigned to produce a factual argument without being given the time or resources to compile conclusive evidence for your claim.

Nevertheless, even where such limitations apply, scientific principles can help you identify whether and to what extent vaguely stated hypotheses are empirical in nature; guide you to the strongest formulation of your argument; suggest kinds of evidence to search out; make your approach to the problem more efficient; and guard you against some of the pitfalls in empirical reasoning.

Writers frequently approach an empirical claim with a tentative formulation of their thesis (although they may not think of it as tentative at the time) and a set of observations that have prompted the claim and seem to support it. For instance, they will argue that "alcoholism is a disease," giving as reasons that it tends to run in families, that it causes damage to organs such as the liver and brain, and that its victims are not responsible for its effects on their lives and the lives of others. Inexperienced writers and thinkers too often stop at this point: They feel that they have produced a passable argument if they present a thesis and three supporting reasons.

In fact, three reasons (or more) can be found in favor of virtually any hypothesis—that the world is flat, that plants can think, that there will be nuclear war within the next two years, that the world's economy is near collapse, and so forth. In a critical approach to an empirical question, it is much more worthwhile to consider what arguments might be found *against* your thesis and what responses to these counterarguments are possible.

If you were beginning with the tentatively formulated hypothesis that alcoholism is a disease and the three items of possible evidence noted above, how might you more profitably proceed towards a cogent argument? First, you should clarify in your own mind whether or to what extent your claim is empirical. It is possible that it is simply a metaphor making not a factual claim but a moral plea to treat alcoholics with greater compassion. (Compare the statement, "Poverty is a disease.")

Can your hypothesis be reduced to observables? Obviously, two concepts, "alcoholism" and "disease," need to be defined in terms of observables. How can you tell which members of any group are alcoholics and which are not? Are all habitual drunkards necessarily alcoholics? Can someone be an alcoholic who yet does not regularly get drunk? And what are the observable defining features of a disease? Clearly it must disadvantage the victim, but what else is requisite for correct application of the term "disease"? Must there be a somatic cause? Can a disease be purely psychological? In this step you are *defining terms,* but in a way that is guided by the task at hand. Too often, inexperienced writers, acting on advice to define their terms, simply go to the dictionary and copy what they find (sometimes having to choose among a number of substantially different meanings of the term). You should by no means rule out use of the dictionary, but use it wisely—that is, choose those aspects of its definitions that will enable you to demonstrate that some of your evidence is compatible with your thesis that alcoholism is a disease as defined.

One good way of clarifying what you intend to assert is to understand fully what you are trying to exclude by your thesis. "Alcoholism is a disease *as opposed to what?*" you might ask, and you might answer, "Well, as opposed to a vice." This questioning process has two benefits. First, it is likely to clarify the rhetorical situation by making you think about your audience. What beliefs and attitudes are likely to characterize those who hold the view that alcoholism is a vice (for these are the people whom you must persuade)? Second, it presents you with a rival hypothesis and thus gives you some guidance as to the kind of evidence you will have to seek, i.e., evidence that will discriminate between the two hypotheses.

The question is: Do the individuals possessing the defining observable characteristics of alcoholism also show the observable symptoms characteristic of diseases but not of vices? You had given as your first reason that alcoholism tends to run in families, but don't vices such as child abuse and laziness tend to run in families too? In other words, this "reason" does not in itself serve to discriminate between our two hypotheses. And yet, though the tendency to run in families characterizes both disease and vice, the mechanisms of transmission are quite different. Poverty runs in families because poor parents are unable to leave large inheritances to their children; because the children of poor parents are less likely to receive the educational advantages that would give them a better chance of success; and for other reasons that are culturally rather than biologically transmitted from parents to offspring. But when diseases run in families, the mechanism of transmission is often genetic. If you could find through library research that a certain genetic abnormality is found in at least some alcoholics, you would have discovered a characteristic that your audience will probably associate more readily with disease than with vice.

Your second reason, that alcoholics cannot control their drinking, may meet with several objections. Some people might accuse you of begging the question. "We know that alcoholics often *do* not control their drinking, but that does not prove that they *cannot* control their drinking. To assert without further proof that they cannot control it is not so much to give a reason for your disease theory of alcoholism as to make the same point in different words." Others might agree that alcoholics cannot control their drinking but point out there there is much compulsive behavior, such as gambling or playing video games, that we do not normally think of as a disease.

But perhaps there is something about the compulsiveness of alcoholism that sets it apart from the compulsiveness of gambling or video games, allying alcoholism with disease, the others with vice. For instance, if there were some physical counterpart of alcoholism—a difference in blood analysis for alcoholics, or a demonstrably different way of metabolising alcohol, we would be strengthening that notion of a medical cause for excessive drinking as opposed to a simple lack of will power, and for most people this distinction is probably the crucial factor that distinguishes a disease from a vice. (Of course, you must beware the *post hoc, ergo propter hoc* fallacy: Consider the possibility that these differences *resulted* from years of drinking rather than *causing* them.)

Consider again your third original reason for considering alcoholism a disease: that it causes organic damage. How would proponents of the vice theory of alcoholism respond to this argument? Surely, they would agree that extremely high consumption of alcohol damages the body, but they would deny that that in itself makes alcoholism a disease. Excessive smoking causes tissue damage, but no one argues that smoking is a disease (though they might agree that it is an addiction). As this counterargument shows, in claiming that "alcoholism is a disease because it causes tissue damage," you were making the hidden assumption that "anything that causes tissue damage is a disease," and this is patently false.

But by this time you have found evidence that some alcoholics have genetic and other physiological differences from people who can consume alcohol without ill effects. The physiological differences, particularly if you can show that they predated heavy drinking in subjects who later became alcoholics, suggest a possible causal mechanism to support the alcoholic's claim that he is subject to compulsions to drink that other people do not suffer, and the genetic correlates suggest that this physiological condition is inborn and not the result of self-indulgence. If these features seem to be true for only some alcoholics, you might at this point have to refine your hypothesis in light of the evidence. Some researchers identify several types of alcoholics—type A, type B, etc. You might find that you can substantiate your argument only for one type.

3 Value

Value Claims and the Value System

Value claims are arguments about matters of judgment. While one might loosely speak of "evaluating" the accuracy of a stopwatch or a student's performance on a multiple choice test, a report on such an evaluation would really be only a factual statement because the results of the test would be precisely measurable. In some cases, though, these empirical measures are not enough for our purposes. If we want to choose the right automobile, we will take into account such measurable qualities as its fuel economy, speed of acceleration, freedom from mechanical breakdowns, and carrying capacity; yet we still have to make a value judgment about which of these qualities will serve us best. At this point our value judgment about the car cannot possibly be made on empirical grounds alone.

The choice of a car is largely a *utilitarian* judgment. We are asking in effect what qualities we should seek to serve the various purposes of our lives. The other two major realms of value judgments are the *aesthetic*, which concerns questions of beauty, and the *ethical*, which concerns questions of right and wrong. It is common for specific value decisions to involve a combination of these three areas, and indeed even the choice of a car involves utilitarian concerns (e.g., carrying capacity), aesthetic concerns (color, lines, trim), and ethical concerns (whether it is American made, whether it is so expensive as to be a selfish purchase). The criteria in these three realms—criteria such as right and wrong, good and bad, beautiful and ugly, rewarding and unrewarding—generally do not lend themselves to precise measurement and cannot be empirically determined.

Sometimes it is difficult to determine whether a claim is factual or evaluative. The claim that "the SAT is biased against women" includes two factual claims: that women receive, on the average, lower scores than men on the test and that lower scores are disadvantageous. But defenders of the SAT deny that these facts alone justify a use of the term "biased," which also implies the value claim that the test is somehow at fault for attributing a lower average scholastic aptitude to women than to men. The Educational Testing Service (ETS) argues that women on the whole take fewer math and science courses than men in high school and that the discrepancy in their SAT math scores is simply a fair, *un*biased reflection of that difference in preparation and practice. By analogy, if a firm were hiring workers to load hundred-pound sacks of flour onto a truck and required applicants for the job to lift several such sacks in succession, this screening device would very probably select more men for the job than women; but we would not call the test "biased."

In testimony at a congressional hearing on sex bias in testing (see reading selection on page 468) Phyllis Rosser provides an interesting argument supporting the ethical charge of bias, but the evidence she offers is wholly factual. She points out that according to the ETS's own statistics, women who, on the average, had scored lower than men on the SAT received, on the average, higher grades in their first year of college. The SAT, she reasons, is supposedly a test of "scholastic aptitude," that is, of students' fitness for studying in school. It professes to predict grades in the first year of college. The SAT, unlike our hypothetical test of aptitude for loading flour sacks, is an indirect measure of this fitness. During it, students do not actually carry out any studies, and many of the tasks they perform are rather artificial (such as completing analogies) and are all within the restrictive confines of the multiple choice format, though surely one mark of aptitude for scholarship is the ability to discover and formulate interesting questions, not just to answer those posed by others. Performance in college classes, on the other hand, is a direct measure of scholastic aptitude. Anyone who has succeeded in a college class is self-evidently fit to take it, and if women receive higher grades than men in their first year of college, they have demonstrated greater aptitude for scholastic study. The element of unfairness in the test, then, according to Rosser, lies in its empirically verifiable underestimation of women's scholastic aptitude. (In another selection, on page 457, a representative of the Educational Testing Service, Carol Anne Dwyer, responds to some of Rosser's arguments.) Many questions about values are like this one. Once all the relevant facts are presented convincingly, the value judgment will be automatic. When this is the case, a strong presentation of the relevant facts is the best way to argue the claim.

But in other cases, even when people agree entirely on the facts, they may be left with a difference of opinion rooted in different values. The long debate about whether or under what circumstances abortion is justified is a case in point. An American president once suggested that the abortion issue could be settled if doctors decided when human life begins. In fact, though, this is not a factual question because no one can say what kind of evidence would be decisive. We already know all the biological evidence (the only kind doctors would be specifically qualified to discover) that is likely to be relevant. "Prochoice" and "prolife" advocates generally agree about when cell division begins, when various organs begin to differentiate themselves, when the heart begins to beat, when brain waves are first registered, etc. They also agree that life is present from the moment of conception and even before conception in the form of the two component gametes. The question is whether we should value biological life at this level, including its potential to develop into a mature human being, enough to extend to it the protections that we extend to a newborn infant. Furthermore, how are the interests of the embryo (if it has interests) to be weighed against the interests of the pregnant woman seeking an abortion? These are value questions.

While some factual claims are controversial, at least there is general agreement about the way of resolving them, or at least about the kind of evidence that would prove the point conclusively to the satisfaction of all rational persons. There is no such generally accepted method for resolving value differences. Yet there are rational and irrational ways of approaching them. Just as the ultimate goal of factual inquiry is to discover a conclusion that conforms to some state of things in nature, the goal of evaluative inquiry is to discover a conclusion that fits consistently into a larger value system.

The Structure of the Value System

Our value system is in part made up of our *principles*. Some of these are extremely general: "All human beings deserve equal opportunity," "It is wrong to cause pain without some pressing cause," "Other things being equal, I should make those choices in life that are likely to bring me the greatest happiness in the long run." Other principles, sometimes called *middle principles*, are intermediate between general principles and specific cases. For instance, the general principle that you should maximize your own happiness as long as you are not hurting others is too broad to guide you in most practical situations. Suppose that you oversleep one day and are late in getting to work. Should you tell the boss the true reason for your lateness or invent a story that your car wouldn't start? You might reason that while the lie would cause you less embarrassment in the short run, in the long run you would be happier if you could regard yourself as an honest person and incidentally ensure your freedom from the danger of being caught in a lie. By adopting this principle, you would also avoid the stress of having to decide on every possible occasion whether or not to tell a self-serving lie. In this case honesty for you would be a middle principle (though for others honesty may well be a general principle; they may regard honesty as a moral imperative regardless of its instrumental value in enhancing their peace of mind.)

Besides general and middle principles, our ethical equipment includes *specific judgments* about people, actions, and things. We may disparage a film as disjointed, feel repugnance toward an acquaintance who has been having an affair with a client, decide against a career change because the added money will not be worth the added stress. All of these responses initially may seem to us not so much judgments, with the deliberate rational balancings that this term implies, as gut reactions. It would be natural to assume that in making specific judgments we deduce them from our principles, but in fact we probably test our principles equally often by our specific judgments.

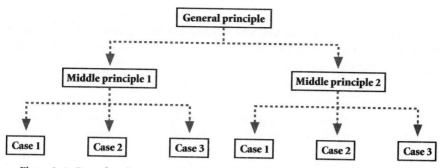

Figure 3–1. Part of a value system, showing the hierarchy from the general to the specific.

We might represent part of a value system as a hierarchy from the general to the specific, as seen in Figure 3–1. This is a part of the system only; the whole might better be represented as a spider's web with specific value judgments ranged around the periphery, principles of increasing generality approaching the center, segments shaped like pie slices devoted to such value areas as the good, the beautiful, and the pleasurable, and ultimate values in the center. A value system also resembles a spider web in that, if any part is touched, the whole trembles. If we are made to realize with a new vividness the cruelty of a specific act of racial discrimination, we may alter our more general principles concerning not only our own behavior, but governmental regulation of a landlord's right to discriminate or perhaps even books and movies that use racial stereotyping.

Whose Value System?

The goal of an evaluative argument, we have said, is to show that a specific evaluative conclusion fits most coherently into a total value system, but we have not specified whose value system we mean. Perhaps the greatest mistake inexperienced writers make is to evaluate their subject solely according to their own principles rather than those of their audience as well. For example, if you are a sales representative responding to an unfavorable job evaluation stating that you have not been "productive" enough, you will not be making an effective response if you talk solely in terms of how many hours you have put in, how much work you carried home on the weekends, or how many phone calls you placed. These may be uppermost in your mind about your performance, and to have them overlooked in an evaluation may deeply offend your sense of fairness; but ultimately the sales manager doesn't care about effort, only results.

The most effective aspect of an evaluative argument may well be facts that your audience has not previously known. If the manager in the above example had been working from outdated or incomplete figures, then simply correcting the record may be all that you have to do. Sometimes, too, disagreements about values may be avoided, at least partially, by clarification of semantic differences. (If the charge that you have not been "productive" enough is based on low sales, can you point to other activities such as developing a product or building good will that might expand the manager's definition of "productiveness"?) In many cases, however, even after factual and semantic questions have been disposed of, there will be a residue of disagreement that can be addressed only by a thoughtful appeal to several levels of your audience's value system.

Fortunately, there is little likelihood that your value system and your audience's will be completely at odds. Generally you will be addressing people who disagree with you in some particulars but who agree that fairness, justice, happiness, and freedom are desirable for all. *Your task is to demonstrate that the claim you are making is more consistent than rival claims with that part of the value system you and your audience share.* A rhetorician once said, "If you want someone to come over to your side of a large room, don't call across to him; go over to his side and lead him by the hand." In other words, in an argument, start with your reader's values and show how they lead to your conclusion.

Often you can strengthen your own arguments by referring to the values of your audience as they themselves have formulated them. For example, organizations often adopt mission statements, codes of ethics, guidelines, statements of purpose, or the like that tend to be forgotten when it is in the organization's interest to forget them. A business may profess its concern for its employees' health and safety but refuse to warn them of suspicious shadows in their lung x-rays through fear that silicon dust or asbestos fibers in the workplace have caused illnesses that might later result in workmen's compensation claims or in lawsuits against the company. Your attempts to persuade such a business to provide proper equipment may be strengthened if you can show that the particular measures you propose are consistent with its professed underlying values.

Justice and Expediency

The point where your value system is most likely to conflict with that of your readers is where their self-interest is at stake. Unfortunately, an argument that urges any readers to undertake some action in the interests of abstract justice or fairness is unlikely to convince if it requires them to surrender any of their own money, rights, or authority. The readings later in this text on the subjects of animal rights and business ethics again and again confront the clash of ethical claims with self-interest. In the area of animal rights, the abstract argument that animals should not be made to suffer in scientific experiments (or, in a milder version, should not be made to suffer "unnecessarily") meets considerable resistance from experimenters whose grant money and careers would be threatened if they were to acknowledge the force of the arguments (though this is not to say that all experimenters protest from self-interested motives). Likewise, corporate officers whose firms' profits are enhanced by the manufacture of a legal but potentially dangerous product may resist arguments that they should stop production altogether or warn consumers more strenuously of the product's hazards. Often those whose self-interest may be threatened by your argument will be ingenious in presenting ethical issues consistent with the position favorable to their self-interest.

Animal researchers point out the advantages of their research not only to human beings but to veterinary medicine, and corporate officers may appeal to their ethical obligations to stockholders in their companies who are mainly or solely interested in profits. The officers may protest that it would be unethical for them to allow their "private morality" to diminish in any way the profits that they are handsomely paid to produce.

There are two lessons for you as a writer in this distinction between the just and the expedient. First, even though you feel that the moral arguments ought to be enough to persuade your reader, make the most of any possible arguments that your position is also consistent with your reader's self-interest. If you write to a corporation about the dangers of one of its profitable products, you should also point out any likelihood of product liability suits or boycotts by angry consumers. Second, be aware that your readers are likely to have their own arsenals of ethical counterarguments which you should attempt to answer if you find them merely self-serving.

On highly controversial questions—ones that bring about deep divisions in society, such as affirmative action, taxation, or abortion—conclusive arguments are likely to be unattainable because any proposed solution will violate some precept buried deep in the collective value system. Any abortion will seem to many people a violation of the fetus' right to life; to proscribe abortions will seem to many others a violation of the pregnant woman's right to control her own body. Often wrenching questions of value are settled not by argument but by circumstance or force. Nevertheless, written analysis of even these intractable issues may well serve the writer in arriving at a consistent position, in defining the issues on which two or more people disagree, or in determining the point at which they must agree to disagree.

Categorizing and Defining in Values Arguments

In discussing categorization and definition in factual claims, we noted that the definitional criteria of empirical classes must be observable. In a values claim, however, there is always at least one *value-laden term*, that is, a term whose meaning cannot be fully specified without including at least one criterion based on a value judgment rather than observation. This is not to say that observable evidence is totally irrelevant, only that it is not sufficient.

For instance, in the spring of 1991 the governor of Connecticut, Lowell Weicker, proposed that the state, which had always relied on a sales tax as its principal source of revenue, now needed an income tax to overcome a deficit from the prior year without hurting businesses. A majority in the legislature opposed this suggestion and passed three successive budgets based on an extended sales tax, all of which the governor vetoed. In letters to the editor and on talk shows throughout the summer, it was clear that state residents were polarized into two factions that polls suggested were about equal in numbers. Those who supported the governor described him as courageous, firm, and decisive, willing to face economic realities, behave responsibly, and exercise true leadership; those who opposed his view described him as dogmatic, arrogant, and inflexible, oblivious to the economic hardships faced by recession-stricken taxpayers, and unresponsive to the wishes of the electorate.

Let us consider one opposing pair from this array: Was the governor "decisive" or "inflexible"? This is a problem of categorization. Both terms have some empirical content; that is, their definitions would include the observable criteria of "tending to reach decisions quickly and then to stick to them," but this definition does not fully express the meaning of either "decisive" or "inflexible" because it does not reflect their opposite connotations. To capture this evaluative dimension in the definition, we would have to say that the governor was "appropriately" quick and tenacious in his decisions (to define "decisive") or "excessively" so (to define "inflexible"). Both "appropriately" and "excessively" are pure value terms.

Notice that some terms that are not value-laden may carry virtually unanimous value judgments with them. If you are told that the liquid you are about to drink is "lethal," you will no doubt react negatively to it, but this value judgment is a *consequence* of the term's meaning in context, not an intrinsic part of it. The word has a totally empirical meaning, "causing death," and the statement may be verified or refuted by reference to empirical tests.

Value arguments generally take the form "X is Y" where Y is a value-laden term. Under what circumstances would you have to define the term, and how would you do it?

Let's say you wanted to nominate a teacher for a teaching award. Your task, then, is to argue that "Ms. Lucas is a good teacher." Let's also imagine a context: At your college, this award has usually gone to dynamic lecturers who keep students on the edge of their seats with trenchant analyses, fascinating information, and flashes of wit. These teachers usually score very high on teacher evaluations, which ask students to rate them on such criteria as "knowledge of subject," "classroom manner," and "organization." If Ms. Lucas fits that description, you may not have to define your value term at all. Your task is essentially to give examples of her brilliance in analysis, informativeness, and wit. It will be evident that by meeting these criteria she meets the prevailing definition of "good teacher."

But suppose you had a teacher of quite opposite style whom you wanted to nominate for the same award, a teacher who chose to teach small discussion classes rather than large lectures, who asked challenging questions rather than imparting information, who tended to let student interests and concerns guide the direction of each class, and who constructed demanding, illuminating assignments for her students on the theory that they learn most by exploring for themselves rather than passively accepting the results of a teacher's explorations. This teacher may not score high on the teacher evaluation because the form favors a teaching style that makes more of a display of the teacher's personal manner, knowledge of the field, and organization. Now your task in writing the recommendation would be in part to redefine for the awards committee what "good teacher" means, and in part to show that your candidate meets these new criteria.

We said earlier that a value term must be defined by reference to the value system of the audience you are addressing, in this case, the awards committee. Wouldn't you be disregarding this advice if you recommended a teacher for the award on the basis of values that distinctly contrast with those of the committee? Not really. Your purpose in defining the term "good teacher" is to show that your proposed redefinition is more consistent with the committee's own deepest values than the conventional definition that has seemed to dominate their value judgments in the past.

The awards committee has shown year after year that within their value system a good teacher is like a skillful entertainer. But you may suspect that the committee, if pressed, would be forced to concede that teaching may be said to have succeeded best when it has best prepared students to exercise the skills and apply the knowledge that the course is intended to impart. The committee might also be brought to agree that a teaching style that forces the student to practice those skills is most likely to succeed in this way. If so, you have shown the committee that there is an inconsistency in their value system. Their conventional image of a good teacher has resembled that of the entertainer who performs for a largely passive audience, while their image of successful teaching implies instead the model of a coach who forces the athletes in his or her charge to do most of the work but who creates the conditions under which that work will most efficiently result in skills.

Unlike the value-laden terms we have been considering—"decisive," "inflexible," "good teacher"—some words have value connotations that are not instantly obvious. Consider the following situation where a definition seems called for: A college English department that has had no teaching vacancies for many years finally succeeds in hiring a new assistant professor directly out of graduate school. She is assigned to teach "American Literature of the Twentieth Century," but her syllabus turns out to include a comic book, two films, a Harlequin romance, a political manifesto, and several rock lyrics. Some of the older members of the department protest, "That's not literature."

One might at first suppose that "literature" is not a value-laden term. After all, we use phrases such as "good literature" and "great literature" to make value judgments, but isn't "literature" itself a value-free term definable in the same way that Howard Gardner defines "intelligence"?

In the essay entitled "What Is Literature?" (see page 289), Terry Eagleton tests the various empirical definitions of literature that have been historically offered and finds all of them wanting. In each case, he finds either

1 Works that have been widely recognized as literature but do not fit the definition, or
2 Works that fit the definition but would not be considered literature.

Both of these strategies are effective in showing that a proposed definition is inadequate.

Eagleton concludes that no empirical definition of "literature" will reflect its actual usage. His final paragraph makes explicit the distinction between the empirical definition of a natural class such as mammals (or, in his own example, insects) and an artificial or "socially constructed" class such as literature. He also shows how the evaluative definition is rooted in the value system:

> *If it will not do to see literature as an "objective," descriptive category, neither will it do to say that literature is just what people whimsically choose to call literature. For there is nothing at all whimsical about such kinds of value-judgement: they have their roots in deeper structures of belief which are as apparently unshakeable as the Empire State Building. What we have uncovered so far, then, is not only that literature does not exist in the sense that insects do, and that the value-judgements by which it is constituted are historically variable, but that these value-judgements themselves have a close relation to social ideologies.*

This is not to say that it is fruitless to propose a definition of literature. It only implies that defining this term will be more like defining "good teacher" than defining "mammal." The definer, that is, will not be describing the discovered boundaries of a natural class, but recommending boundaries for a value class, boundaries that in this case will contain material worthy to be read, studied, criticized, and preserved as determined by a value system shared by the definer and his or her audience.

God Terms and Devil Terms

In approaching an evaluative argument critically, be aware of the key value terms. Consider the following brief argument:

> *You should switch to MotherEarth shampoo because it offers only pure, healthful cleansing action. It contains only natural ingredients. There is nothing artificial about it.*

In this commercial argument, the conclusion ("You should switch to MotherEarth shampoo") is supported by the reason that it consists only of natural ingredients. "Natural" in this case is what one rhetorician has called an *ultimate term,* one which the writer can confidently rely on to carry a powerful value connotation among his audience without the need for further analysis or support.[1] Advertisers have apparently discovered that if they can establish that a shampoo is "natural," that is as far as they have to go. Their audience does not require them to explain why a natural shampoo should be better than an artificial shampoo. It doesn't matter that substances ranging from lard to deadly night-

---

[1] Richard M. Weaver, "Ultimate Terms in Contemporary Rhetoric," *The Ethics of Rhetoric* (Chicago: Henry Regnery Co., 1953), 211–32.

shade are purely natural or that in some sense any material product is made only of natural ingredients (those listed in the periodic table of elements).

Ultimate terms that carry positive connotations without further analysis are called *god terms;* those that carry negative connotations are called *devil terms.* "Artificial," "racist," and "discriminatory" serve the latter function for American writers. To call "racist" a devil term does not imply that racism's negative connotations are undeserved. Racism is a genuine evil. To call it a devil term means that its connotations are so potent that it is liable to abuse. If writers brand a policy or practice they don't like "racist," readers are prone to accept the label even though the recognition of racial differences being stigmatized is not based on racial prejudice. The powerful connotations of a god or devil term can even be transferred to new words formed on their model. For instance, "speciesism" and even "sentiencism" have been coined to capitalize on the current force of terms that stigmatize prejudice against individuals outside one's own group.

Another danger of god terms and devil terms is that they are often used thoughtlessly as vague terms of approval and disapproval. Sometimes this lack of precision can lead to unintentionally comic effects, as when a film is advertised as "a truly unique and original creation in the tradition of *Billy Jack*." A more serious danger is that god and devil terms carry a hidden assumption. In an argument implying that an all-natural shampoo is superior to one that contains artificial ingredients, little is at stake. In other arguments, though, where the god terms may be "profits," "support for our troops," or "national security," uncritical readers may be lulled into accepting political or social actions incompatible with their deepest values.

EXERCISE 1

List terms that you feel operate as god terms or devil terms in your contemporary culture (which you may define as your national culture or a subculture of your choice). Good sources of these terms include statements by advertisers, public relations officers, media commentators, politicians, and evangelists. The terms you list should meet two criteria:

1 They should serve as ultimate terms for those who use them.

2 You should be able to think of exceptions to the assigned value. For instance, if the chief executive officer of a corporation defends some corporate activity because it is "profitable," you should be able to propose an activity which, though "profitable," would not be desirable.

EXERCISE 2

In the spring of 1963, black civil rights groups in Birmingham, Alabama, conducted a series of demonstrations that included sit-ins at segregated lunch counters and marches in the streets after authorities had refused applications for parade permits.

In response, a group of eight Alabama clergymen, Christian and Jewish, issued the public statement below. Identify the god terms and devil terms in their statement.

Public Statement by Eight Alabama Clergymen

(April 12, 1963)

1   We the undersigned clergymen are among those who, in January, issued "An Appeal for Law and Order and Common Sense," in dealing with racial problems in Alabama. We expressed understanding that honest convictions in racial matters could properly be pursued in the courts, but urged that decisions of those courts should in the meantime be peacefully obeyed.

2   Since that time there had been some evidence of increased forbearance and a willingness to face facts. Responsible citizens have undertaken to work on various problems which cause racial friction and unrest. In Birmingham, recent public events have given indication that we all have opportunity for a new constructive and realistic approach to racial problems.

3   However, we are now confronted by a series of demonstrations by some of our Negro citizens, directed and led in part by outsiders. We recognize the natural impatience of people who feel that their hopes are slow in being realized. But we are convinced that these demonstrations are unwise and untimely.

4   We agree rather with certain local Negro leadership which has called for honest and open negotiation of racial issues in our area. And we believe this kind of facing of issues can best be accomplished by citizens of our own metropolitan area, white and Negro, meeting with their knowledge and experience of the local situation. All of us need to face that responsibility and find proper channels for its accomplishment.

5   Just as we formerly pointed out that "hatred and violence have no sanction in our religious and political traditions," we also point out that such actions as incite to hatred and violence, however technically peaceful those actions may be, have not contributed to the resolution of our local problems. We do not believe that these days of new hope are days when extreme measures are justified in Birmingham.

6   We commend the community as a whole, and the local news media and law enforcement officials in particular, on the calm manner in which these demonstrations have been handled. We urge the public to continue to show restraint should the demonstrations continue, and the law enforcement officials to remain calm and continue to protect our city from violence.

7   We further strongly urge our own Negro community to withdraw support from these demonstrations, and to unite locally in working peacefully for a better Birmingham. When rights are consistently denied, a

cause should be pressed in the courts and in negotiations among local leaders, and not in the streets. We appeal to both our white and Negro citizenry to observe the principles of law and order and common sense.

Signed by:

C. C. J. CARPENTER, D.D., LL.D., *Bishop of Alabama*

JOSEPH A. DURICK, D.D., *Auxiliary Bishop, Diocese of Mobile-Birmingham*

Rabbi MILTON L. GRAFMAN, *Temple Emanu-El, Birmingham, Alabama*

Bishop PAUL HARDIN, *Bishop of the Alabama-West Florida Conference of the Methodist Church*

Bishop NOLAN B. HARMON, *Bishop of the North Alabama Conference of the Methodist Church*

GEORGE M. MURRAY, D.D., LL.D., *Bishop Coadjutor, Episcopal Diocese of Alabama*

EDWARD V. RAMAGE, *Moderator, Synod of the Alabama Presbyterian Church in the United States*

EARL STALLINGS, *Pastor, First Baptist Church, Birmingham, Alabama*

Deductive Reasoning and Strategies of Evaluative Arguments

Evaluative arguments relate the question at issue to established decisions and beliefs that already make up part of our value system. We may deduce the position we support from a more general principle; we may argue for our position on the basis of analogies with other established judgments at the same level of generality; or we may use specific cases as counterarguments to principles we disagree with. All three of these strategies rely on deductive reasoning. They will help you to generate arguments, but they are subject to misapplications of which you should also be aware in order to test your own arguments or rebut those of others.

Deduction from More General Principles

Appeal to general principles, or *rules*, is a common form of argument in ordinary discourse. For instance, consider the following dialogue:

> FATHER: No, you can't borrow the car.
> DAUGHTER: But you always said that people should be generous.

The daughter's rejoinder in this interchange makes, in abbreviated form, the following argument:

> Premise 1:   All ungenerous actions are wrong.
> Premise 2:   To refuse to loan the car is an ungenerous action.
>
> Conclusion: Therefore, to refuse to loan the car is wrong.

The first premise states a general rule by attaching a value (wrong) to a criterion (ungenerosity). The second premise asserts that the specific action being evaluated (refusal to loan the car) is a case of the rule because it possesses that criterion. In any argument where the conclusion expresses a value judgment, at least one premise must express a value judgment too.

In ordinary discourse, it is common for one of the premises to be left implicit. Such an abbreviated argument is called an *enthymeme:*

> *I think the state is wrong to run a lottery. Lotteries just tempt people into wasting their money.*

In this argument, the first sentence states a conclusion while the second supports the conclusion by a single premise. This argument assumes a hidden value premise, the general rule that it is wrong for the state to tempt people into wasting their money. The whole argument, made fully explicit, would look like this:

> Rule: It is wrong for the state to tempt people into wasting their
>   money.
> Case: Running a lottery tempts people into wasting their money.
> Conclusion: Therefore it is wrong for the state to run a lottery.

In this argument the hidden premise was the one that stated a general values principle, but it could equally well have been the other premise that was hidden:

> *I think the state is wrong to run a lottery. It isn't right to tempt people into wasting their money.*

Here the general ethical rule that it is wrong to tempt people into wasting their money is made explicit; the premise that state-run lotteries are a case of such temptation is left implicit.

To analyze enthymemes successfully, you should be able to do two things:

1 Recognize which of two explicit statements is the conclusion.
2 Formulate explicitly the assumed premise.

Sometimes the wording of the enthymeme will signal which of the two propositions is the conclusion:

> *That child should not be left unattended at home because she is only ten years old.*

Here the word "because" indicates that the second clause of the sentence ("she is only ten years old") is being used as support for the first clause ("That child should not be left unattended at home"), which is therefore the conclusion. But even if the two clauses had been given with no connective at all, you could determine which was the premise and which the conclusion by supplying the "because" and seeing which order of the clauses makes sense. (It would not make sense to say, "She is only ten years old because she should not be left unattended at home.")

To supply the missing premise of a deductive argument, ask yourself what sentence is required to supply the logical bridge between the explicit premise and the conclusion. In our last example, an alleged fact about the child is given as the reason for a value-laden conclusion. Clearly some value-laden rule is required to make the conclusion follow from the explicit premise:

> Explicit premise: That child is only ten years old.
> Implicit rule: ???
>
> Conclusion: That child should not be left unattended at home.

Common sense will tell you that the conclusion follows from the given reason if we assume the rule that "No child who is only ten years old should be left unattended at home." Of course, the conclusion would follow from the explicit reason also if we assumed the rule that no child under twelve should be left unattended at home, but the enthymeme as stated does not necessarily assume that broad a rule, and our present intention is to reconstitute the hidden premise of the enthymeme.

In advancing your own arguments based on general principles, or in criticizing others', it is important to be able to formulate both of the premises so that you can test them. Both premises should be checked for accuracy. In the argument above you must question the general rule: Are there *no* conditions under which a child of ten might rightly be left unattended at home? But you must also remember to check the truth of the other premise: Are you sure the child is only ten? Perhaps she is older than she looks. (A more precise and systematic procedure for testing the validity of deductive arguments is discussed in the Appendix.)

Testing or Rebutting Arguments From a More General Principle

Rebuttals to arguments from general principles usually take one or more of four forms.

1. Showing That the Principle Doesn't Apply

As we noted earlier, arguments from broader principles take the form:

> All X's are good (or bad, ugly, disadvantageous, etc.).
> Y is an instance of X.
>
> Therefore, Y is good (or bad, etc.).

To deny that a principle applies is to deny the truth of the second premise. For instance, consider one issue in the debate about surrogate motherhood, the practice whereby a couple in which the wife is infertile pays another woman a substantial sum to be artificially inseminated by the husband, then to relinquish to the couple all parental rights to any child that is born.

OPPONENT: Surrogate motherhood should not be legalized. Private adoptions are not and should not be allowed because the child's welfare is better protected when adoptions are regulated by the state.

PROPONENT: I agree with the principle that private adoptions are against the public interest, but the principle doesn't apply here. The husband of the couple who will receive custody of the child is the child's biological father, and it is not possible to "adopt" your own baby.

2. Demonstrating That the Principle, As Stated, Has Unacceptable Consequences

ARNOLD: I am opposed to the killing of whales because I believe with William Blake that "everything that lives is holy."

BARBARA: Everything?

ARNOLD: Everything.

BARBARA: If you really went by that principle, you would have to oppose the chlorination of the water supply or the use of antiseptics, because both procedures kill microorganisms.

Barbara is pointing out that Arnold's principle as stated would lead to what she, at least, considers the absurd consequence that human beings should not be allowed to kill harmful microorganisms. This argumentative strategy is called *reductio ad absurdum*.

3. Producing Counterexamples to the Principle

Once in a Supreme Court case, the accused defended himself against a charge of inciting to riot on the principle that he was constitutionally guaranteed freedom of speech. His argument might be represented formally as follows:

All speech acts are protected by the First Amendment to the Constitution.
Inciting to riot is a speech act.

Therefore, inciting to riot is protected by the First Amendment to the Constitution.

Justice Holmes responded that freedom of speech does not entitle a citizen to shout "Fire!" in a crowded theater. The effect is to show by this counterexample that Premise 1 is wrong; it might have correctly stated that *some* speech acts are protected, but with this alteration the conclusion does not follow because the speaker has not demonstrated that his particular speech act was among those protected by the Constitution. The second version would have committed the fallacy of the *undistributed middle*. (See Appendix, page 504.)

In ordinary discourse, questions beginning "How would you feel if..." generally postulate a hypothetical specific case that the speaker feels will invalidate a principle:

A: Surrogate motherhood is wicked. It is really a form of buying and selling children. Infertile couples are always free to adopt.

B: How would you feel if you desperately wanted a baby, the youngest children available for adoption were three years old, and a willing surrogate mother were available?

Obviously arguments in this form are likely to be emotional and are subject to abuse, but they can also be powerful means of persuasion. The fact that an argument is emotional does not in itself disqualify it. Emotions are a necessary part of the equation in any process of rational evaluation.

4. *Identifying a Conflicting Principle*

Is affirmative action fair? Defenders would argue that provisions whereby certain positions must be filled first by qualified underrepresented minorities are fair because they compensate for a history of discrimination. Opponents attempt to refute this argument by responding that such provisions require "reverse discrimination" against equally qualified — or, in terms of GRE or civil service scores, even better qualified — majority applicants.

Rebuttal by conflicting principle is probably the most common way of attacking an argument from principle. It may succeed if the counterprinciple can be shown to be overriding. For instance, a citizen who has been committed to a mental institution has a powerful argument for release in the principle that individuals are entitled to liberty. But if the state can show that he is a danger to himself or society, then that principle may have overriding force. (Again, in logical terms, this argument works by calling into question the quantifier of the major premise: Perhaps not all, but only some citizens are entitled to liberty.)

Constructive Arguments by Analogy

Analogies are more frequently used than arguments from general principles in making evaluations or proposals. When a new moral dilemma or difficult policy choice arises, we naturally turn to the most closely comparable situations from the past in which we have reached some social consensus. For instance, when it was proposed that persons applying for a marriage license should be tested for the AIDS virus, some people argued that the test would be justified by the precept that measures to protect the public health are desirable. Others, however, cited the precept that people are entitled to privacy. Where general principles conflict like this, as they often do, we naturally seek analogies. Proponents of premarital

HIV testing used a chain of deductive reasoning that is generally representative of any analogical reasoning about value issues:

> AIDS is a sexually transmitted disease (STD).
> In the past we have agreed on the desirability of premarital testing for
>   STD's such as syphilis and gonorrhea.
> Like situations call for like measures.
> _____
> Therefore, we may agree on the desirability of premarital testing for AIDS.

Even our legal system, which is the most deeply and generally supported institution of social evaluation, depends on analogy in the form of legal precedents.

Arguments by analogy are useless in proving an empirical question. If a new species of warm-blooded, milk-producing vertebrate is discovered (in other words, a species that in important respects appears to be a mammal), there is no absolute guarantee that it will prove capable of live birth (think of the platypus). However, arguments by analogy are potent in persuading others of the fairness or justice of rules, requirements, and laws.

Testing or Rebutting Arguments by Analogy

Analogous situations are never identical situations; thus analogies can be refuted by showing that the similarities between them do not warrant the conclusion being argued for. Proponents of surrogate motherhood often argue that it is analogous to another practice generally regarded as moral and beneficial to all concerned, namely, the artificial insemination of a woman whose husband is infertile. In both cases, according to this argument, a couple otherwise incapable of bearing children is able to raise from birth a child who is the biological offspring of one of the parents. This argument has its appeal, but it is vulnerable because a surrogate mother who carries a baby to term is liable to form a stronger bond with the child than a sperm donor, who may not even know whether he has become a father. From the baby's point of view, too, separation from the natural mother may have consequences that have no counterpart in cases of artificial insemination.

To support the validity of your analogies, it helps to relate the analogous cases to some general principle that governs all of them. For instance, in his argument that business bluffing is ethical (see page 183), Albert Carr relies heavily on analogies. No one, says the author, considers bluffing unethical in poker, so why should it be unethical in business? The reader is tempted to object that poker is a game while business is not; that no one has to sit in on a poker game if he doesn't want to or can't afford to, while everyone has to make essential purchases; that poker is in its essence a game of bluffing, and that this essential character is known to and accepted by all players. These objections all question whether the analogy of business to poker is a valid one.

The author counters such objections in two ways. First, he provides other analogies, including diplomacy and legal defense, activities, he says, where society accepts bluffing. These analogies escape some of the objections to which the poker analogy is vulnerable. But in addition he provides a principle whereby, he argues, bluffing becomes ethical in all these situations: "Falsehood ceases to be falsehood when it is understood on all sides that the truth is not expected to be spoken." Of course, the question remains whether this principle applies to business.

Counterarguments from Specific Judgments

Specific judgments, or *specific examples,* are a weak strategy in constructive values arguments. True, Carr seems to support the principle that business bluffing is ethical by reference to specific cases, including those of a Cornell honors graduate who lied (or "bluffed") on a psychological test, a fifty-eight-year-old unemployed salesman who lied about his age on his résumé, and a manufacturer of mouthwash who used a "cheap form of alcohol possibly deleterious to health." However, if Carr used these examples to support the principle that business bluffing is ethical, and if this were his only argument, his essay would be laughably inadequate. A hostile reader might immediately respond that these examples could easily be outweighed by countless examples of business bluffing that were cruel and clearly unethical. If Carr intended these examples in this sense, he would be using a kind of shoddy induction that would be unpersuasive.

In fact, though, his examples are effective because they are being used as *counterexamples* to the common view that all business bluffing is unethical. If you initially agreed with this common view but sympathized with the men in the three sample cases, you would have to reassess your principles. In this rebuttal role, a single example is valid and potent.

Testing or Rebutting Counterarguments from Specific Judgments

1. *Rejecting the Original Value Judgment of the Examples*
   Carr's examples above will be effective only if his audience sympathizes with the three individuals described. Anyone who disapproves of the salesman's lie will not be persuaded.

2. *Showing That the Examples Are Atypical*
   If specific cases are used to support a universal evaluation such as "All males under twenty-five are dangerous drivers," then a single counterexample suffices to refute it. More commonly, though, examples are used to support less sweeping generalizations referring to "many" or "most" of a given class. If you disagree with even such a limited evaluation, you may try to show that the examples proffered are somehow atypical and offer counterexamples of your own. For instance, even if you accept that the three particular business bluffers selected by Carr behaved ethically, you might feel that they do not represent the full range of business bluffing as Carr defines it. If you can think of other instances of business bluffing that are legal but that you would consider unethical, you could advance them as counterexamples to Carr's principle.

Example of an Evaluative Argument

Martin Luther King, Jr.'s "Letter from Birmingham Jail" is a brilliant example of modern rhetoric. It is a rebuttal to the public statement by eight Alabama clergymen that you have already read (page 48) and constitutes a superb example of a critique. Since its publication in 1963, King's letter has become a classic in the literature of civil disobedience. A powerful influence on the civil rights movement, it has been frequently reprinted, and the proposal has even been made that it be adopted as a new book of the Bible to be placed with the other epistles of the New Testament.

MARTIN LUTHER KING, JR.

*Letter from Birmingham Jail**

April 16, 1963

MY DEAR FELLOW CLERGYMEN:

1   While confined here in the Birmingham city jail, I came across your recent statement calling my present activities "unwise and untimely." Seldom do I pause to answer criticism of my work and ideas. If I sought to answer all the criticisms that cross my desk, my secretaries would have little time for anything other than such correspondence in the course of the day, and I would have no time for constructive work. But since I feel that you are men of genuine good will and that your criticisms are sincerely set forth, I want to try to answer your statement in what I hope will be patient and reasonable terms.

2   I think I should indicate why I am here in Birmingham, since you have been influenced by the view which argues against "outsiders coming in." I have the honor of serving as president of the Southern Christian Leadership Conference, an organization operating in every southern state, with headquarters in Atlanta, Georgia. We have some eighty-five affiliated

---

* AUTHOR'S NOTE: This response to a published statement by eight fellow clergymen from Alabama (Bishop C. C. J. Carpenter, Bishop Joseph A. Durick, Rabbi Hilton L. Grafman, Bishop Paul Hardin, Bishop Holan B. Harmon, the Reverend George M. Murray, the Reverend Edward V. Ramage and the Reverend Earl Stallings) was composed under somewhat constricting circumstances. Begun on the margins of the newspaper in which the statement appeared while I was in jail, the letter was continued on scraps of writing paper supplied by a friendly Negro trusty, and concluded on a pad my attorneys were eventually permitted to leave me. Although the text remains in substance unaltered, I have indulged in the author's prerogative of polishing it for publication.

organizations across the South, and one of them is the Alabama Christian Movement for Human Rights. Frequently we share staff, educational and financial resources with our affiliates. Several months ago the affiliate here in Birmingham asked us to be on call to engage in a nonviolent direct-action program if such were deemed necessary. We readily consented, and when the hour came we lived up to our promise. So I, along with several members of my staff, am here because I was invited here. I am here because I have organizational ties here.

3   But more basically, I am in Birmingham because injustice is here. Just as the prophets of the eighth century B.C. left their villages and carried their "thus saith the Lord" far beyond the boundaries of their home towns, and just as the Apostle Paul left his village of Tarsus and carried the gospel of Jesus Christ to the far corners of the Greco-Roman world, so am I compelled to carry the gospel of freedom beyond my own home town. Like Paul, I must constantly respond to the Macedonian call for aid.

4   Moreover, I am cognizant of the interrelatedness of all communities and states. I cannot sit idly by in Atlanta and not be concerned about what happens in Birmingham. Injustice anywhere is a threat to justice everywhere. We are caught in an inescapable network of mutuality, tied in a single garment of destiny. Whatever affects one directly, affects all indirectly. Never again can we afford to live with the narrow, provincial "outside agitator" idea. Anyone who lives inside the United States can never be considered an outsider anywhere within its bounds.

5   You deplore the demonstrations taking place in Birmingham. But your statement, I am sorry to say, fails to express a similar concern for the conditions that brought about the demonstrations. I am sure that none of you would want to rest content with the superficial kind of social analysis that deals merely with effects and does not grapple with underlying causes. It is unfortunate that demonstrations are taking place in Birmingham, but it is even more unfortunate that the city's white power structure left the Negro community with no alternative.

6   In any nonviolent campaign there are four basic steps: collection of the facts to determine whether injustices exist; negotiation; self-purification; and direct action. We have gone through all these steps in Birmingham. There can be no gainsaying the fact that racial injustice engulfs this community. Birmingham is probably the most thoroughly segregated city in the United States. Its ugly record of brutality is widely known. Negroes have experienced grossly unjust treatment in the courts. There have been more unsolved bombings of Negro homes and churches in Birmingham than in any other city in the nation. These are the hard, brutal facts of the case. On the basis of these conditions, Negro leaders sought to negotiate with the city fathers. But the latter consistently refused to engage in good-faith negotiation.

7   Then, last September, came the opportunity to talk with leaders of Birmingham's economic community. In the course of the negotiations, certain promises were made by the merchants—for example, to remove the stores' humiliating racial signs. On the basis of these promises, the Reverend Fred Shuttlesworth and the leaders of the Alabama Christian Movement for Human Rights agreed to a moratorium on all demonstrations. As the weeks and months went by, we realized that we were the victims of a broken promise. A few signs, briefly removed, returned; the others remained.

8   As in so many past experiences, our hopes had been blasted, and the shadow of deep disappointment settled upon us. We had no alternative except to prepare for direct action, whereby we would present our very bodies as a means of laying our case before the conscience of the local and the national community. Mindful of the difficulties involved, we decided to undertake a process of self-purification. We began a series of workshops on nonviolence, and we repeatedly asked ourselves: "Are you able to accept blows without retaliating?" "Are you able to endure the ordeal of jail?" We decided to schedule our direct-action program for the Easter season, realizing that except for Christmas, this is the main shopping period of the year. Knowing that a strong economic-withdrawal program would be the by-product of direct action, we felt that this would be the best time to bring pressure to bear on the merchants for the needed change.

9   Then it occurred to us that Birmingham's mayoral election was coming up in March, and we speedily decided to postpone action until after election day. When we discovered that the Commissioner of Public Safety, Eugene "Bull" Connor, had piled up enough votes to be in the run-off, we decided again to postpone action until the day after the run-off so that the demonstrations could not be used to cloud the issues. Like many others, we waited to see Mr. Connor defeated, and to this end we endured postponement after postponement. Having aided in this community need, we felt that our direct-action program could be delayed no longer.

10   You may well ask: "Why direct action? Why sit-ins, marches and so forth? Isn't negotiation a better path?" You are quite right in calling for negotiation. Indeed, this is the very purpose of direct action. Nonviolent direct action seeks to create such a crisis and foster such a tension that a community which has constantly refused to negotiate is forced to confront the issue. It seeks so to dramatize the issue that it can no longer be ignored. My citing the creation of tension as part of the work of the nonviolent-resister may sound rather shocking. But I must confess that I am not afraid of the word "tension." I have earnestly opposed violent tension, but there is a type of constructive, nonviolent tension which is necessary for growth. Just as Socrates felt that it was necessary to create a tension in the mind so that individuals could rise from the bondage of myths and half-truths to

the unfettered realm of creative analysis and objective appraisal, so must we see the need for nonviolent gadflies to create the kind of tension in society that will help men rise from the dark depths of prejudice and racism to the majestic heights of understanding and brotherhood.

11   The purpose of our direct-action program is to create a situation so crisis-packed that it will inevitably open the door to negotiation. I therefore concur with you in your call for negotiation. Too long has our beloved Southland been bogged down in a tragic effort to live in monologue rather than dialogue.

12   One of the basic points in your statement is that the action that I and my associates have taken in Birmingham is untimely. Some have asked: "Why didn't you give the new city administration time to act?" The only answer that I can give to this query is that the new Birmingham administration must be prodded about as much as the outgoing one, before it will act. We are sadly mistaken if we feel that the election of Albert Boutwell as mayor will bring the millennium to Birmingham. While Mr. Boutwell is a much more gentle person than Mr. Connor, they are both segregationists, dedicated to maintenance of the status quo. I have hope that Mr. Boutwell will be reasonable enough to see the futility of massive resistance to desegregation. But he will not see this without pressure from devotees of civil rights. My friends, I must say to you that we have not made a single gain in civil rights without determined legal and nonviolent pressure. Lamentably, it is an historical fact that privileged groups seldom give up their privileges voluntarily. Individuals may see the moral light and voluntarily give up their unjust posture; but, as Reinhold Niebuhr has reminded us, groups tend to be more immoral than individuals.

13   We know through painful experience that freedom is never voluntarily given by the oppressor; it must be demanded by the oppressed. Frankly, I have yet to engage in a direct-action campaign that was "well timed" in the view of those who have not suffered unduly from the disease of segregation. For years now I have heard the word "Wait!" It rings in the ear of every Negro with piercing familiarity. This "Wait" has almost always meant "Never." We must come to see, with one of our distinguished jurists, that "justice too long delayed is justice denied."

14   We have waited for more than 340 years for our constitutional and God-given rights. The nations of Asia and Africa are moving with jetlike speed toward gaining political independence, but we still creep at horse-and-buggy pace toward gaining a cup of coffee at a lunch counter. Perhaps it is easy for those who have never felt the stinging darts of segregation to say, "Wait." But when you have seen vicious mobs lynch your mothers and fathers at will and drown your sisters and brothers at whim; when you have seen hate-filled policemen curse, kick and even kill your black

brothers and sisters; when you see the vast majority of your twenty million Negro brothers smothering in an airtight cage of poverty in the midst of an affluent society; when you suddenly find your tongue twisted and your speech stammering as you seek to explain to your six-year-old daughter why she can't go to the public amusement park that has just been advertised on television, and see tears welling up in her eyes when she is told that Funtown is closed to colored children, and see ominous clouds of inferiority beginning to form in her little mental sky, and see her beginning to distort her personality by developing an unconscious bitterness toward white people; when you have to concoct an answer for a five-year-old son who is asking: "Daddy, why do white people treat colored people so mean?"; when you take a cross-country drive and find it necessary to sleep night after night in the uncomfortable corners of your automobile because no motel will accept you; when you are humiliated day in and day out by nagging signs reading "white" and "colored"; when your first name becomes "nigger," your middle name becomes "boy" (however old you are) and your last name becomes "John," and your wife and mother are never given the respected title "Mrs."; when you are harried by day and haunted by night by the fact that you are a Negro, living constantly at tiptoe stance, never quite knowing what to expect next, and are plagued with inner fears and outer resentments; when you are forever fighting a degenerating sense of "nobodiness"—then you will understand why we find it difficult to wait. There comes a time when the cup of endurance runs over, and men are no longer willing to be plunged into the abyss of despair. I hope, sirs, you can understand our legitimate and unavoidable impatience.

15   You express a great deal of anxiety over our willingness to break laws. This is certainly a legitimate concern. Since we so diligently urge people to obey the Supreme Court's decision of 1954 outlawing segregation in the public schools, at first glance it may seem rather paradoxical for us consciously to break laws. One may well ask: "How can you advocate breaking some laws and obeying others?" The answer lies in the fact that there are two types of laws: just and unjust. I would be the first to advocate obeying just laws. One has not only a legal but a moral responsibility to obey just laws. Conversely, one has a moral responsibility to disobey unjust laws. I would agree with St. Augustine that "an unjust law is no law at all."

16   Now, what is the difference between the two? How does one determine whether a law is just or unjust? A just law is a man-made code that squares with the moral law or the law of God. An unjust law is a code that is out of harmony with the moral law. To put it in the terms of St. Thomas Aquinas: An unjust law is a human law that is not rooted in eternal law and natural law. Any law that uplifts human personality is just. Any law that degrades human personality is unjust. All segregation statutes are unjust because segregation distorts the soul and damages the personality. It

gives the segregator a false sense of superiority and the segregated a false sense of inferiority. Segregation, to use the terminology of the Jewish philosopher Martin Buber, substitutes an "I–it" relationship for an "I–thou" relationship and ends up relegating persons to the status of things. Hence segregation is not only politically, economically and sociologically unsound, it is morally wrong and sinful. Paul Tillich has said that sin is separation. Is not segregation an existential expression of man's tragic separation, his awful estrangement, his terrible sinfulness? Thus it is that I can urge men to obey the 1954 decision of the Supreme Court, for it is morally right; and I can urge them to disobey segregation ordinances, for they are morally wrong.

17   Let us consider a more concrete example of just and unjust laws. An unjust law is a code that a numerical or power majority group compels a minority group to obey but does not make binding on itself. This is *difference* made legal. By the same token, a just law is a code that a majority compels a minority to follow and that it is willing to follow itself. This is *sameness* made legal.

18   Let me give another explanation. A law is unjust if it is inflicted on a minority that, as a result of being denied the right to vote, had no part in enacting or devising the law. Who can say that the legislature of Alabama which set up that state's segregation laws was democratically elected? Throughout Alabama all sorts of devious methods are used to prevent Negroes from becoming registered voters, and there are some counties in which, even though Negroes constitute a majority of the population, not a single Negro is registered. Can any law enacted under such circumstances be considered democratically structured?

19   Sometimes a law is just on its face and unjust in its application. For instance, I have been arrested on a charge of parading without a permit. Now, there is nothing wrong in having an ordinance which requires a permit for a parade. But such an ordinance becomes unjust when it is used to maintain segregation and to deny citizens the First-Amendment privilege of peaceful assembly and protest.

20   I hope you are able to see the distinction I am trying to point out. In no sense do I advocate evading or defying the law, as would the rabid segregationist. That would lead to anarchy. One who breaks an unjust law must do so openly, lovingly, and with a willingness to accept the penalty. I submit that an individual who breaks a law that conscience tells him is unjust, and who willingly accepts the penalty of imprisonment in order to arouse the conscience of the community over its injustice, is in reality expressing the highest respect for law.

21   Of course, there is nothing new about this kind of civil disobedience. It was evidenced sublimely in the refusal of Shadrach, Meshach and Abednego to obey the laws of Nebuchadnezzar, on the ground that a higher moral law was at stake. It was practiced superbly by the early

Christians, who were willing to face hungry lions and the excruciating pain of chopping blocks rather than submit to certain unjust laws of the Roman Empire. To a degree, academic freedom is a reality today because Socrates practiced civil disobedience. In our own nation, the Boston Tea Party represented a massive act of civil disobedience.

22   We should never forget that everything Adolf Hitler did in Germany was "legal" and everything the Hungarian freedom fighters did in Hungary was "illegal." It was "illegal" to aid and comfort a Jew in Hitler's Germany. Even so, I am sure that, had I lived in Germany at the time, I would have aided and comforted my Jewish brothers. If today I lived in a Communist country where certain principles dear to the Christian faith are suppressed, I would openly advocate disobeying that country's antireligious laws.

23   I must make two honest confessions to you, my Christian and Jewish brothers. First, I must confess that over the past few years I have been gravely disappointed with the white moderate. I have almost reached the regrettable conclusion that the Negro's great stumbling block in his stride toward freedom is not the White Citizen's Counciler or the Ku Klux Klanner, but the white moderate, who is more devoted to "order" than to justice; who prefers a negative peace which is the absence of tension to a positive peace which is the presence of justice; who constantly says: "I agree with you in the goal you seek, but I cannot agree with your methods of direct action"; who paternalistically believes he can set the timetable for another man's freedom; who lives by a mythical concept of time and who constantly advises the Negro to wait for a "more convenient season." Shallow understanding from people of good will is more frustrating than absolute misunderstanding from people of ill will. Lukewarm acceptance is much more bewildering than outright rejection.

24   I had hoped that the white moderate would understand that law and order exist for the purpose of establishing justice and that when they fail in this purpose they become the dangerously structured dams that block the flow of social progress. I had hoped that the white moderate would understand that the present tension in the South is a necessary phase of the transition from an obnoxious negative peace, in which the Negro passively accepted his unjust plight, to a substantive and positive peace, in which all men will respect the dignity and worth of human personality. Actually, we who engage in nonviolent direct action are not the creators of tension. We merely bring to the surface the hidden tension that is already alive. We bring it out in the open, where it can be seen and dealt with. Like a boil that can never be cured so long as it is covered up but must be opened with all its ugliness to the natural medicines of air and light, injustice must be exposed, with all the tension its exposure creates, to the light of human conscience and the air of national opinion before it can be cured.

25   In your statement you assert that our actions, even though peaceful, must be condemned because they precipitate violence. But is this a logical assertion? Isn't this like condemning a robbed man because his possession of money precipitated the evil act of robbery? Isn't this like condemning Socrates because his unswerving commitment to truth and his philosophical inquiries precipitated the act by the misguided populace in which they made him drink hemlock? Isn't this like condemning Jesus because his unique God-consciousness and never-ceasing devotion to God's will precipitated the evil act of crucifixion? We must come to see that, as the federal courts have consistently affirmed, it is wrong to urge an individual to cease his efforts to gain his basic constitutional rights because the quest may precipitate violence. Society must protect the robbed and punish the robber.

26   I had also hoped that the white moderate would reject the myth concerning time in relation to the struggle for freedom. I have just received a letter from a white brother in Texas. He writes: "All Christians know that the colored people will receive equal rights eventually, but it is possible that you are in too great a religious hurry. It has taken Christianity almost two thousand years to accomplish what it has. The teachings of Christ take time to come to earth." Such an attitude stems from a tragic misconception of time, from the strangely irrational notion that there is something in the very flow of time that will inevitably cure all ills. Actually, time itself is neutral; it can be used either destructively or constructively. More and more I feel that the people of ill will have used time much more effectively than have the people of good will. We will have to repent in this generation not merely for the hateful words and actions of the bad people but for the appalling silence of the good people. Human progress never rolls in on wheels of inevitability; it comes through the tireless efforts of men willing to be co-workers with God, and without this hard work, time itself becomes an ally of the forces of social stagnation. We must use time creatively, in the knowledge that the time is always ripe to do right. Now is the time to make real the promise of democracy and transform our pending national elegy into a creative psalm of brotherhood. Now is the time to lift our national policy from the quicksand of racial injustice to the solid rock of human dignity.

27   You speak of our activity in Birmingham as extreme. At first I was rather disappointed that fellow clergymen would see my nonviolent efforts as those of an extremist. I began thinking about the fact that I stand in the middle of two opposing forces in the Negro community. One is a force of complacency, made up in part of Negroes who, as a result of long years of oppression, are so drained of self-respect and a sense of "somebodiness" that they have adjusted to segregation; and in part of a few middle-class Negroes who, because of a degree of academic and economic security and

because in some ways they profit by segregation, have become insensitive to the problems of the masses. The other force is one of bitterness and hatred, and it comes perilously close to advocating violence. It is expressed in the various black nationalist groups that are springing up across the nation, the largest and best-known being Elijah Muhammad's Muslim movement. Nourished by the Negro's frustration over the continued existence of racial discrimination, this movement is made up of people who have lost faith in America, who have absolutely repudiated Christianity, and who have concluded that the white man is an incorrigible "devil."

28   I have tried to stand between these two forces, saying that we need emulate neither the "do-nothingism" of the complacent nor the hatred and despair of the black nationalist. For there is the more excellent way of love and nonviolent protest. I am grateful to God that, through the influence of the Negro church, the way of nonviolence became an integral part of our struggle.

29   If this philosophy had not emerged, by now many streets of the South would, I am convinced, be flowing with blood. And I am further convinced that if our white brothers dismiss as "rabble-rousers" and "outside agitators" those of us who employ nonviolent direct action, and if they refuse to support our nonviolent efforts, millions of Negroes will, out of frustration and despair, seek solace and security in black-nationalist ideologies—a development that would inevitably lead to a frightening racial nightmare.

30   Oppressed people cannot remain oppressed forever. The yearning for freedom eventually manifests itself, and that is what has happened to the American Negro. Something within has reminded him of his birthright of freedom, and something without has reminded him that it can be gained. Consciously or unconsciously, he has been caught up by the *Zeitgeist,* and with his black brothers of Africa and his brown and yellow brothers of Asia, South America and the Caribbean, the United States Negro is moving with a sense of great urgency toward the promised land of racial justice. If one recognizes this vital urge that has engulfed the Negro community, one should readily understand why public demonstrations are taking place. The Negro has many pent-up resentments and latent frustrations, and he must release them. So let him march; let him make prayer pilgrimages to the city hall; let him go on freedom rides—and try to understand why he must do so. If his repressed emotions are not released in nonviolent ways, they will seek expression through violence; this is not a threat but a fact of history. So I have not said to my people: "Get rid of your discontent." Rather, I have tried to say that this normal and healthy discontent can be channeled into the creative outlet of nonviolent direct action. And now this approach is being termed extremist.

31   But though I was initially disappointed at being categorized as an extremist, as I continued to think about the matter I gradually gained a

measure of satisfaction from the label. Was not Jesus an extremist for love: "Love your enemies, bless them that curse you, do good to them that hate you, and pray for them which despitefully use you, and persecute you." Was not Amos an extremist for justice: "Let justice roll down like waters and righteousness like an ever-flowing stream." Was not Paul an extremist for the Christian gospel: "I bear in my body the marks of the Lord Jesus." Was not Martin Luther an extremist: "Here I stand; I cannot do otherwise, so help me God." And John Bunyan: "I will stay in jail to the end of my days before I make a butchery of my conscience." And Abraham Lincoln: "This nation cannot survive half slave and half free." And Thomas Jefferson: "We hold these truths to be self-evident, that all men are created equal . . ." So the question is not whether we will be extremists, but what kind of extremists we will be. Will we be extremists for hate or for love? Will we be extremists for the preservation of injustice or for the extension of justice? In that dramatic scene on Calvary's hill three men were crucified. We must never forget that all three were crucified for the same crime—the crime of extremism. Two were extremists for immorality, and thus fell below their environment. The other, Jesus Christ, was an extremist for love, truth and goodness, and thereby rose above his environment. Perhaps the South, the nation and the world are in dire need of creative extremists.

32   I had hoped that the white moderate would see this need. Perhaps I was too optimistic; perhaps I expected too much. I suppose I should have realized that few members of the oppressor race can understand the deep groans and passionate yearnings of the oppressed race, and still fewer have the vision to see that injustice must be rooted out by strong, persistent and determined action. I am thankful, however, that some of our white brothers in the South have grasped the meaning of this social revolution and committed themselves to it. They are still all too few in quantity, but they are big in quality. Some—such as Ralph McGill, Lillian Smith, Harry Golden, James McBride Dabbs, Ann Braden and Sarah Patton Boyle— have written about our struggle in eloquent and prophetic terms. Others have marched with us down nameless streets of the South. They have languished in filthy, roach-infested jails, suffering the abuse and brutality of policemen who view them as "dirty nigger-lovers." Unlike so many of their moderate brothers and sisters, they have recognized the urgency of the moment and sensed the need for powerful "action" antidotes to combat the disease of segregation.

33   Let me take note of my other major disappointment. I have been so greatly disappointed with the white church and its leadership. Of course, there are some notable exceptions. I am not unmindful of the fact that each of you has taken some significant stands on this issue. I commend you, Reverend Stallings, for your Christian stand on this past Sunday, in welcoming Negroes to your worship service on a nonsegregated basis. I

commend the Catholic leaders of this state for integrating Spring Hill College several years ago.

34   But despite these notable exceptions, I must honestly reiterate that I have been disappointed with the church. I do not say this as one of those negative critics who can always find something wrong with the church. I say this as a minister of the gospel, who loves the church; who was nurtured in its bosom; who has been sustained by its spiritual blessings and who will remain true to it as long as the cord of life shall lengthen.

35   When I was suddenly catapulted into the leadership of the bus protest in Montgomery, Alabama, a few years ago, I felt we would be supported by the white church. I felt that the white ministers, priests and rabbis of the South would be among our strongest allies. Instead, some have been outright opponents, refusing to understand the freedom movement and misrepresenting its leaders; all too many others have been more cautious than courageous and have remained silent behind the anesthetizing security of stained-glass windows.

36   In spite of my shattered dreams, I came to Birmingham with the hope that the white religious leadership of this community would see the justice of our cause and, with deep moral concern, would serve as the channel through which our just grievances could reach the power structure. I had hoped that each of you would understand. But again I have been disappointed.

37   I have heard numerous southern religious leaders admonish their worshipers to comply with a desegregation decision because it is the law, but I have longed to hear white ministers declare: "Follow this decree because integration is morally right and because the Negro is your brother." In the midst of blatant injustices inflicted upon the Negro, I have watched white churchmen stand on the sideline and mouth pious irrelevancies and sanctimonious trivialities. In the midst of a mighty struggle to rid our nation of racial and economic injustice, I have heard many ministers say: "Those are social issues, with which the gospel has no real concern." And I have watched many churches commit themselves to a completely otherworldly religion which makes a strange, un-Biblical distinction between body and soul, between the sacred and the secular.

38   I have traveled the length and breadth of Alabama, Mississippi and all the other southern states. On sweltering summer days and crisp autumn mornings I have looked at the South's beautiful churches with their lofty spires pointing heavenward. I have beheld the impressive outlines of her massive religious-education buildings. Over and over I have found myself asking: "What kind of people worship here? Who is their God? Where were their voices when the lips of Governor Barnett dripped with words of interposition and nullification? Where were they when Governor Wallace gave a clarion call for defiance and hatred? Where were their voices of support when bruised and weary Negro men and women decided to rise

from the dark dungeons of complacency to the bright hills of creative protest?"

39   Yes, these questions are still in my mind. In deep disappointment I have wept over the laxity of the church. But be assured that my tears have been tears of love. There can be no deep disappointment where there is not deep love. Yes, I love the church. How could I do otherwise? I am in the rather unique position of being the son, the grandson and the great-grandson of preachers. Yes, I see the church as the body of Christ. But, oh! How we have blemished and scarred that body through social neglect and through fear of being nonconformists.

40   There was a time when the church was very powerful—in the time when the early Christians rejoiced at being deemed worthy to suffer for what they believed. In those days the church was not merely a thermometer that recorded the ideas and principles of popular opinion; it was a thermostat that transformed the mores of society. Whenever the early Christians entered a town, the people in power became disturbed and immediately sought to convict the Christians for being "disturbers of the peace" and "outside agitators." But the Christians pressed on, in the conviction that they were "a colony of heaven," called to obey God rather than man. Small in number, they were big in commitment. They were too God-intoxicated to be "astronomically intimidated." By their effort and example they brought an end to such ancient evils as infanticide and gladiatorial contests.

41   Things are different now. So often the contemporary church is a weak, ineffectual voice with an uncertain sound. So often it is an archdefender of the status quo. Far from being disturbed by the presence of the church, the power structure of the average community is consoled by the church's silent—and often even vocal—sanction of things as they are.

42   But the judgment of God is upon the church as never before. If today's church does not recapture the sacrificial spirit of the early church, it will lose its authenticity, forfeit the loyalty of millions, and be dismissed as an irrelevant social club with no meaning for the twentieth century. Every day I meet young people whose disappointment with the church has turned into outright disgust.

43   Perhaps I have once again been too optimistic. Is organized religion too inextricably bound to the status quo to save our nation and the world? Perhaps I must turn my faith to the inner spiritual church, the church within the church, as the true *ekklesia* and the hope of the world. But again I am thankful to God that some noble souls from the ranks of organized religion have broken loose from the paralyzing chains of conformity and joined us as active partners in the struggle for freedom. They have left their secure congregations and walked the streets of Albany, Georgia, with us. They have gone down the highways of the South on tortuous rides for freedom. Yes, they have gone to jail with us. Some have been dismissed

from their churches, have lost the support of their bishops and fellow ministers. But they have acted in the faith that right defeated is stronger than evil triumphant. Their witness has been the spiritual salt that has preserved the true meaning of the gospel in these troubled times. They have carved a tunnel of hope through the dark mountain of disappointment.

44   I hope the church as a whole will meet the challenge of this decisive hour. But even if the church does not come to the aid of justice, I have no despair about the future. I have no fear about the outcome of our struggle in Birmingham, even if our motives are at present misunderstood. We will reach the goal of freedom in Birmingham and all over the nation, because the goal of America is freedom. Abused and scorned though we may be, our destiny is tied up with America's destiny. Before the pilgrims landed at Plymouth, we were here. Before the pen of Jefferson etched the majestic words of the Declaration of Independence across the pages of history, we were here. For more than two centuries our forebears labored in this country without wages; they made cotton king; they built the homes of their masters while suffering gross injustice and shameful humiliation— and yet out of a bottomless vitality they continued to thrive and develop. If the inexpressible cruelties of slavery could not stop us, the opposition we now face will surely fail. We will win our freedom because the sacred heritage of our nation and the eternal will of God are embodied in our echoing demands.

45   Before closing I feel impelled to mention one other point in your statement that has troubled me profoundly. You warmly commended the Birmingham police force for keeping "order" and "preventing violence." I doubt that you would have so warmly commended the police force if you had seen its dogs sinking their teeth into unarmed, nonviolent Negroes. I doubt that you would so quickly commend the policemen if you were to observe their ugly and inhumane treatment of Negroes here in the city jail; if you were to watch them push and curse old Negro women and young Negro girls; if you were to see them slap and kick old Negro men and young boys; if you were to observe them, as they did on two occasions, refuse to give us food because we wanted to sing our grace together. I cannot join you in your praise of the Birmingham police department.

46   It is true that the police have exercised a degree of discipline in handling the demonstrators. In this sense they have conducted themselves rather "nonviolently" in public. But for what purpose? To preserve the evil system of segregation. Over the past few years I have consistently preached that nonviolence demands that the means we use must be as pure as the ends we seek. I have tried to make clear that it is wrong to use immoral means to attain moral ends. But now I must affirm that it is just as wrong, or perhaps even more so, to use moral means to preserve immoral ends. Perhaps Mr. Connor and his policemen have been rather nonviolent in public, as was Chief Pritchett in Albany, Georgia, but they have used the moral means of nonviolence to maintain the immoral end of racial

injustice. As T. S. Eliot has said: "The last temptation is the greatest treason: To do the right deed for the wrong reason."

47   I wish you had commended the Negro sit-inners and demonstrators of Birmingham for their sublime courage, their willingness to suffer and their amazing discipline in the midst of great provocation. One day the South will recognize its real heroes. They will be the James Merediths, with the noble sense of purpose that enables them to face jeering and hostile mobs, and with the agonizing loneliness that characterizes the life of the pioneer. They will be old, oppressed, battered Negro women, symbolized in a seventy-two-year-old woman in Montgomery, Alabama, who rose up with a sense of dignity and with her people decided not to ride segregated buses, and who responded with ungrammatical profundity to one who inquired about her weariness: "My feets is tired, but my soul is at rest." They will be the young high school and college students, the young ministers of the gospel and a host of their elders, courageously and nonviolently sitting in at lunch counters and willingly going to jail for conscience' sake. One day the South will know that when these disinherited children of God sat down at lunch counters, they were in reality standing up for what is best in the American dream and for the most sacred values in our Judaeo-Christian heritage, thereby bringing our nation back to those great wells of democracy which were dug deep by the founding fathers in their formulation of the Constitution and the Declaration of Independence.

48   Never before have I written so long a letter. I'm afraid it is much too long to take your precious time. I can assure you that it would have been much shorter if I had been writing from a comfortable desk, but what else can one do when he is alone in a narrow jail cell, other than write long letters, think long thoughts and pray long prayers?

49   If I have said anything in this letter that overstates the truth and indicates an unreasonable impatience, I beg you to forgive me. If I have said anything that understates the truth and indicates my having a patience that allows me to settle for anything less than brotherhood, I beg God to forgive me.

50   I hope this letter finds you strong in the faith. I also hope that circumstances will soon make it possible for me to meet each of you, not as an integrationist or a civil-rights leader but as a fellow clergyman and a Christian brother. Let us all hope that the dark clouds of racial prejudice will soon pass away and the deep fog of misunderstanding will be lifted from our fear-drenched communities, and in some not too distant tomorrow the radiant stars of love and brotherhood will shine over our great nation with all their scintillating beauty.

        Yours for the cause of Peace and Brotherhood,

MARTIN LUTHER KING, JR.

Analysis of King's Letter

King's letter is, of course, a direct rebuttal to another document. While this fact may seem to distinguish it from other evaluative essays, in fact any statement of values proceeds from a felt difference between the author's views and the views he perceives around him. As King says at the beginning of his letter, he seldom paused to answer criticism of his work. But in this case, King was confronted with a document that conveniently summarized the values of white moderates, a group whose allegiance to "Law and Order and Common Sense" made them critics of King's cause but whose basic commitment to decency and racial justice made them potential allies. The authors of the public statement were, moreover, Christian and Jewish clergymen. King felt that the underlying values of the Judeo-Christian religious tradition, with which he as a clergyman was intimately familiar, would be more logically consistent with support for the Birmingham demonstrations than with the "law and order" position that the eight coauthors of the public statement had actually embraced. Throughout his letter he continually cites the actions of biblical figures that the clergymen are vocationally bound to admire as support for the philosophy and actions of his fellow demonstrators.

Beginning his letter with point-by-point rebuttals of issues raised in the public statement, King follows many of the strategies outlined earlier in this chapter.

In the introductory paragraph, King defines the overall point that he intends to rebut, the charge that his "present activities" in Birmingham are "unwise and untimely." Clearly, though, his letter is not merely a personal defense. In the first draft of the letter he refers to "our" present activities rather than "my" present activities.

The next twenty-one paragraphs are point-by-point rebuttals of arguments expressed or implied in the "public statement":

Paragraphs 2–4: King addresses the clergymen's criticism of "outsiders coming in." The clergymen had claimed that the facing of Birmingham's racial issues could "best be accomplished by citizens of our own metropolitan area … meeting with their knowledge and experience of the local situation." King responds using three of the strategies discussed above:

1 **Facts:** King points out that he has organizational affiliations in Birmingham and that he was invited to Birmingham by local citizens.
2 **Analogies:** Since King is addressing both Jewish and Christian clergymen, he points out that both the prophets of the Old Testament and the Apostle Paul of the New Testament left their native villages to spread disconcerting doctrines to other towns. If the clergymen do not reject these biblical precedents, then they must not really extend blanket condemnation to "outside agitators."

Of course, any audience might reject the analogy and protest that King is not St. Paul or anything like him. Thus King must also defend his particular form of outside interference on the basis of…

3 Conflicting principle: In response to the principle that local people have the right to settle their own local problems, King proposes the counterprinciple that "Injustice anywhere is a threat to justice everywhere." Thus he has not only the right but the obligation to intervene.

Paragraphs 5–11: This section of the letter responds to the general tendency to "deplore" the Birmingham demonstrations. King concedes that the civil unrest is "unfortunate," but he argues that "the city's white power structure left the Negro community with no alternative." While the public statement had assumed that people should seek to redress grievances only through court action and negotiation, King here assumes the counterprinciple that where these legal methods fail, the oppressed have the right to engage in "direct action." It remains for him to show that legal methods have indeed failed, and this he does through factual evidence that racial injustice was rife in Birmingham and that the white community had refused to negotiate in good faith. While "tension" was often used as a devil term by opponents of King's demonstrations (though it does not occur in the "public statement"), King points out that tension can be creative, that it is not an alternative to negotiation, but a path to negotiation.

Paragraphs 12–14: Rebuttal of the charge that the demonstrations are "untimely." King's strategies include:

1 Facts: The new administration in Birmingham is segregationist, like the old one. Privileged groups seldom give up their privileges voluntarily. "We have waited for more than 340 years for our constitutional and God-given rights."

2 Principle: "Justice too long delayed is justice denied."

3 Counterexample to the principle that the Negro should "wait": The specific sufferings cataloged in paragraph 14 are intended to demonstrate by their poignancy that further waiting would be intolerable. Anyone counseling the victims of segregation to "wait" would be countenancing a continuation of these abuses. This paragraph, which for many readers will be the most compelling section of the letter, shows the power of the specific example to support the general rule.

Paragraphs 15–22: Rebuttal of the principle that citizens who violate the local ordinances show disrespect for the law. King's strategies here are to

1 Show that the principle, as stated, has unacceptable consequences: King responds that he did not advocate obedience to any law, but only to a just law. If morality were the same as legality, he points out, then to lend aid and comfort to a Jew in Hitler's Germany would have been immoral. Since this conclusion is validly derived from the general principle in question and yet is absurd, the principle itself is demonstrably wrong unless it is qualified. (This obliges King to offer three definitions of the just law, showing how it can be distinguished from the unjust law.)

2 Deny the principle by counterexample: King denies that everyone who violates an ordinance shows disrespect for law. He proposes that one who breaks an unjust law lovingly, openly, and with a willingness to accept the penalty "is in reality expressing the highest respect for law." King also mentions figures from the Bible, from the early history of the Christian church, and from American history as counterexamples to the principle that those who break laws on grounds of conscience are lawless.

EXERCISE

With the foregoing commentaries as a model, you should be able to carry on the analysis to the end of the letter. King structures the rest of his discourse around the expression of his two great "disappointments": the white moderate (paragraphs 23–32) and the white church (paragraphs 33–47). Within this format he continues to rebut specific moderate arguments (some of them articulated in the "public statement," some not); to rebut the implicit rationale of moderate actions; and to present principles of his own. Below is a scratch outline of the rest of the letter listing the topics discussed. In each case:

    1 Expand the topic designation into a proposition.
    2 List King's strategies of proof or rebuttal.

    Paragraphs 23–24: Law, order, peace, and tension
    Paragraph 25: Tendency of demonstrations to precipitate violence
    Paragraph 26: Time
    Paragraphs 27–32: Extremism
    Paragraphs 33–44: Role of the church in desegregation
    Paragraphs 45–47: Deportment of Birmingham police

4 Policy

A policy claim is a proposal that some change should be made in a prevailing practice or policy. Arguments for or against such changes were known to classical rhetoricians as *deliberative rhetoric*. Everyone who leads an active professional or civic life is continually affected by proposals and may frequently be required to write or respond to them. You are likely to encounter proposals of the following sorts frequently:

- Legislative proposals concerning such issues as safety regulations, human rights, weapons systems, highway construction, licensing
- Proposals for municipal projects such as sewer systems, parks, or zoning changes
- Proposals for educational changes such as innovative courses, revised requirements, use of buildings
- Proposals for new products, programs, policies, or organizational structures in your place of business
- Grant proposals in research and other programs

Clearly such proposals can affect your rights, opportunities, obligations, and pocketbook.

Proposals are probably the most natural form for arguments to take. Of course it is possible to write a purely evaluative argument, but as soon as you construct an argument about (say) the moral objections to state-run lotteries or discrimination on the basis of sexual preference, the question immediately arises, "Shouldn't there be a law?" or "Shouldn't the law be changed?" Approving evaluations lead just as readily to proposals. If a public-spirited citizen has started a shelter for the homeless or a boy's choir, it is natural to seek formal recognition, public subsidies, tax exemptions, or the like to maintain the project and provide incentives for emulators. Purely factual arguments are equally possible. The mean global temperature is rising, and this trend is accelerated both by the burning of fossil fuels and the destruction of rain forests. Here are three distinct factual arguments, but obviously they strongly suggest policy reactions. Human beings naturally tend to worry about those issues that they can do something about. Thus factual research tends to be about issues that are a current subject of policy debate, and questions of value (such as the question of whether homosexual relationships are an immoral aberration, an ethically neutral "alternative life-style," or a commendable form of love to be sanctified by church weddings) tend to be more frequently the subject of written arguments when pertinent public or institutional policies are being debated.

While some proposals (such as a university department's proposal to offer a new course) may be noncontroversial and routine, many are highly controversial. Changes in practice or policy often cost money and energy, upset routines, and curtail the rights of one group in order to extend those of another. Thus proponents of change must anticipate and respond to the arguments of those who would be likely to oppose the change.

Affirmative and Negative Policy Claims

Proposals, then, have something of the character of a debate, and several principles of debating are valuable for anyone writing or responding to a proposal. A debate begins with a *proposition,* a resolution that the affirmative team is obliged to defend. *Propositions of policy* always take the form of an assertion that a certain *agent* should effect some *change in the status quo.*
Examples:

> *Resolved:* That the Commonwealth of Massachusetts should impose a mandatory jail sentence for the possession of handguns.
> *Resolved:* That this university should forbid the showing of pornographic films on campus.
> *Resolved:* That Congress should rescind subsidies for tobacco farmers.

The affirmative team in a debate must defend the desirability of the goal expressed and present a specific *plan* for fulfilling that goal. The proposition typically affords the affirmative considerable leeway in the plan it proposes; for instance, if the proposition calls for a certain state to "control handguns," it is the prerogative of the affirmative to propose whatever it believes to be the optimum type and degree of control (confiscate all privately owned handguns? prohibit further sales only? require registration?) and the administrative requirements for implementing the controls.

The negative has three possible responses. First, it could theoretically argue that no change is required in the status quo. In informal debate, proposals to legalize marijuana or surrogate motherhood contracts or gambling or prostitution often encounter this sort of opposition from those who feel no attraction toward the activities to be legalized. However, simple denial of need is a weak position for the negative since topics are usually brought up for debate because of reasonably strong dissatisfaction with the status quo.

The more common negative strategy is to agree that the status quo is imperfect, but to claim that the affirmative's plan would fail to solve the existing problem, would be impractical, or would entail undesirable side effects.

Finally, the negative, though agreeing with the affirmative that a need exists and that the affirmative plan would bring about an improvement over the status quo, can present a *counterplan* that is more effective, more economical, or less disruptive.

The Stock Issues of Debate

Any topic of debate has its own issues that may be debated separately; for instance, the topic of AIDS testing involves such issues as privacy, public health, cost, and the nature of action to be taken in the event of positive results. Some of these issues are peculiar to debates about AIDS testing. But any debate about policy also involves the *stock issues,* so called because the very logic of deliberative rhetoric makes them applicable to any proposition of policy.[1] The stock issues are a set of questions which the negative may use to probe weaknesses in the affirmative case and which the affirmative should use as a checklist to ensure that its case is as well defended as possible. The degree of emphasis which each of the stock issues invites is somewhat dependent on the topic of the debate.

The first two stock issues seek to determine whether any change in the status quo is required.

1. Is There a Serious Need for Change?

Sometimes this issue is thought of as *identifying a disparity* between what is and what could be. The affirmative may be basing its case on a clear need (such as a major threat to health in the environment) or an opportunity (such as a municipality's chance to gain federal funds to build a park). The bare fact that a few people desire a change may be construed as need; think of the fairly small minority who have asked for legalization of surrogate motherhood contracts. When proposing a change which some of the audience may regard as frivolous, such as legalizing the possession and use of marijuana, proponents of the change are well

---

[1] In my use of the stock issues of debate as a heuristic for policy proposals, I am indebted to Richard A. Katula and Richard W. Roth, "A Stock Issues Approach to Writing Arguments," *CCC* 31 (May 1980), 183–96.

advised to keep the audience's value structure in mind and to point to disadvantages in the current situation which the audience may not have considered, such as the enormous untaxed underground economy.

2. Is the Need Inherent?

This question asks, "Is the need which you have pointed out likely to be permanent in the absence of new remedies, or is it being taken care of in some other form?" *Inherency* has been an important issue in the debate over the ERA, because many legislators who are reluctant to tamper with the Constitution except in cases of clear necessity believe that equality of opportunity is being gained already by piecemeal legislation governing sexual discrimination.

The last three issues seek to determine whether the affirmative plan will meet the need effectively. In applying these issues, the most important thing a debater, writer, or evaluator of a plan can do is *visualize* what would happen if the plan were put into effect.

3. Does the Plan Meet the Need?

In other words, assuming that your plan were funded and implemented, would the disparity identified in Issue 1 above disappear? In states that have debated whether to institute (or reinstitute) the death penalty, this issue appears in the question of whether capital punishment will reduce the rate of serious crime.

The "plan-meet-need" issue requires causal reasoning from empirical evidence. That is, it must show that the proposed remedy will cause the desired improvement in the status quo. The affirmative can make a much stronger argument on this issue by citing the favorable effect of similar legislation elsewhere than by simply assuming that the measure will be effective or by deducing the probability of success from vague notions about human nature. The negative may present counterarguments by adducing instances in which similar legislation failed or by denying that the successes cited by the affirmative occurred under comparable conditions.

4. Is the Plan Feasible?

Someone has proposed that all the coin-operated photocopy machines at a large university should be free because (a) the students have already "paid enough" in their various fees and (b) when the machines are out of order, it is usually due to a malfunction of the coin box. To determine whether this plan is feasible, *visualize* what would happen if all the photocopy machines in your library and bookstore were free.

5. Is the Plan Free of Crippling Disadvantages?

This is undoubtedly the most frequently applied of the stock issues. Disadvantages frequently cited include expense, danger, increased red tape, and infringement on someone else's rights. Obviously, the fact that a proposed action carries with it some disadvantages is not necessarily fatal to the proposal; for instance, an effort to reduce air pollution in a given state may put drivers to the trouble and expense of an annual auto emissions test and require the state to build emissions-testing centers. Nevertheless, the reduction of air pollution may make these inconveniences worthwhile.

Discussion of the disadvantage issue may also demand sound causal reasoning, for some of the disadvantages alleged to attend a proposal may be purely conjectural; for instance, proposals to flouridate public drinking waters sometimes confront allegations of health hazards. This issue also demands consideration of values questions, often very sensitive ones, since the enhancement of some people's fortunes under the proposed change will probably require the curtailment of others'. And, again, debaters should be careful to respect the value system of the audience in their arguments.

The affirmative does not win a debate by winning simply a preponderance of the stock issues. It must win them all. Even though the affirmative demonstrates a serious and inherent need for something to be done, presents a plan that will meet the need, and has no disqualifying side effects, if the negative shows that the plan is simply not feasible, the affirmative loses.

These principles of debate have several applications for writers outside the arena of formal debating. When you are called upon to propose some action to be taken, you should be sure that all the stock issues are accounted for. This is not to say that you must discuss them all. If you are proposing a plan for countering a lethal epidemic in progress, you do not have to waste time demonstrating need. If, before you write, you make a preliminary analysis of the question to see which stock issues are relevant, you will know better what form your proposal should take and where you can most profitably focus your energies.

More commonly, you will not be required to present a full proposal but only to discuss some aspect of a proposal under public discussion. Thus, when the debate on the ERA was at its strongest, articles frequently appeared on a variety of issues: Were women actually discriminated against in the workplace, in access to credit and education and the like (need)? Was it desirable for women to have equal rights in these areas (need)? How should the ERA actually be worded (plan)? Would the ERA demand that women serve in armed combat and use the same bathrooms as men (disadvantage)? Would the ERA actually curtail existing discrimination (plan-meet-need)? If greater equality were indeed needed, was a constitutional amendment the best way of securing it or would piecemeal legislation be less disruptive (disadvantage; inherency)? How would the ERA affect family life and child rearing (disadvantage)?

A Checklist for Full Proposals

The following is a checklist for writing full proposals of your own or evaluating those of others. Bear in mind that different topics require different emphases, that not all steps may be required, and that their order may be changed to suit your needs:

1 The proposal should clearly *identify the need for a change in the status quo.* It is generally wise to develop this argument independently of the plan, for if the audience does not accept the specific plan proposed, it may still be willing to consider other means of reaching your general goal.

2 The proposal should *show that the need is not being adequately met* by other existing or contemplated measures (inherency).

3 The proposal should *present a specific plan.* It need not be detailed, but when appropriate it should propose and defend specific answers to such controversial questions as, "How is the plan to be funded?" "Who will make important decisions?" "How will these decision makers be selected?" "What safeguards will be provided?"

4 The proposal should *specify the agent responsible* for implementing the plan. Be sure that this agent has the authority to do so. (For instance, don't propose that the United States government pass laws that violate states' rights; do remember, though, that the federal government can influence state policies by granting or withholding federal funds.)

5 The proposal should *demonstrate that the plan will meet the designated need.*

6 The proposal should *demonstrate that the plan is better than other plans* that might initially be more plausible to the audience.

7 The proposal should *counter any probable objections to its feasibility.*

8 The proposal should *face its own disadvantages squarely and show them to be less onerous than the status quo.*

9 *The proposal should mention any incidental advantages.* For instance, a municipal trash incinerator proposed mainly to dispose of trash might have the side benefit of generating steam power.

10 The proposal should *give fair representation to opposing views in their strongest form.* Avoid the "straw man" fallacy, whereby the writer attacks a weak version of an opponent's argument.

11 Many proposals urge a reversal of a decision previously made. Some propose reconsideration of a plan that was earlier rejected; others propose repeal of a plan that was earlier accepted. In either of these cases, the proposal *should carefully review the reasons for the earlier adverse judgment and carefully describe any new evidence or altered conditions that now make the plan more acceptable.*

Sample Proposal

The eighteenth century saw a great proliferation of proposals in English-speaking countries. Increasing wealth, the growth of science and technology, rapid improvements in literacy, printing, and distribution of printing materials, faith in the power of reason to bring about positive change both in the material and political dimensions of social life—all these forces combined to encourage the publication of proposals on all manner of subjects. In America, Benjamin Franklin wrote proposals on subjects ranging from street sweeping to the defense of Philadelphia, and the *Federalist Papers* presented proposals for various provisions of the Constitution of the United States. In Ireland, Jonathan Swift, the Dean of St. Patrick's Cathedral in Dublin, wrote a number of proposals, many of them on the subject of relieving the terrible poverty in Ireland resulting from the harsh economic regulations imposed by England. Most of his proposals, bound as they were to the problems and conditions of their time, are largely forgotten today, but one of them, his "Modest Proposal," is widely reprinted and read even today for its savage irony. For readers in Swift's day, a great part of its impact would have come from its close adherence to the form, organization, and style of the many contemporary proposals for "the publick good."

JONATHAN SWIFT

A Modest Proposal

For Preventing the Children of Poor People in Ireland from Being a Burden to Their Parents or Country, and for Making Them Beneficial to the Public

1   It is a melancholy object to those who walk through this great town or travel in the country, when they see the streets, the roads, and cabin doors, crowded with beggars of the female-sex, followed by three, four, or six children, all in rags and importuning every passenger for an alms. These mothers, instead of being able to work for their honest livelihood, are forced to employ all their time in strolling to beg sustenance for their helpless infants, who, as they grow up, either turn thieves for want of work, or leave their dear native country to fight for the Pretender in Spain, or sell themselves to the Barbadoes.

2   I think it is agreed by all parties that this prodigious number of children in the arms, or on the backs, or at the heels of their mothers, and frequently of their fathers, is in the present deplorable state of the kingdom a very great additional grievance; and therefore whoever could find out a

fair, cheap, and easy method of making these children sound, useful members of the commonwealth would deserve so well of the public as to have his statue set up for a preserver of the nation.

3   But my intention is very far from being confined to provide only for the children of professed beggars; it is of a much greater extent, and shall take in the whole number of infants at a certain age who are born of parents in effect as little able to support them as those who demand our charity in the streets.

4   As to my own part, having turned my thoughts for many years upon this important subject, and maturely weighed the several schemes of other projectors, I have always found them grossly mistaken in their computation. It is true, a child just dropped from its dam may be supported by her milk for a solar year, with little other nourishment; at most not above the value of two shillings, which the mother may certainly get, or the value in scraps, by her lawful occupation of begging; and it is exactly at one year old that I propose to provide for them in such a manner as instead of being a charge upon their parents or the parish, or wanting food and raiment for the rest of their lives, they shall on the contrary contribute to the feeding, and partly to the clothing, of many thousands.

5   There is likewise another great advantage in my scheme, that it will prevent those voluntary abortions, and that horrid practice of women murdering their bastard children, alas, too frequent among us, sacrificing the poor innocent babes, I doubt, more to avoid the expense than the shame, which would move tears and pity in the most savage and inhuman breast.

6   The number of souls in this kingdom being usually reckoned one million and a half, of these I calculate there may be about two hundred thousand couple whose wives are breeders; from which number I subtract thirty thousand couples who are able to maintain their own children, although I apprehend there cannot be so many under the present distresses of the kingdom; but this being granted, there will remain an hundred and seventy thousand breeders. I again subtract fifty thousand for those women who miscarry, or whose children die by accident or disease within the year. There only remain an hundred and twenty thousand children of poor parents annually born. The question therefore is, how this number shall be reared and provided for, which, as I have already said, under the present situation of affairs, is utterly impossible by all the methods hitherto proposed. For we can neither employ them in handicraft or agriculture; we neither build houses (I mean in the country) nor cultivate land. They can very seldom pick up a livelihood by stealing till they arrive at six years old, except where they are of towardly parts; although I confess they learn the rudiments much earlier, during which time they can however be looked upon only as probationers, as I have been informed by a principal

gentleman in the county of Cavan, who protested to me that he never knew above one or two instances under the age of six, even in a part of the kingdom so renowned for the quickest proficiency in that art.

7   I am assured by our merchants that a boy or a girl before twelve years old is no salable commodity; and even when they come to this age they will not yield above three pounds, or three pounds and half a crown at most on the Exchange; which cannot turn to account either to the parents or the kingdom, the charge of nutriment and rags having been at least four times that value.

8   I shall now therefore humbly propose my own thoughts, which I hope will not be liable to the least objection.

9   I have been assured by a very knowing American of my acquaintance in London, that a young healthy child well nursed is at a year old a most delicious, nourishing, and wholesome food, whether stewed, roasted, baked, or boiled; and I make no doubt that it will equally serve in a fricassee or a ragout.

10   I do therefore humbly offer it to public consideration that of the hundred and twenty thousand children, already computed, twenty thousand may be reserved for breed, whereof only one fourth part to be males, which is more than we allow to sheep, black cattle, or swine; and my reason is that these children are seldom the fruits of marriage, a circumstance not much regarded by our savages, therefore one male will be sufficient to serve four females. That the remaining hundred thousand may at a year old be offered in sale to the persons of quality and fortune through the kingdom, always advising the mother to let them suck plentifully in the last month, so as to render them plump and fat for a good table. A child will make two dishes at an entertainment for friends; and when the family dines alone, the fore or hind quarter will make a reasonable dish, and seasoned with a little pepper or salt will be very good boiled on the fourth day, especially in winter.

11   I have reckoned upon a medium that a child just born will weigh twelve pounds, and in a solar year if tolerably nursed increaseth to twenty-eight pounds.

12   I grant this food will be somewhat dear, and therefore very proper for landlords, who, as they have already devoured most of the parents, seem to have the best title to the children.

13   Infant's flesh will be in season throughout the year, but more plentiful in March, and a little before and after. For we are told by a grave author, an eminent French physician, that fish being a prolific diet, there are more children born in Roman Catholic countries about nine months after Lent than at any other season; therefore, reckoning a year after Lent, the markets will be more glutted than usual, because the number of popish infants is at least three to one in this kingdom; and therefore it will

have one other collateral advantage, by lessening the number of Papists among us.

14   I have already computed the charge of nursing a beggar's child (in which list I reckon all cottagers, laborers, and four fifths of the farmers) to be about two shillings per annum, rags included; and I believe no gentleman would repine to give ten shillings for the carcass of a good fat child, which, as I have said, will make four dishes of excellent nutritive meat, when he hath only some particular friend or his own family to dine with him. Thus the squire will learn to be a good landlord, and grow popular among the tenants; the mother will have eight shillings net profit, and be fit for work till she produces another child.

15   Those who are more thrifty (as I must confess the times require) may flay the carcass; the skin of which artificially dressed will make admirable gloves for ladies, and summer boots for fine gentlemen.

16   As to our city of Dublin, shambles may be appointed for this purpose in the most convenient parts of it, and butchers we may be assured will not be wanting; although I rather recommend buying the children alive, and dressing them hot from the knife as we do roasting pigs.

17   A very worthy person, a true lover of his country, and whose virtues I highly esteem, was lately pleased in discoursing on this matter to offer a refinement upon my scheme. He said that many gentlemen of this kingdom, having of late destroyed their deer, he conceived that the want of venison might be well supplied by the bodies of young lads and maidens, not exceeding fourteen years of age nor under twelve, so great a number of both sexes in every county being now ready to starve for want of work and service; and these to be disposed of by their parents, if alive, or otherwise by their nearest relations. But with due deference to so excellent a friend and so deserving a patriot, I cannot be altogether in his sentiments; for as to the males, my American acquaintance assured me from frequent experience that their flesh was generally tough and lean, like that of our schoolboys, by continual exercise, and their taste disagreeable; and to fatten them would not answer the charge. Then as to the females, it would, I think with humble submission, be a loss to the public, because they soon would become breeders themselves: and besides, it is not improbable that some scrupulous people might be apt to censure such a practice (although indeed very unjustly) as a little bordering upon cruelty; which, I confess, hath always been with me the strongest objection against any project, how well soever intended.

18   But in order to justify my friend, he confessed that this expedient was put into his head by the famous Psalmanazar, a native of the island Formosa, who came from thence to London above twenty years ago, and in conversation told my friend that in his country when any young person happened to be put to death, the executioner sold the carcass to persons of

quality as a prime dainty; and that in his time the body of a plump girl of fifteen, who was crucified for an attempt to poison the emperor, was sold to his Imperial Majesty's prime minister of state, and other great mandarins of the court, in joints from the gibbet, at four hundred crowns. Neither indeed can I deny that if the same use were made of several plump young girls in this town, who without one single groat to their fortunes cannot stir abroad without a chair, and appear at the playhouse and assemblies in foreign fineries which they never will pay for, the kingdom would not be the worse.

19   Some persons of a desponding spirit are in great concern about that vast number of poor people who are aged, diseased, or maimed, and I have been desired to employ my thoughts what course may be taken to ease the nation of so grievous an encumbrance. But I am not in the least pain upon that matter, because it is very well known that they are every day dying and rotting by cold and famine, and filth and vermin, as fast as can be reasonably expected. And as to the younger laborers, they are now in almost as hopeful a condition. They cannot get work, and consequently pine away for want of nourishment to a degree that if at any time they are accidentally hired to common labor, they have not strength to perform it; and thus the country and themselves are happily delivered from the evils to come.

20   I have too long digressed, and therefore shall return to my subject. I think the advantages by the proposal which I have made are obvious and many, as well as of the highest importance.

21   For first, as I have already observed, it would greatly lessen the number of Papists, with whom we are yearly overrun, being the principal breeders of the nation as well as our most dangerous enemies: and who stay at home on purpose to deliver the kingdom to the Pretender, hoping to take their advantage by the absence of so many good Protestants, who have chosen rather to leave their country than to stay at home and pay tithes against their conscience to an Episcopal curate.

22   Secondly, the poorer tenants will have something valuable of their own, which by law may be made liable to distress, and help to pay their landlord's rent, their corn and cattle being already seized and money a thing unknown.

23   Thirdly, whereas the maintenance of an hundred thousand children, from two years old and upwards, cannot be computed at less than ten shillings a piece per annum, the nation's stock will be thereby increased fifty thousand pounds per annum, besides the profit of a new dish introduced to the tables of all gentlemen of fortune in the kingdom who have any refinement in taste. And the money will circulate among ourselves, the goods being entirely of our own growth and manufacture.

24   Fourthly, the constant breeders, besides the gain of eight shillings sterling per annum by the sale of their children, will be rid of the charge of maintaining them after the first year.

25   Fifthly, this food would likewise bring great custom to taverns, where the vintners will certainly be so prudent as to procure the best receipts for dressing it to perfection, and consequently have their houses frequented by all the fine gentlemen, who justly value themselves upon their knowledge in good eating; and a skillful cook, who understands how to oblige his guests, will contrive to make it as expensive as they please.

26   Sixthly, this would be a great inducement to marriage, which all wise nations have either encouraged by rewards or enforced by laws and penalties. It would increase the care and tenderness of mothers toward their children, when they were sure of a settlement for life to the poor babes, provided in some sort by the public, to their annual profit instead of expense. We should see an honest emulation among the married women, which of them could bring the fattest child to the market. Men would become as fond of their wives during the time of their pregnancy as they are now of their mares in foal, their cows in calf, or sows when they are ready to farrow; nor offer to beat or kick them (as is too frequent a practice) for fear of a miscarriage.

27   Many other advantages might be enumerated. For instance, the addition of some thousand carcasses in our exportation of barreled beef, the propagation of swine's flesh, and improvement in the art of making good bacon, so much wanted among us by the great destruction of pigs, too frequent at our tables, which are no way comparable in taste or magnificence to a well-grown, fat, yearling child, which roasted whole will make a considerable figure at a lord mayor's feast or any other public entertainment. But this and many others I omit, being studious of brevity.

28   Supposing that one thousand families in this city would be constant customers for infants' flesh, besides others who might have it at merry meetings, particularly weddings and christenings, I compute that Dublin would take off annually about twenty thousand carcasses, and the rest of the kingdom (where probably they will be sold somewhat cheaper) the remaining eighty thousand.

29   I can think of no one objection that will possibly be raised against this proposal, unless it should be urged that the number of people will be thereby much lessened in the kingdom. This I freely own, and it was indeed one principal design in offering it to the world. I desire the reader will observe, that I calculate my remedy for this one individual kingdom of Ireland and for no other that ever was, is, or I think ever can be upon earth. Therefore let no man talk to me of other expedients: of taxing our absentees at five shillings a pound: of using neither clothes nor household furniture except what is of our own growth and manufacture: of utterly rejecting the materials and instruments that promote foreign luxury: of curing the expensiveness of pride, vanity, idleness, and gaming in our women: of introducing a vein of parsimony, prudence, and temperance: of

learning to love our country, in the want of which we differ even from Laplanders and the inhabitants of Topinamboo: of quitting our animosities and factions, nor acting any longer like the Jews, who were murdering one another at the very moment their city was taken: of being a little cautious not to sell our country and conscience for nothing: of teaching landlords to have at least one degree of mercy toward their tenants: lastly, of putting a spirit of honesty, industry, and skill into our shopkeepers; who, if a resolution could now be taken to buy only our native goods, would immediately unite to cheat and exact upon us in the price, the measure, and the goodness, nor could ever yet be brought to make one fair proposal of just dealing, though often and earnestly invited to it.

30   Therefore I repeat, let no man talk to me of these and the like expedients, till he hath at least some glimpse of hope that there will ever be some hearty and sincere attempt to put them in practice.

31   But as to myself, having been wearied out for many years with offering vain, idle, visionary thoughts, and at length utterly despairing of success, I fortunately fell upon this proposal, which, as it is wholly new, so it hath something solid and real, of no expense and little trouble, full in our own power, and whereby we can incur no danger in disobliging England. For this kind of commodity will not bear exportation, the flesh being of too tender a consistence to admit a long continuance in salt, although perhaps I could name a country which would be glad to eat up our whole nation without it.

32   After all, I am not so violently bent upon my own opinion as to reject any offer proposed by wise men, which shall be found equally innocent, cheap, and effectual. But before something of that kind shall be advanced in contradiction to my scheme, and offering a better, I desire the author or authors will be pleased maturely to consider two points. First, as things now stand, how they will be able to find food and raiment for an hundred thousand useless mouths and backs. And secondly, there being a round million of creatures in human figure throughout this kingdom, whose sole subsistence put into a common stock would leave them in debt two millions of pounds sterling, adding those who are beggars by profession to the bulk of farmers, cottagers, and laborers, with their wives and children who are beggars in effect; I desire those politicians who dislike my overture, and may perhaps be so bold to attempt an answer, that they will first ask the parents of these mortals whether they would not at this day think it a great happiness to have been sold for food at a year old in the manner I prescribe, and thereby have avoided such a perpetual scene of misfortunes as they have since gone through by the oppression of landlords, the impossibility of paying rent without money or trade, the want of common sustenance, with neither house nor clothes to cover them from the inclemencies of the weather, and the most inevitable prospect of entailing the like or greater miseries upon their breed forever.

33   I profess, in the sincerity of my heart, that I have not the least personal interest in endeavoring to promote this necessary work, having no other motive than the public good of my country, by advancing our trade, providing for infants, relieving the poor, and giving some pleasure to the rich. I have no children by which I can propose to get a single penny; the youngest being nine years old, and my wife past childbearing.

Analysis of Swift's Proposal

Paragraphs 1–7 (need): Swift begins the essay with the common strategy of pointing out to his audience those evidences of need that they would most likely have observed for themselves—the many Irish mothers reduced to begging for themselves and their children. He then identifies the area of agreement on this subject and points out that the need extends beyond the children of "professed beggars" to include those of most Irish parents, who are virtual beggars because of the terrible economic problems in Ireland. In paragraph 4 he briefly mentions other views on this subject supplied by "other projectors" (that is, he considers counterplans), but he dismisses them as based on faulty calculations (he attacks their feasibility or ability to meet the need). In paragraphs 4 and 5 he mentions the main benefit of his proposal—to provide for the support of Irish children—and two side benefits, to make them contributors to the economy rather than a drain upon it and to prevent abortions. In paragraphs 6 and 7 he presents some of the factual background about the numbers of children involved and their value. In paragraph 6 he raises the issue of inherency, concluding that the children in question cannot be provided for under any other proposed plans.

Paragraphs 8–19 (plan): Here Swift gives the details of his plan—the ratio of slaughtered children to breeders; the ratio of males in the latter group; the various uses to which the children's meat and hides can be put; the arrangements for butchering; and his rejection of a provision for using older children as a venison substitute.

Paragraphs 20–28 (advantages): Six advantages are specifically enumerated and others hinted at.

Paragraphs 29–33 (possible objections and counterproposals): The only objection to his scheme that Swift professes to foresee is that Ireland may be depopulated, but he transforms this disadvantage into an advantage. He then lists other proposed "expedients" for remedying Ireland's problems (several of which Swift himself introduces in proposals that are not ironic). He pretends that these sensible expedients would not work in Ireland, which he says would not sincerely attempt to put them into practice. In paragraph 32 Swift expresses his willingness to listen to counterproposals but warns their authors of the advantages to his own proposal that they will have to overcome.

EXERCISE

The following newspaper column describes two competing proposals, one by President Bush, the other by members of Congress. Both plans aim at satisfying the same need; they also acknowledge and try to circumvent the same potential disadvantage. Read the essay and answer the questions that follow it.

CHARLES KRAUTHAMMER

*Fetal Tissue Research: Hostage to Abortion Politics**

1   Once more around the block. In 1988, the administration of President Ronald Reagan imposed a ban on federally funded transplantation research that uses fetal tissue taken from abortions. The ban effectively killed U.S. research on fetal tissue transplants, research that may be crucial to the understanding and treatment of Parkinson's, diabetes and other intractable and debilitating diseases. Because fetal tissue is almost magically adaptable and regenerative, there has been pressure from scientists and citizens' groups to lift the ban.

2   Congress is now poised to do exactly that. With several anti-abortion senators coming out in favor of fetal research, there might be enough votes to override a presidential veto. Accordingly, President Bush has tried to defuse the issue and win swing votes with an executive order creating a "Fetal Tissue Bank" to meet research needs with tissue taken only from spontaneous abortions and ectopic pregnancies.

3   The problem is, however, that this will not meet the need. Spontaneous abortions occur, generally speaking, when the fetus is non-viable, often because of chromosomal damage or infection. Only 1 percent of spontaneous abortions produce tissue suitable for transplantation research. And nearly nine out of 10 of that 1 percent occur outside a medical setting, making the tissue unrecoverable for scientific purposes.

4   It makes no sense to try to support transplant research using only spontaneous abortions and ectopic pregnancies. It will cost a fortune and it won't work. Meanwhile, millions of abortions are being performed legally in medical settings throughout the country and the tissue ends up simply being discarded.

---

* Charles Krauthammer is a syndicated columnist.

5   The Fetal Tissue Bank is a transparent device to try to appease the scientific community while remaining on the right side of the more fundamentalist pro-lifers.

6   The Bush position is more than politically cynical. It is intellectually flimsy. When the Bush administration reaffirmed the Reagan ban in 1989 it did so on the stated grounds that allowing the use of aborted fetal tissue encourages abortion. Can you think of one person who would be influenced to have an abortion because of the research value of the tissue? Well, you might say, what about a poor woman? Or a woman whose father needed a fetal tissue transplant for Parkinson's?

7   These are the only conceivable ways in which fetal research might be an inducement to abortion. Accordingly, proponents of fetal research insist on three ironclad safeguards that break any connection between fetal research and the abortion decision.

8   First, maintain and enforce the legal prohibition against the sale of fetuses or parts of fetuses. Second, prohibit any woman from designating the recipient of her fetal tissue. And third, prohibit raising the issue of using aborted tissue for research until after the decision to abort has already been made.

9   The federal government has every right to try to do what it can to discourage abortion, but wrecking fetal transplantation research is a useless and destructive way to go about it.

10   One legitimate avenue of discouragement is, for example, the gag rule. It prohibits all but doctors from discussing abortion with patients in federally financed clinics. A government elected on an openly anti-abortion platform has no obligation to subsidize abortion counseling and referral.

11   Counseling and referral have an obvious and real connection to a woman's decision to abort. Fetal research has only the remotest connection, and even that can be broken with simple safeguards. If the president feels the need to make a stand on abortion, fine. It's a free country and an election year. But fetal research is the wrong place to make that stand. With so much at stake in fetal research, it is a shame to make it hostage to the politics of abortion.

STUDY QUESTIONS

1. At the time this article was written, what was the status quo respecting federally funded research into fetal tissue transplantation?
2. How would the proposal before Congress, supported by scientists and citizens' groups, have changed the status quo?

3. President Bush's proposal for a "Fetal Tissue Bank" is actually a *counterplan* because it addresses the same *need* as the congressional proposal. What is that need?
4. According to Bush, what *disadvantage* in the congressional plan does his counterplan avoid?
5. What provisions did supporters of the congressional proposal include to remove this disadvantage from their own plan?
6. On which of the stock issues does the author of the article believe that the President's plan is weakest?
7. On what (if any) *factual* issues do the opposing positions disagree? on what (if any) *values* issues do the opposing positions disagree?
8. What reasons does the author give for preferring Congress' plan to the President's?
9. Judging from this column, would you characterize the author's position on abortion as conservative, moderate, or liberal? Why?

5 *Writing with Direction*

So far we have been considering chiefly the *logic* of arguments, the structural relationships among evidence, premises, and conclusions in our subject matter. Yet when we produce an extended argument in writing, full understanding of the subject is not enough, for an argument must take its audience into account as well. In order to know how much background and explanation to provide, we must make assumptions about how far our readers already share our values and how much factual knowledge they already possess. But the most complex and difficult aspect of writing for an audience is that, while the component parts of our subject are simultaneously present to our minds in their full structural relations, they can only be conveyed to the reader in a word-by-word trickle.

The point of writing is to change readers' thinking. Sometimes we merely add information, sometimes we want readers to see something from a fresh angle, sometimes we try to persuade them to act, and sometimes, though knowing that they will never accept our conclusions, we try to show them that our position is sincere or respectable or at least sane. In any case, for our writing to succeed, the logical components of our argument must be selected and organized so that our position strikes our readers as understandable, coherent, memorable, and compatible with their other beliefs and values.

Writing that succeeds in these ways has a quality that we may call *direction*, both in the sense that it is headed toward a distinct conclusion and in the sense that it is under control. Argumentative papers with strong direction have the following characteristics:

- They provide a context for the issues discussed, describing the importance of the subject, current views on the subject, and reasons why these positions are unsatisfactory.
- They begin from the reader's standpoint without assuming either knowledge or values that readers may not share.

- They order points efficiently so that those necessary to the intelligibility of later arguments come first.
- They divide the argument into portions of digestible length and complexity. They don't nest one complex argument within another, but rather place them in the most readable sequence.
- They prepare the reader for points by such devices as posing questions and describing problems, paradoxes, and anomalies. A point will be more meaningful and memorable if it resolves a tension created in advance.
- They anticipate and respond to questions or objections that they may provoke in the reader.
- They use examples, comparisons, and analogies to clarify difficult or improbable concepts.

EXERCISE 1

Study Figure 5–1, a diagram of the carbon cycle, and assign a number to each box and to each arrow. Now imagine that you are going to present a lecture in which you will construct this diagram bit by bit on a blackboard as you speak. Write a text for this lecture including an introduction, a conclusion, and stage directions such as "Box 3" and "Arrow 4" to indicate where in the lecture you would draw the corresponding item on the blackboard. Be prepared to explain why you chose the order you did.

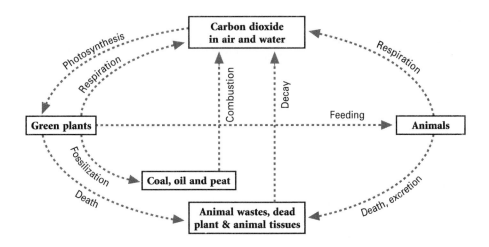

Figure 5–1. The carbon cycle.

EXERCISE 2

Writing is not the only activity in which a temporal sequence is required to present information about and attitudes toward nontemporal subjects. With one or two other people, assume that you are a team assigned to produce a thirty-minute videotape about the architecture of a public building in your locale. Discuss with your partners what aspects of the building you would shoot, whether they would be distance shots or close-ups, how long sequences would last, and in what order the sequences would occur.

The following exerpt is from an essay by Isaac Asimov, a writer who had a passion for conveying scientific concepts clearly to a popular audience. In this essay he is, as he says, "aching to explain," a promising frame of mind for a writer. Here is how he begins:

ISAAC ASIMOV

Time and Tide

1   What with one thing and another, I've gotten used to explaining various subtle puzzles that arise in connection with the scientific view of the universe. For instance, I have disposed of the manner in which electrons and photons can be waves part of the time and particles the rest of the time in a dozen different ways and by use of a dozen different analogies.

2   I've gotten so good at it, in fact, that at dinner parties the word nervously goes about, "For heaven's sake, don't ask Asimov anything about wave-particle duality."

3   And no one ever does. I sit there all primed and aching to explain, and no one ever asks. It kills the party for me.

4   But it's the simple thing that throws me. I've just been trying to write a very small book on the Moon for third-graders and as part of the task I was asked to explain why there are two high tides each day.

5   Simple, I thought, and a condescending smirk passed over my face. I flexed my fingers and bent over the typewriter.

6   As the time passed, the smirk vanished and the hair at my temples grew perceptibly grayer. I managed at last, after a fashion, but if you don't mind, Gentle Reader, I'd like to try again. I need the practice.

Why did Asimov have such difficulty explaining why there are two high tides each day? Not, certainly, because his understanding of the phenomenon was

shaky. Unquestionably he conceptualized the entire structure of forces that produce the tides and could have represented them for himself in visual diagrams
like those in Figure 5–2, where all the components can be present at once:

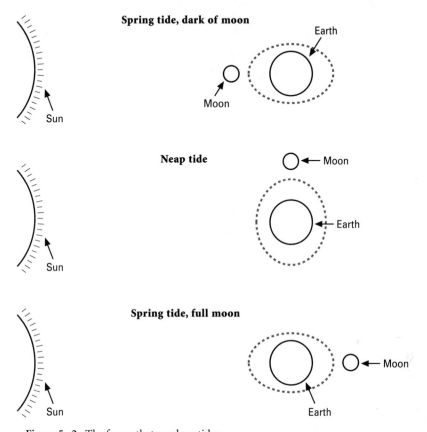

Figure 5–2. The forces that produce tides.

I suspect that Asimov had such difficulty writing out an answer to his question
because he could not convey all the interrelated components of the tidal phenomenon in a lump but had to release them in a trickle. Here is how he solved his
problem:

7   The tides have bothered people for a long
time, but not the good old Greeks, with
reference to whom I start so many articles. The
Greeks, you see, lived (and still live, for that
matter) on the shores of the Mediterranean Sea.
That sea happens to be relatively tideless because
it is so nearly landlocked that high tide can't get
through the Strait of Gibraltar before the time
for it has passed and it is low tide again.

Asimov arouses interest
and directs attention by
an anomaly: Although
the correlation between
spring and neap tides
with the phases of the
moon gave Pytheas
strong reason to believe
that the moon

8   About 325 B.C., however, a Greek explorer, Pytheas of Massalia (the modern Marseilles), ventured out of the Mediterranean and into the Atlantic. There he came across good pronounced tides, with two periods of high water each day and two periods of low water in between. Pytheas made good observations of these, undoubtedly helped out by the inhabitants of the shores facing the open ocean who were used to the tides and took them for granted.

9   The key observation was that the range between high water and low water was not always the same. It increased and decreased with time. Each month there were two periods of particularly large range between high and low tides ("spring tides") and, in between, two periods of particularly small range ("neap tides").

10   What's more, the monthly variations matched the phases of the Moon. The spring tides came at full Moon and new Moon, while the neap tides came at first quarter and third quarter. Pytheas suggested, therefore, that the tides were caused by the Moon. Some of the later Greek astronomers accepted this, but for the most part, Pytheas's suggestion lay fallow for two thousand years.

11   There were plenty of men who believed that the Moon influenced the manner in which crops grew, the rationality or irrationality of men, the way in which a man might turn into a werewolf, the likelihood of encountering spooks and goblins—but that it might influence the tides seemed to be going a bit far!

12   I suspect that one factor that spoiled the Moon/tide connection for thoughtful scholars was precisely the fact that there were two tides a day.

13   For instance, suppose there is a high tide when the Moon is high in the sky. That would make sense. The Moon might well be drawing the water to itself by some mysterious force. No one in ancient and medieval times had any notion of just how such a force might behave, but one could at least give it a name such as

controlled the tides, scholars largely rejected his claim for 2000 years. Readers are prepared to have this odd rejection explained.

The anomalous rejection is explained: Scientists could understand that the "sympathetic attraction" of the moon might account for one

"sympathetic attraction." If the water heaped up under a high Moon, a point on the rotating Earth, passing through the heap, would experience a high tide followed by a low tide.

14   But a little over twelve hours later, there would be another high tide and then the Moon would be nowhere in the sky. It would be, in fact, on the other side of the globe, in the direction of a man's feet. If the Moon were exerting a sympathetic attraction, the water on the man's side of the globe ought to be pulled downward in the direction of his feet. There ought to be a hollow in the ocean, not a heap.

15   Or could it be that the Moon exerted a sympathetic attraction on the side of the Earth nearest itself and a sympathetic repulsion on the side opposite. Then there would be a heap on both sides, two heaps all told. In one rotation of the Earth, a point on the shore would pass through both heaps and there would be two high tides each day, with two low tides in between.

16   The notion that the Moon would pull in some places and push in other places must have been very hard to accept, and most scholars didn't try. So the Moon's influence on the tides was put down to astrological superstition by the astronomers of early modern times.

17   In the early 1600s, for instance, Johannes Kepler stated his belief that the Moon influenced the tides, and the sober Galileo laughed at him. Kepler, after all, was an astrologer who believed in the influence of the Moon and the planets on all sorts of earthly phenomena and Galileo would have none of that. Galileo thought the tides were caused by the sloshing of the oceans back and forth as the Earth rotated—and he was quite wrong.

18   Came Isaac Newton at last! In 1685, he advanced the law of universal gravitation. By using that law it became obvious that the Moon's gravitational field had to exert an influence on the Earth and the tides could well be a response to that field.

tide a day, but not two. Asimov explains why the sympathetic attraction theory "makes sense." The passage makes readers feel secure under Asimov's guidance because the trail of his explanation starts from their own position, even though it is mistaken, rather than from some more accurate assumption that they could not share.

19   But why *two* tides? What difference does it make whether we call the force exerted by the Moon on the Earth "sympathetic attraction" or "gravitational attraction"? How could the Moon, when it was on the other side of the Earth, cause the water on this side to heap upward, *away* from the Moon? The Moon would still have to be pulling in one place and pushing in another, wouldn't it? And that still wouldn't make sense, would it?

We learn that the concept of gravity will explain the tides but that the occurrence of two tides a day still seems to be an obstacle.

20   Ah, but Newton did more than change words and substitute "gravity" for "sympathy." Newton showed exactly how the gravitational force varied with distance, which was more than anyone before him had shown in connection with the vaguely postulated sympathetic force.

21   The gravitational force varied inversely as the square of the distance. That means the force grows smaller as the distance grows larger; and if the distance increases by a ratio of χ, the force decreases by a ratio of χ^2.

The variation of force with distance is shown to be the crucial aspect of gravity that gives it more explanatory power than "sympathetic attraction." A lesser writer might well have considered the explanation complete at this point.

22   Let's take the specific case of the Moon and the Earth. The average distance of the Moon's center from the surface of the Earth nearest itself is 234,000 miles. In order to get the distance of the Moon's center from the surface of the Earth farthest from itself, you must add the thickness of the Earth (8,000 miles) to the first figure, and that gives you 242,000 miles.

23   If we set the distance of the Moon to the near surface of the Earth at 1, then the distance to the far surface is 242,000/234,000 or 1.034. As the distance increases from 1.000 to 1.034, the gravitational force decreases from 1.000 to $1/1.034^2$, or 0.93.

24   There is thus a 7.0 percent difference in the amount of gravitational force exerted by the Moon on the two sides of the Earth.

25   If the Earth were made of soft rubber, you might picture it as yielding somewhat to the Moon's pull, but each part would yield by a different amount depending on the strength of the pull on that particular part.

Asimov provides a clarifying image—if the earth were more pliant, the effects of gravity would be

26   The surface of the Earth on the Moon's side would yield most since it would be most strongly attracted. The parts beneath the surface would be attracted with a progressively weaker force and move less and less toward the Moon. The opposite side of the Earth, being farthest from the Moon would move toward it least of all.

27   There would therefore be two bulges; one on the part of the Earth's surface nearest the Moon, since that part of the surface would move the most; and another on the part of the Earth's surface farthest from the Moon, since that part of the surface would move the least and lag behind all the rest of the Earth.

28   If that's not clear, let's try analogy. Imagine a compact group of runners running a long race. All of them run toward the finish line so that we might suppose some "force" is attracting them toward that finish line. As they run, the speedier ones pull out ahead and the slower ones fall behind. Despite the fact that only one "force" is involved, a "force" directed toward the finish line, there are two "bulges" produced; a bulge of runners extending forward toward the finish line in the direction of the force, and another bulge of runners extending backward in the direction opposite to that of the force.

> Asimov offers an analogy. It adds no new facts or concepts, but merely aims to clarify. Note Asimov's concern for the reader in the first sentence of the paragraph.

29   Actually the solid body of the Earth, held together by strong intermolecular forces, yields only very slightly to the gravitational differential exerted by the Moon on the Earth. The liquid oceans, held together by far weaker intermolecular forces, yield considerably more and make two "tidal bulges," one toward the Moon and one away from it.

30   As the Earth rotates, an individual point on some seacoast is carried past the first tidal bulge and then half a day later through the second. There are thus two high tides and two low tides in one complete rotation of the Earth—or, to put it more simply, in one day.

31   If the Moon were motionless, the tidal bulges would always remain in exactly the same place,

> exaggerated and easier to picture.

> Now Asimov gives readers a more exact

and high tides would be exactly twelve hours apart. The Moon moves in its orbit about the Earth, however, in the same direction that the Earth rotates, and the tidal bulges move with it. By the time some point on Earth has passed through one bulge and is approaching a second, that second bulge has moved onward so that the Earth must rotate an additional half hour in order to pass the point under question through high tide again.

32   The time between high tides is twelve hours and twenty-five minutes, and the time from one high tide to the next but one is twenty-four hours and fifty minutes. Thus, the high tides each day come nearly one hour later than on the day before.

33   But why spring tides and neap tides and what is the connection between tides and the phases of the Moon? For that we have to bring in the Sun. It, too, exerts a gravitational influence on the Earth. The gravitational pull of two separate heavenly bodies on the Earth varies directly with the mass of the bodies in question and inversely with the square of their distance from the Earth.

34   To make things simple, let's use the mass of the Moon as the mass-unit, and the average distance of the Moon from the Earth (center to center) as the distance-unit. The Moon possesses 1 Moon-mass and is at 1 Moon-distance in other words, and the Moon's gravitational pull upon us can therefore be set at $1/1^2$ or 1.

35   The mass of the Sun is 27,000,000 times that of the Moon and its distance from the Earth is 392 times that of the Moon. We can say, then, that the Sun is 27,000,000 Moon-masses and is at 392 Moon-distances. The gravitational pull of the Sun upon the Earth is therefore $27,000,000/392^2$ or 176. This means that the Sun's gravitational pull upon the Earth is 176 times that of the Moon. You would therefore expect the Sun to create tidal bulges on the Earth, and so it does. One bulge on the side toward itself, naturally, and one on the side opposite itself.

image of the two tidal bulges and their relation to the rotation of the earth, freed from some of the misleading tendencies of the images and analogies used earlier to clarify the concepts.

Asimov makes a major transition back to the topic of the spring and neap tides that had originally led Pytheas to suspect the influence of the moon on the tides. Spring and neap tides are more easily explained after readers have digested the ideas that the moon causes the tides and that the presence of a second tidal bulge is owing to the greater proximity of the moon to the near surface of the earth than to the far surface. In like manner, the gravitational force of the sun creates its own tides that can either amplify or counteract the moon's tides.

36   At the new Moon, the Moon is on the same side of the Earth as the Sun, and both Moon and Sun are pulling in the same direction. The bulges they produce separately add to each other, producing an unusually large difference between high and low tide.

35   At the full Moon, the Moon is on the side of the Earth opposite that of the Sun. Both, however, are producing bulges on the side nearest them *and* on the side opposite them. The Sun's near-bulge coincides with the Moon's far-bulge and vice versa. Once again, the bulges produced separately add to each other and another unusually large difference between high and low tide is produced.

38   Therefore the spring tides come at new Moon and full Moon.

39   At first and third quarter, when the Moon has the half-Moon appearance, Moon, Earth, and Sun form a right triangle. If you picture the Sun as pulling from the right and producing a tidal bulge to the right and left of the Earth, then the Moon at first quarter is pulling from above and producing a bulge up and down. (At third quarter, it is pulling from below and still producing a bulge up and down.)

40   In either case, the two sets of bulges tend to neutralize each other. What would ordinarily be the Moon's low tide is partially filled by the existence of the Sun's high tide, so that the range in water level between high and low tide is cut down. Thus we have the neap tides at first and third quarter.

41   Surely, one ought to ask why that should be so. I have said that the Sun's gravitational pull on the Earth is 176 times that of the Moon. Why then should it be the Moon that produces the major tidal effect?

42   The answer is that it is not the gravitational pull itself that produces the tides, but the *difference* in that pull upon different parts of the Earth. The difference in gravitational pull over the Earth's width decreases rapidly as the body

But Asimov immediately anticipates the reader's puzzlement at the apparent anomaly that the sun's

under consideration is moved farther off, since, as the total difference increases, the distance represented by the width of the Earth makes up a smaller and smaller part of the total.

43   Thus, the distance of the Sun's center from the Earth's center is about 92,900,000 miles. The Earth's width makes far less difference in this case than in the case, earlier cited, of the Moon's distance. The distance from the Sun's center to the side of the Earth near it is 92,896,000, while the distance to the far side is 92,904,000. If the distance from the Sun's center to the near side of the Earth is set equal to 1, then the distance to the far side is 1.00009. In that distance, the Sun's gravitational pull drops off to only $1/1.00009^2$ or 0.99982.

44   In other words, where the difference in the Moon's gravitational pull from one side of the Earth to the other is 7.0 percent; the difference of the Sun's gravitational pull is only 0.018 percent. Multiply the Sun's gravitational difference by its greater gravitational pull overall (0.018×176) and you get 3.2 percent. The tide producing effect of the Moon is to that of the Sun as 7.0 is to 3.2 or as 1 is to 0.46.

45   We see then that the Moon's effect on tides is more than twice that of the Sun, despite the Sun's much greater gravitational pull.

gravitational force, though far greater on the earth than the moon's, affects the tides less. Asimov must have been tempted to explain this fact a few paragraphs earlier at the point when he first stated that the sun's gravitational pull on the earth was 176 times that of the moon. Why didn't he do so? Probably because it would have interrupted the explanation then in progress of how the sun's pull sometimes intensifies the moon's and sometimes tends to neutralize it. His restraint in this instance exemplifies his ability to segment a complex conceptual structure into a manageable, logically ordered sequence.

Beginning a Writing Project

The construction of an argument is likely to involve three basic kinds of activity: research, organization, and writing. When you undertake a writing project on a relatively unfamiliar subject, the character of each of these activities will change considerably as you go along. At the outset your research may well be wide-ranging and unsystematic, aiming mainly to discover the range of reading, inter-views, and reference material that may be relevant. Your writing may well func-tion more as self-exploration than communication with others. Your attempts at organization will probably be fragmentary lists and diagrams showing the rela-tionships between ideas that your research and thought suggest will be relevant. If, on the other hand, you are writing on a subject in which you already have considerable expertise, you will skip much of this preliminary groping. But for now, let us consider how a writing project develops in the more difficult case in which you are learning about your subject as you go.

Free Writing

Sometimes the best way to begin a writing project is simply to start writing those parts that come most easily. At this stage, don't edit or censor your writing. Don't even aim at continuity, but feel free to produce discontinuous paragraphs or blocks of paragraphs.

The chunks of material you produce in this way may differ in character and have different functions:

- Some will be expressions of those aspects of the subject about which you feel most certain or most informed.
- Some passages may articulate questions you have about the subject, problems that you foresee, or misgivings about those paragraphs you have already written with apparent conviction. Preliminary writing is in part self-exploration because attempting to write an idea out clearly is often the best way of discovering its full implications, including its flaws. Another important function of these exploratory paragraphs is to record the kinds of questions and confusions a thinking person might have about the subject prior to studying it. It is dangerously easy, once you have researched a topic and thought about it deeply, to forget the elementary questions that your less experienced reader may require to have answered at the outset.
- Include "purple" versions of your own arguments even though you know they will have to be toned down or qualified later. Be as angry, intemperate, gloating, or scornful as you want. Although such emotions, uncensored, usually strike readers as petulant or childish, sometimes it is almost impossible to write an acceptable version until you have undergone this catharsis.
- Try writing out counterarguments to your own position. Adopt the frame of mind of someone who holds the most defensible possible position that is incompatible with your own. This exercise yields several benefits:
  - It forces you to realize fully the strengths of the position you are arguing against. You are never in total command of your own position until you have passed through this stage.
  - It forces you to recognize which of several counterpositions is the strongest. This reduces the danger that you will commit the "straw man" fallacy (i.e., seeking an easy but spurious victory by attacking only a weak form of the opposing argument).
  - You will have drafted material that may well be incorporated in your paper.

Notice that in Asimov's essay on the tides, he paraphrases the views of someone who finds it unbelievable that the moon could produce two tide cycles a day.

Organizing

At the outset, if your project is one in which you are discovering as you write what the boundaries of your subject are, what issues are most urgent, and what angle on the subject you will take, an attempt at a formal outline would be premature. Certainly you should *not* feel obliged to construct a hierarchical topic outline that looks something like this:

> **The Tides**
> I. The Greeks' view of the tides
>   A. Pytheas
>   B. Other Greeks
> II. Effects of gravity on the tides
>   A. The moon's
>   B. The sun's
> III. Correlation of moon phases and tides
>   A. Spring tides
>   1. Full moon
>   2. Dark of moon
>   B. Neap tides

There are several reasons not to begin a writing project with an outline like this.

1 It tends to close off thought by establishing the topics to be discussed before you have had a chance to explore ideas and see where they lead. You should keep an open mind instead.

2 A topic outline offers a partitioning of the *subject,* but it has no regard for the *reader.* It is reasonably well designed to generate an encyclopedia entry, where the goal is to provide an indiscriminate range of facts about a subject for the enlightenment not of a particular audience, but of all audiences. It is not well designed to reflect a particular line of argument addressed to a particular audience.

3 It consists of nouns or noun phrases without the predicates—where the argumentative edge of your essay is always to be found.

But while formal outlines are premature and restrictive during the exploratory stages of composition, a *cluster diagram* can be very helpful. A cluster diagram is created when you jot down key terms to recall concepts that you think you may wish to develop, arranging them on a single page so that associated terms are "clustered" together. Figure 5–1 reproduces a cluster diagram that I developed as a basis for the chapter you are reading now. I began the diagram by writing "sentence outline" near the middle of the page because it is the stage of the writing process that gives your argument direction.

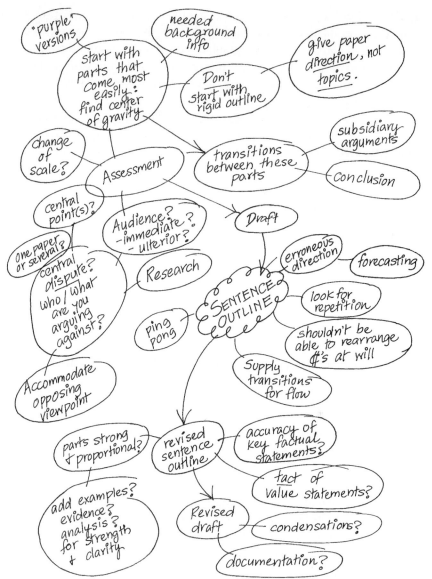

Figure 5–3. Cluster diagram.

In this particular cluster diagram, the progression of the ideas from the top of the page to the bottom roughly matches the order of ideas in the finished chapter. This correspondance is likely to occur when, as in the present instance, the essay describes a temporal process. In other cases a cluster diagram may show the conceptual relations of ideas, but in presenting the clusters to your readers, you will follow such principles of ordering as familiar to unfamiliar, simple to complex, erroneous to true, problem to resolution, or present, flawed state of affairs to proposed, improved state of affairs.

In this beginning stage of your project, free writing, preliminary research, and the development of a cluster diagram proceed together. Often as you write a paragraph, you will see that it leads you to another aspect of the topic that needs to be reflected on the diagram; at other points a term you have entered on the diagram will lead you to write a paragraph or two about it. And in the meantime material you read or hear may prompt adjustments in both your writing and your cluster diagram. In this recursive process your argument "takes shape."

Assessing the Project

At some point in this process you will have a reasonably strong sense that you have a point to make and that you know what issues of fact and value you will need to cover to make that point. (Often, of course, especially if your topic is one that you have frequently read, heard, and thought about, you will begin your composition here.) Since you doubtless have some constraints on the length of the paper you plan to write and the time in which you have to write it, this is a good time to sit back, get some distance on your argument, and pose a few clarifying questions.

In What Discussion Are You Taking Part?

As noted in Chapter 1, every argument has a social context. It is as though you have walked into a room where a discussion is already in progress. As you listen, you begin to pick up on the issues, the crucial difficulties, the personalities of those involved. You learn what factions exist, what are the bases of their alliances, who speaks most authoritatively for each of them. Where is the discussion being conducted to which you intend to become a party? In the national, state, or local media? Your college? A specialized publication to which you subscribe? Among the supporters or critics of a sport, art, or field of entertainment?

The assessment phase of the writing project means being clear about what you are saying, why it is worthwhile, and to whom it is worthwhile. If you are aware how you became acquainted with the discussion in progress, what some of the central documents in its history are (articles, news reports, television stories or interviews, etc.), what factions are involved and who their recognized spokespersons are, you can establish with greater authority the importance of your subject, its problematic aspects, and the relationship of your own position to others.

What Will Your Argument Contribute?

Every real contribution to a discussion adds something new. Simply repeating someone else's point or saying, "I agree with her," does not contribute; but saying, "Here is why her point is crucial," or "I agree with him because . . ." may contribute. While it may not add any new facts, it may show new relationships among the previously known facts or show their previously unrecognized relevance.

Nor, in a written argument, does stating the obvious contribute. If you are writing about AIDS, the point that this disease "causes enormous suffering to individuals and families" is not a very promising point to make since no one could doubt its truth. A point of this kind is said to lack an *argumentative edge*. If you want to write about AIDS, you would do better to focus on genuinely debatable issues, such as mandatory HIV testing, restrictions on the occupations of AIDS victims, or distribution of clean needles on demand to drug users.

One way of finding your argumentative edge is to be clear what position(s) you are arguing against. This is a good practice whether your argument concerns facts, values, or policies. Your argument will have point if it differs concretely and defensibly from some respectable rival position.

Now *write your central point out in a complete sentence phrased as precisely as possible.* You may at this time subscribe only tentatively to this position pending further research. If so, try also to write out those questions that you feel must be answered. Again, phrase both your hypothesis and your questions as clearly and precisely as you can, since their key terms will be crucial to subsequent research.

Obviously arguments that tackle challenging issues in new ways will be difficult or impossible to prove to the satisfaction of every potential reader, but it is a serious mistake to think that an argument is necessarily superior just because everyone accepts it. Sometimes the resistance an argument encounters is a mark not of its weakness but its daring, its freshness, and its challenge to accepted pieties. Unfortunately, political campaigns have accustomed us to rhetoric that seeks out noncontroversial subjects or treats controversial subjects noncommittally. Political rhetoric need not be the model for serious argumentation.

Who Is Your Audience?

Arguments may be addressed to a great variety of audiences. The writer may address a single individual, as in a personal or business letter, or an audience of indefinite size, as in an op-ed item in a newspaper. The audience may already be a part of the discussion that the writer is joining (as in a position paper that someone might write to fellow members on a committee that has met many times) or may have to be informed that such a discussion is going on and why it is important. The audience, while not known personally to the author, may be known from the outset to be friendly; e.g., in the selection on page 282, J. A. Koten addresses the supporters of a symphony orchestra. Is he, then, merely "preaching to the converted"? No, he is both giving them fresh information about how to raise public funds and inspiring them with fresh arguments for a position they already hold. On the other hand, the audience may be known from the start to oppose the writer's position, as is the case in Martin Luther King, Jr.'s letter on page 56 to clergymen who had decried the demonstrations King was leading. If the argument is directed to specified readers, it may or may not have ulterior audiences. For instance, King's letter, though addressed to an ostensible audience of eight clergymen, is surely intended to disturb the segragationist convictions of a broader audience and also to inspire and sustain King's followers.

All of these situations give the writer some guidance in directing their readers. Writers, as we have said, should start the progress toward their conclusions from their readers' original standpoints. They should begin by clearing up misunderstandings and confusion, as Asimov does by acknowledging the reader's natural expectation that the tide will be high only on that part of the earth's surface nearest the moon, and they should likewise begin with the readers' predispositions on questions of value. Writers addressing fellow committee members have the advantage of knowing these predispositions. King, in assessing the values and beliefs of his ostensible audience, the eight Birmingham clergymen, had the advantage of their public statement as well as the deeper values implied by their vocation. Koten knew his audience supported public funding of the arts and that they had encountered problems in raising the funds. But what about the less instructive conditions under which you normally write arguments? Who is your audience and how do you know what that audience's initial beliefs, information, and values are?

First, remember that your "audience" does not necessarily mean the person or persons who will actually read your essay. Your essay may be read only by your teacher or by one or more peer editors, but that does not mean that you have to write directly to them. Instead, try to think of the various kinds of readers to whom your argument might make a difference. If you are disagreeing with a public statement by someone else, you can think of your audience as those who have heard or read the statement and might have been misled by it. If you are offering a solution to a publicly recognized problem, your audience would include everyone with an interest in seeing the problem solved. In either case, do not limit yourself by imagining a single "ideal reader." Remember that your argument may "make a difference" to those initially predisposed in favor of your argument (by giving them arguments to bolster their position), to those initially undecided (by giving them arguments that might break their impasse), and to those initially predisposed against your arguments (by making them question their assumptions, supplying them with previously unknown facts, or perhaps leading them to change their minds outright). This last group is particularly important to keep in mind as a potential audience, for your argument will be stronger if you anticipate and respond to their counterarguments. Even those readers who sympathize with your position will feel it to be a weakness in your argument if you do not show them how to answer embarrassing questions from the opposition.

Do You Have One Paper or Several?

Your paper should be unified and should therefore make one overarching argument. Naturally it can (and, unless it is extremely brief, will) include subordinate arguments. But this is a good moment to consider the constraints of time and space. If you want to tackle the complex question of legalizing drugs such as cocaine and heroin, you will encounter several issues of fact. You would have to exhibit the destructive social effects of drug trafficking today: neighborhoods disrupted by drug pushers and their armed turf battles, the exposure of children to drugs, the incentive to drug addicts to addict others who will become prospective buyers, the presence of high school students with gold chains and beepers who may even be conducting drug sales by cellular phones from their classrooms. Another set of factual issues would concern the effects of your proposed change. You would have to argue that many socially harmful effects of drugs are owing not to the intrinsic effects of the drugs themselves but to their illegality, which raises their price, allows for huge profits, and therefore encourages dealers to extend addiction and battle other dealers. Even if you could argue persuasively that legalizing drugs would eliminate the evils of this illegal traffic, important issues of value would remain to be addressed. What would the legal sanction of drug use mean? Would society be simply capitulating to those who would corrupt it?

Obviously all these issues are important and all could be incorporated into a highly unified paper arguing for the legalization of drugs, but to research the topic and write it up in anything other than a superficial way would require several weeks and at least thirty pages. If your circumstances do not allow this commitment, you might restrict yourself to one of the component issues. Or you might write a series of papers, each one tackling one aspect of the question. (See the essays on mental testing by Walter Lippman on pages 403, 407, and 411, in which he breaks up a large social question to fit the limits of a weekly magazine column.)

Does Lateral Thinking Suggest a Change in Approach or Scope?

When we seek to solve a problem (and argumentation is always problem solving), we can spend all our energy on *vertical thinking,* that is, on working out the implications of our basic assumptions. Suppose you are on the west side of Los Angeles and you have to deliver a document to the other side of the city within two hours. You might quickly and skillfully calculate the advantages of various routes across the city, taking into account relative distances, traffic patterns, construction delays, and even the gas level in your car. But all these calculations, no matter how rationally carried out, are based on the assumption that you must personally drive the document across town. *Lateral thinking,* a phrase coined by Edward de Bono,* asks whether some entirely different solution to the problem is possible. Could you fax the document? employ a motorcycle courier? secure an extension of your deadline and mail it?

---

* Edward de Bono, *New Think: The Use of Lateral Thinking in the Generation of New Ideas* (New York: Basic Books, 1968).

Applying lateral thinking to assess your project means exploring the possibility of major changes in approach through questions such as these:

- Have I used the best arguments to establish the facts of my case?
- Are there avenues of research that I have not explored?
- Have I taken into consideration the most potent analogies and precepts for values arguments?
- In proposals, have I recommended the best and simplest solution for the problem I have identified?

Review the chapters on empirical claims, evaluations, and proposals for more specific suggestions for sharpening your arguments.

All writers like to imagine a reader being favorably impressed by their writing, but at the assessment stage of the project, it is more important to imagine possible critical or skeptical responses. One way to achieve lateral thinking is to imagine the response of someone whose thought patterns you know well—a friend, a family member, a teacher, a media commentator, a newspaper columnist, a writer. If they were going to read your drafts critically, what kinds of objections, questions, or alternative approaches would they offer? If you can think of some such responses, that doesn't mean that you should necessarily adopt their point of view, but it does suggest positions that you might acknowledge in passing or rebut.

Research

We live in the midst of an information explosion. After World War II various information services such as annual bibliographies and citation indexes devised means of collecting and organizing data in various fields for easier and more systematic retrieval. More recently, computer technology, the creation of databases, and communication networks have been increasing the amount of information available, supplying new, more systematic methods of accessing it, and keeping it continuously up to date. This vast set of resources presents two dangers to you as a researcher. You may feel so swamped by information that you feel powerless to inspect it intelligently, or you may feel so pleased at having "enough" information that you assume any selection from it will be adequate. What you mainly need as a researcher is the skill to maintain control over these resources—to find the material that will shape and document your argument and to deploy it in a way that will best serve your own purposes.

By this stage of your project you have done some preliminary reading that has tuned you in to an ongoing social discussion, and you have written out either a tentative position of your own or a question whose answer will clearly help to offer a solution. We shall now see how library resources and your own search strategies can help you build on both these elements. Starting from the documents you have uncovered in your preliminary reading, you can use a citation trail to discover their antecedents and citation indexes and reviews to find how they were subsequently evaluated, confirmed, rebutted or applied. Starting from your questions and hypotheses, you can use a subject guide to search their key terms.

The Citation Trail

Often your interest in the subject you want to write about will have been started or piqued by something you read—a news report, an editorial, an essay in a periodical, a scholarly article, a book, a review. If such a document has reference notes or credits, one of the easiest ways to expand your research resources is to follow up on its bibliography. In selecting which cited documents to pursue, you can be guided both by their titles and by what the author of your immediate source has to say about them. As you look at these cited documents, you may in turn find further references, and in this process you will also begin to see what authors recur, who is most authoritative, and what issues are most contentious or problematic. Sometimes a scholarly article will begin with a review of the prior literature on the question and thus guide you to basic documents you should read. One time-saving device is to photocopy bibliographies and introductory paragraphs from such articles to give you a portable bibliography for further study. Be sure to write in full bibliographic information about your source on these photocopied sheets so you can relocate it if necessary.

Subject Guides

While a citation trail is particularly useful in establishing the context of that part of the subject covered in the document that yielded the citations, this line of inquiry has limitations. The author may have been addressing only a small corner of the subject you wish to research or may have employed only a narrow approach. The author may even have been biased or incompetent. Such potential limitations of any document are one reason to supplement the citation trail with other resources, such as catalogues, indexes, and bibliographies, that list the subject you are pursuing.

A second reason for turning to these sources is that if you have formulated either specific research questions to be answered or hypotheses to be tested, your search will be far more comprehensive and efficient if you search them by their key terms in guides organized by subject. The subject headings of your library's catalogue are one such guide. Others are bibliographies and indexes, which may be available to you in print or database form or both. Your library catalogue may steer you to bibliographies about your subject.

Catalogues or indexes organized by subject are less easy to use than those organized by author or title because the topic you are interested in may not have an immediately obvious name or may go by several names. Some libraries supply volumes entitled *Library of Congress Subject Headings* that will show you what headings are in use and suggest broader and narrower terms. Alternatively, if you know a book that deals squarely with the topic you are researching, check the subject heading on the back of the title page under "Library of Congress Cataloging-in-Publication Data." Other subject indexes, print or database, may have a thesaurus of descriptors from which to choose. If your index lacks such a heading guide, be inventive in thinking of and checking possibilities.

Particularly useful subject guides (which often have also an author-title index) include newspaper indexes and *The Reader's Guide,* which cites items in such popular publications as *Time* and *Harper's.* Scholarly indexes include *The Humanities Index, The Social Sciences Index, The General Science Index, ERIC* (an index covering education and related disciplines), and the *MLA International Bibliography of Books and Articles on the Modern Languages and Literatures* (covering literature and language).

Other useful databases available on CD-ROM are these:

- *Infotrac* includes the *Expanded Academic Index* covering 960 scholarly and general information publications plus the *New York Times;* and the *National Newspaper Index,* which indexes *The Wall Street Journal, Christian Science Monitor, New York Times, Los Angeles Times,* and *Washington Post.*
- *ABI/INFORM* (indexes and abstracts articles contained in over 800 business journals)
- *AGRICOLA* (indexes literature pertaining to agriculture, food science, nutrition, and related life sciences)
- *PsycLIT* (indexes and abstracts the international psychology and behavioral science literature and the related fields of education, business, medicine, and law)
- *Sociofile* (indexes and abstracts more than 1600 journals in sociology, social planning, social policy, and social development)

The *CIS Index* lists and describes working papers of the United States Congress. Hearings by congressional committees include testimony from witnesses whom the committee feels will represent the range of positions that must be heard, and the transcript of the hearings will often show you how witnesses respond to hostile questions about their positions. Detailed instructions for using the index are included at the front of the volume.

The *Left Index* and the *Alternative Press Index* are subject indexes to literature from the alternative press, that is, from periodicals published by small, noncommercial presses devoted to issues associated with the political left—issues such as minority rights, social and economic justice, animal rights, environmentalism, pacifism, and others growing out of "the Movement" that flourished in the 1960s. These publications are outspoken advocates for their various causes, making no pretense of objectivity. They must therefore be used with caution, but the same can be said of any publication. Even those newspapers, journals, and television programs that ostentatiously present "opposing views" must, in selecting the views to be aired, designate some spokespersons on either side as "respectable" and dismiss others as "the lunatic fringe." Often alternative press sources are ahead of the mainstream press in their information and moral positions because they are not bound by the need to please commercial sponsors, the public majority, or government agencies.

When, as is often the case, your interest in a subject begins with or receives a special stimulus from something you read, a citation trail will lead you to the antecedents of that document and an index may lead you to other concurrent and later work on the same subject; but often it is helpful to find later documents that specifically respond to one that you have been interested in. Suppose you read a work published three or four years ago that seems to contain interesting, newsworthy information and ideas. How do you evaluate this material? Is the author reputable? How have his or her ideas fared in the intellectual marketplace since the work was published? It can be embarrassing if you rely heavily on a source that you later discover has been thoroughly debunked, or if you ignore or dismiss a book that is the current authority in its field. This is not to say that you must uncritically accept the views of reviewers, only that your argument will be most rhetorically effective if you show your awareness of the status of writers to whom you refer.

Citation Indexes

Citation indexes are a means of locating an article that cites your source article as a reference. Suppose, for instance, you were interested in tracking the scientific response to the Goldberg article in Chapter 2, "Are Women Prejudiced Against Women?" You could consult the *Social Science Citation Index* for each year following the publication of the study. By looking up Goldberg's name, you would find a number of his publications listed, and under each publication, a list of all articles written in the preceding two years that contain a reference to his article. A separate volume, the source index, will give you complete bibliographic information about the article that cites Goldberg, and will also list all the other citations in the article. Citation indexes are available for the sciences and for the arts and humanities as well.

Citation indexes are increasingly being adapted for CD-ROM access. In this form, not only do they yield citations that cover a number of years rather than only the two most recent years, but they have the additional features of *related records*. This means that if you search a given article in the source index, you will find not only a list of all sources that it cites but a list of other articles whose bibliographies significantly overlap that of your subject article. (The agency publishing the index decides how many references must be shared for two articles to be considered related records.)

Critical evaluations of some sources can also be found in book reviews or review articles. Two reference works are useful as guides to book reviews. The *Book Review Digest* will give you brief summaries of and usually excerpts from two to four different reviews, allowing you to see how much consensus there is about the book in question and what principal objections, if any, have been mounted against it. Often this work is enough to give you confidence that a source you have relied on is authoritative or that an argument you have rejected is rejected by others. If you find that it is a highly controversial book, you will know that you can neither accept nor dismiss it out of hand but must support either of these responses. *The Book Review Index* is another useful guide. It does not print abstracts of reviews, but it provides a more complete list than the *Book Review Digest* of a book's reviews. *Review articles* are articles that very usefully review a number of recent works on the same subject. They often indicate what issues are currently debated and which authors represent distinct positions on the subject.

Summary

The reference materials and research strategies we have discussed should enable you to describe with confidence the place of any source in the ongoing "conversation" about your subject. Figure 5–4 shows how, taking any document you please as a source, you may use these research techniques to trace its antecedents, compare it with other concurrent work in the same field, and follow up on later developments.

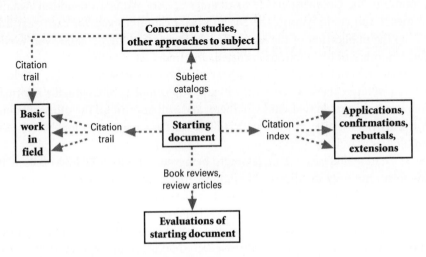

Figure 5–4. The place of a document in the cultural debate.

The First Draft and Sentence Outline

Once you have established the boundaries of your topic, researched the factual background and the range of positions taken by other commentators, decided what audience you are addressing, and clarified how you hope to affect your audience's views, you are in a position to write a first draft of your paper.

Your first draft does not have to be eloquent, graceful, or stylistically correct, but you should try to ensure that all your main ideas along with their supporting arguments and evidence are represented. Aim for fullness, so that subsequent revisions will consist mainly of condensing and reordering your material rather than amplifying it. Sift through the material from your free writing, discarding whatever turns out in retrospect to have been private material for clarifying your own thoughts, retaining or revising whatever seems adaptable to the purpose and audience that have emerged from the planning stage of your project. Use your early notes as a reminder of issues that you may have worked through and forgotten about but that a reader with less experience with the topic might find useful.

Once you have written the first draft of your paper, a sentence outline is the crucial stage of composition that can confer real distinction on your writing. A sentence outline is simply a sequence of sentences, each of which summarizes a paragraph of your paper. By enabling you to treat the paragraph blocks as units, the outline allows you to step back from the sentence-by-sentence detail of your paper and attend to the sequence of paragraphs and transitions between them.

To construct a sentence outline, use a separate slip of paper for each paragraph. The stick-on notes sold under various brand names are ideal because you can provisionally post them at the paragraphs they summarize but later remove them easily to try a different order. Or, if you are used to composing on a computer, you may create a sentence outline file by copying one sentence from each paragraph and manipulating it as needed to make it summarize the paragraph adequately.

Starting at the beginning of your paper, write a single, complete sentence for each paragraph. Be sure that the sentence faithfully reflects the paragraph. If the paragraph seems to contain material that cannot be adequately represented by a single sentence, you probably need to make changes in the paragraph. If the recalcitrant material is simply irrelevant to your paper, delete it; if it is not, you probably need to divide the paragraph into two or more paragraphs. The sentence you write may well be a verbatim repetition of a sentence in your original paragraph. (This will often be true if you are in the habit of including a traditional "topic sentence" in each paragraph.) In your outline, pay attention to the transitions between your sentences. Words or phrases such as "moreover," "on the other hand," "for example," "therefore," "next," and the like indicate the logical relationship of one paragraph to its predecessor.

In its final form, your sentence outline should comprise a smooth, coherent sequence that amounts to an abstract of your paper. Check to be sure that there are no gaps in the sequence; you should be able to explain why each sentence follows from the one before it. Be particularly alert to instances in which two sentences at different points in the outline repeat each other. This is perhaps the most common problem that a sentence outline is likely to reveal. Similarly, look for sentences that raise issues that are clearly related to each other. Are some points so similar that they might be consolidated, or should they at least be placed closer to each other in an order and with transitions that more clearly show their relationship? Finally, check the proportions of your argument. Are you devoting a disproportionate space to any of its components?

Remember that the entire purpose of your paper is to guide the reader from one point to another, perhaps from a point of ignorance to a point of knowledge, perhaps from one side of an issue to the other, perhaps from a state of perplexity to a state of greater understanding. You should have a clear sense of what the reader's starting point is, how the end point differs from the starting point, and how each stage of the argument contributes to the passage from start to finish.

Here is a newspaper article with unusually strong direction that tries to lead the reader by clear steps from one value position to another:

SHANNON STERN-SALB

*Recognize Sexuality Is a Political Issue**

1   Today is National Coming Out Day. This is the day that the national gay community publicly discusses sexual orientation with the recognition that sexuality is a political issue. After learning this, there will, undoubtedly, be those who will maintain that everyone would be better off if gays just stayed in the closet. After all, who minds gays as long as they remain invisible?

2   They will say that not only is sexuality a purely private part of our lives, one which polite company recognizes as an inappropriate subject for the dinner table, but also that coming out (that is, being public about our sexual orientation) subjects us to scorn.

3   My bet is that there are few men or women in the gay community who plan to talk today about what they do in bed (sorry if I disappoint you).

---

* This article first appeared in the University of Connecticut *Daily Campus*. At the time it was written, the author was an undergraduate student at the university and outreach coordinator for the Bisexual, Gay, and Lesbian Association. He spoke frequently on homosexuality.

When people hear the word "homosexual," they think "homo*sexual.*" Realize that being gay affects every part of our lives. When we tell the world that we are gay we are not talking about sex.

4   I challenge my audience to think—and think hard—about their lives and about their sexuality. I propose an experiment for every member of the University of Connecticut community: spend today in the closet. This means more than simply not talking about your great acrobatics last night. I am suggesting that you realize how deeply your sexuality affects your life.

5   Being closeted means that you cannot talk about the person you are dating, you cannot talk about your social life, you cannot talk about your values, you cannot talk about the book you are reading. Hiding the fact that sexuality plays an important part in your life includes hiding fundamental aspects of yourself from your friends, your classmates, your family. Sound easy? Play my game.

6   If you are dating someone, hide it. Don't hold hands, don't smile at each other, and for God's sake, make sure this person's name is not written down anywhere in your room (except maybe in your little black book). Don't mention his or her name. Watch your pronouns. Watch not only your verbal language, but also your body language.

7   But being a minority means more than simply hiding our relationships. It means having constantly to confront ignorance and bigotry. For gay men and lesbians, this means listening with bile rising in our throats as our professors make homophobic comments, refer only to heterosexual relationships, and ignore us and our contributions throughout history. It means dealing with the gay jokes.

8   It means knowing that if the guy in the shower next to me knew that I were gay, I could be attacked—verbally if not physically. It means going to church knowing that if "they knew," they would be disgusted. So not only must we hide from everyone the fact that we date, but we must also ignore every other important aspect of our lives. What results? A ridiculous, one-dimensional parody of a human being.

9   I can barely choke back a laugh when someone asks me how I can talk about my sexuality all the time; after all, they tell me, straight people never talk about theirs. Straights express their sexuality constantly. They hold hands, they kiss in public, they speak comfortably and constantly about their boy/girlfriends. Ironically, after flaunting their sexuality, they tell us not to "flaunt" ours. That is, to pretend we do not exist.

10   Homophobia and heterosexism do not fade of their own accord. It takes activism by gay people (and by straight people) to affect change. I spend a great deal of time and energy being gay—thinking about it and talking about it—not because it so terribly interesting (though it is fun. . .) but because sexuality and politics are inextricably linked.

11   Until homophobia is abolished, Coming Out Days will be necessary. Homophobic comments will never lose their hurt—ask any African-American how it feels to hear "nigger." But the cost of avoiding that scorn by staying in the closet is a price far greater than that I am willing to pay.

Sentence Outline of Stern-Salb's Article

1 While gays use National Coming Out Day to make sexuality a public issue and recognize that it is a political issue, critics will undoubtedly argue that everyone would be better off if gays stayed in the closet.

2 They will say that sexuality is a purely private part of our lives.

3 But sexuality affects all aspects of life, not merely bedroom behavior.

4 Heterosexuals should try the experiment for one day of hiding their sexuality—being closeted.

5 Being closeted means hiding fundamental aspects of yourself from your friends, community, and family.

6 If you are dating someone, it means hiding signs of your affection for that person, evidence of his or her meaning to your life, and even body language that might betray your feelings.

7 For the homosexual minority, sexuality also means enduring homophobic comments, neglect, gay jokes, disgust, and fear of physical or verbal assault.

8 When we must hide not only the fact that we date a member of our own sex, but every other important aspect of our lives, the result is a ridiculous, one-dimensional parody of a human being.

9 Straights ask gays not to flaunt their sexuality, but do not realize that straights flaunt their sexuality constantly.

10 Gays must actively oppose homophobia because sexuality and politics are inextricably linked.

11 Although Coming Out Days expose gays to painful homophobic comments, the cost of staying in the closet is even more painful.

A sentence outline presents the logical skeleton of an argument. The outline above shows that in the article paragraphs 1–2 present what the author believes is a prevalent social conclusion (that gays should stay in the closet) and the premise upon which this conclusion is based (that sexuality is a purely private matter).

The author then attacks the conclusion by attacking the premise. Paragraphs 3–6 all describe ways in which heterosexuals express their sexuality in daily life, thus demonstrating that sexuality is not purely private and that the concealment of one's sexuality is a strain.

The next two paragraphs, 7–8, show the pressures on gays to suppress all the aspects of daily life that betray one's sexuality and thus to become "a ridiculous, one-dimensional parody of a human being."

Paragraph 9 draws together the implications of two sections of the argument. If straights routinely express their own sexuality publicly (paragraphs 3–6) but pressure gays not to do the same (paragraphs 7–8), then, explicitly, a majority is seeking to impose on members of a minority a rule which it is not willing to impose on itself. This situation is self-evidently political and justifies the call to political action that characterizes the conclusion of the article.

The sentence outline, then allows you not only to check that your paragraphs flow gracefully in a determinate direction, but also to discern logical groupings of paragraphs and check that premises and conclusions are intelligibly related to each other. Often, of course, the outline will enable you to see valuable logical connections that you feel might profitably be made more explicit in the essay itself.

The Revised Draft

When you are satisfied that each sentence of your outline states clearly and economically what you intend it to say, that the paragraphs of your paper accurately reflect and develop the sentences of your outline, and that the sequence of ideas is the one best calculated to make your argument intelligible and fluent to your reader, you are ready for the final editing of your paper. This stage includes the following:

- Checking the accuracy of your factual statements
- Checking your value statements for precision and tact
- Adding examples and evidence for support where you feel they are needed; adding explanations and analogies if needed for clarity
- Being sure that the documentation of your paper meets certain standards:
  - It should credit your sources for any analytic insights and evaluative arguments that they have supplied and for factual information that they have discovered. This credit should take the form not only of reference notes, but of quotation marks for directly quoted material and clear indications of the extent of material to which the notes refer.
  - It should enable your readers to locate your source information readily in the event that they wish to follow up on ideas or facts that interest them.
  - It should follow some accepted form of documentation (such as the MLA or APA stylesheets) consistently throughout. Consult with your instructor about the form best suited to your class or your topic.

Before typing your final draft, ask someone to read your paper and note points that were unclear, were unconnected, or raised unanswered questions. If you cannot find someone else obliging enough to do this, try to let your paper sit for a few days and then read it with "strange eyes"—that is, try to put yourself in the position of a reader who lacks your familiarity with the subject and has not read the paper before. Sometimes reading the paper aloud to yourself will reveal awkwardnesses that are not apparent on a silent reading.

Specialized Tasks: Writing in Response to Writing

In both academic and professional situations, you may be asked to produce several kinds of writing in response to other writing. While not everyone means the same thing by some of these terms, the following definitions and guidelines should be of some service:

PARAPHRASE: A paraphrase is a restatement of a discourse in different words. Sometimes in academic classes you may be asked to paraphrase something simply to demonstrate that you understand it. At other times the purpose of a paraphrase is to make the original intelligible to someone else. Try to envision what aspects of the original would be unclear to an intelligent reader and reword with an eye to removing the difficulties. You might use a more familiar word for a less familiar one; straighten out confusing syntax by breaking up a sentence into shorter, more direct sentences; clarify confusing pronoun references; point up the logic of the original by supplying connectives, introducing parallel structure, or inserting ordering devices such as "first," "second," etc.; or identify proper names that may not be known to your audience.

PRECIS OR ABSTRACT: These words mean essentially the same thing: a shortened version of the original that sifts out the main ideas, omitting the supporting detail and illustrations. Often you can retain some wording from the original, though you should put quotation marks around material quoted directly. A precis or abstract should retain the point of view of the original. In other words, if the original is in the first person, your version should be too. The same goes for verb tenses. Be careful not to let your condensation change the meaning. For instance, if the original makes a generalization but then adds several qualifications, you should not simply restate the generalization. You may substitute for the omitted detail by an expression such as "sometimes," or "usually" (be careful to choose one that accurately reflects the strength of the qualification).

SUMMARY: A summary is the same thing as a "precis" or "abstract," except that you are not restricted to retaining the person and tense of the original. Also, while a precis or abstract must cover the main headings point by point, a summary may condense drastically and reorder the points of the original.

ANALYSIS: This differs from the previous items in that it does not purport simply to repeat the original in condensed form but to study and explain the relations of the parts of the discourse to each other and to the whole. To analyze an argument often means to identify its basic assumptions, even though they may not be stated explicitly, and to trace the logic whereby the conclusion is derived from the assumptions and the evidence. An analysis often points up what propositions are most important to the argument. The articles by Neil D. Isaacs and Roland Bartels on pages 320 and 325 are analyses of Eudora Welty's "A Worn Path." Their purpose is to establish the overall theme of the story and show how various details—images, names, events, and symbols—contribute to development of that theme.

CRITICAL ANALYSIS OR CRITIQUE: These add the idea of a judgment or evaluation to an analysis. The purpose of a critique is to explain the significance and important underlying meanings of a piece of writing. Whether or not you agree with the subject of the critique, your decision to discuss it shows that you take the ideas seriously and want to be sure that others recognize their significance. If you admire the subject, you will want to show the importance of the ideas, which other readers may have missed. If you disagree with it, your critique will warn less critical readers not to be taken in. A third possibility, perhaps the most common of all, is that without wholly approving or disapproving of the subject discourse you will want to sort out its valuable aspects from its mistaken or dangerous aspects. Martin Luther King's "Letter from Birmingham Jail" (page 56) is a critique aimed against the letter from eight Alabama clergymen (page 48). Howardena Pindell's "Colonial Culture" (page 353) is a critique aimed against Richard Bernstein's "The Arts Catch up with a Society in Disarray" (page 344).

The kind of material that goes into a critique depends largely on the nature of the argument in the original. The foregoing three chapters have presented the kinds of considerations appropriate in critiquing empirical claims, evaluations, and proposals respectively. But besides these logical standards in writing critiques, keep in mind these general strategic considerations:

- Critiques should ordinarily begin with a concise summary of the work to be discussed. If you are critiquing only one section or aspect of a work, you should summarize that part and briefly indicate how it fits into a larger context. In either case, your summary should be geared to the critique to follow. You should select those aspects of the original to which you intend to respond.
- Avoid the potshot approach. Do not simply offer a sequence of rebuttals to various arguments in the original without organizing them in relation to some central assessment. The piece of writing you are criticizing may contain some very wrong or even silly points without crucial damage to its central argument.
- In the piece you are criticizing, pay attention to *god terms* and *devil terms*. They are often the most convenient indicator of the subject argument's value system, which may be the main focus of your critique.

- Sometimes one of your disagreements with the author will have been anticipated in his or her argument and to some degree rebutted. In such a case, it will not get you anywhere simply to repeat the original objection. You must, so to speak, reenter the dialogue at a higher level, one that acknowledges the author's rebuttal but demonstrates why it fails to overcome the objection.
- If you are critiquing a poorly written or poorly argued statement, your critique will be strongest if you respond to the opposing arguments in their strongest form. Replying to the weaker formulations of opposing arguments is called the *fallacy of the straw man.*

REBUTTAL: A rebuttal is a critical analysis whose purpose is to disprove or discredit the conclusion of the original.

The main mistake students make in fulfilling writing assignments that contain instructions such as "paraphrase," "summarize," or "critique" is to insert their own opinions where they have been instructed to render accurately the flavor of the original or, on the contrary, merely to repeat or condense where they have been asked to adopt a critical perspective on the original. If you are unsure which is wanted, you can minimize the problem by clearly distinguishing your paraphrase or summary of the original from your opinions and by including rational support for whatever opinion you include.

Animal Rights

Every age sees movements to expand the rights of groups newly perceived to be oppressed by some other group. Those aggrieved have sometimes been the victims of an occupying army or colonizing country; a hereditary ruling class or an established religion; another race or the other sex. Often the group in control believes that its privileges are rooted in nature—in the favor of the gods, in racial superiority, in "the blood," in genes, in biologically pre-scribed sex roles, or the like. Liberation movements often express themselves in written documents or in speeches that have a special power because they challenge the most basic assumptions of all—those that validate our social hierarchies and justify differences in liberty, wealth, prestige, and power. The writings of Thomas Paine, Mary Wollstonecraft, Thomas Jefferson, and Martin Luther King, Jr., are among these documents.

It also seems to be true that individuals or cultures capable of produc-ing original and eloquent arguments for liberation of one group are blind to their own complicity in oppressing others. The Constitution of the United States, after all, in its original form countenanced slavery and did not extend the franchise to women. These omissions no doubt seem to many (not all) of those who framed the documents to be aspects of human society that were ordained by biological differences. When these beliefs were challenged, those holding them often responded that those in subordinate positions were happi-est that way.

Since the 1950s the United States has seen many kinds of liberation movements—rights for racial minorities, for women, for the disabled, for ho-mosexuals. Many would regard the animal rights movement as the most ex-treme liberation movement of all. Among the selections below, Peter Singer's essay is a serious and deeply influential examination of our values system and its implications for our treatment of animals, while Coady's is a counterar-gument by a fellow philosopher. Marian Dawkins considers the philosophical problem that besets empirical research pertinent to animal rights. The selec-tions by DeBakey, Noah, and Pacheco bear on various proposals that have been made to regulate the use of animals in medical testing and research.   *121*

PETER SINGER

Animal Liberation

Peter Singer is a philosopher based in Australia. This essay, a review of *Animals, Men, and Morals,* edited by Stanley and Roslind Godlovitch and John Harris, originally appeared in 1973. In 1975, Singer published a book by the same title that has become a central document in the animal rights movement and, because Singer adopts what many consider an extreme position, a favorite target for critics of that movement.

1   We are familiar with Black Liberation, Gay Liberation, and a variety of other movements. With Women's Liberation some thought we had come to the end of the road. Discrimination on the basis of sex, it has been said, is the last form of discrimination that is universally accepted and practiced without pretense, even in those liberal circles which have long prided themselves on their freedom from racial discrimination. But one should always be wary of talking of "the last remaining form of discrimination." If we have learned anything from the liberation movements, we should have learned how difficult it is to be aware of the ways in which we discriminate until they are forcefully pointed out to us. A liberation movement demands an expansion of our moral horizons, so that practices that were previously regarded as natural and inevitable are now seen as intolerable.

2   *Animals, Men and Morals* is a manifesto for an Animal Liberation movement. The contributors to the book may not all see the issue this way. They are a varied group. Philosophers, ranging from professors to graduate students, make up the largest contingent. There are five of them, including the three editors, and there is also an extract from the unjustly neglected German philosopher with an English name, Leonard Nelson, who died in 1927. There are essays by two novelist/critics, Brigid Brophy and Maureen Duffy, and another by Muriel the Lady Dowding, widow of Dowding of Battle of Britain fame and the founder of "Beauty Without Cruelty," a movement that campaigns against the use of animals for furs and cosmetics. The other pieces are by a psychologist, a botanist, a sociologist, and Ruth Harrison, who is probably best described as a professional campaigner for animal welfare.

3   Whether or not these people, as individuals, would all agree that they are launching a liberation movement for animals, the book as a whole amounts to no less. It is a demand for a complete change in our attitudes to nonhumans. It is a demand that we cease to regard the exploitation of other species as natural and inevitable, and that, instead, we see it as a continuing moral outrage. Patrick Corbett, Professor of Philosophy at Sussex University, captures the spirit of the book in his closing words:

...We require now to extend the great principles of liberty, equality and fraternity over the lives of animals. Let animal slavery join human slavery in the graveyard of the past.

4   The reader is likely to be skeptical. "Animal Liberation" sounds more like a parody of liberation movements than a serious objective. The reader may think: We support the claims of blacks and women for equality because blacks and women really are equal to whites and males—equal in intelligence and in abilities, capacity for leadership, rationality, and so on. Humans and nonhumans obviously are not equal in these respects. Since justice demands only that we treat equals equally, unequal treatment of humans and nonhumans cannot be an injustice.

5   This is a tempting reply, but a dangerous one. It commits the nonracist and nonsexist to a dogmatic belief that blacks and women really are just as intelligent, able, etc., as whites and males—and no more. Quite possibly this happens to be the case. Certainly attempts to prove that racial or sexual differences in these respects have a genetic origin have not been conclusive. But do we really want to stake our demand for equality on the assumption that there are no genetic differences of this kind between the different races or sexes? Surely the appropriate response to those who claim to have found evidence for such genetic differences is not to stick to the belief that there are no differences, whatever the evidence to the contrary; rather one should be clear that the claim to equality does not depend on IQ. Moral equality is distinct from factual equality. Otherwise it would be nonsense to talk of the equality of human beings, since humans, as individuals, obviously differ in intelligence and almost any ability one cares to name. If possessing greater intelligence does not entitle one human to exploit another, why should it entitle humans to exploit nonhumans?

6   Jeremy Bentham expressed the essential basis of equality in his famous formula: "Each to count for one and none for more than one." In other words, the interest of every being that has interests are to be taken into account and treated equally with the like interests of any other being. Other moral philosophers, before and after Bentham, have made the same point in different ways. Our concern for others must not depend on whether they possess certain characteristics, though just what concern involves may, of course, vary according to such characteristics.

7   Bentham, incidentally, was well aware that the logic of the demand for racial equality did not stop at the equality of humans. He wrote:

The day may come when the rest of the animal creation may acquire those rights which never could have been withholden from them but by the hand of tyranny. The French have already discovered that the blackness of the skin is no reason why a human being should be abandoned without redress to the caprice of a tormentor. It may one day come to be recognized

that the number of legs, the villosity of the skin, or the termination of the
os sacrum, are reasons equally insufficient for abandoning a sensitive
being to the same fate. What else is it that should trace the insuperable
line? Is it the faculty of reason, or perhaps the faculty of discourse? But a
full-grown horse or dog is beyond comparison a more rational, as well as a
more conversable animal, than an infant of a day, or a week, or even a
month, old. But suppose they were otherwise, what would it avail? The
question is not, Can they reason? nor Can they talk? but, Can they suffer?[1]

Surely Bentham was right. If a being suffers, there can be no moral
justification for refusing to take that suffering into consideration, and,
indeed, to count it equally with the like suffering (if rough comparisons
can be made) of any other being.

8   So the only question is: Do animals other than man suffer? Most
people agree unhesitatingly that animals like cats and dogs can and do
suffer, and this seems also to be assumed by those laws that prohibit
wanton cruelty to such animals. Personally, I have no doubt at all about
this and find it hard to take seriously the doubts that a few people
apparently do have. The editors and contributors of *Animals, Men and*
Morals seem to feel the same way, for although the question is raised more
than once, doubts are quickly dismissed each time. Nevertheless, because
this is such a fundamental point, it is worth asking what grounds we have
for attributing suffering to other animals.

9   It is best to begin by asking what grounds any individual human has for
supposing that other humans feel pain. Since pain is a state of
consciousness, a "mental event," it can never be directly observed. No
observations, whether behavioral signs such as writhing or screaming or
physiological or neurological recordings, are observations of pain itself.
Pain is something one feels, and one can only infer that others are feeling it
from various external indications. The fact that only philosophers are ever
skeptical about whether other humans feel pain shows that we regard such
inference as justifiable in the case of humans.

10   Is there any reason why the same inference should be unjustifiable for
other animals? Nearly all the external signs which lead us to infer pain in
other humans can be seen in other species, especially "higher" animals
such as mammals and birds. Behavioral signs—writhing, yelping, or other
forms of calling, attempts to avoid the source of pain, and many others—
are present. We know, too, that these animals are biologically similar in the
relevant respects, having nervous systems like ours which can be observed
to function as ours do.

---

[1] *The Principles of Morals and Legislation*, ch. XVII, sec. 1, footnote to paragraph 4.

11 So the grounds for inferring that these animals can feel pain are nearly as good as the grounds for inferring other humans do. Only nearly, for there is one behavioral sign that humans have but nonhumans, with the exception of one or two specially raised chimpanzees, do not have. This, of course, is a developed language. As the quotation from Bentham indicates, this has long been regarded as an important distinction between man and other animals. Other animals may communicate with each other, but not in the way we do. Following Chomsky, many people now mark this distinction by saying that only humans communicate in a form that is governed by rules of syntax. (For the purpose of this argument, linguists allow those chimpanzees who have learned a syntactic sign language to rank as honorary humans.) Nevertheless, as Bentham pointed out, this distinction is not relevant to the question of how animals ought to be treated, unless it can be linked to the issue of whether animals suffer.

12 This link may be attempted in two ways. First, there is a hazy line of philosophical thought, stemming perhaps from some doctrines associated with Wittgenstein, which maintains that we cannot meaningfully attribute states of consciousness to beings without language. I have not seen this argument made explicit in print, though I have come across it in conversation. The position seems to me very implausible, and I doubt that it would be held at all if it were not thought to be a consequence of a broader view of the significance of language. It may be that the use of a public, rule-governed language is a precondition of conceptual thought. It may even be, although personally I doubt it, that we cannot meaningfully speak of a creature having an intention unless that creature can use a language. But states like pain, surely, are more primitive than either of these, and seem to have nothing to do with language.

13 Indeed, as Jane Goodall points out in her study of chimpanzees, when it comes to the expression of feelings and emotions, humans tend to fall back on nonlinguistic modes of communication which are often found among apes, such as a cheering pat on the back, an exuberant embrace, a clasp of hands, and so on.[2] Michael Peters makes a similar point in his contribution to *Animals, Men and Morals* when he notes that the basic signals we use to convey pain, fear, sexual arousal, and so on are not specific to our species. So there seems to be no reason at all to believe that a creature without language cannot suffer.

14 The second, and more easily appreciated way of linking language and the existence of pain is to say that the best evidence that we can have that another creature is in pain is when he tells us that he is. This is a distinct

---

[2] Jane van Lawick-Goodall, *In the Shadow of Man* (Boston: Houghton Mifflin, 1971), p. 225.

line of argument, for it is not being denied that a non-language-user conceivably could suffer, but only that we could know that he is suffering. Still, this line of argument seems to me to fail, and for reasons similar to those just given. "I am in pain" is not the best possible evidence that the speaker is in pain (he might be lying) and it is certainly not the only possible evidence. Behavioral signs and knowledge of the animal's biological similarity to ourselves together provide adequate evidence that animals do suffer. After all, we would not accept linguistic evidence if it contradicted the rest of the evidence. If a man was severely burned, and behaved as if he were in pain, writhing, groaning, being very careful not to let his burned skin touch anything, and so on, but later said he had not been in pain at all, we would be more likely to conclude that he was lying or suffering amnesia than that he had not been in pain.

15   Even if there were stronger grounds for refusing to attribute pain to those who do not have a language, the consequences of this refusal might lead us to examine these grounds unusually critically. Human infants, as well as some adults, are unable to use language. Are we to deny that a year-old infant can suffer? If not, how can language be crucial? Of course, most parents can understand the responses of even very young infants better than they understand the responses of other animals, and sometimes infant responses can be understood in the light of later development.

16   This, however, is just a fact about the relative knowledge we have of our own species and other species, and most of this knowledge is simply derived from closer contact. Those who have studied the behavior of other animals soon learn to understand their responses at least as well as we understand those of an infant. (I am not referring to Jane Goodall's and other well-known studies of apes. Consider, for example, the degree of understanding achieved by Tinbergen from watching herring gulls.)[3] Just as we can understand infant human behavior in the light of adult human behavior, so we can understand the behavior of other species in the light of our own behavior (and sometimes we can understand our own behavior better in the light of the behavior of other species).

17   The grounds we have for believing that other mammals and birds suffer are, then, closely analogous to the grounds we have for believing that other humans suffer. It remains to consider how far down the evolutionary scale this analogy holds. Obviously it becomes poorer when we get further away from man. To be more precise would require a detailed examination of all that we know about other forms of life. With fish, reptiles, and other vertebrates the analogy still seems strong, with molluscs like oysters it is much weaker. Insects are more difficult, and it may be that in our present

---

[3] N. Tinbergen, *The Herring Gull's World* (New York: Basic Books, 1961).

state of knowledge we must be agnostic about whether they are capable of suffering.

18   If there is no moral justification for ignoring suffering when it occurs, and it does occur in other species, what are we to say of our attitudes toward these other species? Richard Ryder, one of the contributors to *Animals, Men and Morals,* uses the term "speciesism" to describe the belief that we are entitled to treat members of other species in a way in which it would be wrong to treat members of our own species. The term is not euphonious, but it neatly makes the analogy with racism. The nonracist would do well to bear the analogy in mind when he is inclined to defend human behavior toward nonhumans. "Shouldn't we worry about improving the lot of our own species before we concern ourselves with other species?" he may ask. If we substitute "race" for "species" we shall see that the question is better not asked. "Is a vegetarian diet nutritionally adequate?" resembles the slave-owner's claim that he and the whole economy of the South would be ruined without slave labor. There is even a parallel with skeptical doubts about whether animals suffer, for some defenders of slavery professed to doubt whether blacks really suffer in the way whites do.

19   I do not want to give the impression, however, that the case for Animal Liberation is based on the analogy with racism and no more. On the contrary, *Animals, Men and Morals* describes the various ways in which humans exploit nonhumans, and several contributors consider the defenses that have been offered, including the defense of meat-eating mentioned in the last paragraph. Sometimes the rebuttals are scornfully dismissive, rather than carefully designed to convince the detached critic. This may be a fault, but it is a fault that is inevitable, given the kind of book this is. The issue is not one on which one can remain detached. As the editors state in their Introduction:

> *Once the full force of moral assessment has been made explicit there can be no rational excuse left for killing animals, be they killed for food, science, or sheer personal indulgence. We have not assembled this book to provide the reader with yet another manual on how to make brutalities less brutal. Compromise, in the traditional sense of the term, is simple unthinking weakness when one considers the actual reasons for our crude relationships with the other animals.*

20   The point is that on this issue there are few critics who are genuinely detached. People who eat pieces of slaughtered nonhumans every day find it hard to believe that they are doing wrong; and they also find it hard to imagine what else they could eat. So for those who do not place nonhumans beyond the pale of morality, there comes a stage when further argument seems pointless, a stage at which one can only accuse one's

opponent of hypocrisy and reach for the sort of sociological account of our practices and the way we defend them that is attempted by David Wood in his contribution to this book. On the other hand, to those unconvinced by the arguments, and unable to accept that they are merely rationalizing their dietary preferences and their fear of being thought peculiar, such sociological explanations can only seem insultingly arrogant.

21   The logic of speciesism is most apparent in the practice of experimenting on nonhumans in order to benefit humans. This is because the issue is rarely obscured by allegations that nonhumans are so different from humans that we cannot know anything about whether they suffer. The defender of vivisection cannot use this argument because he needs to stress the similarities between man and other animals in order to justify the usefulness to the former of experiments on the latter. The researcher who makes rats choose between starvation and electric shocks to see if they develop ulcers (they do) does so because he knows that the rat has a nervous system very similar to man's, and presumably feels an electric shock in a similar way.

22   Richard Ryder's restrained account of experiments on animals made me angrier with my fellow men than anything else in this book. Ryder, a clinical psychologist by profession, himself experimented on animals before he came to hold the view he puts forward in his essay. Experimenting on animals is now a large industry, both academic and commercial. In 1969, more than 5 million experiments were performed in Britain, the vast majority without anesthetic (though how many of these involved pain is not known). There are no accurate U.S. figures, since there is no federal law on the subject, and in many cases no state law either. Estimates vary from 20 million to 200 million. Ryder suggests that 80 million may be the best guess. We tend to think that this is all for vital medical research, but of course it is not. Huge numbers of animals are used in university departments from Forestry to Psychology, and even more are used for commercial purposes, to test whether cosmetics can cause skin damage, or shampoos eye damage, or to test food additives or laxatives or sleeping pills or anything else.

23   A standard test for foodstuffs is the "LD50." The object of this test is to find the dosage level at which 50 percent of the test animals will die. This means that nearly all of them will become very sick before finally succumbing or surviving. When the substance is a harmless one, it may be necessary to force huge doses down the animals, until in some cases sheer volume or concentration causes death.

24   Ryder gives a selection of experiments, taken from recent scientific journals. I will quote two, not for the sake of indulging in gory details, but in order to give an idea of what normal researchers think they may legitimately do to other species. The point is not that the individual

researchers are cruel men, but that they are behaving in a way that is allowed by our speciesist attitudes. As Ryder points out, even if only 1 percent of the experiments involve severe pain, that is 50,000 experiments in Britain each year, or nearly 150 every day (and about fifteen times as many in the United States, if Ryder's guess is right). Here then are two experiments:

> *O. S. Ray and R. J. Barrett of Pittsburgh gave electric shocks to the feet of 1,042 mice. They then caused convulsions by giving more intense shocks through cup-shaped electrodes applied to the animals' eyes or through pressure spring clips attached to their ears. Unfortunately some of the mice who "successfully completed Day One training were found sick or dead prior to testing on Day Two."* [Journal of Comparative and Physiological Psychology, *vol. 67, 1969, pp. 110–116]*

> *At the National Institute for Medical Research, Mill Hill, London, W. Feldberg and S. L. Sherwood injected chemicals into the brains of cats — "with a number of widely different substances, recurrent patterns of reaction were obtained. Retching, vomiting, defaecation, increased salivation and greatly accelerated respiration leading to panting were common features."...*
>
>   *The injection into the brain of a large dose of Tubocuraine caused the cat to jump "from the table to the floor and then straight into its cage, where it started calling more and more noisily whilst moving about restlessly and jerkily...finally the cat fell with legs and neck flexed, jerking in rapid clonic movements, the condition being that of a major [epileptic] convulsion...within a few seconds the cat got up, ran for a few yards at high speed and fell in another fit. The whole process was repeated several times within the next ten minutes, during which the cat lost faeces and foamed at the mouth."*
>
>   *The animal finally died thirty-five minutes after the brain injection.* [Journal of Physiology, *vol. 123, 1954, pp. 148–167]*

25   There is nothing secret about these experiments. One has only to open any recent volume of a learned journal, such as the *Journal of Comparative and Physiological Psychology,* to find full descriptions of experiments of this sort, together with the results obtained — results that are frequently trivial and obvious. The experiments are often supported by public funds.

26   It is a significant indication of the level of acceptability of these practices that, although these experiments are taking place at this moment on university campuses throughout the country, there has so far as I know, not been the slightest protest from the student movement. Students have been rightly concerned that their universities should not discriminate on grounds of race or sex, and that they should not serve the purposes of the military or big business. Speciesism continues undisturbed, and many

students participate in it. There may be a few qualms at first, but since everyone regards it as normal, and it may even be a required part of a course, the student soon becomes hardened and, dismissing his earlier feelings as "mere sentiment," comes to regard animals as statistics rather than sentient beings with interests that warrant consideration.

27   Argument about vivisection has often missed the point because it has been put in absolutist terms: Would the abolitionist be prepared to let thousands die if they could be saved by experimenting on a single animal? The way to reply to this purely hypothetical question is to pose another: Would the experimenter be prepared to experiment on a human orphan under six months old, if it were the only way to save many lives? (I say "orphan" to avoid the complication of parental feelings, although in doing so I am being overfair to the experimenter, since the nonhuman subjects of experiments are not orphans.) A negative answer to this question indicates that the experimenter's readiness to use nonhumans is simple discrimination, for adult apes, cats, mice, and other mammals are more conscious of what is happening to them, more self-directing, and, so far as we can tell, just as sensitive to pain as a human infant. There is no characteristic that human infants possess that adult mammals do not have to the same or a higher degree.

28   (It might be possible to hold that what makes it wrong to experiment on a human infant is that the infant will in time develop into more than the nonhuman, but one would then, to be consistent, have to oppose abortion, and perhaps contraception, too, for the fetus and the egg and sperm have the same potential as the infant. Moreover, one would still have no reason for experimenting on a nonhuman rather than a human with brain damage severe enough to make it impossible for him to rise above infant level.)

29   The experimenter, then, shows a bias for his own species whenever he carries out an experiment on a nonhuman for a purpose that he would not think justified him in using a human being at an equal or lower level of sentience, awareness, ability to be self-directing, etc. No one familiar with the kind of results yielded by these experiments can have the slightest doubt that if this bias were eliminated the number of experiments performed would be zero or very close to it.

30   If it is vivisection that shows the logic of speciesism most clearly, it is the use of other species for food that is at the heart of our attitudes toward them. Most of *Animals, Men and Morals* is an attack on meat-eating—an attack which is based solely on concern for nonhumans, without reference to arguments derived from considerations of ecology, macrobiotics, health, or religion.

31   The idea that nonhumans are utilities, means to our ends, pervades our thought. Even conservationists who are concerned about the slaughter of

wild fowl but not about the vastly greater slaughter of chickens for our tables are thinking in this way—they are worried about what we would lose if there were less wildlife. Stanley Godlovitch, pursuing the Marxist idea that our thinking is formed by the activities we undertake in satisfying our needs, suggests that man's first classification of his environment was into Edibles and Inedibles. Most animals came into the first category, and there they have remained.

32   Man may always have killed other species for food, but he has never exploited them so ruthlessly as he does today. Farming has succumbed to business methods, the objective being to get the highest possible ratio of output (meat, eggs, milk) to input (fodder, labor costs, etc.). Ruth Harrison's essay "On Factory Farming" gives an account of some aspects of modern methods, and of the unsuccessful British campaign for effective controls, a campaign which was sparked off by her *Animal Machines* (London: Stuart, 1964).

33   Her article is in no way a substitute for her earlier book. This is a pity since, as she says, "Farm produce is still associated with mental pictures of animals browsing in the fields…of hens having a last forage before going to roost…." Yet neither in her article nor elsewhere in *Animals, Men and Morals* is this false image replaced by a clear idea of the nature and extent of factory farming. We learn of this only indirectly, when we hear of the code of reform proposed by an advisory committee set up by the British government.

34   Among the proposals, which the government refused to implement on the grounds that they were too idealistic, were *"Any animal should at least have room to turn around freely."*

35   Factory farm animals need liberation in the most literal sense. Veal calves are kept in stalls five feet by two feet. They are usually slaughtered when about four months old, and have been too big to turn in their stalls for at least a month. Intensive beef herds, kept in stalls only proportionately larger for much longer periods, account for a growing percentage of beef production. Sows are often similarly confined when pregnant, which, because of artificial methods of increasing fertility, can be most of the time. Animals confined in this way do not waste food by exercising, nor do they develop unpalatable muscle.

36   *"A dry bedded area should be provided for all stock."* Intensively kept animals usually have to stand and sleep on slatted floors without straw, because this makes cleaning easier.

37   *"Palatable roughage must be readily available to all calves after one week of age."* In order to produce the pale veal housewives are said to prefer, calves are fed on an all-liquid diet until slaughter, even though they are long past the age at which they would normally eat grass. They develop a craving for roughage, evidenced by attempts to gnaw wood from their stalls. (For the same reason, their diet is deficient in iron.)

38   *"Battery cages for poultry should be large enough for a bird to be able to stretch one wing at a time."* Under current British practice, a cage for four or five laying hens has a floor area of twenty inches by eighteen inches, scarcely larger than a double page of the *New York Review of Books*. In this space, on a sloping wire floor (sloping so the eggs roll down, wire so the dung drops through) the birds live for a year or eighteen months while artificial lighting and temperature conditions combine with drugs in their food to squeeze the maximum number of eggs out of them. Table birds are also sometimes kept in cages. More often they are reared in sheds, no less crowded. Under these conditions all the birds' natural activities are frustrated, and they develop "vices" such as pecking each other to death. To prevent this, beaks are often cut off, and the sheds kept dark.

39   How many of those who support factory farming by buying its produce know anything about the way it is produced? How many have heard something about it, but are reluctant to check up for fear that it will make them uncomfortable? To nonspeciesists, the typical consumer's mixture of ignorance, reluctance to find out the truth, and vague belief that nothing really bad could be allowed seems analogous to the attitudes of "decent Germans" to the death camps.

40   There are, of course, some defenders of factory farming. Their arguments are considered, though again rather sketchily, by John Harris. Among the most common: "Since they have never known anything else, they don't suffer." This argument will not be put by anyone who knows anything about animal behavior, since he will know that not all behavior has to be learned. Chickens attempt to stretch wings, walk around, scratch, and even dustbathe or build a nest, even though they have never lived under conditions that allowed these activities. Calves can suffer from maternal deprivation no matter at what age they were taken from their mothers. "We need these intensive methods to provide protein for a growing population." As ecologists and famine relief organizations know, we can produce far more protein per acre if we grow the right vegetable crop, soy beans for instance, than if we use the land to grow crops to be converted into protein by animals who use nearly 90 percent of the protein themselves, even when unable to exercise.

41   There will be many readers of this book who will agree that factory farming involves an unjustifiable degree of exploitation of sentient creatures, and yet will want to say that there is nothing wrong with rearing animals for food, provided it is done "humanely." These people are saying, in effect, that although we should not cause animals to suffer, there is nothing wrong with killing them.

42   There are two possible replies to this view. One is to attempt to show that this combination of attitudes is absurd. Roslind Godlovitch takes this course in her essay, which is an examination of some common attitudes to

animals. She argues that from the combination of "animal suffering is to be avoided" and "there is nothing wrong with killing animals" it follows that all animal life ought to be exterminated (since all sentient creatures will suffer to some degree at some point in their lives). Euthanasia is a contentious issue only because we place some value on living. If we did not, the least amount of suffering would justify it. Accordingly, if we deny that we have a duty to exterminate all animal life, we must concede that we are placing some value on animal life.

43   This argument seems to me valid, although one could still reply that the value of animal life is to be derived from the pleasures that life can have for them, so that, provided their lives have a balance of pleasure over pain, we are justified in rearing them. But this would imply that we ought to produce animals and let them live as pleasantly as possible, without suffering.

44   At this point, one can make the second of the two possible replies to the view that rearing and killing animals for food is all right so long as it is done humanely. This second reply is that so long as we think that a nonhuman may be killed simply so that a human can satisfy his taste for meat, we are still thinking of nonhumans as means rather than as ends in themselves. The factory farm is nothing more than the application of technology to this concept. Even traditional methods involve castration, the separation of mothers and their young, the breaking up of herds, branding or ear-punching, and of course transportation to the abattoirs and the final moments of terror when the animal smells blood and senses danger. If we were to try rearing animals so that they lived and died without suffering, we should find that to do so on anything like the scale of today's meat industry would be a sheer impossibility. Meat would become the prerogative of the rich.

45   I have been able to discuss only some of the contributions to this book, saying nothing about, for instance, the essays on killing for furs and for sport. Nor have I considered all the detailed questions that need to be asked once we start thinking about other species in the radically different way presented by this book. What, for instance, are we to do about genuine conflicts of interest like rats biting slum children? I am not sure of the answer, but the essential point is just that we *do* see this as a conflict of interest, that we recognize that rats have interests too. Then we may begin to think about other ways of resolving the conflict—perhaps by leaving out rat baits that sterilize the rats instead of killing them.

46   I have not discussed such problems because they are side issues compared with the exploitation of other species for food and for experimental purposes. On these central matters, I hope that I have said enough to show that this book, despite its flaws, is a challenge to every human to recognize his attitudes to nonhumans as a form of prejudice no

less objectionable than racism or sexism. It is a challenge that demands not just a change of attitudes, but a change in our way of life, for it requires us to become vegetarians.

47   Can a purely moral demand of this kind succeed? The odds are certainly against it. The book holds out no inducements. It does not tell us that we will become healthier, or enjoy life more, if we cease exploiting animals. Animal Liberation will require greater altruism on the part of mankind than any other liberation movement, since animals are incapable of demanding it for themselves, or of protesting against their exploitation by votes, demonstrations, or bombs. Is man capable of such genuine altruism? Who knows? If this book does have a significant effect, however, it will be a vindication of all those who have believed that man has within himself the potential for more than cruelty and selfishness.

STUDY QUESTIONS

1. What broader principles underlie Singer's conclusion that animals are entitled to equality?
2. Locate several passages in which Singer appeals to the reader's specific judgments in real or hypothetical situations as support for his liberationist principles.
3. What analogies does Singer use to show either the evils of speciesism or the merits of animal liberation?
4. Roslind Godlovitch, in the argument cited near the conclusion of Singer's essay, uses the logical strategy of reductio ad absurdum; i.e., she tries to show that two premises to which meat eaters normally subscribe jointly entail a conclusion that they would consider absurd, namely, that "all animal life ought to be exterminated." Her point is that if the absurd conclusion is a valid deduction from the two premises, then at least one of the premises must be false.
   Do you agree with her argument? If not, where is the flaw in her reasoning?
5. Singer uses three rebuttal techniques: analogy, counterexample, and reductio ad absurdum. Explain which of these techniques are used to rebut the following arguments that Singer quotes from speciesists:
   a. That "nothing really bad" could be allowed to happen in factory farms
   b. That the best evidence we can have that another creature is in pain is that he tells us about it
   c. That sexism is the "last remaining form of discrimination"
   d. That since nonhumans are not equal to humans in intelligence and abilities, they are not entitled to equal treatment
   e. That a creature without language cannot feel pain
   f. That to experiment on a single animal, if the experiment could save thousands of human lives, would not be discriminatory

g. That animals raised on factory farms do not suffer because they have never known anything different

h. That what makes experimentation on human infants wrong is that they will develop into adult human beings

6. The early portion of Singer's essay derives animal rights from animals' capacity to suffer. How does Singer justify his claim that even if animals could be killed without physical or mental suffering, they should not be killed for meat?

7. Try using the strategy of reductio ad absurdum to rebut Singer's argument. Do his premises lead to any conclusions that you would consider clearly absurd?

SUGGESTIONS FOR WRITING

1. Singer implies that if you eat meat, you are morally in the position of racists or of "decent Germans" who ignored the Nazi death camps. If you feel after reading his article that you are morally justified in continuing to eat meat, explain where he has made errors in his reasoning. Be careful not to base your case on arguments that Singer has already anticipated and rebutted.

2. If you have any experience with the use of laboratory animals in your institution, write an essay about their care and treatment.

   a. If you agree with Singer on the issue of animal experimentation, write a letter to the head of biological sciences at your institution proposing changes that you feel are necessary and justifying those changes in terms calculated to take his or her presumed values and interests into account. (The essays by Noah and DeBakey in this volume may give you some idea of what your faculty member's value system may be.)

   b. If you believe that some suffering on the part of lab animals is warranted, write a letter to Singer explaining where his argument suffers from falsification or omission.

C. A. J. COADY

Defending Human Chauvinism

C. A. J. Coady is Reader in Philosophy at the University of Melbourne. He has published extensively on ethical issues, particularly those concerned with political violence and nuclear deterrence.

1   My title is a little misleading. Although I shall be offering certain thoughts in defense of a position that some would regard as "human chauvinism" or "speciesism" I am really more concerned with getting clear about just what is being said by those who use those terms in clamorous denunciation and what value their supporting arguments have.

2   The locus of my comments will be the moral concerns and outlooks that have fathered (or mothered?) two political movements—animal liberation and environmentalism. Despite points of tension between the animal and nature liberationists, both have in common that they may be plausibly viewed as calling for a new ethic. The characteristic move of the new ethicists is to declare that the traditional ethic is defective in its emphasis on the importance of human beings. This is speciesism or human chauvinism. The old ethic was human centered, the new will be…well, it will have some other center.

One Bad Argument

3   One bad argument against speciesism consists in drawing attention to the fact that just as we come to realize that moral concern cannot be restricted to the members of our own race ("racism") or of our own sex ("sexism"), so by a sort of analogical extension we come to see that it cannot be restricted to our own species ("speciesism"). But this argument gets things the wrong way round. It is clearly possible for someone who puts special moral importance upon humankind to object to racist policies precisely because they treat their victims as being not human or, in Hitler's classic phrase, subhuman. When we consider that a common element in the usual moral criticism of racism and sexism is precisely that such outlooks ignore the fact that the members of the maltreated class are members of the human species like ourselves, then the condemnation of speciesism can hardly seem a simple extension of those other condemnations.

Justifying Human Superiority

4   Yet, at this point, it will be said that the idea that there is something specially morally important about human beings needs justification. I am of two minds about this demand for justification. I think it can be met but I'm not sure that it has to be. There are various ground floor

considerations in ethics as in any other enterprise for an animal liberationist such things as the "intrinsic good" of pleasure and the "intrinsic evil" of pain are usually ground floor. No further justification is given for them, or needed. It is not clear to me that membership in the human species does not function in a similarly fundamental way in ethics so that there is as much absurdity, if not more, in asking "Why does it matter morally that she is human?" as in asking "Why does it matter morally that she is in pain?" Nonetheless, since justification is preferable to intuition where it can be given let me try to do so.

5   Before trying to provide such a justification let us be clear what it involves. We need some characterization, not necessarily a very precise one, of what it is about humankind that makes it worthy of more moral consideration than other known kinds such as ants, dogs, pine trees, a strain of flu virus, or a type of rock. What we would thereby show, if successful, is that what environmentalists, such as the Routleys, call "the greater value assumption"—the assumption that human beings are of greater value, morally, than individuals of other species—is no mere assumption. We would also perhaps then vindicate a "human-centered ethic" in some sense of that confusing phrase.

6   A further caution is in order about what the task involves. We are trying to exhibit features of humankind that show that the human species is morally distinctive, but these need not be such as to show that no moral respect or even duty is owed to other species. The assumption to be vindicated is a greater value assumption, not an exclusive value assumption. An exclusive value assumption would entail an attitude to nature that sees no value at all in either the animate or inanimate environment except insofar as it subserves rather narrowly conceived human interests.

Intrinsic Values in Nature?

7   The issue of whether there are intrinsic values in the nonanimate world has become a point of serious division between the environmentalists and the animalists because the former object to the latter's emphasis on pain, pleasure, and associated interests as the sole or primary deposit of value. The environmentalists object either that sentience is not a precondition for having interests or that it is not a precondition for having value. They accuse animal liberationists like Peter Singer of the dastardly sin of "sentiencism." The Routleys and others are fond of producing examples our responses to which are supposed to show that there are intrinsic values to nonanimate nature. Let me cite just a few.

8   *1* The last man example. This concerns the last man on earth, sole survivor of the collapse of the world system, who sets to work eliminating

mountains as well. If we think he has acted wrongly, presumably we are recognizing intrinsic value in nonhuman and even in nonanimate entities.

9   *2* The river example. This is to illustrate the idea that natural phenomena can be damaged independently of any human or animal related damage in a way that calls for compensation. The idea is that pollution of a river involves more than damage to the humans affected by it so that compensation requires restoration of the river to its unpolluted state and not merely monetary compensation to any people affected.

10   *3* The noise in the forest example. This concerns an objection to "making unnecessary and excessive noise" in a forest. It is held that the believer in the new ethic's intrinsic values will avoid such noise even if no other humans are around to hear and he will so act "out of respect for the forest and its nonhuman inhabitants." Adherents of the traditional ethic will feel free to shout and howl as the mood takes them.

11   Before I leave these examples for your judgment let me comment briefly on 2. and 3. because I have certain dissatisfactions with them. The river example is defective, as it stands, in placing so much weight on monetary compensation, since the people affected may need to have an unpolluted river in the future so that they do not suffer further damage and they may in any case prefer the appearance of a beautiful, clear, unpolluted stream in which they can catch healthy fish. If we remove these features by paying the people so much that they can move to the banks of another, clean river and then so arrange things (noncoercively) that no humans or even animals are affected by the state of the river, is it so obvious that some moral wrong has been done by continuing to pollute the stream in a good (human) cause? In the forest example we must, I think, exclude noise that might actually cause damage to a wild animal by, say, bursting its eardrums, but if we set that aside can it seriously be claimed that a moral issue about the noise arises?

Speciesism Vindicated

12   Let me now return to my defense of the greater value assumption. Insofar as the Routleys and other advocates of a new ethic rely upon the deliverances of intuition about the morality of shouting in the forest, the last man on earth, and so on, it seems to me that man's greater moral importance over animals, ecosystems, trees, or whatever is far more obvious than any of the intuitions of the new ethic. Consider a small child being attacked by a rat. It is perfectly obvious to anyone not unbalanced by theory that it is morally right to injure or kill the rat if that is necessary to save the child. It makes no difference that the rat may be very smart (for a rat) and the child backward or that the child provoked the attack. Anyone who hesitated to act because of such considerations would be a moral

idiot. Normally, at the level of intuition, serious human welfare clearly outweighs that of animals. I do not know how much we can rely on appeals to intuition, but they seem inescapable in these debates and I think one should be wary of being bluffed out of one's pro-human intuitions. One should be particularly suspicious when marginal intuitions are used to construct an argument which is supposed to disenfranchise more robust intuitions.

13   As for a characterization of the superiority of the human species, my view is that we should not seek to uncover just *one* characteristic such as rationality (though plainly rationality is important) but rather highlight a cluster of interconnected characteristics. So one could cite, in addition to rationality, the capacity for artistic creation, the capacity for theoretical knowledge of the universe and of oneself, the capacity for love including love of one's enemies, and very centrally the capacity for moral goodness. This last provides a crucial distinction between the inanimate, plant, and brute creation on the one side and humanity on the other and makes talk of a moral community among humans, mountains, trees, lakes, fish, and kangaroos a bit one-sided. I should add that I do not here propose a particularly optimistic view of the human species since I recognize that it is an essential concomitant of the capacities listed that they can be abused and that they imply the capacity for irrationality and wickedness. This is what human freedom, which is involved in all these characteristics, typically allows. Nonetheless, that man has this complex of features makes him as a species more morally significant than the nonhuman world as we know it.

Objections Answered

14   There is a strategy employed by the Routleys and also by Peter Singer against claims of the form mine has taken. For any quality that is suggested as giving humans moral superiority the strategy is to declare: (a) that some nonhuman object or process or creature has it, too; (b) that not all humans have it; or (c) that some humans have it in different degrees to others. So in the case of rationality, for instance, we are told that some animals have it, that some defective or immature humans lack it, and that Einstein has more of it than others. In the case of the cluster of properties I have proposed, however, it seems clear that our species is marked by these qualities, and being marked by them is deserving of moral respect, and it is merely delusional to suppose that the cluster is exhibited by any species in the nonhuman world as we know it. The wildest claims on behalf of Washoe, the talking chimpanzee, do not really establish him as an even moderately boring dinner guest. The passion to denigrate the human world has led to very extravagant and ill-founded claims for the linguistic and related achievements of chimpanzees and dolphins. Washoe's exploits have

recently been subjected to much more sober and critical scientific assessment than they received at the hands of the original investigators with alarmingly deflationary results.

15   As to the second and third parts of the strategy, it is of course true that there are immature, senile, and defective members of the species, but only an inordinately individualistic ideology can hold that such members should be given treatment that takes no account of their species membership. We have a vital interest in the immature, the retarded, and the defective of our kind since, apart from anything else, we normal adults have been immature and may become damaged or handicapped. The focus of moral concern upon isolated individuals and their present attributes rather than upon species, groups, kinds, and types is not the only or, one might think, the sanest stance possible for moral theory. As to those members of the species who possess the featured capacities to an outstanding degree, several responses are possible. One is to note that it is very unlikely that many will possess the *complex* to a degree that raises problems of differential respect; a second is to distinguish issues to do with law, politics, and generally civil justice from those that concern other areas of morality—there are well-known reasons for not having legal and political inequalities, but these reasons do not necessarily apply in other areas of moral interest. Perhaps the saint is worthy of special moral respect and even more.

16   A final point about chauvinism. I wonder whether it wouldn't be appropriate to say something here on behalf of artifacts and machines. Are the new ethicists in danger of sliding into a form of nature chauvinism?

STUDY QUESTIONS

1. What Coady calls "ground floor considerations in ethics" in paragraph 4 are what we have referred to as basic principles at the center of the spiderweb values system. What are Coady's ground floor considerations, and how do they differ from those he attributes to the animal liberationists?
2. In the section headed "Intrinsic Values in Nature?" Coady critiques two of the Routleys' hypothetical examples but not the first, "The last man example." Explain just what the Routleys expect this example to prove. Does it succeed? Why, or why not?
3. In paragraph 12 Coady says, "Consider a small child being attacked by a rat. It is perfectly obvious to anyone not unbalanced by theory that it is morally right to injure or kill the rat if that is necessary to save the child." What conclusion does Coady draw from the fact that any normal person would injure or kill the rat?

4. Return to the sentences quoted from Coady in question 3 and change the word "rat" to "man." Would you still agree with the second sentence? If so, is the persuasiveness of Coady's argument affected?
5. In paragraph 13, Coady cites a "complex of features" including the capacity for rationality, love, and moral goodness. Whatever the *capacity* of humans in these areas, we all know—or know of—human beings who rank well below the average golden retriever in *possession* of these traits. Does Coady's argument offer any reason for valuing a brutal or bigoted human being over the golden retriever?

SUGGESTION FOR WRITING

Imagine a private club in South Africa twenty years ago that had for years admitted only white males, but which had recently been persuaded to admit white women and was now being urged to accept nonwhites as well. The president of the club addresses the membership as follows:

> *One bad argument against racism consists in drawing attention to the fact that just as we come to realize that moral concern cannot be restricted to members of our own sex ("sexism"), so by a sort of analogical extension we come to see that it cannot be restricted to our own race ("racism"). But this argument gets things the wrong way round. It is clearly possible for someone who puts special moral importance on Caucasians to object to sexist policies precisely because they treat their victims as being nonwhite or, in Hitler's classic phrase, non-Aryan. When we consider that a common element in the usual moral criticism of sexism is precisely that such outlooks ignore the fact that members of the maltreated class are white like ourselves, then the condemnation of racism can hardly seem a simple extension of those other condemnations.*

Of course, this paragraph is simply a paraphrase of Coady's third paragraph, substituting "sexism" for "racism" and "racism" for "speciesism." The words are changed, but the logic remains the same.

What impact, if any, does the possibility of this substitution have on the validity of Coady's argument?

MARIAN DAWKINS

Do Hens Suffer in Battery Cages?

Much of the debate about the ethical treatment of animals in farming and scientific testing and experimentation hinges on the question of whether animals suffer or undergo any "subjective experience" of any kind. Psychologists and philosophers have also debated whether an answer could conceivably be possible to the question, "Do animals suffer?" Behaviorists, who have been highly influential in scientific inquiries, hold that questions about the mental states of animals (or, for that matter, humans), are not empirical questions. Since any question about mental states must rely for evidence on the observation of behavior (including verbal reports), we may draw conclusions only about behavior. Empirical knowledge cannot extend to mental states.

The following article addresses the general question of whether we can assess suffering in animals and suggests an experimental procedure for studying their subjective experience.

1   **Abstract.** The question "Do hens suffer in battery cages?" is difficult to answer because of the problem of objectively assessing suffering in animals. It is argued that preference tests may be one way of throwing light on this difficult problem. This paper describes some experiments on habitat preference in domestic hens. No preference was observed between a commercial battery cage and a large pen when hens were given continuous access to the two. A simultaneous choice between a battery cage and an outside hen-run showed a clear preference for the run, but choice was strongly influenced by prior experience. The strength of the run preference was investigated by "pitting" the run against food and access to companions.

Introduction

2   To many scientists the question "Do hens suffer in battery cages?" is invalid, as it is a question about an animal's subjective feelings and the subjective feelings of animals are not directly accessible to scientific investigation. We may look for signs of physical ill-health and we can study behaviour, but we can never know for certain whether these observable symptoms are accompanied by subjective consciousness. We may study animals as if they were machines and try to discover what the behaviour machinery is by looking at the relation between inputs and outputs. There will be no place in such models for subjective feelings. But just because we study animals as if they were machines which merely behaved and felt nothing, does not mean that that is all they are. As Griffin (1976) points out: "It is very easy for scientists to slip into the passive assumption that phenomena with which their customary methods cannot deal effectively are unimportant

or even non-existent." There are at least two reasons for believing that the subjective feelings of animals are both important and very far from non-existent.

3   The first reason comes from the way we react to other people. Exactly the same arguments apply to other human beings as to animals. Strictly, we can never know that other people have mental experiences. We cannot do an experiment to demonstrate that another human being is conscious or has feelings remotely like our own any more than we can for a hen or a chimpanzee. But commonsense and intuition tell us that other human beings probably do think and feel as we ourselves do. Their behaviour and physiology are sufficiently similar to our own that we are quite prepared to accept this without the need for logical proof. We base our ideas of morality, such as not to eat people, kill them or torture them, on this commonsense view rather than on strict logic. There is a "common ground": suffering, pleasure, pain, which most people accept as being universals of human experience. But must this common ground stop at the boundaries of our own species? If we accept the evolutionary continuity between man and other animals for physiology, biochemistry and at least some aspects of behaviour, why not mental experiences too (Brophy 1972; Griffin 1976)? Ryder (1971) and Singer (1976) use the term "speciesism" by analogy with racism. Many animals, particularly mammals and birds, seem to have all the basic nervous apparatus for feeling pain and experiencing emotion. Commonsense suggests that they can suffer. Of course, we cannot be certain about this, but neither can we about other people. If animals do suffer from some of our scientific experiments or from the ways in which we keep them for commercial profit, then it seems important on moral grounds to take this into account.

4   The second reason is a more biological one, and comes from consideration of the possible survival value of subjective feelings. We are accustomed to asking questions about the functional significance of the shape, colouring and behaviour of an animal. It is reasonable to assume that subjective feelings too evolved because animals which possessed them were fitter than those which did not. Exactly why they should have been fitter is one of the most profound mysteries of biology, and although various suggestions have been made, e.g. that they aided simulation of the future (Wall 1974), communication or learning, the full reasons are not understood. But whatever the reasons, each of us knows that we have subjective feelings and those feelings must be a product of natural selection. They are part of biology.

5   For these two reasons, questions about the mental states of animals are important: they are important on moral grounds in that if we ignore an animal's subjective feelings, we may be guilty of inflicting or at least condoning suffering in highly sentient and emotional beings; and they are

important on biological grounds since subjective experience is part of an animal's equipment for survival.

6   This seems to bring us to an impasse: subjective feelings are important and yet we apparently cannot study them scientifically. There is, of course, no magic method for solving the major philosophical issues which still exist and gaining direct access into what animals are feeling. But I want to suggest that some behaviours are likely to be good indicators of mental state. The question is: which ones? I would like to discuss this question in relation to one particular problem which has recently aroused a lot of public concern—whether hens in battery cages suffer—but I hope that similar lines of reasoning can also be used for a wider range of problems.

7   Some of the most widely advocated indicators of possible suffering are physical ill-health, poor growth rate, or in the case of laying hens, a substandard number of eggs produced. Presumably physical health is an essential part of mental well-being, and it is often argued that productivity is in itself a sufficient guide on the grounds that animals which are suffering would not produce well. But, as pointed out by the Brambell Committee (Report, 1965), it is quite possible for animals to be growing or laying well, despite periods of acute but transitory physical or mental suffering.

8   Another proposed indicator of suffering has been whether the behaviour patterns of hens in battery cages differ from those of feral fowl, or Burmese red jungle fowl (*Gallus gallus spadiceus*), which is thought to be the wild form (Wood-Gust 1971). Thorpe (1965, 1967) argues that where animals are kept in situations that suppress their natural behaviour patterns, then suffering may well result. Hens in battery cages are physically prevented from performing many behaviours such as roosting, dust-bathing and ground-scratching. The birds cannot flap their wings, walk more than a few steps and are frustrated in their nesting behaviour (Wood-Gush & Gilbert 1969; Wood-Gush 1972). Such a major disruption of the "normal" behaviour patterns should immediately alert us to the possibility of suffering but does not itself constitute evidence that the animals are suffering (Ewbank 1968). Battery-kept hens might, for example, show less anti-predator behaviour than unrestricted fowl, but it would be implausible to argue from this that the birds were suffering from lack of anti-predator behaviour.

9   The Brambell Committee (Report, 1965) argued that the best indicator of suffering in other species was by analogy with the symptoms known to accompany mental suffering in human beings. To draw too close a parallel in this respect is, however, most dangerous. The "fear grimace" of the chimpanzee, which to the human eye looks like a happy smile is in fact given in situations which the animal finds fearful (Jolly 1972). So even in an animal which is very closely related to us there is the possibility of

serious error if the analogy with our own expressions is drawn too closely. How much greater is the possibility of error in animals which are even less like ourselves and have evolved their own independent ways of expressing emotion? At first sight it also seems humane to decry certain husbandry practices on the grounds that we ourselves would not like to be housed in this way. Whilst we must never forget the "common ground" that may exist between us, and other animals, neither should we forget that different species may have genuinely different requirements. Baby jackdaws relish regurgitated worms, which I would not.

10   Physiological measures of "stress" (Selye 1952) such as increased activity of the pituitary and adrenal cortex and development of gastric ulcers have also been used to indicate which conditions animals find stressful. Duncan (1974), in a discussion of this in relation to animal welfare, points out that there are difficulties in measuring physiological changes in living animals. There is also still the problem of relating changed physiological state to the animal's subjective feelings of distress. Animals may suffer before any physiological disturbances are detected or there may be physiological changes totally uncorrelated with suffering.

11   There is, however, another, possibly more direct way of inferring what an animal's feelings are, at least its feelings about a particular environment. This is to allow the animal to express those feelings by being given the opportunity to move out of that environment if it wants to. For example, if we want to know whether hens dislike battery cages, the hens could be given the opportunity to choose between battery cages and some other environment and allowed to "vote with their feet." If it were to turn out that hens have a very strong preference for environments other than battery cages and if they would repeatedly perform some task for the "reward" of being allowed out of a battery cage, then we could say that they disliked battery cages. If, on the other hand, they did not seem to show a very strong preference one way or the other, we might be less inclined to say that they disliked them. Hughes & Black (1973) have shown that hens given the opportunity to stand on different sorts of cage floor spent more time on hexagonal mesh than on coarse rectangular mesh or than on perforated steel sheet. It seems very likely that the hens "like" some floors more than others. The reason why environmental preference is very likely to be closely correlated with an animal's subjective feelings is that natural selection will have favoured such a connection. We should expect co-evolution between an animal's fitness in different environments and the capacity of each environment to evoke escape or settling behaviour (Levins 1968). As Orians (1971) puts it: "birds should evolve to be more 'turned on' by habitats in which their fitness is greater."

12   This paper describes a number of experiments on habitat preference in domestic hens. The experiments could be taken from a strictly behaviourist

viewpoint with no connotations of subjective feelings. However, if the preceding arguments are accepted, they may also be seen as a first step towards developing experimental methods to deal with the mental experiences of animals.

13   The first experiment is an attempt to find out where battery-kept hens choose to spend their time when given the opportunity to be either in a battery cage or in a much bigger pen. The birds were given continuous access to these two environments over a period of 12 h. Where would they go? Would they ever re-enter a battery cage once they had left it? Would their choice be influenced by the time of day or by the lack of familiarity with the pen?

Experiment 1: Where do Battery Kept Hens Go If Given Continuous Access to Battery Cages and a Larger Pen?

Methods

14   Twelve Sykes Tinted hens which had been reared commercially on deep litter by Ross Poultry Ltd, were used for this experiment. At the age of 18 weeks they were put into Patchett battery cages (floor space 0.38 × 0.43 m) with two birds per cage.

15   The birds were housed in a light-proof shed, on a "step-up" system of lighting and fed commercial mash. At the age of 32 weeks they were tested individually by being placed in the centre of a pen (dimensions shown in Figure 1). The floor of the pen was covered with wood shavings. Two Patchett battery cages with the backs removed to permit access were placed at one end of the pen. The floor of the backs of the battery cages was flush with the floor of the pen, so that a hen could walk easily in and out of the battery cages. The position of the two battery cages was changed from one side of the pen to the other for different hens. Food and water were available in equal amounts in similar troughs in the pen and the battery cages. Each bird was tested for 12 h but observations were made only once in each hour for 5 min at regular intervals. At the beginning of a test, an

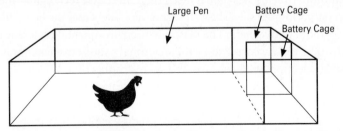

Large Pen   Battery Cage

Battery Cage

Figure 1. Diagram of the large pen and battery cages used in experiment 1. The battery cages had the backs removed so that the hens could wander freely in and out. The floor of the pen was 2.6 × 0.82 m and was covered with wood shavings. The floor space of each battery cage was 0.38 × 0.43 m, the floor being of plastic covered rectangular mesh.

individual bird was placed in the centre of the large pen. It was left to adjust for 5 min and then the first observation session was begun. For subsequent observations, I entered the hut 5 min before an observation was due, to allow the bird to adjust to my presence, and then for 5 min recorded whether the bird was in the pen or one of the battery cages. I also recorded where and when any eggs were laid. In order to separate the effects of time of day from those of familiarity with the test apparatus, the tests of different birds were started at different times of day. One bird would be tested from 08.30 until 20.30 hours, another (on its testing day) from 10.30 to 20.30 hours and then again from 08.30 until 10.30 hours the following morning and so on. This means that many of the birds were removed from the apparatus overnight and restarted in the morning. The birds were at the time of testing on a 14-h light/dark, schedule with the lights coming on from 07.45 hours daily.

Results

16   In order to ensure that the results represent independent observations, the preference of the birds between pen and battery cage were first calculated as where the birds were standing at the beginning of each 5-min observation session (i.e., 12 observations for each of 12 birds). On this measure, 5 out of the 12 birds preferred the battery cages in the sense that the majority of their observation sessions found them standing in one of the battery cages, and 7 preferred the pen. Overall, there was no significant preference one way or the other, using a Wilcoxon Matched Pairs Test on the sign and magnitude of the differences ($N = 12$, $P > 0.05$ two-tailed (Siegel 1956)). This is somewhat surprising in view of the fact that the combined floor area of the two battery cages was so much smaller than the floor area of the pen (See Figure 1) so that by chance one might have expected them to be seen more often in the pen. Through the 12 h of the test (08.30 to 20.30 hours), just under half the birds were seen in one of the battery cages (Figure 2). The data from Figure 2 can be rearranged so that

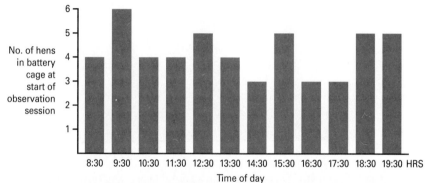

Figure 2. Numbers of hens (out of a total of 12) in one of the battery cages at the beginning of each 5-min observation session throughout a 12-h day.

the position of the hens is seen at different times since the beginning of their own individual tests rather than the time of day (made possible by the design of the experiment in which birds started their tests at different times of their day). Figure 3 shows such a rearrangement and the birds seemed not to change in how likely they were to be in pen or battery cage throughout their tests, even though they might be expected to have become more familiar with the pen the longer they had been in the apparatus.

17   Another measure of preference which makes use of rather more of the data is how many complete minutes of a 5-min observation session a hen spent in pen or battery cage. The maximum possible in any one environment would be 5, but if a hen repeatedly moved between the two, she could score 0 complete minutes for either environment. In any one 5-min observation session, a hen could be said to prefer one environment over the other depending on how many complete minutes she spent in each. Out of her 12 observation sessions she could be said to prefer one environment over the other if the majority of sessions showed a preference for this environment. Using this measure, four hens preferred the battery cages, seven preferred the run and one scored equally for the two environments, but the difference is not significant ($P > 0.05$ Wilcoxon Test, two tailed). Nor was there any tendency for the hens to spend more complete minutes in either environment depending on the time of day (Figure 4) or how long they had been in the apparatus (Figure 5). Nine of the hens laid an egg during the course of being tested, six in the pen and three in one of the battery cages but the figures are too small to draw any conclusions.

Discussion

18   The really rather surprising result of this experiment was the lack of demonstrated preference for either the pen or the battery cages. Of course, such a negative result does not imply that the hens do not have a

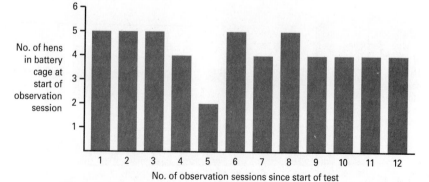

Figure 3. Numbers of hens (out of a total of 12) in one of the battery cages at the beginning of each 5-min observation period throughout a 12-h day.

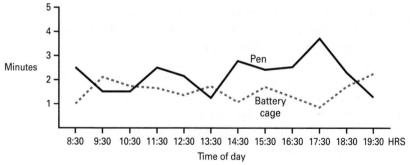

Figure 4. Mean number of complete minutes spent by 12 hens in a battery cage (----) and pen (———) in each of 12 5-min observation sessions throughout the day. There is no significant tendency for the time spent in either environment to be different at different times of the day (Friedman two-way analysis of variance, $P > 0.5$).

preference: it could simply be that the preference was not demonstrated in these particular experimental conditions.

19   One reason why a preference was not demonstrated may have been that the chickens did not regard the pen as sufficiently different from the battery cages to exhibit a preference between them (both pen and battery cage were inside, and the main differences were that the pen was larger and had the floor covered with wood shavings). To meet this possibility, all the experiments described below involve testing a hen's responses to two environments which differed in very many more ways. The two environments were a battery cage and a hen-run outside in the garden.

20   The second reason for the apparent lack of preference may have been the particular method of testing. It is known that a hen's preference may be strongly affected by how the preference is measured. Hughes (1976) tested the preference of domestic hens for wire or litter floors and found that the

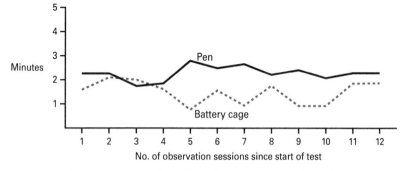

Figure 5. Mean number of complete minutes spent by 12 hens in a battery cage (----) and pen (———) in each of 12 5-min observation sessions throughout the 12-h test. There is no significant tendency for the time spent in either environment to vary depending on how long the birds have been in the apparatus (Friedman two-way analysis of variance, $P > 0.90$).

birds chose differently depending on whether they were given constant access to both floor types or whether they had to make a choice between separate cages, where the choice was irrevocable for several hours. Because of the possibility that the method of testing described above may have given a misleading impression of the kinds of environments that chickens like and dislike, I have adopted two other methods of assessing the relative attractiveness of environments to hens.

21   The first of these methods involved releasing a hen from a starting box and measuring how quickly she moved into either a battery cage or a hen-run. These experiments are described in detail elsewhere (Dawkins 1976). The results showed that using this particular measure of preference, battery-kept hens initially preferred battery cages to a run in the garden in the sense that they moved more quickly into a battery cage than into an outside run. However, this preference was found to be highly dependent on the environment in which the hens had been living before being tested. Hens which had been living outside in a garden hen-run preferred the run, while caged birds preferred the battery cage. So the initial reluctance of a battery-kept hen to enter a run was probably due to its strangeness rather than to its undesirability. It seemed very important, therefore, to investigate precisely how much of the hen's behaviour was due to the unfamiliarity of the environments and to plot the time course of adjustment to the new environment. This was done in the experiment to be described next by repeatedly offering a hen a simultaneous choice between a run and a battery cage. When she had made her first choice, she was then confined for 5 min in whichever environment she had chosen and then replaced in the starting box and offered the same choice again. As the trials progressed, therefore, the hen would gradually accumulate experience of being confined in each of the two environments and by making her choose repeatedly, any changes in her preference could be monitored as a function of this experience.

22   Since the conditions in which the hens had been living before being tested is known to have a profound effect on their performance in a test, (Dawkins 1976), two groups of hens were used, one accustomed to living in battery cages and one group used to living outside in the garden.

Experiment 2: Do Hens Choose a Battery Cage or an Outside Run and Does the Choice Change with Experience?

Methods

23   Fourteen Sykes Tinted hens, aged 48 weeks at the time of testing, were used for this experiment. They had been reared commercially on deep litter by Ross Poultry Ltd, until the age of 20 weeks. On arrival in Oxford

they were randomly divided into two groups: half were put outside into a hen-house and run (house 1.83 × 1.14 m; run area 7.34 m²); half were kept indoors in Patchett battery cages (floor space 0.38 × 0.43 m) with two birds in each cage.

24   The birds were individually given a choice between the two environments presented as the alternatives in a T-maze (see Figure 6): an outside hen-run (1.53 × 0.76 × 0.9 m high) made of wood and chicken wire and supplied by Park Lines Ltd, and a Patchett battery cage with the back removed to allow a hen to enter. For technical reasons it is very difficult to present a choice between a battery hen-house and a garden run, so a compromise in the form of a small hut on wheels that could be moved to any desired position, was adopted. The hut was lit and heated as much as possible like the house in which the hens had been living, and in order to simulate a "battery" of cages, the hut contained three battery cages, the middle one of which was the test cage.

25   Each hen was offered this choice 24 times successively, between the hours of 07.30 to 11.00 and 16.30 to 18.30 daily, extending over several days. Only when one hen had completed her 24 choices was the next hen started. For each choice, an individual hen was placed in the starting box with the door closed for 1 min. The door was then raised and the hen released into a corridor from which she could see simultaneously the run and the battery cage. The time from the raising of the starting box door to when the hen entered one of the two test environments was measured and called the latency of choice. A hen was considered to have made a choice only when she had put both feet in one or other environment. If a hen failed to move out of the starting box within 15 min, she was placed gently in the centre of the corridor (this happened in about 10% of trials). In order to ensure that the hen had a standard and measured amount of time in the environment of her choice, once she had entered it, the door leading to it was closed behind her and she was shut in for 5 min. After this time,

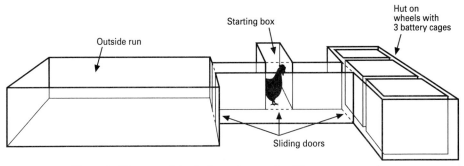

Figure 6. Diagram of the choice test apparatus. The run measured 1.83 × 0.76 × 0.9 m high. The floor space of each battery cage was 0.38 × 0.43 m.

she was returned to the starting box and the next trial begun. In this way, a hen gradually accumulated 5-min blocks of experience of the environments she chose. A hen which had been living inside a battery cage was given its 24 trials following the series of a hen that had been living in the garden so that the test order could not be a confounding variable in the comparison between the two groups. The position of the two environments with respect to the choice corridor was changed daily to avoid position effects. Food was available in similar troughs in both environments.

Results

26   As expected from previous work with latencies to the two environments presented successively (Dawkins 1976), the first choice of the hens was related to the environment in which they had been living. All seven of the hens which had been living in the garden chose the run on their first trial whereas only three of the battery-kept birds did so ($P = 0.05$, Fisher Exact Probability Test). However, the battery-kept hens very quickly began to change their pattern of choice and became more and more likely to choose the run as their trials proceeded (Figure 7). This result is interesting as it would seem to suggest that only a relatively small amount of experience of the run (a matter of minutes) is sufficient to make even battery-kept hens prefer the run.

27   In addition to which environment was chosen, the latency of that choice also provides valuable information about the hens' preferences. These latencies were, however, so variable both between individual birds and from trial to trial even of the same bird to the same environment that graphs for the 14 birds are presented separately in Figure 8. Each graph incorporates two kinds of information: information about which environment the bird chose and information about the latency of choice, plotted cumulatively as the trials progressed. The bird could allocate its testing time between three separate places: the run (5 min at a time), the battery cage (also a maximum of 5 min/trial), and the choice corridor (this time being measured as the latency of response). After each trial, a certain amount of time would have elapsed since the beginning of the series for that bird and that time could have been spent in some or all of those three environments. Each graph plots cumulatively the proportion of the total test time spent in run and battery cage after different numbers of trials. The direction and slope of the graph shows the effect of previous experience, for example, a positively accelerating line would mean that the more time a bird spent in an environment, the more time she would spend in the future in that same place. Figure 8a shows that for six of the hens kept in battery cages the proportion of time spent in the run gradually increased over 24 trials. Only one hen consistently spent more

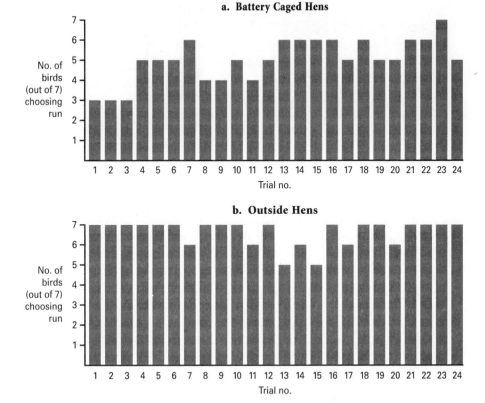

Figure 7. Numbers of (a) battery-caged birds and (b) birds which had been living outside choosing the run in each of 24 trials. The difference between the two groups is significant only for the first three trials (P = 0.05, Fisher Exact Probability test). The battery caged birds become more likely to choose the run as the trials proceed (Spearman rank correlation: $r_s = 0.35$; $N = 24$, $P < 0.05$).

time in the battery cage and even this hen began to spend more time in the run towards the end of the series. On the other hand, the amount of time spent in the battery cage remained roughly constant or dropped off. This implies that whereas the effect of being in the run was to increase the future amount of time the bird spent in run, this was not true of the battery cage. This would seem to be a fairly objective way of saying that hens "liked" the experience of being outside in the run more than they "liked" being in a battery cage. Future experiments might profitably involve recording details of the behaviour of the hens during the 5-min period after each choice.

Hens which had been living outside (Figure 8b) tended to show consistently high levels of time in the run and certainly no tendency to increase time spent in the battery cage as a result of entering the battery cage. Most of them entered once or twice at the most and never again.

28

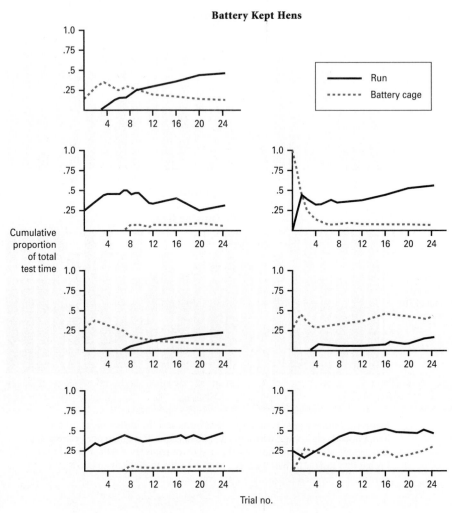

Figure 8a. Cumulative proportion of total test time which seven individual battery-kept hens spent in the run (———) and the battery cage (-----) during the course of their 24 trials (for details see text).

Discussion

29   These results show that battery-kept hens prefer an outside run to a battery cage, once initial unfamiliarity with the run has been overcome. These hens take a very short time to get used to the run (a matter of minutes) and to come to prefer it to their familiar cages. The more experience of the run they have, the more likely they are to choose to spend time in the run in the future. Being in a battery cage, on the other hand, does not seem to increase the likelihood that the hens will choose to spend time in a battery cage in the future, either for battery-kept birds or for hens which have been living outside in a garden run. Birds which have

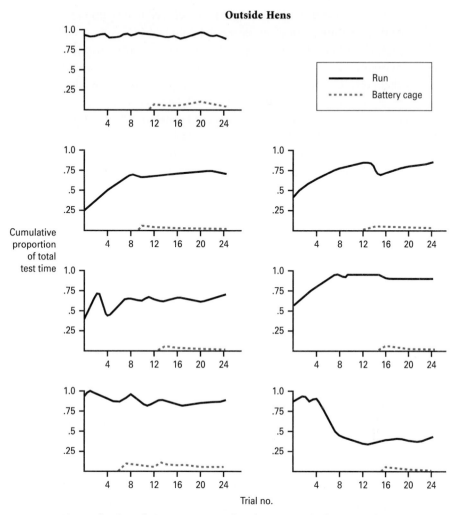

Figure 8b. Cumulative proportion of total test time which seven individual hens which had been living outside in a garden run spent in the run (————) and the battery cage (-----) during the course of their 24 trials.

been living outside consistently prefer the run over the battery cage to a very marked extent.

Although these results give a preliminary indication that hens "like" (as revealed by their behaviour) an outside run more than they "like" a battery cage, there is a long way to go before any conclusions can be drawn about the extent to which hens suffer in battery cages. If a man were to be given a choice between a £1note and a £10 note, for example, and he consistently chose the £10 note, we could hardly be entitled to conclude that he suffered in the presence of single pound notes. Preference per se cannot be used to infer suffering or distress. It can only be used in this way if we can establish how great the preference is in terms of some yardstick, such as how much of some other commodity an animal is prepared to give up in order to obtain something. For example, hens are known to be very social animals and the sight of other hens appears to increase the attractiveness of an environment, since hens moved more quickly into a place where there were other hens (Dawkins 1976). Would hens still choose an outside run if it meant isolation from their flock mates? If they did still prefer an outside run under these circumstances, we could conclude that they "liked" being in the run more than being with other hens. If the opposite result were found, and they chose to be with the other birds, then the conclusion might be that although they prefer a run, other things being equal, this preference is not as strong as their attraction to other birds. In this way it should be possible to get the hens to rank their preferences for different commodities. In the next experiment reported below, hens were offered such a choice between an outside run in which they would be alone, and a battery cage near other birds.

Experiment 3: Do Hens Prefer an Outside Run on Their Own or a Battery Cage Near Other Hens?

Methods

31   Ten Sykes Tinted hens which had been used for the previous experiment were used for this test. Half the birds were from each group, and since being tested previously, had been returned to their original living conditions, i.e. the battery-kept birds had been living in cages and the outside group in the garden. This experiment took place immediately after the previous one, but since this had taken 5 weeks to complete, the time lag between the two was different for different individuals. The choice apparatus was the same as that used in experiment 2 except that the two battery cages on either side of the test cage in the hut (see Figure 6) were not empty as in the previous experiment, but each contained a single bird unfamiliar to the test bird. This meant that the choice presented to test the bird was a battery cage with other birds in cages on either side of it and an outside run in the garden without other hens. In order to make sure that the birds realized that there were other birds in the battery hut but not in the run, the experimental procedure was rather different from the earlier experiment. Before the actual choice was presented, each bird had a series of "training" trials, in which entry to one environment was prevented by closing the sliding door leading to it and the bird had, therefore, to stay in the choice corridor or go into the other environment. All the birds eventually went into the single available environment upon which they were shut in for 5 min. Three of these training trials were given to each environment so that by the end of the six trials, the bird had had at least 15 min experience of both environments. The seventh test was the choice test, with the bird having access to both

environments simultaneously. Only one such choice test was given to each bird. One bird received its six training trials and it choice test in quick succession, the entire test usually taking about 1 h. The latency of responses both during the training trials and the choice test was recorded. The position of the two environments was changed between individuals and each hen received the three training trials for each environment in alternation. Battery-kept and outside hens were tested equally often before and after each other. Another difference from the previous experiment was that there was no food available in either the run or the battery cage (the reason for this will become apparent from the next experiment).

Results

32   In the final choice test, 9 out of the 10 birds chose the run by themselves over the battery cage near other birds. The one bird that chose the battery cage was a bird that had been living outside and was showing pre-egg-laying activity. She laid an egg soon after her test so her choice behaviour may have been temporarily upset. The latency data from the training trials also provides information about the hens' preferences for the two environments. If the latency of response to the battery cage in each of the "battery alone" training trials is compared with the latencies in the "run alone" training trials (Figure 9) it will be seen that the birds took very much longer to enter the battery cage than the run. There was no significant trend for these latencies to change during the training period.

Discussion

33   Both by the criterion of hens choosing in a simultaneous choice test and by that of the latency of response when the environments were presented singly during "training," it would seem that these hens preferred to be in an outside run, even though it meant being by themselves to being in a battery cage near other hens. This was true even though the previous experience of the test birds was rather varied. Half had been living in battery cages, and half outside and all had experienced various degrees of

Figure 9. Median response latency to battery cage presented alone and run presented alone in the training trials before a choice test. There is no significant tendency for these latencies to change over the three trials ($P > 0.1$, Friedman test, $N = 10$).

time in both environments during a previous test. It could be objected to this experiment that the period of "training" was not long enough and that if there had been more training trials, the birds would have had more chance to "take stock" of the two environments and might then have chosen differently. This may indeed be the case, but to judge by the previous experiment even very short periods of time seem to be enough for a hen to learn about two environments. It would certainly be important to repeat this experiment with a longer period of training before we can draw any definite conclusions about how hens rank the opportunity to go into an outside run compared with the opportunity to be in a cage near other hens.

34   Another objection is that the fact that other birds are attractive to hens was inferred from previous work rather than demonstrated in the present experiment, so that, strictly speaking, all that can be concluded from this experiment is that hens prefer a run to a battery cage and this preference still exists even if there are other hens near the battery cage and not in the run. Nevertheless, taking this as a preliminary result, it would certainly seem to suggest that, subject to the objections just mentioned, the preference for the run over the battery cage would seem to be sufficiently strong to override the probable attraction of other hens. Further experiments along these lines are planned.

35   Another way in which it may be possible to assess the strength of hens' preferences for the run is by finding out whether they still choose the run if they can obtain food only in the battery cage. Will the attraction of the run outweigh that of food?

Experiment 4: Do Hens Prefer an Outside Run With No Food or a Battery Cage with Food?

Methods

36   The ten hens which were used for experiment 3 were also used for this experiment. The choice-testing apparatus and procedure were the same as that described for experiment 3, except that the battery hut did not contain the two hens in battery cages. The test battery cage this time had a trough of food and the outside run contained no food. The hens were not deprived of food before being tested, but the daily renewal of their food in their living cages was not carried out until after they had been tested. The hens were given six training trials, three to the battery cage alone and three to the run alone. As before, the seventh trial was the choice test.

Results

37   In the final choice test 3 out of the 10 hens chose the battery cage with food, 7 chose the run without food. This result is not significantly

different from chance ($P > 0.1$ Binomial Test), but the fact that three hens (two-battery-kept and one outside hen) chose the battery cage with food rather than the run means that at the very least, the hens' preferences are not absolutely clear cut, even though they were not deprived of food. Furthermore, the latencies of the response to the two environments presented singly (during the training trials) showed that the run was entered more quickly (Figure 10). There seemed to be some tendency for the latency of response to the battery cage to go down over the three trials, perhaps as the birds learned that there was food in the cage, but this is not significant. However, it would certainly suggest that it would be worth repeating this experiment with a longer period of training and to more accurately "titrate" access to a run against access to food.

Discussion

38   It was argued in the introduction that although it is very difficult, it may not be totally impossible to develop a methodology for dealing with the subjective feelings of animals. The long-term hope is to be able to assess animal suffering in a reasonably objective way. Different methods can all contribute something to our picture, but a particularly important source of evidence may be the kinds of environmental conditions that the animals themselves choose when given the opportunity to do so. The experiments described here, together with others such as those of Hughes (1976) are a first step in developing such a methodology. The experiments do not, and could not, demonstrate the existence of mental events in hens. It would be possible to view these preference tests simply as overt behaviour, with no overtones of mental experiences. However, given that

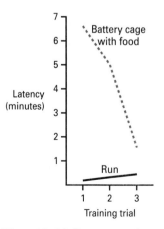

Figure 10. Median response latency to battery cage presented alone and run presented alone in the training trials before a choice test. There is no significant tendency for these latencies to change over the three trials ($P > 0.1$, Friedman test, $N = 10$).

mental experiences will have evolved by natural selection, we would expect that behavioural choice and subjective feelings about the environments chosen would not be completely uncorrelated. If we had a clear idea of the kinds of situations that hens prefer and the extent to which they avoid less preferred environments, then we would be in a much better position to assess the mental states of hens in battery cages. It has been shown that hens prefer an outside run to a battery cage, once initial unfamiliarity with a strange environment has worn off. On the other hand, it is as yet impossible to say how strong this preference is. Hens given continuous access to a battery cage and a larger pen did not show evidence of preference one way or the other and the experiments in which access to a run is possible only if the hen chooses to forgo some other commodity such as food or other hens (experiments 3 and 4), do not enable firm conclusions to be drawn without further work along the same lines.

39   Before these laboratory experiments can be used to say anything one way or the other about the mental state of hens kept under commercial battery cage conditions, it is very important to establish the generality of these results. Is the preference the same whatever the method of testing used? Do different genetic strains of hens show different environmental preferences? Is the nature or extent of the preference affected by the type of battery cage used, for example a four-bird cage, or by the stocking density? These questions can only be answered by further research.

40   I feel strongly that these are preliminary results and should not at the moment be used either to criticize or to support the battery-cage system for keeping laying hens. Anyone who uses these results for either of these purposes is in my view going beyond what our present knowledge warrants. However, I think it is important to continue to research into the question of whether hens suffer in battery cages along the lines that have been started, and I hope that one day such work will enable us to take an objective and humane judgment on life in a battery cage.

Acknowledgments

41   I am very grateful to the Royal Society for Prevention of Cruelty to Animals for financial assistance and to Dr. R. Dawkins for reading the manuscript. I would also like to thank Miss J. Lomer for valuable technical assistance.

References

Brambell, F. R. (Chairman) 1965. *Report of the Technical Committee to Enquire into the Welfare of Animals kept under Intensive Livestock Systems.* Command Paper 2896, H.M.S.O., London.

Brophy, B. 1972. The ethical argument against the use of animals in biomedical research. In: *The Rational Use of Living Systems in Biomedical Research.* U.F.A.W., Potters Bar, Hertfordshire.

Dawkins, M. 1976. Towards an objective method of assessing welfare in domestic fowl. *Appl. Anim. Ethol.,* 2, 245–254.

Duncan, I. J. H. 1974. A scientific assessment of welfare. *Proc. Br. Soc. Anim. Prod.,* 3, 9–19.

Ewbank, R. 1968. The behavior of animals in restraint. In: *Abnormal Behavior in Animals* (Ed. by M. W. Fox), pp. 159–178. Philadelphia: W. B. Saunders.

Griffin, D. R. 1976. *The Question of Animal Awareness.* New York: Rockefeller University Press.

Hughes, B. O. 1976. Preference decisions of domestic hens for wire or litter floors. *Appl. Anim. Ethol.,* 2, 155–165.

Hughes, B. O. & Black, A. J. 1973. The preference of domestic hens for different types of battery cage floor. *Br. Poult. Sci.,* 14, 615–619.

Jolly, A. 1972. *The Evolution of Primate Behavior.* New York: Macmillan Co.

Levins, R. 1968. *Evolution in Changing Environments.* Princeton, N.J.: Princeton University Press.

Orians, G. 1971. Ecological aspects of behavior. In: *Avian Biology.* Vol. I (Ed. by D. S. Farner & J. R. King), pp. 513–546. London and New York: Academic Press.

Ryder, R. 1971. Experiments on animals. In: *Animals, Men and Morals* (Ed. by S. & R. Godlovitch & J. Harris), pp. 41–82. London: Victor Gollancz Ltd.

Selye, H. 1952. *The Story of the Adaptation Syndrome.* Montreal: Acta, Inc.

Siegel, S. 1956. *Nonparametric Statistics for the Behavioral Sciences.* New York: McGraw-Hill.

Singer, P. 1976. *Animals Liberation.* London: Jonathan Cape.

Thorpe, W. H. 1965. The assessment of pain and distress in animals. Appendix III. *Brambell Committee Report,* Command Paper 2896, H.M.S.O., London pp. 71–79.

Thorpe, W. H. 1967. Discussion to Part II. In: *Environmental Control in Poultry Production* (Ed. by T. C. Carter). *British Egg Marketing Board Symposium No. 4.* Edinburgh: Oliver & Boyd.

Wall, P. D. 1974. "My foot hurts me": An analysis of a sentence. In: *Essays on the Nervous System. A Festschrift for Professor J. Z. Young* (Ed. by R. Bellairs & E. G. Gray), pp. 391–406. Oxford: Clarendon Press.

Wood-Gush, D. G. M. 1971. *The Behaviour of the Domestic Fowl.* London: Heinemann.

Wood-Gush, D. G. M. 1972. Strain difference in response to sub-optimal stimuli in the fowl. *Anim. Behav.,* 20, 72–76.

Wood-Gush, D. G. M. & Gilbert, A. B. 1969. Observations on the laying behaviour of hens in battery cages. *Br. Poult. Sci.,* 10, 29–36.

STUDY QUESTIONS

1. Does Dawkins offer an adequate rebuttal to the behaviorist position that she describes in the opening four sentences of the article? Why or why not?
2. Why does Dawkins recommend tests of the sort she proposes in preference to (or at least as a necessary complement to) physiological measures of stress and suffering?

3. Select any one of the four experiments reported. List every aspect of the design of that experiment calculated to avoid a faulty causal attribution and explain what false conclusions the design feature was intended to avoid. (Example: In experiment 1, food and water were placed in both the pen and the cages so that the presence of a hen in one area or the other could not be attributed to the greater availability of such attractions.)

4. The question behind this study is, "Do Hens Suffer in Battery Cages?" Yet, as the author herself points out in her "Discussion" of experiment 2, no demonstration that hens prefer runs to battery cages shows necessarily that the cages cause them suffering—any more, she says, than a man's choice of a £10 note over a £1 note would show that he would suffer by being given a £1 note. Why do you suppose she designed an experiment that she recognized did not answer the question she originally proposed?

SUGGESTION FOR WRITING

Using the basic experimental method proposed by Dawkins, design an experiment that would measure whether hens suffer by confinement in battery cages. Assume that you are justified in imposing on the hens whatever suffering is needed in your experiment, on the grounds that your aim is to benefit by your research a much larger population of chickens. Observe this format in writing your proposal:

> *Background:* Briefly summarize the Dawkins experiments and explain why they do not measure the suffering of the chickens.
> *Procedure:* Describe a procedure that would measure their suffering.
> *Rationale:* Explain how the observed behavior of the chickens allows you to conclude whether or to what degree they suffer.

TIMOTHY NOAH

Monkey Business

Timothy Noah, who writes about a variety of political subjects, has been a regular contributor to the *New Republic* and other periodicals. He has also served on the editorial board of the op-ed page of the *New York Times* and as an editor of the *Washington Monthly*.

In this essay Mr. Noah expresses a view shared by many members of the scientific establishment.

1   "This is vivisection," proclaimed scores of posters that appeared overnight all over Washington to designate April 24 an International Day for Laboratory Animals. "Don't let anyone tell you differently." The posters were illustrated with a lurid photograph of a monkey trapped in an elaborate scaffold, its neck wedged in a narrow aperture and its arms extended, Christ-like, to the outer bars, where they were tightly bandaged. The photograph was a little deceptive. The scaffold was really a restraining chair whose "seat" was obscured by the head-on angle, and though the monkey appeared to be choking, more likely it was simply trying to jerk its head free, and was only seconds short of surrendering. This unmistakable image of suffering, however, was strong enough to lure two hundred demonstrators on the appointed day to a solemn funeral procession, led by a real hearse, that circled the Capitol, drove past the White House, and ended in Bethesda, Maryland, where an empty coffin was unloaded before the National Institutes of Health.

2   In a world of malnutrition, yellow rain, and prison rape, it seems more than a little dilettantish to invoke "animal welfare," "animal rights," or, at the most self-paradistic level, "animal liberation." Despite such silly slogans, however, animal lovers can at least make a dimly plausible case for some of their doctrine. Vegetarianism, for instance, may not rank up there with vaccinating ghetto schoolchildren, but it's a good many ethical notches up from, say, practicing tax law. Even when militancy on behalf of animals leads to socially embarrassing situations, such as the denunciation of an impoverished Eskimo whale hunter by a Scarsdale housewife, one might argue that shining through the wealthy woman's arrogance is the faint glimmering of an ethical principle. After all, didn't the justly admired Albert Schweitzer admonish us to consider a man ethical "only when life as such is sacred to him, that of plants and animals as that of his fellow man"? (Let's ignore for the moment less admirable exemplars like Caligula, who loved his horse so much that he made him a senator, and Hermann Goering, who kept a sign in his Berlin office which read, "He who tortures animals wounds the feelings of the German people.")

3   It's different with anti-vivisectionists. Overtly or implicitly, they reject *in principle* the use of animals in experimentation. (Many will add the caveat, "experimentation that causes pain," but in practice that means just about everything except rats in mazes.) The issue is not human appetites; their concern is not for cattle at the slaughterhouse. Nor is it human vanity. Sealskin coats may be distasteful (though more from an economic point of view than a humanitarian one), but anti-vivisection has nothing to do with the skinning of seals. To be sure, most anti-vivisectionists object to these other forms of cruelty to animals. But by strict definition, anti-vivisection is opposition to animal suffering that may ease human suffering. As philosopher Peter Singer writes in *Animal Liberation,* a very silly 1975 tract that grew out of an article in the *New York Review of Books* and became the bible of the anti-vivisection movement, "An experiment cannot be justifiable unless the experiment is so important that the use of a retarded human being would also be justifiable." In other words, the ethical rules governing animal experimentation are the same thorny rules that govern human experimentation. (See "The Ethics of Human Experimentation," by Charles Krauthammer, TNR, December 12, 1981.)

4   The three major anti-vivisection societies in America—the National, American, and New England "AVs"—are seeking to prevent scientists from harming animals to help human beings. With a combined and partly overlapping membership of under 100,000, their numbers are small. But add to that perhaps as many as ten million members and supporters of various Humane Societies, SPCAs, and other animal welfare groups, which are showing an inclination to join the crusade against animal experimentation, and you have what a prudent futurologist might call an incipient national movement. The Humane Society of America, for instance, is currently seeking to prevent "pound seizure," or the use for medical experiments of animals turned over to local pounds. It recently had a victory in the city of Los Angeles, and is now seeking a statewide ban in California. A spokeswoman for the group argues that these animals are pets—though only a fraction of all pound animals are ever reclaimed by their owners—and denies that the Humane Society is anti-vivisectionist. It may not be in theory, but clamping down on the supply of laboratory animals is an effective way to put anti-vivisection into practice. Another factor that may help anti-vivisection blossom into a nationwide movement is the odd tendency many of us have to care more deeply about cruelty to animals than about cruelty to human beings. This was illustrated vividly in 1973, when Representative Les Aspin, Democrat of Wisconsin, discovered that the Defense Department intended to use two hundred beagle puppies to test poisonous gases. To be sure, this was not an experiment whose benefit to mankind was immediately apparent. But when the volume of mail surpassed the number of letters Defense had received over the bombings of North Vietnam and Cambodia, true humanitarians had cause

to wonder. Anti-vivisectionists, on the other hand, ought to have broken out the champagne. (They were much too surly to do that, of course; Singer gripes that the beagle protest demonstrated "a remarkable ignorance of the nature of quite standard experiments performed by the armed services, research establishments, universities, and commercial firms of many different kinds.") Anti-vivisection has broad appeal insofar as all of us hate the idea of cruelty to animals. But it is, on three levels, a deeply misanthropic movement.

5   The first level is the most familiar: good, old-fashioned hatred of a particular individual. In this case, the individual is a biologist in Silver Spring, Maryland, named Edward Taub. Taub has become a national scapegoat for the anti-vivisection movement because of his alleged (and wholly unproven) mistreatment of seventeen monkeys that were seized from the Institute for Behavioral Research by Montgomery County police last September at the instigation of one of Taub's lab assistants, an undercover animal welfare advocate from People for the Ethical Treatment of Animals. (It was PETA that sponsored the "funeral procession" in April, and one of Taub's monkeys that illustrated the poster. The photograph also appeared in the *Washington Post* the day after the raid.) Taub has received surprisingly unkind treatment from a movement that calls itself humanitarian. "The man was guilty of cruelty on every single count he was charged with," seethes Cleveland Amory, the former *TV Guide* critic and columnist for *Saturday Review,* whose Fund for Animals contributed $20,000 to Taub's legal harassment. Not a very merciful point of view, especially considering that the state of Maryland found Taub *innocent* of all but six of the one hundred and thirteen counts brought against him. And those six counts really amount to one count brought six times, in an odd legal arrangement whereby six wronged monkeys were treated rather more like plaintiffs than like collective property. The charge each of the monkeys brought against their keeper was "unnecessarily failing to provide veterinary care" by an outside vet. For this heinous crime, Taub was fined $3,000.

6   Mild punishment, perhaps, if it had ended there. But with all the awkward publicity, the NIH was compelled to review Taub's $200,000 grant. Two months previous to the September raid, a routine site inspection by the Department of Agriculture had approved Taub's laboratory. Now, however, NIH's eyes were opened to Taub's negligence, and it suspended his grant. Most significant among the reasons, again, was Taub's failure to keep a veterinarian around the lab. The result was that a lot of sores on the monkey's limbs went unbandaged. Some explanation is required here. Taub's experiments involved severing the sensory nerves of monkeys (we'll get to the reason later). Once a limb was numbed, or "deafferented," the monkey had a habit of biting and scratching it. Since the monkey could feel no pain—a point anti-vivisectionists like to

overlook—it tended to bite and scratch so much that bad sores appeared on its deafferented limb. Veterinarians questioned at Taub's trial voiced outrage over his failure to bandage the monkeys. But Taub argued—along with five other scientists, two of them also veterinarians who had had experience with deafferented monkeys—that bandaging only made things worse, because the monkeys tended then to bite and scratch at the *unbandaged* part. The court and NIH rejected Taub's argument. Then NIH, to whom the court assigned custody of the monkeys, proceeded to follow Taub's advice: in its own treatment of the deafferented limbs, it didn't bandage them either.

7   Two other reasons NIH cited for suspension of Taub's grant were poor ventilation and dirty animal cages. Dr. William Raub, Associate Director for Extramural Research and Training, says these were the "major issues." Taub dismisses the criticism of his ventilation system as a technical violation of NIH guidelines that even labs at NIH's research campus in Bethesda routinely violate. NIH guidelines say nothing about cages. Let's assume, however, that ventilation was poor and the cages were dirty. Would Taub routinely expose *himself* to an environment that was unclean enough to threaten health? For if the monkeys were in danger, surely anyone who handled them as much as Taub did might also be in danger. Remember also that a lab that was dirty enough to be unhygenic was not likely to go unnoticed by the inspector from the Department of Agriculture who had dropped by, unannounced, in July. Likelier than not, NIH was troubled by appearances, not by ethics. The best way to keep up appearances was to agree with the anti-vivisectionists that Taub shouldn't be allowed to experiment on monkeys. So NIH suspended Taub's grant.

8   Consequently, Edward Taub can't at the moment experiment with monkeys, as he has for the past twenty-five years. (He claims he has spent more time studying deafferented monkeys than anyone else alive.) Is the world any worse off? The answer is yes, and the reason brings us to the second level of misanthropy in anti-vivisection: to rule out animal suffering is to condone human suffering. Taub's experiments were directed at a phenomenon known as "learned nonuse." It is common among stroke victims, and also occurs sometimes to sufferers of spinal injuries. Learned nonuse is exactly what it sounds like: when life doesn't depend on using a limb deadened to sensation, a person (or monkey) may never make the effort to use it. Although muscles may function normally, the loss of sensation results in a kind of voluntary paralysis. Victims thus must relearn how to use the limbs. Taub says his research may be applicable to roughly one-sixth of all stroke victims, and has already been adapted into clinical technique at two hospitals in the United States. This is the "inhumane" research that anti-vivisectionists have curtailed. They would also like to end the practice of poisoning laboratory animals to determine the lethality of potential drugs and cosmetics. They argue that lethality

varies wildly from species to species, particularly in the oral LD 50 test, in which sixty to a hundred animals are fed enough of a substance to kill 50 percent of them. That's true. But the alternatives they suggest—tests on tissue cultures and computer models—are even more unreliable. Such methods are fine for use in preliminary tests, to weed out obviously toxic substances. But those substances not weeded out inevitably must be tested on whole systems. And, as Dr. Raub testified before the House Subcommittee on Science, Research, and Technology, in the study of "the integrated functions of an intact higher organism or the interaction of organ systems, animal experimentation is inevitable." The only alternative—releasing a drug without such testing—amounts to *human* experimentation.

9   In response to the anti-vivisectionist cry against animal experimentation, Representative Douglas Walgren, Democrat of Pennsylvania and chairman of the Science, Research and Technology Subcommittee, has submitted the Humane Care and Development of Substitutes for Animals in Research Act. The main features of the bill are the addition of red tape in the processing of animal research grants, including the creation of an "animal care committee" on which one place is reserved for an animal welfare advocate, and the appropriation of $75 million over the next three years for development of alternative research methods and "improving animal care facilities." The first provision—red tape—is at best needless (the NIH and Department of Agriculture are already responsible for review and inspection of animal treatment) and at worst a blow to biological (and consequently medical) science. Anti-vivisectionists like to bring up the example of Britain when they try to seem reasonable; licensing for animal experimentation is severely restricted there. British fondness for animals is one of that culture's most endearing qualities. Who among us wasn't touched when the Duke of Edinburgh recently complained that the Falklands conflict might lead to the death of many whales, who emit echoes that sound like Argentine submarines? Deference to the animal kingdom is also, some scientists say, the reason animal research in Britain lags behind in an otherwise impressive tradition of biological research. And as psychiatrist Jeri A. Sechzer has written in the British journal, *Social Science and Medicine,* whatever limits are placed on scientists in Britain would have much worse effect in the U.S., "where there are thousands of research centers and scientists" as compared to the relatively small scientific community in Britain. "Should the use of animals for research and teaching be curtailed as a result of hastily conceived legislation," Sechzer writes, "progress in gaining knowledge crucial to human and animal well-being would be disrupted."

10   The problems inherent in this sort of regulation are illustrated in the troubling issue of anesthesia. Everyone agrees that animals should not be exposed to unnecessary pain. But neither should scientists be hamstrung

by the requirement to use anesthesia in every animal experiment that might cause pain. There are too many experiments — particularly those testing the effects of drugs — that would be impossible to conduct in any scientifically reliable way if this additional chemical variable were made mandatory. The Walgren bill requires "in any case involving surgery or other invasive procedures on animals, appropriate assurances of the proper use of tranquilizers." A subcommittee staffer says the word "proper" allows researchers to fudge when anesthesia might threaten results. But would an "animal care committee" interpret its mandate the same way?

11   The appropriation of $75 million for upgrading facilities and searching for alternatives to animal experimentation is also a blow to the progress of human well-being. No one is anxious to guess where the money will come from, but in the current economic climate it isn't likely this nonsense would be paid for with a new addition to the budget. Rather, the Department of Health and Human Services, which is placed in charge of this program, would have to raid the people kitty. Thus we would witness the absurdity of cutting appropriations for Medicaid, Aid to Families with Dependent Children, and food stamps to pay for welfare for animals. And taking a large view, what benefits would such research provide? Given the likelihood that in 2025 none of us will feel any better about taking pills that haven't been tested on living animals, not much.

12   The third and most ethereal level of misanthropy in the anti-vivisection movement is so intuitive that to launch on an extended attack of it would be sophomoric. It's that, fundamentally, animal welfare makes no distinction between the value of human life and that of animal life. The ease with which anti-vivisectionists pass from one to the other in ethical arguments is downright scary. Peter Singer's equation between the lot of a retarded person and that of a laboratory animal crystallizes the point. "I ask you to recognize that your attitudes to members of other species are a form of prejudice no less objectionable than prejudice about a person's race or sex," writes Singer in introducing the bogeyman of "speciesism," the animal kingdom's equivalent to ethnocentricity. Either this sort of talk makes you angry or it doesn't. An example helps. Alex Pacheco, the undercover animal liberationist who freed Edward Taub's monkeys, argues that the same premise upon which speciesism is based "was used by the slave owners and by white males against blacks and women. And it was used by the Nazis and by Hitler to justify the murder of millions of Jews." Pacheco should ask a ghetto black or an Auschwitz survivor how he likes the analogy. And he shouldn't be surprised when he gets an uncivil answer.

13   Anti-vivisection may never amount to much, although it has already caused Edward Taub some distress. But this is a case where a little paranoia among liberals would be justified. The right has creationism, the know-nothing doctrine that we aren't related to the apes; the left should avoid creationism's mirror image of anti-vivisection, the know-nothing doctrine

that apes are members of the immediate family. Both are anti-scientific ways of thinking that do more harm than good to the prospect that the human race may someday cure its various, far more worrisome ills.

STUDY QUESTIONS

1. Noah calls anti-vivisection "a deeply misanthropic movement" on "three levels." What are the three levels?
2. When Noah discusses the proposal to require anesthesia for every animal experiment that might cause pain, he says that many experiments "would be impossible to conduct in any scientifically reliable way if this additional chemical variable were made mandatory." Why would the reliability of such experiments be compromised?
3. Noah says that "to invoke" phrases such as "animal welfare" is "dilettantish" in a world of malnutrition, yellow rain, and prison rape. What does he mean? Is this criticism of animal welfare proponents valid?
4. Noah refers to Singer's *Animal Liberation* as "a very silly 1975 tract." What arguments does Noah use to rebut Singer's argument? Do you consider Noah's rebuttal effective?
5. Do you feel that Noah has been fair and objective in his defense of Edward Taub? How would you discover more about the Taub case?
6. For what rhetorical purpose do you think Noah defers his explanation of the aim of Taub's experiments until after he has discussed the charges against Taub?
7. Noah says that anti-vivisectionists make "no distinction between the value of human life and that of animal life." If Singer's *Animal Liberation* is a fair representation of the anti-vivisectionist viewpoint on this issue, would you say that Noah is just in his description? What line of reasoning does Noah use to rebut this viewpoint? Is his reasoning persuasive?
8. Noah applies such loaded terms as "silly," "dilettantish," "lurid," "nonsense," and "arrogant" to various aspects of the anti-vivisectionist movement. Identify other terms in the essay that convey value judgments. Does this language impair the rationality of Noah's argument? Is it rhetorically effective?
9. In the next-to-last paragraphs of his essay, Noah criticizes Pacheco's analogy between human victims of the Holocaust and animal victims of speciesism. Do you agree with Pacheco's use of the analogy or Noah's criticism of it?
10. In the final paragraph, Noah makes his own analogy between what he considers to be two "know-nothing" doctrines: creationism and anti-vivisection. Is his analogy well-taken?

SUGGESTION FOR WRITING

Write a rebuttal to Noah's argument based on the premises of Peter Singer.

ALEX PACHECO

Testimony: House Hearings on the Use of Animals in Medical Research and Testing

When evaluations such as Peter Singer's arouse enough public concern, pro-posals arise for counteraction to the abuses described. Often what is proposed is regulatory legislation or changes in existing legislation. The Ninety-Seventh Congress saw the introduction of five bills and a Congressional Resolution aimed at ensuring the humane treatment of animals used in medical research and testing or the development of alternatives to the use of live animals in test-ing. In October 1981, the Subcommittee on Science, Research, and Technology of the House Committee on Science and Technology held two days of hearings on these bills and on the entire question of the treatment of laboratory animals. The following is a transcript of the oral testimony of Alex Pacheco, a volunteer research assistant at the Institute for Behavioral Research in Silver Spring, Maryland, whose charges led police to remove test animals from the facility and the National Institute of Health to suspend grants for experiments on them. At the time of his testimony, Pacheco was also Chairperson of the People for the Ethical Treatment of Animals and the George Washington University Ethics and Animals Society.

1   My name is Alex Pacheco, and I am chairperson for People for the Ethical Treatment of Animals, and I also chair the George Washington University Ethics and Animals Society. First, I have a few photographs that I would like to pass around so you can visualize some of the things I will be describing.

2   I recently worked at a laboratory called the Institute for Behavioral Research (IBR), which is just about twenty-five minutes from here. At this laboratory human research and animal research was conducted. This laboratory, through Dr. Edward Taub, a psychologist, has received roughly $2^1/_4$ million NIH dollars for particular experiments involving the severing of nerves in monkeys.

3   These experiments, which were recently suspended by NIH, involved cutting the nerves at the spine of the monkey, thus rendering a limb useless. Then, through electric shock punishment and other forms of negative stimuli, the animals were forced to try to use their bad arms.

4   So far, I haven't been able to find any evidence that this research has benefited mankind, and I think the best example of this would be the fact that Dr. Taub himself has never specifically made any mention as to how he has really helped or how this research has helped mankind. I think that

is the best example of how much good has really come from the many years of this experimentation.

5   Throughout the four months that I worked at the laboratory, I saw a total disregard for and a total ignorance of the psychological and the physical well-being of all the animals in the laboratory. I saw, for example, animals in the laboratory that were allowed to injure themselves, and injure each other, just because some of the most basic and simple safety precautions were not taken. No consideration was given for the safety of the animals.

6   As an example of this, just four days ago one of the experimental monkeys named Charlie died in the laboratory. He died as a result of improper caging and handling, during which he was allowed to be attacked by another male macaque in the laboratory, and through that attack he suffered some serious injuries. I believe he died needlessly in that laboratory because IBR had been warned in writing about this obvious danger that existed in the caging of the animals.

7   I should mention that Dr. Taub himself has estimated these particular primates to be worth somewhere between 60 and 100,000 tax dollars each.

8   Also, while I was at the laboratory, I saw two of the monkeys, Paul and Hard Times, collapse to their cage floors from not being fed by some of the unsupervised staff. Many of the animals would go for days at a time without being fed. Also, the date on the feed supply used by this laboratory had expired about three months before I began working there. I should point out that there are clear instructions on the bags indicating that it must be supplemented with vitamins after a certain date because it becomes nutritionally deficient. And even though these clear instructions were there, no supplements were ever given to the animals for the entire time I was there.

9   I also saw many primates with open wounds, lacerations, deformed wrists, fingerless hands, and broken bones. Much of this was due to a complete lack of attention to the treatment and even to the prevention of these types of injuries. Improper bandaging by untrained staff took place—not many wounds were bandaged, but when bandaging was done, it was done by untrained staff. And self-mutilation was undiscouraged in this laboratory.

10   The principle of this laboratory was that self-mutilation is just something that can't be avoided, because that's what happens. I think it is an absurd principle.

11   Billy, one of the gentlest of all the primates in the colony room, has lost eight of his ten fingers and, because of that, he has to attempt to feed himself with his feet, or by bending over and eating directly off his cage floor. These animals were never given food bowls or anything to comfort themselves in their cages. Their cages were totally barren. They were given nothing to manipulate—and these are very intelligent and very curious animals.

12   When I asked Dr. Taub, the chief investigator at this laboratory, why
nothing was done to help accommodate some of the crippled animals—
such as why Billy wasn't given a bowl to eat from—Dr. Taub said that
"Billy likes to eat with his feet."

13   Also, because no food bowls were provided, the food would be thrown
into the cage, fall through the wire cage floors and land in the excrement
pans below the cages, where it would immediately begin to absorb urine.
And since the monkeys were only fed, at the most, once a day, whenever
you would pull an excrement pan out, the monkeys would reach down
desperately to try to grab something to eat out of the excrement pan.

14   In the lab the primates were left for weeks and months with injuries,
such as broken bones, lacerations, and draining septic wounds. No
veterinarian had treated any of the animals in this laboratory for at least
two years. In the last ten months alone, three of the animals have died in
incidents unrelated to the experimentation taking place.

15   I would like to say that no one needs a Ph.D. or any other credentials
to recognize the blatant violations of the Animal Welfare Act that were
taking place in this laboratory. No one needs a degree to recognize when
an animal's cage should be cleaned, or that an animal that has just
chewed off all five of his fingers, needs to be seen by a veterinarian. It is
apparently also not necessary to have a degree to conduct research on
primates that were paid for by NIH, because within one week after I first
walked into this laboratory, without any inquiry into my experience or
my health—and health is a serious matter when you're dealing with
nonhuman primates—I was put in charge of an original research project
called "A Pilot Study on Displacement Behavior." I was given two primates
from Dr. Taub's own research group of monkeys and given a separate
room, given video equipment to film everything I did. I was told to
torment, agitate, and frustrate and agitate the animals, and then film
their reactions.

16   When I asked what we hoped to get out of this experiment, I was told
several times that, "It has never been done before and we might find
something interesting." And "something interesting" is what was repeated
to me many times. They said, "If we do come up with something
interesting, we might be able to get funding for it."

17   I need to mention that some of the researchers would go so far as to
torment the animals in their cages. They would do things such as shake the
cages, make harrassing sounds at the animals, verbally threaten the
animals, and at one point one experimenter thrust a pair of surgical pliers
into the mouth of one of the animals and shook them violently against his
teeth. The primate, named Dimition, was immobilized in a restraining
device at the time.

18   For the whole time I was there, the laboratory remained in an
unchanged condition of extreme filth, disrepair, and disarray, and the

whole time the animals remained neglected in their cages. None of the animals were given anything to do inside their cages for the entire three to four years that they have been there, since they were taken from the wild. They used their lame arms as cushions to provide relief from the steel wire floors that they were forced to live on, and they used their own wounds and injuries as things to manipulate, to pick at and chew on.

19   Their lives, in reality, consisted of only hoping for a once-a-day feeding and at other times waiting for electric shock and other negative stimuli in experimental procedures that were conducted on them.

20   Other conditions at the laboratory—which you can see in some of the photographs—included piles of rodent excrement on the floors, in drawers, and on shelves; dirty laundry and discarded tennis shoes in the operating room—the operating room table doubled as a desk—holes in the walls and ceilings; dried blood on the floors and on the ceiling of an experimental chamber—which was a converted refrigerator—piles of molding feces in the cages that were never cleaned. The entire four months I was there, these are the things that I saw, witnessed and photographed, and the things also that the Montgomery County Police photographed when they raided the laboratory.

21   I should mention that in responding to the NIH investigators, a member of the laboratory's animal care committee—a committee that was set up by the laboratory consisting of scientists, a veterinarian, an M.D., and other researchers—the same type that many laboratories have set up in their self-policing system—stated that he assumed IBR was acceptable by all legal and ethical standards because the USDA inspected the laboratory and because NIH had approved its funding.

22   If other animal care committees operate under these same assumptions, we have a serious problem on our hands. I think we should ask NIH how many, if any, of the animal care committees—which are, in effect, composed of fellow researchers appointed by the experimenters themselves—how many of these committees have ever taken independent actions to correct deficiencies or report compliance failures to NIH.

23   I would like to read a few sentences to you here. Of grave concern, is a statement from the IBR animal care committee that it had never considered administering pain killers to any of the animals because analgesics are not required, as far as this scientific committee was aware, by any guide or professional standard.

24   I think perhaps most alarming of all is the statement made to NIH by Dr. David Rioch, M.D., chairman of that animal care committee, that "applying human expectations of pain to animals is inappropriate because pain is primarily a matter of societal conditioning to which animals are not subject."

25   I think this indicates that clearly it is going to take legislation to bring some people in the research community into line with twentieth century

thought on pain in animals and the necessity for administering pain killers in the reduction of animal suffering.

26 I also think this incident at this laboratory has made it clear that neither the NIH peer review system, nor the USDA inspection program, works very well at all.

27 I should mention that in 1977 NIH was informed of the conditions at this laboratory, and at that time the laboratory was found to have been operating for five years without a license. Within one week after this violation was reported to USDA, USDA issued them a license and took no action against the filthy conditions existing at that time.

28 In 1977 NIH promised to investigate and remedy problems at that laboratory. Dr. Taub might well express surprise that the NIH has now, after eleven years of funding and after eleven years of inspections, finally found serious fault in his laboratory. I should mention that this laboratory, the Institute for Behavioral Research, is located less than fifteen minutes from NIH headquarters and main campus in Bethesda.

29 I should mention also that USDA, up to this day, has not taken any action against IBR and has not even admitted that there were any problems at this laboratory other than minor deficiencies, even after Charlie died in the laboratory last Friday.

30 Again, in closing, I would just like to mention, as will be pointed out again and again, anywhere from 60 to 100 million animals exist and die in laboratories in our country alone every single year. I think that even if only one percent of the laboratories in this country are like the Institute for Behavioral Research, then we have a very serious ethical problem that has to be dealt with strongly and in a civilized fashion.

31 Thank you.

STUDY QUESTIONS

1. By underlining passages in pens or pencils of three different colors, identify which statements in this testimony are *statements of fact,* which are *opinions about factual matters,* and which are *value judgments.*
2. Do you find any instances of either opinions about fact or value judgments that lack support? If so, are they too obvious to require support, or do they fail to persuade through lack of substantiation?

SUGGESTIONS FOR WRITING

1. The preceding essay, by Timothy Noah, gives a sharply different evaluation of Dr. Taub and the operation of the Institute for Behavioral Research than does

Alex Pacheco's testimony. Write a brief paper giving a carefully reasoned explanation of which account you find more persuasive. Attempt to be scrupulously fair; do not be afraid to concede some points to the witness with whom you disagree.

2. Write a research paper in which you seek out information from other sources to try to assess which account, Pacheco's or Noah's, describes Taub's laboratory conditions and treatment of test animals more accurately. Be sure to consider the *competency* and *objectivity* of your sources.

MICHAEL E. DEBAKEY

Holding Human Health Hostage

Dr. DeBakey, a world-famous cardiovascular surgeon, is director of the DeBakey Heart Center at Baylor College of Medicine in Houston, Texas. He made pioneer discoveries in the development of blood transfusions, surgical procedures for replacing diseased sections of aorta with synthetic materials, the heart-lung machine, and the artificial heart.

When it was introduced in the House of Representatives on January 27, 1987, the Mrazek bill, which is Dr. DeBakey's immediate subject, attracted over thirty cosponsors. However, it later died in committee.

1   As a patient-advocate, both in and out of the operating room, I feel a responsibility to protect the rights of patients to medical advances resulting from animal research. Had the animal legislation now pending in Congress been enacted when I began my career, it would have prevented me from developing a number of lifesaving procedures in my research laboratory. Instead of restoring thousands of patients to a normal life and a return to productive work, my colleagues and I would have been helpless to offer many of our patients any real hope at all. This legislation, known as the Mrazek bill, seeks to ban the use of pound animals for any research supported by the National Institutes of Health, the chief source of funds for biomedical research in this country. Are we now to hold human health hostage to the rights of abandoned animals to be killed in pounds?

2   Even with today's technology, I could not have developed on a computer the roller pump that made open-heart surgery possible or the artificial artery that restored to health previously doomed patients with aneurysms. Nor could we have attempted the first successful coronary artery bypass or implanted the first temporary mechanical heart with which we saved a patient's life two decades ago. Would animal-rights activists have objected to the first kidney, heart, or liver transplant? Would they forgo the protection humanity enjoys today against poliomyelitis, tetanus, diphtheria, and whooping cough or the treatment for strep throat, ear infections, bronchitis, and pneumonia — all the products of animal research? Would they have denied the 11 million diabetics the right to life that insulin has given them — or victims of cancer the help they have received from radiation and chemotherapy? It was in monkeys that the deadly AIDS virus was isolated, and that isolation is the initial step in the ultimate development of a vaccine. Would the animal-rights activists halt that research and allow an epidemic to rage unopposed? The truth is that there are no satisfactory insentient models at present for certain types of

biomedical research and testing. A computer is not a living system and would not have produced the dramatic medical advances of the past few decades.

3   Only about 1 percent of abandoned dogs are released for research. If pounds are such a meager source of research animals, you may ask, why am I concerned about losing that source? My reasons are well founded, I believe: Not only are pound animals of particular value in research on heart and kidney disease, brain injury, stroke, blindness, and deafness, but a ban on their use could have grave and far-reaching consequences for human and animal health. In addition, such a ban would impose an extra burden on taxpayers and could price many important research projects out of existence. Each dog and cat bred specifically for research costs hundreds of dollars more than a pound animal. The Mrazek bill makes no accommodation in appropriations for this substantial rise in cost. For many of our most productive researchers, the additional expense would shut down their laboratories. Critical work on inducing tolerance in organ grafts, for example, and on minimizing damage to cardiac muscles after heart attacks has been halted in some research laboratories because of soaring costs of dogs.

4   Moreover, eliminating the use of pound animals in research would, paradoxically, cause even more animals to die. According to the American Humane Society, 7 million pet dogs are abandoned to pounds or shelters each year, 5 million of which are killed—600 "trusting pets" killed hourly. Yet some would have you believe that killing animals in a pound is more virtuous than having them help to advance medical knowledge and ultimately benefit human and animal health. I don't like to see life taken from any species unnecessarily, and that would happen if this law is enacted. Every year we would have to breed an additional 138,000 dogs and 50,000 cats for research to replace the pound animals, which would then be put to death anyway because no one wants them. With the current overpopulation of dogs and cats, the logic of such a policy escapes me.

5   It was humane concerns that led me into medicine. I strongly disapprove of cruelty to animals as well as humans. Medical scientists are not engaged in cockfighting, bullfighting, bull-dogging, calf-roping, or any other "sport" imposing stress or violence on animals. Rather, they are searching for ways to relieve suffering and preserve life. Unquestionably, every precaution should be taken, and enforced, to ensure that laboratory animals are treated humanely. Responsible scientists observe humane guidelines, not only because their search for new medical knowledge is motivated by compassion for the suffering, but because they know that improper treatment adversely affects the quality of their research. Scientists are also obligated to use insentient models when these are

satisfactory, but, again, no responsible scientist would incur the substantial expense and devote the considerable space required for housing and caring for animals when other equally satisfactory models were available.

6   If scientists abandon cat and dog experiments for other models that are not as suitable or as well understood, many potential medical breakthroughs may be severely crippled or halted. Grave diseases such as AIDS, cancer, heart disease, muscular dystrophy, Alzheimer's disease, and other serious conditions will, however, continue to plague our families, friends, and fellow citizens, and those patients will properly expect to receive effective treatments and cures.

7   Remember, too, that pets have also profited from animal research. It is doubtful that animals could be treated today for heart or kidney disease, leukemia, or other serious disorders if animal research had been prohibited previously. If an animal is seriously ill or injured, would the animal-rights activist deny him a form of treatment potentially beneficial but never used before—and therefore experimental? Until one is faced with a life-threatening condition of a loved one—human or animal—it is difficult to answer that question truthfully.

8   We have aggressive advocates of the rights of trees, sharks, bats, whales, seals, and other mammals, but what about the rights of ailing humans? Shrill attacks against speciesism are difficult to defend when one observes pit bulldogs mauling and killing children, wolves killing deer, cats consuming rats and birds, and birds consuming worms. And even vegetarians destroy living plants for consumption. Self-preservation is a primary instinct of all members of the animal kingdom, and patients with that instinct deserve our compassion, protection, and assistance as much as other species.

9   Some animal-rights zealots have been quoted as regarding "the right to human life as a perversion," meat-eating as "primitive, barbaric, and arrogant," and pet ownership as an "absolutely abysmal situation brought about by human manipulation." It is difficult to believe that many animal lovers would embrace such an extreme position. There is a difference, moreover, between animal welfare and antisciencism. Infiltrating laboratories surreptitiously by posing as volunteer workers, destroying research records, vandalizing research facilities, bombing, and threatening scientists are all irrational methods of persuasion. At one research institution, damages amounted to more than a half million dollars when computers were destroyed, blood was poured on files, and liberationist slogans were painted on laboratory walls. Research on infant blindness was halted for eight months while claims of animal abuse were investigated, only to be found baseless. Such harassment, demoralization, and interference divert funds from productive research to security and

discourage bright young people from entering research. Once the manpower chain is broken, it will not be easily restored. And where will we then turn for answers to devastating human diseases? Guerrilla tactics, lurid pictures, and sensational headlines may inflame emotions, but they do not lead to rational judgments. More important, should we condone harassment, terrorism, and violence masquerading as concern for animal rights?

10   As a physician, my greatest concern is, of course, for the suffering human beings who will be denied effective treatment because we took action that seems superficially humane but may ultimately render us powerless against certain diseases. What do I tell dying patients who are waiting for the medical advances that these threatened investigations may produce—that there is no hope because we have been prevented from acquiring the new knowledge needed to correct their conditions? As a human being and physician, I cannot conceive of telling parents their sick child is doomed because we cannot use all the tools at our disposal. Surely those who object to animals in research laboratories must be equally distressed at seeing sick children hooked up to tubes. How will those parents feel about a society that legislates the rights of animals above those of humans?

11   Through research, we have made remarkable advances in medicine, but we still do not have all the answers. If the animal-rights activists could witness the heartbreaking suffering of patients and families that I encounter daily, I doubt that they would deliberately pose a direct threat to human and animal health by demanding that we abandon some of our most fruitful methods of medical investigation. The American public must decide: Shall we tell hundreds of thousands of victims of heart attacks, cancer, AIDS, and numerous other dread diseases that the right of abandoned animals to die in a pound supersedes the patients' rights to relief from suffering and premature death? In making that decision, let us use not anger and hatred but reason and good will.

STUDY QUESTIONS

1. Dr. DeBakey's essay is a response to a policy proposal, the Mrazek bill. Which of the stock issues does DeBakey draw on?
2. Paragraph 5 argues that in the prevailing value system, the use of pound animals for medical research deserves a position of honor rather than of shame. What strategies does DeBakey use in this argument? Do they work?
3. In paragraph 8 DeBakey alludes to the killing of animals by other animals. What is the relevance of this argument? Is it persuasive?

4. In paragraphs 4 and 10, how does DeBakey try to show animal rights advocates that *their own* value system, to be consistent, should allow for medical experiments on animals?
5. The immediate target of this editorial is the Mrazek bill. Are DeBakey's arguments limited to the issue of restricting research on pound animals that will be killed anyhow, or does it have implications for the larger competition between animal and human rights?

SUGGESTION FOR WRITING

This essay bears striking parallels with the essay by Charles Krauthammer on page 87. For instance, both concern pending social policy proposals, and both evoke a hostage metaphor in the titles.

Write an essay that develops other parallels between these essays and then goes on to make some point based on the parallels. For instance, if you find both articles persuasive, you might use them as examples to define an effective argumentative strategy for discussing current policy issues. If you find both articles unsuccessful, you might discuss the weaknesses of their common approach. If you like one but not the other, write a comparison/contrast paper that shows why, despite their similarities, one works while the other fails.

Business and
Professional Ethics

The concepts of business and professional ethics arose in response to the recognition that certain spheres of activity involve their participants in ethical dilemmas peculiar to themselves. The golden rule may be an adequate guide for personal behavior, but it cannot apply, at least in any simple way, in competitive business, specially when the businessperson must undertake actions that will affect parties who themselves have conflicting interests—customers, employees, managers, shareholders, competitors, and the surrounding community. Concern for ethical business practices is not new. It goes back at least as far as the Old Testament, which commands merchants to be honest in their weights and measures, and to the Code of Hammurabi, which makes reference to wage and price controls. Early recognition of the need for special ethical codes in the professions also goes back at least as far as the Hippocratic Oath.

But business and professional ethics took on a new urgency in the early 1970s. The Watergate scandal sensitized the country to public immorality, and John Dean, President Nixon's lawyer, observed, "How in God's name could so many lawyers get involved in something like this?" Around the same time, Ralph Nader published *Unsafe at Any Speed,* an indictment of the automobile industry for preferring profits to safety.

The selections that follow address questions of both individual and corporate ethics, and of the special ethical problems of the individual in the corporation. While most of the essays are primarily investigations into values, the cluster of articles and editorials on the marketing of infant formula in developing nations traces a line of development from the empirical claims about the harmful effects of formula under third world economic and social conditions through considerations about how humanitarian values should be weighed against economic values, to proposals for reform drawn up by the World Health Organization.

A second cluster of articles—those by Konner, Fulton, Strong, Hallin, and Corry—concern the ethics of journalism. As social critics such as Bill Moyers and Noam Chomsky have pointed out, modern democracy can succeed only if the populace is informed by a free and responsible press. The articles reprinted here explore some of the threats to an independent press from consumerism, the power of wealthy interest groups to control media outlets or information, and the special pressures of wartime.

The last two articles in the section deal with the ethical concerns of a criminal defense lawyer and a professional athlete.

ALBERT Z. CARR

Is Business Bluffing Ethical?

Albert Carr (1902–1971) was an economist, a business consultant, and the author of short stories, essays, filmscripts, and a number of books, including one entitled *Business as a Game.*

The selection below is a classic statement of one attitude toward the practice of deceit in business.

1   A respected businessman with whom I discussed the theme of this article remarked with some heat, "You mean to say you're going to encourage men to bluff? Why, bluffing is nothing more than a form of lying! You're advising them to lie!"

2   I agreed that the basis of private morality is a respect for truth and that the closer a businessman comes to the truth, the more he deserves respect. At the same time, I suggested that most bluffing in business might be regarded simply as game strategy—much like bluffing in poker, which does not reflect on the morality of the bluffer.

3   I quoted Henry Taylor, the British statesman who pointed out that "falsehood ceases to be falsehood when it is understood on all sides that the truth is not expected to be spoken"—an exact description of bluffing in poker, diplomacy, and business. I cited the analogy of the criminal court, where the criminal is not expected to tell the truth when he pleads "not guilty." Everyone from the judge down takes it for granted that the job of the defendant's attorney is to get his client off, not to reveal the truth; and this is considered ethical practice. I mentioned Representative Omar Burleson, the Democrat from Texas, who was quoted as saying, in regard to the ethics of Congress, "Ethics is a barrel of worms"[1]—a pungent summing up of the problem of deciding who is ethical in politics.

4   I reminded my friend that millions of businessmen feel constrained every day to say *yes* to their bosses when they secretly believe *no* and that this is generally accepted as permissible strategy when the alternative might be the loss of a job. The essential point, I said, is that the ethics of business are game ethics, different from the ethics of religion.

5   He remained unconvinced. Referring to the company of which he is president, he declared: "Maybe that's good enough for some businessmen, but I can tell you that we pride ourselves on our ethics. In 30 years not one customer has ever questioned my word or asked to check our figures. We're loyal to our customers and fair to our suppliers. I regard my handshake on

---

[1] *The New York Times,* March 9, 1967.

a deal as a contract. I've never entered into pricefixing schemes with my competitors. I've never allowed my salesmen to spread injurious rumors about other companies. Our union contract is the best in our industry. And, if I do say so myself, our ethical standards are of the highest!"

6   He really was saying, without realizing it, that he was living up to the ethical standards of the business game—which are a far cry from those of private life. Like a gentlemanly poker player, he did not play in cahoots with others at the table, try to smear their reputations, or hold back chips he owed them.

7   But this same fine man, at that very time, was allowing one of his products to be advertised in a way that made it sound a great deal better than it actually was. Another item in his product line was notorious among dealers for its "built-in obsolescence." He was holding back from the market a much-improved product because he did not want it to interfere with sales of the inferior item it would have replaced. He had joined with certain of his competitors in hiring a lobbyist to push a state legislature, by methods that he preferred not to know too much about, into amending a bill then being enacted.

8   In his view these things had nothing to do with ethics; they were merely normal business practice. He himself undoubtedly avoided outright falsehoods—never lied in so many words. But the entire organization that he ruled was deeply involved in numerous strategies of deception.

Pressure to Deceive

9   Most executives from time to time are almost compelled, in the interests of their companies or themselves, to practice some form of deception when negotiating with customers, dealers, labor unions, government officials, or even other departments of their companies. By conscious misstatements, concealment of pertinent facts, or exaggeration—in short, by bluffing—they seek to persuade others to agree with them. I think it is fair to say that if the individual executive refuses to bluff from time to time—if he feels obligated to tell the truth, the whole truth, and nothing but the truth—he is ignoring opportunities permitted under the rules and is at a heavy disadvantage in his business dealings.

10   But here and there a businessman is unable to reconcile himself to the bluff in which he plays a part. His conscience, perhaps spurred by religious idealism, troubles him. He feels guilty; he may develop an ulcer or a nervous tic. Before any executive can make profitable use of the strategy of the bluff, he needs to make sure that in bluffing he will not lose self-respect or become emotionally disturbed. If he is to reconcile personal integrity

and high standards of honesty with the practical requirements of business, he must feel that his bluffs are ethically justified. The justification rests on the fact that business, as practiced by individuals as well as by corporations, has the impersonal character of a game—a game that demands both special strategy and an understanding of its special ethics.

11   The game is played at all levels of corporate life, from the highest to the lowest. At the very instant that a man decides to enter business, he may be forced into a game situation, as is shown by the recent experience of a Cornell honor graduate who applied for a job with a large company:

12   ▪ This applicant was given a psychological test which included the statement, "Of the following magazines, check any that you have read either regularly or from time to time, and double-check those which interest you most. *Reader's Digest, Time, Fortune, Saturday Evening Post, The New Republic, Life, Look, Ramparts, Newsweek, Business Week, U.S. News & World Report, The Nation, Playboy, Esquire, Harper's, Sports Illustrated.*"

13   His tastes in reading were broad, and at one time or another he had read almost all of these magazines. He was a subscriber to *The New Republic,* an enthusiast for *Ramparts,* and an avid student of the pictures in *Playboy.* He was not sure whether his interest in *Playboy* would be held against him, but he had a shrewd suspicion that if he confessed to an interest in *Ramparts* and *The New Republic,* he would be thought a liberal, a radical, or at least an intellectual, and his chances of getting the job, which he needed, would greatly diminish. He therefore checked five of the more conservative magazines. Apparently it was a sound decision, for he got the job.

14   He had made a game player's decision, consistent with business ethics.

15   A similar case is that of a magazine space salesman who, owing to a merger, suddenly found himself out of a job:

16   ▪ This man was 58, and, in spite of a good record, his chance of getting a job elsewhere in a business where youth is favored in hiring practice was not good. He was a vigorous, healthy man, and only a considerable amount of gray in his hair suggested his age. Before beginning his job search he touched up his hair with a black dye to confine the gray to his temples. He knew that the truth about his age might well come out in time, but he calculated that he could deal with that situation when it arose. He and his wife decided that he could easily pass for 45, and he so stated his age on his résumé.

17   This was a lie; yet within the accepted rules of the business game, no moral culpability attaches to it.

The Poker Analogy

18   We can learn a good deal about the nature of business by comparing it with poker. While both have a large element of chance, in the long run the winner is the man who plays with steady skill. In both games ultimate victory requires intimate knowledge of the rules, insight into the psychology of the other players, a bold front, a considerable amount of self-discipline, and the ability to respond swiftly and effectively to opportunities provided by chance.

19   No one expects poker to be played on the ethical principles preached in churches. In poker it is right and proper to bluff a friend out of the rewards of being dealt a good hand. A player feels no more than a slight twinge of sympathy, if that, when—with nothing better than a single ace in his hand—he strips a heavy loser, who holds a pair, of the rest of his chips. It was up to the other fellow to protect himself. In the words of an excellent poker player, former President Harry Truman, "If you can't stand the heat, stay out of the kitchen." If one shows mercy to a loser in poker, it is a personal gesture, divorced from the rules of the game.

20   Poker has its special ethics, and here I am not referring to rules against cheating. The man who keeps an ace up his sleeve or who marks the cards is more than unethical; he is a crook, and can be punished as such— kicked out of the game or, in the Old West, shot.

21   In contrast to the cheat, the unethical poker player is one who, while abiding by the letter of the rules, finds ways to put the other players at an unfair disadvantage. Perhaps he unnerves them with loud talk. Or he tries to get them drunk. Or he plays in cahoots with someone else at the table. Ethical poker players frown on such tactics.

22   Poker's own brand of ethics is different from the ethical ideals of civilized human relationships. The game calls for distrust of the other fellow. It ignores the claim of friendship. Cunning deception and concealment of one's strength and intentions, not kindness and open-heartedness, are vital in poker. No one thinks any the worse of poker on that account. And no one should think any the worse of the game of business because its standards of right and wrong differ from the prevailing traditions of morality in our society.

Discard the Golden Rule

23   This view of business is especially worrisome to people without much business experience. A minister of my acquaintance once protested that business cannot possibly function in our society unless it is based on the Judeo-Christian system of ethics. He told me:

24   "I know some businessmen have supplied call girls to customers, but there are always a few rotten apples in every barrel. That doesn't mean the rest of the fruit isn't sound. Surely the vast majority of businessmen are ethical. I myself am acquainted with many who adhere to strict codes of ethics based fundamentally on religious teachings. They contribute to good causes. They participate in community activities. They cooperate with other companies to improve working conditions in their industries. Certainly they are not indifferent to ethics."

25   That most businessmen are not indifferent to ethics in their private lives, everyone will agree. My point is that in their office lives they cease to be private citizens; they become game players who must be guided by a somewhat different set of ethical standards.

26   The point was forcefully made to me by a Midwestern executive who has given a good deal of thought to the question:

27   "So long as a businessman complies with the laws of the land and avoids telling malicious lies, he's ethical. If the law as written gives a man a wide-open chance to make a killing, he'd be a fool not to take advantage of it. If he doesn't, somebody else will. There's no obligation on him to stop and consider who is going to get hurt. If the law says he can do it, that's all the justification he needs. There's nothing unethical about that. It's just plain business sense."

28   This executive (call him Robbins) took the stand that even industrial espionage, which is frowned on by some businessmen, ought not to be considered unethical. He recalled a recent meeting of the National Industrial Conference Board where an authority on marketing made a speech in which he deplored the employment of spies by business organizations. More and more companies, he pointed out, find it cheaper to penetrate the secrets of competitors with concealed cameras and microphones or by bribing employees than to set up costly research and design departments of their own. A whole branch of the electronics industry has grown up with this trend, he continued, providing equipment to make industrial espionage easier.

29   Disturbing? The marketing expert found it so. But when it came to a remedy, he could only appeal to "respect for the golden rule." Robbins thought this a confession of defeat, believing that the golden rule, for all its value as an ideal for society, is simply not feasible as a guide for business. A good part of the time the businessman is trying to do unto others as he hopes others will *not* do unto him.[2] Robbins continued:

---

[2] See Bruce D. Henderson, "Brinkmanship in Business," *HBR*, March–April 1967, p. 49.

30   "Espionage of one kind or another has become so common in business that it's like taking a drink during Prohibition—it's not considered sinful. And we don't even have Prohibition where espionage is concerned; the law is very tolerant in this area. There's no more shame for a business that uses secret agents than there is for a nation. Bear in mind that there already is at least one large corporation—you can buy its stock over the counter—that makes millions by providing counterespionage service to industrial firms. Espionage in business is not an ethical problem; it's an established technique of business competition."

"We don't make the laws"

31   Wherever we turn in business, we can perceive the sharp distinction between its ethical standards and those of the churches. Newspapers abound with sensational stories growing out of this distinction:

32   ▪ We read one day that Senator Philip A. Hart of Michigan has attacked food processors for deceptive packaging of numerous products.[3]

33   ▪ The next day there is a Congressional to-do over Ralph Nader's book, *Unsafe At Any Speed,* which demonstrates that automobile companies for years have neglected the safety of car-owning families.[4]

34   ▪ Then another Senator, Lee Metcalf of Montana, and journalist Vic Reinemer show in their book, *Overcharge,* the methods by which utility companies elude regulating government bodies to extract unduly large payments from users of electricity.[5]

35   These are merely dramatic instances of a prevailing condition; there is hardly a major industry at which a similar attack could not be aimed. Critics of business regard such behavior as unethical, but the companies concerned know that they are merely playing the business game.

36   Among the most respected of our business institutions are the insurance companies. A group of insurance executives meeting recently in New England was startled when their guest speaker, social critic Daniel Patrick Moynihan, roundly berated them for "unethical" practices. They had been guilty, Moynihan alleged, of using outdated actuarial tables to obtain unfairly high premiums. They habitually delayed the hearings of lawsuits against them in order to tire out the plaintiffs and win cheap

---

[3] *The New York Times,* November 21, 1966.
[4] New York, Grossman Publishers, Inc., 1965.
[5] New York, David McKay Company, Inc., 1967.

settlements. In their employment policies they used ingenious devices to discriminate against certain minority groups.[6]

37   It was difficult for the audience to deny the validity of these charges. But these men were business game players. Their reaction to Moynihan's attack was much the same as that of the automobile manufacturers to Nader, of the utilities to Senator Metcalf, and of the food processors to Senator Hart. If the laws governing their businesses change, or if public opinion becomes clamorous, they will make the necessary adjustments. But morally they have in their view done nothing wrong. As long as they comply with the letter of the law, they are within their rights to operate their businesses as they see fit.

38   The small business is in the same position as the great corporation in this respect. For example:

39   ▪ In 1967 a key manufacturer was accused of providing master keys for automobiles to mailorder customers, although it was obvious that some of the purchasers might be automobile thieves. His defense was plain and straightforward. If there was nothing in the law to prevent him from selling his keys to anyone who ordered them, it was not up to him to inquire as to his customers' motives. Why was it any worse, he insisted, for him to sell car keys by mail, than for mail-order houses to sell guns that might be used for murder? Until the law was changed, the key manufacturer could regard himself as being just as ethical as any other businessman by the rules of the business game.[7]

40   Violations of the ethical ideals of society are common in business, but they are not necessarily violations of business principles. Each year the Federal Trade Commission orders hundreds of companies, many of them of the first magnitude, to "cease and desist" from practices which, judged by ordinary standards, are of questionable morality but which are stoutly defended by the companies concerned.

41   In one case, a firm manufacturing a well-known mouthwash was accused of using a cheap form of alcohol possibly deleterious to health. The company's chief executive, after testifying in Washington, made this comment privately:

42   "We broke no law. We're in a highly competitive industry. If we're going to stay in business, we have to look for profit wherever the law permits. We don't make the laws. We obey them. Then why do we have to put up with this 'holier than thou' talk about ethics? It's sheer hypocrisy. We're not in business to promote ethics. Look at the cigarette companies,

---

[6] The New York Times, January 17, 1967.
[7] Cited by Ralph Nader in "Business Crime," *The New Republic,* July 1, 1967, p. 7.

for God's sake! If the ethics aren't embodied in the laws by the men who made them, you can't expect businessmen to fill the lack. Why, a sudden submission to Christian ethics by businessmen would bring about the greatest economic upheaval in history!"

43   It may be noted that the government failed to prove its case against him.

Cast Illusions Aside

44   Talk about ethics by businessmen is often a thin decorative coating over the hard realities of the game:

45   ▪ Once I listened to a speech by a young executive who pointed to a new industry code as proof that his company and its competitors were deeply aware of their responsibilities to society. It was a code of ethics, he said. The industry was going to police itself, to dissuade constituent companies from wrongdoing. His eyes shone with conviction and enthusiasm.

46   The same day there was a meeting in a hotel room where the industry's top executives met with the "czar" who was to administer the new code, a man of high repute. No one who was present could doubt their common attitude. In their eyes the code was designed primarily to forestall a move by the federal government to impose stern restrictions on the industry. They felt that the code would hamper them a good deal less than new federal laws would. It was, in other words, conceived as a protection for the industry, not for the public.

47   The young executive accepted the surface explanation of the code; these leaders, all experienced game players, did not deceive themselves for a moment about its purpose.

48   The illusion that business can afford to be guided by ethics as conceived in private life is often fostered by speeches and articles containing such phrases as, "It pays to be ethical, " or, "Sound ethics is good business." Actually this is not an ethical position at all; it is a self-serving calculation in disguise. The speaker is really saying that in the long run a company can make more money if it does not antagonize competitors, suppliers, employees, and customers by squeezing them too hard. He is saying that oversharp policies reduce ultimate gains. That is true, but it has nothing to do with ethics. The underlying attitude is much like that in the familiar story of the shopkeeper who finds an extra $20 bill in the cash register, debates with himself the ethical problem—should he tell his partner?— and finally decides to share the money because the gesture will give him an edge over the s.o.b. the next time they quarrel.

49   I think it is fair to sum up the prevailing attitude of businessmen on ethics as follows:

50 We live in what is probably the most competitive of the world's civilized societies. Our customs encourage a high degree of aggression in the individual's striving for success. Business is our main area of competition, and it has been ritualized into a game of strategy. The basic rules of the game have been set by the government, which attempts to detect and punish business frauds. But as long as a company does not transgress the rules of the game set by law, it has the legal right to shape its strategy without reference to anything but its profits. If it takes a long-term view of its profits, it will preserve amicable relations, so far as possible, with those with whom it deals. A wise businessman will not seek advantage to the point where he generates dangerous hostility among employees, competitors, customers, government, or the public at large. But decisions in this area are, in the final test, decisions of strategy, not of ethics.

The Individual and the Game

51 An individual within a company often finds it difficult to adjust to the requirements of the business game. He tries to preserve his private ethical standards in situations that call for game strategy. When he is obliged to carry out company policies that challenge his conception of himself as an ethical man, he suffers.

52 It disturbs him when he is ordered, for instance, to deny a raise to a man who deserves it, to fire an employee of long standing, to prepare advertising that he believes to be misleading, to conceal facts that he feels customers are entitled to know, to cheapen the quality of materials used in the manufacture of an established product, to sell as new a product that he knows to be rebuilt, to exaggerate the curative powers of a medicinal preparation, or to coerce dealers.

53 There are some fortunate executives who, by the nature of their work and circumstances, never have to face problems of this kind. But in one form or another the ethical dilemma is felt sooner or later by most businessmen. Possibly the dilemma is most painful not when the company forces the action on the executive but when he originates it himself—that is, when he has taken or is contemplating a step which is in his own interest but which runs counter to his early moral conditioning. To illustrate:

54 ▪ The manager of an export department, eager to show rising sales, is pressed by a big customer to provide invoices which, while containing no overt falsehood that would violate a U.S. law, are so worded that the customer may be able to evade certain taxes in his homeland.

55 ▪ A company president finds that an aging executive, within a few years of retirement and his pension, is not as productive as formerly. Should he be kept on?

56   ▪ The produce manager of a supermarket debates with himself whether to get rid of a lot of half-rotten tomatoes by including one, with its good side exposed, in every tomato six-pack.

57   ▪ An accountant discovers that he has taken an improper deduction on his company's tax return and fears the consequences if he calls the matter to the president's attention, though he himself has done nothing illegal. Perhaps if he says nothing, no one will notice the error.

58   ▪ A chief executive officer is asked by his directors to comment on a rumor that he owns stock in another company with which he has placed large orders. He could deny it, for the stock is in the name of his son-in-law and he has earlier formally instructed his son-in-law to sell the holding.

59   Temptations of this kind constantly arise in business. If an executive allows himself to be torn between a decision based on business considerations and one based on his private ethical code, he exposes himself to a grave psychological strain.

60   This is not to say that sound business strategy necessarily runs counter to ethical ideals. They may frequently coincide; and when they do, everyone is gratified. But the major tests of every move in business, as in all games of strategy, are legality and profit. A man who intends to be a winner in the business game must have a game player's attitude.

61   The business strategist's decisions must be as impersonal as those of a surgeon performing an operation—concentrating on objective and technique, and subordinating personal feelings. If the chief executive admits that his son-in-law owns the stock, it is because he stands to lose more if the fact comes out later than if he states it boldly and at once. If the supermarket manager orders the rotten tomatoes to be discarded, he does so to avoid an increase in consumer complaints and a loss of goodwill. The company president decides not to fire the elderly executive in the belief that the negative reaction of other employees would in the long run cost the company more than it would lose in keeping him and paying his pension.

62   All sensible businessmen prefer to be truthful, but they seldom feel inclined to tell the *whole* truth. In the business game truth-telling usually has to be kept within narrow limits if trouble is to be avoided. The point was neatly made a long time ago (in 1888) by one of John D. Rockefeller's associates, Paul Babcock, to Standard Oil Company executives who were about to testify before a government investigating committee: "Parry every question with answers which, while perfectly truthful, are evasive of *bottom* facts."[8] This was, is, and probably always will be regarded as wise and permissible business strategy.

---

[8] Babcock in a memorandum to Rockefeller (Rockefeller Archives).

For Office Use Only

63   An executive's family life can easily be dislocated if he fails to make a sharp distinction between the ethical systems of the home and the office— or if his wife does not grasp that distinction. Many a businessman who has remarked to his wife, "I had to let Jones go today" or "I had to admit to the boss that Jim has been goofing off lately," has been met with an indignant protest. "How could you do a thing like that? You know Jones is over 50 and will have a lot of trouble getting another job." Or, "You did that to Jim? With his wife ill and all the worry she's been having with the kids?"

64   If the executive insists that he had no choice because the profits of the company and his own security were involved, he may see a certain cool and ominous reappraisal in his wife's eyes. Many wives are not prepared to accept the fact that business operates with a special code of ethics. An illuminating illustration of this comes from a Southern sales executive who related a conversation he had had with his wife at a time when a hotly contested political campaign was being waged in their state:

65   "I made the mistake of telling her that I had had lunch with Colby, who gives me about half my business. Colby mentioned that his company had a stake in the election. Then he said, 'By the way, I'm treasurer of the citizens' committee for Lang. I'm collecting contributions. Can I count on you for a hundred dollars?'

66   "Well, there I was. I was opposed to Lang, but I knew Colby. If he withdrew his business I could be in a bad spot. So I just smiled and wrote out a check then and there. He thanked me, and we started to talk about his next order. Maybe he thought I shared his political views. If so, I wasn't going to lose any sleep over it.

67   "I should have had sense enough not to tell Mary about it. She hit the ceiling. She said she was disappointed in me. She said I hadn't acted like a man, that I should have stood up to Colby.

68   "I said, 'Look, it was an either-or situation. I had to do it or risk losing the business.'

69   "She came back at me with, 'I don't believe it. You could have been honest with him. You could have said that you didn't feel you ought to contribute to a campaign for a man you weren't going to vote for. I'm sure he would have understood.'

70   "I said, 'Mary, you're a wonderful woman, but you're way off the track. Do you know what would have happened if I had said that? Colby would have smiled and said, "Oh, I didn't realize. Forget it." But in his eyes from that moment I would be an oddball, maybe a bit of a radical. He would have listened to me talk about his order and would have promised to give it

consideration. After that I wouldn't hear from him for a week. Then I would telephone and learn from his secretary that he wasn't yet ready to place the order. And in about a month I would hear through the grapevine that he was giving his business to another company. A month after that I'd be out of a job.'

71   "She was silent for a while. Then she said, 'Tom, something is wrong with business when a man is forced to choose between his family's security and his moral obligation to himself. It's easy for me to say you should have stood up to him—but if you had, you might have felt you were betraying me and the kids. I'm sorry that you did it, Tom, but I can't blame you. Something is wrong with business!'"

72   This wife saw the problem in terms of moral obligation as conceived in private life; her husband saw it as a matter of game strategy. As a player in a weak position, he felt that he could not afford to indulge an ethical sentiment that might have cost him his seat at the table.

Playing to Win

73   Some men might challenge the Colbys of business—might accept serious setbacks to their business careers rather than risk a feeling of moral cowardice. They merit our respect—but as private individuals, not businessmen. When the skillful player of the business game is compelled to submit to unfair pressure, he does not castigate himself for moral weakness. Instead, he strives to put himself into a strong position where he can defend himself against such pressures in the future without loss.

74   If a man plans to take a seat in the business game, he owes it to himself to master the principles by which the game is played, including its special ethical outlook. He can then hardly fail to recognize that an occasional bluff may well be justified in terms of the game's ethics and warranted in terms of economic necessity. Once he clears his mind on this point, he is in a good position to match his strategy against that of the other players. He can then determine objectively whether a bluff in a given situation has a good chance of succeeding and can decide when and how to bluff, without a feeling of ethical transgression.

75   To be a winner, a man must play to win. This does not mean that he must be ruthless, cruel, harsh, or treacherous. On the contrary, the better his reputation for integrity, honesty, and decency, the better his chances of victory will be in the long run. But from time to time every businessman, like every poker player, is offered a choice between certain loss or bluffing within the legal rules of the game. If he is not resigned to losing, if he

wants to rise in his company and industry, then in such a crisis he will bluff—and bluff hard.

76 Every now and then one meets a successful businessman who has conveniently forgotten the small or large deceptions that he practiced on his way to fortune. "God gave me my money," old John D. Rockefeller once piously told a Sunday school class. It would be a rare tycoon in our time who would risk the horse laugh with which such a remark would be greeted.

77 In the last third of the twentieth century even children are aware that if a man has become prosperous in business, he has sometimes departed from the strict truth in order to overcome obstacles or has practiced the more subtle deceptions of the half-truth or the misleading omission. Whatever the form of the bluff, it is an integral part of the game, and the executive who does not master its techniques is not likely to accumulate much money or power.

STUDY QUESTIONS

1. Make a list of business practices that you feel would come under the rubric of "bluffing" as Carr employs this term. What business practices would Carr consider to be *un*ethical, and what in Carr's analysis enables you to distinguish between mere "bluffing" and immoral acts?
2. To what broader principle(s) does Carr appeal to support his position that business bluffing is ethical?
3. Locate several passages in which Carr appeals to the reader's specific judgments in real or hypothetical situations as support for his approval of business bluffing.
4. What analogies does Carr use to make business bluffing more palatable to the reader?
5. Is Carr simply describing or is he also endorsing the businessman's conception of ethical behavior in his work? How do you know?
6. Is it ethical for businessmen to sell products overseas that are banned for the protection of health in this country? How would Carr presumably answer this question?

SUGGESTIONS FOR WRITING

1. Choose some business practice that you feel to be unethical though legal. Using it as an example, write a rebuttal to Carr's argument. What specific stage(s) of his argument are disproven by your counterexample?

2. Write a brief essay about Carr's use of the poker analogy. Your essay might take a number of approaches: Is the analogy itself a fair and useful one? Could the analysis Carr makes of ethical gradations among poker-playing practices be applied differently to the context of business practices?

ARTHUR KELLY

Case Study: Italian Tax Mores

One ethical problem that faces corporations doing business abroad is whether or not to conform with practices that would be considered unethical at home but that are considered routine in the host country. Such practices frequently include lying, bribery, and kickbacks. Foreign representatives' ethical decisions are also complicated by the knowledge that if they do not accept the local way of doing things, their company will be unable to compete and its niche in the foreign market will immediately be filled by a less scrupulous firm.

The following is a case study of a bank manager caught in such an ethical dilemma. The author, Arthur L. Kelly, has extensive experience as a business executive.

1   The Italian federal corporate tax system has an official, legal tax structure and tax rates just as the U.S. system does. However, all similarity between the two systems ends there.

2   The Italian tax authorities assume that no Italian corporation would ever submit a tax return which shows its true profits but rather would submit a return which understates actual profits by anywhere between 30 percent and 70 percent; their assumption is essentially correct. Therefore, about six months after the annual deadline for filing corporate tax returns, the tax authorities issue to each corporation an "invitation to discuss" its tax return. The purpose of this notice is to arrange a personal meeting between them and representatives of the corporation. At this meeting, the Italian revenue service states the amount of corporate income tax which it believes is due. Its position is developed from both prior years' taxes actually paid and the current year's return; the amount which the tax authorities claim is due is generally several times that shown on the corporation's return for the current year. In short, the corporation's tax return and the revenue service's stated position are the opening offers for the several rounds of bargaining which will follow.

3   The Italian corporation is typically represented in such negotiations by its *commercialista,* a function which exists in Italian society for the primary purpose of negotiating corporate (and individual) tax payments with the Italian tax authorities; thus, the management of an Italian corporation seldom, if ever, has to meet directly with the Italian revenue service and probably has a minimum awareness of the details of the negotiation other than the final settlement.

4   Both the final settlement and the negotiation are extremely important to the corporation, the tax authorities, and the *commercialista.* Since the tax authorities assume that a corporation *always* earned more money this

year than last year and *never* has a loss, the amount of the final settlement, i.e., corporate taxes which will actually be paid, becomes, for all practical purposes, the floor for the start of next year's negotiations. The final settlement also represents the amount of revenue the Italian government will collect in taxes to help finance the cost of running the country. However, since large amounts of money are involved and two individuals having vested personal interests are conducting the negotiations, the amount of *bustarella*—typically a substantial cash payment "requested" by the Italian revenue agent from the *commercialista*—usually determines whether the final settlement is closer to the corporation's original tax return or to the fiscal authority's original negotiating position.

5   Whatever *bustarella* is paid during the negotiation is usually included by the *commercialista* in his lump-sum fee "for services rendered" to his corporate client. If the final settlement is favorable to the corporation, and it is the *commercialista's* job to see that it is, then the corporation is not likely to complain about the amount of its *commercialista's* fee, nor will it ever know how much of that fee was represented by *bustarella* and how much remained for the *commercialista* as payment for his negotiating services. In any case, the tax authorities will recognize the full amount of the fee as a tax deductible expense on the corporation's tax return for the following year.

6   About ten years ago, a leading American bank opened a banking subsidiary in a major Italian city. At the end of its first year of operation, the bank was advised by its local lawyers and tax accountants, both from branches of U.S. companies, to file its tax return "Italian-style," i.e., to understate its actual profits by a significant amount. The American general manager of the bank, who was on his first overseas assignment, refused to do so both because he considered it dishonest and because it was inconsistent with the practices of his parent company in the United States.

7   About six months after filing its "American-style" tax return, the bank received an "invitation to discuss" notice from the Italian tax authorities. The bank's general manager consulted with his lawyers and tax accountants who suggested he hire a *commercialista*. He rejected this advice and instead wrote a letter to the Italian revenue service not only stating that his firm's corporate return was correct as filed but also requesting that they inform him of any specific items about which they had questions. His letter was never answered.

8   About sixty days after receiving the initial "invitation to discuss" notice, the bank received a formal tax assessment notice calling for a tax of approximately three times that shown on the bank's corporate tax return; the tax authorities simply assumed the bank's original return had been based on generally accepted Italian practices, and they reacted accordingly. The bank's general manager again consulted with his lawyers and tax accountants who again suggested he hire a *commercialista* who knew how

to handle these matters. Upon learning that the *commercialista* would probably have to pay *bustarella* to his revenue service counterpart in order to reach a settlement, the general manager again chose to ignore his advisors. Instead, he responded by sending the Italian revenue service a check for the full amount of taxes due according to the bank's American-style tax return even though the due date for the payment was almost six months hence; he made no reference to the amount of corporate taxes shown on the formal tax assessment notice.

9   Ninety days after paying its taxes, the bank received a third notice from the fiscal authorities. This one contained the statement, "We have reviewed your corporate tax return for 19___ and have determined that [the lira equivalent of] $6,000,000 of interest paid on deposits is not an allowable expense for federal tax purposes. Accordingly, the total tax due for 19___ is lira _____." Since interest paid on deposits is any bank's largest single expense item, the new tax assessment was for an amount many times larger than that shown in the initial tax assessment notice and almost fifteen times larger than the taxes which the bank had actually paid.

10   The bank's general manager was understandably very upset. He immediately arranged an appointment to meet personally with the manager of the Italian revenue service's local office. Shortly after the start of their meeting, the conversation went something like this:

GENERAL MANAGER: "You can't really be serious about disallowing interest paid on deposits as a tax deductible expense."

ITALIAN REVENUE SERVICE: "Perhaps. However, we thought it would get your attention. Now that you're here, shall we begin our negotiations?"*

STUDY QUESTIONS

1. Why didn't the bank manager simply go along with local customs? What value assumptions stood in the way of doing so?
2. Had you been in the manager's shoes, would you have followed United States or Italian customs of reporting and negotiating corporate taxes?

SUGGESTION FOR WRITING:

If you believe in some measure of ethical relativism—that is, adjusting your ethical code to cultural circumstances—how do you decide where to draw the line?

---

* NOTE: For readers interested in what happened subsequently, the bank was forced to pay the taxes shown on the initial tax assessment, and the American manager was recalled to the United States and replaced.

For example, if you adjusted your practices to Italian mores in reporting taxable income, would you also follow the prevailing practices of marketing infant formula as described in the article by Leah Margulies in the next selection? If not, why not?

LEAH MARGULIES

Bottle Babies: Death and Business Get Their Market

Within the borders of the United States, corporate behavior that is widely perceived to be unethical is often within a short time made illegal. But corporations dealing with developing nations frequently are faced with deciding what to do when a profitable and legal venture turns out to have consequences that may make it unethical. Two examples of this situation include the marketing of pharmaceuticals that have been banned in the United States and the creation of an overseas market for cigarettes.

Perhaps the best-known challenge to corporations doing business in the Third World has been the protest against the marketing and promotion of infant formula, and particularly the long boycott against all products of the Swiss-based Nestlé corporation, which controlled half the market for infant formula in developing nations. The following article is a statement by a prominent figure in that protest movement. The author, Leah Margulies, directed the Infant Formula Program of the Interfaith Center on Corporate Responsibility, an ecumenical agency of the National Council of Churches.

1   *Caracas, Venezuela, July 1977:* In the emergency room of the Hospital de Niños, a large facility in the center of the city, lie 52 infants. All are suffering from gastroenteritis, a serious inflammation of the stomach and intestines. Many also suffer from pneumonia. According to the doctor in charge, 5000 Venezuelan babies die each year from gastroenteritis, and an equal number die from pneumonia. The doctor further explains that these babies, like many who preceded them and those who would follow, have all been bottle-fed. He remarks. "A totally breast-fed baby just does not get sick like this."

2   Poverty, inadequate medical care, and unsanitary conditions make bottle feeding, to quote a government nurse in Peru, "poison" for babies in the developing countries. Yet bottle feeding is rapidly becoming the norm in Third World countries. In 1951, almost 80 percent of all three-month-old babies in Singapore were being breast-fed at the age of three months; twenty years later, only 5 percent of them were at the breast. In 1966, 40 percent fewer mothers in Mexico nursed their six-month-old babies than had done so six years earlier.

3   The end result of this significant change in human behavior is higher morbidity and mortality rates among bottle-fed babies. Many well-known studies provide evidence of the relation between bottle feeding and infant malnutrition, disease, and death. Of course, it is impossible to know how many babies are getting sick or dying because of bottle feeding, but the

number is large and growing throughout the developing world. Dr. Derrick Jelliffe, head of the Department of Population, Health, and Family Planning at the UCLA School of Public Health, conservatively estimates that about 10 million babies a year suffer from malnutrition related to bottle feeding. The phenomenon is literally worldwide. According to medical reports of malnutrition among Eskimo children in the Baffin Zone of Canada, almost 5 percent of the infants born there in 1973–74 had to be flown to Montreal for emergency treatment, and doctors believe that one of the major causes of this tragic development was bottle feeding.

4   At the center of the bottle-feeding controversy are the promotional practices of the corporations who sell bottles and powdered baby milks in the Third World. Critics believe that promotion of these powders to mothers who do not have the facilities to properly prepare the feeds is a deadly way to make a profit. However, despite the increased activity of critics and acknowledgments by industry that improper bottle feeding can be dangerous, sales of infant formulas in poor countries are still escalating.

5   The corporations that sell infant formula in the Third World run the gamut from prestigious American, Swiss, British, and Japanese multinational corporations—like Abbott, American Home products, Bristol-Myers, Nestlés, and Cow and Gate—to local fly-by-night manufacturers trying to cash in. The concentrated campaign to attract Third World consumers began in the late 1950s. Soon a body of literature arose to help business conquer this almost virgin territory. For example, various articles advised foreign marketers that in the absence of a middle class, they should consider the urban poor as an important potential market.

6   Business began to understand the market potential of a poor population with many unfulfilled needs. Often the real needs of the poor could be obscured by a corporate sales strategy which promised the satisfaction of newly created needs. Mass media—TV, radio, and newspapers—could convey the promise that new products would meet these new needs. *Fortune* magazine heralded this new age with an article entitled, "Welcome to the Consumption Community." It was therefore not surprising that when the "Community" of infant formula consumers in the United States began to shrink as postwar birth rates declined and middle-class women in the developed countries decided they had been deprived of the experience of breast-feeding and began turning to the more natural way, the corporations turned to the ripe Third World market.

7   For the companies, baby formula sales strategies have paid off. Unfortunately no reliable statistics on infant formula sales are publicly available, although sometimes companies have inadvertently revealed the

extent of their commitment to the product. Worldwide sales of formula are estimated to total around $1 billion, with Nestlé's figure at roughly $300–400 million. Nestlé reportedly controls approximately half of the formula market in developing countries.

8   Whatever the sales figures at present, they will undoubtedly increase in the future. Bristol-Myers, for instance, has consistently reported sales gains for its Enfamil infant formula. Moreover, the upward trend, for the other companies as well as for Bristol-Myers, shows few signs of abating. Of course, sales figures do not tell the full story. Profit rates for infant formulas are also thought to be quite high. According to a 1977 supermarket sales printout from Brazil, commercial formula enjoyed a 72 percent profit margin, while all other supermarket products ranged between 15 percent and 25 percent.

What Is It?

9   What kind of product is infant formula? It is a highly processed food, based primarily on cow's milk. While the fat content and sugar source are patterned after mothers' milk, the company's claim that it is "nearly identical to mother's milk" is ridiculous. Maternal milk is a living substance, unique in many ways. Besides supplying the proper quantities of protein, fats, and other nutrients, it protects the infant from disease by providing antibodies important to the development of the immunization system. Formula does not have the digestibility of mothers' milk. Sometimes the product is sold premixed, but in the Third World it is more often sold as a powder that requires measured amounts of *pure* water for the proper reconstitutions. Sterilized bottles and nipples are also necessary.

10   There are a number of reasons why infant formula sells so well in the Third World. A mother in a developing country often finds herself in situations totally unlike those her mother ever experienced. She may, for instance, work outside the home, listen to the radio, or watch TV. These situations can be disorienting, and new values and attitudes must be formed in order to deal with them. Newly acquired values such as social mobility, as well as a high regard for modern products and medical expertise, make her a particularly vulnerable target for sophisticated formula marketing campaigns. The smiling white babies pictured on the front of formula tins can lead her to think that rich, white mothers feed their baby this product and that therefore it must be better.

11   Going into a hospital to give birth can be an especially frightening situation for a young Third World woman. Since in many countries only a small proportion of women attend the prenatal clinic (if there is one), a mother's maternity stay may be one of the few times in her life that she will

go into a hospital. Any products given to her in this environment will seem
to carry medical endorsement.

12   Imagine the reaction of a Third World mother in her home, or a group
of mothers in a clinic or hospital attending a class, to a woman in a crisp
nurse's uniform. The woman may or may not be a nurse. She begins her
speech, tactfully enough, by reassuring them that "breast is best," but she
ends by extolling the virtues of her company's product over the natural
method. Capitalizing on the respect given a nurse, the use of a "milk
nurse" implies a connection between the health care profession and the
commercial product.

13   In developed and developing countries alike, one of the hospital
practices most damaging to breast-feeding efforts—and one implicitly
supported by company promotional practices—is the separation of
mothers and infants shortly after birth. During the twelve to forty-eight
hours of separation, the infants are bottle fed in the nursery. Mothers are
sometimes given antilactation shots during this period. Thus when a
mother is finally reunited with her baby, switching from bottle to breast is
made more difficult. Furthermore, if the hospital has no incentive to teach
her, the woman is even less likely to breast-feed. Formula companies create
a strong climate for their products with their constant offers to set up
bottle sterilization and preparation facilities, to equip nurseries, and to
provide free supplies of formula. Busy doctors and nurses are led to adopt
the postnatal separation strategy by the willingness of formula companies
to make this approach easier than breast-feeding.

14   Medical personnel are a prime target for promotion because they are
the direct link to mothers. Although it is the patient who ultimately pays
for the product, doctors tell her what to buy, and the difference in
backgrounds of doctor and patient may well lead to an inappropriate
choice. As Dr. John Knowles, president of the Rockefeller Foundation,
stated in a letter to the chairman of Bristol-Myers:

> *The problem is not a "scientific" one. The problem is poverty and the
> inadequate home environment which makes the use of prepared formulae
> so lethal. This the physician is not uniquely qualified to understand. In
> fact, he may be precisely the most unqualified to understand since he
> undoubtedly comes from a different socio-economic background and may
> have no idea of the home conditions of the poorest mothers of his own
> society.*

15   Many dedicated physicians face a real dilemma when dealing with the
promotion efforts of formula companies. Their hospitals and clinics are
often woefully short of medical equipment and supplies. Under such
circumstances, it may seem harmless, indeed charitable, to agree to give

away free samples of infant formula to mothers in exchange for the company's gift of medical stocks or a new nursery. One hospital administrator in Malaysia has explained. "It is a very corrupting influence. You are always aware that you could have virtually anything you ask for."

Marketing for Babies

16   These marketing strategies are consciously decided upon and implemented through instructions to sales personnel, milk nurses, and distributors. Note the following extract from American Home Products selling instructions for 1975:

> Selected Doctors: *40–50 doctors per territory including 5 or 6 VIP's. These doctors should all be selected on the basis of their known influence on the selection of formula by mothers and by hospital or clinic maternity services. Sampling… Maternity services should be given primary allocation of free samples, geared to producing potential sales.*

Companies believe, and with good reason, that the product a mother goes home with is the product she will be loyal to. A 1969 study of 120 mothers in Barbados showed that 82 percent of the mothers given free samples, whether in a hospital or at home, later purchased the same brand. Thirty-two percent of them admitted that they were influenced by the free sample.

17   This aggressive market penetration and consumer creation are particularly destructive because they affect the most important resource developing countries have—people. In Chile in 1973, three times as many deaths occurred among infants who were bottle fed before three months old than among wholly breast-fed infants. A research team inspecting feeding bottles there discovered a bacterial contamination rate of 80 percent. Poverty and underdevelopment lead to abuse of even legitimate baby milk substitutes. Poor mothers cannot afford them in the quantities needed. Water is often contaminated, and the necessary boiling is rarely possible. Illiteracy makes it difficult to follow proper directions. Early weaning of infants from the breast to bottled infant formula is accompanied by increasing cases of diarrhea and gastroenteritis. Improperly attended—as they are likely to be due to inadequate medical care—these disorders result in many deaths.

18   Malnutrition is another common result and has been described as "commerciogenic malnutrition." This is not meant to imply that the manufacturers are solely responsible but simply that this type of malnutrition has nothing directly to do with underdevelopment and lack of food resources. As Dr. Michael Latham, a pediatrician and Cornell University professor of nutrition stated, "Placing a baby on the bottle in

the Third World might be tantamount to signing that baby's death certificate."

19   A 1975 Pan American Health Organization study found that childhood deaths from malnutrition peaked in the third and fourth months of life, because of the early abandonment of breast-feeding. The study covered some 35,00 deaths in fifteen countries. Medical studies linking bottle feeding with infant mortality and morbidity cover practically all areas of the Third World and some developed countries as well. A 1977 study in Cooperstown, New York, compared 164 breast-fed infants with 162 formula-fed infants; significant illnesses increased as breast-feeding declined. In 1970 a study of Jamaica, West Indies, revealed a higher incidence of gastroenteritis in the first four months of life among partly or wholly bottle-fed babies than among breast-fed babies. Other studies have reported similar results from Chile, Lebanon, Israel, Lagos, and others.

20   Hospital reports and personal testimony from doctors and nurses confirm these findings. Doctors in Jamaica have reviewed the records of thirty-seven seriously ill infants admitted in 1975 into their hospital, the Tropical Metabolism Research Unit in 1975. Twenty-five of the thirty-seven patients had been fed a brand-name infant formula. The average body weight of the babies was only 58 percent of the normal value. Their families were simply not equipped to safely bottle feed. About one fifth of the mothers were illiterate. The remainder were able to sign their names but were functionally illiterate. It was highly unlikely that they would be able to read, much less understand, written directions.

21   Nearly all the families lived in cramped, overcrowded, and unsanitary conditions, with an average weekly income of sixteen dollars. A tin of baby formula costs approximately two dollars and a baby needs two cans a week if exclusively formula-fed. Despite optimal medical care, five of these babies died. The case studies graphically show the inevitability of bottle contamination and dilution—the key culprits leading to illness and malnutrition.

22   Since 1970 when the Protein Advisory Group (recently dismantled) of the United Nations first met with the baby formula industry, there has been a growing international campaign aimed at stopping unethical promotional practices. In 1973, the Protein Advisory Group published guidelines for promoting infant nutrition and included the need for restrictions in advertising. In 1974, the World Health Assembly called for a critical review of company promotion, and the issue has been discussed extensively at medical conferences, international seminars, in U.N. papers, etc. Most recently, on January 31, 1978, the World Health Organization, announced, "The advertising of food for nursing infants or older babies and young children is of particular importance and should be prohibited

on radio and television…finally, the distribution of free samples and other sales promotion practices for baby foods should be generally prohibited."

23   In 1975 the International Pediatrics Association issued a series of recommendations to encourage breast-feeding. The section entitled "Curtailing Promotion of Artificial Feeding" reads:

1 Sales promotion activities of organizations marketing baby milks and feeding bottles, that run counter to the general intent expressed in this document, must be curtailed by every means available to the profession, including, where necessary and feasible, legislation to control unethical practice.

2 Dissemination of propaganda about artificial feeding and distribution of samples of artificial baby foods in maternity units should be banned immediately.

24   In the U.S. recently, considerable interest has centered around the stockholder lawsuit against Bristol-Myers (Mead Johnson Division). The Sisters of the Precious Blood have charged the company with making "false and misleading statements" about their overseas promotion and sales of infant formula. The statements appeared in a proxy report to stockholders, which is required by law to be accurate. In May 1977, a U.S. district court judge dismissed the case, stating that the Sisters had not shown that they, as shareholders, had been caused "irreparable harm" by the alleged misstatements. The judge declined to comment on the accuracy of the company's proxy report. The nuns appealed this decision.

25   Then, in the first weeks of 1978, the Sisters signed an out-of-court settlement with Bristol-Myers. The settlement stipulates that a report be sent to all shareholders of the company, outlining the legal action and the positions of both parties. The Sisters' statement in the report contains affidavits from five countries and an analysis of their current criticisms of company practices. The company's statement announces a more stringent interpretation of its Code of Policies and Practices and the fact that it has discontinued the use of milk nurses in Jamaica. Industry critics view the settlement as an important step toward convincing the companies that public opinion has changed the social climate in which marketing takes place. What was at one time an "acceptable" social cost no longer is the case, primarily because of increased public knowledge and protest.

26   The findings of the lawsuit have prompted local consumer advocacy groups in the United States to join forces in a coalition called INFACT (Infant Formula Action). These groups believe it vital to keep pressuring Nestlé—the largest manufacturer of baby formula in the Third World—to desist from its promotion tactics. The Minnesota-based Third World Institute has initiated a consumer boycott which is quietly spreading

throughout the U.S. In addition, church groups, acting in their capacity as stockholders in the American companies, are continuing their efforts to further restrict the promotion these companies engage in. This year two new shareholder resolutions were filed with American Home Products and Carnation, both of whom widely advertise their condensed milk in the Third World.

27   Because of this growing condemnation of industry practices, the companies have made some attempts to deal with their critics. In most cases however, the concessions do not significantly alter the outcome of formula promotion. There have been a number of changes:

28   ▪ After blatant advertising (especially mass-media promotion) had made some of the companies highly vulnerable to criticism, these companies switched the focus of their promotion efforts to the medical profession. This new marketing approach is more sophisticated, less risky, and far more effective. Via mass media, everyone heard the message, whether they were potential customers or not. Now marketing focuses more directly on the consumer through the use of health workers. For example, in a poverty hospital in the Philippines, name tags with a prominent brand-name logo are found on each crib in the nursery. Nestlé wrist labels have also been provided. There and elsewhere, while the most blatant ads have been curtailed, direct consumer promotion continues in the hospitals themselves and appears to be sanctioned by the medical authorities.

29   ▪ In the past, critics charged that companies encouraged the abandonment of breast-feeding. Now the companies agree that bottle feeding to the exclusion of breast-feeding is not desirable. They talk about "supplementation." However, mixed feeding has also been shown to be quite dangerous. Consuming smaller amounts of contaminated and diluted formula is preferable, one assumes, but it is not the answer. Furthermore, the encouragement of supplementation in fact undermines breast-feeding. According to most medical experts, supplementation negatively affects the production of human milk.

30   ▪ Critics have also complained about milk nurses and the ethics involved in employing nurses as a company sales force. Again, the companies have adapted. They often change the colors of the uniforms, add belts, call them "company representatives," and may even agree to alter somewhat milk-nurse sales techniques. But visits to hospitals and homes continue, and the nurses are still being lured away from government
health services.

31   ▪ A more significant adaptive technique is that of employing nutritionists and other highly trained professionals. In Venezuela, for

example, Nestlé employs no milk nurses but several nutritionists. These nutritionists interact on a regular basis with Ministry of Health, nutrition, and hospital personnel. One Nestlé nutritionist in Caracas appears to have been totally integrated into the health care team at Maternidad Hospital as she made her rounds with the paid hospital staff. This type of interaction between government and business personnel raises serious ethical questions about the extent to which industry's point of view should be institutionalized within government health services.

32   ▪ When critics argued that formula was being promoted to the poor, the companies responded that formula is priced above the income of poor people and is purchased almost exclusively by upper-income groups. But the companies have provided no evidence to confirm this argument. Indeed, there is more than adequate proof that the products are being promoted and sold indiscriminately to mothers who have neither the financial nor the sanitary facilities to use the products safely. Since July 1977 alone, documentation confirms the presence of promotional displays in markets, pharmacies, and grocery stores in the mountain villages of India, the barrios of Caracas, and the slums of Manila.

33   ▪ In response to these kinds of intense promotion efforts, the critics finally called for regulation of the formula industry. The industry, in turn, has responded with "self-regulation," which mainly consists of business codes. There are now several codes of ethics, some more stringent than others. All, however, share two inherent weaknesses.

34   ▪ First, the codes legitimize promotion to the medical profession and characterize the latter as "intermediaries" between the baby food industry and the mother. However, given the desperate shortages of medical personnel in developing countries and the constant pressure exerted on existing workers by the companies, it is very difficult for these intermediaries to be impartial.

35   ▪ Second, insuring that the companies will adhere to their self-imposed restrictions is virtually impossible in the absence of regular scrutiny by an independent body. In August 1977, a Bristol-Myers milk nurse was interviewed by this author on the ward of the largest public hospital in Jamaica. The milk nurse had in her hand a list of mothers she intended to visit in their homes. She had copied the names from ward lists. In an interview just two days before, the chief medical officer of Jamaica had explained that government policy prohibited milk nurses from entering public hospitals. The milk nurse's actions were therefore doubly in violation of Bristol-Myers's code of ethics which specifically requires cooperation with government health policies as well as the solicitation of references from medical professionals for all home visits. The publicity surrounding this incident most likely influenced Bristol-Myers's decision

because the existing social and economic conditions make proper usage virtually impossible. An end to malnutrition will ultimately require massive changes in the distribution of wealth, land, and power. But that is no reason not to take intermediate steps. The shifts in promotion thus far are adaptations to a new business climate and clearly prove that the formula industry is vulnerable to pressure.

37   If promotion could be eliminated entirely, health care institutions and governments would be freer to develop their own capacity to handle the monumental health problems that face Third World countries. To accomplish this, the public needs a strategy. It must include the continuous monitoring and disclosure of corporate activity; cooperation between concerned health professionals, international agencies, and advocacy groups; and the development of an increasingly larger audience of people who share the belief that business must be held accountable for unethical practices, however costly and inconvenient. As Dr. Alan Jackson of the Tropical Metabolism Research Unit in Jamaica stated in a recent interview:

> *When you spend your time working with children who are malnourished and you see children dying because they are either getting wrong food or food prepared improperly, it has a devastating effect upon you. It's very hard to think that people who are involved in selling, encouraging people to buy infant preparation, can carry on in this kind of a way, and at the same time pretend that they are not involved in the end results, which is malnutrition, malnourished children.*

STUDY QUESTIONS

1. The success of this article depends on establishing a causal connection between bottle feeding of infant formula and infant mortality, malnutrition, and disease. Identify the factual claims made in the article about infant disease and death and evaluate the strength of the argument linking these facts to the use of infant formula.

2. Identify two or three points in the article at which the argument rests on correlations between infant illness or death and the use of infant formula. The baby food industry has often responded that correlation does not prove cause. In the arguments you have identified, what alternative causal arguments might they propose?

3. Does the author claim or imply that formula companies deliberately exploit the Third World market knowing the hazards of using their products in that environment? Where are these claims or implications made? Are claims about industry motivation supported by facts?

4. What steps had already been taken to forestall the abuses Margulies details? Why did she consider these steps inadequate? What steps does she propose in their place?

SUGGESTION FOR WRITING

The next selection, the testimony of Oswaldo Ballarin before a Senate subcommittee, is in large measure an industry response to the kind of arguments presented in the Margulies article. Write an essay weighing the two arguments against each other. Structure your article in three parts: factual claims, value assumptions, and proposals for action. Do not get lost in detail: Try to cut through the welter of facts and contentions to focus on the facts you feel are sustained by the evidence and the values you feel should prevail. The thesis of your argument should be the crucial question of what kind of social or legal action you feel is required.

OSWALDO BALLARIN

Prepared Statement to the United States Subcommittee on Health and Scientific Research

On May 23, 1978, the Senate Subcommittee on Health and Scientific Research, chaired by Senator Edward Kennedy, conducted a hearing on the marketing and promotion of infant formula in the developing nations. The members of the subcommittee received prepared statements from expert witnesses and interested parties and held panel discussions with them.

The early witnesses were mostly concerned doctors, nurses, and other workers in developing nations who testified to the harmful effects of infant formula when improperly prepared and stored and who also testified about promotional practices of companies selling infant formula. They were followed by a panel of representatives of various corporations marketing infant formula in developing nations. Oswaldo Ballarin, the first industry spokesman to testify, was Chairman of the Board of the Brazilian branch of Nestlé, the Swiss-based company that commanded about half the Third World infant formula market and that was the subject of a growing boycott by church groups and others in the United States and Europe.

1   Senator Kennedy, Senator Javits, and members of the Health and Scientific Research Subcommittee:

2   My name is Oswaldo Ballarin and I am Chairman of the Board of the company that manufactures and sells Nestlé products in Brazil. I have been concerned with problems of nutrition in the Third World for many years, having been a member of the Protein Advisory Group of United Nations System.

3   Senator Kennedy's invitation to testify here today was directed to The Nestlé Company, Inc. of White Plains, N.Y. The White Plains company is a New York corporation and it does not manufacture or sell infant formula products. Since I have more than fifty years of experience in this field, my friends at White Plains asked me to appear before you to discuss the manufacture and distribution of infant formula products in the developing countries.

4   I came here of my own free will with the understanding that this Committee does not have jurisdiction over me or over the Nestlé parent company in Switzerland.

5   Although the U.S. Nestlé company does not manufacture or sell any infant food products, it is my understanding that certain groups are boycotting the sale of U.S. Nestlé products such as coffee and chocolate.

The boycott is for the avowed purpose of putting pressure on Nestlé's Swiss parent company to stop alleged misconduct in the marketing of infant formula in the Third World.

6   I am aware of the specific charges made by these groups and can state that they are quite misleading and inaccurate, based on my personal experience in many developing countries.

7   The U.S. Nestlé company has advised me that their research indicates this is actually an indirect attack on the free world's economic system. A worldwide church organization with the stated purpose of undermining the free enterprise system is in the forefront of this activity.

8   To this end, the European and American working affiliates of this organization, including the activist group called INFACT, have been distributing a completely distorted and misleading film entitled "Bottle Babies" to many local churches and schools to incite the emotional responses necessary for the boycott attempt. Literature and advertisements I have seen, with equally erroneous data, have also been distributed in the U.S.

9   Because of the very questionable credibility of the accusations, it is somewhat difficult to give them recognition. However, I am happy that the U.S. Nestlé company has invited me to speak about my personal knowledge of Nestlé activities in a developing country.

10   Nestlé started operations in the Third World nearly sixty years ago with the main purpose of making milk of good quality available wherever it was needed. Doctors had been concerned by the use of inadequate foods when breast milk alone was insufficient to meet the needs of babies. In those days bottle-feeding was already practiced and was not introduced by the infant food companies. Many mothers bottle-fed their babies with a milky-looking fluid obtained by simply extracting manioc flour with water, or sometimes with fresh cow's milk of poor quality. The results were adverse because of the complete inadequacy of the food, both from the nutritional and hygienic standpoint. Doctors therefore welcomed the possibility of prescribing a safe and nutritious product for babies whose mothers had to supplement or replace breast milk. This is a well-known fact to which any doctor in those regions could testify.

11   In Brazil, and in many other developing countries, Nestlé responded to the challenge by pioneering the establishment of local milk processing facilities based on the encouragement of local dairy farming. This made a positive contribution to the development of the country and helped to raise standards of living. There is no correlation therefore, as has been suggested in some quarters, between Nestlé's presence in Brazil and other developing countries and the declining birth rates in the industrialized countries.

12   Nestlé recognized that even the best products will not give the desired

results if used incorrectly. We, therefore, placed great weight on educational efforts aimed at explaining the correct use of our products. Our work in this field has received the public recognition and approval of the official Pediatric Associations in many countries. Such educational efforts never attempt to infer that our product is superior to breast milk. Indeed, we have devoted much attention to the promotion of breast-feeding, and educational material has always insisted that breast-feeding is best for the baby.

13   Nevertheless, many factors militate against exclusive breast-feeding in the rapidly growing cities of Brazil as well as other developing countries, and our products are seen today as filling a valid need, just as they did when they were first introduced over fifty years ago. In recognition of this, all such products are subject to strict price control, while in many countries which do not have a local dairy industry, they are classified as essential goods and imported free of duty. In many cases, official agencies establish what they consider to be a fair margin for the manufacturers.

14   It must be stressed that many problems remain to be solved. Our production is far from reaching the total needs of the population. Hence, many mothers in the poorer population groups continue to supplement breast-feeding with foods of doubtful quality. Owing to the lack of adequate medical services, especially in the rural areas, misuse of any supplement can occur and we are very conscious of the need to improve our efforts. These efforts depend on continued cooperation between the infant food industry and health professionals. We have to be more and more conscious of our responsibility to encourage breast-feeding while researching new foods and safer methods for feeding babies who cannot be exclusively breast-fed. The dilemma facing industry and the health services alike, is how to teach these methods without discouraging breast-feeding.

15   It is precisely for this reason that the International Council of Infant Food Industries (ICIFI) was established in order to reach international agreement on the role and "modus operandi" of the Infant Food Industry. Nestlé is a founder member of the Council which has commenced consultation with a view to implementing the recommendations to the Infant Food Industry. These recommendations were contained in PAG Statement No. 23 and constitute the only official United Nations guidelines directed at governments, the health professions, and industry on their responsibilities in promoting the use of supplementary foods to the vulnerable groups.

16   Nestlé makes no claim to perfection, and we are always willing to accept valid suggestions and criticism and make changes accordingly. As Dr. Jelliffe's successor at the Caribbean Food and Nutrition Institute in Jamaica said in a letter to Nestlé, "This Institute with the international agencies supporting it (PAHO/WHO, FAO, and UNICEF) feels that public

out that the Institute's aim is cooperation with the infant formula companies rather than conflict. We agree with these sentiments and feel that it is counterproductive to cater to the demands of those who distort facts and oversimplify the complex issues of infant health as a means to attack the free world's economic system.

STUDY QUESTIONS:

1. In reading this prepared statement to the subcommittee, Ballarin reached only the end of paragraph 7 before he was angrily interrupted by Senator Kennedy in a scene that appeared that night on the national news and that has often been cited as an important stimulus to the Nestlé boycott. Why should this portion of the statement have been considered objectionable?
2. What empirical claims does this statement offer to defend the sale and promotion of infant formula in developing nations?
3. At the end of paragraph 11, what is the alleged "correlation" that Ballarin seeks to refute?
4. What aspect of Ballarin's value system would not be shared by his adversaries in the Nestlé boycott movement?
5. Protests against the marketing of formula cite misuse of the product as the cause of infant malnutrition, illness, and death. Protesters argue that in areas of high illiteracy, poor sanitation, contaminated water, and lack of refrigeration, such misuse is inevitable unless marketing and promotion of formula are strictly controlled or forbidden altogether. Does Ballarin answer these charges directly? If so, how effective is his answer?

Editorials on the U.S. Vote against the WHO Code of Ethics for Companies Marketing Infant Foods

Reports of abuses in the marketing of infant formula in developing nations prompted various proposals for corrective measures. An International Council of Infant Food Industries drew up its own code of ethics, and some member corporations instituted their own more stringent codes as well; but these attempts by the industry at self-regulation did not satisfy critics, who often felt that it was a self-serving and unenforceable measure to avoid regulation from outside. Unilateral action by the United States would have been ineffective, since many of the companies marketing the formula were not based in the United States.

Therefore, in May of 1981 the World Health Organization (WHO), in consultation with medical experts and industry representatives, proposed a code of ethics to govern the sale and advertising of infant formulas. The code was non-binding; it urged nations to apply its stipulations in ways "appropriate to their social and legislative framework."

The code was put to a committee vote on May 20 and a final vote on May 21, where it passed 118 to 1 with three abstentions. The only "no" vote was cast by the United States.

The following are a sample of editorials from around the country (and from Vancouver) in response to the United States vote.

Chicago Tribune
Chicago, Ill., May 27, 1981

1   It's inevitable that the United States will be tarred as a sort of heartless Uncle Son of Sam killer of Third World babies for its vote against the adoption by the World Health Organization of a code to ban promotion of infant formulas.

2   The American delegation stood alone in opposing the code, except for Chad and Bangladesh, whose delegates later explained their vote was a protest against curtailing debate on the bitter issue.

3   But it's not just a matter of the U.S. callously supporting exploitive multinational formula manufacturers who want to push an expensive product on poor Third World mothers whose babies die because they lack the sanitation, clean water, and money to use formula safely and in adequate amounts, as supporters of the WHO code protest. There are some good reasons for the unpopular American stand.

4   The code, which is voluntary but which WHO wants all nations to incorporate into their laws and regulations, sharply curtails the way baby formula can be advertised and marketed. For example, it would prohibit health care workers from telling women about using formula except when

medically necessary. Such restrictions on business and on free speech aren't acceptable in the United States, especially when the product involved is safely and widely used here. The U.S. is right to vote against a code it would not incorporate into American law—and right to oppose this initial adventure into the regulation of international marketing of products.

5   The hundreds of protest groups which have urged boycotting the baby formula manufacturers over this issue say from 1 to 10 million babies a year die because the companies persuade mothers to abandon breast-feeding. But the statistics are unsubstantiated. And they ignore the fact that infant morbidity and mortality are high in Third World countries. They are high because breast-feeding by malnourished mothers may be inadequate, because sanitation is poor, and because mothers are often forced to use such locally-available milk-substitutes as rice gruel. Rather than restrict the availability and knowledge of commercial formulas, WHO might do better by finding ways to make such products safely and affordably available to mothers whose infants they could help.

6   It's surprising that women's groups have not protested against the WHO code. In one light, it can be seen as an attempt by a mostly male organization to dictate to women on an international scale how they must use their bodies—by restricting access to information that would permit them to make their own choices and in effect by limiting their ability to hold jobs until their babies are weaned. Many American women would be furious if the U.S. passed a law saying no one could tell them about baby formula or how to get it or how to use it unless a doctor (most of whom are male) decided it was medically necessary. Yet this is what the WHO code prescribes.

7   Breast-feeding is best for babies. The WHO code affirms it. Formula makers concur. In a voluntary agreement worked out with WHO in 1979, the companies pledged to end objectionable sales promotion to consumers; while there have been some violations of the accord, it remains preferable to the new, much more restrictive code. Gerald B. Helman, who represents the U.S., emphasized after the WHO vote that the Reagan administration endorses "efforts to promote and protect breast-feeding as the ideal form of infant nutrition." But women are entitled to an informed choice in the matter, which the WHO code will not give them.

The Commercial Appeal
Memphis, Tenn., May 24, 1981

1   Now that the U.S. delegation to the Joint World Health Organization/United Nations International Children's Emergency Fund meeting in Geneva has embarrassed the United States and made Americans appear heartless by casting the only vote against an

international code for marketing infant formulas, maybe the nutritionists can get down to dealing with the real problem.

2   The Reagan administration has defended its lonely position on this issue as an overstepping of bounds by the WHO and an uncalled-for interference with private business activities. Besides, the administration argues, there would be no way to enforce the restrictions on advertising and promotion.

3   The formula manufacturers have defended their promotions on the ground that many mothers in those countries suffer malnutrition themselves and as a result are unable to breast-feed their infants. The opponents of the formulas say they must be mixed with polluted water and that as a result the infants die of infections instead of malnutrition.

4   In the last analysis, the question is not whether the formulas themselves are good or bad.

5   Everybody agrees infant formulas are good if properly used.

6   But too often in Third World situations those formulas are not and cannot be used properly. The women simply don't have the kind of sterile equipment—or, for that matter, even simply clean equipment—as do mothers in the United States or in Europe. It is not unusual to find a Third World mother mixing the dry formula with the polluted native water in a discarded, filthy soft-drink bottle. And lacking the plastic or rubber nipples for the bottles, the mother will simply plug the bottle with an old rag for the baby to suck.

7   Under such conditions, the bottled formula serves as a culturing medium for the polluted water, causing bacteria to multiply and become lethal.

8   One challenge to the nutritionist and the infant formula manufacturers, therefore, is to devise a better means of delivering the necessary nutrients to the needy infants. Surely a nation which found ways to deliver processed rations to its soldiers under the most difficult of field conditions can find a way to deliver safe bottled infant formula to Third World children.

9   Beyond that, would it not seem logical for the makers of those infant formulas to devote some of their efforts and promotions to devising food supplements for the women in those undernourished nations for use in their prenatal and postnatal periods? That would enable mothers to breast-feed their children and thus given them the natural immunities breast-fed infants get.

The Charleston Gazette
Charleston, W. Va., May 20, 1981

1   The United States has indicated its intention of casting what will probably be the only "no" vote in Geneva May 21 against a proposed U.N. code of ethics designed to encourage breast-feeding of infants.

2   Among other prohibitions the measure would ban the advertising of artificial formulas designed to supplant breast-feeding.

3   The administration's stance on this issue, given Reagan's ties to Big Business, must be viewed with suspicion. Significantly, U.S. firms manufacture much infant formula sold in Third World countries.

4   Consumption of these artificial formulas—with the resultant discouragement of natural breast-feeding—has been promoted through overseas advertising as a sort of low-budget conspicuous consumption for status-conscious mothers in the world's poor countries.

5   When rich corporations are permitted to persuade starving mothers to substitute an expensive, less-nutritious, store-bought commodity for a natural, healthy and absolutely free alternative that has served well for millennia, a great wrong has been committed.

6   The U.S. contingent has objected to the code—which is endorsed by the World Health Organization—on grounds that it would be hypocritical for us to suggest a rule we would not permit in our own country. A ban on advertising is a restraint on free trade and is therefore intolerable, the argument goes.

7   Nonsense. Television and radio advertising of cigarettes, to cite just one example, is banned here at home to protect the public health.

8   Health advantages of breast-feeding are as well-established as dangers of cigarette use. No hypocrisy exists here.

9   The Reagan administration's willingness to discourage breast-feeding would literally sacrifice the health—perhaps the lives—of Third World babies for the financial health of industry in the developed countries.

10   Surely Reagan's debt to Big Business isn't that BIG.

The Sun
Baltimore, Md., May 14, 1981

1   Though breast-feeding evangelists sometimes overstate their case, mother's milk is still so close to being the perfect infant food that practically all responsible health experts today would agree that breast feeding usually is far superior to bottle feeding. For that reason, the United States should support a World Health Organization code aimed at encouraging mothers in developing countries to rely primarily on breast-feeding rather than bottle feeding. That the administration instead is opposing the code makes it appear to be callous toward the welfare of infants in the Third World.

2   Breast milk is "designed" for human consumption. It contains, in exactly the right proportions, exactly those nutrients needed for human infants. It also immunizes infants against various diseases. Breast feeding is a natural contraceptive, because it often suppresses ovulation in mothers. In developing countries, where sanitation is poor, breast-feeding is much less likely to transmit infections.

3   But various U.S. baby food manufacturers oppose U.S. support of the WHO guidelines, which come up for a vote in Geneva Monday. These companies earlier had adopted their own guidelines to discourage the inappropriate "pushing" of their own infant formula products on Third World mothers. In many cases where these abuses continue, the perpetrators are smaller local companies. Why then do the large U.S. companies oppose the WHO guidelines? Two possibilities exist, say public health experts: 1) The companies stopped pushing inappropriate bottle feeding only temporarily, in response to now-ended Carter administration pressures, and/or 2) U.S. multinational corporations in general are frightened of an "entering wedge" of international control of marketing practices that, though illegal in the U.S., are still practiced in the Third World.

4   What the companies seem not to recognize is that the Third World may well be on the brink of a revolution in infant health care (part of the theoretical base of which was laid at the Johns Hopkins School of Hygiene and Public Health in Baltimore). Adoption of the WHO guidelines could be a first—and probably necessary—step in the revolution, which also would include supplemental feeding with locally grown cereals and lentils, control of infant diseases and infant infections, and help for parents in spacing their children farther apart. The latter would reduce the rate of population growth. One Hopkins researcher says the revolution could be accomplished for an affordable $2 per year per infant. When they oppose the WHO code, the U.S. companies and the U.S. government appear to oppose a public health revolution which could yield immense benefits for the world's poor.

St. Petersburg Times
St. Petersburg, Fla., May 23, 1981

1   Two astonishing things happened Wednesday at the meeting of the World Health Organization in Geneva, Switzerland.

2   Ninety-five countries voted for the adoption of a voluntary code urging restraints in the marketing of powdered milk formulas for infants. Such solid unanimity among so many countries with diverse interests is quite unusual.

3   The United States' no vote, making it the lone dissenter, was also astonishing. The Reagan administration's shameful decision to vote against the code ignores world opinion, insults Third World countries, and casts the United States as an enemy of mothers and babies.

4   Some companies have been accused of using high-powered sales tactics to discourage breast-feeding in Third World countries where conditions make it likely that baby formulas will be misused, causing the deaths of innocent infants. Most experts agree that breast feeding is the healthiest

way to nurture a baby. Mother's milk is nutritious, safe and helps immunize against disease.

5   The nonbinding code is only a recommendation that different countries could modify to fit local circumstances and customs. There was no good reason for the United States to oppose it, but many good reasons to support it.

6   Unfortunately, there is little chance that the Reagan administration will change the United States' vote today when the final tally is taken.

The Des Moines Register
Des Moines, Iowa, May, 22, 1981

1   On orders from the White House, the United States cast the only vote against World Health Organization guidelines to protect babies in underdeveloped nations from the malnutrition and disease that often accompany the use of infant formula by uninformed users.

2   The vote at the WHO assembly in Geneva was 118–1. The U.S. government thus presents itself to the world as a captive of the Grocery Manufacturers Association and the U.S. formula manufacturers (Abbott Laboratories, American Home Products, Bristol-Meyers—the biggest, Nestlé, is a Swiss corporation). Two U.S. Agency for International Development officials, Stephen Joseph and Eugene Babb, are being forced to resign for their protest.

3   The guidelines are advisory. This had been insisted upon by the Carter administration as necessary for U.S. support. Now, just as it did on the international-law-of-the-sea treaty, the Reagan administration has reneged.

4   The groups comprising the Infant Formula Action Coalition accuse manufacturers and dealers of misleading mothers in Third World countries into trying the formula rather than breast-feeding. Then, after her milk has dried, the mother must continue with formula even though she may be too poor to afford it and lack facilities to use it safely.

5   Four of the five practices the code seeks to prohibit have been major targets of criticism in the Third World distribution of free samples to pregnant women, sales persons contacting mothers directly, use of premiums, and product labels that promote the use of formula in various ways.

6   The guidelines call, as well, for prohibition of all advertising and promotion of formula. Administration spokesmen have seized upon this as grounds for voting "no," arguing that advertising regulations would be unconstitutional. But the rules are only advisory and acknowledge that each nation may enforce them within its own "social and legislative framework."

7   The WHO guidelines grew out of problems that exist primarily in the Third World. Contaminated water and infant formula, for example, make a

deadly mix. If sales of infant formula in this country pose little or no problem, Congress and regulatory agencies would do nothing.

8   U.S. opposition may have one beneficial effect. The anti-U.S. anger it is inspiring may cause underdeveloped nations to enact laws implementing the code more promptly than they otherwise would have done. Unfortunate effects may include increased reluctance of these nations to cooperate with the United States in health-regulated matters, including regulation of the narcotics traffic.

9   By appearing to put ideology and corporate profit ahead of babies' welfare in the affected countries, the Reagan administration is further isolating itself from the world community of nations, an isolation it can ill afford.

The Sun
Vancouver, B.C., May 22, 1981

1   The World Health Organization and UNICEF, the United Nations children's fund, obviously would not counsel women to breast-feed their babies if they didn't feel it was the healthy thing to do.

2   But is it healthy to lay down a rigid worldwide set of rules making it, if not exactly mandatory, certainly the only acceptable method of nourishing children at birth?

3   The code adopted by the World Health Organization this week—over the objections of the United States but with the approval of Canada and 94 other nations—is undoubtedly well-intentioned, but the effect is spoiled by the restrictions it attempts to place on artificial substitutes for mother's milk.

4   It is one thing to say, as UNICEF does, that "it is likely that at least one million children in the developing world die each year from inadequate artificial feeding," but is that necessarily the fault of the manufacturers of baby formula?

5   Other proponents of the code seem to accept that it isn't, and that the danger in Third World countries, particularly, comes mainly from local misuse—where the formula is mixed with polluted water under poor health conditions.

6   In trying to impose a global ban on promotion and advertising of baby formula, on distribution of free product samples, and on gifts promoting the use of formula as a substitute for breast milk, the WHO is seriously challenging a mother's right to choose for herself.

7   Not all mothers in all the countries prepared to go along with the code like breast-feeding. Not all of them can. Where would such a code leave them, if not in as much ignorance and desperation as those who have already fallen prey to high-pressure salesmanship?

8   If, as seems to be the case, the WHO is concerned about the aggressive and successful sales tactics of manufacturers in weaning gullible mothers onto the bottle, which in certain countries holds health risks for the child, the answer surely is for governments to do a better job of educating the people.

9   It should not have the result, which the code aspires to achieve, of making any substitute for breast-feeding unthinkable.

Oklahoma City Times
Oklahoma City, Okla., May 22, 1981

1   On the heels of the uproar over its proposals to stave off Social Security insolvency by reducing benefits in the future, the Reagan administration is tackling another no-win issue—breast-feeding vs. bottled formula for Third World infants.

2   The United States voted in the World Health Organization meeting in Geneva this week against a nonbinding eight-page code encouraging women, especially those in poor countries, to breast-feed their babies rather then give them manufactured substitutes.

3   It urges a global ban on the promotion and advertising of baby formula, on distribution of free product samples, and on gifts for promoting the use of formula as a substitute for breast milk. Although the code was adopted only as a recommendation, the member governments of WHO were urged to "translate" it into national law and regulations.

4   The problem, say proponents of the code, is that aggressive sales tactics by the makers of formula discourage mothers from breast-feeding their babies. It is argued that the formula, while medically good, is dangerously misused in backward countries beset by poverty, illiteracy and poor sanitation. Label instructions are not followed and the formula is mixed with polluted water. The result is a high incidence of infant deaths, WHO officials say.

5   The U.S. delegate was careful to point out that the Reagan administration endorses efforts to promote breast-feeding. But that reassurance was ignored in the predictable adverse reaction on the home front.

6   Sen. Edward Kennedy, D-Mass., already had a forum going to air objections to the U.S. vote. Self-proclaimed experts were only too willing to express their shock and shame. Naturally, the official position provides one more excuse for an outpouring of antibusiness venom.

7   While the Reagan administration showed courage in taking a stance certain to stir an emotional response, it was based on sound reasoning. The WHO has no business trying to regulate, or even to promote the idea of regulating, international trade. From the U.S. standpoint, the code,

which apparently went beyond guidelines issued two years ago, would violate constitutional provisions on speech freedom and laws barring restraint of trade.

8   The simple solution seems to be for the formula makers to go the "extra mile" and undertake an extensive educational campaign in the Third World countries on the proper use of their product. They might even offer to help provide better sanitation and good water.

The Charlotte Observer
Charlotte, N.C., May 26, 1981

1   It is unfair to characterize the United States as a callous enemy of Third World babies because it opposed an international code on marketing infant formula. It's also unfair to cast proponents of the code as dogooders who want to restrict trade.

2   It's distressing that the debate over the code passed last week by the World Health Organization (WHO) consisted of so much simplistic name-calling—and so little serious discussion of a complex issue.

3   The WHO, an agency of the United Nations, endorsed the code advising nations to curtail aggressive marketing of formula and encourage infant health through breast-feeding. Proponents argue that formula manufacturers have used hard-sell tactics in poor nations, discouraging breast-feeding and allowing illiteracy and poor sanitation to cause dangerous misuse of their products.

4   The Reagan administration—against the advice of some high-ranking U.S. health officials—opposed the code. The administration said it objected to "rigid rules" on global trade and to making the WHO an "international Federal Trade Commission." That's a principle worth defending, but it isn't clear that it really applied in this case. The proposed code, at one time more rigid, was made voluntary to gain support from the Carter administration. It now directs nations to implement its recommendations in ways "appropriate to their social and legislative framework."

5   The code says, in essence, that manufacturers should exercise responsibility in countries where mothers cannot read instructions; where formula may be excessively diluted to stretch supplies; where it may be mixed with contaminated water.

6   There is no attempt to ban the distribution or use of formula. Rather, the code urges that it be used under supervision of health authorities—and not promoted in such a way as to dispute the universally agreed-upon superiority of breast-feeding.

7   Those are reasonable goals. Improper use of formula is unquestionably a public health problem, and has caused malnutrition and death in poor

nations. UNICEF estimates that a million children die each year in developing nations from misuse of formula; manufacturers dispute that figure. No one disagrees, however, that the problem exists.

8 Formula manufacturers did accede to a voluntary WHO agreement in 1979 to limit over-enthusiastic promotion: dressing salespeople in white to imply medical authority, for example, and distributing free formula samples to illiterate mothers. But it's questionable how well that agreement has succeeded.

9 The greater issues are how far member nations should now go in limiting manufacturers' marketing—and in limiting women's choice of how they will feed their children.

10 Will the code drive up the price of formula and make it inaccessible to women in poor nations, even those who may be unable to breast-feed? Will some nations use the code as a basis for laws that unfairly restrain free trade?

11 These are serious questions that demand further discussion by WHO and its member nations. We hope the United States won't allow its opposition to shut it out of the debate.

Democrat Chronicle
Rochester, N.Y., May 21, 1981

1 America gives the impression that it's trying to tell the world how to feed its babies.

2 Babies of the world—not just American babies—should be fed powdered formula mixed with water, not breast-fed natural milk by their mothers. That's the implication coming out of the White House.

3 The administration's intent isn't to turn the world's mothers from breast-feeding or to ignore the dangers to babies. But that's the impression it is creating by its stand, which is to fight limitation of world trade.

4 The Reagan administration has said it intends to cast its vote at the United Nations World Health Assembly in Geneva against an international code urging curtailment of marketing infant formulas in poorer nations. The Americans are expected to cast the only negative vote, with 156 countries expected to vote yes.

5 The code doesn't have the effect of a law. It spells out the real dangers to babies in those countries where water is contaminated and where people aren't aware of sterilization and other sanitary methods.

6 The intention of the code is to stop large international companies such as Nestlé from engaging in marketing promotions to increase sales of breast milk substitutes. The World Health Organization already has said that poor infant feeding is "one of the world's major problems and a serious obstacle to social and economic development."

7   Nestlé, with $12 billion annual sales across the world, operates in the developing nations of Africa, South America and Asia where the infant mortality rate is high.

8   Adoption of the U.N. code wouldn't toss Nestlé or any other company out of these countries. It would urge those countries to make people aware of the advantages of breast-feeding and the dangers of mixing formula in polluted water. The code says that each country should take action that's "appropriate to their social and legislative framework."

9   The Reagan administration opposes the United Nations code on grounds that it might have to be applied in America as well as the developing nations. Two officials in the U.S. Agency for International Development said they will quit unless the administration changes its vote.

10   One of those officials, Dr. Stephen Joseph, said that a no vote by the United States would be damaging to the health of the world's children. Joseph, head of the agency, said one million baby deaths a year are associated with artificial formula feeding.

11   Putting aside the politics and the lobbying from both sides, America is in an unenviable position at the United Nations. A negative vote will indicate that we don't have concern for children of developing nations, although we have been the leader in aid. The no vote will say that America is telling mothers not to breast-feed their babies.

12   Our position in the world is shaky enough without giving the false impression that we are telling mothers how they must feed their babies.

The Dispatch
Columbus, Ohio, May 20, 1981

1   Many adults are crying louder than babies over the refusal of the United States to join most of the rest of the world in voting for a World Health Organization code for the marketing of infant formula.

2   That is understandable. The International Code of Marketing for Breastmilk Substitutes is a well-intended, nonbinding document.

3   Its aim is to prevent advertising and promotions that entice mothers who could breast-feed their babies to use formula instead, especially where formula is very apt to be mixed with contaminated water.

4   Proponents of the code, drafted by the Joint World Health Organization/UNICEF Meeting on Infant and Young Child Feeding, say formula is misused in the Third World and thus causes thousands of cases of infant morbidity and mortality.

5   To combat this, the code recommended a ban on

- All promotion of breast milk substitutes, supplements, and feeding bottles directly to the general public
- The distribution of all free samples

> ▪ Any promotional devices which suggest the superiority of any
> product over natural mother's milk

6   No one questions that mother's milk is best when mother is eating
properly and can nurse her baby.

7   Opponents of the code, however, say it is an impractical attack on the
wrong part of the problem.

8   The opponents say there is little scientific evidence to justify the notion
that marketing practices of the baby formula industry have been a primary
cause of infant deaths in the Third World. They also say the code directs
the attack at infant formula instead of at the real killers—disease, unsanitary
living conditions, impure water and lack of nutritious diet supplements.

9   The opponents further argue that mothers who cannot or who do not
want to nurse their babies should have ready access to information on how
to supplement their babies' diets. To believe that mothers who are poor and
live in out-of-the-way villages will travel many miles to consult health
officials about how to feed babies is impractical, say opponents to the code.

10   Further, many in the infant formula industry put labels on their
products clearly stating it is not as good as mother's milk. The industry is
already policing its own ranks.

11   The United States has also taken the position the code sets a dangerous
precedent in attempting to regulate industry and the free market.

12   We are on the side of the mothers and their babies. We do not think the
Reagan administration has set a course against them.

The Oregonian
Portland, Ore., May 23, 1981

1   The United States' negative and futile vote in the World Heath
Organization infant formula controversy does not mean the Reagan
administration should be cast as the enemy of mothers and babies in the
Third World. It does indicate the administration myopically overlooked
international corporate misbehavior in a strained effort to defend free
trade principles that were not seriously at risk.

2   Former Sen. Sam Ervin, Jr., recently testified to Congress that the
WHO baby formula marketing code was a totalitarian document that
could undermine American constitutional values of free speech, free press
and free competition. Ervin's assessment is as extreme and distorted in its
way as opposing statements that portray infant formula companies as
conscienceless baby-killers.

3   The pertinent points are:

> ▪ The infant formulas of the major international producers generally
> are conceded to be beneficial substitutes if mother's milk is
> unavailable.

- The products are nutritionally superior to common local substitutes such as gruels made of water and maize, rice or millet flours, cracker-sugar-water or mashed fruits.
- The problems with the mother's milk substitutes sent into international trade (1) are not inherent in the products themselves but in their misuse, as in mixing them with polluted water or, owing to their high cost, diluting them excessively, contributing to the malnourishment of babies; and (2) are associated with sales techniques that place poor and uneducated mothers in a crossfire of slick advertising arguments they do not understand to persuade them, needlessly and often to their children's detriment, to stop breast-feeding.

4   UNICEF links misuse of the infant formula to an estimated 1 million baby deaths yearly in the Third World. There is no way to prove or disprove the estimate, but to reject the association is as absurd as denying a relationship exists between the 55 mph speed limit and reduced traffic deaths.

5   The Reagan administration's negative vote was the only one at variance with 118 affirmative votes for the model legislation to curb unnecessary formula advertising and sales. Its ideological rationale—opposition to allowing WHO to become an international equivalent of the Federal Trade Commission—is bankrupt because the rules are voluntary: Member nations are bound to follow only those portions of the code to which they do not file individual objections within 18 months. This procedural safeguard to national sovereignty also makes a mockery of the administration's contention that it would be hypocritical to urge the code on others since the United States would be unwilling to adopt all of its provisions itself.

6   What the vote has done is to leave the world with the impressions that the United States cares more about corporate health than the health of the world's children and that this administration is insensitive to the most elemental concerns of others. Those impressions may yet interfere with well-intended U.S. efforts to help developing countries.

The Hartford Courant
Hartford, Ct., May 21, 1981

1   The Reagan administration has taken an adamant and ideological stand at the meeting of the World Health Assembly in Geneva. It will not support a proposed code to limit marketing of infant formula. The code is being advocated by the World Health Organization (WHO), the United Nations Children's Fund, and most national health authorities.

2   Perhaps the most distressing aspect of the controversy is that how a mother feeds her child has become a political and ideological issue. This is, or should be, a health matter. The misuse of bottle formula affects the lives of millions of children around the world, especially in developing countries.

3   Nearly 100 governments were willing to endorse the conclusions and recommendations of the international health community. The only, and embarrassing, exception was the United States.

4   The code, to encourage the "protection and promotion of breast-feeding," prohibits direct advertising of formula to mothers. Free samples are not to be distributed to mothers or health workers, and companies are forbidden from having their sales personnel dress like nurses in white uniforms or to pay commissions based on sales.

5   The Reagan White House claims it does not want WHO to be turned into an "international Federal Trade Commission." The code would interfere in free market economics, according to the ideologues in Washington.

6   The code, however, is meant to be implemented through governments, legislatures, and regulatory agencies of individual countries. The code is a model, which could be adopted, discarded, or revised by each nation. No nation would be forced to accept it. Governments already regulate food labeling, and how food should be transported, stored, and sold.

7   Clever and unscrupulous marketing in the past has taken its toll. Mothers have been given free samples of the powdered formula until their own milk supply dried up. Manufacturers' representatives dressed in nurse uniforms have dispensed the product freely and authoritatively.

8   Mothers then were forced to depend on the formula. Estimates are that millions of babies have died when formula was mixed with contaminated water or overdiluted to save money.

9   Even the infant formula manufacturers admit that a mother's milk is superior to any substitute. It has nutritional advantages and also helps immunize babies against disease.

10   But the Reagan administration has bought the corporate arguments that no evidence exists to link formula use to infant mortality and that companies should be allowed to sell their products, free from government intervention.

11   Even though most governments are willing to accept the proposed code, their responsibilities do not end there. Governments that decide to discourage formula feeding should also help make breast-feeding a realistic option. The code in that sense does not go far enough.

12   Infant formula sales have made their greatest inroads in urban areas where women must work away from home and the family plot. Facilities must be provided so these women can nurse their children. An alternative

would be to have governments distribute premixed formula free or at affordable cost to eliminate the hazards of bottle feeding.

13   The code, which the Reagan administration opposes for ideological reasons, is only a partial but necessary step toward protecting the health and welfare of mothers and children.

SUGGESTIONS FOR WRITING

1. First try to put these editorials into useful categories. "Pro" and "con" are two broad categories that come readily to mind, but within each of these you may find other criteria for distinguishing subgroups. After arriving at your categories, write an essay about the range of opinion in this country about the U.S. vote, classifying the editorial responses and analyzing the reasons underlying the differences in opinion. Conclude by stating and defending your own view on the subject.

2. If your library subscribes to the periodical *Editorials on File,* you will find in it collections of editorials like these on a great number of controversial issues. Choose an issue that interests you, briefly describe the nature and background of that issue, and write an analytic essay describing, classifying, and explaining the editorial responses from around the country. Conclude by stating and defending your own view on the subject.

JOAN KONNER

From *"Women in the Marketplace"*

Joan Konner is Dean of the Columbia University School of Journalism. This selection is an excerpt from a speech she delivered to the New Jersey Press Women's Association in Paterson, New Jersey, on May 5, 1990.

1   Last fall the Columbia Journalism School Alumni chose the topic "Is News Getting Too Soft?" for its annual fall meeting. The subject, and the title, were picked by one of the men. Of course. "Hard" and "soft" are terms only a man would have invented. It goes with the sports metaphor of most news. Who's winning? Who's losing? In politics, business, culture. Who's up? Who's down? If you're winning, you're "hard" news. If you're losing, you're a "soft" feature for the inside pages.

2   I didn't know exactly what the title — "Is News Getting Too Soft" — meant. It turned out there was concern about changes brought about by different perspectives in the newsrooms—from women and minorities— that are beginning to alter the definition of news.

3   Soma Golden, national editor for The New York *Times,* an alumna of our School, gave her analysis of the change in the front page of her paper. On a given day in 1959 there were 18 stories, all hard news. On the same day in 1969, there were 23 stories, again all hard news. By 1979, the format had changed so there were fewer stories, but even so, what was called "new" news stories made it to the front page along with hard news. In 1989, the trend continued with as many as three "new" news stories mingled with dateline news. A new story was a series on care of the elderly or Public School 94 in the Bronx or an analysis of social trends. The position of these stories in The *Times* tells us that the distinction between soft news and hard news is blurring.

4   Is this happening because there are more women in the newsrooms?

5   Probably, but who knows? Clearly a shift of values and priorities is taking place.

6   Are women better equipped to cover this "new" news? It is possible we are. The psychologist Carol Gilligan, in her book, *In A Different Voice,* described a difference between the moral development of men and women.

7   Women, she says, develop an ethic of care, an empathy based on their identification with the primary parent, usually the mother. Women define themselves in terms of relationship and responsibility.

8   Men develop an ethic of justice as they separate from the mother. They define themselves in terms of difference, position and hierarchy. If we accept this, then I think we can assume the responsibility that comes with

our capacity to adopt a broader perspective and show the human, caring side of the news.

9   The feminine sensibility is growing everywhere in our culture today—in literature, in art, in history, politics, and the media. It coincides with concerns about the environment, a growing awareness of Mother Earth, as our life support system. There is talk of the Gaia principle, a world view that says we are all part of one living body. We find the principle expressed in the mythology of the Goddess, in which there is also a revival of interest today. The Goddess was worshipped for thousands of years in agrarian, egalitarian societies in which there was a love of life, of nature and beauty.

10   There seems at this time to be a great hunger in the American culture for the values of the goddess—the values of life, generation, and creation. There seems to be a growing reverence for nature, for a collective spirit, and relationship based on the awareness of the interconnectedness of life. We are becoming more concerned that our competitive Western culture that developed along the lines of the Darwinian principle of the survival of the fittest may have been a life-supporting pattern for one period of human evolution but it may no longer be a life-supporting pattern for another—this one. Human intelligence creates systems to protect human life. Today those very systems are threatening it—industrial development which threatens the environment; nuclear weapons that threaten all of life. In such a world, those with a wider perspective and greater awareness are turning out to be the fittest.

11   We are coming around a bend, and we realize there is a need for other values, values of collaboration, community, care. These are the values that used to belong to the private sphere of home and family. But we are beginning to see these values in the workplace and in public life as well. One hypothesis is that women, as they succeed in the marketplace, retain what is valuable from what used to be considered the domestic sphere and bring that wider perspective into view. It does seem some of us—women and men—have had enough of the instinct for the jugular. I think that women in position of power—in politics, public service, and the media—are helping to make that difference.

STUDY QUESTIONS

1. In the first two paragraphs, the author is somewhat hesitant in defining "hard" and "soft" news and the difference between them. Using the context of the article as a whole, try to define these two terms so that the difference is apparent.
2. How does the term "'new' news" relate to the terms "hard" and "soft" news?

3. Do you agree with the factual contention in paragraph 3 that news has gotten softer since 1969? If you wanted to seek further empirical testing of this claim, how would you go about it?

4. Konner offers two levels of causal explanation in this essay: one arguing that the change in the definition of news has been caused by the heightened presence of women and minorities in the newsroom; the other that women's perspective on news differs from men's because the two sexes follow different paths of moral development. Are these two causal explanations sound? How would you go about testing them?

SUGGESTION FOR WRITING

1. Briefly summarize Konner's view about the role of "the feminine sensibility" in our culture today. Then discuss its validity by referring either to examples of "women in the marketplace" that you know of or to a few of the female authors represented in this anthology.

2. What counts as "news" or "hard news"? Select one issue of a newspaper from the past two weeks and find in it any two articles whose relative importance seems to you to have been reversed by editorial choices such as placement on the front page or the "living" section, size of headlines, or the like. Explain why you feel the editors should have assigned reverse priorities.

KATHERINE FULTON

From *"Writing and Liberty in a Consumer Culture"*

The following is an excerpt from a speech to the North Carolina Women Writers' Conference on March 15, 1992. The speech in its entirety was reprinted in the *AWP Chronicle* 24 (May, 1992), page 1.

1   Nearly 10 years ago, after working several years for the Greensboro daily newspapers, I faced a dilemma in my own life. I had become a journalist because I wanted to learn about the world, about how power is exercised, by whom and why. I had come of age after Vietnam and Watergate, when journalists had helped shape this nation's history. I believed, and believe still, in the power of facts. All the opinions in the world about Vietnam couldn't match the pictures that were brought into Americans' living rooms. And no matter how many columnists and liberals hated Richard Nixon, their collective opinions about his behavior mattered not, compared to the power of the facts journalists revealed about the Watergate burglary and coverup.

2   By 1982, I had learned my craft, as journalists like to say. I had learned how to write and edit news stories—how to gather facts, test my assumptions, probe conventional interpretations, be suspicious of the way ideology can manipulate and distort truth. I had been promoted, anointed at the age of twenty-six, to be the only female editor among some eleven middle-aged men running a medium-sized newspaper. And I learned a little too much about how easily influenced I was both by my environment and my own ambition.

3   I had begun to develop my own ideas about how news should be defined, how more diverse voices should be included in the debate. But I had also begun to learn about the subtle ways my own private commitments were shaped by my public environment, by the fact that I was trying to get along and get ahead in a corporation. I began to wonder who I would be and what I would believe if and when I ever accumulated enough power to enact my agenda.

4   Now, I happen to think that the world will be a better place when more women have more power, and I applaud the fact that North Carolina's two largest newspapers now have female managing editors. But I was afraid I was moving too far too fast, that my spine wasn't yet strong enough to resist the pull of my own ambition. I had also learned that as they say, the power of the press belongs to him who owns one—that no matter how much power you have as an editor, you usually don't have the power that

matters the most, the power to set the profit margin. In a typical American newspaper, at least before the recession set in, the difference between say, a 10 percent profit margin, and a 15 percent one can be the difference between a mediocre newspaper and a great one.

5   So I jumped ship and joined forces with two men in Durham who wanted to start a small alternative newspaper, two '60s activists who were the antithesis of corporate businessmen, and as such, were likely to do battle with my journalist's skepticism while testing my political spine. I figured if I was ever going to do anything crazy, I might as well do it in my twenties. And believe me, everybody I knew thought we were crazy, believed that six months later we would be out of luck and out of business.

6   Nearly a decade and 300 issues later, this week, I found in my files the forty-page "Working Paper for a new newspaper" that we wrote in November 1981. I smiled — a tired, wry smile — as I spotted, for the first time in years, our manifesto leading off the first page, a quote from *New York Times* columnist Russell Baker about the state of American society. "We are," he wrote, "in the hands of men who make no music and have no dream."

7   Here we were, the three of us, daring to dream of the kind of newspaper the South had never seen, an alternative newspaper committed to journalistic excellence, social justice, and commercial success. We pledged ourselves to serious, thoughtful print journalism, twice a month, just as *USA Today* and CNN were emerging. We devoted ourselves to selling subscriptions all over North Carolina even though the newspaper business had become the business of selling advertising, targeted to specific local audiences. And in the new Reagan era, on Jesse Helms's turf, we gave ourselves to rallying the weakened opposition. We wanted to write about private lives as well as public agendas, to bring a rich array of voices into the open by breaking down the barriers between the academy and the general audience, between professional writers and non-professionals, between reporters and activists. We wanted to report facts about friends and foes, not propaganda, to present the news honestly in a context that would allow people to make sense out of it.

8   We were engaged in the kind of imaginative act any writer engages in. We were trying to create something out of nothing. We were trying to succeed in the world while changing it. We were trying to disturb the peace.

9   We had no idea what we were getting into; I guess if we had, we wouldn't have been able to do it. For our courage was rooted in our ignorance.

10   Let me give you a few examples of what we didn't know about how difficult it would be to claim a new media voice in North Carolina.

11   We didn't know the commercial consequences of simple, editorial decisions, like putting a photograph of a black, female textile worker on

our cover. The woman, who had injured her arms from repetitive motion, adorned the front of the 20,000 issues we distributed free in Greensboro in the late summer of 1983. It was our first issue in Greensboro; we were breaking into a new market, making a first impression. And we never recovered. The story may have been true, its facts accurate, its point important. But to the Greensboro retail establishment—the people we had to convince to buy ads in our paper—we were a communist newspaper for blacks. Two years and $75,000 in losses later, we decided to pull out of Greensboro. These kinds of commercial pressures have been a constant, never more so than during the Gulf War last year. Integrity can exact a price.

12   But so too, of course, can compromising integrity. We didn't understand the ways we *would* have to give in to certain relentless commercial pressures in order to survive. If you read *The Independent,* you have seen this evolution, nowhere more prominently than in our classified ad section, where for the past two years we have been publishing one or two pages of "sex ads" each issue. These are the 1–900 classified ads, made possible by new technology and attractive as safe sex in the age of AIDS. You dial a number, and pay to hear, as the ads proclaim, "Live Virgins who won't let you down," or "X-rated fantasies." Many people are offended by these ads, and feel that they are degrading and exploitative, especially to women. Some readers have given up on us altogether because we publish them. They can't understand why we would demean ourselves for the sake of a buck.

13   Well folks, it ain't that simple. As you might imagine, we've had passionate battles within our staff, and in our pages about the moral and practical issues these sex ads raise. For journalists, there are clear free speech/censorship issues that cannot easily be pushed aside: After all, no one was being forced to look at the pages, and some of our readers use the ads, otherwise the advertisers wouldn't buy them. Why should some of our readers tell others of our readers what to do with their private lives?

14   But even more important to us, it was a question of balancing one kind of hurt against another. Those ads paid the salaries of 5 people at *The Independent* last year; they helped a very fragile business that has never made a profit survive during a recession, so that it might continue to provide meaningful jobs for twenty-two people and publish investigative reporting on slum lords, and hazardous waste incinerators and creepy politicians.

15   When does the means justify the ends? When have you compromised too much, given up something valuable, like your principles, or your reputation, that you can never have back? How do you know? What does it feel like?

didn't want to live on the margins, powerless. We wanted to join the fight, to swell the ranks of the dissenters…by the mere fact that we're together.

17   But we didn't know how much it would hurt to be under attack, fairly constantly, from both sides of the line — for maintaining our principles here, sacrificing them to gain strength there. Always, always, it seems, the letter writers know they would do a better job drawing the line. And maybe they could, though few of them have ever had the guts or the fortitude to live on the line, year after year.

18   These are the kinds of things you face when you decide to disturb the peace.

STUDY QUESTIONS

1. Apart from her desire to join *The Independent,* what motives did the author have for leaving the Greensboro dailies, where her career was doing well? (See paragraphs 3–4.)
2. In what ways did "commercial pressures" influence editorial policies on *The Independent?*
3. Given the kind of newspaper *The Independent* is, why do you suppose commercial pressures were particularly strong during the Gulf War of 1991, and what form do you think these pressures took?
4. Review the arguments for and against *The Independent*'s accepting "sex ads." Do you agree with the editor that the benefits of this policy decision outweighed the ethical costs?
5. How do Katherine Fulton's views on the role of women in the press compare with Joan Konner's in the previous selection?

SUGGESTION FOR WRITING

Write a concise essay about some situation in which you did something you found ethically distasteful though you still believe the end justified the means. Your essay will be interesting insofar as you can make as clear and emphatic as possible the wrongful aspects of your behavior and yet argue as convincingly as possible that this behavior was justified.

JOHN CORRY

TV News and the Neutrality Principle

John Corry, formerly a television critic for the *New York Times,* now teaches at the College of Communications at Boston University and is at work on a book about the media. This article appeared in the May 1991 issue of *Commentary.*

1 Almost unremarked, we have passed a turning point in journalism, particularly as journalism is practiced on television. Exactly when this happened is unclear—although by the 1980's there were hints—but American broadcasts from Baghdad while American war-planes flew overhead finally made it certain. The old journalistic ideal of objectivity— the sense that reporting involves the gathering and presentation of relevant facts after appropriate critical analysis—has given way to a more porous standard. According to this new standard, reporters may—indeed should—stand midway between two opposing sides, even when one of the two sides is their own.

2 This is no academic matter. Neutrality is now a principle of American journalism, explicitly stated and solemnly embraced. After Dan Rather of CBS reported from Saudi Arabia last August that "our tanks are arriving," the Washington *Post* gave him a call: wasn't it jingoistic, perhaps xenophobic, to say "our tanks"? Rather apologized and promised he would never say such a thing again. He should have known better in the first place. After all, Mike Wallace, Rather's CBS colleague, made the new standard clear well before the Gulf crisis started. At a conference on the military and the press at Columbia University on October 31, 1987, Wallace announced that it would be appropriate for him as a journalist to accompany enemy troops into battle, even if they ambushed American soldiers.* And during the war itself, Bernard Shaw of CNN, explaining why he had refused to be debriefed by American officials after he left Baghdad, declared that reporters must be "neutral."

3 As it happens, Shaw once said that the late Edward R. Murrow of CBS was his great hero. Indeed, a whole generation of television newsmen

---

* A Marine colonel at the conference, George M. Connell, had a different perspective. "I feel utter contempt," he said when responding to Wallace, who had been supported in his declaration of neutrality, even if hesitantly, by Peter Jennings of ABC. "Two days later they're both [Wallace and Jennings] walking off my hilltop: they're 200 yards away, and they get ambushed, and they're lying there wounded—and they're going to expect that I send Marines up there to get them.... But I'll do it, and that's what makes me so contemptuous of them. And Marines will die going to get a couple of journalists." Colonel Connell was not being fanciful. When the correspondent Bob Simon vanished with his crew near the Kuwait border, CBS called the Pentagon to help.

regard Murrow as their hero, invoking his name every time they give one another an award. They ought to go back now and listen to his broadcasts. In the Battle of Britain and other engagements, Murrow was outspoken about which side he was on, and he was never a neutral reporter. It would have been unthinkable for him in 1944, say, to make his way to Berlin, check into the Adlon Hotel, and pass on pronouncements by Hitler.

4   Still, this is the New World Order, and rules everywhere are changing. The great place to be for television journalists this winter was the Al Rashid Hotel in Baghdad, in the basement of which, according to the Pentagon, was a command-and-control center, although the journalists holed up there were (neutrally) unable to find it.

5   Colleagues did complain when Peter Arnett of CNN stayed on in Baghdad after other journalists had been expelled; the complaints, however, were not so much about whether CNN (which has outlets in 104 countries) was acting as a broadcasting service for Saddam Hussein as about whether it was taking advantage of its competitors. When CBS, ABC, and NBC got their own correspondents into Baghdad, the complaints ended.

6   "You must avoid the appearance of cheerleading," Ed Turner, the vice president of CNN, said during the war. "We are, after all, at CNN, a global network." Turner, no relation to his boss Ted Turner, although obviously they think alike, went on to stress that CNN wanted to be fair to *all* nations. But the truth was that CNN had a mission. Speaking from Baghdad, Arnett told us what it was:

> *I know it's Ted Turner's vision to get CNN around the world, and we can prevent events like this from occurring in the future. I know that is my wish after covering wars all over and conflicts all over the world. I mean, I am sick of wars, and I am here because maybe my contribution will somehow lessen the hostilities, if not this time, maybe next time.*

7   Old-style journalists grew sick of wars, too, although few thought their presence would prevent them. New-style neutral journalists, however, have their conceits, and the constraints that bind fellow citizens are not necessarily binding on them. At the Columbia conference, Mike Wallace was asked if a "higher duty as an American citizen" did not take precedence over the duty of a journalist. "No," Wallace replied, "you don't have that higher duty—no, no." But if a neutral journalist does not owe a higher duty to citizenship, where does his higher duty lie? Old-style journalists seldom thought about that. A story was a story, and a reporter went out and reported it. Our age is self-consciously moral, though, and higher duties now weigh on us all. Arnett was clear about his higher duty, even without being asked. "I don't work for the national interest," he asserted in another broadcast from Baghdad. "I work for the public interest."

8   And it may be here that neutral journalism flies apart and breaks up into shards. What is this public interest, and who determines it, anyway? The

national interest is determined by consensus and people are elected to serve it. The recent consensus was that the U.S. national interest lay in driving Iraq out of Kuwait and decimating its war machine. But the public interest is amorphous, and usually it turns out to be closer to the interest of its advocates than to that of the public.

9 Consider the performances in Baghdad. The correspondents there could not gather relevant facts, and if they had tried, they would have been expelled, or worse, from Iraq. What the correspondents did was listen to government-controlled Baghdad Radio (with a translator, presumably; none of the correspondents seemed to speak Arabic), tour Baghdad neighborhoods (with government guides and monitors), and, in the fashion of journalists everywhere, pick up what they could from other correspondents they met.

10 There is not much chance to do real reporting in a situation like that, and most of the time, one suspects, the correspondents knew it. Anchormen pressed them on questions they could not possibly answer. Tell me, Peter (or Bill, or Tom, or Betsy), an anchor would ask, how do Iraqis feel about this statement from President Bush? And Peter (or Bill, or Tom, or Betsy), from a cubicle in a hotel, an eight-hour time difference away, in a country whose language he did not understand, would reply as best he could.

11 The most accurate reply would have been, "I don't know," but you cannot say that very often and keep your job in television. So the reporting from Baghdad inevitably turned into an exercise by the correspondent in appearing to know something when he probably did not know much, while bearing in mind that he could not offend the host government.

12 Obvious questions arise: what if a correspondent in Baghdad had discovered something the host government did not want revealed? What if a correspondent had uncovered news about a party purge, or an outbreak of civil disorder, or the whereabouts of Saddam Hussein? Or—and this is not far-fetched—what if a correspondent, being bused from Baghdad to Basra, had come across an artillery battery with shells loaded with nerve gas and pointed toward U.S. Marines? The profession was uncomfortable with questions like that. Nonetheless, they could not be entirely ignored, and obliquely the correspondents in Baghdad addressed them. Were they, for example, holding back information?

13 "There are lots of things that you can't report," Betsy Aaron of CBS acknowledged. "If you do, you are asked to leave the country, and I don't think we want to do that. I think you do a very valuable service reporting, no matter what you are allowed to report."

14 No matter what you are allowed to report? Imagine Ed Murrow saying that. Neutral journalism assumes that what the reporter reports is not nearly as important as the fact that the reporter is there to report it.

Journalism becomes a symbolic act, distinguished by form and not content. Operate under that standard, and censorship will not be a problem. Here is Bill Blakemore, speaking over ABC from Baghdad:

> *The script process is very normal for wartime, I would say. We write our scripts. We find one of the censors who's down in the hotel lobby, and we show it to the censor who reads it, and sometimes there's a slight change of a word here or there. Very often you may say something you didn't realize would touch a sensitivity, but there's not been any kind of heavy censorship in my experience here so far. It's a fairly easy understanding we have.*

15   Clearly, the "fairly easy understanding" between correspondents and one of the world's most repressive governments meant that the correspondents simply censored themselves. If they were uncertain how to do this, they could always get help. Here is Blakemore again, in an exchange with his anchorman, Peter Jennings:

16   "Bill, are you operating on a completely uncensored basis?" Jennings whimsically asked.

17   No, Blakemore responded, "we got organized just now and managed to get somebody over here to listen and make sure we don't have any military or strategic information."

18   Neutral status means that a journalist does not report objectively; he reports selectively. Arnett, visiting what had been Baghdad's two main power plants, now destroyed by bombs and missiles, spoke of "relentless attacks on civilian installations." He did not mention that those installations had been covered in camouflage paint. When he reported on the famous target that the Pentagon said was a biological-weapons factory and the Iraqis claimed was a "baby-milk plant" — "innocent enough from what we could see," observed Arnett — he did not notice the camouflage there, either. (Visiting German peace activists, of all people, did notice it and talked about it when they got back to Europe.) After being taken to another bombed-out site, Arnett reported that "while we were there, a distraught woman shouted insults at the press and vented anger at the West." Then we saw and heard the woman, who was standing next to a crater. "All of you are responsible, all of you, bombing the people for the sake of oil," she screamed in perfect English. She also turned up on French television speaking perfect French. Several days later, a CNN anchor in Atlanta identified her as an employee of the Iraqi Foreign Ministry.

19   Arnett, an old hand at covering wars and seeing through propaganda, presumably knew that when the "distraught woman" was shouting. Surely he at least noticed that her jogging suit had "United Nations" printed down one leg. A neutral journalist must narrow his vision and report with one eye closed.

20   The Baghdad correspondents, as individuals or as a group, most likely

will sweep this year's television-journalism prizes. A claque formed almost immediately for Arnett, heaping encomiums on his head (especially after his patriotism was questioned by Senator Alan Simpson). He was a "dukes-up guy," "brave" and "independent," and an ornament to his profession. In the true spirit of neutral journalism, government-controlled Iraqi newsmen joined the claque, too. "The Iraqi press wrote favorably about me," Arnett told Larry King, the CNN talk-show host, who interviewed him when the war was over. Arnett also said he had become a "third-world hero."

21   Certainly Arnett and the other Baghdad correspondents displayed physical bravery in placing themselves in a war zone; and they did report, loosely speaking, to the best of their abilities. On the other hand, the correspondents as individuals were incidental. If there had not been Peter, Bill, Tom, or Betsy, there would have been John, Morton, Arthur, or Susan, and the "reporting" would have been much the same. For them, the great thing was that anyone was in Baghdad at all, and it did not matter that a great many other Americans were disturbed. When a Washington *Post*-ABC News poll asked if we should bomb a communications center in the Baghdad hotel where the reporters were staying, 62 percent of the respondents said we should issue a warning and then bomb even if the reporters were still there; 5 percent said we should forget the warning and just go ahead with the bombing.

22   In fact, the press as a whole did not come off well in the war. Television tarred more reliable print, and polls showed a huge dislike of the media. The essential reason was captured by the headline over a story in *Time* about disenchantment with the press: "Just Whose Side Are They On?" The "they," of course, were journalists, and simply by raising the question *Time* went a long way toward providing the answer, even though the story itself predictably took a different position: "The attacks from both sides probably mean that the press is situated just about where it usually is: in the even-handed middle ground."

23   Well, perhaps, but the even-handed middle ground becomes an increasingly elusive place in the television age. There were no American reporters in Kuwait when Iraq salted and pillaged that country; it was not in Iraq's interest to have them there. It was in Iraq's interest, however, to have reporters in Baghdad; when the war was over, Iraq kicked them out. Could the press have found a more even-handed middle ground here? Why, yes. It could have insisted that if it was going to be in Baghdad it must also be in Kuwait. Obviously, no network did insist on that.

24   The principal signs of television's search for a middle ground were "cleared by censor" titles; they were even-handedly applied to film approved by either American or Iraqi censors, showing skepticism of both sides. But the new neutral journalism also went a long way toward

suggesting which side it was the more skeptical of. As long ago as last August, Michael Gartner, the president of NBC News, in a piece for the op-ed page of the *Wall Street Journal,* had alerted us to danger: "Here's something should know about the war that's going on in the Gulf: much of the news that you read or hear or see is being censored."

25   Actually, the American part of the war had not begun yet, but that did not deter Gartner. He went on to quote, disdainfully, from a list of things the Pentagon did not want us to know. These included:

1 Number of troops

2 Number of aircraft

3 Number of other equipment (e.g., artillery, tanks, radars, trucks, water "buffaloes," etc.)

4 Names of military installations/geographic locations of U.S. military units in Saudi Arabia

5 Information regarding future operations

6 Information concerning security precautions at military installations in Saudi Arabia

26   And so on, ending with "*9.* Photography that would show level of security at military installations in Saudi Arabia" and "*10.* Photography that would reveal the name of specific locations of military forces or installations."

27   While it would be easy to dismiss Gartner as merely frivolous, it may be assumed that his peculiar ideas about censorship and war and the military and the press got passed on to his reporters. Surely they were reflected in an NBC special, "America: The Realities of War," when Arthur Kent, the NBC correspondent in Saudi Arabia, took on Pete Williams, the Pentagon spokesman in Washington.

28   "Why are you trying to put your hands so far into our business?" Kent asked peevishly. "We're not trying to tell you how to run the war. We're just trying to cover it. Why do you want to control us so completely?"

29   Williams did not mention Gartner's laundry list of complaints, although if he had he would have made a reasonable argument not just for controlling the press but for banning it altogether. Williams did not say either that some of the television coverage was so goofy the Pentagon might have thought its higher duty was to straighten it out. In an interview when the war was over, General H. Norman Schwarzkopf remarked that he had "basically turned the television off in the headquarters very early on because the reporting was so inaccurate I did not want my people to get confused."

30   On the same program in which he attacked Williams, Kent also offered a choice specimen of the reporting General Schwarzkopf probably had

31   "Saddam Hussein is a cunning man and nowhere does he show that more clearly than on a battlefield when he's under attack," Kent told Faith Daniels, who was anchoring the special.

32   "And that, Arthur, really seems to be this administration's greatest miscalculation," Daniels replied.

33   "That's right, Faith," Kent continued. "He is ruthless, but more than ruthless. In the past eleven days, he's surprised us. He's shown us a capable military mind, and he still seems to know exactly what he's doing."

34   With "reporting" like that, is it any wonder that 57 percent of the respondents in one poll said the military should exercise more, not less, control over the press, and that 88 percent in another poll supported censorship? For, in addition to the other problems—moral, political, and professional—it has created, the neutrality principle has evidently turned many otherwise intelligent people into fools.

STUDY QUESTIONS

1. In the first two paragraphs, Corry describes two opposing ideals of journalism: "objectivity" and "neutrality." In his view, what is the difference between them?
2. In paragraph 18, Corry says that a "neutral" journalist does not report "objectively," but rather "selectively." Yet, in the opening paragraph, he had said that the more traditional, "objective" journalist reported "relevant facts after appropriate critical analysis." How in Corry's view do these two modes of selectivity differ? Do you find the distinction valid?
3. Explain the distinction between the "public interest" and the "national interest" that is drawn in paragraphs 7 and 8.
4. Is Corry making or implying a proposal for the ethical behavior of journalists? If so, what guidelines are suggested by his article?

SUGGESTION FOR WRITING

Paragraphs 7 and 8 show that Peter Arnett and John Corry disagree about the desirability of the journalist's allegiance to the "public interest" as opposed to "the national interest." Write a short paper defining these two terms in a way that clarifies the difference between them. Then describe where you stand on this point of contention and justify your view by reference to news coverage of the 1991 Gulf War or some other news event.

DANIEL HALLIN

TV's Clean Little War

Daniel Hallin is Associate Professor of Communication at the University of California at San Diego and author of *The "Uncensored War": The Media and Vietnam*. This article appeared in the May 1991 issue of *The Bulletin of the Atomic Scientists*.

1   In the introduction to *Living-Room War,* a book about television coverage of the Vietnam War, Michael Arlen wrote: "I can't say I completely agree with people who think that when battle scenes are brought into the living room the hazards of war are necessarily made 'real' to the civilian audience. It seems to me that by the same process they are also made less 'real'—diminished, in part, by the physical size of the television screen, which, for all the industry's advances, still shows one picture of men three inches tall shooting at other men three inches tall, and trivialized, or at least tamed, by the enveloping cozy alarums of the household."

2   But Arlen knew that what diminished and prettified television's portrayal of Vietnam was more than the size of the television screen and its location in the domestic space of the home. The nature of television journalism and its relation to its audience, its military sources, and the wider American culture also pushed strongly in this direction. Americans went into Vietnam with a romantic view of war derived largely from the representation of World War II in popular culture. For readers of the *New York Times* and the *Washington Post* the war may have been above all a political policy, part of the global struggle between East and West; television accepted the political rationale, but its focus was different. On television, war was an arena of individual action, a place where men— there was no room for women—could show courage and mastery in a way that was rarely possible in everyday life.

3   Eventually Vietnam forced a more sober view of war into American culture. *Combat* gave way to *M*A*S*H,* and *The Green Berets* to *Full Metal Jacket.* Older images lived on in such films as *Rambo* but they no longer dominated the culture. But television coverage of the war in the Persian Gulf has brought back much of the guts and glory tradition. And this may prove one of the second living-room war's greatest costs: that it restored war to a place of pride in American culture.

4   Five interconnected images dominated television coverage of the Gulf War:

5   ▪ **Technology.** Surely the most powerful images of this war were of triumphant technology: smart-bomb videos, tanks rolling across the desert, cruise missiles flaming into the sky in a graceful arc, the homely

desert, cruise missiles flaming into the sky in a graceful arc, the homely but lovable A-10 Warthog. "Deadly streaks of fire in the night sky," ABC's Sam Donaldson reported on January 21. "A Scud missile is headed for Dhahran in eastern Saudi Arabia. And rising to intercept it, a U.S. Patriot missile. Bull's eye! No more Scud!"

6   The pictures were compelling: it is hard to imagine better video than the explosion of a mine-clearing line charge. And the technical accomplishments were stunning enough to impress journalists, as when CNN anchor David French was "honored" by the air force with a ride on an F-15E Strike Eagle and gushed about its high-tech effectiveness.

7   The pictures would be different if the cameras were on the ground, where the bombs landed. But in a technological war, especially one in which most of the dying is on one side, this is rarely possible. Even if Iraq had granted the media full freedom to cover the war from its side, journalists would not be interested in experiencing a B-52 attack first-hand. So technological war appears "clean" most of the time, more so when both sides exercise military restrictions on coverage.

8   Network coverage of the aftermath of the Gulf War, when journalists finally could see its human results, often seemed tamer than print coverage, which was full of references to charred and dismembered bodies. In Vietnam, self-censorship was also significant. Network policies limited the use of the most graphic footage, particularly of American casualties.

9   ▪ **Experts.** These appeared in two guises. First there were the military briefers, standing calm and assured before the clamoring throng of reporters. Their role was much more important in the Gulf War than in Vietnam, where the daily press briefing in Saigon was grist for wire stories but rarely shown on television. It is not hard to see why—military control of the media in the Gulf, especially restrictions on movement, gave journalists there few other channels of information. In Vietnam, journalists were free to visit any unit that would have them and to travel without an official escort. In the Gulf, until the last days of the war when the pool arrangement broke down, small numbers of reporters were shepherded around under carefully controlled conditions. The military managed the media much as a modern presidential campaign does, releasing carefully controlled doses of information, setting up carefully planned photo opportunities, and minimizing reporters' access to any other source of information.

10   It is interesting that despite complaints and finally evasion by reporters in the field, major news organizations declined to join in legal challenges to the rules. The networks may well have been so wary of appearing adversarial that they were happy to be able to put on the screen, "Cleared by the U.S. Military."

11   The tightness of these restrictions was by no means purely a matter of

protecting military security. According to a number of reviews of the press in Vietnam, including studies by the Twentieth Century Fund and the army's Office of Military History, the looser rules that prevailed in Vietnam worked well for that purpose. Journalists in Vietnam accepted guidelines for restricting sensitive information as a condition of accreditation to accompany troops in the field. But they neither had to submit their copy for censorship nor travel in pools organized and supervised by the military.

12   The networks also had their own experts, retired military and Defense Department officials for the most part, whose function was to put the war "into context." This meant that the war was seen from the strategist's point of view, in essentially technical terms sanitized from reference to violence or death. "We have the initiative in the air," reported ABC consultant Tony Cordesman on January 21. Cordesman is a military specialist who has also served as an aide to Republican Sen. John McCain of Arizona. "We can use our aircraft as long as we think we can keep finding valuable targets and killing them before we commit the land forces." (Killing targets is different from killing people.) "We're going to wait...as we let air power take what is an inevitable toll and we can undermine and almost destroy the cohesiveness of Iraq's forces." Cordesman stumbled for a moment before saying "destroy," as though he were uncomfortable with a word that connoted violence.

13   Journalists quickly picked up the language. "From the air, sea, and with artillery they pounded Iraqi troops and armor concentrations in southern Kuwait for three hours," NBC's Tom Brokaw said on February 12. "It was the real thing, yet it was also a useful test of the complexities of mounting an all-out attack with so many forces from many different nations." Again there is the parallel with coverage of presidential elections, the focus on candidates' "game plans" which keeps journalists clear of divisive questions of ideology and policy. The parallel to sports reporting is also clear: one of the most prominent visuals of the Gulf War was the computerized "chalkboard," used to diagram military strategy as it is used to diagram football plays.

14   ▪ **The fighting men and women.** On August 23 Dan Rather opened the *CBS Evening News* broadcast with a report on the First Tactical Air Wing of the U.S. Air Force: "These are the warplanes and these are the fighting men and women who are the heart of the massive U.S. military buildup in the area. We'll show it to you up close and from the inside on tonight's broadcast." The central characters in television's drama of war, in the Gulf as in Vietnam, were the American soldiers, and their moods set the tone of the reporting.

15   Troops went into Vietnam with high morale, and the gung-ho attitude pervaded the living-room war in the early years. Later, as the troops began to sour on the war, television's image of the war became more negative. In

the Gulf crisis the reverse was true. During the troop buildup, soldiers in the Gulf would often be heard expressing doubts about the prospect of war. Once policymakers decided to go to war, however, the troops put aside doubts and focused on doing their job. "Can't wait to do it," said one marine in a typical report on the impending ground war (CBS, January 28). "This is what we have been training for—myself for 13 years." Television reflected and celebrated their enthusiasm, and the war came to be identified with them.

16   War brings out "valor and grit," in the melodramatic phrase Rather invoked repeatedly the night President Bush announced a cease-fire. But it also brings out hatred—more intensely in a war like Vietnam which had substantial casualties on both sides—and cold indifference to human life. But television cannot speak of this other side of the war culture, because it would show disrespect to the fighting men and women.

17   A gunner on the battleship *Wisconsin* said with a big laugh to CBS correspondent Eric Engberg on February 9: "The 16-inch is of course a great counter to the other guy's firepower weapon. It's an anti-materiel weapon. And we prefer shooting at their artillery, their structures. Don't waste the 16-inch on people; you can do that with other things!" But his attitude had to be assimilated to the image of skill and bravery, and its moral implications passed over.

18   There is an important connection between the images of the fighting men and women and technology. The troops took pride in their mastery of technology, and their skill was an important theme in news coverage. But mastering technology generally means accepting its logic, and the soldiers often added to the chorus of sanitized, technological language.

19   ▪ **The enemy.** War reporting usually turns the enemy into the incarnation of absolute evil, and one of the reasons the Gulf War played so well in the media is that Saddam Hussein's regime fit the image better than most. Nevertheless, the tendency to portray war as good versus evil distorted Gulf coverage in important ways.

20   The enemy is considered to practice a kind of evil we could never practice; his actions and ours belong to different moral orders. Reporting on the release of oil into the Gulf, Alan Pizzey of CBS said on January 28: "This is the first time in history that nature has been a direct target." He forgot that the United States defoliated nearly five million acres of forest during the Vietnam War, spraying almost half of South Vietnam's forest area at least once.

21   Although the presence of television cameras in Iraq added a new dimension to this second living-room war, the effect on public opinion in the West was probably minimal. Images of dead and grieving Iraqis filled the television screens for a few brief but powerful minutes in the aftermath of the bombing of the shelter in Baghdad in which many civilians died.

But those images were sandwiched between, and overwhelmed in volume of coverage by, other images: the experts, assuring us that we, unlike the enemy, care about human life; and the fighting men and women, expressing gratitude that planes, not they, were doing the fighting.

22   If the war had dragged on, Iraq might have taken on a human face different from that of its hated leader. Television has the power to do that, and more so as it becomes a more global institution whose presence is accepted across political lines. American TV never had the kind of access to North Vietnam that CNN had to Iraq.

23   ▪ **The flag.** The flag never figured prominently in television coverage of Vietnam, in an era when patriotism—or nationalism—was taken for granted. Those who questioned the war were excoriated, but only very late in the war did part of the public feel the need to, literally, wave the flag.

24   For television, the flag is as sacred as the fighting men and women. These symbols are close to the hearts of ordinary Americans, to whose sentiments television is closely tuned. The flag must be celebrated and is above politics. The patriotism stories were often found at the end of the news and treated with a heavy dose of symbolic visuals, even becoming part of the network's signature. NBC sent a reporter to Mount Rushmore on Presidents Day to interview people about the war, closing the evening news with their unanimous expressions of support for it and for the president, and a lingering shot of the "American shrine."

25   Producers of network news shows were no doubt sincerely caught up, like most of the nation, in the wave of community feeling, closely connected to solidarity with the troops, which was labeled patriotism. But the flag was also a convenient political protection from charges that the networks were helping the enemy by reporting from Baghdad.

26   And the flag provided an upbeat closing to the news, something apparently of concern to advertisers. Despite the increase in viewing during the war, advertisers were reluctant to sponsor war news. The *New York Times* reported on February 7: "CBS executives had even offered advertisers assurances that…war specials could be tailored to provide better lead-ins to commercials. One way would be to insert the commercials after segments that were specially produced with up-beat images like patriotic views from the home front." Advertisers, according to the *Times,* were not impressed. But the networks' preoccupation with this problem may partly explain the flag's prominence in coverage.

27   NBC adopted as its logo a picture of a fighter/bomber superimposed on the American flag with the words, "America at War." This is a good summary of the Gulf War on television: the good feelings and sacred aura of the flag have been attached once again to war. There has been much commentary about the Gulf War "exorcising the ghosts of Vietnam," as ABC's Jeff Greenfield put it the day after the cease-fire, and this is assumed

Vietnam, and if exorcising the ghosts means forgetting that war is not a parade, this is a dangerous turn for American culture.

STUDY QUESTIONS

1. What significant difference does Hallin see between the wars in Vietnam and the Persian Gulf as they were reflected on TV? Show how the last paragraph returns to the theme of the opening three paragraphs.
2. How, in Hallin's view, was TV coverage of the Gulf War influenced by commercial sponsors of the news?
3. Does Hallin feel that government's less stringent control of the press during the Vietnam War was more or less desirable than its control during the Gulf War? Why?
4. One would think that use of experts to comment on the strategy and direction of the Gulf War could only enhance viewers' knowledge and understanding. What does Hallin find to criticize in this use of experts?
5. Hallin says in paragraph 18, "Mastering technology generally means accepting its logic." What does this mean?

SUGGESTION FOR WRITING

This essay appeared in the same month, May 1991, as the essay by John Corry that precedes it. Write an analytic essay highlighting the sharp contrast in their views on the media's proper role in wartime.

MORGAN STRONG

Portions of the Gulf War Were Brought to You by...the Folks at Hill and Knowlton

Morgan Strong is a freelance reporter specializing in the Middle East. This article originally appeared in *TV Guide* in February of 1992.

1   By now, it is well known that some portions of the Persian Gulf war effort were stage-managed in an effort to rally public opinion for military action against Iraq. The two leading television newsmagazines, ABC's *20/20* and CBS's *60 Minutes,* devoted segments last month to the fact that an emotional appeal in 1990 before a Congressional caucus hearing, supposedly by an anonymous Kuwaiti refugee girl called Nayirah, was in fact delivered by the daughter of Kuwait's ambassador to the U.S. Both stories followed a *New York Times* op-ed piece that exposed Nayirah's true identity, by John R. MacArthur, publisher of *Harper's Magazine.*

2   Further, it was revealed that the public relations firm of Hill and Knowlton, headed at the time by Craig Fuller, former chief of staff to George Bush when he was vice president, helped to package and rehearse the young woman's appearance on behalf of their client, Citizens for a Free Kuwait, an exile organization primarily funded by the Emir of Kuwait. Nayirah's testimony was that Iraqi soldiers had stormed hospitals and torn newborn babies from their incubators, leaving them to die. Her story, which received wide network coverage—and was invoked on numerous occasions by President Bush—had, in fact, been rehearsed before video cameras by Hill and Knowlton. But according to Kuwaiti doctors interviewed by *20/20* and *60 Minutes,* no such incident had occurred.

3   If this had been the only occurrence of packaged war reporting broadcast in the heat of war hysteria, it might be excusable. But what I found during my long stint in Saudi Arabia (I was a consultant for both PBS's *Frontline* and England's Thames Television) was a far more systematic manipulation of news by the PR firm than is generally known:

- Following the August 1990 invasion of Kuwait by Iraq, refugees with stories about their country were selected and coached by Hill and Knowlton. Those with the most compelling tales—and the ones most in keeping with the agenda of Hill and Knowlton's client— were made available to news organizations, thus limiting journalists' ability to independently assess claims of brutalities. Indeed, the PR firm's operatives were given free rein to travel unescorted throughout Saudi Arabia, while journalists were severely restricted.

- Hill and Knowlton also was the source for a large number of the amateur videos shot inside Kuwait and smuggled out. The videos were collected, screened and edited at the PR firm's TV studios in the Saudi capital, Riyadh, and in the coastal city of Dharan. The packaged videotapes were then distributed free of charge to the networks, ostensibly by Citizens for a Free Kuwait. In the U.S., Hill and Knowlton also distributed the tapes to affiliated and independent stations.
- A second woman who was identified as simply another Kuwaiti refugee, and who made an appearance before a widely televised session of the UN Security Council on Nov. 27, 1990, turned out to be a close relative of a senior Kuwaiti official. The woman, Fatima Fahed, came before the world body as it was debating the use of force to oust the Iraqis from Kuwait. She gave harrowing details of Iraqi atrocities inside her country.

7   What was not reported is that Fahed was, in fact, the wife of Sulaiman Al-Mutawa, Kuwait's minister of planning, and herself a well-known TV personality in Kuwait. Surprised that a high-profile Kuwaiti could be labeled, and accepted as just another "refugee," I asked one of the leaders of Citizens for a Free Kuwait, Fawzi Al-Sultan, why Fahed had been chosen to speak to the UN. "Because of her professional experience," he said, "she is more believable."

8   But, like the story related by Nayirah, Fahed's testimony was not necessarily true. In testifying to the UN, she implied that her information was firsthand. "Such stories...I personally have experienced," she said. But when I had interviewed her in Jedda, Saudi Arabia, before her UN appearance, she told me that she had *no* firsthand knowledge of the events she was describing. Some weeks later, in advance of her UN testimony, she and other witnesses were coached—including rehearsals, wardrobe and prepared scripts—extensively by employees of Hill and Knowlton.

- A tape from inside Kuwait, supplied to journalists by the PR firm before the U.S.–led invasion, purported to show peaceful Kuwaiti demonstrators being fired upon by the occupying Iraqi troops.

10   But, on the ground in Saudi Arabia, I managed to interview a Kuwaiti refugee present at the demonstration whose story was quite different. The man, a Kuwaiti policeman, said that no demonstrators were injured, and that gunshots captured on tape were, in fact, those of Iraqi troops firing on nearby resistance fighters, who had fired first at the Iraqis. When I asked him to appear on camera and tell the true story, he refused. "I do not want to harm the resistance," he said.

11   None of this is to suggest that the Iraqis did not perpetrate atrocities while occupying Kuwait, nor does it underestimate the difficulties facing

the media in obtaining original material under censorship conditions. However, these examples are but a few of the incidents of outright misinformation that found their way onto the network news. It is an inescapable fact that much of what Americans saw on their news broadcasts, especially leading up to the Allied offensive against Iraqi-occupied Kuwait, was in large measure the contrivance of a public relations firm.

STUDY QUESTIONS

1. In the series of instances reported in this article, did Hill and Knowlton behave unethically?
2. Did those responsible for the network broadcasts neglect their obligations?
3. Is it significant that the head of Hill and Knowlton at the time of this misinformation was the former chief of staff to George Bush when he was vice president?
4. What does this article suggest about the organization known as "Citizens for a Free Kuwait"?

JACK TATUM WITH BILL KUSHNER

I Plead Guilty, But Only to Aggressive Play

Jack Tatum, a former professional linebacker for the Oakland Raiders, became well known in 1978 when Darryl Stingley, an opposing player, was permanently paralyzed by one of his tackles. The following essay, the first chapter of Tatum's book *They Call Me Assassin*, expresses the ethical code of one professional athlete.

1   When you're a two-time all-American from Ohio State, you expect to be drafted into professional football. I certainly felt that one of the NFL teams would draft me, and in the first round, too. In college, and even in high school, I had developed a reputation as a devastating hitter. Whenever I'd hit a running back or receiver with a good shot, the man usually didn't get up. I've always had an affinity for controlled violence and contact sports. Professional scouts look for athletes who have an appetite for contact, so they were looking at me.

2   Before the draft, the All-American team did a television show with Mr. Bob Hope. He introduced the team members and cracked jokes about each player. When my turn came, he said, "Jack Tatum…what a hitter. Tatum can straighten your spine quicker than Ben Casey. Why, he's so tough that even his fingernails have muscles. I became a Jack Tatum fan when I saw him play in the Rose Bowl. Jack hit O. J. [Simpson] so hard that he knocked me out of my fifty-yard line seat and into the parking lot. Imagine how the Juice felt…squeezed. Jack's mother told me that he was just a normal kid…except he liked to ram his head into fire hydrants. Normal kid, eh?"

3   Mr. Hope glanced at me and saw that I was laughing and enjoying his teasing. He paused for a second and then said, "Sorry we don't have any fire hydrants on stage, Jack. Oh, what the hell, if you want to have some of your kind of fun, then go ahead and ram your head into the walls."

4   Neither Mr. Hope nor anyone in the audience realized what was really making me laugh, but the conception most people have of aggressive football players seems so funny to me. They think a man has to be mentally unbalanced to play football violently. I know me better than anyone else knows me, and I'm no psychopath. But I and others like myself learned early in our careers that in football, the name of the game is hitting, and to play it well, you have to play it hard.

5   High school football was the beginning of my career. I quickly learned that it hurt more to get hit than it did to actually do the hitting. That might sound strange, but let me explain. Most high school defensive

players are passive. They sit back and wait for the opposition to come to them. This is bad, because a young player can get seriously hurt. When you lay back, the offensive man builds up his momentum and is doing the hitting while the defensive man is getting hit.

6   Good defensive football amounts to mass times velocity. The faster I can move toward impact, and the more violently I can drive my body through a target, the more effective my hit will be. This way I'm doing the hitting and the offensive player is absorbing the punishment. Most running backs and receivers never run full speed. They're either cutting or dodging tacklers. So once I figure out where the man is trying to go, it just becomes a matter of building up a full head of speed and driving through him. My method is similar to a karate punch. I concentrate on a point one yard or so beyond the man I'm going after, and on impact, I drive hard to that point.

7   I played my first game of football as a sophomore in high school, and even then I was effective. My coach, John Federici, said, "Jack, when you see the quarterback dropping back to pass, go after him."

8   I did something right because in the fourth quarter, the team we were playing ran out of quarterbacks. They had to finish the game with a tight end taking the snaps from the center. After the game, I was a hero. The fans loved my style of play.

9   In college I developed quickly. I grew stronger and faster, and became a more aggressive and vicious tackler. Naturally, I still practiced the basics of sound football, but in addition, I also learned other important defensive fundamentals. Coach Woody Hayes was a teacher of body control. He believed that a great athlete could thoroughly control his body. Through Woody's drills I learned how to start and stop on a dime and generate maximum power in my tackles. An important part of body control was also, as Woody called it, mind control. This meant no late hits or cheap shots out of bounds. It was still rough and violent football, but my style of aggressive play was within the rules and regulations of the game.

10   In my first collegiate game I won no All-American honors, but I did make the other teams on our schedule wary of me. I was only a sophomore, but I had earned a starting assignment as a linebacker. We were playing Southern Methodist, a school known for putting the ball in the air. That meant people would be running pass patterns in my area looking for the ball instead of the linebackers. Believe me, when you catch someone with a good shot who isn't expecting it, you're going to hurt him.

11   Early in the first quarter I spotted a wide receiver running a quick slant over the middle. The receiver was concentrating on making the catch and never saw me coming. He was my first collegiate knockout victim.

12   Later in the same period, I saw a running back slip over the middle and look back for the pass. He became my second knockout. The 85,000 fans

watching the game were delighted. The action was gruesome, but that's what the fans love, violent contact. The Ohio State fans loved the action I had provided and so did my coaches. Once again I was a hero.

13   By the time my college career ended, I had more knockouts than Joe Louis and Muhammad Ali combined. I won every defensive award the Big Ten had to offer and more. Three times I was among the top vote getters for the Heisman Trophy, and twice I was voted the nation's best defensive player. I was certain that my next adventure would be professional football.

14   I have mentioned a word that is synonymous with boxing: Knockout. Actually, though, knockouts do occur in many of the nonpassive sports. It's just that the very purpose of a boxing match is built around one's ability to knock his opponent into a senseless mass of blood and flesh. Football and the other contact sports do have a different purpose. In football there are various degrees of violence and contact, but the two basic objectives of the game are to score points and prevent points from being scored, and not to knock people out cold. However, when you put an offensive team on the field for the purpose of advancing the ball forward, and the defensive team has quite the opposite purpose, it all becomes a war, and I am simply a warrior in a very physical way. As a warrior I must discourage running backs and receivers whenever they attempt to gain yardage against the defense. It is a physical and a violent job, and quite often the end results are knockouts or serious injuries to my opponent. But it is just part of a very risky business.

15   The first round of the college draft went as I expected, and I became the property of the Oakland Raiders. After eight years of hard work in high school and college, I was at last part of the NFL.

16   Several weeks after the draft, I flew out to Oakland for contract talks with Al Davis, a partner and general manager of the Raiders. Al Davis talked my language. I asked, "How much?" and he answered with a $50,000 bonus check and a three-year, no-cut contract worth six attractive figures. I signed the contract.

17   When the paperwork was finished, there was a statement in the press to the effect the Raiders had just hired the Assassin that no winning team could be without…and his name was Jack Tatum.

18   "Assassin?" I thought. "That makes me sound like a gangster." But, actually, I was a "hit man." I didn't run out and buy a dark suit or fedora, but I did think about my career. The Raiders had invested in me and I had to produce. Professional football is vicious and brutal; there's not much time for sentiment. I was being paid well for a service, and if I didn't deliver, they'd go and find someone else who would.

19   I was committed to play my first professional game with the College All-Stars against the World Champion Baltimore Colts. The game was an annual charity affair held each year in Chicago, but it was also much more.

20   As All-Americans we wanted to prove to the Colts that we belonged in the NFL. We weren't concerned with showing off or pretending that we were already professional superstars. We just wanted to go out, play a good game, and earn the respect of the best team in professional football. But for some reason the old pros turned nasty and tried to beat our heads in. Every time they got off a good play, they would smart-mouth us or cuss. I thought it was very unfair of them to treat us as if we didn't belong in the same stadium. We had only played together for ten days, and the Colts had years behind them. I don't think that any of the All-Stars seriously believed that we could win the game, but still, we didn't expect to be disgraced.

21   Before very long, the Colts had a seven-point lead but were acting as though they had a seventy-point lead. On a third down and eight play, I started thinking that maybe Earl Morrall would look for his tight end, John Mackey. Earlier in the game Morrall tried a quick pass to the tight end, and it had worked for good yardage. That first time, as I went after Mackey, someone had partially blocked me and I hadn't made good contact. Mackey got up, shrugged his shoulders, and walked back to the huddle laughing and hollering in my direction, "Hard hitting rookie...what a joke."

22   Morrall took the snap and dropped straight back looking for the tight end. I carefully avoided the blind side blocks and drew a bead on Mackey's rib cage. Morrall hadn't thrown one of his better passes, and I could have easily intercepted, but I had other plans. I wondered if John Mackey would still think I was a joke after he was really hit. As Mackey reached back for the ball, I drove my helmet into his ribs and knocked him to the ground. It was a good hit. Mackey was on the ground flopping around like a wounded duck and gasping for air. Standing over him, I glared down and asked, "How funny was that joke?" Of course, I admit I cussed at him, too.

23   John Mackey wasn't the only Colt I ran into on that particular night. Later in the game I found another tight end, Tom Mitchell, roaming in my area trying to catch one of Morrall's terrible wobbly passes. I introduced myself to Tom, but I don't think he heard the name. Tom was my second professional knockout.

24   Immediately, sportswriters started comparing me with Dick Butkus, a linebacker for the Chicago Bears. Butkus was supposedly the meanest, dirtiest, hardest-hitting football player to ever put on a pair of cleats and walk out onto the field. I resented the comparison because I had seen Butkus play. I admit that Butkus was mean and there was strong evidence he played dirty (teeth marks on running backs' ankles), but for anyone to think he was a hitter was absurd. Butkus even admitted that he couldn't hit. When he traveled across the country doing TV shows, he said, "Whenever I get a clear shot at the ball carrier. I don't want him turning to see who did the hitting. I want him to know without looking that it was Dick Butkus."

25   Any fool knows that when you hit someone with your best shot and he is still able to think, then you're not a hitter. My idea of a good hit is when the victim wakes up on the sidelines with train whistles blowing in his head and wondering who he is and what ran over him. I'm not saying that Butkus wasn't a fair linebacker, because after all, he was an All-Pro. But in my estimation Butkus was most definitely not a hitter.

26   As a defensive player I had resigned myself to the fact that I would never rush for 1000 yards during a season and I would never score many touchdowns. But at the same time I vowed to earn my reputation in professional football with aggressive tackling. I knew that in professional football or even high school football, the team that can dominate physically will usually win. Punishment is demoralizing, and few teams can withstand a painful beating without it warping their will to win. I never make a tackle just to bring someone down. I want to punish the man I'm going after and I want him to know that it's going to hurt every time he comes my way.

27   Violent play can make a defensive team much sharper, but there is a limit. I believe that running backs and receivers are fair game once they step onto the field. If they want to run out of bounds to avoid the tackle, then fine, let them run away from the action. But anyone that comes near me is going to get hit. I like to believe that my best hits border on felonious assault, but at the same time everything I do is by the rule book. I don't want to be the heir to Butkus's title, because his career had shadows. Some people say that Butkus bit, while others say he didn't. My style of play is mean and nasty and I am going to beat people physically and mentally, but in no way am I going down in the record book as a cheap-shot artist.

28   After the All-Star game I joined the Raider training camp at Santa Rosa, California. I guess it was surprising that my helmet still fit over my head. I was starting to believe everything the press wrote about me, and I'm afraid I became overconfident. After all, I was considered a superstar in high school and was a collegiate All-American three times. Then came the All-Star game and my two professional knockouts. It was a lot for a twenty-one-year-old man to grasp and still keep both feet on the ground. The Oakland Raiders had a man named Fred Biletnikoff, now retired, who put things in proper perspective for me, however.

29   Fred Biletnikoff was a balding but hippy-looking wide receiver for the Oakland Raiders. When I was instructed by my coaches to cover Fred one-on-one during a pass defense drill, I laughed to myself. Fred Biletnikoff had a great pair of hands and could catch anything near him, but he was slow by NFL standards. I've played against big receivers, small receivers, and fast receivers, and they couldn't burn me. Now, for my first test in an Oakland Raider camp, they put me against a slow receiver.

30   Fred ran his first pattern and I showed him why I was all All-American. Covering him like a blanket, I nearly intercepted the ball, and after the play I told Fred, "You're lucky that we aren't hitting."

31   On the next play Fred drove off the line hard and made a good move to the outside. I was too quick for him though and reacted like an All-Pro. But then he broke back across the middle and left me tripping over my own feet. Needless to say, the quarterback laid a perfect pass into Fred's hands, and he scored. On the way back to the huddle, Fred showed me the football and asked, "Were you looking for this, Rookie?"

32   That got me upset and I started cussing. I told him, "Try me again and see what happens, Chump!"

33   Fred came at me again with about five different fakes and just as I went left, he went right and scored again. Fred Biletnikoff started running patterns that quickly deflated my ego and taught me humiliation. He burned me time and time again so bad that I went back to the locker room feeling very uncertain as to whether or not I had what it takes to make it in professional football. Deep down inside my pride was scorched.

34   Later that same evening I bumped into Fred and we started talking about practice. Fred turned out to be a pretty good guy. After a few minutes we were talking like old friends. Fred told me that he grew up in Erie, Pennsylvania, and it didn't sound like paradise. While he was talking about the mills and factories of Erie, I was picturing the filth and dirt of my home town, Passaic, New Jersey. After a great high school career in Erie, Fred accepted a scholarship to attend Florida State University, and there earned All-American honors. The more we talked, the better I liked the man.

35   "A man has to adjust," Fred was saying about the NFL, "and if he doesn't, he's gone. The difference today was that I knew you could knock me out if you hit me with a good shot but you didn't know that I could burn you. Now it comes down to respecting each other and adjusting."

36   I listened to everything Fred told me, because he had the experience and wanted to help my career. He told me that receivers are the biggest bunch of cons going. Fred warned, "Some receivers will fake with their hips, feet, head, shoulders, eyes, or anything to gain a liberated step. Don't be sucked in by a fake; go after what's real. Remember, Jack, all the quarterbacks in this league can hit the one-on-one pass. If some receiver gives you a fake and you trip over your own feet going after nothing, then it's just God and green grass between that man and six points."

37   Fred started working with me and taught me how to think like a receiver. By the time the exhibition season opened up, I didn't have all the answers, but I gave my best. Maybe if Fred hadn't given me some of his time, my stay in the NFL would have been a short one.

38   I got burned a few times, but luck was with me. It seemed that if a receiver caught a pass over me, I was able to stick the next attempt in his rib cage. Still, though, I was undisciplined enough to be hazardous. Aggressiveness is as common to football as helmets and shoulder pads, but I had yet to learn how to channel my aggressive style of play into aspects of the game where it would do the team the most good.

39   In one game we were holding a 21–14 lead over the New Orleans Saints. Late in the fourth period the Saints quarterback threw over the middle for his wide receiver, Danny Abramowicz, who was well covered by our strong safety, George Atkinson. In my eagerness to assist, I blasted in from the weak side and creamed everyone. It was a double knockout. I got Abramowicz, but I got George too.

40   After that my play became sloppy. I'd go after the ball and slam into anyone that got in the way. It was early in the season and I had already knocked out seven men. That would have been a good start, except that four of those knockouts were Oakland Raiders. I knocked out our Captain, Willie Brown, got Nemiah Wilson and cut his eye pretty bad, too, and then there was George Atkinson. I knocked out George twice. It got to the point where our defensive people were starting to worry more about me than the real enemy.

41   After George recovered from his second knockout, he took me aside and said, "Damn, Tate, are you colorblind or something? I wear the same color jersey as you do. I'm on your side and the deal is gettin' the other team."

42   After he felt that I was sure which team I played for, George started teaching me some of his techniques. I learned how to anticipate the offensive man. For example, if a running back went wide on a play and there was good outside pursuit, then I'd position myself inside and hope the back would cut against the flow. That way I'd be waiting, and from there it was a matter of building up my speed and hitting the enemy. On passing situations I talked with the other defensive backs and asked how they were going to play a particular receiver. That way I sort of knew where my people were going to be and how they were going to play the situation. For example, if Willie Brown said he was going to play his man loose and go for the ball, then I went for the receiver. It started working so well that most of the time I let the other backs go for the interception and I'd punish the receiver.

43   George Atkinson started teaching me a few more of his other tricks. George said, "I was going to teach you the 'Hook' when you first came into the league but you were having identification problems. Now that you seem to know who's who, let me show you the best intimidator in the business, the Hook." Of course, the rules governing the Hook have changed recently, but back then it wasn't just legal but an important weapon in a good hitter's arsenal.

44   The Hook is simply flexing your biceps and trying to catch the receiver's head in the joint between the forearm and upper arm. It's like hitting with the biceps by using a head-lock type of action. The purpose of the Hook was to strip the receiver of the ball, his helmet, his head, and his courage. Of course, you only use the hook in full-speed contact, and usually from the blind side. Using the Hook effectively was not as easy as it may sound. Very few defensive backs used the Hook because if you were a little high with your shot, the receiver would slip under and get away. Also, if you weren't careful and you hit with the forearm, it became an illegal tactic.

45   Another trick that George taught me was the "Groundhog." The Groundhog is a perfectly timed hit to the ankles just as the receiver is leaping high to catch a pass. The Groundhog isn't as devastating as it looks on TV but it does have a tendency to keep the receiver closer to the ground on high passes.

46   As the free safety for the Raiders, I never have a specific responsibility. I am given the freedom to help out wherever we feel the offense is going to concentrate its attack. If a team is running good against us, then I move closer to the line of scrimmage and try to get a good hit on a running back. Most of the time one good hit will slow down any running back and wake up the defense. That's what I meant about punishment demoralizing and warping a team's will to win.

47   I started feeling comfortable about halfway into the season. It seemed as though everything was falling into place rather nicely, and best of all, I hadn't knocked out any of my teammates for three games. I worked hard at practice, studied game films of coming opponents, and showed improvement weekly. My career was getting off to a solid start, and I felt good about the overall development I had shown. I was doing my job, getting well-paid, and no one had any complaints. At least no one on the Oakland Raiders had any complaints.

48   If ever a man did have a reason to complain about my style of play, it had to be Riley Odoms, a tight end with the Denver Broncos. During a game at Denver's Mile High Stadium, I leveled the best shot of my career against Riley. It was a clean hit, not a cheap shot, but I was upset because I really thought I had killed the man.

49   Late in the game we had built a 27–16 lead, but Denver's offense was getting fancy. They singled out Nemiah Wilson, our left cornerback, as the man in the secondary to exploit. Nemo was small, only about 170 pounds, and he was playing with an injured leg. This seemed to be an invitation for Charley Johnson, Denver's quarterback, to do his passing around Nemo. Denver positioned both of their wide receivers on opposite sides of the field, away from Nemo, and put him one-on-one with Riley Odoms. Riley is one of the best tight ends in professional football. He's big, standing

6 feet 4 inches and weighing 235 pounds; he would be a lot of man for Nemo on this particular Sunday, or any day of the week, for that matter.

50   Since I had the option of roaming around and policing the secondary, I decided to help Nemo. When the play started to develop, I dropped back a few steps to give Riley the impression I had deep coverage. Riley saw me dropping off and made a quick move over the middle. It was a great move because Riley had Nemo off balance and he broke open by five yards. Quarterbacks love to see that type of a situation, and Charley Johnson wasted little time releasing the ball toward Riley. I just timed my hit. When I felt I could zero in on Riley's head at the same time the ball arrived in his hands, I moved. It was a perfectly timed hit, and I used my Hook on his head. Because of the momentum built up by the angles and speed of both Riley and myself, it was the best hit of my career. I heard Riley scream on impact and felt his body go limp. He landed flat on his back, and the ball came to rest on his chest for a completion, but Riley's eyes rolled back in his head and he wasn't breathing. I had another knockout, and maybe this time, I had even killed a man. God knew that I didn't want something like that to happen.

51   I've used the word "kill," and when I'm hitting someone I really am trying to kill, but not like forever. I mean I'm trying to kill the play or the pass, but not the man. Football is a violent game, and people are seriously injured; sometimes they are killed. But any man that puts on a uniform and doesn't play hard is cheating. The players of the NFL are paid good money and risk serious injuries because the structure of football is based on punishing your opponent. There is nothing humorous or even vaguely cheerful about playing in the NFL. It is a high risk but high-salaried job.

52   Riley was scraped off the field and carried to the sidelines. He was shaken and hurt, but thank God he was still alive. After the game I went over to the Denver locker room and talked with Riley. He said, "Damn, Tate, don't ever hit me like that again. You nearly killed me." Then he laughed and I slapped him on the back and smiled with relief. Very few people understand the camaraderie and mutual respect professional athletes feel for each other. We admire each other's abilities and appreciate the man who had the guts to do his job well. My coaches, sportswriters, and even football fans talked about how hard I hit Riley. People called that hit everything from vicious to brutal but I never heard anyone say it was a cheap shot.

53   During the years that have followed I have continued my style of play and have registered many more knockouts. I remember one game, again it was against Denver, when the Broncos' best running back, Floyd Little, took a hand-off and swept around left end with a herd of blockers leading the way. As he turned the corner, the reds and blues of Denver had gone south and I was coming up fast. Floyd didn't see me coming and there was

a collision at mid-field near the sidelines, right in front of the Denver bench. I whipped my Hook up under Floyd's face mask and landed a solid shot flush on his jaw. Floyd looked like a magician practicing levitation just before all the lights went out. His head snapped back, his feet straightened out, and the ball and one of his shoes shot into the stands. I was coming so hard that my momentum carried both of us into the Denver bench.

54   The play had started close to the sidelines and I could have pushed Floyd out of bounds, but instead, I hit him with everything I had to offer because if you just push a guy like Floyd Little out of bounds, then he'll start getting some bad ideas about you. Floyd would probably start thinking that I was soft, and that would lead to him wanting to take advantage of me. Before long every team in the NFL would be gunning their game plans at me, and when that happened the Raiders would get someone else, someone that would beat a running back out of bounds rather than give him a sissy push.

55   Some of the players moaned when I hit Floyd and a few of them even cussed at me, but once again no one even suggested that I hit Floyd with a cheap shot.

56   My ferocity seemed to influence the entire Raider defense. Everyone started talking about getting a "knockout." Guys who used to tackle just to bring someone down started to punish people, and that made the defense much sharper. If a running back got off a good play and picked up, say, fifteen yards but got his head rattled so badly that he had to leave the game, it was worth the fifteen yards. I started taking shots at everyone wearing a different colored uniform. I'd take shots at every receiver and running back. They didn't like it, and sometimes they'd send a lineman after me, but I didn't care; I'd take a shot at him, too. I would initiate a demoralizing kind of punishment on the opposing offense and it picked our defensive team up. The Raiders had become a nasty group of men. The Oakland Raiders have never tried to look loveable. As soon as they run onto the field, they radiate villainy. The black-shirted Raiders, with their crossed swords and pirate decals, immediately bring to mind the bad guys in the old movies. Every team in professional football seems to consider the Raiders their arch-rival. They all treat the Raider malice with a special intensity, and football fans love it. I was enjoying my job with the Raiders and proud to be a part of the organization regardless of what the national image was. I knew in my heart that it was professional football and there wasn't any on-field charm connected with the game.

57   During my second year George Atkinson suggested that he and I start a contest for who would get the most knockouts over the course of the season. It sounded like a good idea, and we agreed on a set of rules. First of all, neither of us wanted to get penalties called against us so we agreed that our hits must be clean shots and legal. Next, the man you hit would have to

be down for an official injury time-out and he had to be helped off the field. That would be considered a "knockout" and it was worth two points. Sometimes, one of us would hit a man and he'd take the injury time-out but would limp off the field under his own power. We called that a "limp-off" and it was worth one point. When the season started, so did we. Actually, it was all part of our job, but we made a game out of it. Guess who won?

58 　The seasons had a way of piling up, and before I knew it, I was a veteran of seven years. When I stopped to look back and see what had happened over the course of my career, I was shocked. I came into the NFL wanting to be the most intimidating hitter in the history of the game. At this stage of my career, people were scared of me because they knew I was accomplishing my objective. But something else was also happening and I resented it. Some people considered me a dirty player and a cheap-shot artist. I can live with rumors, but when I see my name published in the San Diego *Union* along with football's top ten dirty players, I get upset. When my attorney calls me from Pittsburgh and tells me that Sam Nover of Channel 2 and Myron Cope of Channel 4 are doing specials on my dirty tactics, I become angry. After a few questionable incidents, everything has mushroomed into a problem serious enough for Howard Cosell to dedicate one of his halftime shows on "Monday Night Football" to George Atkinson and me and our "cheap shots." Even NBC Sports used prime time for a special, "Violence in Sports."

59 　It started with a normal football game, a few good hits, a knockout, and a certain coach's "criminal element" speech. From there it was picked up by the press and traveled into the office of the Commissioner of the NFL. From there some fines were issued, which then I refused to pay, and now every official in the NFL is throwing quick flags in my general direction. However, I doubt that I'm going to change how I live my life and how I play the game because, as I told the Commissioner, "I plead guilty, but only to aggressive play."

STUDY QUESTIONS

1. Tatum uses the word "tackle" only infrequently. What term does he use instead? Why?
2. In paragraph 14, Tatum at first distinguishes between boxing, where knockouts are the purpose of the sport, and football, where they are not. How in the rest of the same paragraph does he justify his attempts to knock out his opponents?
3. List Tatum's "god terms" and "devil terms" (see pages 46–47).

4. Write a list of precepts that you believe would constitute Jack Tatum's code of ethics as a professional football player. Include items that describe what the player must always do and what he must never do. Be prepared to indicate passages in the article that would support your formulation of these precepts.

5. Does Tatum persuasively defend his own motives and behavior in the "hits" directed at John Mackey, Riley Odoms, and Floyd Little and in his knockout contest with George Atkinson?

6. To what degree does moral responsibility for violence in professional football, boxing, and hockey rest with individual contestants? coaches? club owners? the media? the fans? legislators?

SUGGESTION FOR WRITING

Is Tatum's professional ethic compatible with good sportsmanship? If not, which ethic do you feel exerts the stronger claim, and why?

MONROE H. FREEDMAN

Professional Responsibility of the Criminal Defense Lawyer: The Three Hardest Questions

The conduct of lawyers is governed by the "Canons of Professional Ethics" of the American Bar Association. The code was adopted by the association in 1908 and has been expanded and amended several times since. The Bar Association has a Committee on Professional Ethics and Grievances whose function is to interpret the canons, that is, to determine how they apply to specific practices. In addition, similar inquiries are conducted by local bar associations.

However, the canons, even as clarified by decisions of various ethics committees, do not offer a completely unambiguous guide to professional conduct. In this classic essay, Monroe Freedman, a professor of law and Co-Director of the Criminal Trial Institute of Washington, D.C., considers what he calls the three hardest ethical questions facing the criminal defense lawyer. As he points out in footnote 1, this essay was so controversial when he first presented it to fellow members of the Bar Association that a group of judges demanded an inquiry to consider his possible suspension or disbarment.

Professor Freedman has amplified his views and modified them somewhat in *Lawyers' Ethics in an Adversary System* (1975) (ABA Gavel Award Certificate of Merit, 1976), and in "Personal Responsibility in a Professional System," 27, *Cath. Univ. L. Rev.* 191 (1978) (Pope John XXIII Lecture).

1   In almost any area of legal counseling and advocacy, the lawyer may be faced with the dilemma of either betraying the confidential communications of his client or participating to some extent in the purposeful deception of the court. This problem is nowhere more acute than in the practice of criminal law, particularly in the representation of the indigent accused. The purpose of this article is to analyze and attempt to resolve three of the most difficult issues in this general area:

> *1* Is it proper to cross-examine for the purpose of discrediting the reliability or credibility of an adverse witness whom you know to be telling the truth?
>
> *2* Is it proper to put a witness on the stand when you know he will commit perjury?
>
> *3* Is it proper to give your client legal advice when you have reason to believe that the knowledge you give him will tempt him to commit perjury?

2   These questions present serious difficulties with respect to a lawyer's ethical responsibilities. Moreover, if one admits the possibility of an affirmative answer, it is difficult even to discuss them without appearing to some to be unethical.[1] It is not surprising, therefore, that reasonable, rational discussion of these issues has been uncommon and that the problems have for so long remained unresolved. In this regard it should be recognized that the Canons of Ethics, which were promulgated in 1908 "as a general guide,"[2] are both inadequate and self-contradictory.

I. The Adversary System and the Necessity for Confidentiality

3   At the outset, we should dispose of some common question-begging responses. The attorney is indeed an officer of the court, and he does participate in a search for truth. These two propositions, however, merely serve to state the problem in different words: As an officer of the court, participating in a search for truth, what is the attorney's special responsibility, and how does that responsibility affect his resolution of the questions posed above?

4   The attorney functions in an adversary system based upon the presupposition that the most effective means of determining truth is to present to a judge and jury a clash between proponents of conflicting views. It is essential to the effective functioning of this system that each adversary have, in the words of Canon 15, "entire devotion to the interest of the client, warm zeal in the maintenance and defense of his rights and the exertion of his utmost learning and ability." It is also essential to maintain the fullest uninhibited communication between the client and his attorney, so that the attorney can most effectively counsel his client and advocate the latter's cause. This policy is safeguarded by the requirement that the lawyer must, in the words of Canon 37, "preserve his client's confidences." Canon 15 does, of course, qualify these obligations by stating that "the office of attorney does not permit, much less does it demand of him for any client, violations of law or any manner of fraud or chicane." In addition, Canon 22 requires candor toward the court.

---

[1] The substance of this paper was recently presented to a Criminal Trial Institute attended by forty-five members of the District of Columbia Bar. As a consequence, several judges (none of whom had either heard the lecture or read it) complained to the Committee on Admissions and Grievances of the District Court for the District of Columbia, urging the author's disbarment or suspension. Only after four months of proceedings, including a hearing, two meetings, and a *de novo* review by eleven federal district court judges, did the Committee announce its decision to "proceed no further in the matter."

[2] American Bar Association, Canons of Professional Ethics, Preamble (1908).

5   The problem presented by these salutary generalities of the Canons in the context of particular litigation is illustrated by the personal experience of Samuel Williston, which was related in his autobiography.[3] Because of his examination of a client's correspondence file, Williston learned of a fact extremely damaging to his client's case. When the judge announced his decision, it was apparent that a critical factor in the favorable judgment for Williston's client was the judge's ignorance of this fact. Williston remained silent and did not thereafter inform the judge of what he knew. He was convinced, and Charles Curtis[4] agrees with him, that it was his duty to remain silent.

6   In an opinion by the American Bar Association Committee on Professional Ethics and Grievances, an eminent panel headed by Henry Drinker held that a lawyer should remain silent when his client lies to the judge by saying that he has no prior record, despite the attorney's knowledge to the contrary.[5] The majority of the panel distinguished the situation in which the attorney has learned of the client's prior record from a source other than the client himself. William B. Jones, a distinguished trial lawyer and now a judge in the United States District Court for the District of Columbia, wrote a separate opinion in which he asserted that in neither event should the lawyer expose his client's lie. If these two cases do not constitute "fraud or chicane" or lack of candor within the meaning of the Canons (and I agree with the authorities cited that they do not), it is clear that the meaning of the Canons is ambiguous.

7   The adversary system has further ramifications in a criminal case. The defendant is presumed to be innocent. The burden is on the prosecution to prove beyond a reasonable doubt that the defendant is guilty. The plea of not guilty does not necessarily mean "not guilty in fact," for the defendant may mean "not legally guilty." Even the accused who knows that he committed the crime is entitled to put the government to its proof. Indeed, the accused who knows that he is guilty has an absolute constitutional right to remain silent.[6] The moralist might quite reasonably understand this to mean that, under these circumstances, the defendant and his lawyer are privileged to "lie" to the court in pleading not guilty. In my judgment, the moralist is right. However, our adversary system and related notions of the proper administration of criminal justice sanction the lie.

---

[3] Williston, *Life and Law,* 271 (1940).
[4] Curtis, *Its Your Law,* 17–21 (1954). See also Curtis, "The Ethics of Advocacy," 4 Stan. L. Rev. 3, 9–10 (1951); Drinker, "Some Remarks on Mr. Curtis's *The Ethics of Advocacy,*" 4 Stan. L. Rev., 349, 350–51 (1952).
[5] Opinion 287, Committee on Professional Ethics and Grievances of the American Bar Association (1953).
[6] Escobedo v. Illinois, 378 U.S. 478, 485, 491 (1964).

8   Some derive solace from the sophistry of calling the lie a "legal fiction," but this is hardly an adequate answer to the moralist. Moreover, this answer has no particular appeal for the practicing attorney, who knows that the plea of not guilty commits him to the most effective advocacy of which he is capable. Criminal defense lawyers do not win their cases by arguing reasonable doubt. Effective trial advocacy requires that the attorney's every word, action, and attitude be consistent with the conclusion that his client is innocent. As every trial lawyer knows, the jury is certain that the defense attorney knows whether his client is guilty. The jury is therefore alert to, and will be enormously affected by, any indication by the attorney that he believes the defendant to be guilty. Thus, the plea of not guilty commits the advocate to a trial, including a closing argument, in which he must argue that "not guilty" means "not guilty in fact."[7]

9   There is, of course, a simple way to evade the dilemma raised by the not guilty plea. Some attorneys rationalize the problem by insisting that a lawyer never knows for sure whether his client is guilty. The client who insists upon his guilt may in fact be protecting his wife, or may know that he pulled the trigger and that the victim was killed, but not that his gun was loaded with blanks and that the fatal shot was fired from across the street. For anyone who finds this reasoning satisfactory, there is, of course, no need to think further about the issue.

10   It is also argued that a defense attorney can remain selectively ignorant. He can insist in his first interview with his client that, if his client is guilty, he simply does not want to know. It is inconceivable, however, that an attorney could give adequate counsel under such circumstances. How is the client to know, for example, precisely which relevant circumstances his lawyer does not want to be told? The lawyer might ask whether his client has a prior record. The client, assuming that this is the kind of knowledge that might present ethical problems for his lawyer, might respond that he has no record. The lawyer would then put the defendant on the stand and, on cross-examination, be appalled to learn that his client has two prior convictions for offenses identical to that for which he is being tried.

11   Of course, an attorney can guard against this specific problem by telling his client that he must know about the client's past record. However,

---

[7] "The failure to argue the case before the jury, while ordinarily only a trial tactic not subject to review, manifestly enters the field of incompetency when the reason assigned is the attorney's conscience. It is as improper as though the attorney had told the jury that his client had uttered a falsehood in making the statement. The right to an attorney embraces effective representation throughout all stages of the trial, and where the representation is of such low caliber as to amount to no representation, the guarantee of due process has been violated," Johns v. Smyth, 176 F. Supp. 949, 953 E.D. Va. 1959); Schwartz, *Cases on Professional Responsibility and the Administration of Criminal Justice* 79 (1962).

a lawyer can never anticipate all of the innumerable and potentially critical factors that his client, once cautioned, may decide not to reveal. In one instance, for example, the defendant assumed that his lawyer would prefer to be ignorant of the fact that the client had been having sexual relations with the chief defense witness. The client was innocent of the robbery with which he was charged, but was found guilty by the jury—probably because he was guilty of fornication, a far less serious offense for which he had not even been charged.

12   The problem is compounded by the practice of plea bargaining. It is considered improper for a defendant to plead guilty to a lesser offense unless he is in fact guilty. Nevertheless, it is common knowledge that plea bargaining frequently results in improper guilty pleas by innocent people. For example, a defendant falsely accused of robbery may plead guilty to simple assault, rather than risk a robbery conviction and a substantial prison term. If an attorney is to be scrupulous in bargaining pleas, however, he must know in advance that his client is guilty, since the guilty plea is improper if the defendant is innocent. Of course, if the attempt to bargain for a lesser offense should fail, the lawyer would know the truth and thereafter be unable to rationalize that he was uncertain of his client's guilt.

13   If one recognizes that professional responsibility requires that an advocate have full knowledge of every pertinent fact, it follows that he must seek the truth from his client, not shun it.[8] This means that he will have to dig and pry and cajole, and, even then, he will not be successful unless he can convince the client that full and confidential disclosure to his lawyer will never result in prejudice to the client by any word or action of the lawyer. This is, perhaps, particularly true in the case of the indigent defendant, who meets his lawyer for the first time in the cell block or the rotunda. He did not choose the lawyer, nor does he know him. The lawyer has been sent by the judge and is part of the system that is attempting to punish the defendant. It is no easy task to persuade this client that he can talk freely without fear of prejudice. However, the inclination to mislead one's lawyer is not restricted to the indigent or even to the criminal defendant. Randolph Paul has observed a similar phenomenon among the wealthier class in a far more congenial atmosphere:

> *The tax advisor will sometimes have to dynamite the facts of his case out of the unwilling witnesses on his own side—witnesses who are nervous, witnesses who are confused about their own interest, witnesses who try to*

---

[8] "Counsel cannot properly perform their duties without knowing the truth." Opinion 23, Committee on Professional Ethics and Grievances of the American Bar Association (1930).

be too smart for their own good, and witnesses who subconsciously do not want to understand what has happened despite the fact that they must if they are to testify coherently.[9]

Paul goes on to explain that the truth can be obtained only by persuading the client that it would be a violation of a sacred obligation for the lawyer ever to reveal a client's confidence. Beyond any question, once a lawyer has persuaded his client of the obligation of confidentiality, he must respect that obligation scrupulously.

II. The Specific Questions

14   The first of the difficult problems posed above will now be considered: Is it proper to cross-examine for the purpose of discrediting the reliability or the credibility of a witness whom you know to be telling the truth? Assume the following situation. Your client has been falsely accused of a robbery committed at 16th and P Streets at 11:00 p.m. He tells you at first that at no time on the evening of the crime was he within six blocks of that location. However, you are able to persuade him that he must tell you the truth and that doing so will in no way prejudice him. He then reveals to you that he was at 15th and P Streets at 10:55 that evening, but that he was walking east, away from the scene of the crime, and that, by 11:00 p.m., he was six blocks away. At the trial, there are two prosecution witnesses. The first mistakenly, but with some degree of persuasion identifies your client as the criminal. At that point, the prosecution's case depends on this single witness, who might or might not be believed. Since your client has a prior record, you do not want to put him on the stand, but you feel that there is at least a chance for acquittal. The second prosecution witness is an elderly woman who is somewhat nervous and who wears glasses. She testifies truthfully and accurately that she saw your client at 15th and P Streets at 10:55 p.m. She has corroborated the erroneous testimony of the first witness and made conviction virtually certain. However, if you destroy her reliability through cross-examination designed to show that she is easily confused and has poor eyesight, you may not only eliminate the corroboration, but also cast doubt in the jury's mind on the prosecution's entire case. On the other hand, if you should refuse to cross-examine her because she is telling the truth, your client may well feel betrayed, since you knew of the witness's veracity only because your client confided in you, under your assurance that his truthfulness would not prejudice him.

15   The client would be right. Viewed strictly, the attorney's failure to cross-examine would not be violative of the client's confidence because it

---

[9] Paul, "The Responsibilities of the Tax Adviser," 63 Harv. L. Rev. 377, 383 (1950).

would not constitute a disclosure. However, the same policy that supports the obligation of confidentiality precludes the attorney from prejudicing his client's interest in any other way because of knowledge gained in his professional capacity. When a lawyer fails to cross-examine only because his client, placing confidence in the lawyer, has been candid with him, the basis of such confidence and candor collapses. Our legal system cannot tolerate such a result.

> *The purposes and necessities of the relation between a client and his attorney require, in many cases, on the part of the client, the fullest and freest disclosures to the attorney of the client's objects, motives and acts.... To permit the attorney to reveal to others what is so disclosed, would be not only a gross violation of a sacred trust upon his part, but it would utterly destroy and prevent the usefulness and benefits to be derived from professional assistance.[10]*

The client's confidences must "upon all occasions be inviolable," to avoid the "greater mischiefs" that would probably result if a client could not feel free "to repose [confidence] in the attorney to whom he resorts for legal advice and assistance."[11] Destroy that confidence, and "a man would not venture to consult any skillful person, or would only dare to tell his counsellor half his case."[12]

16   Therefore, one must conclude that the attorney is obligated to attack, if he can, the reliability or credibility of an opposing witness whom he knows to be truthful. The contrary result would inevitably impair the "perfect freedom of consultation by client with attorney," which is "essential to the administration of justice."[13]

17   The second question is generally considered to be the hardest of all: Is it proper to put a witness on the stand when you know he will commit perjury? Assume, for example, that the witness in question is the accused himself, and that he has admitted to you, in response to your assurances of confidentiality, that he is guilty. However, he insists upon taking the stand to protect his innocence. There is a clear consensus among prosecutors and defense attorneys that the likelihood of conviction is increased enormously when the defendant does not take the stand. Consequently, the attorney who prevents his client from testifying only because the client has confided

---

[10] 2 Mechem, Agency § 2297 (2d ed. 1914).
[11] Opinion 150, Committee on Professional Ethics and Grievances of the American Bar Association (1936), quoting Thornton, *Attorneys at Law* § 94 (1914). See also Opinion 23, *supra* note 8.
[12] Greenough v. Gaskell, 1 Myl. & K. 98, 103, 39 Eng. Rep. 618, 621 (Ch. 1833) (Lord Chancellor Brougham).
[13] Opinion 91, Committee on Professional Ethics and Grievances of the American Bar Association (1933).

his guilt to him is violating that confidence by acting upon the information in a way that will seriously prejudice his client's interests.

18   Perhaps the most common method for avoiding the ethical problem just posed is for the lawyer to withdraw from the case, at least if there is sufficient time before trial for the client to retain another attorney.[14] The client will then go to the nearest law office, realizing that the obligation of confidentiality is not what it has been represented to be, and withhold incriminating information or the fact of his guilt from his new attorney. On ethical grounds, the practice of withdrawing from a case under such circumstances is indefensible, since the identical perjured testimony will ultimately be presented. More important, perhaps, is the practical consideration that the new attorney will be ignorant of the perjury and therefore will be in no position to attempt to discourage the client from presenting it. Only the original attorney, who knows the truth, has that opportunity, but he loses it in the very act of evading the ethical problem.

19   The problem is all the more difficult when the client is indigent. He cannot retain other counsel, and in many jurisdictions, including the District of Columbia, it is impossible for appointed counsel to withdraw from a case except for extraordinary reasons. Thus, appointed counsel, unless he lies to the judge, can successfully withdraw only by revealing to the judge that the attorney has received knowledge of his client's guilt. Such a revelation in itself would seem to be a sufficiently serious violation of the obligation of confidentiality to merit severe condemnation. In fact, however, the situation is far worse, since it is entirely possible that the same judge who permits the attorney to withdraw will subsequently hear the case and sentence the defendant. When he does so, of course, he will have had personal knowledge of the defendant's guilt before the trial began.[15] Moreover, this will be knowledge of which the newly appointed counsel for the defendant will probably be ignorant.

20   The difficulty is further aggravated when the client informs the lawyer for the first time during trial that he intends to take the stand and commit

---

[14] See Orkin, "Defense of One Known To Be Guilty," 1 Crim. L.Q. 170, 174 (1958). Unless the lawyer has told the client at the outset that he will withdraw if he learns that the client is guilty, "it is plain enough as a matter of good morals and professional ethics" that the lawyer should not withdraw on this ground. Opinion 90, Committee on Professional Ethics and Grievances of the American Bar Association (1932). As to the difficulties inherent in the lawyer's telling the client that he wants to remain ignorant of crucial facts, see note 8 *supra* and accompanying text.

[15] The judge may infer that the situation is worse than it is in fact. In the case related in note 23 *infra*, the attorney's actual difficulty was that he did not want to permit a plea of guilty by a client who was maintaining his innocence. However, as is commonly done, he told the judge only that he had to withdraw because of "an ethical problem." The judge reasonably inferred that the defendant had admitted his guilt and wanted to offer a perjured alibi.

perjury. The perjury in question may not necessarily be a protestation of innocence by a guilty man. Referring to the earlier hypothetical of the defendant wrongly accused of a robbery at 16th and P, the only perjury may be his denial of the truthful, but highly damaging, testimony of the corroborating witness who placed him one block away from the intersection five minutes prior to the crime. Of course, if he tells the truth and thus verifies the corroborating witness, the jury will be far more inclined to accept the inaccurate testimony of the principal witness, who specifically identified him as the criminal.[16]

21   If a lawyer has discovered his client's intent to perjure himself, one possible solution to this problem is for the lawyer to approach the bench, explain his ethical difficulty to the judge, and ask to be relieved, thereby causing a mistrial. This request is certain to be denied, if only because it would empower the defendant to cause a series of mistrials in the same fashion. At this point, some feel that the lawyer has avoided the ethical problem and can put the defendant on the stand. However, one objection to this solution, apart from the violation of confidentiality, is that the lawyer's ethical problem has not been solved, but has only been transferred to the judge. Moreover, the client in such a case might well have grounds for appeal on the basis of deprivation of due process and denial of the right to counsel, since he will have been tried before, and sentenced by, a judge who has been informed of the client's guilt by his own attorney.

22   A solution even less satisfactory than informing the judge of the defendant's guilt would be to let the client take the stand without the attorney's participation and to omit reference to the client's testimony in closing argument. The latter solution, of course, would be as damaging as to fail entirely to argue the case to the jury, and failing to argue the case is "as improper as though the attorney had told the jury that his client had uttered a falsehood in making the statement."[17]

23   Therefore, the obligation of confidentiality, in the context of our adversary system, apparently allows the attorney no alternative to putting a perjurious witness on the stand without explicit or implicit disclosure of the attorney's knowledge to either the judge or the jury. Canon 37 does not proscribe this conclusion; the canon recognizes only two exceptions to the

---

[16] One lawyer, who considers it clearly unethical for the attorney to present the alibi in this hypothetical case, found no ethical difficulty himself in the following case. His client was prosecuted for robbery. The prosecution witness testified that the robbery had taken place at 10:15, and identified the defendant as the criminal. However, the defendant had a convincing alibi for 10:00 to 10:30. The attorney presented the alibi, and the client was acquitted. The alibi was truthful, but the attorney knew that the prosecution witness had been confused about the time, and that his client had in fact committed the crime at 10:45.

[17] See note 7 *supra.*

obligation of confidentiality. The first relates to the lawyer who is accused by his client and may disclose the truth to defend himself. The other exception relates to the "announced intention of a client to commit a crime." On the basis of the ethical and practical considerations discussed above, the Canon's exception to the obligation of confidentiality cannot logically be understood to include the crime of perjury committed during the specific case in which the lawyer is serving. Moreover, even when the intention is to commit a crime in the future, Canon 37 does not require disclosure, but only permits it. Furthermore, Canon 15, which does proscribe "violation of law" by the attorney for his client, does not apply to the lawyer who unwillingly puts a perjurious client on the stand after having made every effort to dissuade him from committing perjury. Such an act by the attorney cannot properly be found to be subornation— corrupt inducement— of perjury. Canon 29 requires counsel to inform the prosecuting authorities of perjury committed in a case in which he has been involved, but this can only refer to perjury by opposing witnesses. For an attorney to disclose his client's perjury "would involve a direct violation of Canon 37."[18] Despite Canon 29, therefore, the attorney should not reveal his client's perjury "to the court or to the authorities."[19]

24   Of course, before the client testifies perjuriously, the lawyer has a duty to attempt to dissuade him on grounds of both law and morality. In addition, the client should be impressed with the fact that his untruthful alibi is tactically dangerous. There is always a strong possibility that the prosecutor will expose the perjury on cross-examination. However, for the reasons already given, the final decision must necessarily be the client's. The lawyer's best course thereafter would be to avoid any further professional relationship with a client whom he knew to have perjured himself.

25   The third question is whether it is proper to give your client legal advice when you have reason to believe that the knowledge you give him will tempt him to commit perjury. This may indeed be the most difficult problem of all, because giving such advice creates the appearance that the attorney is encouraging and condoning perjury.

26   If the lawyer is not certain what the facts are when he gives the advice, the problem is substantially minimized, if not eliminated. It is not the lawyer's function to prejudge his client as a perjurer. He cannot presume that the client will make unlawful use of his advice. Apart from this, there is a natural predisposition in most people to recollect facts, entirely

---

[18] Opinion 287, Committee on Professional Ethics and Grievances of the American Bar Association (1953).
[19] *Ibid.*

honestly, in a way most favorable to their own interest. As Randolph Paul has observed, some witnesses are nervous, some are confused about their own interests, some try to be too smart for their own good, and some subconsciously do not want to understand what has happened to them.[20] Before he begins to remember essential facts, the client is entitled to know what his own interests are.

27   The above argument does not apply merely to factual questions such as whether a particular event occurred at 10:15 or at 10:45.[21] One of the most critical problems in a criminal case, as in many others, is intention. A German writer, considering the question of intention as a test of legal consequences, suggests the following situations.[22] A young man and a young woman decide to get married. Each has a thousand dollars. They decide to begin a business with these funds, and the young lady gives her money to the young man for this purpose. Was the intention to form a joint venture or a partnership? Did they intend that the young man be an agent or a trustee? Was the transaction a gift or a loan? If the couple should subsequently visit a tax attorney and discover that it is in their interest that the transaction be viewed as a gift, it is submitted that they could, with complete honesty, so remember it. On the other hand, should their engagement be broken and the young woman consult an attorney for the purpose of recovering her money, she could with equal honesty remember that her intention was to make a loan.

28   Assume that your client, on trial for his life in a first-degree murder case, has killed another man with a penknife but insists that the killing was in self-defense. You ask him, "Do you customarily carry the penknife in your pocket, do you carry it frequently or infrequently, or did you take it with you only on this occasion?" He replies, "Why do you ask me a question like that?" It is entirely appropriate to inform him that his carrying the knife only on this occasion, or infrequently, supports an inference of premeditation, while if he carried the knife constantly, or frequently, the inference of premeditation would be negated. Thus, your client's life may depend upon his recollection as to whether he carried the knife frequently or infrequently. Despite the possibility that the client or a third party might infer that the lawyer was prompting the client to lie, the lawyer must apprise the defendant of the significance of his answer. There is no conceivable ethical requirement that the lawyer trap his client into a hasty and ill-considered answer before telling him the significance of the question.

---

[20] See Paul, *supra* note 9.
[21] Even this kind of "objective fact" is subject to honest error. See note 16 *supra*.
[22] Wurzel, *Das Juristische Denken* 82 (1904), translated in Fuller, *Basic Contract Law* 67 (1964).

29   A similar problem is created if the client has given the lawyer incriminating information before being fully aware of its significance. For example, assume that a man consults a tax lawyer and says, "I am fifty years old. Nobody in my immediate family has lived past fifty. Therefore, I would like to put my affairs in order. Specifically, I understand that I can avoid substantial estate taxes by setting up a trust. Can I do it?" The lawyer informs the client that he can successfully avoid the estate taxes only if he lives at least three years after establishing the trust or, should he die within three years, if the trust is found not to have been created in contemplation of death. The client then might ask who decides whether the trust is in contemplation of death. After learning that the determination is made by the court, the client might inquire about the factors on which such a decision would be based.

30   At this point, the lawyer can do one of two things. He can refuse to answer the question, or he can inform the client that the court will consider the wording of the trust instrument and will hear evidence about any conversations which he may have or any letters he may write expressing motives other than avoidance of estate taxes. It is likely that virtually every tax attorney in the country would answer the client's question, and that no one would consider the answer unethical. However, the lawyer might well appear to have prompted his client to deceive the Internal Revenue Service and the courts, and this appearance would remain regardless of the lawyer's explicit disclaimer to the client of any intent so to prompt him. Nevertheless, it should not be unethical for the lawyer to give the advice.

31   In a criminal case, a lawyer may be representing a client who protests his innocence, and whom the lawyer believes to be innocent. Assume, for example, that the charge is assault with intent to kill, that the prosecution has erroneous but credible eyewitness testimony against the defendant, and that the defendant's truthful alibi witness is impeachable on the basis of several felony convictions. The prosecutor, perhaps having doubts about the case, offers to permit the defendant to plead guilty to simple assault. If the defendant should go to trial and be convicted, he might well be sent to jail for fifteen years; on a plea of simple assault, the maximum penalty would be one year, and sentence might well be suspended.

32   The common practice of conveying the prosecutor's offer to the defendant should not be considered unethical, even if the defense lawyer is convinced of his client's innocence. Yet the lawyer is clearly in the position of prompting his client to lie, since the defendant cannot make the plea without saying to the judge that he is pleading guilty because he is guilty. Furthermore, if the client does decide to plead guilty, it would be improper for the lawyer to inform the court that his client is innocent, thereby

compelling the defendant to stand trial and take the substantial risk of
fifteen years' imprisonment.[23]

33   Essentially no different from the problem discussed above, but
apparently more difficult, is the so-called *Anatomy of a Murder*
situation.[24] The lawyer, who has received from his client an incriminating
story of murder in the first degree, says, "If the facts are as you have stated
them so far, you have no defense, and you will probably be electrocuted.
On the other hand, if you acted in a blind rage, there is a possibility of
saving your life. Think it over, and we will talk about it tomorrow." As in
the tax case, and as in the case of the plea of guilty to a lesser offense, the
lawyer has given his client a legal opinion that might induce the client to
lie. This is information which the lawyer himself would have, without
advice, were he in the client's position. It is submitted that the client is
entitled to have this information about the law and to make his own
decision as to whether to act upon it. To decide otherwise would not only
penalize the less well-educated defendant, but would also prejudice the
client because of his initial truthfulness in telling his story in confidence to
the attorney.

III. Conclusion

34   The lawyer is an officer of the court, participating in a search for truth. Yet
no lawyer would consider that he had acted unethically in pleading the
statute of frauds or the statute of limitations as a bar to a just claim.
Similarly, no lawyer would consider it unethical to prevent the
introduction of evidence such as a murder weapon seized in violation of
the fourth amendment or a truthful but involuntary confession, or to

---

[23] In a recent case, the defendant was accused of unauthorized use of an automobile, for
which the maximum penalty is five years. He told his court-appointed attorney that he
had borrowed the car from a man known to him only as "Junior," that he had not
known the car was stolen, and that he had an alibi for the time of the theft. The
defendant had three prior convictions for larceny, and the alibi was weak. The
prosecutor offered to accept a guilty plea to two misdemeanors (taking property
without right and petty larceny) carrying a combined maximum sentence of eighteen
months. The defendant was willing to plead guilty to the lesser offenses, but the
attorney felt that, because of his client's alibi, he could not permit him to do so. The
lawyer therefore informed the judge that he had an ethical problem and asked to be
relieved. The attorney who was appointed in his place permitted the client to plead
guilty to the two lesser offenses, and the defendant was sentenced to nine months. The
alternative would have been five or six months in jail while the defendant waited for his
jury trial, and a very substantial risk of conviction and a much heavier sentence.
Neither the client nor justice would have been well served by compelling the defendant
to go to trial against his will under these circumstances.
[24] See Traver, *Anatomy of a Murder* (1958).

defend a guilty man on grounds of denial of a speedy trial.[25] Such actions are permissible because there are policy considerations that at times justify frustrating the search for truth and the prosecution of a just claim. Similarly, there are policies that justify an affirmative answer to the three questions that have been posed in this article. These policies include the maintenance of an adversary system, the presumption of innocence, the prosecution's burden to prove guilt beyond a reasonable doubt, the right to counsel, and the obligation of confidentiality between lawyer and client.

STUDY QUESTIONS

1. In his first paragraph the author lists the three "hardest questions" he means to take up. Why does he delay discussion of these questions until after he establishes the "necessity for confidentiality" in Section I?
2. When Freedman alludes to the lawyer's obligation to "preserve his client's confidences," what does he mean (beyond the obvious signification of not verbally disclosing information given in confidence)?
3. In the first paragraph of Section II, the author poses the hypothetical situation of an innocent client whose case may be damaged by truthful testimony. Is it legitimate for the author to use such an example?
4. Suppose the case in this same paragraph were the same except that the client was in fact guilty and had told his lawyer so. Would the author still countenance a cross-examination designed to discredit a witness known to be telling the truth? How might an affirmative answer to this question be defended morally?
5. As the author points out twice in this essay, once in the opening sentences of Section I and again in the first sentence of the Conclusion, The lawyer is "an officer of the court, participating in a search for truth." Yet if his advice in the body of the essay is followed, the lawyer, as the author is well aware, will become an agent of falsehood deliberately frustrating the search for truth in the interests of his client. What ultimate values does the author appeal to in order to defend his argument?

---

[25] *Cf.* Kamisar, "Equal Justice in the Gatehouses and Mansions of American Criminal Procedure," in *Criminal Justice in Our Time* 77–78 (Howard ed. 1965):

Yes, the presence of counsel in the police station may result in the suppression of truth, just as the presence of counsel at the trial may, when a client is advised not to take the stand, or when an objection is made to the admissibility of trustworthy, but illegally seized, "real" evidence.

If the subject of police interrogation not only cannot be "coerced" into making a statement, but need not volunteer one, why shouldn't he be so advised? And why shouldn't court-appointed counsel, as well as retained counsel, so advise him?

Literature and
the Arts

The arts, including the literary arts, present us with two persistently puzzling kinds of questions, the interpretive and the evaluative.

Interpretive questions ask what a work means. Some interpreters equate meaning with the intention of the artist. An interpretation in this mode is essentially an empirical investigation, with the interpreter drawing evidence from the work itself, letters or recorded remarks of the artist, interpretations by the artist's contemporaries, and the like. Other critics argue, however, not only that the artist's intention is altogether hidden from us by time or cultural difference, but that it may not be a true index to the achieved meaning of the work. The artist may have failed to convey the intended meaning or may, perhaps through the operation of subconscious or archetypal forces, have produced richer meanings than he or she consciously recognized. While these latter critics often assume that the work has a determinate meaning even though they deny that it is identical with the author's intention, a third group would deny that any single meaning inheres in the art. They regard meaning as subjective, something existing not in the work itself or the mind of its author, but in that of the percipient. A number of recent critics have argued that a work of art lends itself to a number of interpretations that may be incompatible with each other, and that the greater the work, the greater the range of possible interpretations. Criticism based on this theory is not an empirical argument but a creative endeavor in its own right.

Several of the following selections deal with meaning and the interpretation of meaning. Laura Bohannan reports on the cross-cultural reception of a work she had considered to be universal in its meanings, and Robert Penn Warren discusses the role of meaning in our reading of fiction. Eudora Welty offers a well-known short story, which is followed by two conflicting interpretations of it and the author's own comment on one aspect of its intended meaning. Finally, Susan Sontag challenges the whole enterprise of interpretation.

Other perennial problems in criticism of the arts concern evaluation. Thirty
years ago, the evaluation of works of art tended to invoke purely aesthetic criteria,

most of which were in fact formal. In recent years, critics have stressed the moral functions of art and the moral obligations of museums, theaters, college courses involving the arts, granting agencies, and other arenas where value judgments determine what artists will be encouraged and what works of art will be presented to the public. Some critics have questioned whether aesthetic and ethical values can ever be disentangled. For instance, can a novel with majestic imagery, deeply evocative symbolism, and engrossing characters be considered great if it is tainted with racism? Questions about artistic values and their relationship to other social values are especially charged when public funds are involved, as in subsidies to museums or in grants by the National Endowment for the Arts. Among the selections in this section, those by J. A. Koten, Katha Pollitt, Richard Bernstein, Howardena Pindell, and Suzi Gablik all investigate aspects of the arts in relation to other social values.

J. A. KOTEN

Music Hath Charms to Soothe a Savage Breast but Can It Put Bread on the Table?

The following is a speech delivered to the American Symphony Orchestra League of Highland Park, Illinois, on August 11, 1982. At that time the author was Vice President for Corporate Communications of Illinois Bell. The speech is not so much a proposal in itself as advice to the audience about how to present a proposal for public support of the arts to those who control the public purse.

1   In a frequently quoted verse, the poet William Congreve tells us that music has charms to soothe a savage breast, to soften rocks, or bend a knotted oak.

2   I wouldn't go so far as to characterize the typical politician as having a savage breast. But convincing a representative of the people to vote in favor of an appropriation for the arts — for example, a symphony orchestra — just might take the ability to soften a rock or bend that knotted oak.

3   It can, however, be done. And that's what we're here to discuss today.

4   How does one go about approaching a city council, state legislature or the federal government to get funds for art groups and orchestras? What is the case for government funding? How best can the case be presented in a legislative forum or to the proper administrative branch?

5   That's the problem — and a tough one it is.

6   Recently there has been a steady erosion of public funding for the arts. This has sent cultural groups scrambling to compete for private and corporate support.

7   Support has not been lacking. In 1980, for example, in Chicago, private and corporate foundations contributed 10.8 million dollars to the arts.

8   Current wisdom — in view of the federal administration's economic policies — suggests the private sector must do more and more. It must take care of the unemployed and the aged…of the ill and infirm…provide cheap housing, cheap transportation and quality education…and raise money for museums, artists, dancers, and symphony orchestras.

9   Isn't it evident that the private sector won't do everything? That the private sector *can't* do everything?

10   Not long ago the complaint in state and local government was "Washington is taking too much away from us!" — too much power, too much autonomy, too much discretion about the distribution of resources. Cities were begging for local control of federal funding.

11   Now Washington proposes to give much of the autonomy and responsibility back to the states and the cities. And suddenly the states and cities are not overjoyed at the prospect.

12   They have their own priorities—and problems.

13   The National Conference of State Legislatures met last July in Chicago and the atmosphere was one of extreme concern. The legislators are running scared. They worry about taking care of a variety of social needs, funding for which is being decreased—or eliminated—on the federal level. Under the New Federalism they have to look at every source of possible revenue enhancement. And they must look for ways to hold the line or reduce expenses to match their diminished revenues.

14   Considering the circumstances, it is not surprising that arts and culture suffer neglect—and perhaps will be left entirely out in the cold.

15   This year in Illinois, Governor James Thompson proposed a one million dollar cut in the existing 3.8 million dollar budget for the Illinois Arts Council for fiscal 1983.

16   As recently as May, state legislators were predicting that the budget cut would pass when it was voted on in June.

17   The proposal's chief sponsor was House Appropriations Committee Chairman Representative Jacob Wolf of Chicago. He pretty much summed up the general feeling about money for the arts when he said, "The Earth is not going to end if there are no poems on the CTA (Chicago Transit Authority)." And he added—with reason—"The arts are low priority in Illinois."

18   In fact, Illinois ranks 36th among the 50 states, spending 25.1 cents per person annually on the arts.

19   The *Chicago Reporter* in May expressed concern that groups devoted to the promotion of minority culture would suffer most from the proposed cut-back in funds.

20   In response, Governor Thompson wrote a letter in which he pointed out how difficult the decisions are that must be made today to keep Illinois solvent and to avoid bankruptcy. "As long as I am governor of Illinois," he said, "this state will not go broke."

21   Who can say this is not a healthy attitude for the state's chief executive? I hope your chief executive feels the same about balancing the budget in your state or community.

22   Faced with these prospects, a number of folks involved in the arts in Illinois were feeling mighty glum about the future.

23   But, as it turned out, there was *good* news.

24   A number of individuals who put a high value on the arts, on museums, and on the symphony, engaged in some effective lobbying. They wrote letters, spoke to legislators, defended their interests to the governor.

25   Eventually, the governor withdrew his proposal to eliminate state support for the arts from the budget he proposed to the General Assembly in March.

26   The turnaround was significant. It occurred because a few people were determined to make it happen.

27   In a letter to corporate presidents and others who had helped change the governor's mind, House Democratic Leader Michael J. Madigan said this "represents a major victory for our educational and cultural institutions at a time when many other important state programs have been drastically cut back." He added—significantly—"It is a victory that would have been impossible without your support."

28   "It wouldn't have been possible without *your* support."

29   That's the cue to successful advocacy on behalf of the arts. The answer is *involvement.*

30   Involvement means more than hand-wringing or bemoaning the neglect of culture and the dearth of public funds. It means more than meeting in committee or making speeches about the glories of the arts.

31   It means we have to stop talking to one another and get out and enlist others to help support our efforts.

32   The involvement I'm talking about is *political* involvement, and it is intensely practical. To effectively convince legislators and move them to action you have to (1) understand and (2) make intelligent use of the political process.

33   The first condition for effective action is to find a sponsor for the needed appropriation—identify an individual or group of individuals willing and able to carry the ball.

34   The sponsor or sponsors ought to be people with real interest in the arts and with genuine influence with their colleagues in the legislature.

35   Now, interest can be of at least two kinds. A legislator may happen to have a sincere interest in music or the arts, or he may have a deep personal commitment to bettering the quality of life in the state. On the other hand, he may be motivated to support by the knowledge that his *constituents* have such a commitment—or that some of *his* principal supporters do.

36   If the choice of chief sponsor lies between a refined, cultured individual with season tickets to the symphony and a cigar chomper with a pinky ring, it's possible the cigar chomper will make the better sponsor. He may be the more effective because he knows his way around the political arena. The key is to make him see the practical advantages to him in championing the cause—in this case votes. If he can't see any benefit to him or his constituents, you're probably wasting your time.

37   Don't ignore the season ticket holder—there's always room for co-sponsors, and in a pinch they may have to carry the ball. But you need a lead person with political savvy.

38   Having found a sponsor, someone willing to toss a bill into the hopper, the next hurdle is committee hearings. At this point knowledgeable people of prominence and influence must be willing to testify before the committee. They must be armed with arguments calculated to convince legislators that funding of an activity like the symphony is needed, that there is a demand for it, that it will pay off in terms of a satisfied constituency…and that it makes good economic sense.

39   Meantime, it is well to remember that, having passed the legislature, an appropriations bill still requires the governor's signature. Again, there is a need for people who will exercise advocacy in both their official and social contacts. The change of mind about the arts bill I mentioned earlier was brought about largely by personal contacts with the governor—visits, letters, phone calls, casual encounters.

40   The sponsor, the witnesses, and the other advocates, must have a convincing rationale. They must be able to articulate the *reasons* why the state should devote money to the symphony.

41   The arguments *against* voting to spend money on the arts can be reduced to three: (1) There are more pressing priorities, (2) Cultural institutions, such as the symphony, are elitist, and (3) Support of the arts doesn't provide much economic benefit.

42   The arguments *in favor* of appropriating money for the arts must, therefore, demonstrate that (1) The availability of the fine arts is important to the community environment, (2) Cultural events, such as concerts, are wanted and enjoyed by the general public, and (3) There are strong economic reasons for giving money to symphonies.

43   It is easy enough for opponents to say, "Why worry about spending money on an orchestra when we don't have enough available funds to finance health care, take care of our senior citizens, and provide adequate public transportation? Who needs music when there's not enough bread on the table? First things first. So don't ask us for money for the frills."

44   How can we deal with that argument?

45   It has been known for a long time that man does not live by bread alone. Mere subsistence is not life—at least, it is not *human* life. A dog or a cat may be fat and happy if it has enough to eat and drink, but men and women need something more.

46   Human nature includes intelligence and it includes sensitivities that transcend the need for meat and potatoes, a roof overhead, and protection from predators.

47   In some of our large cities there is a religious order called the Little Brothers of the Poor. The brothers devote their life to the service of the destitute, the miserably poor.

48   Interestingly enough, when they visit a poor family, they don't come with a loaf of bread and a basket of canned goods. They spread the table

with a linen table cloth and set it with bone china and sterling silver. They provide a centerpiece of fresh flowers.

49 The meal they serve is not hamburger or hot dogs. It is more likely to be beef burgundy, or Chateaubriand, or chicken Kiev.

50 Is this an extravagance? Is it wasteful? Not if you consider how few such pleasures the poor experience in a lifetime. A gourmet meal—even if it is available but rarely—can be an enriching experience.

51 So can an opportunity to enjoy good music. It is a great mistake to think that those who patronize the symphony are only the wealthy.

52 It is neither the monied elite nor the intellectual elite who attend the concerts in Grant Park on Chicago's lakefront.

53 It is not just the elite who listen to the opera on the radio.

54 It is not a small group of cognoscenti who patronize the tours our great symphony orchestras take into towns and villages throughout the country.

55 Music is a source of enrichment to the entire population. It contributes to the quality of life in society at large.

56 Illinois, for example, is rapidly changing from an industrial state to a high technology state. Good music has a special appeal to the kind of people who will be in the high tech work force. People want to live and work where there are pleasant surroundings, good schools, and opportunities to enjoy a full measure of life.

57 Live, in-person music does reach many people—and in a way that can't be duplicated by recordings, or radio, or television. The Chicago Symphony, in any given year, reaches more than 165,000 individuals of all ages through its educational programs.

58 The Symphony touches more than 3,500 youngsters between the ages of 5 to 8...7,000 blind, hearing impaired, and physically disabled...6,000 young people through its Youth Concerts...10,000 high school students...15,000 college students...and 70,000 men, women and children from schools, hospitals, senior citizens' homes and neighborhood centers.

59 That is hardly the story of an enterprise that appeals to a small number of elitists.

60 They come because they sense there is more to life than the bare necessities. And they come from the whole spectrum of our society.

61 There is a practical sense, too, in which the arts contribute to the quality of life of a community. They aid economic development in an area—economic development which eventually provides the funds, public and private, for the high-priority, basic social programs.

62 The presence of museums, art institutes, opera, symphonies, and the like, make any area attractive to industry. An evaluation of the cultural facilities is high on the list of any organization seeking a place in which to locate or to expand.

63   It is a fallacy to think that support for the arts is money spent without hope of economic return.

64   Government may provide money for symphonies, but symphonies help generate revenues for government, too. When people travel, near or far, to hear concerts, they pay taxes—gasoline taxes for their cars, sales taxes for their food and lodging.

65   It stands to reason that a portion of this revenue should flow back to help perpetuate the source that generated it.

66   Cultural institutions also attract tourists.

67   The U.S. Chamber of Commerce estimates that the money that as few as 24 tourists a day spend in a community is equivalent to a small factory or business with an annual payroll of $100,000. That's roughly equivalent to 10 people earning an average of $10,000 per year.

68   Municipalities benefit from the property taxes businesses pay that deal with tourists or visitors.

69   The direct benefits of visitors to the private sector are income and employment to retail and service establishments in the area. Those employees extend the benefits to other sectors of the local economy through re-spending of the visitors' dollars.

70   The United States Travel Data Center in Washington reports that in 1980 (the latest year for which figures are available) the tourist trade in Illinois amounted to $5.2 billion. In the United States the figure was $160.8 billion!

71   So, if we believe business and individuals should help support symphonies—there's ample reason, strictly from a dollars and cents standpoint, for governments to do likewise.

72   Financial support of a symphony, therefore, is not a one-way street.

73   Such is the nature of our advocacy. The arguments, when advanced by proper spokespersons, can be persuasive. Successful advocates understand that politics is a practical, not a theoretical science.

74   It is possible to gain government support of symphony orchestras by pointing out that they are not just a luxury…that they fill a genuine need in the minds and hearts of all people, rich or poor…that symphonies do enhance the quality of life by making a community a better place to live and work…that symphonies do generate additional tax revenues…and that there are people—voters, if you will—who are interested in good music and will reward on election day those who recognize the great value that a symphony orchestra represents.

75   That is the essence of our case. It works. It works best when there are many who are willing to take a few moments of their time to present it in the proper forums.

STUDY QUESTIONS

1. In the middle of his speech, Koten lists three arguments why state legislators should *not* vote to appropriate money for support of the arts and three arguments why they *should*. Are the items on the second list supposed to demonstrate the falsity of those on the first or simply to counterbalance them?

2. Show how the paragraphs following the second list are organized to support its three contentions.

3. Among the reasons Koten proposes for extending public support to the arts, which are effective because they present facts that might otherwise have been overlooked? Would these facts be likely to influence a legislator favorably?

4. Which of Koten's reasons favoring public support of the arts are based on values rather than on facts?

5. Which of Koten's arguments are based on the inherent justice or fairness of the proposals and which are based on arguments from expediency (see page 42).

6. Koten describes dinners given to the poor by the Little Brothers of the Poor. What analogy is intended by this example? Is the analogy fair and effective?

SUGGESTION FOR WRITING

Write a proposal that some authority fund an activity to which they might normally be opposed on the grounds of hidden benefits to them.

TERRY EAGLETON

What Is Literature?

Terry Eagleton, a fellow and tutor in English at Wadham College, Oxford, is one of the best-known contemporary exponents of Marxist criticism and literary theory. Recently scholars have debated the nature of the literary canon, that is, the body of works generally accepted as "literature." Here, by attempting to define "literature," Eagleton mounts a challenge to the widely accepted ideas that "literature" is an objective category like "mammals." Instead, he argues, our very notion of what constitutes the literary canon is a product of the power-relations in our society.

1   If there is such a thing as literary theory, then it would seem obvious that there is something called literature which it is the theory of. We can begin, then, by raising the question: what is literature?

2   There have been various attempts to define literature. You can define it, for example, as "imaginative" writing in the sense of fiction — writing which is not literally true. But even the briefest reflection on what people commonly include under the heading of literature suggests that this will not do. Seventeenth-century English literature includes Shakespeare, Webster, Marvell and Milton; but it also stretches to the essays of Francis Bacon, the sermons of John Donne, Bunyan's spiritual autobiography and whatever it was that Sir Thomas Browne wrote. It might even at a pinch be taken to encompass Hobbes's *Leviathan* or Clarendon's *History of the Rebellion.* French seventeenth-century literature contains, along with Corneille and Racine, La Rochefoucauld's maxims, Bossuet's funeral speeches, Boileau's treatise on poetry, Madame de Sévigné's letters to her daughter and the philosophy of Descartes and Pascal. Nineteenth-century English literature usually includes Lamb (though not Bentham), Macaulay (but not Marx), Mill (but not Darwin or Herbert Spencer).

3   A distinction between "fact" and "fiction," then, seems unlikely to get us very far, not least because the distinction itself is often a questionable one. It has been argued, for instance, that our own opposition between "historical" and "artistic" truth does not apply at all to the early Icelandic sagas.[1] In the English late sixteenth and early seventeenth centuries, the word "novel" seems to have been used about both true and fictional events, and even news reports were hardly to be considered factual. Novels and news reports were neither clearly factual nor clearly fictional: our own sharp discriminations between these categories simply did not apply.[2]

---

[1] See M. I. Steblin-Kamenskij, *The Saga Mind* (Odense, 1973).
[2] See Lennard J. Davis, 'A Social History of Fact and Fiction: Authorial Disavowal in the Early English Novel,' in Edward W. Said (ed.) *Literature and Society* (Baltimore and London, 1980).

Gibbon no doubt thought that he was writing the historical truth, and so perhaps did the authors of Genesis, but they are now read as "fact" by some and "fiction" by others; Newman certainly thought his theological meditations were true but is now for many readers "literature." Moreover, if "literature" includes much "factual" writing, it also excludes quite a lot of fiction. *Superman* comic and Mills and Boon novels are fictional but not generally regarded as literature, and certainly not as Literature. If literature is "creative" or "imaginative" writing, does this imply that history, philosophy and natural science are uncreative and unimaginative?

4   Perhaps one needs a different kind of approach altogether. Perhaps literature is definable not according to whether it is fictional or "imaginative," but because it uses language in peculiar ways. On this theory, literature is a kind of writing which, in the words of the Russian critic Roman Jakobson, represents an "organized violence committed on ordinary speech." Literature transforms and intensifies ordinary language, deviates systematically from everyday speech. If you approach me at a bus stop and murmur "Thou still unravished bride of quietness," then I am instantly aware that I am in the presence of the literary. I know this because the texture, rhythm and resonance of your words are in excess of their abstractable meaning—or, as the linguists might more technically put it, there is a disproportion between the signifiers and the signifieds. Your language draws attention to itself, flaunts its material being, as statements like "Don't you know the drivers are on strike?" do not.

5   This, in effect, was the definition of the "literary" advanced by the Russian formalists, who included in their ranks Viktor Shklovsky, Roman Jakobson, Osip Brik, Yury Tynyanov, Boris Eichenbaum and Boris Tomashevsky. The Formalists emerged in Russia in the years before the 1917 Bolshevik revolution, and flourished throughout the 1920s, until they were effectively silenced by Stalinism. A militant, polemical group of critics, they rejected the quasi-mystical symbolist doctrines which had influenced literary criticism before them, and in a practical, scientific spirit shifted attention to the material reality of the literary text itself. Criticism should dissociate art from mystery and concern itself with how literary texts actually worked: literature was not pseudo-religion or psychology or sociology but a particular organization of language. It had its own specific laws, structures and devices, which were to be studied in themselves rather than reduced to something else. The literary work was neither a vehicle for ideas, a reflection of social reality nor the incarnation of some transcendental truth: it was a material fact, whose functioning could be analyzed rather as one could examine a machine. It was made of words, not of objects or feelings, and it was a mistake to see it as the expression of an author's mind. Pushkin's *Eugene Onegin*, Osip Brik once

airily remarked, would have been written even if Pushkin had not lived.

6   Formalism was essentially the application of linguistics to the study of literature; and because the linguistics in question were of a formal kind, concerned with the structures of language rather than with what one might actually say, the Formalists passed over the analysis of literary "content" (where one might always be tempted into psychology or sociology) for the study of literary form. Far from seeing form as the expression of content, they stood the relationship on its head: content was merely the "motivation" of form, an occasion or convenience for a particular kind of formal exercise. *Don Quixote* is not "about" the character of that name: the character is just a device for holding together different kinds of narrative technique. *Animal Farm* for the Formalists would not be an allegory of Stalinism; on the contrary, Stalinism would simply provide a useful opportunity for the construction of an allegory. It was this perverse insistence which won for the Formalists their derogatory name from their antagonists; and though they did not deny that art had a relation to social reality—indeed some of them were closely associated with the Bolsheviks—they provocatively claimed that this relation was not the critic's business.

7   The Formalists started out by seeing the literary work as a more or less arbitrary assemblage of "devices," and only later came to see these devices as interrelated elements or "functions" within a total textual system. "Devices" included sound, imagery, rhythm, syntax, metre, rhyme, narrative techniques, in fact the whole stock of formal literary elements; and what all of these elements had in common was their "estranging" or "defamiliarizing" effect. What was specific to literary language, what distinguished it from other forms of discourse, was that it "deformed" ordinary language in various ways. Under the pressure of literary devices, ordinary language was intensified, condensed, twisted, telescoped, drawn out, turned on its head. It was language" made strange," and because of this estrangement, the everyday world was also suddenly made unfamiliar. In the routines of everyday speech, our perceptions of and responses to reality become stale, blunted, or, as the Formalists would say, "automatized." Literature, by forcing us into a dramatic awareness of language, refreshes these habitual responses and renders objects more "perceptible." By having to grapple with language in a more strenuous, self-conscious way than usual, the world which that language contains is vividly renewed. The poetry of Gerard Manley Hopkins might provide a particularly graphic example of this. Literary discourse estranges or alienates ordinary speech, but in doing so, paradoxically, brings us into a fuller, more intimate possession of experience. Most of the time we breathe in air without being conscious of it: like language, it is the very medium in

which we move. But if the air is suddenly thickened or infected we are forced to attend to our breathing with new vigilance, and the effect of this may be a heightened experience of our bodily life. We read a scribbled note from a friend without paying much attention to its narrative structure; but if a story breaks off and begins again, switches constantly from one narrative level to another and delays its climax to keep us in suspense, we become freshly conscious of how it is constructed at the same time as our engagement with it may be intensified. The story, as the Formalists would argue, uses "impeding" or "retarding" devices to hold our attention; and in literary language, these devices are "laid bare." It was this which moved Viktor Shklovsky to remark mischievously of Laurence Sterne's *Tristram Shandy,* a novel which impedes its own story-line so much that it hardly gets off the ground, that it was "the most typical novel in world literature."

8   The Formalists, then, saw literary language as a set of deviations from a norm, a kind of linguistic violence: literature is a "special" kind of language, in contrast to the "ordinary" language we commonly use. But to spot a deviation implies being able to identify the norm from which it swerves. Though "ordinary language" is a concept beloved of some Oxford philosophers, the ordinary language of Oxford philosophers has little in common with the ordinary language of Glaswegian dockers. The language both social groups use to write love letters usually differs from the way they talk to the local vicar. The idea that there is a single "normal" language, a common currency shared equally by all members of society, is an illusion. Any actual language consists of a highly complex range of discourses, differentiated according to class, region, gender, status and so on, which can by no means be neatly unified into a single homogeneous linguistic community. One person's norm may be another's deviation: "ginnel" for "alleyway" may be poetic in Brighton but ordinary language in Barnsley. Even the most "prosaic" text of the fifteenth century may sound "poetic" to us today because of its archaism. If we were to stumble across an isolated scrap of writing from some long-vanished civilization, we could not tell whether it was "poetry" or not merely by inspecting it, since we might have no access to that society's "ordinary" discourses; and even if further research were to reveal that it was "deviatory," this would still not prove that it was poetry as not all linguistic deviations are poetic. Slang, for example. We would not be able to tell just by looking at it that it was not a piece of "realist" literature, without much more information about the way it actually functioned as a piece of writing within the society in question.

9   It is not that the Russian Formalists did not realize all this. They recognized that norms and deviations shifted around from one social or historical context to another—that "poetry" in this sense depends on where you happen to be standing at the time. The fact that a piece of language was "estranging" did not guarantee that it was always and everywhere so: it was estranging only against a certain normative linguistic

background, and if this altered then the writing might cease to be perceptible as literary. If everyone used phrases like "unravished bride of quietness" in ordinary pub conversation, this kind of language might cease to be poetic. For the Formalists, in other words, "literariness" was a function of the *differential* relations between one sort of discourse and another; it was not an eternally given property. They were not out to define "literature," but "literariness" — special uses of language, which could be found in "literary" texts but also in many places outside them. Anyone who believes that "literature" can be defined by such special uses of language has to face the fact that there is more metaphor in Manchester than there is in Marvell. There is no "literary" device — metonymy, synecdoche, litotes, chiasmus and so on — which is not quite intensively used in daily discourse.

10   Nevertheless, the Formalists still presumed that "making strange" was the essence of the literary. It was just that they relativized this use of language, saw it as a matter of contrast between one type of speech and another. But what if I were to hear someone at the next pub table remark "This is awfully squiggly handwriting!" Is this "literary" or "non-literary" language? As a matter of fact it is "literary" language, because it comes from Knut Hamsun's novel *Hunger.* But how do I know that it is literary? It doesn't, after all, focus any particular attention on itself as a verbal performance. One answer to the question of how I know that this is literary is that it comes from Knut Hamsun's novel *Hunger.* It is part of a text which I read as "fictional," which announces itself as a "novel," which may be put on university literature syllabuses and so on. The *context* tells me that it is literary; but the language itself has no inherent properties or qualities which might distinguish it from other kinds of discourse, and someone might well say this in a pub without being admired for their literary dexterity. To think of literature as the Formalists do is really to think of all literature as *poetry.* Significantly, when the Formalists came to consider prose writing, they often simply extended to it the kinds of technique they had used with poetry. But literature is usually judged to contain much besides poetry — to include, for example, realist or naturalistic writing which is not linguistically self-conscious or self-exhibiting in any striking way. People sometimes call writing "fine" precisely because it *doesn't* draw undue attention to itself: they admire its laconic plainness or low-keyed sobriety. And what about jokes, football chants and slogans, newspaper headlines, advertisements, which are often verbally flamboyant but not generally classified as literature?

11   Another problem with the "estrangement" case is that there is no kind of writing which cannot, given sufficient ingenuity, be read as estranging. Consider a prosaic, quite unambiguous statement like the one sometimes seen in the London underground system: "Dogs must be carried on the escalator." This is not perhaps quite as unambiguous as it seems at first

sight: does it mean that you *must* carry a dog on the escalator? Are you likely to be banned from the escalator unless you can find some stray mongrel to clutch in your arms on the way up? Many apparently straightforward notices contain such ambiguities: "Refuse to be put in this basket," for instance, or the British road-sign "Way Out" as read by a Californian. But even leaving such troubling ambiguities aside, it is surely obvious that the underground notice could be read as literature. One could let oneself be arrested by the abrupt, minatory *staccato* of the first ponderous monosyllables; find one's mind drifting, by the time it had reached the rich allusiveness of "carried," to suggestive resonances of helping lame dogs through life; and perhaps even detect in the very lilt and inflection of the word "escalator" a miming of the rolling, up-and-down motion of the thing itself. This may well be a fruitless sort of pursuit, but it is not significantly more fruitless than claiming to hear the cut and thrust of the rapiers in some poetic description of a duel, and it at least has the advantage of suggesting that "literature" may be at least as much a question of what people do to writing as of what writing does to them.

12   But even if someone were to read the notice in this way, it would still be a matter of reading it as *poetry*, which is only part of what is usually included in literature. Let us therefore consider another way of "misreading" the sign which might move us a little beyond this. Imagine a late-night drunk doubled over the escalator handrail who reads the notice with laborious attentiveness for several minutes and then mutters to himself "How true!" What kind of mistake is occurring here? What the drunk is doing, in fact, is taking the sign as some statement of general, even cosmic significance. By applying certain conventions of reading to its words, he prises them loose from their immediate context and generalizes them beyond their pragmatic purpose to something of wider and probably deeper import. This would certainly seem to be one operation involved in what people call literature. When the poet tells us that his love is like a red rose, we know by the very fact that he puts this statement in metre that we are not supposed to ask whether he actually had a lover who for some bizarre reason seemed to him to resemble a rose. He is telling us something about women and love in general. Literature, then, we might say, is "non-pragmatic" discourse: unlike biology textbooks and notes to the milkman it serves no immediate practical purpose, but is to be taken as referring to a general state of affairs. Sometimes, though not always, it may employ peculiar language as though to make this fact obvious—to signal that what is at stake is a *way of talking* about a woman, rather than any particular real-life woman. This focusing on the way of talking, rather than on the reality of what is talked about, is sometimes taken to indicate that we mean by literature a kind of *self-referential* language, a language which talks about itself.

13   There are, however, problems with this way of defining literature too. For one thing, it would probably have come as a surprise to George Orwell to hear that his essays were to be read as though the topics he discussed were less important than the way he discussed them. In much that is classified as literature, the truth-value and practical relevance of what is said *is* considered important to the overall effect. But even if treating discourse "non-pragmatically" is part of what is meant by "literature," then it follows from this "definition" that literature cannot in fact be "objectively" defined. It leaves the definition of literature up to how somebody decides to *read*, not to the nature of what is written. There are certain kinds of writing—poems, plays, novels—which are fairly obviously intended to be "non-pragmatic" in this sense, but this does not guarantee that they will actually be read in this way. I might well read Gibbon's account of the Roman empire not because I am misguided enough to believe that it will be reliably informative about ancient Rome but because I enjoy Gibbon's prose style, or revel in images of human corruption whatever their historical source. But I might read Robert Burns's poem because it is not clear to me, as a Japanese horticulturalist, whether or not the red rose flourished in eighteenth-century Britain. This, it will be said, is not reading it "as literature"; but am I reading Orwell's essays as literature only if I generalize what he says about the Spanish civil war to some cosmic utterance about human life? It is true that many of the works studied as literature in academic institutions were "constructed" to be read as literature, but it is also true that many of them were not. A piece of writing may start off life as history or philosophy and then come to be ranked as literature; or it may start off as literature and then come to be valued for its archaeological significance. Some texts are born literary, some achieve literariness, and some have literariness thrust upon them. Breeding in this respect may count for a good deal more than birth. What matters may not be where you came from but how people treat you. If they decide that you are literature then it seems that you are, irrespective of what you thought you were.

14   In this sense, one can think of literature less as some inherent quality or set of qualities displayed by certain kinds of writing all the way from *Beowulf* to Virginia Woolf, than as a number of ways in which people *relate themselves* to writing. It would not be easy to isolate, from all that has been variously called "literature," some constant set of inherent features. In fact it would be as impossible as trying to identify the single distinguishing feature which all games have in common. There is no "essence" of literature whatsoever. Any bit of writing may be read "non-pragmatically," if that is what reading a text as literature means, just as any writing may abe read "poetically." If I pore over the railway timetable not to discover a train connection but to stimulate in myself general reflections on the speed

and complexity of modern existence, then I might be said to be reading it as literature. John M. Ellis has argued that the term "literature" operates rather like the word "weed": weeds are not particular kinds of plant, but just any kind of plant which for some reason or another a gardener does not want around.[3] Perhaps "literature" means something like the opposite: any kind of writing which for some reason or another somebody values highly. As the philosophers might say, "literature" and "weed" are *functional* rather than *ontological* terms: they tell us about what we do, not about the fixed being of things. They tell us about the role of a text or a thistle in a social context, its relations with and differences from its surroundings, the ways it behaves, the purposes it may be put to and the human practices clustered around it. "Literature" is in this sense a purely formal, empty sort of definition. Even if we claim that it is a non-pragmatic treatment of language, we have still not arrived at an "essence" of literature because this is also so of other linguistic practices such as jokes. In any case, it is far from clear that we can discriminate neatly between "practical" and "non-practical" ways of relating ourselves to language. Reading a novel for pleasure obviously differs from reading a road sign for information, but how about reading a biology textbook to improve your mind? Is that a "pragmatic" treatment of language or not? In many societies, "literature" has served highly practical functions such as religious ones; distinguishing sharply between "practical" and "non-practical" may only be possible in a society like ours, where literature has ceased to have much practical function at all. We may be offering as a general definition a sense of the "literary" which is in fact historically specific.

15   We have still not discovered the secret, then, of why Lamb, Macaulay and Mill are literature but not, generally speaking, Bentham, Marx and Darwin. Perhaps the simple answer is that the first three are examples of "fine writing," whereas the last three are not. This answer has the disadvantage of being largely untrue, at least in my judgement, but it has the advantage of suggesting that by and large people term "literature" writing which they think is *good.* An obvious objection to this is that if it were entirely true there would be no such thing as "bad literature." I may consider Lamb and Macaulay overrated, but that does not necessarily mean that I stop regarding them as literature. You may consider Raymond Chandler "good of his kind," but not exactly literature. On the other hand, if Macaulay were a *really* bad writer—if he had no grasp at all of grammar and seemed interested in nothing but white mice—then people might well not call his work literature at all, even bad literature. Value-judgements would certainly seem to have a lot to do with what is judged literature and

---

[3] *The Theory of Literary Criticism: A Logical Analysis* (Berkeley, 1974), pp. 37–42.

what isn't—not necessarily in the sense that writing has to be "fine" to be literary, but that it has to be *of the kind* that is judged fine: it may be an inferior example of a generally valued mode. Nobody would bother to say that a bus ticket was an example of inferior literature, but someone might well say that the poetry of Ernest Dowson was. The term "fine writing," or *belles lettres,* is in this sense ambiguous: it denotes a sort of writing which is generally highly regarded, while not necessarily committing you to the opinion that a particular specimen of it is "good."

16   With this reservation, the suggestion that "literature" is a highly valued kind of writing is an illuminating one. But it has one fairly devastating consequence. It means that we can drop once and for all the illusion that the category "literature" is "objective," in the sense of being eternally given and immutable. Anything can be literature, and anything which is regarded as unalterably and unquestionably literature—Shakespeare, for example—can cease to be literature. Any belief that the study of literature is the study of a stable, well-definable entity, as entomology is the study of insects, can be abandoned as a chimera. Some kinds of fiction are literature and some are not; some literature is fictional and some is not; some literature is verbally self-regarding, while some highly-wrought rhetoric is not literature. Literature, in the sense of a set of works of assured and unalterable value, distinguished by certain shared inherent properties, does not exist. When I use the words "literary" and "literature" from here on in this book, then, I place them under an invisible crossing-out mark, to indicate that these terms will not really do but that we have no better ones at the moment.

17   The reason why it follows from the definition of literature as highly valued writing that it is not a stable entity is that value-judgments are notoriously variable. "Times change, values don't," announces an advertisement for a daily newspaper, as though we still believed in killing off infirm infants or putting the mentally ill on public show. Just as people may treat a work as philosophy in one century and as literature in the next, or vice versa, so they may change their minds about what writing they consider valuable. They may even change their minds about the grounds they use for judging what is valuable and what is not. This, as I have suggested, does not necessarily mean that they will refuse the title of literature to a work which they have come to deem inferior: they may still call it literature, meaning roughly that it belongs to the *type* of writing which they generally value. But it does mean that the so-called "literary canon," the unquestioned "great tradition" of the "national literature," has to be recognized as a *construct,* fashioned by particular people for particular reasons at a certain time. There is no such thing as a literary work or tradition which is valuable *in itself,* regardless of what anyone might have said or come to say about it. "Value" is a transitive term: it

means whatever is valued by certain people in specific situations, according to particular criteria and in the light of given purposes. It is thus quite possible that, given a deep enough transformation of our history, we may in the future produce a society which was unable to get anything at all out of Shakespeare. His works might simply seem desperately alien, full of styles of thought and feeling which such a society found limited or irrelevant. In such a situation, Shakespeare would be no more valuable than such present-day graffiti. And though many people would consider such a social condition tragically impoverished, it seems to me dogmatic not to entertain the possibility that it might arise rather from a general human enrichment. Karl Marx was troubled by the question of why ancient Greek art retained an "eternal charm," even though the social conditions which produced it had long passed; but how do we know that it will remain "eternally" charming, since history has not yet ended? Let us imagine that by dint of some deft archaeological research we discovered a great deal more about what ancient Greek tragedy actually meant to its original audiences, recognized that these concerns were utterly remote from our own, and began to read the plays again in the light of this deepened knowledge. One result might be that we stopped enjoying them. We might come to see that we had enjoyed them previously because we were unwittingly reading them in the light of our own preoccupations; once this became less possible, the drama might cease to speak at all significantly to us.

18   The fact that we always interpret literary works to some extent in the light of our own concerns—indeed that in one sense of "our own concerns" we are incapable of doing anything else—might be one reason why certain works of literature seem to retain their value across the centuries. It may be, of course, that we still share many preoccupations with the work itself; but it may also be that people have not actually been valuing the "same" work at all, even though they may think they have. "Our" Homer is not identical with the Homer of the Middle Ages, nor "our" Shakespeare with that of his contemporaries; it is rather that different historical periods have constructed a "different" Homer and Shakespeare for their own purposes, and found in these texts elements to value or devalue, though not necessarily the same ones. All literary works, in other words, are "rewritten," if only unconsciously, by the societies which read them; indeed there is no reading of a work which is not also a "re-writing." No work, and no current evaluation of it, can simply be extended to new groups of people without being changed, perhaps almost unrecognizably, in the process; and this is one reason why what counts as literature is a notably unstable affair.

19   I do not mean that it is unstable because value-judgments are "subjective." According to this view, the world is divided between solid

facts "out there" like Grand Central station, and arbitrary value-judgments "in here" such as liking bananas or feeling that the tone of a Yeats poem veers from defensive hectoring to grimly resilient resignation. Facts are public and unimpeachable, values are private and gratuitous. There is an obvious difference between recounting a fact, such as "This cathedral was built in 1612," and registering a value-judgment, such as "This cathedral is a magnificent specimen of baroque architecture." But suppose I made the first kind of statement while showing an overseas visitor around England, and found that it puzzled her considerably. Why, she might ask, do you keep telling me the dates of the foundation of all these buildings? Why this obsession with origins? In the society I live in, she might go on, we keep no record at all of such events: we classify our buildings instead according to whether they face north-west or south-east. What this might do would be to demonstrate part of the unconscious system of value-judgments which underlies my own descriptive statements. Such value-judgements are not necessarily of the same kind as "This cathedral is a magnificent specimen of baroque architecture," but they are value-judgements nonetheless, and no factual pronouncement I make can escape them. Statements of fact are after all *statements,* which presumes a number of questionable judgements: that those statements are worth making, perhaps more worth making than certain others, that I am the sort of person entitled to make them and perhaps able to guarantee their truth, that you are the kind of person worth making them to, that something useful is accomplished by making them, and so on. A pub conversation may well transmit information, but what also bulks large in such dialogue is a strong element of what linguists would call the "phatic," a concern with the act of communication itself. In chatting to you about the weather I am also signalling that I regard conversation with you as valuable, that I consider you a worthwhile person to talk to, that I am not myself anti-social or about to embark on a detailed critique of your personal appearance.

20   In this sense, there is no possibility of a wholly disinterested statement. Of course stating when a cathedral was built is reckoned to be more disinterested in our own culture than passing an opinion about its architecture, but one could also imagine situations in which the former statement would be more "value-laden" than the latter. Perhaps "baroque" and "magnificent" have come to be more or less synonymous, whereas only a stubborn rump of us cling to the belief that the date when a building was founded is significant, and my statement is taken as a coded way of signalling this partisanship. All of our descriptive statements move within an often invisible network of value-categories, and indeed without such categories we would have nothing to say to each other at all. It is not just as though we have something called factual knowledge which may then be distorted by particular interests and judgements, although this is certainly

possible; it is also that without particular interests we would have no knowledge at all, because we would not see the point of bothering to get to know anything. Interests are *constitutive* of our knowledge, not merely prejudices which imperil it. The claim that knowledge should be "value-free" is itself a value-judgement.

21   It may well be that a liking for bananas is a merely private matter, though this is in fact questionable. A thorough analysis of my tastes in food would probably reveal how deeply relevant they are to certain formative experiences in early childhood, to my relations with my parents and siblings and to a good many other cultural factors which are quite as social and "non-subjective" as railway stations. This is even more true of that fundamental structure of beliefs and interests which I am born into as a member of a particular society, such as the belief that I should try to keep in good health, that differences of sexual role are rooted in human biology or that human beings are more important than crocodiles. We may disagree on this or that, but we can only do so because we share certain "deep" ways of seeing and valuing which are bound up with our social life, and which could not be changed without transforming that life. Nobody will penalize me heavily if I dislike a particular Donne poem, but if I argue that Donne is not literature at all then in certain circumstances I might risk losing my job. I am free to vote Labour or Conservative, but if I try to act on the belief that this choice itself merely masks a deeper prejudice—the prejudice that the meaning of democracy is confined to putting a cross on a ballot paper every few years—then in certain unusual circumstances I might end up in prison.

22   The largely concealed structure of values which informs and underlies our factual statements is part of what is meant by "ideology." By "ideology" I mean, roughly, the ways in which what we say and believe connects with the power-structure and power-relations of the society we live in. It follows from such a rough definition of ideology that not all of our underlying judgements and categories can usefully be said to be ideological. It is deeply ingrained in us to imagine ourselves moving forwards into the future (at least one other society sees itself as moving backwards into it), but though this way of seeing *may* connect significantly with the power-structure of our society, it need not always and everywhere do so. I do not mean by "ideology" simply the deeply entrenched, often unconscious beliefs which people hold; I mean more particularly those modes of feeling, valuing, perceiving and believing which have some kind of relation to the maintenance and reproduction of social power. The fact that such beliefs are by no means merely private quirks may be illustrated by a literary example.

23   In his famous study *Practical Criticism* (1929), the Cambridge critic I. A. Richards sought to demonstrate just how whimsical and subjective literary value-judgements could actually be by giving his undergraduates a

set of poems, withholding from them the titles and authors' names, and asking them to evaluate them. The resulting judgements, notoriously, were highly variable: time-honoured poets were marked down and obscure authors celebrated. To my mind, however, much the most interesting aspect of this project, and one apparently quite invisible to Richards himself, is just how tight a consensus of unconscious valuations underlies these particular differences of opinion. Reading Richards' undergraduates' accounts of literary works, one is struck by the habits of perception and interpretation which they spontaneously share—what they expect literature to be, what assumptions they bring to a poem and what fulfilments they anticipate they will derive from it. None of this is really surprising: for all the participants in this experiment were, presumably, young, white, upper- or upper-middle-class, privately educated English people of the 1920s, and how they responded to a poem depended on a good deal more than purely "literary" factors. Their critical responses were deeply entwined with their broader prejudices and beliefs. This is not a matter of *blame:* there is no critical response which is not so entwined, and thus no such thing as a "pure" literary critical judgement or interpretation. If anybody is to be blamed it is I. A. Richards himself, who as a young, white, upper-middle-class male Cambridge don was unable to objectify a context of interests which he himself largely shared, and was thus unable to recognize fully that local, "subjective" differences of evaluation work within a particular, socially structured way of perceiving the world.

24   If it will not do to see literature as an "objective," descriptive category, neither will it do to say that literature is just what people whimsically choose to call literature. For there is nothing at all whimsical about such kinds of value-judgement: they have their roots in deeper structures of belief which are as apparently unshakeable as the Empire State building. What we have uncovered so far, then, is not only that literature does not exist in the sense that insects do, and that the value-judgements by which it is constituted are historically variable, but that these value-judgements themselves have a close relation to social ideologies. They refer in the end not simply to private taste, but to the assumptions by which certain social groups exercise and maintain power over others. If this seems a far-fetched assertion, a matter of private prejudice, we may test it out by an account of the rise of "literature" in England.

STUDY QUESTIONS

1. The early pages of this essay are organized into blocks, each discussing one of the definitions of "literature" that Eagleton proposes and rejects. What are these definitions?

2. What definition, if any, does Eagleton finally accept?
3. At different points Eagleton compares the definition of literature to the definition of "game" and the definition of "weeds." What points is he making by these comparisons?
4. What does Eagleton mean by "ideology," and how is a person's (or a society's) notion of the "literary canon" an ideological matter?

SUGGESTION FOR WRITING

If, unlike Eagleton, you believe that "literature" can be successfully defined in terms of essential characteristics, (so that, for example, we could say that *Hamlet* is literature while the *Origin of Species* is not, because the one embodies the defining features while the other does not), write an essay proposing your definition and arguing against the objections that you think Eagleton might raise.

LAURA BOHANNAN

Shakespeare in the Bush

Laura Bohannan, an American anthropologist who received a doctorate from Oxford, originally wrote this article for the BBC's Third Programme. It was republished in *Natural History* in 1966 and has been reprinted several times since.

The story may be considered a report of an investigation into an empirical question about literary interpretation: Will a classic tragedy have essentially the same meaning for readers the whole world over?

1   Just before I left Oxford for the Tiv in West Africa, conversation turned to the season at Stratford. "You Americans," said a friend, "often have difficulty with Shakespeare. He was, after all, a very English poet, and one can easily misinterpret the universal by misunderstanding the particular."

2   I protested that human nature is pretty much the same the whole world over; at least the general plot and motivation of the greater tragedies would always be clear—everywhere—although some details of custom might have to be explained and difficulties of translation might produce other slight changes. To end an argument we could not conclude, my friend gave me a copy of *Hamlet* to study in the African bush: it would, he hoped, lift my mind above its primitive surroundings, and possibly I might, by prolonged meditation, achieve the grace of correct interpretation.

3   It was my second field trip to that African tribe, and I thought myself ready to live in one of its remote sections—an area difficult to cross even on foot. I eventually settled on the hillock of a very knowledgeable old man, the head of a homestead of some hundred and forty people, all of whom were either his close relatives or their wives and children. Like the other elders of the vicinity, the old man spent most of his time performing ceremonies seldom seen these days in the more accessible parts of the tribe. I was delighted. Soon there would be three months of enforced isolation and leisure, between the harvest that takes place just before the rising of the swamps and the clearing of new farms when the water goes down. Then, I thought, they would have even more time to perform ceremonies and explain them to me.

4   I was quite mistaken. Most of the ceremonies demanded the presence of elders from several homesteads. As the swamps rose, the old men found it too difficult to walk from one homestead to the next, and the ceremonies gradually ceased. As the swamps rose even higher, all activities but one came to an end. The women brewed beer from maize and millet. Men, women, and children sat on their hillocks and drank it.

5   People began to drink at dawn. By midmorning the whole homestead was singing, dancing, and drumming. When it rained, people had to sit

inside their huts: there they drank and sang or they drank and told stories. In any case, by noon or before, I either had to join the party or retire to my own hut and my books. "One does not discuss serious matters when there is beer. Come, drink with us." Since I lacked their capacity for the thick native beer, I spent more and more time with *Hamlet*. Before the end of the second month, grace descended on me. I was quite sure that *Hamlet* had only one possible interpretation, and that one universally obvious.

6   Early every morning, in the hope of having some serious talk before the beer party, I used to call on the old man at his reception hut—a circle of posts supporting a thatched roof above a low mud wall to keep out wind and rain. One day I crawled through the low doorway and found most of the men of the homestead sitting huddled in their ragged cloths on stools, low plank beds, and reclining chairs, warming themselves against the chill of the rain around a smoky fire. In the center were three pots of beer. The party had started.

7   The old man greeted me cordially. "Sit down and drink." I accepted a large calabash full of beer, poured some into a small drinking gourd, and tossed it down. Then I poured some more into the same gourd for the man second in seniority to my host before I handed my calabash over to a young man for further distribution. Important people shouldn't ladle beer themselves.

8   "It is better like this," the old man said, looking at me approvingly and plucking at the thatch that had caught in my hair. "You should sit and drink with us more often. Your servants tell me that when you are not with us, you sit inside your hut looking at a paper."

9   The old man was acquainted with four kinds of "papers": tax receipts, bride price receipts, court fee receipts, and letters. The messenger who brought him letters from the chief used them mainly as a badge of office, for he always knew what was in them and told the old man. Personal letters for the few who had relatives in the government or mission stations were kept until someone went to a large market where there was a letter writer and reader. Since my arrival, letters were brought to me to be read. A few men also brought me bride price receipts, privately, with requests to change the figures to a higher sum. I found moral arguments were of no avail, since in-laws are fair game, and the technical hazards of forgery difficult to explain to an illiterate people. I did not wish them to think me silly enough to look at any such papers for days on end, and I hastily explained that my "paper" was one of the "things of long ago" of my country.

10   "Ah," said the old man. "Tell us."

11   I protested that I was not a storyteller. Storytelling is a skilled art among them; their standards are high, and the audiences critical—and vocal in their criticism. I protested in vain. This morning they wanted to

hear a story while they drank. They threatened to tell me no more stories until I told them one of mine. Finally, the old man promised that no one would criticize my style "for we know you are struggling with our language." "But," put in one of the elders, "you must explain what we do not understand, as we do when we tell you our stories." Realizing that here was my chance to prove *Hamlet* universally intelligible, I agreed.

12   The old man handed me some more beer to help me on with my storytelling. Men filled their long wooden pipes and knocked coals from the fire to place in the pipe bowls; then, puffing contentedly, they sat back to listen. I began in the proper style, "Not yesterday, not yesterday, but long ago, a thing occurred. One night three men were keeping watch outside the homestead of the great chief, when suddenly they saw the former chief approach them."

13   "Why was he no longer their chief?"

14   "He was dead," I explained. "That is why they were troubled and afraid when they saw him."

15   "Impossible," began one of the elders, handing his pipe on to his neighbor, who interrupted, "Of course it wasn't the dead chief. It was an omen sent by a witch. Go on."

16   Slightly shaken, I continued. "One of these three was a man who knew things" — the closest translation for scholar, but unfortunately it also meant witch. The second elder looked triumphantly at the first. "So he spoke to the dead chief saying, 'Tell us what we must do so you may rest in your grave,' but the dead chief did not answer. He vanished, and they could see him no more. Then the man who knew things—his name was Horatio—said this event was the affair of the dead chief's son, Hamlet."

17   There was a general shaking of heads round the circle. "Had the dead chief no living brothers? Or was this son the chief?"

18   "No," I replied. "That is, he had one living brother who became the chief when the elder brother died."

19   The old men muttered: such omens were matters for chiefs and elders, not for youngsters; no good could come of going behind a chief's back; clearly Horatio was not a man who knew things.

20   "Yes, he was," I insisted, shooing a chicken away from my beer. "In our country the son is next to the father. The dead chief's younger brother had become the great chief. He had also married his elder brother's widow only about a month after the funeral."

21   "He did well," the old man beamed and announced to the others, "I told you that if we knew more about Europeans, we would find they really were very like us. In our country also," he added to me, "the younger brother marries the elder brother's widow and becomes the father of his

children. Now, if your uncle, who married your widowed mother, is your father's full brother, then he will be a real father to you. Did Hamlet's father and uncle have one mother?"

22   His question barely penetrated my mind; I was too upset and thrown too far off balance by having one of the most important elements of *Hamlet* knocked straight out of the picture. Rather uncertainly I said that I thought they had the same mother, but I wasn't sure—the story didn't say. The old man told me severely that these genealogical details made all the difference and that when I got home I must ask the elders about it. He shouted out the door to one of his younger wives to bring his goatskin bag.

23   Determined to save what I could of the mother motif, I took a deep breath and began again. "The son Hamlet was very sad because his mother had married again so quickly. There was no need for her to do so, and it is our custom for a widow not to go to her next husband until she has mourned for two years."

24   "Two years is too long," objected the wife, who had appeared with the old man's battered goatskin bag. "Who will hoe your farms for you while you have no husband?"

25   "Hamlet," I retorted without thinking, "was old enough to hoe his mother's farms himself. There was no need for her to remarry." No one looked convinced. I gave up. "His mother and the great chief told Hamlet not to be sad, for the great chief himself would be a father to Hamlet. Furthermore, Hamlet would be the next chief: therefore he must stay to learn the things of a chief. Hamlet agreed to remain, and all the rest went off to drink beer."

26   While I paused, perplexed at how to render Hamlet's disgusted soliloquy to an audience convinced that Claudius and Gertrude had behaved in the best possible manner, one of the younger men asked me who had married the other wives of the dead chief.

27   "He had no other wives," I told him.

28   "But a chief must have many wives! How else can he brew beer and prepare food for all his guests?"

29   I said firmly that in our country even chiefs had only one wife, that they had servants to do their work, and that they paid them from tax money.

30   It was better, they returned, for a chief to have many wives and sons who would help him hoe his farms and feed his people; then everyone loved the chief who gave much and took nothing—taxes were a bad thing.

31   I agreed with the last comment, but for the rest fell back on their favorite way of fobbing off my questions: "That is the way it is done, so that is how we do it."

32   I decided to skip the soliloquy. Even if Claudius was here thought quite right to marry his brother's widow, there remained the poison motif, and I

knew they would disapprove of fratricide. More hopefully I resumed, "That night Hamlet kept watch with the three who had seen his dead father. The dead chief again appeared, and although the others were afraid, Hamlet followed his dead father off to one side. When they were alone, Hamlet's dead father spoke."

33   "Omens can't talk!" The old man was emphatic.

34   "Hamlet's father wasn't an omen. Seeing him might have been an omen, but he was not." My audience looked as confused as I sounded. "It *was* Hamlet's dead father. It was a thing we call a 'ghost.'" I had to use the English word, for unlike many of the neighboring tribes, these people didn't believe in the survival after death of any individuating part of the personality.

35   "What is a 'ghost?' An omen?"

36   "No, a 'ghost' is someone who is dead but who walks around and can talk, and people can hear him and see him but not touch him."

37   They objected. "One can touch zombis."

38   "No, no! It was not a dead body the witches had animated to sacrifice and eat. No one else made Hamlet's dead father walk. He did it himself."

39   "Dead men can't walk," protested my audience as one man.

40   I was quite willing to compromise. "A 'ghost' is the dead man's shadow."

41   But again they objected. "Dead men cast no shadows."

42   "They do in my country," I snapped.

43   The old man quelled the babble of disbelief that arose immediately and told me with that insincere, but courteous, agreement one extends to the fancies of the young, ignorant, and superstitious, "No doubt in your country the dead can also walk without being zombis." From the depths of his bag he produced a withered fragment of kola nut, bit off one end to show it wasn't poisoned, and handed me the rest as a peace offering.

44   "Anyhow," I resumed, "Hamlet's dead father said that his own brother, the one who became chief, had poisoned him. He wanted Hamlet to avenge him. Hamlet believed this in his heart, for he did not like his father's brother." I took another swallow of beer. "In the country of the great chief, living in the same homestead, for it was a very large one, was an important elder who was often with the chief to advise and help him. His name was Polonius. Hamlet was courting his daughter, but her father and her brother...[I cast hastily about for some tribal analogy] warned her not to let Hamlet visit her when she was alone on her farm, for he would be a great chief and so could not marry her."

45   "Why not?" asked the wife, who had settled down on the edge of the old man's chair. He frowned at her for asking stupid questions and growled, "They lived in the same homestead."

46   "That was not the reason," I informed them. "Polonius was a stranger who lived in the homestead because he helped the chief, not because he was a relative."

47   "Then why couldn't Hamlet marry her?"

48   "He could have," I explained, "but Polonius didn't think he would. After all, Hamlet was a man of great importance who ought to marry a chief's daughter, for in his country a man could have only one wife. Polonius was afraid that if Hamlet made love to his daughter, then no one else would give a high price for her."

49   "That might be true," remarked one of the shrewder elders, "but a chief's son would give his mistress's father enough presents and patronage to more than make up the difference. Polonius sounds like a fool to me."

50   "Many people think he was," I agreed. "Meanwhile Polonius sent his son Laertes off to Paris to learn the things of that country, for it was the homestead of a very great chief indeed. Because he was afraid that Laertes might waste a lot of money on beer and women and gambling, or get into trouble by fighting, he sent one of his servants to Paris secretly to spy out what Laertes was doing. One day Hamlet came upon Polonius's daughter Ophelia. He behaved so oddly he frightened her. Indeed" — I was fumbling for words to express the dubious quality of Hamlet's madness — "the chief and many others had also noticed that when Hamlet talked one could understand the words but not what they meant. Many people thought that he had become mad." My audience suddenly became much more attentive. "The great chief wanted to know what was wrong with Hamlet, so he sent for two of Hamlet's age mates [school friends would have taken long explanation] to talk to Hamlet and find out what troubled his heart. Hamlet, seeing that they had been bribed by the chief to betray him, told them nothing. Polonius, however, insisted that Hamlet was mad because he had been forbidden to see Ophelia, whom he loved."

51   "Why," inquired a bewildered voice, "should anyone bewitch Hamlet on that account?"

52   "Bewitch him?"

53   "Yes, only witchcraft can make anyone mad, unless, of course, one sees the beings that lurk in the forest."

54   I stopped being a storyteller, took out my notebook and demanded to be told more about these two causes of madness. Even while they spoke and I jotted notes, I tried to calculate the effect of this new factor on the plot. Hamlet had not been exposed to the beings that lurk in the forests. Only his relatives in the male line could bewitch him. Barring relatives not mentioned by Shakespeare, it had to be Claudius who was attempting to harm him. And, of course, it was.

55   For the moment I staved off questions by saying that the great chief also refused to believe that Hamlet was mad for the love of Ophelia and nothing else. "He was sure that something much more important was troubling Hamlet's heart."

56   "Now Hamlet's age mates," I continued, "had brought with them a famous storyteller. Hamlet decided to have this man tell the chief and all his homestead a story about a man who had poisoned his brother because he desired his brother's wife and wished to be chief himself. Hamlet was sure the great chief could not hear the story without making a sign if he was indeed guilty, and then he would discover whether his dead father had told him the truth."

57   The old man interrupted, with deep cunning, "Why should a father lie to his son?" he asked.

58   I hedged: "Hamlet wasn't sure that it really was his dead father." It was impossible to say anything, in that language, about devil-inspired visions.

59   "You mean," he said, "it actually was an omen, and he knew witches sometimes send false ones. Hamlet was a fool not to go to one skilled in reading omens and divining the truth in the first place. A man-who-sees-the-truth could have told him how his father died, if he really had been poisoned, and if there was witchcraft in it; then Hamlet could have called the elders to settle the matter."

60   The shrewd elder ventured to disagree. "Because his father's brother was a great chief, one-who-sees-the-truth might therefore have been afraid to tell it. I think it was for that reason that a friend of Hamlet's father—a witch and an elder—sent an omen so his friend's son would know. Was the omen true?"

61   "Yes," I said, abandoning ghosts and the devil; a witch-sent omen it would have to be. "It was true, for when the storyteller was telling his tale before all the homestead, the great chief rose in fear. Afraid that Hamlet knew his secret he planned to have him killed."

62   The stage set of the next bit presented some difficulties of translation. I began cautiously. "The great chief told Hamlet's mother to find out from her son what he knew. But because a woman's children are always first in her heart, he had the important elder Polonius hide behind a cloth that hung against the wall of Hamlet's mother's sleeping hut. Hamlet started to scold his mother for what she had done."

63   There was a shocked murmur from everyone. A man should never scold his mother.

64   "She called out in fear, and Polonius moved behind the cloth. Shouting, 'A rat!' Hamlet took his machete and slashed through the cloth." I paused for dramatic effect. "He had killed Polonius!"

65   The old men looked at each other in supreme disgust. "That Polonius truly was a fool and a man who knew nothing! What child would not know enough to shout, 'It's me!'" With a pang, I remembered that these people are ardent hunters, always armed with bow, arrow, and machete; at the first rustle in the grass an arrow is aimed and ready, and the hunter

shouts "Game!" If no human voice answers immediately, the arrow speeds on its way. Like a good hunter Hamlet had shouted, "A rat!"

66   I rushed in to save Polonius's reputation. "Polonius did speak. Hamlet heard him. But he thought it was the chief and wished to kill him to avenge his father. He had meant to kill him earlier that evening..." I broke down, unable to describe to these pagans, who had no belief in individual afterlife, the difference between dying at one's prayers and dying "unhousell'd, disappointed, unaneled."

67   This time I had shocked my audience seriously. "For a man to raise his hand against his father's brother and the one who has become his father— that is a terrible thing. The elders ought to let such a man be bewitched."

68   I nibbled at my kola nut in some perplexity, then pointed out that after all the man had killed Hamlet's father.

69   "No," pronounced the old man, speaking less to me than to the young men sitting behind the elders. "If your father's brother has killed your father, you must appeal to your father's age mates; *they* may avenge him. No man may use violence against his senior relatives." Another thought struck him. "But if his father's brother had indeed been wicked enough to bewitch Hamlet and make him mad that would be a good story indeed, for it would be his fault that Hamlet, being mad, no longer had any sense and thus was ready to kill his father's brother."

70   There was a murmur of applause. *Hamlet* was again a good story to them, but it no longer seemed quite the same story to me. As I thought over the coming complications of plot and motive, I lost courage and decided to skim over dangerous ground quickly.

71   "The great chief," I went on, "was not sorry that Hamlet had killed Polonius. It gave him a reason to send Hamlet away, with his two treacherous age mates, with letters to a chief of a far country, saying that Hamlet should be killed. But Hamlet changed the writing on their papers, so that the chief killed his age mates instead." I encountered a reproachful glare from one of the men whom I had told undetectable forgery was not merely immoral but beyond human skill. I looked the other way.

72   "Before Hamlet could return, Laertes came back for his father's funeral. The great chief told him Hamlet had killed Polonius. Laertes swore to kill Hamlet because of this, and because his sister Ophelia, hearing her father had been killed by the man she loved, went mad and drowned in the river."

73   "Have you already forgotten what we told you?" The old man was reproachful. "One cannot take vengeance on a madman; Hamlet killed Polonius in his madness. As for the girl, she not only went mad, she was drowned. Only witches can make people drown. Water itself can't hurt anything. It is merely something one drinks and bathes in."

74   I began to get cross. "If you don't like the story, I'll stop."

75   The old man made soothing noises and himself poured me some more beer. "You tell the story well, and we are listening. But it is clear that the elders of your country have never told you what the story really means. No, don't interrupt! We believe you when you say your marriage customs are different, or your clothes and weapons. But people are the same everywhere; therefore, there are always witches and it is we, the elders, who know how witches work. We told you it was the great chief who wished to kill Hamlet, and now your own words have proved us right. Who were Ophelia's male relatives?"

76   "There were only her father and her brother." Hamlet was clearly out of my hands.

77   "There must have been many more; this also you must ask of your elders when you get back to your country. From what you tell us, since Polonius was dead, it must have been Laertes who killed Ophelia, although I do not see the reason for it."

78   We had emptied one pot of beer, and the old men argued the point with slightly tipsy interest. Finally one of them demanded of me, "What did the servant of Polonius say on his return?"

79   With difficulty I recollected Reynaldo and his mission. "I don't think he did return before Polonius was killed."

80   "Listen," said the elder, "and I will tell you how it was and how your story will go, then you may tell me if I am right. Polonius knew his son would get into trouble, and so he did. He had many fines to pay for fighting, and debts from gambling. But he had only two ways of getting money quickly. One was to marry off his sister at once, but it is difficult to find a man who will marry a woman desired by the son of a chief. For if the chief's heir commits adultery with your wife, what can you do? Only a fool calls a case against a man who will someday be his judge. Therefore Laertes had to take the second way: he killed his sister by witchcraft, drowning her so he could secretly sell her body to the witches."

81   I raised an objection. "They found her body and buried it. Indeed Laertes jumped into the grave to see his sister once more—so, you see, the body was truly there. Hamlet, who had just come back, jumped in after him."

82   "What did I tell you?" The elder appealed to the others. "Laertes was up to no good with his sister's body. Hamlet prevented him, because the chief's heir, like a chief, does not wish any other man to grow rich and powerful. Laertes would be angry, because he would have killed his sister without benefit to himself. In our country he would try to kill Hamlet for that reason. Is this not what happened?"

83   "More or less," I admitted. "When the great chief found Hamlet was still alive, he encouraged Laertes to try to kill Hamlet and arranged a fight with machetes between them. In the fight both the young men were

wounded to death. Hamlet's mother drank the poisoned beer that the chief meant for Hamlet in case he won the fight. When he saw his mother die of poison, Hamlet, dying, managed to kill his father's brother with his machete."

84   "You see, I was right!" exclaimed the elder.

85   "That was a very good story," added the old man, "and you told it with very few mistakes. There was just one more error, at the very end. The poison Hamlet's mother drank was obviously meant for the survivor of the fight, whichever it was. If Laertes had won, the great chief would have poisoned him, for no one would know that he arranged Hamlet's death. Then, too, he need not fear Laertes' witchcraft; it takes a strong heart to kill one's only sister by witchcraft.

86   "Sometime," concluded the old man, gathering his ragged toga about him, "you must tell us some more stories of your country. We, who are elders, will instruct you in their true meaning, so that when you return to your own land your elders will see that you have not been sitting in the bush, but among those who know things and who have taught you wisdom."

STUDY QUESTIONS

1. In paragraph 2, Bohannan makes the claim that since "human nature is pretty much the same the whole world over," the meaning of *Hamlet* should be largely the same for readers everywhere, "although some details of custom might have to be explained." Do the Tiv tribesmen interpret the play so differently from Bohannan because her thesis was false, because she did not adequately explain English customs, because the Tiv were unwilling to accept the explanations, or for some other reason?

2. Do the Tiv elders also believe that human nature is pretty much the same everywhere and that the story has a single determinate meaning?

SUGGESTION FOR WRITING

In the last paragraph of "Shakespeare in the Bush," the tribesmen offer to instruct Bohannan in the "true meaning" of her country's stories. Do you agree that stories have a "true meaning" and how does Bohannan's experiment in interpretation bear on this question? (If you believe that literary works generally do have a determinate meaning, how do you explain the discrepancy between Bohannan's interpretation of *Hamlet* and the Africans'? If you do not believe that stories have a determinate meaning, are you willing to say that the tribesmen's interpretation is as valid as Bohannan's?)

EUDORA WELTY

A Worn Path

Eudora Welty is a well-known Southern writer. She received the Pulitzer Prize in 1973 for her novel, *The Optimist's Daughter.* In 1991 she was awarded the National Book Foundation Medal and a prize of $10,000 for Distinguished Contribution to American Letters. "A Worn Path," one of her earlier stories, has often been reprinted. Although it appears to be a simple story, it has given rise to very diverse interpretations, two of which are reprinted here along with Eudora Welty's own comment on the meaning of the story.

1   It was December—a bright frozen day in the early morning. Far out in the country there was an old Negro woman with her head tied in a red rag, coming along a path through the pinewoods. Her name was Phoenix Jackson. She was very old and small and she walked slowly in the dark pine shadows, moving a little from side to side in her steps, with the balanced heaviness and lightness of a pendulum in a grandfather clock. She carried a thin, small cane made from an umbrella, and with this she kept tapping the frozen earth in front of her. This made a grave and persistent noise in the still air, that seemed meditative like the chirping of a solitary little bird.

2   She wore a dark striped dress reaching down to her shoe tops, and an equally long apron of bleached sugar sacks, with a full pocket: all neat and tidy, but every time she took a step she might have fallen over her shoelaces, which dragged from her unlaced shoes. She looked straight ahead. Her eyes were blue with age. Her skin had a pattern all its own of numberless branching wrinkles and as though a whole little tree stood in the middle of her forehead, but a golden color ran underneath, and the two knobs of her cheeks were illumined by a yellow burning under the dark. Under the red rag her hair came down on her neck in the frailest of ringlets, still black, and with an odor like copper.

3   Now and then there was a quivering in the thicket. Old Phoenix said, "Out of my way, all you foxes, owls, beetles, jack rabbits, coons and wild animals!...Keep out from under these feet, little bob-whites...Keep the big wild hogs out of my path. Don't let none of those come running my direction. I got a long way." Under her small black-freckled hand her cane, limber as a buggy whip, would switch at the brush as if to rouse up any hiding things.

4   On she went. The woods were deep and still. The sun made the pine needles almost too bright to look at, up where the wind rocked. The cones dropped as light as feathers. Down in the hollow was the mourning dove—it was not too late for him.

5   The path ran up a hill. "Seem like there is chains about my feet, time I get this far," she said, in the voice of argument old people keep to use with themselves. "Something always take a hold of me on this hill—pleads I should stay."

6   After she got to the top she turned and gave a full, severe look behind her where she had come. "Up through pines," she said at length. "Now down through oaks."

7   Her eyes opened their widest, and she started down gently. But before she got to the bottom of the hill a bush caught her dress.

8   Her fingers were busy and intent, but her skirts were full and long, so that before she could pull them free in one place they were caught in another. It was not possible to allow the dress to tear. "I in the thorny bush," she said. "Thorns, you doing your appointed work. Never want to let folks pass, no sir. Old eyes thought you was a pretty little green bush."

9   Finally, trembling all over, she stood free, and after a moment dared to stoop for her cane.

10   "Sun so high!" she cried, leaning back and looking, while the thick tears went over her eyes. "The time getting all gone here."

11   At the foot of this hill was a place where a log was laid across the creek.

12   "Now comes the trial," said Phoenix.

13   Putting her right foot out, she mounted the log and shut her eyes. Lifting her skirt, leveling her cane fiercely before her, like a festival figure in some parade, she began to march across. Then she opened her eyes and she was safe on the other side.

14   "I wasn't as old as I thought," she said.

15   But she sat down to rest. She spread her skirts on the bank around her and folded her hands over her knees. Up above her was a tree in a pearly cloud of mistletoe. She did not dare to close her eyes, and when a little boy brought her a plate with a slice of marble-cake on it she spoke to him. "That would be acceptable," she said. But when she went to take it there was just her own hand in the air.

16   So she left that tree, and had to go through a barbed-wire fence. There she had to creep and crawl, spreading her knees and stretching her fingers like a baby trying to climb the steps. But she talked loudly to herself: she could not let her dress be torn now, so late in the day, and she could not pay for having her arm or her leg sawed off if she got caught fast where she was.

17   At last she was safe through the fence and risen up out in the clearing. Big dead trees, like black men with one arm, were standing in the purple stalks of the withered cotton field. There sat a buzzard.

18   "Who you watching?"

19   In the furrow she made her way along.

20   "Glad this not the season for bulls," she said, looking sideways, "and the good Lord made his snakes to curl up and sleep in the winter. A pleasure I

don't see no two-headed snake coming around that tree, where it come once. It took a while to get by him, back in the summer."

21   She passed through the old cotton and went into a field of dead corn. It whispered and shook and was taller than her head. "Through the maze now," she said, for there was no path.

22   Then there was something tall, black, and skinny there, moving before her.

23   At first she took it for a man. It could have been a man dancing in the field. But she stood still and listened, and it did not make a sound. It was as silent as a ghost.

24   "Ghost," she said sharply, "who be you the ghost of? For I have heard of nary death close by."

25   But there was no answer—only the ragged dancing in the wind.

26   She shut her eyes, reached out her hand, and touched a sleeve. She found a coat and inside that an emptiness, cold as ice.

27   "You scarecrow," she said. Her face lighted. "I ought to be shut up for good," she said with laughter. "My senses is gone. I too old. I the oldest people I ever know. Dance, old scarecrow," she said, "while I dancing with you."

28   She kicked her foot over the furrow, and with mouth drawn down, shook her head once or twice in a little strutting way. Some husks blew down and whirled in streamers about her skirts.

29   Then she went on, parting her way from side to side with the cane, through the whispering field. At last she came to the end, to a wagon track where the silver grass blew between the red ruts. The quail were walking around like pullets, seeming all dainty and unseen.

30   "Walk pretty," she said. "This the easy place. This the easy going."

31   She followed the track, swaying through the quiet bare fields, through the little strings of trees silver in their dead leaves, past cabins silver from weather, with the doors and windows boarded shut, all like old women under a spell sitting there. "I walking in their sleep," she said, nodding her head vigorously.

32   In a ravine she went where a spring was silently flowing through a hollow log. Old Phoenix bent and drank. "Sweet-gum makes the water sweet," she said, and drank more. "Nobody know who made this well, for it was here when I was born."

33   The track crossed a swampy part where the moss hung as white as lace from every limb. "Sleep on, alligators, and blow your bubbles." Then the track went into the road.

34   Deep, deep the road went down between the high green-colored banks. Overhead the live-oaks met, and it was as dark as a cave.

35   A black dog with a lolling tongue came up out of the weeds by the ditch. She was meditating, and not ready, and when he came at her she

only hit him a little with her cane. Over she went in the ditch, like a little puff of milkweed.

36   Down there, her senses drifted away. A dream visited her, and she reached her hand up, but nothing reached down and gave her a pull. So she lay there and presently went to talking. "Old woman," she said to herself, "that black dog come up out of the weeds to stall you off, and now there he sitting on his fine tail, smiling at you."

37   A white man finally came along and found her—a hunter, a young man, with his dog on a chain.

38   "Well, Granny!" he laughed. "What are you doing there?"

39   "Lying on my back like a June-bug waiting to be turned over, mister," she said, reaching up her hand.

40   He lifted her up, gave her a swing in the air, and set her down. "Anything broken, Granny?"

41   "No sir, them old dead weeds is springy enough," said Phoenix, when she had got her breath. "I thank you for your trouble."

42   "Where do you live, Granny?" he asked, while the two dogs were growling at each other.

43   "Away back yonder, sir, behind the ridge. You can't even see it from here."

44   "On your way home?"

45   "No sir, I going to town."

46   "Why, that's too far! That's as far as I walk when I come out myself, and I get something for my trouble." He patted the stuffed bag he carried, and there hung down a little closed claw. It was one of the bob-whites, with its beak hooked bitterly to show it was dead. "Now you go on home, Granny!"

47   "I bound to go to town, mister," said Phoenix. "The time come around."

48   He gave another laugh, filling the whole landscape. "I know you old colored people! Wouldn't miss going to town to see Santa Claus!"

49   But something held old Phoenix very still. The deep lines in her face went into a fierce and different radiation. Without warning, she had seen with her own eyes a flashing nickel fall out of the man's pocket onto the ground.

50   "How old are you, Granny?" he was saying.

51   "There is no telling mister," she said, "no telling."

52   Then she gave a little cry and clapped her hands and said, "Git on away from here, dog! Look! Look at that dog!" She laughed as if in admiration. "He ain't scared of nobody. He a big black dog." She whispered; "Sic him!"

53   "Watch me git rid of that cur," said the man. "Sic him, Pete! Sic him!"

54   Phoenix heard the dogs fighting, and heard the man running and throwing sticks. She even heard a gunshot. But she was slowly bending forward by that time, further and further forward, the lids stretched down over her eyes, as if she were doing this in her sleep. Her chin was lowered

almost to her knees. The yellow palm of her hand came out from the fold of her apron. Her fingers slid down and along the ground under the piece of money with the grace and care they would have in lifting an egg from under a setting hen. Then she slowly straightened up, she stood erect, and the nickel was in her apron pocket. A bird flew by. Her lips moved, "God watching me the whole time. I come to stealing."

55   The man came back, and his own dog panted about them. "Well, I scared him off that time," he said, and then he laughed and lifted his gun and pointed it at Phoenix.

56   She stood straight and faced him.

57   "Doesn't the gun scare you?" he said, still pointing it.

58   "No, sir, I seen plenty go off closer by, in my day, and for less than what I done," she said, holding utterly still.

59   He smiled, and shouldered the gun. "Well, Granny," he said, "you must be a hundred years old, and scared of nothing. I'd give you a dime if I had any money with me. But you take my advice and stay home, and nothing will happen to you."

60   "I bound to go on my way, mister," said Phoenix. She inclined her head in the red rag. Then they went in different directions, but she could hear the gun shooting again and again over the hill.

61   She walked on. The shadows hung from the oak trees to the road like curtains. Then she smelled wood-smoke, and smelled the river, and she saw a steeple and the cabins on their steep steps. Dozens of little black children whirled around her. There ahead was Natchez shining. Bells were ringing. She walked on.

62   In the paved city it was Christmas time. There were red and green electric lights strung and criss-crossed everywhere, and all turned on in the daytime. Old Phoenix would have been lost if she had not distrusted her eyesight and depended on her feet to know where to take her.

63   She paused quietly on the sidewalk where people were passing by. A lady came along in the crowd, carrying an armful of red-, green- and silver-wrapped presents; she gave off perfume like the red roses in hot summer, and Phoenix stopped her.

64   "Please, missy, will you lace up my shoe?" She held up her foot.

65   "What do you want, Grandma?"

66   "See my shoe," said Phoenix. "Do all right for out in the country, but wouldn't look right to go in a big building."

67   "Stand still then, Grandma," said the lady. She put her packages down on the sidewalk beside her and laced and tied both shoes tightly.

68   "Can't lace 'em with a cane," said Phoenix. "Thank you, missy. I doesn't mind asking a nice lady to tie up my shoe, when I gets out on the street."

69   Moving slowly and from side to side, she went into the big building, and into a tower of steps, where she walked up and around and around until her feet knew to stop.

70   She entered a door, and there she saw nailed up on the wall the document that had been stamped with the gold seal and framed in the gold frame, which matched the dream that was hung up in her head.

71   "Here I be," she said. There was a fixed and ceremonial stiffness over her body.

72   "A charity case, I suppose," said an attendant who sat at the desk before her.

73   But Phoenix only looked above her head. There was sweat on her face, the wrinkles in her skin shone like a bright net.

74   "Speak up, Grandma," the woman said. "What's your name? We must have your history, you know. Have you been here before? What seems to be the trouble with you?"

75   Old Phoenix only gave a twitch to her face as if a fly were bothering her.

76   "Are you deaf?" cried the attendant.

77   But then the nurse came in.

78   "Oh, that's just old Aunt Phoenix," she said. "She doesn't come for herself—she has a little grandson. She makes these trips just as regular as clockwork. She lives away back off the Old Natchez Trace." She bent down. "Well, Aunt Phoenix, why don't you just take a seat? We won't keep you standing after your long trip." She pointed.

79   The old woman sat down, bolt upright in the chair.

80   "Now, how is the boy?" asked the nurse.

81   Old Phoenix did not speak.

82   "I said, how is the boy?"

83   But Phoenix only waited and stared straight ahead, her face very solemn and withdrawn into rigidity.

84   "Is his throat any better?" asked the nurse. "Aunt Phoenix, don't you hear me? Is your grandson's throat any better since the last time you came for the medicine?"

85   With her hands on her knees, the old woman waited, silent, erect and motionless, just as if she were in armor.

86   "You mustn't take up our time this way, Aunt Phoenix," the nurse said. "Tell us quickly about your grandson, and get it over. He isn't dead, is he?"

87   At last there came a flicker and then a flame of comprehension across her face, and she spoke.

88   "My grandson. It was my memory had left me. There I sat and forgot why I made my long trip."

89   "Forgot?" The nurse frowned. "After you came so far?"

90   Then Phoenix was like an old woman begging a dignified forgiveness for waking up frightened in the night. "I never did go to school, I was too old at the Surrender," she said in a soft voice. "I'm an old woman without an education. It was my memory fail me. My little grandson, he is just the same, and I forgot it in the coming."

91   "Throat never heals, does it?" said the nurse, speaking in a loud, sure voice to old Phoenix. By now she had a card with something written on it, a little list. "Yes. Swallowed lye. When was it?—January—two-three years ago—"

92   Phoenix spoke unasked now. "No, missy, he not dead, he just the same. Every little while his throat begin to close up again, and he not able to swallow. He not get his breath. He not able to help himself. So the time come around, and I go on another trip for the soothing medicine."

93   "All right. The doctor said as long as you came to get it, you could have it," said the nurse. "But it's an obstinate case."

94   "My little grandson, he sit up there in the house all wrapped up, waiting by himself." Phoenix went on, "We is the only two left in the world. He suffer and it don't seem to put him back at all. He got a sweet look. He going to last. He wear a little patch quilt and peep out holding his mouth open like a little bird. I remembers so plain now. I not going to forget him again, no, the whole enduring time. I could tell him from all the others in creation."

95   "All right." The nurse was trying to hush her now. She brought her a bottle of medicine. "Charity," she said, making a check mark in a book.

96   Old Phoenix held the bottle close to her eyes, and then carefully put it into her pocket.

97   "I thank you," she said.

98   "It's Christmas time, Grandma," said the attendant. "Could I give you a few pennies out of my purse?"

99   "Five pennies is a nickel," said Phoenix stiffly.

100   "Here's a nickel," said the attendant.

101   Phoenix rose carefully and held out her hand. She received the nickel and then fished the other nickel out of her pocket and laid it beside the new one. She stared at her palm closely, with her head on one side.

102   Then she gave a tap with her cane on the floor.

103   "This is what come to me to do," she said. "I going to the store and buy my child a little windmill they sells, made out of paper. He going to find it hard to believe there such a thing in the world. I'll march myself back where he waiting, holding it straight up in this hand."

104   She lifted her free hand, gave a little nod, turned around, and walked out of the doctor's office. Then her slow step began on the stairs, going down.

Two Interpretations of "A Worn Path"

The following two arguments are examples of the "New Criticism," a style of interpretation that prevailed in American criticism from the 1940s through most of the 1960s. The New Criticism rested on the faith that a work of literature was a self-sufficient object independent of the author's biography or intention. Meaning was created by devices of language such as imagery, symbolism, irony, allusion to earlier literary works, and ambiguity. Often the New Critics ascribed the richness of literature about the modern world to echoes of ancient myths and rituals, as in Joyce's *Ulysses* or T. S. Eliot's *The Waste Land.* Though the two following articles employ much the same critical method, they arrive at very different interpretations.

NEIL D. ISAACS

Life for Phoenix

1   The first four sentences of "A Worn Path" contain simple declarative statements using the simple past of the verb "to be": "It was December…," "…there was an old Negro woman…," "Her name was Phoenix Jackson," "She was very old and small…." The note of simplicity thus struck is the keynote of Eudora Welty's artistic design in the story. For it is a simple story (a common reaction is "simply beautiful"). But it is also a story which employs many of the devices which can make of the modern short story an intricate and densely complex form. It uses them, however, in such a way that it demonstrates how a single meaning may be enriched through the use of various techniques. Thus, instead of various levels of meaning, we have here a single meaning reinforced on several levels of perception. Moreover, there is no muddying of levels and techniques; they are neatly arranged, straightforwardly presented, and simply perceived.

2   The plot-line follows Phoenix Jackson, who is graphically described in the second paragraph, on her long walk into Natchez where she has to get medicine for her grandson. The trek is especially difficult because of her age, and in the process of struggling on she forgets the reason for the struggle. At the end she has remembered, received the medicine, and decided to buy the child a Christmas present with the ten cents she has acquired during the day.

3   What makes this a story? It barely appears to fulfill even Sidney Cox's generous criterion of "turning a corner or at least a hair." But it does belong to a specific story-teller's genre familiar from Homer to Fielding to Kerouac—"road" literature. This form provides a ready-made plot pattern

with some inherent weaknesses. The story concerns the struggle to achieve a goal, the completion of the journey; and the story's beginning, middle, and end are the same as those of the road. The primary weakness of this structure is its susceptibility to too much middle.

4   A traditional concept of road literature, whether the mythical journey of the sun across the heavens or a boy's trip down the Mississippi or any other variation, is its implicit equation with life: the road of life, life's journey, ups and downs, the straight and narrow, and a host of other clichés reflect the universality of this primitive metaphor. "A Worn Path" makes explicit, beginning with the very title, Eudora Welty's acceptance of the traditional equation as a basic aspect of the story. In fact, the whole meaning of "A Worn Path" will rely on an immediate recognition of the equation—the worn path equals the path of life—which is probably why it is so explicit. But we needn't start with a concept which is metaphorical or perhaps primitively allegorical. It will probably be best for us to begin with the other literal elements in the story: they will lead us back to the sub- or supra-literal eventually anyway.

5   An important part of the setting is the time element, that is, the specific time of the year. We learn immediately that it is "a bright frozen day" in December, and there are several subsequent, direct statements which mark it more precisely as Christmas time. The hunter talks about Santa Claus and the attendant at the hospital says that "It's Christmas time," echoing what the author has said earlier. There are several other references and images forming a pattern to underline the idea of Christmas time, such as "Up above her was a tree in a pearly cloud of *mistletoe.*" [Italics in this paragraph all mine.] Notice especially the elaborate color pattern of red, green, and silver, the traditional colors of Christmas. It begins with Phoenix's head "in a *red* rag, coming along a path through the pinewoods" (which are green as well as Christmas trees). Later she sees "a wagon track, where the *silver grass* blew between the *red* ruts" and "little strings of trees *silver* in their dead leaves" (reddish brown?). This pattern comes to a climax in the description of the city and the lady's packages, which also serves to make explicit its purpose, return it to the literal: "There were red and green electric lights strung and criss-crossed everywhere.... ...an armful of red-, green-, and silver-wrapped presents."

6   From the plot-line alone the idea of Christmas doesn't seem to be more than incidental, but it is obvious from the persistent references that Christmas is going to play an important part in the total effect of the story. Besides the direct statements already mentioned, there proliferates around the pattern throughout the story a dense cluster of allusions to and suggestions of the Christmas myth at large and to the *meanings* of Christmas in particular. For instance, as Phoenix rests under a tree, she has a vision of a little boy offering her a slice of marble-cake on a little plate, and she says, "That would be acceptable." The allusion here is to

Communion and Church ritual. Later, when a bird flies by, Phoenix says, "God watching me the whole time." Then there are references to the Eden story (the ordering of the species, the snake in summer to be avoided), to the parting of the Red Sea (Phoenix walking through the field of corn), to a sequence of temptations, to the River Jordan and the City of Heaven (when Phoenix gets to the river, sees the city shining, and hears the bells ringing; then there is the angel who waits on her, tying her shoes), to the Christ-child in the manger (Phoenix describing her grandson as "all wrapped up" in "a little patch quilt... like a little bird" with "a sweet look"). In addition, the whole story is suggestive of a religious pilgrimage, while the conclusion implies that the return trip will be like the journey of the Magi, with Phoenix following a star (the marvelous windmill) to bring a gift to the child (medicine, also windmill). Moreover, there's the hunter who is, in part, a Santa Claus figure himself (he carries a big sack over his shoulder, he is always laughing, he brings Phoenix a gift of a nickel).

7   The richness of all this evocation of a Christianity-Christmas frame of reference heightens the specific points about the meanings of Christmas. The Christmas spirit, of course, is the Christian ethic in its simplest terms: giving, doing for others, charity. This concept is made explicit when the nurse says of Phoenix, "She doesn't come for herself." But it had already been presented in a brilliant piece of ironic juxtaposition [Emphasis mine]:

> *She entered a door, and there she saw* nailed up, on the wall *the document that had been stamped with the* gold seal *and framed in the* gold frame *which* matched the dream that was hung up in her head.
>   "Here I be," *she said. There was a* fixed and ceremonial stiffness *over her body.*
>   "A charity *case, I suppose," said an attendant....*

Amid the Christmas season and the dense Christmas imagery, Phoenix, with an aiding intuitive faith, arrives at the shrine of her pilgrimage, beholds a symbolic crucifixion, presents herself as a celebrant in the faith, and is recognized as an embodiment of the message of the faith. This entire scene, however, with its gold trimming and attitude of the attendant, is turned ironically to suggest greed, corruption, cynicism—the very opposite of the word used, charity. Yet the episode, which is Phoenix's final and most severe trial, also results in her final emergence as a redeemer and might be called her Calvary.

8   Perhaps a better way to get at the meaning of Christmas and the meaning of "A Worn Path" is to talk about life and death. In a sense, the meaning of Christmas and that of Easter are the same—a celebration of life out of death. (Notice that Phoenix refers to herself as a *June* bug and that the woman with the packages "gave off perfume like the *red roses in hot summer.*") [Italics mine.] Christ is born in the death of the year and in a near-dead nature-society situation in order to rejuvenate life itself,

naturally and spiritually. He dies in order that the life of others may be saved. He is reborn out of death, and so are nature, love, and the spirit of man. All this is the potent Christian explanation of the central irony of human existence, that life means death and death is life. One might state the meaning of "A Worn Path" in similar terms, where Phoenix endures a long, agonizing dying in order to redeem her grandson's life. So the medicine, which the nurse calls charity as she makes a check in her book, is a symbol of love and life. The windmill represents the same duality, but lighter sides of both aspects. If the path is the path of life, then its end is death and the purpose of that death is new life.

9 It would be misleading, however, to suggest that the story is merely a paralleling of the Christian nature-myth. It is, rather, a miniature nature-myth of its own which uses elements of many traditions. The most obvious example is the name Phoenix from the mythological Egyptian bird, symbol of immortality and resurrection, which dies so that a new Phoenix may emerge from its ashes. There is a reference to the Daedalus labyrinth myth when Phoenix walks through the corn field and Miss Welty puns: "'Through the maze now,' she said, for there was no path." That ambivalent figure of the hunter comes into play here as both a death figure (killer, bag full of slain quail) and a life figure (unconscious giver of life with the nickel, banisher of Cerberus-like black dog who is attacking Phoenix), but in any case a folk-legend figure who can fill "the whole landscape" with his laugh. And there are several references to the course of the sun across the sky which gives a new dimension to the life-road equation; e.g., "Sun so high!... The time getting all gone here."

10 The most impressive extra-Christian elements are the patterns that identify Phoenix as a creature of nature herself and as a ritual-magic figure. Thus, Phoenix makes a sound "like the chirping of a solitary little bird," her hair has "an odor like copper," and at one point "with [her] mouth drawn down, [she] shook her head once or twice in a little strutting way." Even more remarkable is the "fixed and ceremonial stiffness" of her body, which moves "like a festival figure in some parade." The cane she carries, made from an umbrella, is tapped on the ground like a magic wand, and she uses it to "switch at the brush as if to rouse up any hiding things." At the same time she utters little spells:

> *Out of my way, all you foxes, owls, beetles, jack rabbits, coons, and wild animals!...Keep out from under these feet, little bob-whites...keep the big wild hogs out of my path. Don't let none of those come running my direction...Ghost,...who be you the ghost of?...Sweetgum makes the water sweet....Nobody know who made this well for it was here when I was born....Sleep on, alligators, and blow your bubbles.*

11 Other suggestions of magic appear in the whirling of cornhusks in streamers about her skirts, when she parts "her way from side to side with

the cane, through the whispering field," when the quail seem "unseen," and when the cabins are "all like old women under a spell sitting there." Finally, ironically, when Phoenix swings at the black dog, she goes over "in the ditch, like a little puff of milk-weed."

12   More or less remote, more or less direct, all these allusions are used for the same effect as are the references to Christianity, to reinforce a statement of the meaning of life. This brings us back to the basic life-road equation of the story, and there are numerous indications that the path is life and that the end of the road is death and renewal of life. These suggestions are of three types; statements which relate the road, the trip, or Phoenix to time: Phoenix walks "with the balanced heaviness and lightness of a pendulum in a grandfather clock"; she tells the hunter, "I bound to go.... The time come around"; and the nurse says "She makes these trips just as regular as clockwork." Second (the most frequent type), there are descriptions of the road or episodes along the way which are suggestive of life, usually in a simple metaphorical way: "I got a long way" (ambiguously referring to past and future); "I in the thorny bush"; "Up through pines.... Now down through oaks"; "This is the easy place. This the easy going." Third, there are direct references to death, age, and life: Phoenix says to a buzzard, "Who are you watching?" and to a scarecrow, "Who be you the ghost of? For I have heard of nary death close by"; then she performs a little dance of death with the scarecrow after she says, "My senses is gone. I too old. I the oldest people I ever know."

13   This brings us full circle in an examination of the design of the story, and it should be possible now to say something about the total meaning of "A Worn Past." The path is the path of life, and the story is an attempt to probe the meaning of life in its simplest, most elementary terms. Through the story we arrive at a definition of life, albeit a teleological one. When the hunter tells Phoenix to "take my advice and stay home, and nothing will happen to you," the irony is obvious and so is the metaphor: don't live and you can't die. When Phoenix forgets why she has made the arduous trek to Natchez, we understand that it is only a rare person who knows the meaning of his life, that living does not imply knowing. When Phoenix describes the Christ-like child waiting for her and says, "I not going to forget him again, no, the whole enduring time. I could tell him from all the others in creation," we understand several things about it: her life is almost over, she sees clearly the meaning of life, she has an abiding faith in that meaning, and she will share with her grandson this great revelation just as together they embody its significance. And when Phoenix's "slow step began on the stairs, going down," as she starts back to bring the boy the medicine and the windmill, we see a composite symbol of life itself, dying so that life may continue. Life is a journey toward death, because one must die in order that life may go on.

ROLAND BARTEL

Life and Death in Eudora Welty's "A Worn Path"

1   I have found Saralyn Daly's interpretation of "A Worn Path" to be basically sound (*Studies in Short Fiction,* 1 [Winter 1964], 133–139), but the more I teach the story the more I become convinced that an additional comment is needed to bring out the richness of the central character, Phoenix Jackson.

2   As most critics have noted, Phoenix Jackson's first name links her to the Egyptian myth of the bird that renews itself periodically from its own ashes. Equally obvious is the quest motif associated with her annual journey to Natchez. What concerns me about these discussions is that they treat Phoenix Jackson as a stereotype and allow the obvious archetypal significance of her name and her journey to overshadow the uniqueness of one of the most memorable women in short fiction.

3   Phoenix Jackson is a very old woman who walks from the Old Natchez Trace into Natchez at Christmas time to get medicine for her grandson. Previous critics have noted the many ways in which the renewal myth applies to the frail grandmother and to the grandson for whom she undertakes the hazardous journey each year. I want to add the suggestion that the story operates on the psychological level also, that Phoenix Jackson must make the journey to sustain her own life, that her character becomes unusually poignant if we consider seriously the possibility that her grandson is, in fact, dead. The journey to Natchez then becomes a psychological necessity for Phoenix, her only way of coping with her loss and her isolation. As she says to the white hunter who twice urges her to give up the journey: "I bound to go to town, mister, the time come around" and "I bound to go on my way, mister." Having at first made the journey to save the life of her grandson, she now follows the worn path each Christmas season to save herself. Her survival depends on her going through a ritual that symbolically brings her grandson back to life.

4   The assumption that the grandson is dead helps to explain Phoenix Jackson's stoical behavior in the doctor's office. She displays a "ceremonial stiffness" as she sits "bolt upright" staring "straight ahead, her face solemn and withdrawn into rigidity." This passiveness suggests her psychological dilemma—she cannot explain why she made the journey. Her attempt to blame her lapse of memory on her illiteracy is unconvincing. Her lack of education is hardly an excuse for forgetting her grandson, but it goes a long way toward explaining her inability to articulate her subconscious motives for her journey.

5   When the nurse asks whether the grandson is dead, Phoenix suddenly remembers and then overcompensates. In her imagination she brings him back to life, her concluding comment sounding very much like the language of a person trying to revive the image of someone who has died: "I remember so plain now. I not going to forget him again, no, the whole enduring time. I could tell him from all others in creation."

6   The story ends with Phoenix going down the stairs. Ascending a stairway is associated in folklore and religion with entering a new level of life, with achieving one's destination. Descending a stairway has the opposite implication and has, since *Dante's Inferno,* often been associated with a descent into hell. When Phoenix ascends the stairs she knows she has reached her destination when she sees hanging on the wall the gold seal in the gold frame, "which matched the dream that was hung up in her head." After she gets the medicine from the nurse and the nickel from the attendant, she talks briefly about a paper windmill for her grandson, but then the story ends abruptly with her going down the stairs, a fact that suggests the end of her hope, possibly the end of her life. This interpretation strengthens the thematic unity and symmetry of the story by beginning and ending with references to death. At the beginning of the story Phoenix taps the frozen ground with her cane. At the end of the story, just before she goes down the stairs, she taps the wooden floor with her cane, an action reminiscent of the old man in Chaucer's *Pardoner's Tale,* who taps the earth with his cane seeking death.

7   Phoenix has to make herself and others believe that her grandson lives so that she can endure her hardships and her subconscious awareness of the imminence of her own death. Literally she seeks the city to give life to her grandson, but symbolically she needs the city to support her own life. Carl Jung has interpreted the city as the feminine principle in general and more specifically as a woman who cares for the inhabitants as if they were her children. When Phoenix enters the city she cannot trust her eyes, so she relies on her feet to take her to her destination, another indication of the subconscious element of her journey.

8   If the journey is as much a necessity for the grandmother as for the grandson, then the episodes along the way take on added significance. After she crosses the creek with her eyes closed, she has a vision of a boy offering her a cake, quite possibly her deceased grandson. Her desperate need for companionship is demonstrated not only by this vision but also by her practice of talking to animals and objects, most of which she imagines rather than sees.

9   Phoenix Jackson thus emerges from the story as a distinctive person, a feeble old woman whose active imagination rescues her from the harshest aspects of her existence. She is driven to the necessity of inventing such details as make the last portion of her life bearable. If her grandson is dead,

then the rebirth implied in her name is doubly pathetic: she unwittingly makes the journey to meet her own needs rather than her grandson's, and what begins as a life-sustaining journey seems to end in a journey of death. If the white hunter was right in saying that she hardly had enough time to return home if she started back immediately, she certainly will not make it back, literally or symbolically, after the passing of the additional time required to get to the city and the doctor's office. During the first part of the journey we get flashes of her sense of humor, but by the end of the story her senility seems to overcome her. The second sentence of the story, "Her name was Phoenix Jackson," seems to suggest by its brevity that all she has left in life is her name and all it implies. At the end of the story the impression prevails that she has risen from the ashes for the last time.

STUDY QUESTIONS

1. Isaacs assumes Phoenix's grandson is alive; Bartel argues (along with many other readers) that he is dead. How does the truth of this matter affect the meaning of the story as a whole?
2. Which interpretation better accounts for the various elements of the story?
3. Why does Bartel consider that Phoenix is a "richer" character if we assume that her grandson is dead? Do you agree?

EUDORA WELTY

"Is Phoenix Jackson's Grandson Really Dead?"

When the distinguished journal *Critical Inquiry* began publication in 1974, its editors decided to include periodically a feature entitled, "Artists on Criticism of Their Art." For the first appearance of this feature, they invited Eudora Welty to offer a commentary, and she chose to discuss the question that had most frequently been sent to her by interested readers, "Is Phoenix Jackson's Grandson Really Dead?" Her essay offers a rare look not only at a distinguished writer's reading of her own story, but at her views on other readers' interpretations as well.

1   A story writer is more than happy to be read by students; the fact that these serious readers think and feel something in response to his work he finds life-giving. At the same time, he may not always be able to reply to their specific questions in kind. I wondered if it might clarify something, for both the questioners and myself, if I set down a general reply to the question that comes to me most often in the mail, from both students and their teachers, after some classroom discussion. The unrivaled favorite is this: "Is Phoenix Jackson's grandson really *dead?*"

2   It refers to a short story I wrote years ago called "A Worn Path," which tells of a day's journey an old woman makes on foot from deep in the country into town and into a doctor's office on behalf of her little grandson; he is at home, periodically ill, and periodically she comes for his medicine; they give it to her as usual, she receives it and starts the journey back.

3   I had not meant to mystify readers by withholding any fact; it is not a writer's business to tease. The story is told through Phoenix's mind as she undertakes her errand. As the author at one with the character as I tell it, I must assume that the boy is alive. As the reader, you are free to think as you like, of course: the story invites you to believe that no matter what happens, Phoenix, for as long as she is able to walk and can hold to her purpose, will make her journey. The *possibility* that she would keep on even if he were dead is there in her devotion and its single-minded, single-track errand. Certainly the *artistic* truth, which should be good enough for the fact, lies in Phoenix's own answer to that question. When the nurse asks, "He isn't dead, is he?" she speaks for herself: "He still the same. He going to last."

4   The grandchild is the incentive. But it is the journey, the going of the errand, that is the story, and the question is not whether the grandchild is in reality alive or dead. It doesn't affect the outcome of the story or its meaning from start to finish. But it is not the question itself that has struck me as much as the idea, almost without exception implied in the

asking, that for Phoenix's grandson to be dead would somehow make the story "better."

5   It's *all right,* I want to say to the students who write to me, for things to be what they appear to be, for words to mean what they say. It's all right too for words and appearances to mean more than one thing—ambiguity is a fact of life. But it is not all right, not in good faith, for things *not* to mean what they say. A fiction writer's responsibility covers not only what he presents as the facts of a given story but what he chooses to stir up as their implications. In the end, these implications too become facts, in the larger, fictional sense.

6   The grandson's plight was real and it made the truth of the story, which is the story of an errand of love carried out. If the child no longer lived, the truth would persist in the "wornness" of the path. But his being dead can't increase the truth of the story, can't affect it one way or the other. I think I signal this, because the end of the story has been reached before old Phoenix gets home again: she simply starts back. To the question "Is the grandson really dead?" I could reply that it doesn't make any difference. I could also say that I did not make him up in order to let him play a trick on Phoenix. But my best answer would be: "*Phoenix* is alive."

7   The origin of a story is sometimes a trustworthy clue to the author—or can provide him with the clue—to its key image: maybe in this case it will do the same for the reader. One day I saw a solitary old woman like Phoenix. She was walking: I saw her, at middle distance, in a winter country landscape, and watched her slowly make her way across my line of vision. That sight of her made me write the story. I invented an errand for her, but that only seemed a living part of the figure she was herself: what errand other than for someone else could be making her go? And her going was the first thing, her persisting in her landscape was the real thing, and the first and the real were what I wanted and worked to keep. I brought her up close enough, by imagination, to describe her face, make her present to the eyes, but the full-length figure moving across the winter fields was the indelible one and the image to keep, and the perspective extending into the vanishing distance the true one to hold in mind.

8   I invented for my character, as I wrote, some passing adventures—some dreams and harassments and a small triumph or two, some jolts to her pride, some flights of fancy to console her, one or two encounters to scare her, a moment that gave her cause to feel ashamed, a moment to dance and preen—for it had to be a *journey,* and all these things belonged to that, parts of life's uncertainty.

9   A narrative line is in its deeper sense, of course, the tracing out of a meaning, and the real continuity of a story lies in this probing forward. The real dramatic force of a story depends on the strength of the emotion that has set it going. The emotional value is the measure of the reach of the

story. What gives any such content to "A Worn Path" is not its circumstances but its *subject:* the deep-grained habit of love.

10   What I hoped would come clear was that in the whole surround of this story, the world it threads through, the only certain thing at all is the worn path. The habit of love cuts through confusion and stumbles or contrives its way out of difficulty, it remembers the way even when it forgets, for a dumbfounded moment, its reason for being. The path is the thing that matters.

11   *Her* victory—old Phoenix's—is when she sees the diploma in the doctor's office, when she finds "nailed up on the wall the document that had been stamped with the gold seal and framed in the gold frame, which matched the dream that was hung up in her head." The return with the medicine is just a matter of retracing her own footsteps. It is the part of the journey, and of the story, that can now go without saying.

12   In the matter of function, old Phoenix's way might even do as a sort of parallel to your way of work if you are a writer of stories. The way to get there is the all-important, all-absorbing problem, and this problem is your reason for undertaking the story. Your only guide, too, is your sureness about your subject, about what this subject is. Like Phoenix, you work all your life to find your way, through all the obstructions and the false appearances and the upsets you may have brought on yourself, to reach a meaning—using inventions of your imagination, perhaps helped out by your dreams and bits of good luck. And finally, too, like Phoenix, you have to assume that what you are working in aid of is life, not death.

13   But you would make the trip anyway, wouldn't you?—just on hope.

STUDY QUESTIONS

1. Does Welty ever give a direct answer to the question posed in the title of her essay? If so, what is her answer?
2. In paragraph 5, Welty says "it is not all right, not in good faith, for things *not* to mean what they say." Does this mean that stories should not have limited narrators who fail to see the truth, or at least the whole truth?
3. Welty says that many students and teachers who write to her assume that the story would be "better" if the grandson were dead. Why would a reader assume this about the story? Does Welty agree?
4. Although this essay ostensibly undertakes to address only a limited aspect of the story, the question whether the grandson is dead, it actually implies a good deal more about the meaning of the story as Welty sees it. What does she see as the central meaning of the story? How does her interpretation compare with those of Isaacs and Bartel?

5. Where does Welty seem to feel the meaning of the story resides: in the author's intention? in the formal relationships of the text? in the mind of the reader?

SUGGESTION FOR WRITING

Having read interpretations of "A Worn Path" by Isaacs, Bartel, and Welty herself, write an essay giving your considered opinion on the central questions of meaning in this story: Does it have one meaning or many? Can an interpretation be wrong? Is the interpretation of the author privileged?

ROBERT PENN WARREN

From *"Why Do We Read Fiction?"*

Robert Penn Warren (1905–1991) wrote not only fiction but poetry, drama, and essays as well. He also taught at Yale and was the winner of three Pulitzer prizes. He is probably best known for his novel *All the King's Men.*

The following is an excerpt from a longer essay first printed in *The Saturday Evening Post* in 1962.

1   Why do we read fiction? The answer is simple. We read it because we like it. And we like it because fiction, as an image of life, stimulates and gratifies our interest in life. But whatever interests may be appealed to by fiction, the special and immediate interest that takes us to fiction is always our interest in a story.

2   A story is not merely an image of life, but life in motion—specifically, the presentation of individual characters moving through their particular experiences to some end that we may accept as meaningful. And the experience that is characteristically presented in a story is that of facing a problem, a conflict. To put it bluntly: no conflict, no story.

3   It is no wonder that conflict should be at the center of fiction, for conflict is at the center of life. But why should we, who have the constant and often painful experience of conflict in life and who yearn for inner peace and harmonious relation with the outer world, turn to fiction, which is the image of conflict? The fact is that our attitude toward conflict is ambivalent. If we do find a totally satisfactory adjustment in life, we tend to sink into the drowse of the accustomed. Only when our surroundings— or we ourselves—become problematic again do we wake up and feel that surge of energy which is life. And life more abundantly lived is what we seek.

4   So we, at the same time that we yearn for peace, yearn for the problematic. The adventurer, the sportsman, the gambler, the child playing hide-and-seek, the teen-age boys choosing up sides for a game of sandlot baseball, the old grad cheering in the stadium—we all, in fact, seek out or create problematic situations of greater or lesser intensity. Such situations give us a sense of heightened energy, of life. And fiction, too, gives us the fresh, uninhibited opportunity to vent the rich emotional charge—tears, laughter, tenderness, sympathy, hate, love, and irony—that is stored up in us and short-circuited in the drowse of the accustomed. Furthermore, this heightened awareness can be more fully relished now, because what in actuality would be the threat of the problematic is here tamed to mere

imagination, and because some kind of resolution of the problem is, owing to the very nature of fiction, promised.

5   The story promises us a resolution, and we wait in suspense to learn how things will come out. We are in suspense, not only about what will happen, but even more about what the event will mean. We are in suspense about the story in fiction because we are in suspense about another story far closer and more important to us—the story of our own life as we live it. We do not know how that story of our own life is going to come out. We do not know what it will mean. So, in that deepest suspense of life, which will be shadowed in the suspense we feel about the story in fiction, we turn to fiction for some slight hint about the story in the life we live. The relation of our life to the fictional life is what, in a fundamental sense, takes us to fiction.

6   Even when we read, as we say, to "escape," we seek to escape not *from* life but *to* life, to a life more satisfying than our own drab version. Fiction gives us an image of life—sometimes of a life we actually have and like to dwell on, but often and poignantly of one we have had and do not have now, or one we have never had and can never have.

STUDY QUESTIONS

1. The title poses a causal question. What is the answer Warren gives?
2. Why does Warren regard our desire to read fiction as problematic? What sentence in his essay articulates this problem?
3. Many people, if asked why they read fiction, would answer, "For fun," or "For excitement." Would either of these answers be substantially the same as or different from Warren's response?

SUGGESTION FOR WRITING

Warren says that we read a story to discover not only how it will turn out, but what it means. In a paragraph or two, test Warren's characterization of story-reading by applying it to "A Worn Path" by Eudora Welty. Does the plot have a satisfying resolution?

SUSAN SONTAG

Against Interpretation

Susan Sontag is an essayist, novelist, and film director. During the 1960s, she was an influential exponent of the avant-garde, reacting in several ways against traditional ways of appreciating and criticizing literature and art. In 1964, when this essay was written, she also became famous for her essay "Notes on Camp."

"Against Interpretation" is a proposal for a radically different approach to literature.

> *Content is a glimpse of something, an encounter like a flash. It's very tiny — very tiny, content.*
>
> **Willem de Kooning,** in an interview

> *It is only shallow people who do not judge by appearances. The mystery of the world is the visible, not the invisible.*
>
> **Oscar Wilde,** in a letter

I

1   The earliest experience of art must have been that it was incantatory, magical; art was an instrument of ritual (cf. the paintings in the caves at Lascaux, Altamira, Niaux, La Pasiega, etc.). The earliest *theory* of art, that of the Greek philosophers, proposed that art was mimesis, imitation of reality.

2   It is at this point that the peculiar question of the *value* of art arose. For the mimetic theory, by its very terms, challenges art to justify itself.

3   Plato, who proposed the theory, seems to have done so in order to rule that the value of art is dubious. Since he considered ordinary material things as themselves mimetic objects, imitations of transcendent forms or structures, even the best painting of a bed would be only an "imitation of an imitation." For Plato, art is neither particularly useful (the painting of a bed is no good to sleep on), nor, in the strict sense, true. And Aristotle's arguments in defense of art do not really challenge Plato's view that all art is an elaborate *trompe l'oeil,* and therefore a lie. But he does dispute Plato's idea that art is useless. Lie or no, art has a certain value according to Aristotle because it is a form of therapy, Art is useful, after all, Aristotle counters, medicinally useful in that it arouses and purges dangerous emotions.

4   In Plato and Aristotle, the mimetic theory of art goes hand in hand with the assumption that art is always figurative. But advocates of the

mimetic theory need not close their eyes to decorative and abstract art. The fallacy that art is necessarily a "realism" can be modified or scrapped without ever moving outside the problems delimited by the mimetic theory.

5 The fact is, all Western consciousness of and reflection upon art have remained within the confines staked out by the Greek theory of art as mimesis or representation. It is through this theory that art as such— above and beyond given works of art—becomes problematic, in need of defense. And it is the defense of art which gives birth to the odd vision by which something we have learned to call "form" is separated off from something we have learned to call "content," and to the well-intentioned move which makes content essential and form accessory.

6 Even in modern times, when most artists and critics have discarded the theory of art as representation of an outer reality in favor of the theory of art as subjective expression, the main feature of the mimetic theory persists. Whether we conceive of the work of art on the model of a picture (art as a picture of reality) or on the model of a statement (art as the statement of the artist), content still comes first. The content may have changed. It may now be less figurative, less lucidly realistic. But it is still assumed that a work of art *is* its content. Or, as it's usually put today, that a work of art by definition *says* something. ("What X is saying is…", "What X is trying to say is…", "What X said is…", etc., etc.)

II

7 None of us can ever retrieve that innocence before all theory when art knew no need to justify itself, when one did not ask of a work of art what it *said* because one knew (or thought one knew) what it *did*. From now to the end of consciousness, we are stuck with the task of defending art. We can only quarrel with one or another means of defense. Indeed, we have an obligation to overthrow any means of defending and justifying art which becomes particularly obtuse or onerous or insensitive to contemporary needs and practice.

8 This is the case, today, with the very idea of content itself. Whatever it may have been in the past, the idea of content is today mainly a hindrance, a nuisance, a subtle or not so subtle philistinism.

9 Though the actual developments in many arts may seem to be leading us away from the idea that a work of art is primarily its content, the idea still exerts an extraordinary hegemony. I want to suggest that this is because the idea is now perpetuated in the guise of a certain way of encountering works of art thoroughly ingrained among most people who take any of the arts seriously. What the overemphasis on the idea of content entails is the perennial, never consummated project of *interpretation*. And, conversely, it

is the habit of approaching works of art in order to *interpret* them that sustains the fancy that there is such a thing as the content of a work of art.

III

10   Of course, I don't mean interpretation in the broadest sense, the sense in which Nietzsche (rightly) says, "There are no facts, only interpretations." By interpretation, I mean here a conscious act of the mind which illustrates a certain code, certain "rules" of interpretation.

11   Directed to art, interpretation means plucking a set of elements (the X, the Y, the Z, and so forth) from the whole work. The task of interpretation is virtually one of translation. The interpreter says, Look, don't you see that X is really—or, really means—A? That Y is really B? That Z is really C?

12   What situation could prompt this curious project for transforming a text? History gives us the materials for an answer. Interpretation first appears in the culture of late classical antiquity, when the power and credibility of myth had been broken by the "realistic" view of the world introduced by scientific enlightenment. Once the question that haunts post-mythic consciousness—that of the *seemliness* of religious symbols—had been asked, the ancient texts were, in their pristine form, no longer acceptable. Then interpretation was summoned, to reconcile the ancient texts to "modern" demands. Thus, the Stoics, to accord with their view that the gods had to be moral, allegorized away the rude features of Zeus and his boisterous clan in Homer's epics. What Homer really designated by the adultery of Zeus with Leto, they explained, was the union between power and wisdom. In the same vein, Philo of Alexandria interpreted the literal historical narratives of the Hebrew Bible as spiritual paradigms. The story of the exodus from Egypt, the wandering in the desert for forty years, and the entry into the promised land, said Philo, was really an allegory of the individual soul's emancipation, tribulations, and final deliverance. Interpretation thus presupposes a discrepancy between the clear meaning of the text and the demands of (later) readers. It seeks to resolve that discrepancy. The situation is that for some reason a text has become unacceptable; yet it cannot be discarded. Interpretation is a radical strategy for conserving an old text, which is thought too precious to repudiate, by revamping it. The interpreter, without actually erasing or rewriting the text, is altering it. But he can't admit to doing this. He claims to be only making it intelligible, by disclosing its true meaning. However far the interpreters alter the text (another notorious example is the Rabbinic and Christian "spiritual" interpretations of the clearly erotic Song of Songs), they must claim to be reading off a sense that is already there.

13   Interpretation in our own time, however, is even more complex. For the contemporary zeal for the project of interpretation is often prompted not

by piety towards the troublesome text (which may conceal an aggression), but by an open aggressiveness, an overt contempt for appearances. The old style of interpretation was insistent, but respectful; it erected another meaning on top of the literal one. The modern style of interpretation excavates, and as it excavates, destroys; it digs "behind" the text, to find a sub-text which is the true one. The most celebrated and influential modern doctrines, those of Marx and Freud, actually amount to elaborate systems of hermeneutics, aggressive and impious theories of interpretation. All observable phenomena are bracketed, in Freud's phrase, as *manifest content*. This manifest content must be probed and pushed aside to find the true meaning—the *latent content*—beneath. For Marx, social events like revolutions and wars; for Freud, the events of individual lives (like neurotic symptoms and slips of the tongue) as well as texts (like a dream or a work of art)—all are treated as occasions for interpretation. According to Marx and Freud, these events only *seem* to be intelligible. Actually, they have no meaning without interpretation. To understand *is* to interpret. And to interpret is to restate the phenomenon, in effect to find an equivalent for it.

14   Thus, interpretation is not (as most people assume) an absolute value, a gesture of mind situated in some timeless realm of capabilities. Interpretation must itself be evaluated, with a historical view of human consciousness. In some cultural contexts, interpretation is a liberating act. It is a means of revising, of transvaluing, of escaping the dead past. In other cultural contexts, it is reactionary, impertinent, cowardly, stifling.

IV

15   Today is such a time, when the project of interpretation is largely reactionary, stifling. Like the fumes of the automobile and of heavy industry which befoul the urban atmosphere, the effusion of interpretations of art today poisons our sensibilities. In a culture whose already classical dilemma is the hypertrophy of the intellect at the expense of energy and sensual capability, interpretation is the revenge of the intellect upon art.

16   Even more. It is the revenge of the intellect upon the world. To interpret is to impoverish, to deplete the world—in order to set up a shadow world of "meanings." It is to turn *the* world into *this* world. ("This world!" As if there were any other.)

17   The world, our world, is depleted, impoverished enough. Away with all duplicates of it, until we again experience more immediately what we have.

V

18   In most modern instances, interpretation amounts to the philistine refusal to leave the work of art alone. Real art has the capacity to make us nervous.

By reducing the work of art to its content and then interpreting *that*, one tames the work of art. Interpretation makes art manageable, comfortable.

19   This philistinism of interpretation is more rife in literature than in any other art. For decades now, literary critics have understood it to be their task to translate the elements of the poem or play or novel or story into something else. Sometimes a writer will be so uneasy before the naked power of his art that he will install within the work itself—albeit with a little shyness, a touch of the good taste of irony—the clear and explicit interpretation of it. Thomas Mann is an example of such an over-co-operative author. In the case of more stubborn authors, the critic is only too happy to perform the job.

20   The work of Kafka, for example, has been subjected to a mass ravishment by no less than three armies of interpreters. Those who read Kafka as a social allegory see case studies of the frustrations and insanity of modern bureaucracy and its ultimate issuance in the totalitarian state. Those who read Kafka as a psycho-analytic allegory see desperate revelations of Kafka's fear of his father, his castration anxieties, his sense of his own impotence, his thraldom to his dreams. Those who read Kafka as a religious allegory explain that K. in *The Castle* is trying to gain access to heaven, that Joseph K. in *The Trial* is being judged by the inexorable and mysterious justice of God…. Another *oeuvre* that has attracted interpreters like leeches is that of Samuel Beckett. Beckett's delicate dramas of the withdrawn consciousness—pared down to essentials, cut off, often represented as physically immobilized—are read as a statement about man's alienation from meaning or from God, or as an allegory of psycho-pathology.

21   Proust, Joyce, Faulkner, Rilke, Lawrence, Gide… one could go on citing author after author; the list is endless of those around whom thick encrustations of interpretation have taken hold. But it should be noted that interpretation is not simply the compliment that mediocrity pays to genius. It is, indeed, *the* modern way of understanding something, and is applied to works of every quality. Thus, in the notes that Elia Kazan published on his production of *A Streetcar Named Desire*, it becomes clear that, in order to direct the play, Kazan had to discover that Stanley Kowalski represented the sensual and vengeful barbarism that was engulfing our culture, while Blanche Du Bois was Western civilization, poetry, delicate apparel, dim lighting, refined feelings and all, though a little the worse for wear to be sure. Tennessee William's forceful psychological melodrama now became intelligible: it was *about* something, about the decline of Western civilization. Apparently, were it to go on being a play about a handsome brute named Stanley Kowalski and a faded mangy belle named Blanche Du Bois, it would not be manageable.

VI

22   It doesn't matter whether artists intend, or don't intend, for their work to be interpreted. Perhaps Tennessee Williams thinks *Streetcar* is about what Kazan thinks it to be about. It may be that Cocteau in *The Blood of a Poet* and in *Orpheus* wanted the elaborate readings which have been given these films, in terms of Freudian symbolism and social critique. But the merit of these works certainly lies elsewhere than in their "meanings." Indeed, it is precisely to the extent that Williams's plays and Cocteau's films do suggest these portentous meanings that they are defective, false, contrived, lacking in conviction.

23   From interviews, it appears that Resnais and Robbe-Grillet consciously designed *Last Year at Marienbad* to accommodate a multiplicity of equally plausible interpretations. But the temptation to interpret *Marienbad* should be resisted. What matters in *Marienbad* is the pure, untranslatable, sensuous immediacy of some of its images, and its rigorous if narrow solutions to certain problems of cinematic form.

24   Again, Ingmar Bergman may have meant the tank rumbling down the empty night street in *The Silence* as a phallic symbol. But if he did, it was a foolish thought. ("Never trust the teller, trust the tale," said Lawrence.) Taken as a brute object, as an immediate sensory equivalent for the mysterious abrupt armored happenings going on inside the hotel, that sequence with the tank is the most striking moment in the film. Those who reach for a Freudian interpretation of the tank are only expressing their lack of response to what is there on the screen.

25   It is always the case that interpretation of this type indicates a dissatisfaction (conscious or unconscious) with the work, a wish to replace it by something else.

26   Interpretation, based on the highly dubious theory that a work of art is composed of items of content, violates art. It makes art into an article for use, for arrangement into a mental scheme of categories.

VII

27   Interpretation does not, of course, always prevail. In fact, a great deal of today's art may be understood as motivated by a flight from interpretation. To avoid interpretation, art may become parody. Or it may become abstract. Or it may become ("merely") decorative. Or it may become non-art.

28   The flight from interpretation seems particularly a feature of modern painting. Abstract painting is the attempt to have, in the ordinary sense, no content; since there is no content, there can be no interpretation. Pop Art works by the opposite means to the same result; using a content so blatant, so "what it is," it, too, ends by being uninterpretable.

29   A good deal of modern poetry as well, starting from the great experiments of French poetry (including the movement that is misleadingly called Symbolism) to put silence into poems and to reinstate the *magic* of the word, has escaped from the rough grip of interpretation. The most recent revolution in contemporary taste in poetry—the revolution that has deposed Eliot and elevated Pound—represents a turning away from content in poetry in the old sense, an impatience with what made modern poetry prey to the zeal of interpreters.

30   I am speaking mainly of the situation in America, of course. Interpretation runs rampant here in those arts with a feeble and negligible avant-garde: fiction and the drama. Most American novelists and playwrights are really either journalists or gentlemen sociologists and psychologists. They are writing the literary equivalent of programme music. And so rudimentary, uninspired, and stagnant has been the sense of what might be done with *form* in fiction and drama that even when the content isn't simply information, news, it is still peculiarly visible, handier, more exposed. To the extent that novels and plays (in America), unlike poetry and painting and music, don't reflect any interesting concern with changes in their form, these arts remain prone to assault by interpretation.

31   But programmatic avant-gardism—which has meant, mostly, experiments with form at the expense of content—is not the only defense against the infestation of art by interpretations. At least, I hope not. For this would be to commit art to being perpetually on the run. (It also perpetuates the very distinction between form and content which is, ultimately, an illusion.) Ideally, it is possible to elude the interpreters in another way, by making works of art whose surface is so unified and clean, whose momentum is so rapid, whose address is so direct that the work can be...just what it is. Is this possible now? It does happen in films, I believe. This is why cinema is the most alive, the most exciting, the most important of all art forms right now. Perhaps the way one tells how alive a particular art form is, is by the latitude it gives for making mistakes in it, and still being good. For example, a few of the films of Bergman—though crammed with lame messages about the modern spirit, thereby inviting interpretations—still triumph over the pretentious intentions of their director. In *Winter Light* and *The Silence,* the beauty and visual sophistication of the images subvert before our eyes the callow pseudo-intellectuality of the story and some of the dialogue. (The most remarkable instance of this sort of discrepancy is the work of D. W. Griffith.) In good films, there is always a directness that entirely frees us from the itch to interpret. Many old Hollywood films, like those of Cukor, Walsh, Hawks, and countless other directors, have this liberating anti-symbolic quality, no less than the best work of the new European directors, like Truffaut's

Shoot the Piano Player and *Jules and Jim*, Godard's *Breathless* and *Vivre Sa Vie*, Antonioni's *L'Avventura*, and Olmi's *The Fiancés*.

32   The fact that films have not been overrun by interpreters is in part due simply to the newness of cinema as an art. It also owes to the happy accident that films for such a long time were just movies; in other words, that they were understood to be part of mass, as opposed to high, culture, and were left alone by most people with minds. Then, too, there is always something other than content in the cinema to grab hold of, for those who want to analyse. For the cinema, unlike the novel, possesses a vocabulary of forms—the explicit, complex, and discussable technology of camera movements, cutting, and composition of the frame that goes into the making of a film.

VIII

33   What kind of criticism, of commentary on the arts, is desirable today? For I am not saying that works of art are ineffable, that they cannot be described or paraphrased. They can be. The question is how. What would criticism look like that would serve the work of art, not usurp its place?

34   What is needed, first, is more attention to form in art. If excessive stress on *content* provokes the arrogance of interpretation, more extended and more thorough descriptions of *form* would silence. What is needed is a vocabulary—a descriptive, rather than prescriptive, vocabulary—for forms.[1] The best criticism, and it is uncommon, is of this sort that dissolves considerations of content into those of form. On film, drama, and painting respectively, I can think of Erwin Panofsky's essay, "Style and Medium in the Motion Pictures," Northrop Frye's essay, "A Conspectus of Dramatic Genres," Pierre Francastel's essay, "The Destruction of a Plastic Space." Roland Barthes's book *On Racine* and his two essays on Robbe-Grillet are examples of formal analysis applied to the work of a single author. (The best essays in Erich Auerbach's *Mimesis*, like "The Scar of Odysseus," are also of this type.) An example of formal analysis applied simultaneously to genre and author is Walter Benjamin's essay, "The Story Teller: Reflections on the Works of Nicolai Leskov."

---

[1] One of the difficulties is that our idea of form is spatial (the Greek metaphors for form are all derived from notions of space). This is why we have a more ready vocabulary of forms for the spatial than for the temporal arts. The exception among the temporal arts, of course, is the drama: perhaps this is because the drama is a narrative (i.e. temporal) form that extends itself visually and pictorially, upon a stage....What we don't have yet is a poetics of the novel, any clear notion of the forms of narration. Perhaps film criticism will be the occasion of a breakthrough here, since films are primarily a visual form, yet they are also a subdivision of literature.

35   Equally valuable would be acts of criticism which would supply a really accurate, sharp, loving description of the appearance of a work of art. This seems even harder to do than formal analysis. Some of Manny Farber's film criticism, Dorothy Van Ghent's essay, "The Dickens World: A View from Todgers'," Randall Jarrell's essay on Walt Whitman are among the rare examples of what I mean. These are essays which reveal the sensuous surface of art without mucking about in it.

IX

36   *Transparence* is the highest, most liberating value in art—and in criticism—today. Transparence means experiencing the luminousness of the thing in itself, of things being what they are. This is the greatness of, for example, the films of Bresson and Ozu and Renoir's *The Rules of the Game.*

37   Once upon a time (say, for Dante), it must have been a revolutionary and creative move to design works of art so that they might be experienced on several levels. Now it is not. It reinforces the principle of redundancy that is the principal affliction of modern life.

38   Once upon a time (a time when high art was scarce), it must have been a revolutionary and creative move to interpret works of art. Now it is not. What we decidedly do not need now is further to assimilate Art into Thought, or (worse yet) Art into Culture.

39   Interpretation takes the sensory experience of the work of art for granted, and proceeds from there. This cannot be taken for granted, now. Think of the sheer multiplication of works of art available, to every one of us, superadded to the conflicting tastes and odors and the sights of the urban environment that bombard our senses. Ours is a culture based on excess, on overproduction; the result is a steady loss of sharpness in our sensory experience. All the conditions of modern life—its material plentitude, its sheer crowdedness—conjoin to dull our sensory faculties. And it is in the light of the condition of our senses, our capabilities (rather than those of another age), that the task of the critic must be assessed.

40   What is important now is to recover our senses. We must learn to *see* more, to *hear* more, to *feel* more.

41   Our task is not to find the maximum amount of content in a work of art, much less to squeeze more content out of the work than is already there. Our task is to cut back content so that we can *see* the thing at all.

42   The aim of all commentary on art now should be to make works of art—and, by analogy, our own experience—more, rather than less, real to us. The function of criticism should be to show *how it is what it is,* even *that it is what it is,* rather than to show *what it means.*

X

43   In place of a hermeneutics we need an erotics of art.

STUDY QUESTIONS

1. How do the two epigraphs function in relation to the essay?
2. Why is Sontag "against interpretation?"
3. How does she believe art should be experienced?
4. What does she believe the proper function of critics is, if not to interpret?
5. Do you agree with this essay, or do you feel that those who experience art have a psychological need for interpretation?
6. Consider Sontag's metaphors for interpretation and for art that invites interpretation. What are these metaphors? What are their implications? Are they just?

SUGGESTIONS FOR WRITING

1. Pick some work of art as a test case for Sontag's ideas—possibly one of the works mentioned in the essay (such as a story by Kafka or a Beckett play). Does interpretation enhance or inhibit your appreciation of the work?
2. Respond to Sontag's essay as above, but using Welty's "A Worn Path" and the three essays that follow it in this volume as your test cases.

RICHARD BERNSTEIN

The Arts Catch Up with a Society in Disarray

The following was the lead article in the Arts and Leisure section of the *New York Times* on Sunday, September 2, 1990. It is one of several articles in major publications at about the same period to react against demands that art museums, college art history courses, public exhibitions and performances, and grants to artists reflect more fully the cultural diversity of the arts community.

1   The words come from the nineteenth century, and you have to wonder if they could be said today. Henrik Ibsen, the author of *A Doll's House,* was being honored for his contribution to women's rights. "I thank you for the toast but must disclaim the honor of having consciously worked for the women's rights movement," the playwright said. "My task has been the description of humanity."

2   Ibsen's sentiment seems apt in light of headline-grabbing episodes of the past few weeks, episodes of what has been called a new tribalism, a heightened awareness of ethnic and racial separateness. If Ibsen took all of humanity as his subject, the tendency now is toward a division of the society into a myriad of small cultures—an ethnic culture, a racial culture, a woman's, a gay's, a black's culture. Everybody seems to be looking at the world through the brightly colored lens of his or her own particular group.

3   In the unfolding of what might be called the *Miss Saigon* affair, Actors' Equity described the casting of a Caucasian actor in the role of a Eurasian pimp in the Broadway version of the hit London musical as an affront to Asians, thereby creating one of Broadway's biggest political incidents in years.

4   Spike Lee, the celebrated creator of *Do the Right Thing* and *Mo' Better Blues,* told a television interviewer that he could not do "some anti-Semitic thing," because "a large part of the people that run Hollywood are Jewish. I mean that's a basic fact."

5   Last year some black city councilmen in Chicago tore down a caricature of Harold Washington, the city's first black mayor, from a show at the Art Institute of Chicago, arguing that it constituted a racist slur. Similar trouble erupted in Chicago a few months later when a jury for an exhibition of local artists chose works by only 6 minority artists out of 120 altogether. "The dominant white culture has excluded my culture," said Carlos Tortoleno, the head of the Mexican Fine Arts Center and a leader of the protest that ensued. Meanwhile, in another long-brewing issue,

homosexuals were complaining that the attack on the National Endowment for the Arts stemmed from a blatant hatred of homosexuality felt by conservative and religious groups.

6   Are these incidents mere bumps on the running graph of a pluralistic society that is inevitably in a state of constant flux? Or are they signs of more seismic stirrings? Lloyd Richards, the director of the Yale Drama School, thinks they're to be expected. "The norm has been disturbed, but the norm was unbalanced and needed to be disturbed," he said. "Change is inevitable. It's not always comfortable, but it's inevitable."

7   Mr. Richards was speaking, with approval, of the "strength and presence" of minorities on the arts scene in recent years. There are more Asian, black and other minority actors, directors, musicians, authors and impresarios dealing with the minority experience than ever before in American history. Equity's own figures reveal that 50 percent of shows produced last year by the League of American Theaters had a significant number of actors belonging to ethnic minorities. Asian actors can expect a bonanza of roles when the Broadway musical *Shogun* comes to Broadway.

8   And yet there continue to be real, deep-seated inequities in the larger society, reflected by an intense racial unease in the air, a sense of mutual watchfulness, and it is not only in the arts. The debates taking place inside the corridors of Actors' Equity in New York reflect the minority assertiveness, the raw sensibilities, the demands for change that are affecting many aspects of American life, from politics to literary criticism to historical research to employment. Some of this derives from what might be called the French Revolutionary principle. It is that the demand for more does not come from the dispossessed; it comes from those who feel matters getting better and want the pace to quicken. But there seems to be far more here than can be explained by a revolution of rising expectations.

From Melting Pot to Tower of Babel

9   The country is in the grip of what might be called a cult of otherness, the word otherness being highly fashionable in academic circles these days. Twenty-five years ago the civil rights movement began to erase differences imposed by race and ethnic origin. Now the cult of otherness asserts that the differences are unbridgeable.

10   "The contemporary ideal is not assimilation but ethnicity," the historian Arthur Schlesinger Jr. wrote recently in an essay in *The Wall Street Journal.* "We used to say *e pluribus unum.* Now we glorify *pluribus* and belittle *unum.* The melting pot yields to the Tower of Babel."

11   At the same time, there seems to be a close connection, a kind of
natural synergy, between artistic matters and the harsh world of the streets,
where things seem to be getting conspicuously worse.

12   Even as Mr. Lee was making his remarks about Jews, racial relations in
New York were acrimonious. The trial of three black and Hispanic youths
for the rape and assault of the Central Park jogger was rolling toward its
eventual verdict of guilty. Only recently, New York went through the
enormously divisive trials of whites convicted of killing a black youth
who came into their Brooklyn neighborhood of Bensonhurst to look at a
used car.

13   All during this period, Tawana Brawley, the black teenager who caused
turmoil when she told a story of rape and racial abuse by six white
policemen (a story later shown to have been fabricated), was being lionized
by such black leaders as the Rev. Louis Farrakhan and the Rev. Al Sharpton,
who have tried to turn her into a martyr to what they term, with no approval
intended, "white justice." In an intra-minority twist to the picture, a
Korean grocery store in Brooklyn has been boycotted by blacks for months.

14   In Washington, Mayor Marion Barry was on trial, protesting that he
was being prosecuted because he was black. In Boston, a man who told
police that his wife had been killed by a black mugger was immediately
believed — until the evidence showed that he was lying. At Harvard Law
School, the only tenured black professor, Derek Bell, went on a leave of
absence to protest the university's failure to hire a black woman to a
tenured faculty post.

15   In short, ethnic tensions are enflamed as they have rarely been since the
race riots of the 1960s. It sometimes seems as though there is no such thing
as an objective truth, either on the streets or in the arts. There are only
beliefs shaped by ethnic experience and identity. Crowds of blacks and
Hispanics shouting "slut" and "K.K.K." outside the courtroom hounded
the prosecutor in the jogger case. When it turned out that she had been
having marital difficulties during the trial, Mr. Sharpton declared that her
situation "added to her hostility," as though it is unfair for a prosecutor to
be hostile toward a defendant.

16   Similarly, when Spike Lee told his television interviewer that he could
not make an anti-Semitic film because the Jews "run" Hollywood, he
seemed to lose sight of one thing: that in these days of raw nerves and
heightened sensitivity, you cannot make an anti-black film or an anti-gay
film, and it has nothing to do with who "runs" Hollywood.

17   Even the movie-makers live in the real world, after all, and the world
today has placed a strict taboo on stereotypes of just about anybody well
enough organized to fight back. Mr. Lee's statement about the Jews was
not so much anti-Semitic as ethnically one-sided, a view of the world

refracted by that narrow particularist prism, an obverse of a problem felt by many blacks, Asians and others—that for many decades whites controlled the way they were portrayed in the arts.

Who Controls Art? Artists or Social Goals?

18   If the animosities of the real world are extending their grip into artistic matters, some fundamental issues are raised. One of them is nothing less than who controls a society's cultural life. Few disagree that society has an obligation to guard against legitimate discrimination and to hear all the voices in what New York's Mayor David Dinkins has called a "gorgeous mosaic."

19   But are culture and the arts obliged to be socially responsible? Who, or what, should determine art—the untrammeled visions of the artist or society's political goals and strivings for social justice? And, if society's political goals prevail, isn't there a very real danger that the result will be a kind of "politically correct" art, an art suffocated by a requirement that nobody be either offended or excluded?

20   On college campuses across the country faculties have been passing regulations forbidding certain kinds of speech—racial slurs, misogynous comments, anti-homosexual remarks—that might offend others. The American Civil Liberties Union has been fighting these efforts on the well-established ground that speech must be free even when it offends.

21   The issue is similar in the arts. The independence of the artist can be compromised by the requirement of sensitivity to social goals. The quest for diversity can turn into its opposite, a conformity that masquerades as diversity, or just plain mediocrity. And given the sanctimonious current atmosphere that surrounds the issue of race and minorities, it seems possible that nobody will point the mediocrity out.

22   These are difficult and confusing issues in the arts, largely because of the conflict of principles involved. Nobody wants to relinquish the moral high ground of ethnic diversity or greater opportunity for groups that have been excluded in the past. Nobody wants to turn the clock back to the days when such things as nontraditional casting—by which a black actor, for example, might play a white character—were considered controversial.

23   As the *Miss Saigon* ruckus was reaching a crescendo two weeks ago, the New York Shakespeare Festival was featuring Denzel Washington, the award-winning black actor, as Richard III. Earlier this summer, Morgan Freeman, the chauffeur in the film *Driving Miss Daisy,* played Petruchio in the festival's production of *The Taming of the Shrew.* A welcome colorblindness—once the goal of the "gorgeous mosaic"—seemed to prevail in those productions. More commonly, however, colorblindness is giving way to a demand for ethnic representation.

24   The very vocabulary that emerged from recent cultural disputes suggests the extent to which ethnic politics can mingle with the arts. During the *Miss Saigon* affair, Mr. Dinkins, whose most pressing task may be to keep the ethnic peace, spoke of "nontraditional and culturally appropriate casting" and of "appropriate casting where ethnicity is critical to the role."

25   What exactly "culturally appropriate" casting is Mr. Dinkins did not say. But the New York Human Rights Commission announced that it would hold hearings on employment practices in the theater, implying that government might start considering how directors choose casts and whether playwrights are creating enough roles for minorities. Artists themselves would probably be unanimous in rejecting government suasion on such issues, but they differ among themselves on how much place such goals as ethnic representativeness should have in their own decisions.

26   "I think that trying to develop minority performers can be one of the parameters within which one does one's work, one of the contingencies by which one makes decisions, and it should be that way," said Zelda Fichandler, producing director of the Arena Stage Company in Washington. "I think we're closer to recognizing that we have to provide the opportunities for actors from minority groups to compete artistically with the people who have evolved through our system to stardom. Major actors just don't fall from sky."

'The Mad Intellect of Democracy'

27   Robert Brustein, the director of the American Repertory Theater in Cambridge, Mass., and a theater critic for *The New Republic,* agreed that every effort should be made to encourage all talent. "The more you explore for talent, the happier any art form is," he said.

28   But Mr. Brustein sees a danger in the possibility that applying affirmative action to the arts will exact a price in excellence.

29   "Everyone's in the casting business," he said. "You have to cast a black woman in a law school as a law professor. You have to cast Asians, homosexuals, everyone, in order to get sufficiently diverse multicultural representation. That is what Yeats called the 'mad intellect of democracy,' thinking that democracy means there has to be equal representation for everything that happens.

30   "You have to have certain standards when you make your judgments," Mr. Brustein said. "If you stop making the judgments, you are in cultural anarchy."

Is Integration Out of Fashion?

31   Certainly, this is a time of surgent minorities. The ethnic consciousness movements that began in the 1960s intensified in the late 1980s, so that

there is a host of subgroups—including blacks, Hispanics, women, homosexuals and lesbians, the handicapped, American Indians, Asians, people of color (as nonwhites are referred to)—all paying close attention to the way they are portrayed in books and movies, on television, and in other domains of American life. This new assertiveness can be seen in many other ways as well.

32   Indeed, the clamor in the arts, including the episodes involving Mr. Lee, *Miss Saigon,* the Chicago aldermen, merely reflect deep movements taking place elsewhere in our society, the rise of what the syndicated columnist Charles Krauthammer, has called a new tribalism. Until recently, most groups accepted the idea that public life provided a certain common identity, even as individual characteristics were maintained in private life.

33   It was over such notions that the fight for civil rights in the 1960s was waged. The goal of the movement, as the Rev. Dr. Martin Luther King, Jr., used to say, was integration. But the tendency now is for individuals, particularly members of minority groups, to identify primarily with their groups rather than with the common culture—often pushed into it by the radicalism of militant leaders. In academic circles these days the very idea of a common culture is under assault, seen merely as a tool used by what is called the white, male, heterosexual establishment to exercise its "hegemony."

The Common Ground Is Shrinking Fast

34   At the same time, the degree of common ground seems to be shrinking. Whites cannot understand blacks, this reasoning goes; blacks owe it to themselves to reject the "white Eurocentric culture" in favor of their own, more authentic visions. Molefi Kete Asante, a professor of African-American studies at Temple University in Philadelphia, has written that black students should "move away from a Eurocentric framework" because "it is difficult to create freely when you use someone's else's motifs, styles, images, and perspectives."

35   "Whenever black people want to move off the plantation white people see it as a threat," Professor Asante said in an interview. "Nobody gets upset over Chinatown, but if blacks created a Nigeria-town, they would be called separatist, rather than people trying to reinforce cultural roots that are significant for them."

36   A radical minority assertiveness, that cult of otherness, permeates the mainstream. Every minority group has its own sub-specialty within each department. Women are expected to study women; homosexuals study homosexuals. The notion of scholarly neutrality has given way to a contrary notion, which is that minority group members or women are supposed to find in, say, history some glory for their group.

37   These trends are summed up in the determined assault on college campuses against required courses in Western culture, which minority

students feel should be dropped on the ground that they are "Eurocentric." They are demeaning to other cultures, the argument goes, and they ignore the contributions to American life of "women, minorities and people of color" — as the litany of the ethnic militants has it.

38   "A Beirutization of American higher education is taking place," said Chester Finn, the director of the Education Excellence Network in Washington. "More and more we are identifying ourselves in terms of race, ethnicity and sexual preference, and we are beginning to group ourselves accordingly. We are conferring benefits, rights and resources according to group identification, and gradually we are beginning to dislike or to envy other groups."

Myth of the Permanent Victim

39   What begins as rebellion often ends up as a new orthodoxy. That is what threatens to happen now as the potent ethnic-consciousness movement moves into the arts. What makes the movement so irresistible, so confounding, is the fact that there is so much idealism, so many laudable intentions in it, so much healthy recognition of a profoundly flawed and unfair past. When some Asian actors, speaking of the *Miss Saigon* controversy, complain that for decades they have been portrayed in prefabricated fashion by whites, they are right. It is when they insist on that as a description of the present that a myth of permanent victimization seems to be in the making.

40   Here, too, there is a strange reversal. The artist, the creative personality, has in modern times often been a rebel against prevailing morals and conventions. When a performing artist like Karen Finley rails against what she characterizes as the degradation of women in society, she seems to be in that tradition, presenting herself as a lonely rebel, one with the courage to be different. Her theatrical pose is that of the victim of the violence of male-dominated society.

41   But Ms. Finley's message, with its evocations of injustice, is what has become the "politically correct attitude," encouraging audiences, critics and artists alike in reverent support of the cause of the "oppressed."

42   "I think there's an atmosphere of fear abroad, where people are afraid to evaluate work correctly because somehow they'll be accused of being anti-feminist, anti-black, or anti-gay," Mr. Brustein said. "Lionel Trilling once said that when a lie introduced into society is not exposed, then the society begins to fester. I think there are a lot of lies being expressed in our society these days, or, at least, the whole truth is not being expressed."

43   The last thing needed is a cultural consensus, even a consensus dressed in the mantle of diversity. The experience of Eastern Europe has made it clear that there is nothing so boring as "politically correct" art, nice art, art whose purpose is to make everybody with a grievance feel good.

STUDY QUESTIONS

1. Bernstein opens with a quotation from Ibsen. From Bernstein's point of view, why are Ibsen's words "apt"? What aspect of his argument do they support? Discuss the range of ways in which feminists might react to Ibsen's remark.

2. In paragraph 8 Bernstein describes the "French Revolutionary principle." How, in his view, does this apply to conditions in the arts today?

3. In paragraph 17 Bernstein says, "Even the movie-makers live in the real world, after all, and the world today has placed a strict taboo on stereotypes of just about anybody well enough organized to fight back." Does Bernstein regard this taboo on stereotypes as a healthy or unhealthy trend? What are his reasons? Do you agree with him?

4. Bernstein describes the trend toward "otherness" as a constraining influence on artistic expression. Those who disagree with him, of course, would argue that this trend has aimed at opening up the arts to new subject matter (e.g., homosexuality, minority cultures) and to new artistic voices. Which viewpoint do you support, and why?

5. In the section titled "Who Controls Art? Artists or Social Goals?" Bernstein expresses the fear that "the sanctimonious current atmosphere" surrounding the issue of race and minorities will produce an art that is suffocating and mediocre by substituting politically correct social goals for the "untrammeled visions of the artist."

   Which of the following do you think Bernstein would consider mechanisms of social control: censorship? government funding? boycotts? corporate sponsorship? advertising? critical reviews? decisions by private consumers about which events to buy tickets for or which art objects or recordings to buy? Can you think of others?

6. Bernstein says that members of minority groups now tend to identify primarily with their groups rather than with "the common culture." Is there a "common culture"? How is it defined? How is it distinguished from the culture of males of European descent?

SUGGESTIONS FOR DISCUSSION AND WRITING

1. One of the incidents that Bernstein lists (in paragraph 5) as illustrating the trend toward "tribalism" is the controversy that arose in Chicago when "a jury for an exhibition of local artists chose works by only 6 minority artists out of 120 altogether." In paragraph 15 Bernstein says, "It sometimes seems as though there is no such thing as an objective truth, either on the streets or in the arts. There are only beliefs shaped by ethnic experience and identity." In the selection of artworks to be exhibited (or of literary works to be included in a course or curriculum), can decisions be based on "objective truth," or are such decisions all inevitably political?

2. Write an essay examining the five specific incidents that Bernstein lists in the third, fourth, and fifth paragraphs of his article as troubling examples of the "new tribalism." What mechanisms of "social control" over art operate in each of these instances? Do you agree that this social control has been unhealthy in these cases? Would it have been possible to eliminate social control over the artist? Would it have been desirable? (See question 5 above.)

3. Bernstein asks, "Are culture and the arts obliged to be socially responsible?" This question concerns the intersection of moral and aesthetic values. A corollary question is whether a work of art can ever achieve artistic greatness if it includes morally repugnant values. This approach has been used to explore the aesthetic consequences of antisemitism in Pound's *Cantos,* alleged racism in Conrad's *Heart of Darkness,* obliviousness to the inequitable British economic system in Jane Austen's *Emma,* and the glorification of drugs, violence, and self-destructiveness in various recent recordings. Write an essay about some work of art with some plausible claim to artistic excellence that you feel is diminished by socially irresponsible content; or defend the aesthetic excellence of a work of art that has been criticized for social irresponsibility.

HOWARDENA PINDELL

Colonial Culture

In the fall of 1990, when the *New York Times* published the preceding selection and a companion piece, also by Richard Bernstein, entitled "The Rising Hegemony of the Politically Correct," the journal *Lies of Our Times* solicited responses from three cultural critics. The following selection is one of those responses. Its author, Howardena Pindell, is a painter, professor of art at the State University of New York at Stony Brook, and the author of several articles denouncing racism and sexism in the art world.

1   The chilling effect of Richard Bernstein's piece on the "new tribalism" stems both from his calculated omission of valuable information and from his trivialization of the cultural contributions of what he calls "sub-groups." His narrow, clubby approach to the arts is racist, sexist, homophobic, and above all paternalistic. The essay's underlying ideology—that of the *New York Times*—is an affront to women and people of color and to all of us who are lumped into "sub-groups." It is designed to comfort the privileged who see themselves threatened by what they feel to be cultural militancy, even cultural terrorism.

2   Bernstein writes as if the only "objective" voice is the white male voice. For example, he uses terms such as "tribalism," "ethnic," "sub-group," "minority," and "cult of otherness" as if they do not apply to him. Indeed, a woman artist of color was recently taken to task by her *New York Times* reviewer for "an affinity for an obnoxious word like 'Euroethnic'" (Michael Brenson, "Adrian Piper's Head-on Confrontation of Racism," October 26, 1990, p. C36). Everyone, of course, beyond being members of the human race, is ethnic one way or another, and can be put in various "sub-groups," large and small. But what Bernstein does—and this is the Big Lie here—is use terms like "sub-group" and "minority" for every category he discusses *except* white males. Only about a quarter of the people of the world are white, and fewer than half of those are men, so who then is the real minority? He writes, with some concern, of "what might be called a cult of otherness," while he is a part of, and a mouthpiece for, a white, male, western, corporate cult, complemented in the spiritual arena by a god portrayed over hundreds of years by European artists spreading the propaganda that god *must* be white and male.

3   Bernstein resents authentic voices and implies that the art produced by the "sub-group" members is both mediocre and obsessed with victimization. Neither assertion is true, but they help to deflect and trivialize the critical questions of racism and sexism—the censorship of artists who are not white and male. Bernstein's frequent references to the

civil rights movement of the 1960s and his discussion of a "myth of permanent victimization" imply that these "sub-groups" are now rarely victimized. Bernstein says that "few disagree that society has an obligation to guard against legitimate [*sic*] discrimination"; but, he adds, "are culture and the arts obliged to be socially responsible?" By qualifying discrimination, he implies that a lot of what we misguided folks see as discrimination and censorship is simply the triumph of "objective" quality.

4   Bernstein's fear of "the rising hegemony of the politically correct," described in his "news" article on academia, demonstrates again his mirror-image view of reality. With respect to art and culture, for example, he ignores the existence, much less the meaning, of the lucrative links between large corporations, auction houses, galleries, collectors, museum trustees and acquisition committees, country clubs, private clubs. This is the manipulative power structure that launders its corporate images through culture. The concept of being politically correct has always existed, and, in fact, in conservative circles has generally meant *exactly the opposite* of what Bernstein depicts. In the art world for decades, to be politically correct in most instances has meant to ignore issues of social and human concern. It has meant to be white and male and socially graceful, or to try very hard to be so. It has meant stroking stereotypes about people of color in an arena that was closed to artists of color and to critics of color.

5   How many critics of color have worked regularly for the *Times?*

STUDY QUESTIONS

1. Pindell sees Bernstein's essay as intended to "comfort the privileged." What does she mean, and do you agree with her?
2. What "meaning" do you think Pindell ascribes to the "lucrative links" between corporations, galleries, auction houses, and the like? How do these links bear on Bernstein's argument about "political correctness"?
3. Pindell says that the "concept of being politically correct has always existed." Discuss some forms that "political correctness" has taken in the past.

SUGGESTION FOR WRITING

Pindell's rebuttal of Bernstein essentially makes only three points:

   1 Bernstein appropriates "objectivity" for white males and patronizingly dismisses others as "sub-groups."

2 He ignores the censorship of artists who are not white males or else misrepresents it as the "objective" rejection of the mediocre.
3 He ascribes "hegemony of the politically correct" to academia, leftists, and minorities while ignoring the real hegemony of the white corporate world which, through its money and power, controls the galleries and museums that limit access to artists who express an altogether opposite notion of political correctness.

Are these three points valid? Are they potshots at peripheral aspects of Bernstein's essay, or do they attack the heart of his argument?

KATHA POLLITT

Why We Read

Katha Pollitt, a poet and contributing editor to *The Nation*, first presented an expanded form of this essay as part of a panel discussion on "The Politics of Culture" at the Columbia University Center for American Culture Studies. The complete text was published in the September 23, 1991, issue of *The Nation*, then reprinted in this condensed form in *Harper's Magazine*, December 1991.

1   What are we to make of the current, spluttering debate over the canon, in which charges of imperialism are met by equally passionate accusations of vandalism, in which each side hates the others and yet each one seems to have its share of reason? Perhaps what we have here is one of those debates in which the opposing sides, unbeknownst to themselves, share a myopia that will turn out to be the most telling feature of the whole discussion.

2   Something is indeed being overlooked: the state of reading, and books, and literature in our country at this time. Why, ask yourself, is everyone so hot under the collar about what to put on the required-reading shelf? It is because while we have been arguing so fiercely about which books make the best medicine, the patient has been slipping deeper and deeper into a coma.

3   Let us imagine a country in which reading is a popular voluntary activity. There, parents read books for their own edification and pleasure, and also read to their children, give them books for presents, talk to them about books, and underwrite, with their taxes, a public library system that is open all day, every day. In school—where an attractive library is invariably to be found—the children study certain books together but also have an active reading life of their own. Years later it may even be hard for them to remember if they read *Jane Eyre* at home and Judy Blume in class, or the other way around. In college young people continue to be assigned certain books, but far more important are the books they discover for themselves—browsing in the library, in bookstores, on the shelves of friends, one book leading to another, back and forth in history and across languages and cultures. After graduation they continue to read, and in the fullness of time produce a new generation of readers. O happy land! I wish we all lived there.

4   In that other country of real readers—voluntary, active, self-determined readers—a debate like the current one over the canon would not be taking place. Or if it did, it would be as a kind of parlor game: What books would *you* take to a desert island? Everyone would know that the top-ten list was merely a tiny fraction of the books one would read in a lifetime. It would not seem racist or sexist or hopelessly hidebound to put

Hawthorne on the syllabus and not Toni Morrison. It would be more like putting oatmeal and not noodles on the breakfast menu—a choice part arbitrary, part a nod to the national past, part, dare one say it, a kind of reverse affirmative action: School might frankly be the place where you read the books that are a little off-putting, that have gone a little cold, that you might pass over because they do not address, in reader-friendly contemporary fashion, the issues most immediately at stake in modern life, but that, with a little study, turn out to have a great deal to say. Being on the list wouldn't mean so much. It might even add to a writer's cachet *not* to be on the list, to be in one way or another too heady, too daring, too exciting to be ground up into institutional fodder for teenagers.

5   In America today the assumption underlying the canon debate is that the books on the list are the only books that are going to be read. Becoming a textbook is a book's only chance; all sides take that for granted. And so all agree not to mention certain things that they themselves, as highly educated people and, one assumes, devoted readers, know perfectly well: That if you read only twenty-five, or fifty, or a hundred books, you can't understand them, however well chosen they are. That if you don't have an independent reading life—and very few students do—you won't *like* reading the books on the list and will forget them the minute you finish them. And that books have, or should have, lives beyond the syllabus— thus, the totally misguided attempt to put current literature in the classroom. How strange to think that people need professional help to read John Updike or Alice Walker, writers people actually do read for fun. But all sides agree: If it isn't taught, it doesn't count.

6   Let's look at the canon question from another angle. Instead of asking what books we want others to read, let's ask why we read books ourselves. I think the canon debaters are being a little disingenuous here, are suppressing, in the interest of their own agendas, their personal experience of reading. Sure, we read to understand our American culture and history, and to rediscover wrongly neglected masterpieces, and to learn more about the accomplishments of our subgroup and thereby increase our self-esteem. But what about reading for the aesthetic pleasures of language, form, image? What about reading to learn something new, to have a vicarious adventure, to follow the workings of an interesting, if possibly skewed, narrow, and ill-tempered mind? What about reading for the story? For an expanded sense of sheer human variety? There are a thousand reasons why a book might have a claim on our time and attention other than its canonization. I once infuriated an acquaintance by asserting that Trollope, although in many ways a lesser writer than Dickens, possessed some wonderful qualities Dickens lacked: a more realistic view of women, a more skeptical view of good intentions, a subtler sense of humor, a drier

vision of life that I myself found congenial. You'd think I'd advocated throwing Dickens out and replacing him with a toaster. Because Dickens is a certified Great Writer, and Trollope is not.

7   All sides in the canon debate seem to agree that the purpose of reading is none of the many varied and delicious satisfactions I've mentioned; it's medicinal. The chief end of reading is to produce a desirable kind of person and a desirable kind of society. A respectful, high-minded citizen of a unified society for the conservatives, an up-to-date and flexible sort for the liberals, a subgroup-identified, robustly confident one for the radicals. How pragmatic, how moralistic, how American! The culture debaters turn out to share a secret suspicion of culture itself, as well as the antipornographer's belief that there is a simple, one-to-one correlation between books and behavior. Read the conservatives' list and produce a nation of sexists and racists—or a nation of philosopher kings. Read the liberals' list and produce a nation of spineless relativists—or a nation of open-minded world citizens. Read the radicals' list and produce a nation of psychobabblers and ancestor worshipers—or a nation of stalwart proud-to-be-me pluralists.

8   But is there any list of a few dozen books that can have such a magical effect, for good or for ill? Of course not. It's like arguing that a perfectly nutritional breakfast cereal is enough food for the whole day. And so the canon debate is really an argument about what books to cram down the resistant throats of a resentful captive populace of students; and the trick is never to mention the fact that, in such circumstances, one book is as good, or bad, as another. Because, as the debaters know from their own experience as readers, books are not pills that produce health when ingested in measured doses. Books do not shape character in any simple way—if, indeed, they do so at all—or the most literate would be the most virtuous instead of just the ordinary run of humanity with larger vocabularies. Books cannot mold a common national purpose when, in fact, people are honestly divided about what kind of country they want—and are divided, moreover, for very good and practical reasons, as they always have been.

9   For these burly purposes, books are all but useless. The way books affect us is an altogether more subtle, delicate, wayward, and individual, not to say private, affair. And that reading is being made to bear such an inappropriate and simplistic burden speaks to the poverty both of culture and of frank political discussion in our time.

10   On his deathbed, Dr. Johnson—once canonical, now more admired than read—is supposed to have said to a friend who was energetically rearranging his bedclothes, "Thank you, this will do all that a pillow can do." One might say that the canon debaters are all asking of their handful of chosen books that they do a great deal more than any handful of books can do.

STUDY QUESTIONS

1. Pollitt asserts that in a land where everyone voluntarily read for his or her own edification and pleasure, a debate about the canon would not take place. Paraphrase the argument she gives in support of this contention. Do you agree with it?
2. Pollitt raises the analogy of breakfast cereal in paragraph 4 and then again in paragraph 8. What is the point of this analogy, and does it work?
3. In paragraph 6, Pollitt raises the same question that Warren raises: Why do we read books? Is her answer essentially the same as his or different?

SUGGESTION FOR WRITING

The main focus of the canon debate, as far as literature is concerned, is the curriculum of courses in high school and college. If we were to accept Pollitt's argument, what implications would it have on choices about the curriculum? Write a brief proposal for policy governing the choice of readings in some English course at your school, a proposal that either accepts Pollitt's argument and implements it or that rejects it in favor of some other attitude toward the canon. If you like, you may also refer to the views of Bernstein, Pindell, and Eagleton, all of whose arguments are pertinent to the canon debate.

SUZI GABLIK

Toward an Ecological Self

Suzi Gablik is the author of *Has Modernism Failed?* This essay is an abstract from her book, *The Re-enchantment of Art.*

1   We seem to have reached a critical threshold between survival and ecocide, where to continue on our consumerist course is no longer viable. But how does a culture redefine itself? Modernism was the art of the rise and fall of the industrial age. Problems that Modernists were fascinated by, and attached great importance to, were without question linked to a certain view of the world and concern about what was important, which I believe is now changing. I believe that in the ecological future, art may come to signify a different set of behaviors and attitudes than it has within the Modern aesthetic paradigm.

2   The critic Arthur Danto has referred to the end of art history as a time when art does not end, but continues in a new realm that is characterized by nonpatriarchal, non-Eurocentric ideals. A new narrative is being created in which the old guidelines, based on the notion of masterpieces, the styles of the masters, originality, and aesthetics are no longer useful. The aesthetic, autonomous, and stylistic values of Modernism have ended. One could find devastation in the phrase "art history is dead," as a student of mine in Boulder said, but the repercussions are far from devastating. Although the end to art history is threatening to some, to others it is a step in the redefining of our values that will further assist the change into a new paradigm.

3   All of us, to varying degrees, have internalized the dominator system and its ideal of autonomous, self-determining personalities, so that to speak of the end of a certain infrastructure of autonomous individualism—or what we have been calling Cartesian selfhood—is to threaten the axiomatic foundation of modern aesthetic practice and art history. "Our present idea of freedom," Wendell Berry has written in *The Hidden Wound*, "is only the freedom to do as we please: to sell ourselves for a high salary, a home in the suburbs, and idle weekends. But that is a freedom dependent upon affluence, which is in turn dependent upon the rapid consumption of exhaustible supplies. The other kind of freedom is the freedom to take care of ourselves and each other." It is the other kind of freedom which I shall try to address here.

4   Within modern culture, society has been characterized as a hostile rather than a resonant environment for the self-unfolding of the individual. A deep dualism existed within Modernism, between public and

private, that severed any connections between them and colored our view of art as basically a "private" affair. The politics of a contextual/connective aesthetics is very different; it tries to move beyond social passivity, culturally conditioned modes of distancing, and the denial of responsibility. The prestige of individualism has been so high in our culture that even in an artist like Christo, whose environmental projects such as *Running Fence* require the participation of *thousands* of people, the feeling of being independent and separate still dominates the psyche. In a recent interview in *Flash Art* (March/April 1990), Christo stated: "The work is irrational and perhaps irresponsible. Nobody needs it. The work is a huge individualistic gesture that is entirely decided by me....One of the greatest contributions of modern art is the notion of individualism....I think that the artist can do anything he wants to do. This is why I would never accept a commission. Independence is most important to me. The work of art is a scream of freedom." In a year fraught with art politics, sexual censorship, and the tyrannical Senator Jesse Helms (who seems almost singlehandedly to have undermined the durability of government support for the arts), Christo's "scream of freedom" continues to be the unwavering, ever-present, moral imperative that is always brandished politically as well as philosophically in the great tradition of Western thought. The entire structure of our thinking and experience has been pervasively shaped by this assumption of separateness as the absolute foundation on which we live our lives.

5   From the vantage point of individuality—the vision of a self in ultimate control, whose innermost impulse is self-assertion—it is virtually impossible to imagine the relational pattern between individuals and society changing. Individual freedom and individual uniqueness were cultural ideals summed up and embodied in the motifs of Romanticism; today, however, we find that a different cultural imperative is being argued and fought. "Today," states the ecofeminist writer Charlene Spretnak in *Reweaving the World*, "we work for ecopeace, ecojustice, ecoeconomics, ecopolitics, ecoeducation, ecophilosophy, ecotheology, and for the evolution of ecofeminism....to refuse to let the dominant culture pave them over any longer with a value system of denial distancing, fear and ignorance."

6   At the 1989 Mountain Lake Symposium held in Virginia, one of the presenters, artist Sidney Tillim, asked: "Do intentions matter? Does art, or do intentions, really matter if you can't make a living from them?" In a free society, he added, one has almost to improvise convictions. I should like to try and answer these questions by discussing the work of a young artist that evokes, at least for me, the essence of a new paradigm of intentions which, as I see it, presents art in a radically revised relationship with

society, and tests its meaningfulness beyond the disinterested, disembodied, free play of the mind.

7   I first met Bradley McCallum when he was in the undergraduate sculpture department at Virginia Commonwealth University in Richmond, where he was making large, rather distinctive objects in welded steel. Somewhere along the way his consciousness changed, as did his basic commitments. He began thinking about how an audience would view and experience his work and realized that a lot of the experience was missing. He felt a need to engage the audience more directly and became interested in collaboration, feeling drawn at the same time to work with the homeless community in Richmond. Brad wanted to do this *as art,* that is, capitalizing on the same skills he used in making sculpture. He was not searching for independence, autonomy, or freedom so much as for the social need he sensed that art was meant to fulfill. His art soon became pragmatic, goal-directed, purposive, and charged with ethical sensitivity, all things that run counter to the teachings of aesthetic autonomy. He began to care less for originality than for results.

8   His studio was in an old Richmond carriage house near some alleys where the homeless hang out and pass by with their carts. In time Brad was able to make friends with some of them. His art emerged from these relationships. Brad observed that, at least in Richmond, ordinary grocery carts do not roll well on the bumpy cobblestone streets. He was aware of the prototype designs for shopping carts, the *Homeless Vehicles,* pioneered by Krzysztof Wodiczko, which at this point still exist primarily in the realm of art, not (yet) having been manufactured or provided in any numbers to the homeless. Brad decided on a different path, since his fundamental concern was with how to translate helping the homeless into a living artistic practice, an actual *modus operandi* that would go beyond a merely symbolic potential.

9   He, too, began by building a prototype cart, using a softer wire mesh than is found in commercial carts and welding it entirely by hand to make a deeper, more pliant basket. Most of the materials he was able to obtain free, from scrap metal companies and hospitals, whom he approached for donations of specially sized wheels, removed from broken wheelchairs and other disused medical equipment, that would be sturdy enough to make it over the cobblestones. Then he offered the prototype for a week to some of his homeless friends for use on a trial basis, inviting suggestions for its greater effectiveness from each potential user. This became the catalyst for further collaborations. One man, for instance, who had skin cancer, requested a little awning over his head that would shield his face from the sun while he pushed the cart around collecting cans. In order to accommodate the different needs of each person, Brad had to develop a certain trust and fluidity; to be open to interpenetration and blending, he

had to develop a more transparent and permeable ego structure that would be receptive to an intertwining of self and other. Then he would create another cart, incorporating the new features, and give it to the person. Before Brad left Richmond for graduate school in New Haven, he had constructed and given away a total of 11 carts. For him, the finished carts are sculptures; for his senior thesis exhibition in downtown Richmond, he invited his homeless friends to bring their carts along for the opening if they wanted to.

10   During his first term at Yale in 1989, Brad introduced himself to Jackie, a middle-aged black woman who had been living in a small, abandoned city park, used temporarily to store materials for street repairs. Brad told Jackie that he was a sculptor and showed her photographs of the work he'd done with the homeless in Virginia. Initially, Jackie explained that she had no need for the mobile carts he'd made; later, in other conversations, she expressed a wish that the city would make park benches with awnings. This sparked an idea that they began to work on together. An aluminum structure with a backrest that jutted over at the top like a shelf was built and bolted to the park bench. Jackie was unhappy with certain features of the construction, but other homeless people liked it and said that they would happily use it in her place. The wondered why Brad felt the need to keep changing it, continuing to work with Jackie until both of them were satisfied with the result. Brad explained to them what he felt was important to collaboration: the freedom that comes from being unattached to the outcome. "Simply put," he said, "if I were to ignore Jackie and leave the awning as it was, I would violate a trust that is essential to the collaboration: the potential for learning from one another is realized by honoring this trust and listening. With Jackie, it meant reworking the awning to satisfy both our intentions." The actual object exchanged is secondary, for Brad, to the ethical values that are explicitly shared.

11   What finally emerged was far more functional and, in Brad's view, a more powerful image than the first attempt. The rigid back panel was removed and a tarpaulin attached to the remaining overhang in such a way that it could be rolled up and down on pulleys like a Mozart curtain to create a tent around the bench that was adaptable to all weathers. Ten days after the tarpaulin was added, the New Haven Recreation and Parks Department removed the whole structure and moved Jackie's belongings to a parking lot across the street, their justification being that no one is allowed to make a permanent shelter in a city park. On one level, Brad was pleased that the structure had stayed up unmolested as long as it did; on another, he was worried that his work with Jackie had brought unnecessary attention to her place of refuge.

12   That same week, Brad was asked to participate in a First Year Students' Show at the Yale School of Art. As a way of documenting his collaboration

with Jackie, he got permission to do a performance on the night of the opening. Jackie had many plastic bags filled with clothes that she and Brad decided to wash and use in the installation, which turned out to be ten washloads at the laundromat. In the exhibition space at school, slides of the park-bench construction were projected, with a statement on the wall describing the nature of the collaboration and questioning the extent to which artists should involve themselves in the community. The performance took place in a room adjacent to the main gallery, where Brad strung up a series of temporary wash lines and hung Jackie's clothes up to dry. During the opening he stayed in the room, ironing and then folding the clothes into neat piles. The piece was over when he had placed all the clothes into plastic bags and returned them to Jackie (which was long after the opening had ended). The intention was to demonstrate through a commonplace ritual that his interaction with Jackie continues beyond the making of functional sculpture, but also to provide a way for the audience to relate to Jackie's homelessness through her striving for identity by collecting clothes—which she then distributes to other homeless people.

13   Art which heals rather than confronts has not been highly valued by our society and the students at Yale were duly critical. They wondered, for instance, if by becoming involved in these people's lives, Brad might not be creating false hopes for them and even subtly exploiting their plight for his own good. Some felt that if he really wanted to help the homeless he ought to work in soup kitchens or for other institutions already addressing this problem. Also, wouldn't politics be a more effective medium than sculpture? And couldn't the problems of homeless people be solved just as well by buying them tents and camping gear, if indeed temporary shelters were the answer?

14   So why do I like this work so much? First of all, because it is not counterphobically tough. Nor does it aestheticize homelessness. Rather, it breaks the trance of economic thinking and legitimates another kind of motivation. It offers our society a different image of itself that is not based on the conspicuous consumption of valuable goods or the inevitability of self-interest. The quality of the response is crucial—it moves away from alienation and the mode of the helpless, isolated individual submissive to things as they are, which tends to shape all our interactions. To use ecologist Bill Devall's wonderful phrase, the work is "simple in means, rich in ends." In a consumption-oriented culture, the most important thing is to buy and own objects; the more things that can be bought and sold the better. This intense involvement with things, with consumption and one's own standard of living, seems to go hand-in-hand with a lack of involvement in social problems and relationships. "The mechanical division between self and world," writes Wendell Berry, "involves an

emotional dynamics that has disordered the heart of both the society as a whole and of every person in the society."

15   What is really at stake in the changes being discussed here cannot be totally divorced from the kind of beings individuals take themselves to be. In moving beyond conventional notions of self and self-interest, as the Buddhist scholar and ecologist Joanna Macy argues in *Sacred Interconnections,* and shedding them like an old skin or confining shell in order to engage more effectively with the forces and pathologies that imperil planetary survival, we are awakening to our larger, ecological self. For Macy, as for many others, the crisis that is threatening our planet, whether in its military, ecological, or social aspects, derives from a dysfunctional and pathogenic notion of the self. In awakening to our larger, ecological self, we will find new powers, according to Macy, undreamed of in our squirrel cage of separate ego. But, she adds, because these potentialities are interactive in nature, they manifest only to the extent that we recognize and act upon our interexistence. Through the power of his caring, Brad is able to extend his sense of self so that it also encompasses the self of Jackie; it is a real shift in identity. What we are really talking about is cultivating a new sort of person, one which includes patterns of interaction and interdependence that extend the self beyond the narrow ego and into the larger whole.

16   The possibility of constellating a self beyond the egoic one which has risen to power in the modern world and is maintained by our social consensus has been compellingly raised by David Michael Levin in all of his books, each of which argues in turn for "practices of the self" that do not separate the self from society and withdraw it from social responsibility. Many people find it difficult to imagine a self that is not shaped by the concept of an isolated individual fending for herself in the marketplace. They believe that economic self-interest is a given of human nature. In a recent issue of the newsletter *New Options,* however, editor Mark Satin wrote that during the 1980s, American culture began to move away from a focus on the rugged individual toward a focus on the caring individual. Caring individuals are less driven by materialistic values and status and have been described by Abraham Maslow as "meta-motivated" — they are not so preoccupied with basic needs such as security and survival. Theories of social Darwinism have led our culture to view the whole of existence as a competitive struggle for survival "of the fittest" and to falsely regard the environment as an object for exploitation. These ideas have been pumped into us from every direction. If a historically new kind of self — the ecological self — is truly emerging, it will eventually challenge our present society's primary assumption that human beings are basically selfish and motivated entirely by economics. Obviously what is being suggested is a revolution in consciousness as far

sweeping as the emergence of individualism itself was in the Renaissance. Our whole notion of what it means to be human may prove to have been inadequate and counterproductive.

17   The next evolutionary stage in consciousness will see a more integrated relationship between the masculine and feminine components in the psyche, which will replace the one-sided rule of the masculine as the dominant human consciousness. This is the inner basis of the ecological self. As Levin puts it in *The Opening of Vision*: "Archetypes which for too long have been constitutive only of femininity must be seen and valued as essential for the fulfillment of masculinity...[and] be integrated into its network of practices and institutions, transforming them accordingly." In the post-Cartesian, postpatriarchal identity, the so-called feminine values of caring and compassion will play leading roles. Levin has argued still further that since any change in cultural premises or dominant values begins in the individual's self-image, to redefine the self as relational rather than as self-contained could actually bring about a new stage in our social and cultural evolution. The restructuring of the Cartesian self, and its rebirth as an ecological self-plus-other or self-plus-environment, not only thoroughly transfigures our world view (and self-view) but, as I have been arguing myself, it is the basis for the reenchantment of art.

18   To see beyond the individual's perspective is to engage with the world from a participating consciousness rather than an observing one. The mode of distanced, objective knowing, removed from moral and social responsibility, has been the animating motif of both science and art in the modern world. As a form of thinking, it is now proving to be something of an evolutionary dead end. Indeed, cultural historian Morris Berman goes so far as to claim that the reenchantment of the world may necessitate the end of ego-consciousness altogether, for the reason that it may not be viable for our continuation on this planet.

19   Once we have changed the mode of our thinking to the methodology of participation we are not so detached. For the participating consciousness, things are no longer removed, separate, "out there." Objectivity serves as a distancing device, offering the illusion of impregnable strength, certainty, and control. Knowledge can then be used as an instrument of power and domination. Objective thinking negates the entire dimension of our visionary being. The self which challenges us to see beyond merely personal existence to intersubjective coexistence and community, the self expanded beyond a concern for one's own personal welfare, is the ecological self. If we strive for rather than give up on it, there is at least a possibility, Levin suggests, that we may move beyond the prevailing historical conditions, beyond the socialized ego and open up to our radical relatedness. Then being uniquely ourselves need not be cast in the category of the separate, Cartesian ego. Care and compassion are the tools

of the soul, but they are often ridiculed by our society, which has been
weak in the empathic mode. The feminine values of feeling, relatedness,
and soul-consciousness have been virtually driven out of our culture by
our patriarchal mentality. Gary Zukav puts it very concisely when he
states, in *The Seat of the Soul,* that there is currently no place for
spirituality, or the concerns of the heart, within science, politics, business,
or academia. Zukav doesn't mention art, but there is no particular
hospitality there either.

20   "If you're out, you're out — you simply don't count," the artist Sandro
Chia declared recently in an interview with Lilly Wei in *Art in America.*
"Anything that happens must happen within this system…I work for a few
months, then I go to a gallery and show the dealer my work. The work is
accepted, the dealer makes a selection, then an installation. People come
and say you're good or not so good, then they pay for these paintings and
hang them on other walls. They give cocktail parties and we all go to
restaurants and meet girls. I think this is the weirdest scene in the world."

21   Most of us work within a system of categories provided by society.
Patriarchal structures are especially strong in the art world. Becoming
aware of how much they enslave us is the first step toward breaking the
cultural trance. So far, as Lester Milbraith points out in *Envisioning a
Sustainable Society,* this awareness is still confined primarily to women and
now needs to spread to men. Many men will be receptive, he claims,
especially if they perceive that a change in beliefs is essential for saving our
ecosystem and society. We can be sure, however, that many other men will
feel threatened by partnership ideas and values and will vigorously oppose
the change. Sandro Chia's candid description of professional life in the art
world is all too familiar, but it is a routine part of the trajectory of
competition in our culture, where success is scoring and artists distinguish
themselves through selling or not selling. Other distinctions, such as moral
or immoral, are foreign to the enterprise and are likely to be pushed aside.
It is hardly surprising that more and more artists are recoiling from this
debilitating ideology.

22   How, then, can we shift our usual way of thinking so that we create
more compassionate structures in our culture? The compassionate,
ecological self will need to be cultivated with as much thoroughness as we
have cultivated, in long years of abstract thinking, the mind geared to
scientific and aesthetic objectivity: distant, cold, neutral, value-free. In *Has
Modernism Failed?* I wrote, "generally speaking, the dynamics of
professionalization do not dispose artists to accept their moral role;
professionals are conditioned to avoid thinking about problems that do not
bear directly on their work." Since writing this nearly a decade ago, it
seems as if the picture is changing. The search for a new agenda for art has
become a conscious one. Chicago artist Othello Anderson, who has been

painting images of the world's forests burning and the effects of deforestation through acid rain, comments:

> *Carbon and other pollutants are emitted into the air in such massive quantities that large areas of forest landscapes are dying from the effects of acid rain. Millions of tons of toxic waste are being poured into our lakes, rivers and oceans, contaminating drinking water and killing off aquatic life. Slash-and-burn forest clearing and forest fires are depleting the forests worldwide. Recognizing this crisis, as an artist I can no longer consider making art that is void of moral consciousness, art that carries no responsibility, art without spiritual content, or art that ignores the state of the world in which it exists.*

23   All of this is not to say that the social change envisioned here will happen quickly. The status quo is deeply entrenched and no new paradigm will suddenly eliminate the present order. Nevertheless, a social process can be accelerated or retarded. My impression is that artists who have restructured their personal reality away from the competitive mechanisms of the art world do not represent merely the response of isolated individuals to the dead-endedness of our present situation. They are prototypes living out the next epistemology of self. An increasing number of individuals understand the need for an ethical stance as central to the recovery of a meaningful society—and a meaningful art.

24   It is true that the value-based art they are trying to create still exists only at the margins of social change, but eventually a critical threshold is finally reached when enough people change their self-images and beliefs to begin the realignment of an entire society. It has been suggested that only five to ten percent of people need to change in order to create change in the whole. As social ecologist Murray Bookchin points out in *The Modern Crisis,* it is precisely to the "periphery" and the "margins" that we must look, if we are to find the "cores" that will be central to society in the future, for it is here that they will be found to be emerging. No doubt the previously entrenched paradigm will continue to exist alongside the later one, even after the other has more fully emerged, but with certain limitations, perhaps, in its relevance. Given the differences among us, we can safely assume that not everyone will agree that a relational, participatory, and ecocentric aesthetic is a good thing for all art.

STUDY QUESTIONS

1. In parallel columns, list the qualities that Gablik attaches to Modernism and the opposite qualities that she attaches to the new aesthetic that she sees emerging.

2. Why has Gablik selected the work of Bradley McCallum to illustrate her view of the new movement in art?

3. If McCallum is a sculptor, how does his work extend conventional notions of sculpture?

4. Gablik says that McCallum's art "does not aestheticize homelessness." What does she mean, and do you agree with her?

SUGGESTION FOR WRITING

Some politically involved art is criticized as preachy and sanctimonious, and when it involves problems like poverty, homelessness, and illness, it is sometimes accused of exploiting the people it professes concern for. Using Gablik's article as a point of reference, but also any other examples of art or art theory that you have had experience with, either flesh out this counterargument to Gablik's or defend her viewpoint against it.

Intelligence and

Aptitude

Through much of the nineteenth century, the social rank of most Europeans was hereditary. The last two centuries have seen the emergence of a "meritocracy," an ideal of distributing wealth, authority, and prestige according to merit rather than birth. The kind of merit that often determines who may pursue academic or professional pathways to high social rank is "intelligence," which means that as a cultural value it rates very high.

While the general notion of intelligence is an ancient one, the notion of intelligence as a measurable attribute originated in the early twentieth century with the work of the French psychologist, Binet, who invented an intelligence test as, in his own opinion, a crude device for identifying students whose intelligence was so low that they would require special schooling.

Binet's test was revised for use in the United States by Lewis Terman of Stanford University in 1916. Terman and two other pioneers of "mental testing," Henry Goddard of the Vineland Training School and Robert Yerkes at Harvard, believed that intelligence was largely or wholly hereditary, that "feeble-mindedness" was responsible for much crime, degeneracy, and pauperism, and that mental tests could help identify the feeble-minded in order to discourage their procreation and their opportunity for criminal acts. From about 1908 well into the 1920s, American scientists at some of the most distinguished universities subscribed to a science of "mental levels" with such labels as "idiot," "imbecile," and "moron." Their followers advocated social programs in which mental level as determined by intelligence tests would decide who would be allowed to immigrate into the United States, who should be confined involuntarily, and even who should be subject to involuntary sterilization.

During the First World War, the U.S. Army employed Yerkes and other experts to administer intelligence tests to all recruits for the purpose of identifying those most suitable for officer rank and suggesting proper military assignment for the others. The selection by Gould below describes these tests and the way the
370 testers interpreted their results. The following selections by Lippmann and Cutten

come from this early period of intelligence testing and suggest the range of response. The selection by Gardner outlines a more recent approach that carries different implications for social and educational policy.

While the connection of intelligence testing with eugenics and immigration has subsided, intelligence continues to be highly valued, and tests of intelligence and "aptitude" continue to play important but highly controversial roles in American life and in the life of many other nations as well. The articles by Owen, Dwyer, Rosser, and Seligman all examine the value and fairness of the standardized tests administered by the Educational Testing Service, while Gahagan's relates testing to educational priorities and the social values underlying them. Finally, Machado offers a view of intelligence from a different cultural perspective altogether.

STEPHEN JAY GOULD

From "*The Hereditarian Theory of IQ*"

Stephen Jay Gould is respected both as a researcher and as a scientific writer who presents scientific ideas and history to the layman in clear, lively prose, making them understandable without oversimplification. For some years he has written a regular column in *Natural History,* and he has published several books on science including *Ever Since Darwin, The Panda's Thumb,* and *The Flamingo's Smile.* Throughout these writings Gould stresses that science is not a purely rational or coldly mechanical method, but that its findings are often affected by the metaphorical and ideological assumptions through which scientists see the world.

This selection is taken from a chapter in Gould's 1981 book *The Mismeasure of Man,* which won the National Book Critics Circle Award for general nonfiction. Here Gould outlines the results of the army's intelligence testing program during the First World War—results that led to empirical claims that the average mental age of Americans was only about thirteen; that the performances of European immigrants confirmed the intellectual superiority of blond Nordic types over darker southern types; and that blacks were markedly inferior in intelligence, having an average mental age of ten and a half. Gould then goes on to critique these claims by revealing the nature of the raw data on which they were based and by suggesting an alternative interpretation.

R. M. Yerkes and the Army Mental Tests: IQ Comes of Age

Psychology's Great Leap Forward

1   Robert M. Yerkes, about to turn forty, was a frustrated man in 1915. He had been on the faculty of Harvard University since 1902. He was a superb organizer of men, and an eloquent promotor of his profession. Yet psychology still wallowed in its reputation as a "soft" science, if a science at all. Some colleges did not acknowledge its existence; others ranked it among the humanities and placed psychologists in departments of philosophy. Yerkes wished, above all, to establish his profession by proving that it could be as rigorous a science as physics. Yerkes and most of his contemporaries equated rigor and science with numbers and quantification. The most promising source of copious and objective numbers, Yerkes believed, lay in the embryonic field of mental testing. Psychology would come of age, and gain acceptance as a true science worthy of financial and institutional support, if it could bring the question of human potential under the umbrella of science:

> *Most of us are wholly convinced that the future of mankind depends in no small measure upon the development of the various biological and social sciences....We must...strive increasingly for the improvement of our methods of mental measurement, for there is no longer ground for doubt concerning the practical as well as the theoretical importance of studies of human behavior. We must learn to measure skillfully every form and aspect of behavior which has psychological and sociological significance (Yerkes, 1917a, p. 111).*

2   But mental testing suffered from inadequate support and its own internal contradictions. It was, first of all, practiced extensively by poorly trained amateurs whose manifestly absurd results were giving the enterprise a bad name. In 1915, at the annual meeting of the American Psychological Association in Chicago, a critic reported that the mayor of Chicago himself had tested as a moron on one version of the Binet scales. Yerkes joined with critics in discussions at the meeting and proclaimed: "We are building up a science, but we have not yet devised a mechanism which anyone can operate" (quoted in Chase, 1977, p. 242).

3   Second, available scales gave markedly different results even when properly applied....Half the individuals who tested in the low, but normal range on the Stanford-Binet, were morons on Goddard's version of the Binet scale. Finally, support had been too inadequate, and coordination too sporadic, to build up a pool of data sufficiently copious and uniform to compel belief (Yerkes, 1917b).

4   Wars always generate their retinue of camp followers with ulterior motives. Many are simply scoundrels and profiteers, but a few are spurred by higher ideals. As mobilization for World War I approached, Yerkes got one of those "big ideas" that propel the history of science: could psychologists possibly persuade the army to test all its recruits? If so, the philosopher's stone of psychology might be constructed: the copious, useful, and uniform body of numbers that would fuel a transition from dubious art to respected science. Yerkes proselytized within his profession and within government circles, and he won his point. As Colonel Yerkes, he presided over the administration of mental tests to 1.75 million recruits during World War I. Afterward, he proclaimed that mental testing "helped to win the war." "At the same time," he added, "it has incidentally established itself among the other sciences and demonstrated its right to serious consideration in human engineering" (quoted in Kevles, 1968, p. 581).

5   Yerkes brought together all the major hereditarians of American psychometrics to write the army mental tests. From May to July 1917 he worked with Terman, Goddard, and other colleagues at Goddard's Training School in Vineland, New Jersey.

6   Their scheme included three types of tests. Literate recruits would be given a written examination, called the Army Alpha. Illiterates and men who had failed Alpha would be given a pictorial test, called the Army Beta. Failures in Beta would be recalled for an individual examination, usually some version of the Binet scales. Army psychologists would then grade each man from A to E (with plusses and minuses) and offer suggestions for proper military placement. Yerkes suggested that recruits with a score of C– should be marked as "low average intelligence—ordinary private." Men of grade D are "rarely suited for tasks requiring special skill, forethought, resourcefulness or sustained alertness." D and E men could not be expected "to read and understand written directions."

7   I do not think that the army ever made much use of the tests. One can well imagine how professional officers felt about smart-assed young psychologists who arrived without invitation, often assumed an officer's rank without undergoing basic training, commandeered a building to give the tests (if they could), saw each recruit for an hour in a large group, and then proceeded to usurp an officer's traditional role in judging the worthiness of men for various military tasks. Yerkes's corps encountered hostility in some camps; in others, they suffered a penalty in many ways more painful: they were treated politely, given appropriate facilities, and then ignored.[1] Some army officials became suspicious of Yerkes's intent and launched three independent investigations of the testing program. One concluded that it should be controlled so that "no theorist may...ride it as a hobby for the purpose of obtaining data for research work and the future benefit of the human race" (quoted in Kevles, 1968, p. 577).

8   Still, the tests did have a strong impact in some areas, particularly in screening men for officer training. At the start of the war, the army and national guard maintained nine thousand officers. By the end, two hundred thousand officers presided, and two-thirds of them had started their careers in training camps where the tests were applied. In some camps, no man scoring below C could be considered for officer training.

9   But the major impact of Yerkes's tests did not fall upon the army. Yerkes may not have brought the army its victory, but he certainly won his battle. He now had uniform data on 1.75 million men, and he had devised, in the Alpha and Beta exams, the first mass-produced written tests of

---

[1] Yerkes continued to complain throughout his career that military psychology had not achieved its due respect, despite its accomplishments in World War I. During World War II the aging Yerkes was still grousing and arguing that the Nazis were upstaging America in their proper use and encouragement of mental testing for military personnel. "Germany has a long lead in the development of military psychology....The Nazis have achieved something that is entirely without parallel in military history....What has happened in Germany is the logical sequel to the psychological and personnel services in our own Army during 1917–1918" (Yerkes, 1941, p. 209).

intelligence. Inquiries flooded in from schools and businesses. In his massive monograph (Yerkes, 1921) on *Psychological Examining in the United States Army,* Yerkes buried a statement of great social significance in an aside on page 96. He spoke of "the steady stream of requests from commercial concerns, educational institutions, and individuals for the use of army methods of psychological examining or for the adaptation of such methods to special needs." Binet's purpose could now be circumvented because a technology had been developed for testing all pupils. Tests could now rank and stream everybody; the era of mass testing had begun.

Results of the Army Tests

10   The primary impact of the tests arose not from the army's lackadaisical use of scores for individuals, but from general propaganda that accompanied Yerkes's report of the summary statistics (Yerkes, 1921, pp. 553–875). E. G. Boring, later a famous psychologist himself but then Yerkes's lieutenant (and the army's captain), selected one hundred sixty thousand cases from the files and produced data that reverberated through the 1920s with a hard hereditarian ring. The task was a formidable one. The sample, which Boring culled himself with the aid of only one assistant, was very large; moreover, the scales of three different tests (Alpha, Beta, and individual) had to be converted to a common standard so that racial and national averages could be constructed from samples of men who had taken the tests in different proportions (few blacks took Alpha, for example).

11   From Boring's ocean of numbers, three "facts" rose to the top and continued to influence social policy in America long after their source in the tests had been forgotten.

12   1. The average mental age of white American adults stood just above the edge of moronity at a shocking and meager thirteen. Terman had previously set the standard at sixteen. The new figure became a rallying point for eugenicists who predicted doom and lamented our declining intelligence, caused by the unconstrained breeding of the poor and feeble-minded, the spread of Negro blood through miscegenation, and the swamping of an intelligent native stock by the immigrating dregs of southern and eastern Europe. Yerkes[2] wrote:

> It is customary to say that the mental age of the average adult is about 16 years. This figure is based, however, upon examinations of only 62 persons; 32 of them high-school pupils from 16–20 years of age, and 30 of them "business men of moderate success and of very limited educational

---

[2] I doubt that Yerkes wrote all parts of the massive 1921 monograph himself. But he is listed as the only author of this official report, and I shall continue to attribute its statements to him, both as shorthand and for want of other information.

> *advantages." The group is too small to give very reliable results and is furthermore probably not typical....It appears that the intelligence of the principal sample of the white draft, when transmuted from Alpha and Beta exams into terms of mental age, is about 13 years (13.08) (1921, p. 785).*

Yet, even as he wrote, Yerkes began to sense the logical absurdity of such a statement. An average is what it is; it cannot lie three years below what it should be. So Yerkes thought again and added:

> *We can hardly say, however, with assurance that these recruits are three years mental age below the average. Indeed, it might be argued on extrinsic grounds that the draft itself is more representative of the average intelligence of the country than is a group of high-school students and business men (1921, p. 785).*

13   If 13.08 is the white average, and everyone from mental age 8 through 12 is a moron, then we are a nation of nearly half-morons. Yerkes concluded (1921, p. 791): "It would be totally impossible to exclude all morons as that term is at present defined, for there are under 13 years 37 percent of whites and 89 percent of negroes."

14   2. European immigrants can be graded by their country of origin. The average man of many nations is a moron. The darker peoples of southern Europe and the Slavs of eastern Europe are less intelligent than the fair peoples of western and northern Europe. Nordic supremacy is not a jingoistic prejudice. The average Russian has a mental age of 11.34; the Italian, 11.01; the Pole, 10.74. The Polish joke attained the same legitimacy as the moron joke — indeed, they described the same animal.

15   3. The Negro lies at the bottom of the scale with an average mental age of 10.41. Some camps tried to carry the analysis a bit further, and in obvious racist directions. At Camp Lee, blacks were divided into three groups based upon intensity of color; the lighter groups scored higher (p. 531). Yerkes reported that the opinions of officers matched his numbers (p. 742):

> *All officers without exception agree that the negro lacks initiative, displays little or no leadership, and cannot accept responsibility. Some point out that these defects are greater in the southern negro. All officers seem further to agree that the negro is a cheerful, willing soldier, naturally subservient. These qualities make for immediate obedience, although not necessarily for good discipline, since petty thieving and venereal disease are commoner than with white troops.*

16   Along the way, Yerkes and company tested several other social prejudices. Some fared poorly, particularly the popular eugenical notion that most offenders are feeble-minded. Among conscientious objectors for

political reasons, 59 percent received a grade of A. Even outright disloyals scored above the average (p. 803). But other results buoyed their prejudices. As camp followers themselves, Yerkes's corps decided to test a more traditional category of colleagues: the local prostitutes. They found that 53 percent (44 percent of whites and 68 percent of blacks) ranked at age ten or below on the Goddard version of the Binet scales. (They acknowledge that the Goddard scales ranked people well below their scores on other versions of the Binet tests.) Yerkes concluded (p. 808):

> *The results of Army examining of prostitutes corroborate the conclusion, attained by civilian examinations of prostitutes in various parts of the country, that from 30 to 60 percent of prostitutes are deficient and are for the most part high-grade morons; and that 15 to 25 percent of all prostitutes are so low-grade mentally that it is wise (as well as possible under the existing laws in most states) permanently to segregate them in institutions for the feeble-minded.*

One must be thankful for small bits of humor to lighten the reading of an eight-hundred-page statistical monograph. The thought of army personnel rounding up the local prostitutes and sitting them down to take the Binet tests amused me no end, and must have bemused the ladies even more.

17   As pure numbers, these data carried no inherent social message. They might have been used to promote equality of opportunity and to underscore the disadvantages imposed upon so many Americans. Yerkes might have argued that an average mental age of thirteen reflected the fact that relatively few recruits had the opportunity to finish or even to attend high school. He might have attributed the low average of some national groups to the fact that most recruits from these countries were recent immigrants who did not speak English and were unfamiliar with American culture. He might have recognized the link between low Negro scores and the history of slavery and racism.

18   But scarcely a word do we read through eight hundred pages of any role for environmental influence. The tests had been written by a committee that included all the leading American hereditarians discussed in this chapter. They had been constructed to measure innate intelligence, and they did so by definition. The circularity of argument could not be broken. All the major findings received hereditarian interpretations, often by near miracles of special pleading to argue past a patent environmental influence. A circular issued from the School of Military Psychology at Camp Greenleaf proclaimed (do pardon its questionable grammar): "These tests do not measure occupational fitness nor educational attainment; they measure intellectual ability. This latter has been shown to be important in estimating military value" (p. 424). And the boss himself argued (Yerkes, quoted in Chase, 1977, p. 249):

> *Examinations Alpha and Beta are so constructed and administered to minimize the handicap of men who because of foreign birth or lack of education are little skilled in the use of English. These group examinations were originally intended, and are now definitely known, to measure native intellectual ability. They are to some extent influenced by educational acquirement, but in the main the soldier's inborn intelligence and not the accidents of environment determines his mental rating or grade in the army.*

A Critique of the Army Mental Tests

THE CONTENT OF THE TESTS

19   The Alpha test included eight parts, the Beta seven; each took less than an hour and could be given to large groups. Most of the Alpha parts presented items that have become familiar to generations of test-takers ever since: analogies, filling in the next number in a sequence, unscrambling sentences, and so forth. This similarity is no accident; the Army Alpha was the granddaddy, literally as well as figuratively, of all written mental tests. One of Yerkes's disciples, C. C. Brigham, later became secretary of the College Entrance Examination Board and developed the Scholastic Aptitude Test on army models. If people get a peculiar feeling of déjà-vu in perusing Yerkes's monograph, I suggest that they think back to their own College Boards, with all its attendant anxiety.

20   These familiar parts are not especially subject to charges of cultural bias, at least no more so than their modern descendants. In a general way, of course, they test literacy, and literacy records education more than inherited intelligence. Moreover, a schoolmaster's claim that he tests children of the same age and school experience, and therefore may be recording some internal biology, didn't apply to the army recruits—for they varied greatly in access to education and recorded different amounts of schooling in their scores. A few of the items are amusing in the light of Yerkes's assertion that the tests "measure native intellectual ability." Consider the Alpha analogy: "Washington is to Adams as first is to...."

21   But one part of each test is simply ludicrous in the light of Yerkes's analysis. How could Yerkes and company attribute the low scores of recent immigrants to innate stupidity when their multiple-choice test consisted entirely of questions like:

> *Crisco is a: patent medicine, disinfectant, toothpaste, food product*
> *The number of a Kaffir's legs is: 2, 4, 6, 8*
> *Christy Mathewson is famous as a: writer, artist, baseball player, comedian*

I got the last one, but my intelligent brother, who, to my distress, grew up in New York utterly oblivious to the heroics of three great baseball teams then resident, did not.

22   Yerkes might have responded that recent immigrants generally took Beta rather than Alpha, but Beta contains a pictorial version of the same theme. In this complete-a-picture test, early items might be defended as sufficiently universal: adding a mouth to a face or an ear to a rabbit. But later items required a rivet in a pocket knife, a filament in a light bulb, a horn on a phonograph, a net on a tennis court, and a ball in a bowler's hand (marked wrong, Yerkes explained, if an examinee drew the ball in the alley, for you can tell from the bowler's posture that he has not yet released the ball). Franz Boas, an early critic, told the tale of a Sicilian recruit who added a crucifix where it always appeared in his native land to a house without a chimney. He was marked wrong.

23   The tests were strictly timed, for the next fifty were waiting by the door. Recruits were not expected to finish each part; this was explained to the Alpha men, but not to Beta people. Yerkes wondered why so many recruits scored flat zero on so many of the parts (the most telling proof of the tests' worthlessness—see pp. 213–214). How many of us, if nervous, uncomfortable, and crowded (and even if not), would have understood enough to write anything at all in the ten seconds allotted for completing the following commands, each given but once in Alpha, Part 1?

> *Attention! Look at 4. When I say "go" make a figure 1 in the space which is in the circle but not in the triangle or square, and also make a figure 2 in the space which is in the triangle and circle, but not in the square. Go.*
>
>   *Attention! Look at 6. When I say "go" put in the second circle the right answer to the question: "How many months has a year?" In the third circle do nothing, but in the fourth circle put any number that is a wrong answer to the question that you have just answered correctly. Go.*

INADEQUATE CONDITIONS

24   Yerkes's protocol was rigorous and trying enough. His examiners had to process men rapidly and grade the exams immediately, so that failures could be recalled for a different test. When faced with the added burden of thinly veiled hostility from the brass at several camps, Yerkes's testers were rarely able to carry out more than a caricature of their own stated procedure. They continually compromised, backtracked, and altered in the face of necessity. Procedures varied so much from camp to camp that results could scarcely be collated and compared. The whole effort, through no fault of Yerkes's beyond impracticality and overambition, became something of a shambles, if not a disgrace. The details are all in Yerkes's monograph, but hardly anyone ever read it. The summary statistics became an important social weapon for racists and eugenicists; their rotten core lay exposed in the monograph, but who looks within when the surface shines with such a congenial message.

25   The army mandated that special buildings be supplied or even constructed for Yerkes's examinations, but a different reality prevailed

(1921, p. 61). The examiners had to take what they could get, often rooms in cramped barracks with no furnishings at all, and inadequate acoustics, illumination, and lines of sight. The chief tester at one camp complained (p. 106): "Part of this inaccuracy I believe to be due to the fact that the room in which the examination is held is filled too full of men. As a result, the men who are sitting in the rear of the room are unable to hear clearly and thoroughly enough to understand the instructions."

26   Tensions rose between Yerkes's testers and regular officers. The chief tester of Camp Custer complained (p. 111): "The ignorance of the subject on the part of the average officer is equalled only by his indifference to it." Yerkes urged restraint and accommodation (p. 155):

> *The examiner should strive especially to take the military point of view. Unwarranted claims concerning the accuracy of the results should be avoided. In general, straightforward commonsense statements will be found more convincing than technical descriptions, statistical exhibits, or academic arguments.*

As friction and doubt mounted, the secretary of war polled commanding officers of all camps to ask their opinion of Yerkes's tests. He received one hundred replies, nearly all negative. They were, Yerkes admitted (p. 43), "with a few exceptions, unfavorable to psychological work, and have led to the conclusion on the part of various officers of the General Staff that this work has little, if any, value to the army and should be discontinued." Yerkes fought back and won a standoff (but not all the promotions, commissions, and hirings he had been promised); his work proceeded under a cloud of suspicion.

27   Minor frustrations never abated. Camp Jackson ran out of forms and had to improvise on blank paper (p. 78). But a major and persistent difficulty dogged the entire enterprise and finally, as I shall demonstrate, deprived the summary statistics of any meaning. Recruits had to be allocated to their appropriate test. Men illiterate in English, either by lack of schooling or foreign birth, should have taken examination Beta, either by direct assignment, or indirectly upon failing Alpha. Yerkes's corps tried heroically to fulfill this procedure. In at least three camps, they marked identification tags or even painted letters directly on the bodies of men who failed—a ready identification guide for further assessment (p. 73, p. 76): "A list of D men was sent within six hours after the group examination to the clerk at the mustering office. As the men appeared, this clerk marked on the body of each D man a letter P" (indicating that the psychiatrist should examine them further).

28   But standards for the division between Alpha and Beta varied substantially from camp to camp. A survey across camps revealed that the minimum score on an early version of Alpha varied from 20 to 100 for

assignment to further testing (p. 476). Yerkes admitted (p. 354):

> *This lack of a uniform process of segregation is certainly unfortunate. On account of the variable facilities for examining and the variable quality of the groups examined however, it appeared entirely impossible to establish a standard uniform for all camps.*

C. C. Brigham, Yerkes's most zealous votary, even complained (1921):

> *The method of selecting men for Beta varied from camp to camp, and sometimes from week to week in the same camp. There was no established criterion of literacy, and no uniform method of selecting illiterates.*

29   The problem cut far deeper than simple inconsistency among camps. The persistent logistical difficulties imposed a systematic bias that substantially lowered the mean scores of blacks and immigrants. For two major reasons, many men took only Alpha and scored either zero or next to nothing, not because they were innately dumb, but because they were illiterate and should have taken Beta by Yerkes's own protocol. First, recruits and draftees had, on average, spent fewer years in school than Yerkes had anticipated. Lines for Beta began to lengthen and the entire operation threatened to clog at this bottleneck. At many camps, unqualified men were sent in droves to Alpha by artificial lowering of standards. Schooling to the third grade sufficed for Alpha in one camp; in another, anyone who said he could read, at whatever level, took Alpha. The chief tester at Camp Dix reported (p. 72): "To avoid excessively large Beta groups, standards for admission to examination Alpha were set low."

30   Second, and more important, the press of time and the hostility of regular officers often precluded a Beta retest for men who had incorrectly taken Alpha. Yerkes admitted (p. 472): "It was never successfully shown, however, that the continued recalls…were so essential that repeated interference with company maneuvers should be permitted." As the pace became more frantic, the problem worsened. The chief tester at Camp Dix complained (pp. 72–73): "In June it was found impossible to recall a thousand men listed for individual examination. In July Alpha failures among negroes were not recalled." The stated protocol scarcely applied to blacks who, as usual, were treated with less concern and more contempt by everyone. Failure on Beta, for example, should have led to an individual examination. Half the black recruits scored D– on Beta, but only one-fifth of these were recalled and four-fifths received no further examination (p. 708). Yet we know that scores for blacks improved substantially when the protocol was followed. At one camp (p. 736), only 14.1 percent of men who had scored D– on Alpha failed to gain a higher grade on Beta.

31   The effects of this systematic bias are evident in one of Boring's experiments with the summary statistics. He culled 4,893 cases of men

who had taken both Alpha and Beta. Converting their scores to the common scale, he calculated an average mental age of 10.775 for Alpha, and a Beta mean of 12.158 (p. 655). He used only the Beta scores in his summaries; Yerkes procedure worked. But what of the myriads who should have taken Beta, but only received Alpha and scored abysmally as a result—primarily poorly educated blacks and immigrants with an imperfect command of English—the very groups whose low scores caused such a hereditarian stir later on?

DUBIOUS AND PERVERSE PROCEEDINGS: A PERSONAL TESTIMONY

32   Academicians often forget how poorly or incompletely the written record, their primary source, may represent experience. Some things have to be seen, touched, and tasted. What was it like to be an illiterate black or foreign recruit, anxious and befuddled at the novel experience of taking an examination, never told why, or what would be made of the results: expulsion, the front lines? In 1968 (quoted in Kevles), an examiner recalled his administration of Beta: "It was touching to see the intense effort...put into answering the questions, often by men who never before had held a pencil in their hands." Yerkes had overlooked, or consciously bypassed, something of importance. The Beta examination contained only pictures, numbers, and symbols. But it still required pencil work and, on three of its seven parts, a knowledge of numbers and how to write them.

33   Yerkes's monograph is so thorough that his procedure for giving the two examinations can be reconstructed down to the choreography of motion for all examiners and orderlies. He provides facsimiles in full size for the examinations themselves, and for all explanatory material used by examiners. The standardized words and gestures of examiners are reproduced in full. Since I wanted to know in as complete a way as possible what it felt like to give and take the test, I administered examination Beta (for illiterates) to a group of fifty-three Harvard undergraduates in my course on biology as a social weapon. I tried to follow Yerkes's protocol scrupulously in all its details. I feel that I reconstructed the original situation accurately, with one important exception: my students knew what they were doing, didn't have to provide their names on the form, and had nothing at stake. (One friend later suggested that I should have required names—and posted results—as just a small contribution to simulating the anxiety of the original.)

34   I knew before I started that internal contradictions and a priori prejudice thoroughly invalidated the hereditarian conclusions that Yerkes had drawn from the results. Boring himself called these conclusions "preposterous" late in his career (in a 1962 interview, quoted in Kevles, 1968). But I had not understood how the Draconian conditions of testing made such a thorough mockery of the claim that recruits could have

been in a frame of mind to record anything about their innate abilities. In short, most of the men must have ended up either utterly confused or scared shitless.

35   The recruits were ushered into a room and seated before an examiner and demonstrator standing atop a platform, and several orderlies at floor level. Examiners were instructed to administer the test "in a genial manner" since "the subjects who take this examination sometimes sulk and refuse to work" (p. 163). Recruits were told nothing about the examination or its purposes. The examiner simply said: "Here are some papers. You must not open them or turn them over until you are told to." The men then filled in their names, age, and education (with help for those too illiterate to do so). After these perfunctory preliminaries, the examiner plunged right in:

> *Attention. Watch this man (pointing to demonstrator). He (pointing to demonstrator again) is going to do here (tapping blackboard with pointer) what you (pointing to different members of the group) are to do on your papers (here examiner points to several papers that lie before men in the group, picks up one, holds it next to the blackboard, returns the paper, points to demonstrator and the blackboard in succession, then to the men and their papers). Ask no questions. Wait till I say "Go ahead!" (p. 163).*

36   By comparison, Alpha men were virtually inundated with information (p. 157), for the Alpha examiner said:

> *Attention! The purpose of this examination is to see how well you can remember, think, and carry out what you are told to do. We are not looking for crazy people. The aim is to help find out what you are best fitted to do in the Army. The grade you make in this examination will be put on your qualification card and will also go to your company commander. Some of the things you are told to do will be very easy. Some you may find hard. You are not expected to make a perfect grade, but do the very best you can....Listen closely. Ask no questions.*

37   The extreme limits imposed upon the Beta examiner's vocabulary did not only reflect Yerkes's poor opinion of what Beta recruits might understand by virtue of their stupidity. Many Beta examinees were recent immigrants who did not speak English, and instruction had to be as pictorial and gestural as possible. Yerkes advised (p. 163): "One camp has had great success with a 'window seller' as demonstrator. Actors should also be considered for the work." One particularly important bit of information was not transmitted: examinees were not told that it was virtually impossible to finish at least three of the tests, and that they were not expected to do so.

38   Atop the platform, the demonstrator stood in front of a blackboard roll covered by a curtain; the examiner stood at his side. Before each of the seven tests, the curtain was raised to expose a sample problem (all reproduced in Figure 1), and examiner and demonstrator engaged in a bit of pantomime to illustrate proper procedure. The examiner then issued an order to work, and the demonstrator closed the curtain and advanced the roll to the next sample. The first test, maze running, received the following demonstration:

> *Demonstrator traces path through first maze with crayon, slowly and hesitatingly. Examiner then traces second maze and motions to demonstrator to go ahead. Demonstrator makes one mistake by going into the blind alley at upper left-hand corner of maze. Examiner apparently does not notice what demonstrator is doing until he crosses line at end of alley; then examiner shakes his head vigorously, says "No-no," takes demonstrator's hand and traces back to the place where he may start right again. Demonstrator traces rest of maze so as to indicate an attempt at haste, hesitating only at ambiguous points. Examiner says "Good." Then holding up blank, "Look here," and draws an imaginary line across the page from left to right for every maze on the page. Then, "All right. Go ahead. Do it (pointing to men and then to books). Hurry up."*

39   This paragraph may be naively amusing (some of my students thought so). The next statement, by comparison, is a bit diabolical.

> *The idea of working fast must be impressed on the men during the maze test. Examiner and orderlies walk around the room, motioning to men who are not working, and saying, "Do it, do it, hurry up, quick." At the end of 2 minutes examiner says, "Stop! Turn over the page to test 2."*

40   The examiner demonstrated test 2, cube counting, with three-dimensional models (my son had some left over from his baby days). Note that recruits who could not write numbers would receive scores of zero even if they counted all the cubes correctly. Test 3, the X-O series, will be recognized by nearly everyone today as the pictorial version of "what is the next number in the sequence." Test 4, digit symbols, required the translation of nine digits into corresponding symbols. It looks easy enough, but the test itself included ninety items and could hardly be finished by anybody in the two minutes allotted. A man who couldn't write numbers was faced with two sets of unfamiliar symbols and suffered a severe additional disadvantage. Test 5, number checking, asked men to compare numerical sequences, up to eleven digits in length, in two parallel columns. If items on the same line were identical in the two columns, recruits were instructed (by gestures) to write an X next to the item. Fifty sequences occupied three minutes, and few recruits could finish. Again, an

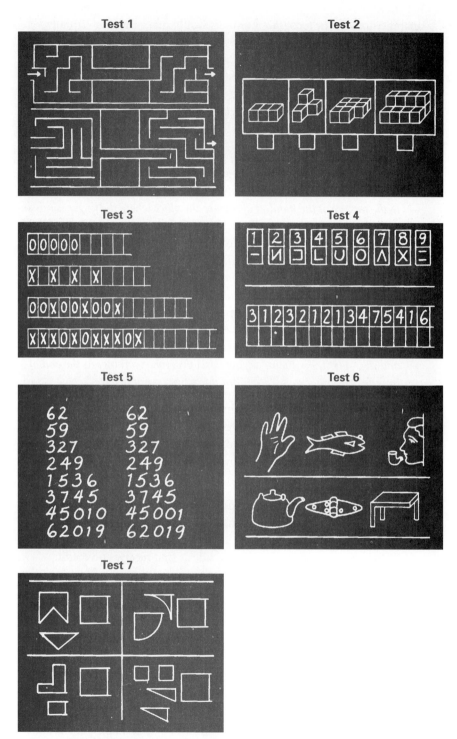

Figure 1. The blackboard demonstrations for all seven parts of the Beta test. *(From Yerkes, 1921.)*

inability to write or recognize numbers would make the task virtually impossible.

41   Test 6, pictorial completion, is Beta's visual analogue of Alpha's multiple-choice examination for testing innate intelligence by asking recruits about commercial products, famous sporting or film stars, or the primary industries of various cities and states. Its instructions are worth repeating:

> *"This is test 6 here. Look. A lot of pictures." After everyone has found the place, "Now watch." Examiner points to hand and says to demonstrator, "Fix it." Demonstrator does nothing, but looks puzzled. Examiner points to the picture of the hand, and then to the place where the finger is missing and says to demonstrator, "Fix it; fix it." Demonstrator then draws in finger. Examiner says, "That's right." Examiner then points to fish and place for eye and says, "Fix it." After demonstrator has drawn missing eye, examiner points to each of the four remaining drawings and says, "Fix them all." Demonstrator works samples out slowly and with apparent effort. When the samples are finished examiner says, "All right. Go ahead. Hurry up!" During the course of this test the orderlies walk around the room and locate individuals who are doing nothing, point to their pages and say, "Fix it. Fix them," trying to set everyone working. At the end of 3 minutes examiner says. "Stop! But don't turn over the page."*

The examination itself is also worth reprinting (Figure 2). Best of luck with pig tails, crab legs, bowling balls, tennis nets, and the Jack's missing diamond, not to mention the phonograph horn (a real stumper for my students). Yerkes provided the following instructions for grading:

> *Rules for Individual Items*
> Item 4.—Any spoon at any angle in right hand receives credit. Left hand, or unattached spoon, no credit.
> Item 5.—Chimney must be in right place. No credit for smoke.
> Item 6.—Another ear on same side as first receives no credit.
> Item 8.—Plain square, cross, etc., in proper location for stamp, receives credit.
> Item 10.—Missing part is the rivet. Line of "ear" may be omitted.
> Item 13.—Missing part is leg.
> Item 15.—Ball should be drawn in hand of man. If represented in hand of woman, or in motion, no credit.
> Item 16.—Single line indicating net receives credit.
> Item 18.—Any representation intended for horn, pointing in any direction, receives credit.
> Item 19.—Hand and powder puff must be put on proper side.
> Item 20.—Diamond is the missing part. Failure to complete hilt on sword is not an error.

Figure 2. Part 6 of examination Beta for testing innate intelligence.

42   The seventh and last test, geometrical construction, required that a square be broken into component pieces. Its ten parts were allotted two and a half minutes.

43   I believe that the conditions of testing, and the basic character of the examination, make it ludicrous to believe that Beta measured any internal state deserving the label intelligence. Despite the plea for geniality, the examination was conducted in an almost frantic rush. Most parts could not be finished in the time allotted, but recruits were not forewarned. My students compiled the following record of completions on the seven parts (see table below). For two of the tests, digit symbols and number checking (4 and 5), most students simply couldn't write fast enough to complete the ninety and fifty items, even though the protocol was clear to all. The third test with a majority of incompletes, cube counting (number 2), was too difficult for the number of items included and the time allotted.

TEST	FINISHED	NOT FINISHED
1	44	9
2	21	32
3	45	8
4	12	41
5	18	35
6	49	4
7	40	13

44   In summary, many recruits could not see or hear the examiner; some had never taken a test before or even held a pencil. Many did not understand the instructions and were completely befuddled. Those who did comprehend could complete only a small part of most tests in the allotted time. Meanwhile, if anxiety and confusion had not already reached levels sufficiently high to invalidate the results, the orderlies continually marched about, pointing to individual recruits and ordering them to hurry in voices loud enough, as specifically mandated, to convey the message generally. Add to this the blatant cultural biases of test 6, and the more subtle biases directed against those who could not write numbers or who had little experience in writing anything at all, and what do you have but a shambles.

45   The proof of inadequacy lies in the summary statistics, though Yerkes and Boring chose to interpret them differently. The monograph presents frequency distributions for scores on each part separately. Since Yerkes believed that innate intelligence was normally distributed (the "standard" pattern with a single mode at some middle score and symmetrically deceasing frequencies away from the mode in both directions), he expected that scores for each test would be normally distributed as well.

But only two of the tests, maze running and picture completion (1 and 6), yielded a distribution even close to normal. (These are also the tests that my own students found easiest and completed in highest proportion.) All the other tests yielded a bimodal distribution, with one peak at a middle value and another squarely at the minimum value of zero (Figure 3).

46   The common-sense interpretation of this bimodality holds that recruits had two different responses to the tests. Some understood what they were supposed to do, and performed in varied ways. Others, for whatever reasons, could not fathom the instructions and scored zero. With high levels of imposed anxiety, poor conditions for seeing and hearing, and general inexperience with testing for most recruits, it would be fatuous to interpret the zero scores as evidence of innate stupidity below the intelligence of men who made some points—though Yerkes wormed out of the difficulty this way (see pp. 213–214). (My own students compiled lowest rates of completion for the tests that yield the largest secondary modes at zero in Yerkes's sample—tests 4 and 5. As the only exception to this pattern, most of my students completed test 3, which produced a strong zero mode in the army sample. But 3 is the visual analog of "what is the next number in this series," a test that all my students have taken more times than they care to remember.)

47   Statisticians are trained to be suspicious of distributions with multiple modes. Such distributions usually indicate inhomogeneity in the system,

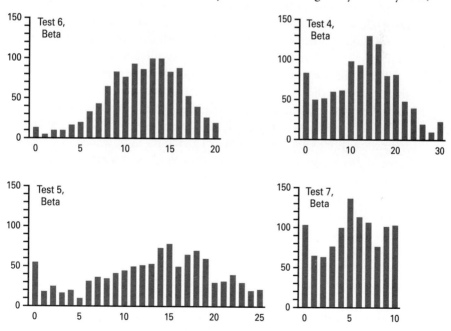

Figure 3. Frequency distributions for four of the Beta tests. Note the prominent mode at zero for tests 4, 5, and 7.

or, in plainer language, different causes for the different modes. All familiar proverbs about the inadvisibility of mixing apples and oranges apply. The multiple modes should have guided Yerkes to a suspicion that his tests were not measuring a single entity called intelligence. Instead, his statisticians found a way to redistribute zero scores in a manner favorable to hereditarian assumptions (see next section).

48   Oh yes, was anyone wondering how my students fared? They did very well of course. Anything else would have been shocking, since all the tests are greatly simplified precursors of examinations they have been taking all their lives. Of fifty-three students, thirty-one scored A and sixteen B. Still, more than 10 percent (six of fifty-three) scored at the intellectual borderline of C; by the standards of some camps, they would have been fit only for the duties of a buck private.

FINAGLING THE SUMMARY STATISTICS: THE PROBLEM OF ZERO VALUES

49   If the Beta test faltered on the artifact of a secondary mode for zero scores, the Alpha test became an unmitigated disaster for the same reason, vastly intensified. The zero modes were pronounced in Beta, but they never reached the height of the primary mode at a middle value. But six of eight Alpha tests yielded their highest mode at zero. (Only one had a normal distribution with a middle mode, while the other yielded a zero mode lower than the middle mode.) The zero mode often soared above all other values. In one test, nearly 40 percent of all scores were zero (Figure 4, test 4). In another, zero was the only common value, with a flat distribution of other scores (at about one-fifth the level of zero values) until an even decline began at high scores (Figure 4, test 5).

50   Again, the common-sense interpretation of numerous zeros suggests that many men didn't understand the instructions and that the tests were invalid on that account. Buried throughout Yerkes's monograph are numerous statements proving that testers worried greatly about the high frequency of zeros and, in the midst of giving the tests, tended to interpret zeros in this common-sense fashion. They eliminated some tests from the Beta repertoire (p. 372) because they produced up to 30.7 percent zero scores (although some Alpha tests with a higher frequency of zeros were retained). They reduced the difficulty of initial items in several tests "in order to reduce the number of zero scores" (p. 341). They included among the criteria for acceptance of a test within the Beta repertoire (p. 373): "ease of demonstration, as shown by low percentage of zero scores." They acknowledged several times that a high frequency of zeros reflected poor explanation, not stupidity of the recruits: "The large number of zero scores, even with officers, indicates that the instructions were unsatisfactory" (p. 340). "The main burden of the early reports was to the

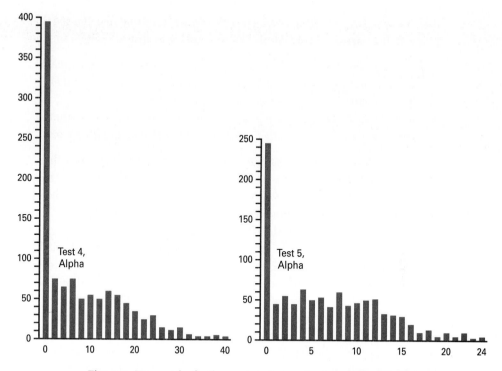

Figure 4. Zero was by far the most common value in several of the Alpha tests.

effect that the most difficult task was 'getting the idea across.' A high percentage of zero scores in any given test was considered an indication of failure to 'get that test across'" (p. 379).

51   With all these acknowledgments, one might have anticipated Boring's decision either to exclude zeros from the summary statistics or to correct for them by assuming that most recruits would have scored some points if they had understood what they were supposed to do. Instead, Boring "corrected" zero scores in the opposite way, and actually demoted many of them into a negative range.

52   Boring began with the same hereditarian assumption that invalidated all the results: that the tests, by definition, measure innate intelligence. The clump of zeros must therefore be made up of men who were too stupid to do any items. Is it fair to give them all zero? After all, some must have been just barely too stupid, and their zero is a fair score. But other dullards must have been rescued from an even worse fate by the minimum of zero. They would have done even more poorly if the test had included enough easy items to make distinctions among the zero scores. Boring distinguished between a true "mathematical zero," an intrinsic minimum that cannot logically go lower, and a "psychological zero," an arbitrary beginning

defined by a particular test. (As a general statement, Boring makes a sound point. In the particular context of the army tests, it is absurd):

> *A score of zero, therefore, does not mean no ability at all; it does not mean the point of discontinuance of the thing measured; it means the point of discontinuance of the instrument of measurement, the test…The individual who fails to earn a positive score and is marked zero is actually thereby given a bonus varying in value directly with his stupidity (p. 622).*

Boring therefore "corrected" each zero score by calibrating it against other tests in the series on which the same man had scored some points. If he had scored well on other tests, he was not doubly penalized for his zeros; if he had done poorly, then his zeros were converted to negative scores.

53   By this method, a debilitating flaw in Yerkes's basic procedure was accentuated by tacking an additional bias onto it. The zeros only indicated that, for a suite of reasons unrelated to intelligence, vast numbers of men did not understand what they were supposed to do. And Yerkes should have recognized this, for his own reports proved that, with reduced confusion and harassment, men who had scored zero on the group tests almost all managed to make points on the same or similar tests given in an individual examination. He writes (p. 406): "At Greenleaf it was found that the proportion of zero scores in the maze test was reduced from 28 percent in Beta to 2 percent in the performance scale, and that similarly zero scores in the digit-symbol test were reduced from 49 to 6 percent."

54   Yet, when given an opportunity to correct this bias by ignoring or properly redistributing the zero scores, Yerkes's statisticians did just the opposite. They exacted a double penalty by demoting most zero scores to a negative range.

FINAGLING THE SUMMARY STATISTICS: GETTING AROUND OBVIOUS CORRELATIONS WITH ENVIRONMENT

55   Yerkes's monograph is a treasure-trove of information for anyone seeking environmental correlates of performance on "tests of intelligence." Since Yerkes explicitly denied any substantial causal role to environment, and continued to insist that the tests measured innate intelligence, this claim may seem paradoxical. One might suspect that Yerkes, in his blindness, didn't read his own information. The situation, in fact, is even more curious. Yerkes read very carefully; he puzzled over every one of his environmental correlations, and managed to explain each of them away with arguments that sometimes border on the ridiculous.

56   Minor items are reported and dispersed in a page or two. Yerkes found strong correlations between average score and infestation with hookworm in all 4 categories:

	INFECTED	NOT INFECTED
White Alpha	94.38	118.50
White Beta	45.38	53.26
Negro Alpha	34.86	40.82
Negro Beta	22.14	26.09

These results might have led to the obvious admission that state of health, particularly in diseases related to poverty, has some effect upon the scores. Although Yerkes did not deny this possibility, he stressed another explanation (p. 811): "Low native ability may induce such conditions of living as to result in hookworm infection."

57   In studying the distribution of scores by occupation, Yerkes conjectured that since intelligence brings its own reward, test scores should rise with expertise. He divided each job into apprentices, journeymen, and experts and searched for increasing scores between the groups. But he found no pattern. Instead of abandoning his hypothesis, he decided that his procedure for allocating men to the three categories must have been flawed (pp. 831–832):

> It seems reasonable to suppose that a selection process goes on in industry which results in a selection of the mentally more alert for promotion from the apprentice stage to the journeyman stage and likewise from the journeyman stage to the expert. Those inferior mentally would stick at the lower levels of skill or be weeded out of the particular trade. On this hypothesis one begins to question the accuracy of the personnel interviewing procedure.

58   Among major patterns, Yerkes continually found relationships between intelligence and amount of schooling. He calculated a correlation coefficient of 0.75 between test score and years of education. Of 348 men who scored below the mean in Alpha, only 1 had ever attended college (as a dental student), 4 had graduated from high school, and only 10 had ever attended high school at all. Yet Yerkes did not conclude that more schooling leads to increasing scores per se; instead, he argued that men with more innate intelligence spend more time in school. "The theory that native intelligence is one of the most important conditioning factors in continuance in school is certainly borne out by this accumulation of data" (p. 780).

59   Yerkes noted the strongest correlation of scores with schooling in
considering the differences between blacks and whites. He made a
significant social observation, but gave it his usual innatist twist (p. 760):

> The white draft of foreign birth is less schooled; more than half of this
> group have not gone beyond the fifth grade, while one-eighth, or 12.5
> percent, report no schooling. Negro recruits though brought up in this
> country where elementary education is supposedly not only free but
> compulsory on all, report no schooling in astonishingly large proportion.

Failure of blacks to attend school, he argued, must reflect a disinclination
based on low innate intelligence. Not a word about segregation (then
officially sanctioned, if not mandated), poor conditions in black schools,
or economic necessities for working among the impoverished. Yerkes
acknowledged that schools might vary in quality, but he assumed that such
an effect must be small and cited, as primary evidence for innate black
stupidity, the lower scores of blacks when paired with whites who had
spent an equal number of years in school (p. 773):

> The grade standards, of course, are not identical all over the country,
> especially as between schools for white and for negro children, so that
> "fourth-grade schooling" doubtless varies in meaning from group to group,
> but this variability certainly cannot account for the clear intelligence
> differences between groups.

60   The data that might have led Yerkes to change his mind (had he
approached the study with any flexibility) lay tabulated, but unused,
within his monograph. Yerkes had noted regional differences in black
education. Half the black recruits from Southern states had not attended
school beyond the third grade, but half had reached the fifth grade in
Northern states (p. 760). In the North, 25 percent completed primary
school; in the South, a mere 7 percent. Yerkes also noted (p. 734) that "the
percentage of Alphas is very much smaller and the percentage of Betas very
much larger in the southern than in the northern group." Many years later,
Ashley Montagu (1945) studied the tabulations by state that Yerkes had
provided. He confirmed Yerkes's pattern: the average score on Alpha was
21.31 for blacks in thirteen Southern states, and 39.90 in nine Northern
states. Montagu then noted that average black scores for the four highest
Northern states (45.31) exceeded the *white* mean for nine Southern states
(43.94). He found the same pattern for Beta, where blacks of six Northern
states averaged 34.63, and whites of fourteen Southern states, 31.11.
Hereditarians had their pat answer, as usual: only the best Negroes had
been smart enough to move North. To people of good will and common

sense an explanation in terms of educational quality has always seemed more reasonable, especially since Montagu also found such high correlations between a state's expenditure for education and the average score of its recruits.

61   One other persistent correlation threatened Yerkes's hereditarian convictions, and his rescuing argument became a major social weapon in later political campaigns for restricting immigration. Test scores had been tabulated by country of origin, and Yerkes noted the pattern so dear to the hearts of Nordic supremacists. He divided recruits by country of origin into English, Scandinavian, and Teutonic on one side, and Latin and Slavic on the other, and stated (p. 699): "the differences are considerable (an extreme range of practically two years mental age)"—favoring the Nordics, of course.

62   But Yerkes acknowledged a potential problem. Most Latins and Slavs had arrived recently and spoke English either poorly or not at all; the main wave of Teutonic immigration had passed long before. According to Yerkes's protocol, it shouldn't have mattered. Men who could not speak English suffered no penalty. They took Beta, a pictorial test that supposedly measured innate ability independent of literacy and language. Yet the data still showed an apparent penalty for unfamiliarity with English. Of white recruits who scored E in Alpha and therefore took Beta as well (pp. 382–383), speakers of English averaged 101.6 in Beta, while nonspeakers averaged only 77.8. On the individual performance scale, which eliminated the harassment and confusion of Beta, native and foreign-born recruits did not differ (p. 403). (But very few men were ever given these individual tests, and they did not affect national averages.) Yerkes had to admit (p. 395): "There are indications to the effect that individuals handicapped by language difficulty and illiteracy are penalized to an appreciable degree in Beta as compared with men not so handicapped."

63   Another correlation was even more potentially disturbing. Yerkes found that average test scores for foreign-born recruits rose consistently with years of residence in America.

YEARS OF RESIDENCE	AVERAGE MENTAL AGE
0–5	11.29
6–10	11.70
11–15	12.53
16–20	13.50
20–	13.74

Didn't this indicate that familiarity with American ways, and not innate intelligence, regulated the differences in scores? Yerkes admitted the possibility, but held out strong hope for a hereditarian salvation (p. 704):

> *Apparently then the group that has been longer resident in this country does somewhat better[3] in intelligence examination. It is not possible to state whether the difference is caused by the better adaptation of the more thoroughly Americanized group to the situation of the examination or whether some other factor is operative. It might be, for instance, that the more intelligent immigrants succeed and therefore remain in this country, but this suggestion is weakened by the fact that so many successful immigrants do return to Europe. At best we can but leave for future decision the question as to whether the differences represent a real difference of intelligence or an artifact of the method of examination.*

The Teutonic supremacists would soon supply that decision: recent immigration had drawn the dregs of Europe, lower-class Latins and Slavs. Immigrants of longer residence belonged predominantly to superior northern stocks. The correlation with years in America was an artifact of genetic status.

64
　　The army mental tests could have provided an impetus for social reform, since they documented that environmental disadvantages were robbing from millions of people an opportunity to develop their intellectual skills. Again and again, the data pointed to strong correlations between test scores and environment. Again and again, those who wrote and administered the tests invented tortuous, ad hoc explanations to preserve their hereditarian prejudices.

65
　　How powerful the hereditarian biases of Terman, Goddard, and Yerkes must have been to make them so blind to immediate circumstances! Terman seriously argued that good orphanages precluded any environmental cause of low IQ for children in them. Goddard tested confused and frightened immigrants who had just completed a grueling journey in steerage and thought he had captured innate intelligence. Yerkes badgered his recruits, obtained proof of confusion and harassment in their large mode of zero scores, and produced data on the inherent abilities of racial and national groups. One cannot attribute all these conclusions to some mysterious "temper of the times," for contemporary critics saw through the nonsense as well. Even by standards of their own era, the American hereditarians were dogmatists. But their dogma wafted up on favorable currents into realms of general acceptance, with tragic consequences.

---

[3] Note how choice of language can serve as an indication of bias. This 2.5 year difference in mental ages (13.74–11.29) only represents "somewhat better" performance. The smaller (but presumably hereditary) difference of 2 years between Nordic-Teutonic and Latin-Slav groups had been described as "considerable."

Works Cited

Chase, A. 1977. *The Legacy of Malthus.* New York: A. Knopf, 686 pp.

Kevles, D. J. 1968. Testing the army's intelligence: psychologists and the military in World War I. *Journal of American History* 55: 565–581.

Montagu, Ashley. 1945. Intelligence of northern Negroes and southern whites in the First World War. *American Journal of Psychology* 58: 161–188.

Yerkes, R. M. 1917a. The Binet version versus the point scale method of measuring intelligence. *Journal of Applied Psychology* 1: 111–122.

————1917b. How may we discover the children who need special care. *Mental Hygiene* 1: 252–259.

Yerkes, R. M. (ed.). 1921. Psychological examining in the United States army. *Memoirs of the National Academy of Sciences,* vol. 15, 890 pp.

STUDY QUESTIONS

1. What evidence does Gould offer that the conclusions of Yerkes, Boring, and their followers were determined by "hereditarian prejudice" rather than by the implications of the data themselves?

2. How does Gould's interpretation of the data differ from that of Yerkes and his colleagues? Which interpretation is more probable?

3. "To avoid excessively large Beta groups, standards for admission to examination Alpha were set low" (paragraph 29). How did this fact affect the conclusions of the army study?

4. In paragraphs 55–59 Gould discusses correlations that Yerkes had discovered between performance on the intelligence tests and various other facts about those tested. What correlations did Yerkes discover between intelligence and infestation with hookworm? intelligence and level of occupational expertise? intelligence and amount of schooling? How did Yerkes account for these correlations? What counter-explanation does Gould give?

5. Northern blacks did better on the test than Southern blacks (paragraph 60). How did this difference pose a threat to hereditarian theorists? How did they explain the difference away?

6. Why is it misleading to discuss the "average" scores or "mean" scores of the test results graphed in Figure 4?

SUGGESTION FOR WRITING

Write a critique of Beta test 6 (shown in Figure 2), including the rules for scoring individual items. Does it test intelligence? What kinds of flaws do you find in the test? Are these flaws peculiar to the particular items selected for this test (including the rules for scoring) or would any test of picture completion have the same problems?

GEORGE B. CUTTEN

From "*The Reconstruction of Democracy*"

The empirical claims of the psychologists who administered intelligence tests to the U. S. Army in 1917 and 1918 led to many proposals for change in social policy. The following essay is one of them. Like several others that appeared during the early 1920s, it proposes changes in the governance of the United States. (Another on the same theme was a famous address by the chairman of Harvard's psychology department, entitled, "Is America Safe for Democracy?") The author of the selection below was by no means a crank or a fanatic. George B. Cutten (1874–1962) was a Baptist minister who later became a respected college administrator. This selection is an excerpt from his inaugural address as president of Colgate University on October 7, 1922. He held this office for twenty years.

1   If all men were born free and equal, democracy would not only be possible, but it would be very desirable. Whether fortunately or unfortunately this is not so. The mental tests recently made on one and three quarters million men in the United States Army showed us not only an inequality, but revealed even larger proportions in the extreme classes than we thought likely or perhaps possible. With only $13^1/_2$ per cent. of the population able to get through college well, 15 per cent. able to get through at all, and 25 per cent. unable to comprehend the significance of the ballot, democracy is out of the question. The real tariff experts of this country could probably be counted on the fingers of one hand, and these do not agree, because they either have not all the same facts or else do not interpret them the same way, and yet we calmly submit the subject of the tariff to the people as a whole, 25 per cent. of whom are mentally subnormal, and the average mentality of whom is slightly over thirteen years. The subject of the League of Nations is one, the ramifications of which are too numerous and complicated for any one expert to grasp, and yet we can readily have an election on this. It may be a wise course to treat the people like children and let them play at governing themselves, but would it probably not be as wise to recognize the truth? The play goes on until a problem arises and then we call for a "leader." What we mean, of course, is a ruler. The ruler, thus called, rules autocratically during the period of the difficulty and then lets us play again....

2   Let us look the question fairly in the face and be honest with ourselves. We are ruled in industry, in commerce, in professions, in government by an intellectual aristocracy. We have never had a true democracy, and the low level of the intelligence of the people will not permit of our having one. We can not conceive of any worse form of chaos than a real democracy in a population of an average intelligence of a little over thirteen years. If the

war was fought to make the world safe for democracy, the success of the object would be a ghastly failure. Fortunately no one thought that it was fought for that purpose, except those who were unfit to be a part of a democracy.

3   Even Lord Bryce in his great work on Modern Democracies admits that the rule is never by the many but always by the few. I shall quote somewhat fully from him, for while he talks continually about democracy, he practically admits there is no such thing. In his chapter on "Oligarchies within Democracies" he says, "No one can have had some years' experience of the conduct of affairs in a legislature or an administration without observing how extremely small is the number of persons by whom the world is governed." (p. 542). "In large democratic countries like England and France, and above all in the United States, the number of persons who count, swelled as it is by journalists and by the leaders of various organizations that can influence votes, is very much larger in proportion to the population [than in Germany and Austria] but that proportion is still infinitesimally small." (p. 544). "But the most striking illustration of the law that the larger the body the fewer those who rule it, is furnished by the great Labor Unions that now exist in all industrial countries. The power which the members of the unions entrust to their delegates to trade congresses, and the docility with which in some countries they follow whatever lead is given them by a strong will, can, as an able writer who had given special study to the subject remarks, be in those countries paralleled only by the religious veneration given to saints." (p. 545 f.). "Thus free government can not but be, and has in reality always been, an oligarchy within a democracy. But it is oligarchy not in the historical sense of the rule of a class, but rather in the original sense of the word, the rule of few instead of many individuals, to wit, those few whom neither birth nor wealth nor race distinguishes from the rest, but only nature in having given to them qualities or opportunities she had denied to others." (p. 550). He concludes that the only functions of the many in contrast to the few are possibly three, viz: 1, "Though the people can not choose and guide the means administration employs, they can prescribe the ends, and so although government may not be by the people, it may be for the people"; 2, "They commit the means for attaining that end to the citizens whom they select for the purpose"; and 3, "They watch these selected citizens to make sure that they do not misuse the authority entrusted to them." Bryce then continues, "Of these three functions the most important and most difficult is that of choosing leaders, for though it seems simple to say that government must pursue the common good, the power to discern and decide in any given case what is that good, and what means best conduce thereto, needs a wisdom and an unselfishness possessed by few. Since the people can seldom do this for themselves, their leaders must do it for them, and be held responsible for the consequences." In effect this means that all

the many can do is to choose their ruler, but in how few cases is even this possible! In most cases the best offered to a voter is a choice between two persons, neither one of whom he wishes to have for a ruler. Some have their rulers born, some have them chosen, but most people in democratic countries have their rulers thrust upon them....

4   There must be some solution to the problem of government, and we must find it. What is it? We must first recognize that we are and have been, since the revolt against autocracy, ruled by the intelligentsia; more than ever the rule must be by an aristocracy, i.e., a rule by the best. . . .

5   This aristocracy must inevitably be the most intelligent, but it must also be well trained, benevolently inclined, and willing to admit any others to its membership who are fitted to belong. Democracy then comes to be a government of the people, for the people, by all those of their number fitted by intellectual ability, moral ideals, and carful training. The ruling has always been by the few intelligent members of the community or the nation, and in America the aristocracy has always had the "open shop." The training has also been a factor, even if an accidental factor, but the element most lacking has been the moral ideals. Government for the people, instead of for the governors, must be the key note of the future, and the task of the colleges and the universities is the training of this aristocracy.

6   It may be interesting to speculate concerning the effect of mental tests upon the problem of democracy. If the present hopes and expectations are realized they will result in a caste system as rigid as that of India, but on a rational and just basis. We are now examining children in the public schools, and find all ranges of intelligence from imbecility to genius. We are told that the intelligence quotient of a child rarely changes, so that we are enabled to tell early in his life what the limit of intelligence of any person will be, and in a general way to what class of vocation he is best fitted, and, to a certain extent, destined. When the tests for vocational guidance are completed and developed, each boy and girl in school will be assigned to the vocation for which he is fitted, and, presuming that the tests are really efficient, he will in the future not attempt any work too advanced for his ability and hence make a failure of it, neither will he be found in an occupation too elementary for his ability and hence be dissatisfied. Economically nothing could be more desirable. All differences in accomplishments or results from that which the intelligence quotients would indicate would be due to certain traits of character which intelligence tests do not measure, viz.: industry, perseverance, thoroughness, honesty.

7   One's intelligence quotient will eventually be known and persons will be classed thereby. Those of high intelligence will be directed into lines of occupation which call for leadership. Those persons will naturally be

placed in the professions, and in leading positions in industry, commerce, and politics. Each person will then be directed on a scale of intelligence down to those whose work is of the most routine character of which an imbecile is capable. But what effect will this have on our so-called democracy? It must inevitably destroy universal adult suffrage, by cutting off at least 25 per cent. of the adults, those whose intelligence is so low as to be incapable of comprehending the significance of the ballot. On the other hand, it will throw the burden and responsibility of government where it belongs, on those of high intelligence, and we come back again to the rule of the aristocracy—this time the real and total aristocracy. For its own salvation the state must assume the obligation and responsibility of selecting this intellectual aristocracy, and having selected it see that it is properly trained.

8   Some further questions naturally arise from this new state of affairs, the chief among which is this: would not those of low mentality rebel, and cause a revolution which would throw the government into their hands and thus cause a condition of affairs worse, even, than could be imagined? There are three reasons why this would not likely be so. In the first place that portion of the population of lower mentality would be engaged in occupations for which they would be perfectly fitted and consequently they would be contented—contented people do not rebel. In the second place it has been shown quite conclusively, that people of low mentality do not object to being governed by others, provided the government is benevolent. In the third place they would lack leaders of intelligence to incite or to direct any rebellion, and consequently it would not be started, or if started would not be successful. Of course, there would always be the possibility of some one of the aristocracy descending to become a demagogue, and leading those of low mentality for the sake of personal gain, but this simply emphasizes the necessity of moral training along with the intellectual.

9   The value of an intellectual aristocracy would be that it would be open, the intellectually superior being selected early in life and trained for special service, and not an aristocracy dependent upon accident of birth, wealth, or favor. Of all bases for an aristocracy none better could be found. In such a society it would then be seen whether the aristocracy would accept the responsibility of parenthood in order to perpetuate itself, and at the same time if the mentally unfit and those of low mentality would be prevented from propagating their kind, for in such a scheme only is there hope for the race. There is only one objection to this last statement, viz: "that in such a scheme only is there hope of the race," and that is the general scheme of development of the race. Man has not always been as intelligent as now; he has developed this intelligence, and if this individual development is still continuing, there may yet be another basis for hope; but we know the scheme of breeding to be a far more rapid method of obtaining results, and

if both methods are still to be depended upon they are both needed to bring the race to a high intellectual plane.

10   For many years we have heard of the great advantage of education because so many college graduates occupied positions of influence and power. It has been frequently pointed out that although only a very small percentage of persons go to college, a very large percentage of those who are sufficiently successful to have their names in "Who's Who" are college graduates. In the past we have credited this almost wholly to the training received in college, and undoubtedly this was a factor, but the discovery that only 15 per cent. of the people have sufficient intelligence to get through college is enlightening. These men and women are the intellectual aristocracy, and those who have graduated from college, in addition to belonging to this class, have had a training which should better fit them for successful endeavor.

11   Our college men must be a part of the 15 per cent. necessarily, so while the intelligentsia may be found elsewhere they are sure to be found, and to be found in greater proportions, in our colleges. There comes, then, the recognition of the heavy responsibility of the colleges to train these men— these choice, selected men—so as to enable them to render the greatest service. This training must be along two lines, general training and moral training, and both should be thoroughly adapted to fit this intellectual aristocracy to do the work and to encourage them to accept the responsibility.

STUDY QUESTIONS

1. List the empirical claims that Cutten advances in this speech as the basis of his social and political proposals. What assumptions does he make about the accuracy and power of intelligence tests?
2. Summarize Cutten's evaluation of democracy.
3. Exactly what changes in American government does Cutten propose?
4. List those aspects of government that Cutten seems to value most. Do his priorities differ from your own?
5. Express the argument of this speech in a syllogism in which the first premise is an empirical claim about the intelligence of Americans and the conclusion is a statement about the kind of government we ought to have. What premise is required to combine these into a syllogism? Since you have molded the second premise to the first premise and the conclusion, the syllogism is bound to be valid. If you disagree with the conclusion, what do you disagree with in the premises? Are you disagreeing with facts, values, or both?

WALTER LIPPMANN

Three Essays on Intelligence Tests

Walter Lippmann (1889–1974) was an American political analyst, editor, columnist, political advisor, and winner of the Pulitzer Prize. In 1922 he published in the pages of the *New Republic* (of which he was a cofounder) a series of six articles responding in part to claims by Yerkes and his colleagues in the intelligence testing enterprise, but even more to popularizers who reported the findings of the psychologists in sometimes exaggerated or garbled form.

The following are the first three articles in Lippmann's series. They are primarily empirical arguments, for they are concerned with the kinds of claims about "intelligence" or "mental age" that can be drawn from the raw data provided by the army intelligence tests.

The Mental Age of Americans

1   A startling bit of news has recently been unearthed and is now being retailed by the credulous to the gullible. "The *average* mental age of Americans," says Mr. Lothrop Stoddard in *The Revolt Against Civilization,* "is only about fourteen."

2   Mr. Stoddard did not invent this astonishing conclusion. He found it ready-made in the writings of a number of other writers. They in their turn got the conclusion by misreading the data collected in the army intelligence tests. For the data themselves lead to no such conclusion. It is impossible that they should. It is quite impossible for honest statistics to show that the average adult intelligence of a representative sample of the nation is that of an immature child in that same nation. The average adult intelligence cannot be less than the average adult intelligence, and to anyone who knows what the words "mental age" mean, Mr. Stoddard's remark is precisely as silly as if he had written that the average mile was three-quarters of a mile long.

3   The trouble is that Mr. Stoddard uses the words "mental age" without explaining either to himself or to his readers how the conception of "mental age" is derived. He was in such an enormous hurry to predict the downfall of civilization that he could not pause long enough to straighten out a few simple ideas. The result is that he snatches at a few scarifying statistics and uses them as a base upon which to erect a glittering tower of generalities. For the statement that the average mental age of Americans is only about fourteen is not inaccurate. It is not incorrect. It is nonsense.

4   Mental age is a yardstick invented by a school of psychologists to measure "intelligence." It is not easy, however, to make a measure of

intelligence and the psychologists have never agreed on a definition. This quandary presented itself to Alfred Binet. For years he had tried to reach a definition of intelligence and always he had failed. Finally he gave up the attempt, and started on another tack. He then turned his attention to the practical problem of distinguishing the "backward" child from the "normal" child in the Paris schools. To do this he had to know what was a normal child. Difficult as this promised to be, it was a good deal easier than the attempt to define intelligence. For Binet concluded, quite logically, that the standard of a normal child of any particular age was something or other which an arbitrary percentage of children of that age could do. Binet therefore decided to consider "normal" those abilities which were common to between 65 and 75 percent of the children of a particular age. In deciding on these percentages, he thus decided to consider at least 25 percent of the children as backward. He might just as easily have fixed a percentage which would have classified 10 percent of the children as backward, or 50 percent.

5   Having fixed a percentage which he would henceforth regard as "normal," he devoted himself to collecting questions, stunts, and puzzles of various sorts, hard ones and easy ones. At the end he settled upon fifty-four tests, each of which he guessed and hoped would test some element of intelligence; all of which together would test intelligence as a whole. Binet then gave these tests in Paris to 200 school children who ranged from three to fifteen years of age. Whenever he found a test that about 65 percent of the children of the same age could pass he called that a Binet test of intelligence for that age. Thus a mental age of seven years was the ability to do all the tests which 65 to 75 percent of a small group of seven-year-old Paris schoolchildren had shown themselves able to do.

6   This was a promising method, but of course the actual tests rested on a very weak foundation indeed. Binet himself died before he could carry his idea much further, and the task of revision and improvement was then transferred to Stanford University. The Binet scale worked badly in California. The same puzzles did not give the same results in California as in Paris. So about 1910, Professor L. M. Terman undertook to revise them. He followed Binet's method. Like Binet he would guess at a stunt which might indicate intelligence, and then try it out on about 2,300 people of various ages, including 1,700 children "in a community of average social status." By editing, rearranging, and supplementing the original Binet tests he finally worked out a series of tests for each age which the average child of that age in about one hundred Californian children could pass.

7   The puzzles which this average child among one hundred Californian children of the same age about the year 1913 could answer are the yardstick by which mental age is measured in what is known as the Stanford Revision of the Binet-Simon scale. Each correct answer gives a

credit of two months' mental age. So if a child of seven can answer all tests up to the seven-year-old tests perfectly, and cannot answer any of the eight-year-old tests, his total score is seven years. He is said to test "at age," and his "intelligence quotient" or "IQ" is unity or 100 percent. Anybody's IQ can be figured, therefore, by dividing his mental age by his actual age. A child of five who tests at four years' mental age has an IQ of 80 ($^4/_5$ = .80). A child of five who tests at six years' mental age has an IQ of 120 ($^6/_5$ = 1.20).

8   The aspect of all this which matters is that mental age is simply the average performance with certain rather arbitrary problems. The thing to keep in mind is that all the talk about "a mental age of fourteen" goes back to the performance of eighty-two California school children in 1913–1914. Their success and failures on the days they happened to be tested have become embalmed and consecrated as the measure of human intelligence. By means of that measure writers like Mr. Stoddard fix the relative values of all the peoples of the earth and of all social classes within the nations. They don't know they are doing this, however, because Mr. Stoddard at least is quite plainly taking everything at second hand.

9   However, I am willing for just a moment to grant that Mr. Terman in California has worked out a test for the different ages of a growing child. But I insist that anyone who uses the words "mental age" should remember that Mr. Terman reached his test by seeing what the average child of an age group could do. If his group is too small or is untypical, his test is in the same measure inaccurate.

10   Remembering this, we come to the army tests. Here we are dealing at once with men all of whom are over the age of the mental scale. For the Stanford-Binet scale ends at "sixteen years." It assumes that intelligence stops developing at sixteen, and everybody sixteen and over is therefore treated as "adult" or as "superior adult." Now the adult Stanford-Binet tests were "standardized chiefly on the basis of results from 400 adults [Terman, p. 13] of moderate success and of very limited educational advantages" and also thirty-two high school pupils from sixteen to twenty years of age. Among these adults, those who tested close together have the honor of being considered the standard of average adult intelligence.

11   Before the army tests came along, when anyone talked about the average adult he was talking about a few hundred Californians. The army tested about 1,700,000 adult men. But it did not use the Binet system of scoring by mental ages. It scored by a system of points which we need not stop to describe. Naturally enough, everyone interested in mental testing wanted to know whether the army tests agreed in any way with the Stanford-Binet mental-age standard. So by another process, which need also not be described, the results of the army tests were translated into Binet terms. The result of this translation is the table which has so badly misled poor Mr. Stoddard. This table showed that the average of the army did not agree

at all with the average of Mr. Terman's Californians. There were then two things to do. One was to say that the average intelligence of 1,700,000 men was a more representative average than that of 400 men. The other was to pin your faith to the 400 men and insist they gave the true average.

12   Mr. Stoddard chose the average of 400 rather than the average of 1,700,000 because he was in such haste to write his own book that he never reached page 785 of *Psychological Examining in the United States Army,* the volume of the data edited by Major Yerkes.* He would have found there a clear warning against the blunder he was about to commit, the blunder of treating the average of a small number of instances as more valid than the average of a large number.

13   But instead of pausing to realize that the army tests had knocked the Stanford-Binet measure of adult intelligence into a cocked hat, he wrote his book in the belief that the Stanford measure is as good as it ever was. This is not intelligent. It leads one to suspect that Mr. Stoddard is a propagandist with a tendency to put truth not in the first place but in the second. It leads one to suspect, after such a beginning, that the real promise and value of the investigation which Binet started is in danger of gross perversion by muddle-headed and prejudiced men.

STUDY QUESTIONS

1. In paragraph 2, Lippmann contests the psychometricians' claim that the average mental age of Americans is only about fourteen. Does he rebut this claim

---

* "For norms of adult intelligence, the results of the Army examinations are undoubtedly the most representative. It is customary to say that the mental age of the average adult is about sixteen years. This figure is based, however, upon examinations of only 62 persons....This group is too small to give very reliable results and is furthermore probably not typical." *Psychological Examining in the United States Army,* p. 785.

The reader will note that Major Yerkes and his colleagues assert that the Stanford standard of adult intelligence is based on only sixty-two cases. This is a reference to page 49 of Mr. Terman's book on the Stanford Revision of the Binet-Simon Scale. But page 13 of the same book speaks of 400 adults being the basis on which the adult tests were standardized. I have used this larger figure because it is more favorable to the Stanford-Binet scale.

It should also be remarked that the army figures are not the absolute figures but the results of a "sample of the white draft" consisting of nearly 100,000 recruits. In strictest accuracy, we ought to say then that the disagreement between army and Stanford-Binet results derives from conclusions drawn from 100,000 cases as against 400.

If these 100,000 recruits are not a fair sample of the nation, as they probably are not, then in addition to saying that the army tests contradict the Stanford-Binet Scale, we ought to add that the army tests are themselves no reliable basis for measuring the average American mentality.

by advancing contradictory empirical evidence or by some other means? Is his rebuttal logically sound?

2. In paragraph 4 Lippmann discusses Binet's attempt to identify "backward" children in the Paris schools. After reading Lippmann's analysis, do you think the question, "What percentage of children in the Paris schools are backward?" is an empirical question?

3. Why does Lippmann believe that the army tests "knocked the Stanford-Binet measure of adult intelligence into a cocked hat"?

The Mystery of the "A" Men

1   Because the results are expressed in numbers, it is easy to make the mistake of thinking that the intelligence test is a measure like a foot rule or a pair of scales. It is, of course, a quite different sort of measure. For length and weight are qualities which men have learned how to isolate no matter whether they are found in an army of soldiers, a heap of bricks, or a collection of chlorine molecules. Provided the foot rule and the scales agree with the arbitrarily accepted standard foot and standard pound in the Bureau of Standards at Washington they can be used with confidence. But intelligence is not an abstraction like length and weight; it is an exceedingly complicated notion which nobody has as yet succeeded in defining.

2   When we measure the weight of a schoolchild we mean a very definite thing. We mean that if you put the child on one side of an evenly balanced scale, you will have to put a certain number of standard pounds in the other scale in order to cancel the pull of the child's body toward the center of the earth. But when you come to measure intelligence you have nothing like this to guide you. You know in a general way that intelligence is the capacity to deal successfully with the problems that confront human beings, but if you try to say what those problems are, or what you mean by "dealing" with them, or by "success," you will soon lose yourself in a fog of controversy. This fundamental difficulty confronts the intelligence tester at all times. The way in which he deals with it is the most important thing to understand about the intelligence test, for otherwise you are certain to misinterpret the results.

3   The intelligence tester starts with no clear idea of what intelligence means. He then proceeds by drawing upon his common sense and experience to imagine the different kinds of problems men face which might in a general way be said to call for the exercise of intelligence. But these problems are much too complicated and too vague to be reproduced in the classroom. The intelligence tester cannot confront each child with

the thousand and one situations arising in a home, a workshop, a farm, an office or in politics, that call for the exercise of those capacities which in a summary fashion we call intelligence. He proceeds, therefore, to guess at the more abstract mental abilities which come into play again and again. By this rough process the intelligence tester gradually makes up his mind that situations in real life call for memory, definition, ingenuity, and so on. He then invents puzzles which can be employed quickly and with little apparatus, that will, according to his best guess, test memory, ingenuity, definition, and the rest. He gives these puzzles to a mixed group of children and sees how children of different ages answer them. Whenever he finds a puzzle that, say, 60 percent of twelve-year-old children can do, and 20 percent of the eleven-year-olds, he adopts that test for the twelve-year-olds. By a great deal of fitting, he gradually works out a series of problems for each age group which 60 percent of his children can pass, 20 percent cannot pass and, say, 20 percent of the children one year younger can also pass. By this method he has arrived, under the Stanford-Binet system, at a conclusion of this sort: Sixty percent of children twelve years old should be able to define three out of the five words: pity, revenge, charity, envy, justice. According to Professor Terman's instructions, a child passes this test if he says that "pity" is "to be sorry for someone"; the child fails if he says "to help" or "mercy." A correct definition of "justice" is as follows: "It's what you get when you go to court"; an incorrect definition is "to be honest."

4   A mental test, then, is established in this way: The tester himself guesses at a large number of tests which he hopes and believes are tests of intelligence. Among these tests, those finally are adopted by him which 60 percent of the children under his observation can pass. The children whom the tester is studying select his tests.

5   There are, consequently, two uncertain elements. The first is whether the tests really test intelligence. The second is whether the children under observation are a large enough group to be typical. The answer to the first question—whether the tests are tests of intelligence—can be determined only by seeing whether the results agree with other tests of intelligence, whatever they may be. The answer to the second question can be had only by making a very much larger number of observations than have yet been made. We know that the largest test made, the army examinations, showed enormous error in the Stanford test of adult intelligence. These elements of doubt are, I think, radical enough to prohibit anyone from using the results of these tests for large generalization about the quality of human beings. For when people generalize about the quality of human beings, they assume an objective criterion of quality, and for testing intelligence there is no such criterion. These puzzles may test intelligence, and they may not. They may test an aspect of intelligence. Nobody knows.

6   What then do the tests accomplish? I think we can answer this question best by starting with an illustration. Suppose you wished to judge all the

pebbles in a large pile of gravel for the purpose of separating them into three piles, the first to contain the extraordinary pebbles, the second the normal pebbles, the third the insignificant pebbles. You have no scales. You first separate from the pile a much smaller pile and pick out one pebble which you guess is the average. You hold it in you left hand and pick up another pebble in your right hand. The right pebble feels heavier. You pick up another pebble. It feels lighter. You pick up a third. It feels still lighter. A fourth feels heavier than the first. By this method, you can arrange all the pebbles from the smaller pile in a series running from the lightest to the heaviest. You thereupon call the middle pebble the standard pebble, and with it as a measure you determine whether any pebble in the larger pile is a subnormal, a normal, or a supernormal pebble.

7   This is just about what the intelligence test does. It does not weigh or measure intelligence by any objective standard. It simply arranges a group of people in a series from best to worst by balancing their capacity to do certain arbitrarily selected puzzles, against the capacity of all the others. The intelligence test, in other words, is fundamentally an instrument for classifying a group of people. It may also be an instrument for measuring their intelligence, but of that we cannot be at all sure unless we believe that M. Binet and Mr. Terman and a few other psychologists have guessed correctly when they invented their tests. They may have guessed correctly but, as we shall see later, the proof is not yet at hand.

8   The intelligence test, then, is an instrument for classifying a group of people, rather than "a measure of intelligence." People are classified within a group according to their success in solving problems which may or may not be tests of intelligence. They are classified, according to the performance of some Californians in the years 1910 to about 1916, with Mr. Terman's notion of the problems that reveal intelligence. They are not classified according to their ability in dealing with the problems of real life that call for intelligence.

9   With this in mind, let us look at the army results as they are dished up by writers like Mr. Lothrop Stoddard and Professor McDougall of Harvard. The following table is given:

$4^1/_2$% of the army were A men
9% of the army were B men
$16^1/_2$% of the army were C+ men
25% of the army were C men
20% of the army were C− men
15% of the army were D men
10% of the army were D− men

10   But how, you ask, did the army determine the qualities of an "A" man? For an "A" man is supposed to have "very superior intelligence," and of course, mankind has wondered for at least two thousand years what were

the earmarks of very superior intelligence. McDougall and Stoddard are quite content to take the army's word for it, or at least they never stop to explain, before they exploit the figures, what the army meant by "very superior intelligence." The army, of course, had no intention whatever of committing itself to a definition of very superior intelligence. The army was interested in classifying recruits. It therefore asked a committee of psychologists to assemble from all the different systems, Binet and otherwise, a series of tests. The committee took this series and tried it out in a few camps. They timed the tests. "The number of items and the time limits were so fixed that five percent or less in any average group would be able to finish the entire series of items in the time allowed."[1] It is not surprising, therefore, that five percent or less ($4^{1}/_{2}$ percent actually) of the army made a top score. It is not surprising that tests devised to pass 5 percent or less "A" men should have passed $4^{1}/_{2}$ percent "A" men.

11   The army was quite justified in doing this because it was in a hurry and was looking for about 5 percent of the recruits to put into officers' training camps. I quarrel only with the Stoddards and McDougalls who, solemnly talk about the $4^{1}/_{2}$ percent of "A" men in the American nation without understanding how these $4^{1}/_{2}$ percent were picked. They do not seem to realize that if the army had wanted half the number of officers, it could by shortening the time have made the scarcity of "A" men seem even more alarming. If the army had wanted to double the "A" men, it could have done that by lengthening the time. Somewhere, of course, in the whole group would have been found men who could not have answered all the questions correctly in any length of time. But we do not know how many men of the kind there were because the tests were never made that way.[2]

12   The army was interested in discovering officers and in eliminating the feeble-minded. It had no time to waste, and so it adopted a rough test which would give a quick classification. In that, it succeeded on the whole very well. But the army did not measure the intelligence of the American nation, and only very loose-minded writers imagine that it did. When men write as Mr. Stoddard does that "only four and a half millions [of the whole population] can be considered 'talented,'" the only possible comment is that the statement has no foundation whatsoever. We do not know how many talented people there are: first, because we have no measure of talent, and second, because we have never made the attempt to devise one or apply one. But when we see how men like Stoddard and McDougall have exploited the army tests, we realize how necessary, but

---

[1] Yoakum and Yerkes, *Army Mental Tests,* p. 3.
[2] *Psychological Examining in the United States Army,* p. 419. "The high frequencies of persons gaining at the upper levels (often 100%) indicate for the people making high scores on single time the 'speed' element is predominant."

how unheeded, is the warning of Messrs. Yoakum and Yerkes that "the ease with which the army group test can be given and scored makes it a dangerous method in the hands of the inexpert. It was not prepared for civilian use, and is applicable only within certain limits to other uses than that for which it was prepared."

STUDY QUESTIONS

1. What does Lippmann mean by saying (in paragraph 4), "The children whom the tester is studying select his tests"? Does this fact (if it is a fact) discredit the tests, and if so why?
2. Lippmann says that measures of intelligence are unlike measures of length and weight, which compare an object under investigation with an arbitrarily accepted standard in the Bureau of Standards. But doesn't the sample used for norming the intelligence test (as described in Lippmann's first essay) serve as such an arbitrary standard against which any group being tested can be measured? If not, why not?
3. Is Lippmann derogating the tests when he describes the correct and incorrect definitions of words at the end of paragraph 3? Do you feel that the test items as described (including the guidelines for scoring answers) accurately measure intelligence?
4. Paragraph 8, which summarizes the foregoing part of the essay, makes several distinct criticisms of the tests. What are they?
5. Stoddard and other popularizers of the army results find it very alarming that only 5 percent of men in the army were judged to possess "very superior intelligence." How does Lippmann make this finding seem less alarming?

The Reliability of Intelligence Tests

1　　Suppose, for example, that our aim was to test athletic rather than intellectual ability. We appoint a committee consisting of Walter Camp, Percy Haughton, Tex Rickard, and Bernard Darwin; and we tell them to work out tests which will take no longer than an hour and can be given to large numbers of men at once. These tests are to measure the true athletic capacity of all men anywhere for the whole of their athletic careers. The order would be a large one, but it would certainly be no larger than the pretensions of many well-known intelligence testers.

2　　　Our committee of athletic testers scratch their heads. What shall be the hour's test, they wonder, which will "measure" the athletic "capacity" of

Dempsey, Tilden, Sweetser, Siki, Suzanne Lenglen, and Babe Ruth; of all sprinters, Marathon runners, broad jumpers, high divers, wrestlers, billiard players, marksmen, cricketers, and pogo bouncers? The committee has courage. After much guessing and some experimenting, the committee works out a sort of condensed Olympic games which can be held in any empty lot. These games consist of a short sprint, one or two jumps, throwing a ball at a bull's eye, hitting a punching machine, tackling a dummy, and a short game of clock golf. They try out these tests on a mixed assortment of champions and duffers and find that on the whole the champions do all the tests better than the duffers. They score the result and compute statistically what is the average score for all the tests. This average score then constitutes normal athletic ability.

3   Now it is clear that such tests might really give some clue to athletic ability. But the fact that in any large group of people 60 percent made an average score would be no proof that you had actually tested their athletic ability. To prove that, you would have to show that success in the athletic test correlated closely with success in athletics. The same conclusion applies to the intelligence tests. Their statistical uniformity is one thing; their reliability another. The tests might be a fair guess at intelligence, but the statistical result does not show whether they are or not. You could get a statistical curve very much like the curve of "intelligence" distribution if, instead of giving each child from ten to thirty problems to do, you had flipped a coin the same number of times for each child and had credited him with the heads. I do not mean, of course, that the results are as chancy as all that. They are not, as we shall soon see. But I do mean that there is no evidence for the reliability of the tests as tests of intelligence in the claim, made by Terman,[1] that the distribution of intelligence quotients corresponds closely to "the theoretical normal curve of distribution (the Gaussian curve)." He would, in a large enough number of cases, get an even more perfect curve if these tests were tests not of intelligence but of the flip of a coin.

4   Such a statistical check has its uses of course. It tends to show, for example, that in a large group, the bias and errors of the tester have been canceled out. It tends to show that the gross result is reached in the mass by statistically impartial methods, however wrong the judgment about any particular child may be. But the fairness in giving the tests and the reliability of the tests themselves must not be confused. The tests may be quite fair applied in the mass, and yet be poor tests of individual intelligence.

5   We come then to the question of the reliability of the tests. There are many different systems of intelligence testing and, therefore, it is important

---

[1] *Stanford Revision of Binet-Simon Scale,* p. 42.

to find out how the results agree if the same group of people take a number of different tests. The figures given by Yoakum and Yerkes[2] indicate that people who do well or badly in one are likely to do more or less equally well or badly in the other tests. Thus the army test for English-speaking literates, known as Alpha, correlates with Beta, the test for non-English speakers or illiterates at .80. Alpha with a composite test of Alpha, Beta, and Stanford-Binet gives .94. Alpha, with Trabue B and C completion-tests, combined gives .72. On the other hand, as we noted in the first article of this series, the Stanford-Binet system of calculating "mental ages" is in violent disagreement with the results obtained by the army tests.

6   Nevertheless, in a rough way the evidence shows that the various tests in the mass are testing the same capacities. Whether these capacities can fairly be called intelligence, however, is not yet proved. The tests are all a good deal alike. They all derive from a common stock, and it is entirely possible that they measure only a certain kind of ability. The type of mind which is very apt in solving Sunday newspaper puzzles, or even in playing chess, may be specially favored by these tests. The fact that the same people always do well with puzzles would in itself be no evidence that the solving of puzzles was a general test of intelligence. We must remember, too, that the emotional setting plays a large role in any examination. To some temperaments the atmosphere of the examination room is highly stimulating. Such people "outdo themselves" when they feel they are being tested; other people "cannot do themselves justice" under the same conditions. Now in a large group these differences of temperament may neutralize each other in the statistical result. But they do not neutralize each other in the individual case.

7   The correlation between the various systems enables us to say only that the tests are not mere chance, and that they do seem to seize upon a certain kind of ability. But whether this ability is a sign of general intelligence or not, we have no means of knowing from such evidence alone. The same conclusion holds true of the fact that when the tests are repeated at intervals on the same group of people they give much the same results. Data of this sort are as yet meager, for intelligence testing has not been practiced long enough to give results over long periods of time. Yet the fact that the same child makes much the same score year after year is significant. It permits us to believe that some genuine capacity is being tested. But whether this is the capacity to pass tests or the capacity to deal with life, which we call intelligence, we do not know.

8   This is the crucial question, and in the nature of things there can as yet be little evidence one way or another. The Stanford-Binet tests were set in

---

[2] *Army Mental Tests*, p. 20

order about the year 1914. The oldest children of the group tested at that time were 142 children ranging from fourteen to sixteen years of age. Those children are now between twenty-two and twenty-four. The returns are not it. The main question of whether the children who ranked high in the Stanford-Binet tests will rank high in real life is now unanswerable, and will remain unanswered for a generation. We are thrown back, therefore, for a test of the tests on the success of these children in school. We ask whether the results of the intelligence test correspond with the quality of school work, with school grades, and with school progress.

9   The crude figures, at first glance, show a poor correspondence. In Terman's studies,[3] the intelligence quotient correlated with school work, as judged by teachers, only .45 and with intelligence as judged by teachers, only .48. But that in itself proves nothing against the reliability of the intelligent tests. For after all the test of school marks, of promotion or the teacher's judgments, is not necessarily more reliable. There is no reason certainly for thinking that the way public school teachers classify children is any final criterion of intelligence. The teachers may be mistaken. In a definite number of cases Terman has shown that they are mistaken, especially when they judge a child's intelligence by his grade in school and not by his age. A retarded child may be doing excellent work, an advanced child poorer work. Terman has shown also that teachers make their largest mistakes in judging children who are above or below the average. The teachers become confused by the fact that the school system is graded according to age.

10   A fair reading of the evidence will, I think, convince anyone that as a *system of grading* the intelligence tests may prove superior in the end to the system now prevailing in the public schools. The intelligence test, as we noted in an earlier article, is an instrument of classification. When it comes into competition with the method of classifying that prevails in school, it exhibits many signs of superiority. If you have to classify children for the convenience of school administration, you are likely to get a more coherent classification with the tests than without them. I should like to emphasize this point especially, because it is important that in denying the larger pretensions and misunderstanding we should not lose sight of the positive value of the tests. We say, then, that none of the evidence thus far considered shows whether they are reliable tests of the capacity to deal intelligently with the problems of real life. But as gauges of the capacity to deal intelligently with the problems of the classroom, the evidence justifies us in thinking that the tests will grade the pupils more accurately than do the traditional school examinations.

---

[3] *Stanford Revision of Binet-Simon Scale,* chap. 6.

11   If school success were a reliable index of human capacity, we should be able to go a step further and say that the intelligence test is a general measure of human capacity. But of course no such claim can be made for school success, for that would be to say that the purpose of the schools is to measure capacity. It is impossible to admit this. The child's success with school work cannot be a measure of the child's success in life. On the contrary, his success in life must be a significant measure of the school's success in developing the capacities of the child. If a child fails in school and then fails in life, the school cannot sit back and say: You see how accurately I predicted this. Unless we are to admit that education is essentially impotent, we have to throw back the child's failure at the school, and describe it as a failure not by the child but by the school.

12   For this reason, the fact that the intelligence test may turn out to be an excellent administrative device for grading children in school cannot be accepted as evidence that it is a reliable test of intelligence....The whole claim of the intelligence testers to have found a reliable measure of human capacity rests on an assumption, imported into the argument, that education is essentially impotent because intelligence is hereditary and unchangeable. This belief is the ultimate foundation of the claim that the tests are not merely an instrument of classification but a true measure of intelligence. It is this belief which has been seized upon eagerly by writers like Stoddard and McDougall. It is a belief which is, I am convinced, wholly unproved, and it is this belief which is obstructing and perverting the practical development of the tests.

STUDY QUESTIONS

1. This essay begins with an evaluation based on an analogy between a test of intelligence and a hypothetical test of athletic capacity. What point is Lippmann trying to prove about intelligence tests through the use of this analogy? Is the analogy fair and persuasive?

2. On the basis of positive correlations between various intelligence tests, Lippmann concedes that they measure *something*, but he insists that we cannot know whether it is intelligence that they are measuring. What might they be measuring if not intelligence? What do you think Lippmann means by "intelligence," and what do you think he would consider an ideal means of testing it?

HOWARD GARDNER

What Is an Intelligence?

Howard Gardner is one of several contemporary developmental and cognitive psychologists who reject the notion of a single intelligence that is innate, largely constant throughout life, measurable in an hour or two by a question-and-answer test,
and reducible to a single number, the I.Q. Instead, Gardner argues for the existence
of "several *relatively autonomous* human intellectual competences," or "multiple
intelligences." While Gardner considers it impossible to compile a "single,
irrefutable, and universally accepted list" of these intelligences, he argues for the
analytic and practical utility of a classification into six: the linguistic, the musical,
the logical-mathematical, the spatial, the bodily-kinesthetic, and the personal.
Gardner's theory draws on his studies of normal children and adults, gifted children, prodigies, *idiots savants,* and brain-damaged adults. He also makes frequent
reference to those considered highly intelligent by cultures very different from ours
(for example, a twelve-year-old boy from the Caroline Islands selected by his elders
for training in navigation around the hundreds of islands within sailing range of the
Carolines). The essay, a chapter from Gardner's book *Frames of Mind,* represents
one phase of an empirical investigation: the process of determining which phenomena are included in the subject to be investigated and which excluded.

Prerequisites of an Intelligence

1   To my mind, a human intellectual competence must entail a set of skills of
problem solving—enabling the individual *to resolve genuine problems or
difficulties* that he or she encounters and, when appropriate, to create an
effective product—and must also entail the potential for *finding or
creating problems*—thereby laying the groundwork for the acquisition of
new knowledge. These prerequisites represent my effort to focus on those
intellectual strengths that prove of some importance within a cultural
context. At the same time, I recognize that the ideal of what is valued will
differ markedly, sometimes even radically, across human cultures, with the
creation of new products or posing of new questions being of relatively
little importance in some settings.

2   The prerequisites are a way of ensuring that a human intelligence must
be genuinely useful and important, at least in certain cultural settings.
This criterion alone may disqualify certain capacities that, on other
grounds, would meet the criteria that I am about to set. For instance, the
ability to recognize faces is a capacity that seems to be relatively
autonomous and to be represented in a specific area of the human nervous
system. Moreover, it exhibits its own developmental history. And yet, to my
knowledge, while severe difficulties in recognizing faces might pose
embarrassment for some individuals, this ability does not seem highly

valued by cultures. Nor are there ready opportunities for problem finding in the domain of face recognition. Acute use of sensory systems is another obvious candidate for a human intelligence. And when it comes to keen gustatory or olfactory senses, these abilities have little special value across cultures. (I concede that people more involved than I in the culinary life might disagree with this assessment!)

3   Other abilities that are certainly central in human intercourse also do not qualify. For instance, the abilities used by a scientist, a religious leader, or a politician are of great importance. Yet, because these cultural roles can (by hypothesis) be broken down into collections of particular intellectual competences, they do not themselves qualify as intelligences. From the opposite end of analysis, many skills tested for perennially by psychologists—ranging from recall of nonsense syllables to production of unusual associations—fail to qualify, for they emerge as the contrivances of an experimenter rather than as skills valued by a culture.

4   There have, of course, been many efforts to nominate and detail essential intelligences, ranging from the medieval trivium and quadrivium to the psychologist Larry Gross's list of five modes of communication (lexical, social-gestural, iconic, logico-mathematical, and musical), the philosopher Paul Hirst's list of seven forms of knowledge (mathematics, physical sciences, interpersonal understanding, religion, literature and the fine arts, morals, and philosophy). On an *a priori* basis, there is nothing wrong with these classifications; and, indeed, they may prove critical for certain purposes. The very difficulty with these lists, however, is that they are *a priori*—an effort by a reflective individual (or a culture) to devise meaningful distinctions among types of knowledge. What I am calling for here are sets of intelligences which meet certain biological and psychological specifications. In the end, the search for an empirically grounded set of faculties may fail; and then we may have to rely once more on *a priori* schemes, such as Hirst's. But the effort should be made to find a firmer foundation for our favorite faculties.

5   I do not insist that the list of intelligences presented here be exhaustive. I would be astonished if it were. Yet, at the same time, there is something awry about a list that leaves glaring and obvious gaps, or one that fails to generate the vast majority of roles and skills valued by human cultures. Thus, a prerequisite for a theory of multiple intelligences, as a whole, is that it captures a reasonably complete gamut of the kinds of abilities valued by human cultures. We must account for the skills of a shaman and a psychoanalyst as well as of a yogi and a saint.

Criteria of an Intelligence

6   So much, then, for the prerequisites of this undertaking and onward to criteria, or "signs." Here, I outline those considerations that have weighed

most heavily in the present effort, those desiderata on which I have come to rely in an effort to nominate a set of intelligences which seems general and genuinely useful. The very use of the word *signs* signals that this undertaking must be provisional: I do not include something merely because it exhibits one or two of the signs, nor do I exclude a candidate intelligence just because it fails to qualify on each and every account. Rather, the effort is to sample as widely as possible among the various criteria and to include within the ranks of the chosen intelligences those candidates that fare the best. Following the suggestive model of the computer scientist Oliver Selfridge, we might think of these signs as a group of demons, each of which will holler when an intelligence resonates with that demon's "demand characteristics." When enough demons holler, an intelligence is included; when enough of them withhold approbation, the intelligence is, if regrettably, banished from consideration.

7   Ultimately, it would certainly be desirable to have an algorithm for the selection of an intelligence, such that any trained researcher could determine whether a candidate intelligence met the appropriate criteria. At present, however, it must be admitted that the selection (or rejection) of a candidate intelligence is reminiscent more of an artistic judgment than of a scientific assessment. Borrowing a concept from statistics, one might think of the procedure as a kind of "subjective" factor analysis. Where my procedure does take a scientific turn is in the making public of the grounds for the judgment, so that other investigators can review the evidence and draw their own conclusions.

8   Here then, in unordered fashion, are the eight "signs" of an intelligence:

Potential Isolation by Brain Damage

9   To the extent that a particular faculty can be destroyed, or *spared* in isolation, as a result of brain damage, its relative autonomy from other human faculties seems likely. In what follows I rely to a considerable degree on evidence from neuropsychology and, in particular, on that highly revealing experiment in nature—a lesion to a specific area of the brain. The consequences of such brain injury may well constitute the single most instructive line of evidence regarding those distinctive abilities or computations that lie at the core of a human intelligence.

The Existence of Idiots Savants, Prodigies, and Other Exceptional Individuals

10   Second only to brain damage in its persuasiveness is the discovery of an individual who exhibits a highly uneven profile of abilities and deficits. In the case of the prodigy, we encounter an individual who is extremely precocious in one (or, occasionally, more than one) area of human competence. In the case of the *idiot savant* (and other retarded or

exceptional individuals, including autistic children), we behold the unique sparing of one particular human ability against a background of mediocre or highly retarded human performances in other domains. Once again, the existence of these populations allows us to observe the human intelligence in relative—even splendid—isolation. To the extent that the condition of the prodigy or the *idiot savant* can be linked to genetic factors, or (through various kinds of non-invasive investigative methods) to specific neural regions, the claim upon a specific intelligence is enhanced. At the same time, the selective absence of an intellectual skill—as may characterize autistic children or youngsters with learning disabilities—provides a confirmation-by-negation of a certain intelligence.

An Identifiable Core Operation or Set of Operations

11 Central to my notion of an intelligence is the existence of *one or more* basic information-processing operations or mechanisms, which can deal with specific kinds of input. One might go so far as to define a human intelligence as a neural mechanism or computational system which is genetically programmed to be activated or "triggered" by certain kinds of internally or externally presented information. Examples would include sensitivity to pitch relations as one core of musical intelligence, or the ability to imitate movement by others as one core of bodily intelligence.

12 Given this definition, it becomes crucial to be able to identify these core operations, to locate their neural substrate, and to prove that these "cores" are indeed separate. Simulation on a computer is one promising way of establishing that a core operation exists and can in fact give rise to various intellectual performances. Identification of core operations is at this point still largely a matter of guesswork, but it is no less important on that account. Correlatively, resistance to the detection of core operations is a clue that something is amiss: one may be encountering an amalgam which calls for decomposition in terms of its own constituent intelligences.

A Distinctive Developmental History, Along with a Definable Set of Expert "End-State" Performances

13 An intelligence should have an identifiable developmental history, through which normal as well as gifted individuals pass in the course of ontogeny. To be sure, the intelligence will not develop in isolation, except in an unusual person; and so it becomes necessary to focus on those roles or situations where the intelligence occupies a central place. In addition, it should prove possible to identify disparate levels of expertise in the development of an intelligence, ranging from the universal beginnings through which every novice passes, to exceedingly high levels of competence, which may be visible only in individuals with unusual talent and/or special forms of training. There may well be distinct critical periods

in the developmental history, as well as identifiable milestones, linked either to training or to physical maturation. Identification of the developmental history of the intelligence, and analysis of its susceptibility to modification and training, is of the highest import for educational practitioners.

An Evolutionary History and Evolutionary Plausibility

14   All species display areas of intelligence (and ignorance), and human beings are no exception. The roots of our current intelligences reach back millions of years in the history of the species. A specific intelligence becomes more plausible to the extent that one can locate its evolutionary antecedents, including capacities (like bird song or primate social organization) that are shared with other organisms; one must also be on the lookout for specific computational abilities which appear to operate in isolation in other species but have become yoked with one another in human beings. (For example, discrete aspects of musical intelligence may well appear in several species but are only joined in human beings.) Periods of rapid growth in human prehistory, mutations that may have conferred special advantages upon a given population, as well as evolutionary paths that did not flourish, are all grist for a student of multiple intelligences. Yet it must be stressed that this is an area where sheer speculation is especially tempting, and firm facts especially elusive.

Support from Experimental Psychological Tasks

15   Many paradigms favored in experimental psychology illuminate the operation of candidate intelligences. Using the methods of the cognitive psychologist, one can, for example, study details of linguistic or spatial processing with exemplary specificity. The relative autonomy of an intelligence can also be investigated. Especially suggestive are studies of tasks that interfere (or fail to interfere) with one another, tasks that transfer (and those that do not) across different contexts, and the identification of forms of memory, attention, or perception that may be peculiar to one kind of input. Such experimental tests can provide convincing support for the claim that particular abilities are (or are not) manifestations of the same intelligences. To the extent that various specific computational mechanisms—or procedural systems—work together smoothly, experimental psychology can also help demonstrate the ways in which modular or domain-specific abilities may interact in the execution of complex tasks.

Support from Psychometric Findings

16   Outcomes of psychological experiments provide one source of information relevant to intelligences; the outcomes of standard tests (like I.Q. tests)

provide another clue. While the tradition of intelligence testing has not emerged as the hero of my earlier discussion, it is clearly relevant to my pursuit here. To the extent that the tasks that purportedly assess one intelligence correlate highly with one another, and less highly with those that purportedly assess other intelligences, my formulation enhances its credibility. To the extent that psychometric results prove unfriendly to my proposed constellation of intelligences, there is cause for concern. It must be noted, however, that intelligence tests do not always test what they are claimed to test. Thus many tasks actually involve the use of more than their targeted ability, while many other tasks can be solved using a variety of means (for example, certain analogies or matrices may be completed by exploiting linguistic, logical, and/or spatial capacities). Also, the stress on paper-and-pencil methods often precludes the proper test of certain abilities, especially those involving active manipulation of the environment or interaction with other individuals. Hence, interpretation of psychometric findings is not always a straightforward matter.

Susceptibility to Encoding in a Symbol System

17   Much of human representation and communication of knowledge takes place via symbol systems—culturally contrived systems of meaning which capture important forms of information. Language, picturing, mathematics are but three of the symbol systems that have become important the world over for human survival and human productivity. In my view, one of the features that makes a raw computational capacity useful (and exploitable) by human beings is its susceptibility to marshaling by a cultural symbol system. Viewed from an opposite perspective, symbol systems may have evolved *just in those cases* where there exists a computational capacity ripe for harnessing by the culture. While it may be possible for an intelligence to proceed without its own special symbol system, or without some other culturally devised arena, a primary characteristic of human intelligence may well be its "natural" gravitation toward embodiment in a symbolic system.

18   These, then, are criteria by which a candidate intelligence can be judged....It is germane here to remark on certain considerations that might cause one to rule out an otherwise plausible candidate intelligence.

Delimiting the Concept of an Intelligence

19   One group of candidate intelligences includes those that are dictated by common parlance. It may seem, for example, that the *capacity to process auditory sequences* is a strong candidate for an intelligence; indeed, many experimentalists and psychometrians have nominated this capacity.

However, studies of the effects of brain damage have repeatedly documented that musical and linguistic strings are processed in different ways and can be compromised by different lesions. Thus, despite the surface appeal of such a skill, it seems preferable not to regard it as a separate intelligence. Other abilities frequently commented upon in specific individuals—for example, remarkable common sense or intuition—might seem to exhibit such signs as "prodigiousness." In this case, however, the categorization seems insufficiently examined. More careful analysis reveals discrete forms of intuition, common sense, or shrewdness in various intellectual domains, intuition in social matters predicts little about intuition in the mechanical or musical realm. Again, a superficially appealing candidate does not qualify.

20   It is, of course, possible that our list of intelligences is adequate as a baseline of core intellectual abilities, but that certain more general abilities may override, or otherwise regulate, the core intelligences. Among candidates that have frequently been mentioned are a "sense of self," which derives from one's peculiar blend of intelligences; an "executive capacity," which deploys specific intelligences for specific ends; and a synthesizing ability, which draws together conclusions residing in several specific intellectual domains. Beyond challenge, these are important phenomena, which demand to be considered, if not explained. Such discussion, however, is a task best left until later....

21   On the other hand, the question of how specific intelligences come to be linked, supplemented, or balanced to carry out more complex, culturally relevant tasks, is one of the utmost importance....

22   Once one has set forth the criteria or signs most crucial for the identification of an intelligence, it is important to state as well what intelligences are *not*. To begin with, intelligences are not equivalent to sensory systems. In no case is an intelligence completely dependent upon a single sensory system, nor has any sensory system been immortalized as an intelligence. The intelligences are by their very nature capable of realization (at least, in part) through more than one sensory system.

23   Intelligences should be thought of as entities at a certain level of generality, broader than highly specific computational mechanisms (like line detection) while narrower than the most general capacities, like analysis, synthesis, or a sense of self (if any of these can be shown to exist apart from combinations of specific intelligences). Yet it is in the very nature of intelligences that each operates according to its own procedures and has its own biological bases. It is thus a mistake to try to compare intelligences on all particulars; each must be thought of as its own system with its own rules. Here a biological analogy may be useful. Even though the eye, the heart, and the kidneys are all bodily organs, it is a mistake to

try to compare these organs in every particular: the same restraint should be observed in the case of intelligences.

24   Intelligences are not to be thought of in evaluative terms. While the word *intelligence* has in our culture a positive connotation, there is no reason to think that an intelligence must necessarily be put to good purposes. In fact, one can use one's logical-mathematical, linguistic, or personal intelligences for highly nefarious purposes.

25   Intelligences are best thought of apart from particular programs of action. Of course, intelligences are most readily observed when they are being exploited to carry out one or another program of action. Yet the possession of an intelligence is most accurately thought of as *a potential:* an individual in possession of an intelligence can be said to have no circumstance that prevents him from using that intelligence....

26   In the study of skills and abilities, it is customary to honor a distinction between *know-how* (tacit knowledge of how to execute something) and *know-that* (propositional knowledge about the actual set of procedures involved in execution). Thus, many of us know how to ride a bicycle but lack the propositional knowledge of how that behavior is carried out. In contrast, many of us have propositional knowledge about how to make a soufflé without knowing how to carry this task through to successful completion. While I hesitate to glorify this rough-and-ready distinction, it is helpful to think of the various intelligences chiefly as *sets of know-how*—procedures for doing things. In fact, a concern with propositional knowledge about intelligences seems to be a particular option followed in some cultures, while of little or no interest in many others.

Conclusion

27   ...There is a universal human temptation to give credence to a word to which we have become attached, perhaps because it has helped us to understand a situation better. As noted at the beginning of this book, *intelligence* is such a word; we use it so often that we have come to believe in its existence, as a genuine tangible, measurable entity, rather than as a convenient way of labeling some phenomena that may (but may well not) exist.

28   This risk of reification is grave in a work of exposition, especially in one that attempts to introduce novel scientific concepts. I, and sympathetic readers, will be likely to think—and to fall into the habit of saying—that we here behold the "linguistic intelligence," the "interpersonal intelligence," or the "spatial intelligence" at work, and that's that. But it's not. These intelligences are fictions—at most, useful fictions—for discussing processes and abilities that (like all of life) are continuous with

one another; Nature brooks no sharp discontinuities of the sort proposed here. Our intelligences are being separately defined and described strictly in order to illuminate scientific issues and to tackle pressing practical problems. It is permissible to lapse into the sin of reifying *so long as we remain aware that this is what we are doing.* And so....I must repeat that they exist not as physically verifiable entities but only as potentially useful scientific constructs.

STUDY QUESTIONS

1. In paragraph 4, Gardner expresses his desire to discover "empirically grounded" rather than "a priori" sets of faculties that meet the prerequisites of an intelligence. What does this distinction mean, and what kinds of empirical evidence favor Gardner's categories?
2. Does Garner believe that an intelligence can be trained?
3. This selection presents a definition of "an intelligence." Is this definition purely arbitrary, or can it somehow be defended as more scientific than the definition implied by the work of Binet and other psychologists who followed his line of investigation?
4. How might educational policies based on Gardner's theory of intelligence differ from those based on Binet's?
5. Pick two or three of Gardner's criteria of an intelligence and explain why they are appropriate to this theory as a whole. How would the process of selecting from among candidate intelligences be altered if the criteria you consider were excluded?

SUGGESTION FOR WRITING

We have all heard stories of exceptionally talented college athletes who performed academic tasks very poorly and who are therefore written off as "dumb." Make a case for the intelligence of a standout athlete based simply on the competencies necessary for his or her sport. Do you agree with Gardner that bodily-kinesthetic competency should be classed as an "intelligence?"

DAVID OWEN

The Last Days of ETS

The Scholastic Aptitude Test administered by the Educational Testing Service is a rite of passage for many college-bound Americans. While it is not called an "intelligence" test, it was originally developed from the army Alpha test and, like intelligence tests, claims to make valid predictions about the subject's "aptitude" for college work on the basis of a two-hour multiple-choice test. Owen's article provides a close look at sample items from the SAT in order to enquire whether responses to these items constitute reasonable evidence for predictions of the students' college performance, and if so, whether they are the best, fairest, and most efficiently gathered evidence.

I. Brigadoon

1   Tennis courts, a swimming pool, a baseball diamond, a private hotel, 400 acres of woods and rolling hills, cavorting deer, a resident flock of Canadian geese—I'm loving every minute here at the Educational Testing Service, the great untaxed, unregulated, unblinking eye of the American meritocracy.

2   ETS is best known as the Princeton, New Jersey, manufacturer of the Scholastic Aptitude Test, the two-and-a-half-hour multiple-choice examination that helps determine where (or whether) more than a million young Americans will go to college every year. ETS is also responsible for, among other things, the Graduate Record Examinations (for graduate school candidates), the Graduate Management Admission Test (for business school candidates), and part of the Law School Admission Test (for future attorneys, many of whom will later take ETS-written bar exams). But let's not talk about tests for a moment.

3   Just now I'm stretched out in ETS's co-ed sauna, dabbing my beaded forehead with a hankie. Less than an hour ago, as the sun was sinking in the west, I stood beside the skating pond and watched a pair of distant riders cross a snowy field on horseback. In the early 1970s ETS had plans to build a golf course here. During an hour of tramping around I managed to find neither it nor the Laurie Chauncey Nature Path, a meandering forest byway that, according to an ETS brochure, "provides an idyllic setting for a quiet stroll or conversation." The late Laurie Chauncey (beloved wife of Henry, ETS's first president and abiding institutional deity) is immortalized not only in the sylvan jogging trail that bears her name but also in Laurie House. This is an enlarged and lavishly renovated nineteenth-century dwelling that served as the Stoney Brook Hunt Club during much of the Great Depression and as the Chauncey family

residence from 1955 to 1970. Today Laurie House is part of the Henry Chauncey Conference Center, a 100-room, $100-a-night convention facility whose pillowcases, bath towels, and shoeshine mitts are emblazoned with ETS insignia, and whose rooms are decorated with artwork of the signed-and-numbered variety. Guests at the conference center are invited to enjoy both "a variety of potables" and "a proud selection of comestibles," the splendor of the latter being "limited only by a client's imagination."

4   Historically and in spirit, ETS is a product of the American Century (circa 1945–1973). When returning soldiers besieged American campuses at the end of World War II, the College Entrance Examination Board, an institution that had been quietly administering an admissions test for a few selective colleges, found itself with more testing traffic than it could handle. In 1947 it got together with the American Council on Education and the Carnegie Foundation for the Advancement of Teaching and created the nonprofit Educational Testing Service to take care of the new demand.

5   In the beginning ETS was a nickel-and-dime operation that did little more than administer the College Board's Scholastic Aptitude Test, which in 1948 was taken by 75,000 students. But ETS grew quickly, soon dwarfing the College Board. (Today many ETS people refer to the board as though it were some mildly retarded younger brother only reluctantly included in big-boy games.) By 1954 ETS had outgrown its tiny Princeton headquarters and become wealthy enough to move to bigger digs. The change of address was prompted by a Christmas gift from Laurie Chauncey to her husband. "The gift was a $1.25 knapsack to carry the lunch they often took with them on hikes," says an ETS brochure published in 1977. "The Chaunceys, who then lived on the other side of Stoney Brook, crossed the stream the following Sunday — 'a bleak, raw December day' — and coming through the woods, discovered the open farmland area where ETS buildings now stand." Ah, Brigadoon. Chauncey persuaded ETS to buy the entire 400-acre spread and to plant him and his family, free of charge, in the house that stood on it.

6   In the innocence of youth, a No. 2 pencil trembling in my fingers, I pictured the Educational Testing Service not as the passable vacation spot it is but as a dusty, cramped, and spinster-staffed department of Princeton University. In truth, ETS owes Princeton only the scholarly heft of its return address, which itself is a mere postal courtesy: ETS's rustic headquarters actually lie in Lawrenceville, not in Princeton. Nor are the company's employees the crotchety old maids I once imagined; they're smooth-talking ministers of mental measurement, people who more than once have taken solemn pleasure in describing their company as "the nation's gatekeeper."

7   The business of deciding who goes where in American society is so vast and various that during peak grading season ETS's "scanners," the machines that score answer sheets at the rate of 200 a minute, are never turned off. Day after day, night after night, ETS's computers process and consume an unceasing stream of information, giving the company one of the largest compilations of private data about individuals in the world. "Maybe only the CIA," an ETS memorandum once asserted with pride, "has greater and better capacities."

8   The Central Intelligence Agency may have greater capacities, but even that resourceful institution knows when it needs outside help. The CIA buys ETS tests. So do the Defense Department, the National Security Council, the government of Trinidad and Tobago, the Institute for Nuclear Power Operations, the National Contact Lens Examiners, the International Council for Shopping Centers, the American Society of Heating, Refrigerating and Air-Conditioning Engineers, the Commission on Graduates of Foreign Nursing Schools, the Malaysian Ministry of Education, the National Board of Podiatry Examiners, and the Institute for the Advancement of Philosophy for Children.

9   You can't become a golf pro without passing an ETS exam (sample item: "The distance from the center line of a shaft hole to the farthest front portion of the face is the (A) hosel offset (B) loft (C) lie (D) face progression (E) length"*). In at least some parts of the country you also can't become a real-estate salesman, a certified moving consultant, a certified auto mechanic, a merchant marine officer (the same holds true in Liberia), a fireman, a travel agent ("with the ultimate expectation of improving public confidence in the travel industry," according to ETS), a certified business-form consultant, or, in Pennsylvania, a beautician or a barber.

10   Old-fashioned thinkers may wonder whether a multiple-choice test is really a better measure of barbering skills than a haircut is, or what great social cost would be exacted if a few untutored individuals were suffered to trim the sideburns of Pennsylvanians. But no such befuddlement hampers executives at ETS. A COPA promotional pamphlet makes prominent mention of the barber exam, and also tests for, among others, office managers, architects, social workers, and gynecologists.

11   ETS had revenues of $115 million in 1981. As a "nonprofit" institution, ETS does not make profits as such. But these revenues support a very comfortable life and generous salaries for ETS's 2,200 employees. They also support research studies to further the cause of testing.

12   Just about half of ETS's annual revenues come from the SAT and related college admissions tests conducted for the College Board. Every

---

* Answer: (D).

penny of that sum, $55 million in 1981, as well as much of the College Board's revenues, came from students who paid to take the test. Most of the rest of ETS's budget also came from people required to pay for the privilege of submitting to ETS exams in order to pass various checkpoints in America's social hierarchy.

13   ETS is a monopoly, probably the most powerful unregulated monopoly in America. People who wish to advance in almost all walks of life have no choice but to pay its fees and take its exams. Corporations and institutions with far less power have had to submit, in the public interest, to government regulation over the last half century, but ETS has managed to resist, flourish, and spread into markets where none but the brave would have imagined a need.

14   What started as a small organization performing a narrow service has taken on a life of its own. Although ETS does not hire its own executives on the basis of test scores, its guiding philosophy is that people's selection of comestibles on the buffet of life should be governed by a series of multiple-choice exams. In evangelizing its tests, ETS may merely be following the institutional imperative of survival and growth. But at the same time, it is promoting the notion that human superiority and inferiority can and should be measured scientifically and rewarded accordingly.

15   ETS has big plans for the future. Its researchers are working on a computerized version of the SAT that will take only a few minutes to administer. "We have the technology virtually ready to go," an ETS executive told College Board members at a conference last fall. "We expect we're going to be getting rapidly out of the paper transfer business." ETS president George Anrig is looking forward to a day when Americans will be able to take ETS tests on their television sets. Other people at ETS are working on computerized teaching programs that will make the testing company a powerful presence in schools, enabling it both to teach what it tests and to test what it teaches. Still others are tinkering with scoring systems that will replace numbers with "narrative," providing test-takers with computer-written paragraphs detailing all there is to know about their "aptitude." The day is coming, the company hopes, when you'll scarcely be able to get out of bed without some ETS statistician offering his considered opinion as to whether you've really got what it takes.

16   On the other hand, perhaps not. In fact, we may be seeing the beginning of the end of the Educational Testing Service. After several decades of steady growth in tax-free revenues, ETS suffered its first small deficit in fiscal 1980. The company more than made up for the shortfall in 1981, but that brief encounter with red ink put the fear of the almighty dollar in ETS executives. The company substantially reduced its research staff in a series of large-scale firings. As recently as two or three years ago,

ETS executives were known to grow pale if unthinking workers described their employer as a "company" instead of an "institution." But in 1982, President Anrig inaugurated his term of office by commissioning a $500,000 "strategic plan" from Booz, Allen & Hamilton, Inc., a New York-based management consulting firm. In connection with the study, Anrig divided key ETS personnel into a dozen "revenue growth teams" charged with identifying new opportunities for short-term profits. Anrig also issued a confidential "corporate plan" calling for, among other things, "corporate intelligence gathering, external relations, and government relations focused to provide a positive climate and receptive clients for ETS marketing initiatives."

17   The hard times at ETS aren't just economic. In recent years the company has endured its first sustained public criticism in areas it had come to believe were sacrosanct: the quality, meaning, and use of its tests. Vocal critics of standardized testing have been around for years, arguing that tests like the SAT measure little more than absorption of white upper-middle-class culture and penalize both the economically disadvantaged and the unusually bright. But the new onslaught caught ETS by surprise. In the late 1960s, researchers at the University of Michigan discovered a blood test that appeared to be better than the SAT at predicting which students would ultimately graduate from school. The Federal Trade Commission released a report taking issue with ETS's long-standing claim that the SAT could not be coached. A group funded by Ralph Nader published a 500-plus–page report accusing ETS of misrepresenting its tests.

18   Several ETS employees I spoke with told me they resented the tendency of people like Nader to compare ETS to the CIA. But readers with above-average verbal aptitude will remember that the CIA comparison I quoted several paragraphs ago originated not with a detractor but with ETS itself. In fact, ETS has always cultivated its image as an organization whose ways passeth all understanding and whose methodology is not only above reproach but also exempt from public scrutiny. In 1979 it published a pamphlet called "The War on Testing," in which criticism of standardized tests was referred to as "an attack on truth itself."

19   Because this aura of mystery is so important to ETS, the greatest blow came in 1979, when New York State passed a "truth-in-testing" law. This law required, among other things, that ETS make test questions and graded answer-sheets available to the students who take its tests. Until 1980, when the law went into effect, no one besides ETS could check whether the scores that could determine people's places in life had even been added up correctly, let alone whether the questions were faulty. ETS has since admitted under challenge that several of its "right" answers have, in fact, been wrong.

20   When ETS cites "scientific studies" supporting its side of various controversies, it is almost always referring to research performed by people in its own employ. Until 1980, nobody besides ETS could assess the value of the tests for their ostensible purposes, since nobody but ETS could see them except while actually taking them. To make outside assessment possible, the New York truth-in-testing law also required ETS to publish information about the "validity" of its exams, and about the correlation between test scores and family background, income, race, and other factors.

21   While the bill was being considered, ETS and the College Board pelted college presidents, high school principals, headmasters, and legislators with letters, mailgrams, and phone calls warning of dire results that would ensue if the New York legislature had its way. Their most serious charge was that disclosing SAT tests would lead to huge increases in test fees and sharp reductions in the number of times tests could be given, since ETS would no longer to able to reuse test questions. ETS itself, though, had compiled the figures that refute this claim: a 1972 study had shown that less than 5 percent of student fees go into the writing of tests and that few questions were ever reused. In a memorandum labeled URGENT and dated May 11, 1979, the College Board also alleged that "the bill encroaches on institutional autonomy by requiring testing agencies to disclose confidential information, such as validity information, which is *the property of the colleges and universities.*" (My emphasis.) This is a curious claim, since ETS's "validity" studies are paid for entirely out of students' fees and provided free of charge, along with reams of other information, to colleges and universities that want them. If ETS's "validity" information is the property of anyone, it is the property of the students who pay for it.

22   Having predicted the collapse of civilization if the truth-in-testing law passed, ETS did not, in the event, collapse itself. In fact, it adapted easily. Test fees in New York are only fifty cents higher than in other states and test schedules were not dramatically changed.

23   Smiling ETS executives today claim that the furious response to the truth-in-testing law was the work of a few excitable individuals and not representative of the company as a whole. This argument is not persuasive to anyone who has sifted through the reams of official documents ETS and the College Board churned out while the bill was being considered. In fact, ETS *still* hands out a pamphlet, published in 1981 (a year after the bill went into effect), that purports to tell "The Truth about Truth-in-Testing." The pamphlet, which is printed in the form of a multiple-choice test, points out, among other things, that less than 2 percent "of students identifying themselves as black, Mexican-American or Puerto Rican have requested copies of their SAT questions and answers," a statistic perhaps not entirely unrelated to the fact that ETS charges $6.50 for every such report. For the

final question in the brochure—"Should other states considering legislation similar to the New York Sate testing law approve it?"—ETS offers only one possible response: "(A) The only reasonable answer is 'no.'"

24   ETS has responded to every challenge to its mission and methods the same way it responded to truth-in-testing. This response takes the form of a series of contradictory assertions, known to lawyers as "arguing in the alternative." A man is accused of borrowing and breaking his neighbor's kettle. His lawyer argues in his defense: 1) he didn't take the kettle; 2) it was already broken when he took it; 3) he returned it in perfect condition. Whatever the issue, ETS argues: 1) it has done nothing wrong; 2) it has fixed the problem; 3) nothing has changed. Truth-in-testing makes this elusive stance increasingly hard to maintain.

25   It would be impolitic for ETS, as a semipublic institution, to refuse all outside scrutiny, but it is extremely cautious about outsiders. I was accompanied on all my interviews in Lawrenceville by at least one emissary from the company's bustling Information Division, who generally took copious notes. Employees of the Information Division do not hesitate to inject themselves into conversations if they perceive that the actual interviewee is being insufficiently ingenious in his defense of his employer. After a while I almost expected passing secretaries to come sailing through open doorways, thrusting sheaves of paper at me and saying, "What he *really* means is…" When I interviewed President Anrig, I was preceded by a bundle of my previous articles, which someone in Information had dutifully dug up. Anrig had also requested a list of the questions I intended to ask him. I replied that ETS doesn't hand out its questions ahead of time, and neither do I.

II. None of the Above

26   The oldest controversy involving ETS concerns the validity of multiple-choice tests. Without such tests, which can be graded and scored by machines, assessing the abilities of millions of people every year would be impossible, and ETS would go out of business. More important, widespread acceptance of testing depends on the perception that it is scientifically neutral and objective, which only a test with "right" and "wrong" answers can be.

27   In the early 1950s, ETS was criticized in educational circles for presuming to assess writing skills with a multiple-choice "achievement" exam called (then as now) the English Composition Test. Still at its peak of institutional self-confidence, ETS set out to silence the critics by demonstrating that a multiple-choice test is actually a better measure of essay-writing ability than writing an essay is. Together with the College Board, ETS designed a three-year experiment to compare the ECT with

both an all-essay achievement exam (called the General Composition Test) and the verbal portion of the SAT. These three tests were judged against general essay writing ability as measured over a year or more by actual teachers of the students taking the tests.

28   Now, ETS has long held that teachers' opinions are deceiving, since they are highly subjective and reflect all sorts of unconscious prejudices and expectations. This, indeed, is the justification for giving Scholastic Aptitude Tests. But faced with the need to measure the validity of its tests against *something*, ETS had nowhere else to turn.

29   In 1957, when ETS tallied the results of its experiment, the all-essay GCT, as ETS had predicted, came in last. The two multiple-choice tests, the verbal SAT and the ECT, came in first and second, respectively. ETS and the College Board announced the findings triumphantly, and proceeded as before.

30   But there was something very odd about these results, as Banesh Hoffmann, a distinguished mathematician, pointed out a few years later in a wonderful book called *The Tyranny of Testing*. If the experiment proved to ETS's satisfaction that its multiple-choice English Composition Test was better than an essay test, it also proved that the verbal part of the SAT was a better test of English composition ability than the ECT. Yet ETS continued to administer the ECT (to customers who'd already paid to take the SAT), perhaps realizing that if necessary an experiment could be devised to demonstrate the superiority of the ECT. ETS is singularly adept at proving the excellence of whatever test it happens to be peddling at the moment, even if these proofs perforce contradict one another.

31   In later years, ETS retreated to the position that multiple-choice tests are only *just as good* as essay tests, and it offered new experimental results to prove this thesis. In a 1980 article about standardized testing in the *Atlantic Monthly*, James Fallows wrote: "Hunter Breland, an ETS research psychologist, explained that to get statistically reliable results from an essay exam, students had to write five separate essays, with five readers each. 'We found we could do as well with fifty multiple choice questions in a thirty-minute test,' Breland said. '*We got the same people in the same order.*'" (My emphasis.)

32   The same people in the same order? This must be a typical ETS exaggeration. After all, ETS calculates that one SAT-taker in three will score more than thirty-three points higher or lower than his hypothetical "true score." Not even two administrations of the SAT would produce "the same people in the same order." Hunter Breland, it seems, was trying to make his argument sound stronger than it was.

33   But let's ignore this point and address Breland's major assertion, which is that a statistically reliable essay exam requires five separate essays, each of them evaluated by five graders.

34   Strange to report, ETS has been giving essay exams for years. Back in the 1960s, the company bowed to continued criticism from educators and began offering students the option of writing an essay as part of the English Composition Test. The essay was not graded, because ETS had proved that a grade on a single writing sample was not reliable. Student compositions were merely passed along to college admissions officers, who apparently could be trusted to submit them to five separate readers before passing judgment.

35   But the critics were not appeased, and ETS was eventually forced to take the next step down this fatal road. In 1977, it began to offer, once a year, an optional version of the ECT with one graded twenty-minute essay question in place of some of the usual multiple-choice items. Both versions of the test last an hour overall, and scores on both are reported as single numerical grades on ETS's familiar 600-point scale. On tests with an essay, the essay counts for one third of the score.

36   The single ECT essay is graded not by the five readers Breland calls for, but by two. "Readers are instructed to read essays quickly," a College Board publication explains, "and to score immediately while the impression the total essay creates remains fresh." Time is money in the testing business. ETS refers to this grading system as "holistic." It instructs graders to read each essay only once and not to be overly concerned with spelling, punctuation, or grammar. "The first thing we tell our readers," an ETS executive told me, "is that this is not creative writing. We don't expect a brilliant political essay." Each reader assigns a grade of 1, 2, 3, or 4. The two readers' scores are then added together to produce a final range of 2–8, which, when multiplied by 100, provides a no-frills approximation of the standard ETS scale.

37   Contrary to what you may believe, ETS essay tests are not graded by Irving Howe, Northrop Frye, and whatever other distinguished scholars happen to be passing through New Jersey at scoring time. In fact, ECTs are graded by the sort of high school English teachers and low-level college instructors who can be tempted away from Shakespeare and Milton by the prospect of spending five days in a gymnasium reading 1,500 or so one-page adolescent responses to a single question in return for $310. Periodic calibrating sessions are held in which all the graders read sample answers and indicate their grades with a show of hands. This continues until everyone's back on the same wavelength.

38   Let's take a holistic look at a College Board booklet called "The English Composition Test with Essay," which contains the essay assignment from the 1978 exam, along with some responses. The 1978 assignment was to discuss the quotation "We have met the enemy and he is us." ("What does this quotation imply about human beings? Do you agree or disagree with its implications?") The first sample essay, which the booklet describes as "a well-written response taking a psychological approach," begins: "The

quotation I am to discuss implies a dual nature for human beings, both at the individual and at the collective level." A bit thick, that, when you consider that the quotation under discussion was originally uttered by a talking possum in a cartoon strip about the animal inhabitants of a swamp. On the other hand, the student has clearly demonstrated a thorough knowledge of how to sucker a high school English teacher.

39   Is the ECT with essay a better measure of writing skills than the ECT without? This is a thorny question, since giving a definite answer would require throwing out one or the other version. If one test is better, why give the other? If the tests are the same, why give both? In an exercise that is supposed to rank people scientifically on a scale from 200 to 800, how can you offer a choice of tests? But throwing out the all-multiple-choice version would imply what ETS has always denied: that an essay test, especially a teeny one, is *better* than a multiple-choice test. On the other hand, getting rid of the essay would amount to a confession that all this "holistic grading" business is just a bunch of hooey; it would also defeat the *true* purpose of the essay, which is to pacify all those skeptics out there who don't believe you can learn very much about students' ability to write without asking them to write something.

40   So does the essay make the ECT better, worse, or what? "Essentially, we're looking at writing style, not creativity, conceptualization, and what have you," says Richard Noeth, director of ETS's Admissions and Guidance Programs. "That's different, I think—though I'm not saying better or worse—different than an item-by-item analysis of ability to recognize something in a particular sentence, or the ability to restate something in a different way, or what have you. We're looking at essentially a very holistic analysis of a student's ability in this area. So I think that's different, and I think that adds a different component to what we can assess."

41   The test was fine all along; but the essay adds something; but it makes no difference to your score.

42   Lock up the kettle, folks.

III. The Cabbage Questions

43   In contrast to messy essay tests, ETS would have you think, its multiple-choice questions and answers are designed by scientific methods so complex and so exacting that outsiders can't hope to comprehend them. In fact, ETS tests are written by ordinary people who quite possibly didn't do as well on their SATs as you did on yours. Until 1980, it was impossible for any outsider to evaluate ETS's tests, since only a few sample questions were made available. But New York's truth-in-testing law changed that.

44   The first challenge came almost immediately, when a high school student named Daniel Lowen protested ETS's scoring of the now famous "pyramid problem." The problem showed a picture of two pyramids, one

with a square base and four triangular sides, the other with a triangular base and three triangular sides. All the triangles were equilateral, and all were the same size. The question asked: "If the two pyramids were placed together face-to-face with the vertices of the equal-sized equilateral triangles coinciding, how many exposed faces would the resulting solid have?" The answer ETS wanted was seven, since the two touching faces would disappear when the pyramids were joined, leaving seven of the original nine. But Lowen realized that there would actually be only five faces left, since four of the original triangles would merge into two parallelograms. (Try it yourself if you don't believe him.) ETS admitted its mistake and raised 240,000 scores, even though few of these 240,000 could have gotten the answer "wrong" for the "right" reason. On the other hand, ETS did not *lower* any scores, apparently reasoning that students shouldn't be punished for failing to see something ETS didn't see either. Nor did ETS go back and rescore any of the earlier tests that included the same question.

45   ETS eventually took steps to tighten its question checking procedures (without, of course, admitting that it had been negligent before, or that truth-in-testing laws might be a good thing), but bad questions continue to surface. Not many, of course, since few students will bother to make the enormous effort required to challenge a question. But even a few errors tarnish ETS's claims to scientific perfection, and the impossibility of ETS's making a logically consistent response when a faulty question is found puts those claims in a nice comic light.

46   No one has ever successfully challenged an SAT verbal question. The reason is obvious: outside mathematics, ETS's "right" answer cannot be proved definitely "wrong," because the questions are inherently ambiguous, precisely what ETS must deny in defending the scientific accuracy of its tests. But a study of SAT verbal questions confirms the obvious.

47   One of the first tasks the creator of a multiple-choice test faces is how to make people miss questions whose subject matter they actually understand. This sounds silly, but it's important. One way it's done is by limiting the time allowed. (Veteran test-takers know, for instance, that the key to doing well on SAT math items lies in finding *quick* solutions; if you have to perform a complex or lengthy calculation, you've probably missed the trick.) Another way is to write questions that are misleading. Test-makers don't always do this intentionally, but they always do it, in part because it's very hard not to. Many of the verbal items ETS calls most difficult are in fact merely ambiguous, since writing a genuinely difficult multiple-choice item is much harder than writing a confusing one. This was one of Banesh Hoffmann's main points in *The Tyranny of Testing.*

48   In order to get people to miss the right answer, as of course some must if the test is to be useful, it's necessary to make another answer look equally

or more attractive. One way to do this is to make the question so hard that students have no idea what the desired response is. The drawback to this method is that if only a very few students understand the question, more will get it right for the wrong reason or through luck than for the right reason, and it won't be testing what it's supposed to test. The alternative is to make the question ambiguous. It's revealing to note, as Hoffmann points out, that in the jargon of standardized testing, "incorrect" answers are known as "distractors."

49   One of the few scientific studies of test ambiguity was performed in 1980 by Walt Haney and Laurie Scott of the Huron Institute in Cambridge, Massachusetts. Haney and Scott did something that ETS never does in checking its tests, which was to ask a group of children *why* they had chosen their answers. In one of the experimental items, for example, taken from a published Stanford Achievement Test, young children were shown a picture of a potted flower, a cabbage, and a potted cactus and asked, "Which plant needs the least amount of water?" The desired answer was the cactus, which nine of eleven children chose. But one child chose the head of cabbage, explaining that it would need water "only when you clean it." Since there was nothing in the drawing to indicate that the cabbage was growing in a garden and not sitting in a refrigerator, the child's answer was at least as rational as the desired answer, and it was arguably a good bit more intelligent, since it indicated that the child had delved further into the question than the other children had. But on an actual administration of the test, of course, his score would have been lower. That clever child will have to learn, in his test-taking career, that delving further is a fatal mistake.

50   If ETS allowed challenges to nonmathematical questions, there'd be no end to it. Only in math can the occasional Daniel Lowen be allowed to dig deeper and mess up the test results. But the principle that ambiguous questions undermine ETS's claims to be measuring something with scientific precision is the same, no matter what the topic.

51   How many cabbage questions are there on, say, a Scholastic Aptitude Test, ETS's biggest seller? ETS would say virtually none, and can haul out statistical studies to "prove" it. But the statistics only show that people who did well on the rest of the exam tended to get this question "right"—that is, to see the question the way the testmakers saw it. Indeed, this is the way ETS assures itself of the quality of all its tests. But statistics cannot spot errors of the sort Daniel Lowen found.

52   The only reliable way to evaluate the testmakers is to look at an actual test. The purpose is not to suggest that ETS discriminates against the brilliant Daniel Lowens of the world (they generally figure out how to give ETS what it wants), but to assess ETS's claims to scientific accuracy, and to ask whether what ETS tests is anything other than the ability to take ETS tests. (See box, page 437.)

TAKE THIS SIMPLE TEST

To help convince you that what ETS tests test is the ability to take ETS tests, I've composed a short Scholastic Aptitude Test Aptitude Test (SATAT). The five items below are taken from a reading-comprehension portion of an actual SAT. In answering them, reach back in your mind to the days when you took your own SATs and then look for the kinds of answers that you think would appeal to a test writer at ETS.

Oh, yes: I've left out the reading passage that the items refer to. I've also mixed up the order of the items and eliminated all references to the actual novelist and books the reading passage discusses. You need to know only that the novelist, though dead, has a name you would recognize, and that "the author" referred to in several of the items is the author of the reading passage, not the author of the novels.

So that you will approach this test in a properly anxious frame of mind, I will tell you that when I administered it to myself, after many hours spent reading SATs, I had no trouble getting all of the answers right. And I *still* haven't read the passage.

1 The main idea of the passage is that
   (A) a constricted view of [this novel] is natural and acceptable
   (B) a novel should not depict a vanished society
   (C) a good novel is an intellectual rather than an emotional experience
   (D) many readers have seen only the comedy in [this novel]
   (E) [this novel] should be read with sensitivity and an open mind

2 The author's attitude toward someone who "enjoys [this novel] and then remarks 'but of course it has no relevance today'" (lines 21–22) can best be described as one of

(A) amusement
(B) astonishment
(C) disapproval
(D) resignation
(E) ambivalence

3 The author [of the passage] implies that a work of art is properly judged on the basis of its
   (A) universality of human experience truthfully recorded
   (B) popularity and critical acclaim in its own age
   (C) openness to varied interpretations, including seemingly contradictory ones
   (D) avoidance of political and social issues of minor importance
   (E) continued popularity through different eras and with different societies

4 It can be inferred that the author [of the passage] considers the question stated and restated in lines 8–13 to be unsatisfactory because it
   (A) fails to assume that society and its standards are the proper concern of a novel
   (B) neglects to assume that the novel is a definable art form
   (C) suggests that our society and [this novelist's] are quite different
   (D) fails to emphasize [this novelist's] influence on modern writers
   (E) wrongly states the criteria for judging a novel's worth

5 The author [of the passage] would probably disagree with those critics or readers who find that the society in [this novelist's] novels is
   (A) unsympathetic
   (B) uninteresting
   (C) crude
   (D) authoritarian
   (E) provincial

When I administered this test to four people at a *Harper's* editorial meeting, the youngest member of the staff, who has just emerged from the world of ETS exams, also got all the answers. Two older editors got three correct. The worst score—one out of five—was that of an editor from England, who has never taken (or even seen) an SAT test. Thus there was a perfect (1.0) correlation between test scores and familiarity with the ETS mentality.

CORRECT ANSWERS: 1. E 2. C 3. A 4. E 5. B

53   In the days before ETS was required by law to disclose its tests, actually
examining the questions was impossible. But nowadays people who can
spare $6 can order a College Board publication called *6 SATs*. This booklet,
which was published in 1982, contains six SAT tests that were administered
a year or two before. Since ETS has never thrown out a verbal item, we'll
confine our investigation to verbal items. So ETS won't be able to claim
we're nitpicking, let's look only at the first section of the first test in the
booklet. This section contains forty-five items and has a time limit of
thirty minutes.

54   Here's the first item that caught my eye, a sentence completion:

> *Unfortunately, certain aspects of democratic government sometimes put*
> *pressure on politicians to take the easy way out, allowing —— to crowd*
> *out —— .*
> (A) *exigencies…necessities*
> (B) *immediacies…ultimates*
> (C) *responsibilities…privileges*
> (D) *principles…practicalities*
> (E) *issues…problems*

This is a particularly interesting item, because it is an example not only of
ambiguity but also of cultural bias.

55   How you respond to this item will depend on what you think
politicians do when they "take the easy way out." Unlike most ETS sentence
completions, this one doesn't contain a contextual clue. We are told only
that "certain aspects" are at fault, that they only "sometimes" have an
effect, and that when they are in force all they do is allow one thing to
"crowd out" another.

56   The answer ETS is looking for here is (B). This produces a plausible
sentence, and one that is only slightly vaguer and more badly written than
the uncompleted version. (Back in my test-taking days, I used to think that
badly written items and reading passages in ETS tests served some diabolical
but scientifically precise assessment purpose; it was thus something of a
shock to learn, as I did on visiting Lawrenceville, that ETS actually tries
hard to write sturdy, well-crafted prose.) "Immediacies" and "ultimates"
are two words that, in this context at least, don't willingly divulge much
solid meaning. I suppose, however, that the finished sentence could be
translated into English as something like this: "In a democratic society,
considerations of the moment unfortunately sometimes distract politicians
from contemplating fundamental principles." Certainly we've all heard a
sentiment like this before, perhaps from our high school civics teacher, who
was also, quite possibly, the football coach. To get this question "right"
requires a dead ear for the language combined with a belief in conventional
wisdom (or, of course, a wily understanding of the ETS mentality).

57   Is the ETS answer correct? Consider an example from contemporary political life. The United States government is currently running a large deficit. Politicians from both parties agree this is bad. What should be done? One possibility would be to do something "immediate": raise taxes, slash spending. But these steps affect voters' lives and are unpopular. So instead we have a president who wants neither to raise taxes nor to slash spending but rather to add a balance-the-budget amendment to the Constitution. This doesn't affect anybody right now. It is a fundamental statement of principle. President Reagan is unfortunately taking the easy way out, letting an "ultimate" crowd out "immediacies."

58   By this reasoning, a better answer is (D). President Reagan is letting the principle of a balanced budget crowd out the practicalities of actually balancing the budget.

59   For that matter, why not (E)? Nuclear disarmament is an extremely popular issue at the moment. Overcrowded prisons are a tenacious and unpopular problem. If you invite Teddy Kennedy to speak to your breakfast club next week, which topic do you think he'll be more likely to address? The fact that unglamorous problems like prison reform almost always take a backseat to (important but) nebulous and generally intractable issues like nuclear disarmament is, I would argue, an unfortunate aspect of democratic government. When a politician wants to avoid a problem, there's always an issue to hide behind.

60   A case could even be made for (A). The point, though, is that getting this question "correct" depends less on understanding its verbal content than on subscribing to ETS's locker-room idealism about the way things ought to work. If—for cultural, ideological, or practical reasons—you think it's just fine that elected representatives don't spend more time lounging on the steps of the Capitol asking, "And what is Truth, Socrates?" then you're just plain out of luck. Yet ETS contends that, through questions like this one, it can rank people precisely on a 600-point scale of "aptitude."

61   Let's try another. Here's an analogy. In SAT analogy items, students are given a pair of words and asked to select, from among five choices, another pair "that *best* expresses a relationship similar to that expressed in the original pair." (Original emphasis.) This one reads as follows:

> THREAT: HOSTILITY::
> (A) plea: clemency
> (B) promise: benevolence
> (C) lampoon: praise
> (D) capitulation: malice
> (E) compliment: admiration

ETS suggests that students approach analogy questions by forming a sentence using the words in capital letters (known to testmakers as the "stem") and then plugging in the lettered choices to see which fits best. If we form our sentence as "A threat is an expression of hostility," we probably won't have much difficulty in settling on (E), which is the desired answer, or "key." A compliment, after all, is an expression of admiration.

62   But suppose we form our sentence in a slightly different way and say, "A threat produces hostility." Isn't this every bit as true as the other sentence is? Working from this statement, (A) now seems like the best choice (with [D] a nearly elegant and possibly profound runner-up).

63   When I discussed this and other questions with Pamela Cruise, an ETS official in charge of putting together verbal SAT tests, she told me that an analogy is no good "if you have to use 'sometimes'" (even though ETS itself hides behind a "sometimes" in the sentence-completion question discussed above). A threat only *sometimes* produces hostility. But ETS's answer doesn't work without "sometimes" either. After all, a compliment is only *sometimes* an expression of admiration. Compliments are uttered for all sorts of reasons, and sincere admiration may not even be the most common one. Can ETS honestly argue that a student who understood all of the words in this item, and could formulate the possible relationships between them, might not be justified in selecting (A) as his answer?

64   Let's try another. Here is part of a reading-comprehension passage, along with one of the questions that follow it:

> *Suppose that a rod is moving at very high speed. At first it is oriented perpendicular to its line of motion. Then it is turned through a right angle so that it is along the line of motion. The rod contracts. This contraction* [is] *known as the FitzGerald contraction....*
>
> [This] *may seem surprising....If the rod is thought of as continuous substance, extending in space because it is the nature of substance to occupy space, then there seems to be no valid cause for a change of dimensions. But the rod is really a swarm of electrical particles moving about and widely separated from one another. The marvel is that such a swarm should tend to preserve any definite extension....*
>
> *30. When the author refers to the idea that a solid rod is "continuous substance" (lines 13–14), he implies that this idea is which of the following?*
> *I. A common conception of the nature of solid matter*
> *II. A concept that is not particularly useful for explaining the FitzGerald contraction*
> *III. An accurate description of some kinds of matter*
> *(A) I only (B) III only (C) I and II only (D) II and III only (E) I, II, and III*

65   We have no trouble agreeing with I and eliminating III. But what about II? We could agree with it immediately if it were worded differently: "A

concept that does not explain the FitzGerald contraction." But ETS says "not particularly useful." Is ETS getting at something? Why, after all, does the author bring up the "continuous substance" idea? Surely because he finds it useful, if only in a negative way, for explaining the FitzGerald contraction. Writers, orators, and advertisers do this all the time. It's a run-of-the-mill rhetorical device.

66   When I administered this test to myself, I pondered Item 30 for a very long time and then finally settled on (A) as my answer. I knew that the author of the passage didn't think the "continuous substance" idea *explained* the FitzGerald contraction, but that wasn't what the item asked. The item asked whether *referring* to the "continuous substance" idea helped *the author* to explain the FitzGerald contraction.

67   As you must have guessed already, this line of thinking didn't win me any points with ETS. The "correct" response is (C). I am left to conclude that ETS didn't realize how sloppily the item was written. Perhaps ETS ought to be required to print, on the cover of every SAT test, the names and SAT scores of all the people who contributed to it.

68   Here's one last item:

MAGNET:IRON::
(A) tank:fluid
(B) hook:net
(C) sunlight:plant
(D) spray:tree
(E) flame:bird

You probably didn't have any trouble in selecting (C), the answer ETS wants. But if you thought harder (a mistake, of course), you might notice that the analogy is stated incorrectly: magnet*ism* is to iron as sunlight is to plant—or magnet is to iron as *sun* is to plant.

69   In an ETS pamphlet called "Preparing for Tests," students who are about to take the SAT are told, "Be careful to eliminate those relationships that are not exactly parallel to the relationship of the original pair."

70   Is there a better answer? How about (B)? You can pick up a net with a hook, just as you can pick up a piece of iron with a magnet. You can also pick up a hook with a net, as you can a magnet with a piece of iron. Plants, by contrast, do *not* attract sunlight. Unlike a plant and sunlight, but like a magnet and iron, the relationship between hook and net remains true no matter how long you keep them apart. Hook and net are both inanimate and both made of matter. And so on and so on.

71   Why is (B) a worse answer than (C)? Pamela Cruise of ETS: "It doesn't really strike me as an analogy. I mean, there's a reason for pairing magnet and iron. I mean, that's the kind of thing that seems to go together. You've done it yourself, you've picked up pieces of iron or pins or something with

a magnet. God, I've done it millions of times. But you don't really think of hook and net in that same kind of sense. I mean, if you had suggested that as a stem and key for an analogy, I would say that doesn't really strike me as an analogy."

72   In other words, it's so *obvious* what the answer is.

73   To see the inherent flaw in questions like this, all you have to do is put them in a different context. Suppose I typed out the magnet item on a piece of paper, handed it to you, and said, "Here's an analogy problem that's got all the fellas up at MIT bamboozled. See what you can make of it." Wouldn't you hesitate before selecting (C) as your answer? Might you not discover that you could make a case for one of the other choices? Might you not begin to lean toward this new answer if you thought the tester was looking for something more than an ability to think conventionally? And what is an item like this doing in a test of *verbal* skills in the first place? All you need to answer it is a little first-grade physics, so that you know how magnets work, and a little fourth-grade biology, so that you know how plants grow.

74   A student of even moderate ability who chooses an "incorrect" response for this item (and ETS considers it fairly difficult) probably does so not because he doesn't understand the words or the relationships among them, but because his ability to read the mind of Pamela Cruise has momentarily faltered and he has read more into the item than was intended.

75   Let's suppose, for the sake of argument, that I really have found four bad items in a single section of a single SAT verbal test (and I think there are more than four). The test may not be perfect, but it's still useful if the majority of ETS's other questions are valid, isn't it? Not really. The great drawback of a multiple-choice test is that you can't use a single item to measure a *range* of performance. Every question you add to your test increases the *test's* range of measurement (assuming that each new question measures something different from what the previous one did), but each *question* adds only a single piece of information to the total picture. Suppose, for instance, you want to find out how high a group of test-takers can count, up to an upper limit of, say, eighty-five. In a free-response test you could simply say, "Write out all the whole numbers between 0 and 86 in order." But in a multiple-choice test (that is, a test that can be given to millions and graded by a machine) you'll need eighty-five items ("The first whole number larger than 0 is (A) 5 (B) 44 (C) 1 (D) 20 (E) 13; The second whole number is..." and so on). Assuming you remember not to number your questions, you'll end up with a similar picture of your group's counting ability. But the quality of your results will depend on how well you wrote all your questions. If "85" is not one of the choices on the eighty-fifth item, you won't be able to distinguish a person

who can count up to eighty-five from one who can only count up to eighty-four. (A flaw like this will cause other measurement errors, too.)

76   A verbal SAT test, as it happens, consists of eighty-five items. Each of these has its own difficulty rating, known as its "delta," which is just a fancy-sounding way of expressing the percentage of test-takers who get it "correct." Since each item has its own delta, you can take all eighty-five items and line them up, from 1 to 85, in order of their difficulty ratings, the same way we arranged the items in our counting test. In fact, ETS does essentially this in building its exams. Every SAT test is constructed according to a standard set of specifications that dictate how many items of a certain difficulty rating will be included, what their subject matter will be, and where they will be placed. Every test, section, and subsection is arranged so that it tends to increase in difficulty from beginning to end. Test-takers who understand this know that it is foolish to spend a lot of time puzzling over the last few items in a given subsection, since the first few items in the next subsection will almost certainly be easier.

77   It may seem crudely simplistic to compare an SAT test to the multiple-choice counting test I described earlier, but the two tests are intended to perform in exactly the same way. If the SAT test is functioning just as it is supposed to, each student will climb the delta ladder, answering questions correctly precisely up to the limit of his "aptitude," and then he will be able to answer no more.

78   Even ETS does not expect a real test to behave in this ideal manner. But by ETS's own criteria, a test must be viewed as flawed precisely to the extent that it fails to do so. Suppose, for instance, that you and I take an SAT verbal exam and that we each miss five items. We'll both receive the same score, in this case 750. But suppose that the five items you missed were the five "easiest" items on the test, while the ones I missed were the five most "difficult." In my case, the test behaved exactly as it was supposed to. I missed the items that a person who scores 750 is supposed to miss. But in your case, something went wrong. Our performances on the test don't mean the same thing. In the test's own terms, my score is more reliable than yours is, because the "errors" I made—once again in the test's own terms—were more meaningful than yours. But of course there's no way to tell us apart by looking at our scores.

79   On any single SAT test that is functioning exactly as it should, there are only two important items: the last one on the delta ladder that the student gets correct, and the first one that he misses. For a student who scores 750 on an ideal SAT, the first seventy-nine items on the delta scale are superfluous, because all the information his score conveys about him is conveyed exclusively by his performance on the eightieth and eighty-first items. We can now think of a verbal SAT test not as a single eight-five-item

exam but as a large number of very much smaller exams, all of which have been lumped together in a single booklet in order to make it more convenient for ETS to measure, at one sitting, more than a million people of widely disparate backgrounds, abilities, and levels of education. All those easy "tests" at the bottom of the scale don't add any reliability to the score of someone who performs at the very top; all they can do is subtract from it, by failing to convey the information that the logic of the test says they should. And for someone who scores near the bottom of the scale, the questions at the top can only reduce the reliability of his score, by giving him the opportunity to beat chance in guessing at the answers.

80   For any given SAT-taker, the true "test" that determines ETS's assessment of his "scholastic aptitude" is actually very much smaller than the entire eighty-five-item example. If the real business of determining your score is actually being done by five or ten difficult questions, the quality and content of individual items begin to take on an immense significance.

81   No college would ever consider creating, say, a ten-minute, ten-item multiple-choice test (with two sentence completions, two analogies, two antonyms, and two reading-comprehension passages with two questions each) and then using it to determine anything at all about its applicants, much less their "scholastic aptitude." The idea is ridiculous. And yet all selective schools do essentially this very thing every time they allow an admissions decision to be affected by an SAT score.

82   To get an idea of what ETS *really* thinks about the "accuracy" of SAT tests, all you have to do is look at its method of detecting cheating. ETS's scoring computers are programmed to set aside the answer sheets of students who, in taking the SAT for the second time, score suspiciously higher or lower than they did the first. In order to set off the computers in this way, there has to be a 250-point difference between the first verbal or math score and the second.

83   If you take the SAT verbal and score 500 on it, and then you take it again and score either 260 or 740—scores that encompass all but 120 points of the total scale—ETS's computers won't bat an eye. (If the difference is more than 250 points, ETS will look for irregularities in your signature or similarities to the answer sheets of students who sat near you. In most cases, ETS says, no damaging evidence is found and the scores are allowed to stand.) If a 250-point difference in scores on two versions of the same test isn't cheating, what is it? Does ETS think that "scholastic aptitude" is so volatile that it can grow or shrink by 50 percent in less than a year?

IV. A Hard, Smooth Nut

84   ETS's recent history as a public institution has consisted almost entirely of a not always orderly retreat from prior enthusiasms. On no subject has the

retreat been more dramatic than on the issue of what exactly it is that the SAT tests. Carl Campbell Brigham's two great contributions to Western civilization were the Scholastic Aptitude Test, of which he was the primary author, and the Immigration Restriction Act of 1924, for which his book *A Study of American Intelligence* provided the major theoretical justification. Both these monuments to his insight grew out of the infamous Army Alpha and Army Beta examinations of "innate intelligence," which Brigham helped administer to new recruits at the time of America's entry into World War I. Brigham's work with the soldiers convinced him that Catholics, Greeks, Hungarians, Italians, Jews, Negroes, Poles, Russians, Turks, and a great many others were innately less intelligent than people whose ancestors were born in countries that abounded in natural blonds. After the war he addressed himself to the problem of how to keep these people out of the American mainstream, if not out of America entirely, and the SAT and the Immigration Act were two of the results. Today Brigham is little remembered, except by historians of mental measurement and by users of the Carl Campbell Brigham Library, the principal repository of enlightenment and learning at the Educational Testing Service.

85   The army mental tests were ludicrously flawed, relying on questions like the following: "Crisco is a: —patent medicine, —disinfectant, — toothpaste, —food product." But Brigham rubbed his hands and drew dark conclusions from his results. "We must face a possibility of racial admixture here that is infinitely worse than that faced by any European country today," he wrote, "for we are incorporating the negro into our racial stock, while all of Europe is comparatively free from this taint."

86   The idea of mental measurement struck a chord deep in the American psyche and had a profound effect on the life of the nation. The innate superiority of individuals, countries, races, and even entire hemispheres could now be proven scientifically. "Within two or three years after the war," writes Brigham's biographer in a celebratory volume published by ETS in 1961, "intelligence testing had developed a new and wide popularity in secondary schools, colleges, and universities across the country."

87   Brigham field-tested the Army Alpha exam on students at Princeton University, then created a more challenging version of his own. In 1925 Princeton made Brigham's test a requirement for admission.

88   Brigham's experiments sent a shiver of foreboding through the College Entrance Examination Board. The College Board had been established in 1900 to prepare and administer standardized admissions exams for a handful of prestigious Eastern colleges. High school students across the country could take a single essay test and have the results accepted at any school that participated in the program (973 young people took the College Board's first exam, in 1901). But now that intelligence testing had

taken hold in the popular imagination, the board's very existence was in danger. It took the only logical step and put Brigham on its payroll. His first "Scholastic Aptitude Test," the direct descendant of the Army Alpha exam, was administered, alongside the board's usual essay exam, in 1926. The two tests were given together until 1942, when the essay exam was discontinued for the duration of World War II, and never resumed.

89   Brigham, who died in 1943 at the age of fifty-two, created the culture of standardized testing. He is responsible for the 200–800 scale, the "delta" difficulty rating system, the practice of testing new questions by burying them in actual tests, the statistical "equating" of tests from one year to another, and so on.

90   Carl Brigham publicly recanted the racism of his youth in 1930, seven years after the publication of *A Study of American Intelligence,* four years after the first SAT. His interpretation of the army data, Brigham conceded, had been wrong. His recantation was properly applauded as the act of courage that it was. But it had virtually no effect on the new social attitudes, now widely held, that Brigham had been instrumental in creating. The Immigration Restriction Act was not repealed. The Scholastic Aptitude Test was not abandoned. The methodology of testing did not change.

91   Henry Chauncey, ETS's president from its founding in 1947 until 1970, was a bony-jawed New England aristocrat and former Harvard dean who was fascinated with the idea of assessing mental powers. In the Army Alpha exam and other intelligence tests, he whiffed the inebriating spoor of *science.* Writing in 1963 about the early intelligence experiments of Alfred Binet, Chauncey commented:

> [Binet's] *method was truly scientific and remarkably like the method used by physicists forty years later to detect and measure the forces released by the atom. The cloud chamber does not permit the physicist to see the atom or its electrically charged components, but it does reveal the tracks of ionizing particles and thus permits the scientist to deduce the nature of the atom from which the particles emanate.*

92   Intelligence, for Chauncey, was a hard, smooth nut, buried somewhere deep in the brain, that cast off particles of merit. One might never hope to squirrel out the thing itself, but if one were scientific enough, the nature of the nut might be deduced from its "emanations." Chauncey did not doubt the significance of his mission. In ETS's *Annual Report* for 1949–50, he described "an urgent need for a national census of human abilities," which, he said, would be "of critical importance for the National Military Establishment" and would also provide information about "the ability difference between men and women, and the trends of employment as between the sexes…." ETS's tests, furthermore, would serve society by

dampening the unreasonable aspirations of the unfit. "Life may have less mystery," Chauncey wrote, "but it will also have less disillusionment and disappointment. Hope will not be a lost source of strength, but it will be kept within reasonable bounds."

93   Chauncey thought of the SAT as essentially an IQ test. No one at ETS would publicly claim that today. Indeed, the company is reluctant even to refer to the Scholastic Aptitude Test as an *aptitude* test. You can read "Taking the SAT" from cover to cover and not find the word "aptitude" in it anywhere except in the name of the test the booklet purports to describe. The new euphemism is "developed ability," and ETS is now careful to say, for instance, that the SAT "is not a test of some inborn and unchanging capacity."

94   ETS hasn't always been so careful. In 1959 it published a booklet called "YOU: Today and Tomorrow" to help *grade school* students plan out the rest of their lives on the basis of their performance on ETS aptitude tests. "Your scholastic ability is like the engine," the booklet said: "it is the source of your power and speed in school. It tells you how fast and how far you *can* go." (Original emphasis.) Everything was so simple in those days. "Can you measure scholastic ability?" the booklet asked. "This is where you can use your 'magic mirror!' Take a good look at the facts about your scholastic ability *now*." These days ETS often says that it abhors the "common misconception" that the company's aptitude tests measure something innate and unchanging. But if this is a misconception, no one has worked harder to make it a common one than ETS.

V. Thermometer and Fever

95   ETS's slow abandonment of the notion of innate aptitude has required any number of dike-plugging operations as the foundations sink and the floodwalls start to crack. One involves the issue of coaching. In recent years, a lively and profitable industry has grown up offering coaching books, live training, and practice sessions for the SAT, LSAT, and other ETS exams. Many high schools have also started coaching programs. These developments threaten ETS in at least two ways. First, they add weight to the frequent charge that ETS tests simply reinforce social and economic advantages. The students who get coaching are the ones whose parents are disposed toward it and can afford to pay. Second, and more important, coaching lends credence to the suspicion that all ETS really tests is the trick of taking ETS tests. Should major decisions about people's lives really turn on scores that can be affected by a few weeks' (some would say a few hours') practice?

96   ETS's traditional position, therefore, has been that SAT scores cannot be improved by coaching. More recently, as numerous independent

researchers have published findings to the contrary, ETS has retreated a bit. ETS officers are now careful to say that coaching "as we define it" is ineffective, and coaching as ETS now defines it is "the short drill." How short is short? Answers to this question tend to be vague. Last year in *The New York Times,* George Hanford, the president of the College Board, said, "Coaching is at one end of a continuum, with teaching and a good education at the other. The distinctions are hard to make."

97   The short drill may not help, but in 1978 ETS itself began publishing a practice booklet called "Taking the SAT," which was intended, according to an ETS document, "to improve candidates' familiarity with the Scholastic Aptitude Test." Then, with that imperviousness to irony so necessary to an authentic kettle defense, ETS set about proving that this new coaching tool doesn't do students any good. An experiment was hastily designed. About 1,000 high school juniors were mailed prepublication copies of the booklet; their SAT scores were later compared with those of a group of students who had not received it. Although relatively few of the students who had received the booklet bothered to take and score the sample test that it contained, the comparison was based on the entire group. ETS proudly announced that the students who had not received the booklet scored slightly higher on their SATs than the students who had. The gentlemanly response to this discovery, certainly, would have been to recall all extant copies of the booklet and burn them. But ETS continues to publish "Taking the SAT." And ETS officials continue to cite their "study" as proof that coaching doesn't work.

98   Of course it's perfectly obvious to anyone who's ever taken an ETS test that coaching and practice help. In 1981, for example, ETS did something it had never done before: it analyzed, item by item, an entire school's performance on a PSAT (Preliminary SAT, given to high school juniors) and compared the results with the national average. One unexpected discovery was that the students at this particular school apparently weren't guessing the answers to items they didn't know. It turned out that the administrator of their exam had told them not to. In fact, you *are* supposed to guess, if you can eliminate one obviously wrong answer. A student who doesn't do this will earn a lower score than a student who does. The students at this school were penalized because they hadn't known the proper way to take the test. That's one thing they drill into you in coaching school.

99   The SAT wouldn't enjoy the stature it does today if college admissions officers didn't think of it as something not unlike an absolute measure of intellectual worth. (Admissions officers refer to people who do well in school but poorly on SAT tests as "overachievers," not as "undertesters.") But ETS has never officially claimed more for the SAT than that it is a slightly less reliable predictor of freshman grades than an applicant's high

school performance is. "Your high school record," says "Taking the SAT," "is probably the best evidence of your preparation for college." How well does the SAT actually predict freshman grades?

100   George Hanford, president of the College Board, was quoted in *The New York Times* last year as saying, "Most studies show validities for the SAT and for the high school record of .52 (each, separately)." The number Hanford mentioned is known as a correlation coefficient. I don't know where he got his figure, unless he did a study of his own. In a booklet ETS published in 1980 in response to the Nader report, the correlation between SAT scores and freshman grades was given as .41. An ETS statistician told me it has since risen to about .43. A perfect positive correlation—which would exist if you could line up everybody at any given college according to their SATs and the order turned out be exactly the same as if you'd lined them up by grades—is 1.0. A correlation of under .5 is pretty modest.

101   If the SAT is not even as good a predictor as high school grades of the one thing it claims to predict—college freshman grades—what's the purpose of it? The correct function of the SAT, many people would say, is to enable college admissions officers to find promising students who might otherwise be lost in the shuffle. The SAT, this argument goes, puts minority students on an equal footing with white students, giving a uniform, color-blind test on which to demonstrate "aptitude."

102   This is a cheerful thought, but I challenge anyone to prove it. As ETS finally acknowledged with published statistics in 1982, there is a considerable gap between the average SAT performance of whites and that of blacks, Mexican-Americans, and Puerto Ricans, and between that of people whose families have a lot of money and people whose families don't. In 1981, 8,239 whites scored 700 or above on the verbal SAT; so did 70 blacks. In the same year, 57,686 whites scored 600 or above on the verbal SAT; so did 887 blacks. (The test population included 719,383 whites and 75,434 blacks.) The mean score for whites on the verbal SAT was 442; the mean score for blacks was 332.

103   If colleges actually used the SAT as a "color-blind" indicator of academic ability, you wouldn't find many minority students enrolled in selective schools. Most minority applicants who are admitted to selective colleges are admitted *in spite of* their SAT scores, not because of them. Admission to college in these circumstances carries with it a built-in slap in the face: you can come to our school, but you're not really entitled to.

104   Whether the SAT is culturally biased against minorities is another hardy perennial controversy in which ETS takes the kettle position: the tests were never biased; they've now been fixed; but the changes have had no effect. ETS naturally says that it has proved statistically that its tests aren't biased. Just to make sure, for the last few years it has used "an actual

member of a minority" (as one ETSer told me) to read every test before it's published. This minority reader presumably scours each test booklet, scrupulously scratching out the word "nigger" wherever he finds it, and then affixes his actual-minority-member seal of approval. All this has less to do with test integrity than with public relations. The same is true of ETS's decision in 1970 to add "minority-oriented" reading passages to SAT verbal tests.

105   While making both of these gestures, ETS continues to insist that its tests can be "equated": this month's SAT is supposed to perform just like last month's SAT, which allegedly performs just like last year's SAT, which allegedly performs just like the SAT in 1965. This is why ETS claims it can actually compare average SAT scores from 1982 with average SAT scores from, say, 1969. But if this is true, you can't add a "minority-oriented" reading passage to an SAT unless it performs just like a non-minority-oriented reading passage, since non-minority-oriented passages are what the SAT always *used* to have. In the same sense, you can't remove the word "nigger" from one item unless you find some way to sneak it into another. Otherwise, you couldn't "equate" the tests over time, and editorial writers wouldn't be able to moan about one-point SAT-score declines.

106   In 1974, a writer for *New York* magazine interviewed ETS executive Marion Epstein about the new "minority-oriented" reading passages.

> Q: *If the texts weren't culturally biased in the first place, why did you make the change?*
> A: *Because minorities feel at ease reading this kind of passage.*
> Q: *If they feel at ease reading this one, does that mean they* don't *feel at ease reading the six or seven other passages in the text?*
> A: *No. It just means they feel more comfortable with this one.*
> Q: *Well, if they feel more comfortable, does that mean their scores will be higher?*
> A: *No, I don't think there will be any difference in "scores."*

107   Is the SAT biased against blacks? A senior research scientist at ETS, who asked not to be identified, told me that black students tend to do better in college than their SAT scores predict they will. If you have a black student and a white student with identical scores, he said, you can expect the black student to earn a higher grade-point average than the white student. No doubt the motive for this assertion is high-minded: to rebut accusations that unqualified blacks are getting into selective schools because of favored treatment. But if the assertion is true, the SAT test is literally racist: it systematically gives black students lower SAT scores than they deserve in terms of the sole criterion by which the test's validity is judged.

108   But maybe the research scientist was wrong. When I asked Arthur M. Kroll, an ETS vice president in charge of College Board programs, if the

SAT penalized blacks, he said, "If you mean, Does the SAT predict as well how minority students are going to do in college as majority students, then the SAT has done as effective a job for blacks as for whites." If I understand Kroll correctly (why do so many people at ETS seem to have so much trouble with syntax?), this means that the SAT is not biased either for or against blacks. A different story. So I asked the same question of Ernest Kimmel, who's in charge of test development for ETS's College Board programs. "I guess I'll disagree slightly with my boss," he said. "The scores do not work exactly the same with whites and blacks. If an admissions officer uses a single admissions equation based on a mix of white and black students with the same scores and the same high school rank, he's going to predict the same grade averages. But in actuality the black students in about 80 percent of the studies seem to do a bit worse." In other words, blacks get worse grades than their SATs would predict; the test is biased against whites.

109   I now had three apparently contradictory explanations. I took them to Richard Noeth, the ETS official who had told me that essay exams are different from multiple-choice exams, but are neither better nor worse.

110   "The thing is," Noeth said, "to my knowledge, there's supporting evidence for each of the three positions that you mentioned. I tend to—I believe them all. I'm sure they're all true."

111   Well, we've certainly cleared up this bias business. But we're left with the disparity in scores. Now that ETS has abandoned "aptitude" in favor of "developed ability" as its rallying cry, no one seriously disputes the explanation. Obviously a student's SAT scores are very heavily affected by the quality of the education he has received up until the time he takes the test. Private school students do better on SATs than public school students, and so on. Since most black children attend worse schools than most white children, it would indeed be surprising if black children did as well as white children on SATs.

112   It's equally obvious (though ETS cannot concede this) that white middle- and upper-class children have a big advantage because they are familiar with the ins and outs of ETS-test-taking. Students in good schools pick up test-taking skills almost by osmosis, because standardized tests are a constant presence in their lives. They know when to guess and when not to, they know where to find easy items, they know the kind of predictable answers ETS usually looks for, they know not to give up if they run into a string of questions they can't answer, they know the instructions and the different types of questions.

113   ETS regards the disadvantages some children bring to the SAT as part of the hard facts of life. It says that it bears no more responsibility for the low scores that result than a thermometer does for a fever. But what is left

of the rationale for the SAT if it cannot filter out the hard facts of life? Remember, ETS concedes that the SAT does not predict college freshman grades (the only thing ETS claims the test *does* predict) as well as high school grades do. The rationale for the SAT has been that it could see past the prejudices and disadvantages and lift up promising students who haven't had the opportunities they deserve. But if black students do poorly on the SAT because they've gotten a lousy education, or because they haven't mastered the code the test is written in, their scores won't tell you a thing about their "scholastic aptitude." All the scores will do is to make it a bit less likely that they'll ever be given the chance to find out what the big secret was all about.

VI. The Big Secret

114   In March 1980, the *Bulletin of the American Association for Higher Education* published a paper that, in cautious academic prose, threatens the very existence of the Educational Testing Service. The paper, written by Rodney T. Hartnett and Robert A. Feldmesser, two senior research scientists at ETS, was entitled "College Admissions Testing and the Myth of Selectivity." It pointed out the curious fact that although virtually all American colleges require their applicants to take a standardized admissions test, hardly any actually use the scores in making admissions decisions.

115   "Many of the institutions that accept large proportions of their applicants nevertheless require the applicants to submit an admissions-test score," the paper said. "Ninety-two percent of all institutions in the random sample from the [College Board's] *College Handbook* had such a requirement; even among those accepting at least 90 percent of their applicants, 88 percent had such a requirement.... These figures put admissions tests in a new light and raise interesting questions about the role they are playing in the admissions policies and practices of particular colleges and universities, and in higher education generally."

116   The overwhelming majority of colleges and universities in this country require standardized admissions tests, but aren't using the results. "There's no way they could be," Hartnett says. "If you look at the distribution of American institutions of higher education with regard to selectivity, you'd probably be amazed to learn how many of them are either open-door institutions or ones that accept virtually everybody who applies. They may turn away kids who have some record of drug abuse or something."

117   Hartnett and Feldmesser's paper was really a call for further research, a call that ETS was understandably reluctant to heed. ETS and the College Board, Hartnett says, pressured them to reconsider their findings. They refused. Later, both were given the choice of either leaving the company or accepting new jobs outside of research. Hartnett, who had been at ETS

fifteen years, quit. Feldmesser decided to stay and was put to work writing test questions, something ETS also hires college students to do. Both actions were officially described as cost-cutting moves, but because ETS has a university-style tenure system, Hartnett had to be given a generous severance settlement and Feldmesser continued to be paid his old salary. More recently, he also quit.

118   ETS essentially confirms Hartnett and Feldmesser's thesis. Ernest Kimmel, the director of test development for ETS's College Board programs, told me that there are only "fifty or sixty colleges and universities that are still selective." But ETS, characteristically, shies away from the implications.

119   What are the implications? Well, as we've seen, the entire meaning (whatever it may be) of an SAT score, if the test is functioning the way ETS says it is supposed to, derives not from the entire test but from just a few questions. Now it turns out that SAT scores are used not by the hundreds of colleges that require them but by just a few dozen schools. All of those schools use other factors besides the SAT in deciding whom to admit, factors (like grades) that correlate roughly with the SAT anyway; so the SAT makes the crucial difference in only a fraction of admissions decisions even at selective schools.

120   In other words, the entire portentous and expensive apparatus of the Scholastic Aptitude Test is irrelevant for its stated purpose of determining who should go to which college, except for a very few questions asked of a very few students applying to a very few schools. If colleges required only the scores they really used, the cost would be prohibitive. The SAT— cornerstone of the testing establishment and of ETS's finances—would go bust.

121   Why do colleges demand SAT scores that they don't really use? "We came to the conclusion," Hartnett says, "that most institutions require the test scores to maintain this aura of selectivity. One other reason they do it is that it doesn't cost them anything. It costs the kids. If, in fact, the institutions had to pay, you'd better believe they'd stop it in a hurry."

122   Contrary to what many people think, it doesn't cost an institution anything to require and receive your SAT scores, or your Achievement Test scores, or any other ETS score. In New York State in 1982–83, ETS charged you $11 for every SAT you took and $18.25 for every Achievement Test. (When I applied to college, I was told to take the SAT twice, and three different Achievements.) There is a slew of extra charges for things like late registration and extra score results. (If you apply to more than three colleges, you pay so the extra schools can find out your score.) Advanced Placement tests cost $42 each. And so on.

123   That's what you paid. What did you pay for? You paid for things like the subsidized lunches in ETS's employee cafeteria, and for mowing the

grass on the baseball diamond, and for tidying up the little island in the middle of the goose pond. You also paid for dozens of ancillary studies and services that ETS provides to high schools and colleges—the real "customers"—free of charge, along with scores. You also paid for all those "validity" studies that ETS performs every year for the 200 or so colleges that request them. All of this information is less useful to the colleges than it is to ETS. ETS floods institutions with statistics in order to make itself seem indispensable and to uphold the "scientific" façade it has erected around its tests. If the colleges had to pay, few of them would bother.

124   An ETS employee I spoke to disagreed. "The colleges would just pay for it," he said, "and then pass the cost along to the students. It's no big deal. It's like: General Motors has to have airbags? Sure. So we'll add $300 to the cost of the car."

125   If memory serves, there are no airbags in General Motors cars. GM didn't think it could pass the cost along to consumers, so it resisted regulations requiring passive restraints in cars. The ETS employee's analogy does not best express the relationship between standardized tests and airbags.

126   Bowdoin College, a top liberal arts school in Maine, stopped requiring SAT scores in 1970, having found that it could build a better student body without them. If a college like Bowdoin can get by without SATs, how many schools in the country can convincingly argue that they can't? And if those schools really *do* believe they can't do without the SATs, shouldn't they have to pay for the luxury of requiring students to take them? Where is Milton Friedman when you need him?

127   One of the reasons Bowdoin got rid of SATs was that in the two years before its decision, only 31 percent of all its honors graduates had scored above the class average on both SATs, while 24 percent had scored below. SAT scores weren't telling Bowdoin much of anything it couldn't have figured out by simply, say, asking applicants how much their parents earned and whether their mothers had gone to college and where they spent their summer vacations.

128   Hartnett and Feldmesser's hypothesis that colleges require test scores they don't really need for reasons of "prestige" is on the right track, but perhaps too narrow. Life without the SATs and other such tests is simply hard to imagine. Ever since the Army Alpha exams of World War I, American society has been hypnotized by mental measurement. And no matter how much ETS protests that this isn't what it intends, test scores are taken by society and by the recipients themselves as proxies for "merit" and therefore for their proper place in the social hierarchy.

129   The more important test scores become, the more they tend to become self-fulfilling prophecies. A high score can give a great boost to self-confidence, giving a young person the courage to trust his judgment. But a

low score has the opposite effect. A study at Duke University last year showed that the grades of struggling freshmen could be improved simply by telling them that their sophomore grades would probably be better. We'll never truly be able to discover how strong this effect is with ETS tests because ETS, like a bad doctor, buries its mistakes.

130   Leaving aside the technical debate over bias, the simple fact is that from the beginning—the Army Alpha exams—standardized testing has been associated with racial and cultural prejudice and has served to reinforce the established hierarchy rather than to shake it up. And even apart from who in particular is helped or hurt, the question remains as to why, in a democracy, it should be considered desirable to rank people from 200 to 800 every time they turn around.

131   Sprawled in the sauna at the Henry Chauncey Conference Center, mopping my humid brow, I reflect that there's no reason to accuse the people at ETS of some nefarious plot to enforce the social status quo. Institutional self-preservation is a more likely explanation for their eagerness to expand testing into new and ever less likely aspects of life, for their refusal to inquire what good all this testing does, for their casual indifference to the harm, and for the jerry-built reinforcements they construct every time another chunk of their ideological foundation collapses.

132   It can't last.

STOP

If you finish before time is called, you may check your work on this section only.
Do not work on any other section in the test.

STUDY QUESTIONS

1. In paragraph 24 Owen accuses ETS of using the logical fallacy of "arguing in the alternative" (fallacious because self-contradictory). According to Owen, how is ETS guilty of this fallacy?
2. Why does Owen accuse the sentence completion item quoted in paragraph 54 of "cultural bias"? Do you agree that this item is also ambiguous?
3. The remarks of Pamela Cruise quoted in paragraph 71 utterly fail, of course, to defend her contention that the best answer to the analogy question in paragraph 68 (magnet:iron) is answer C, sunlight:plant. Can you think of a better defense of the item? If so, do you feel that the item is unambiguous?
4. In paragraphs 82–83, Owen discusses the great differences that sometimes occur between a student's first and second testing. What point is he trying to make? Do you think such differences demonstrate a flaw in the SAT?

5. According to Owen (paragraph 93), the ETS now prefers to say that the SAT measures "developed ability" rather than "aptitude." What is the difference, and why should the ETS make this change?

6. Paragraphs 101–110 claim racial bias in the SAT. Is this an empirical claim? Since Owen does not analyze actual items for racial bias, what kind of evidence does he offer? What is ETS's response? Who's right?

7. Owen's tone often includes parody, exaggeration, sarcasm, and ad hominem attack. Do these rhetorical qualities affect the persuasiveness of the article either positively or negatively?

SUGGESTION FOR WRITING

Does your own knowledge of the SAT—either through your personal experience or information provided by others—tend to confirm or contradict Owen's charges?

CAROL ANNE DWYER

Testimony at the House Subcommittee Hearings on Sex and Race Differences on Standardized Tests, April 23, 1987

At these Congressional hearings, where various witnesses testified against standardized college aptitude tests, Carol Anne Dwyer, Executive Director for Test Development, School and Higher Education Programs, of the Educational Testing Service in Princeton, defended them. She holds a Ph.D. in Educational Psychology from the University of California in Berkeley and began her affiliation with the ETS in 1972.

1   Good morning, Mr. Chairman and members of the subcommittee. My name is Carol Anne Dwyer. For the past fifteen years, I have worked at the Educational Testing Service as a developer of tests. ETS is a measurement and research organization headquartered in New Jersey. We are most widely known for our standardized admissions tests, including the Scholastic Aptitude Test (SAT), which we develop for the College Board, the Graduate Record Examination (GRE), the Graduate Management Admissions Test (GMAT) and the Test of English as a Foreign Language (TOEFL), which we also conduct for sponsoring boards. I am presently in charge of test development for elementary school, secondary school, and higher education testing programs.

2   I am a psychologist, a Fellow of the American Psychological Association, and a member of its Educational Psychology Division's Executive Board. I have also served on the Executive Council of the American Educational Research Association and have been Vice President for Measurement and Research Methodology with that organization.

3   My primary professional research interests, beginning with my doctoral dissertation at the University of California, Berkeley, have been the fairness of tests, the relationship between gender and achievement, and the interface of technology and social values. I have conducted training activities for AERA, APA, and other associations and institutions on bias in testing, and have chaired and served on numerous womens' committees for AERA and APA. I was one of the founders of AERA's Special Interest Group on Research on Women in Education.

4   Understanding bias, and knowing how to avoid it, is at the heart of what we do at ETS. Fairness is integral to the term "standardized." In every aspect of our work, from the development of questions, to the administration of tests, to the scoring of answer sheets, to the reporting of

scores, and to the use of our tests in society, we are involved in the constant pursuit of equity. The contributions of ETS to the test bias literature over many decades show clearly that ETS is a leader in research and development in this field.

5   This morning, I would like to talk about four major issues concerning the fairness of tests. First, a word or two about why we have standardized tests; next, the question of "bias" on tests. Then I would like to share with you some of the recent trends in standardized test scores for females and minorities (which are often mistakenly assumed to be evidence of bias). Finally, I'll discuss admissions tests and what we do to ensure their fairness.

Why Standardized Tests

6   Now, about standardized tests....One of the primary purposes of developing standardized educational tests, which have a history in this country back to the past century, was to ensure the fair treatment of every test-taker. "Standardizing" means that each student is exposed to the same or equivalent tasks, administered under the same conditions, in the same amount of time, with scoring as objective as possible. These methods overcome problems that would otherwise exist in comparing students from different grades, schools, or areas. Without standardized tests, their performance could only be evaluated by different teachers using different methods, according to different criteria for success, and this would create questions about equivalency. For example, a "B" from one teacher in one classroom may indicate more knowledge than an "A" from a different teacher in a different classroom. Or the top class rank in one school may represent the same level of achievement as an average rank in another.

7   Standardization has been particularly helpful in the college admissions situation. Previous methods of selection were sometimes based upon such considerations as family ties to the college, the potential of large alumni gifts, and other criteria such as race, religion, and sex. Standardized tests became—and still are—a major vehicle for promoting equity in admissions and thus access to higher education for women and ethnic, racial, and religious minorities.

8   Standardized tests, along with high school grades, have proven useful to both students and colleges as an important element in effecting appropriate matches between them. Students benefit by their ability to select a college that will fit their academic preparation and expectations. Colleges make optimum use of their resources by admitting students whose test performance and high school record suggest that they are likely to be able to handle the work required and thus continue beyond the first year.

9   Decisions about selection and admission, however, are not the only reason for standardized tests. Uniform tests used by school systems or states provide helpful information that can lead to improved teaching and

learning by pinpointing where deficiencies exist and where special efforts and funds should be targeted. Scores from repeated assessments of samples of a state's or the nation's students are also extremely valuable as indicators of educational trends. They provide some of the best and most useful information we have about what our students know and can do. Without these uniform tools, we would find it difficult to judge objectively whether boys and girls, or Blacks, Whites, and Hispanics across the nation, for example, perform the same or differently on important school tasks. We wouldn't know for sure what proportion of our young adults are literate, and we would have great difficulty determining whether our youth are prepared for the technological age and for the competitive world economy they face. Even if we guessed that our schools need reform—and were right—without standard measures, we would lack essential data for determining whether the reforms had worked.

10   Thus, there are extremely important reasons for having, and keeping, standardized tests in this country. The important issue that we are addressing today is the fairness of these tests. There is a great deal being said these days about bias in tests, and next I'd like to say a few words about that.

The Question of Bias

11   Some people think that a test is biased if different groups of people get different average scores. However, score differences in and of themselves do not mean that a test is biased; they may simply mean that the groups on average know different amounts about what is being tested. Measuring instruments that show differences are not necessarily biased. The average height of men, for example, is not the same as the average height of women, but this does not mean that yardsticks used to measure them are biased. Individual differences, whatever their source, are also recognized as inherent in the human condition. No two people are identical; no two groups are exactly alike.

12   In our educational system, individuals and groups differ in such respects as background, interests, quality of education they receive, types of courses taken, attitudes toward these subjects, kinds of non-school experiences, and school grades received. We expect these differences; we are enriched by the diversity that many of them bring to our culture. We are alerted by other differences to important problems to be solved. Tests are not intended to eliminate or disguise these differences; they are intended to identify them, if they exist, as accurately as possible, whether the results are judged to be positive or negative.

13   It is important to distinguish between test results that *show* differences, and the factors that *cause* the differences. Scales, for example, do not cause people to gain or lose weight. Tampering with the instruments to cover up

differences is tempting, but dangerous and wrong. Tests are an easy target when they reveal unwanted or unexpected results, but they are the wrong target. Changing tests simply to hide differences in achievement could lead us to ignore real problems that should be addressed.

14   There are, of course, ways in which tests can be biased or unfair. Avoiding bias is central to a test-maker's main concern — that of developing a valid test. By "validity" I simply mean the extent to which the test accomplishes its intended purpose.

15   A test itself, for example, could conceivably contain questions that are unfair to a group of test-takers because of offensive language or inappropriate presentation of group members. It could also contain content that is not accurately representative of the ability being tested or questions that are poorly worded or unnecessarily confusing. It is extremely important that tests be free of such bias, and I will tell you later in my presentation what we at ETS do to ensure that our tests are fair in all respects.

16   It is also possible that a particular use of a test, rather than the test itself, may be biased. Use of a spelling test to select people for jobs that require no spelling — such as assembling electronic parts — is a biased use. That same test used to select secretaries may be perfectly appropriate — even if the average scores of the secretaries and the electronics assemblers are the same. Potential bias can also occur when test scores are used to predict performance on an inappropriate criterion measure (i.e., an outcome we would like to predict, such as class leadership or future income). This can occur if the criterion measure itself is invalid or biased for certain groups, for example. Tests can also simply be used for the wrong reason.

17   How tests are most equitably used in society is not primarily a technical or statistical question. Test makers have a responsibility to supply technical assistance, make recommendations, and set standards of good practice for the services they supply; but fair test use is a question of values that goes beyond the test itself and its makers. The purpose of testing and the best strategy for dealing with any group differences should be defined before any use is made of tests. If a stated policy goal is to increase the number of minority nurses on a hospital staff, for example, a racially balanced group of trainees might be selected from a pool of qualified applicants all of whom passed a nursing exam, rather than being selected simply in rank order of their test scores. Or if a college admissions staff's primary need is to predict as precisely as possible (without over- or under-prediction) the performance of a group of applicants' first year grades, they could use estimation procedures that will maximize that precision. Validity studies provide valuable information to help colleges in making decisions as to which technical procedures to use in their admissions practices to

accomplish their goals. Charges that the SAT cheats women by under-predicting their performance are not supported by the facts. These charges are based on a misinterpretation of the role of the test in prediction and selection. The SAT, when used appropriately, is a valid predictor for both men and women.

Trends in Score Differences

18   Although differences in test scores of different groups of people do not in themselves mean a test is biased, it is nevertheless important to examine score differences carefully. They could point to an area of *potential* bias, warranting further investigation. They could also point to areas where curriculum or instructional change is needed. Let's take a look at some of these group differences.

19   Compelling evidence now exists of *diminishing differences* between men's and women's verbal test scores. This finding is based on results from a host of measures, and is not merely function of performance on the SAT. A recently-completed, but not yet published meta-analysis by Janet Hyde and Marcia Linn of 165 studies (not including the SAT) reports that the long-observed tendency toward higher verbal performance for females (about .25 of a standard deviation) has nearly disappeared. The difference was evident prior to 1974, but from that time onward, no meaningful general sex differences in verbal performance have been shown to exist within any age group they studied.

20   It is extremely unlikely that this trend was a result of changes in tests, for a wide variety of tests show the same effect, and many of them had not been revised at all throughout the time period when scores changed. As many of us remember well, the early and mid-70's were a period of great social and educational change.

21   Since 1972, women's scores on the SAT verbal section have also declined in comparison to men's. In the years just prior to 1972, women scored between two and seven points (out of a total of 600 points) higher than men on the SAT verbal section. Now, however, women are scoring lower than men on that section by 11 points. A difference of about 50 points between men's and women's SAT math scores observed since the mid-70's still remains today. In a slightly older age group, the American women electing to take the Graduate Record Examination perform less well on average than men on its verbal section. However, we need to remember that students decide whether to take tests like the SAT, ACT and GRE. The nature of the group of people taking these tests has changed, as I will discuss later.

22   The best and most representative evidence of the true reading and writing achievement of all American men and women comes from the National Assessment of Educational Progress (NAEP). NAEP tells us that

17-year-old women continue to read and write better than men, although the margin of difference in reading achievement has become smaller over the years since 1975. Most of the decrease in the difference on the NAEP students' performance is accounted for by increases in men's scores, rather than a decline in the women's.

23   Studies now in progress show that one major cause of the decline in women's average scores on admission tests relative to men's are demographic changes in the self-selected group of people who take the tests. The most important of these is that many more women are now taking the SAT than ever before. Whereas women constituted only 44.5% of the test-takers in 1965, now at 52%, they have become the majority. This no doubt means that more women are aspiring to higher education. However, there is evidence that these women on the average are not as well prepared academically as the women who previously took the test. Therefore, their mean scores should not be expected to be as high as those of their predecessors. The net effect of this is that when the "new" group of women is included in the score average for all women, the average goes down. There has been no corresponding trend for young male high school graduates.

24   We are also investigating the possibility that changes in test content could have contributed to the decline in women's verbal scores. The amount of science reading in the SAT changed during the 1970's, for example; however our initial research does not indicate that the dates of these changes coincide with the dates of the observed score changes.

25   The ACT Assessment program is the other large college admission testing program that, like the SAT, tests over a million students each year. Users of the ACT and SAT tend to be clustered in certain regions, with those using the ACT concentrated primarily in the midwest and the southern region. The ACT Assessment tests college skills somewhat differently than the SAT, but the general trends in males' and females' scores are highly similar in both testing programs. ACT also has experienced a growth in the proportion of women taking the test and has also seen evidence that the women taking that test have had on the average fewer courses in math and science than the male ACT test-takers.

26   Many of the issues that I have discussed today with an emphasis on women are issues for racial and ethnic minority group members as well. We should also remember that these are not separate categories: very substantial numbers of test-takers are minority women.

27   Very often minority group members score lower on tests than the majority group. It is generally observed, for example, that Black test-takers, regardless of sex, score well below White test-takers on many educational tests. The magnitude of the difference between Black and White candidates' scores is larger than all but a very few gender differences. Hispanic test-takers as a group, tend to achieve scores somewhere between

those of Blacks and Whites. Asian-American test-takers, as a group, excel in mathematics and science tests, but do less well than majority group members on verbal tests. Again, none of these differences in themselves indicates bias in the test, but may simply reveal continuing disparities in the education of minority students of all ages. For example, we know that Black and Hispanic students are less likely than White students to be enrolled in an academic program in high school.

28   These broad generalizations hold true on major admission tests such as the SAT and the ACT Assessment. However, there is some encouraging news. A number of statistics from admissions tests, large-scale longitudinal surveys, and the National Assessment of Educational Progress suggest that the gap between majority and minority group scores is narrowing, particularly in reading. Different tests show differences in the rate of this progress but the overall trend is clear.

29   Mathematics represents a special problem area for both women and Black test-takers as a group. Black students, like women, tend to take less coursework in mathematics than majority males and to be underrepresented in higher-level math courses. This is, not surprisingly, correlated with their mathematics test scores, and is an important area where further affirmative efforts to increase women's and minority group members' participation in mathematics and science activities are greatly needed in order to improve their academic and employment options.

Ensuring Fairness in Tests

30   As we have seen, differences in performance on standardized tests by different groups have long been observed and are closely monitored by educational researchers and testing companies. A necessary first step in investigating score differences is to examine the test itself for any possible bias. I want to take a little time now to talk about how we at ETS try to ensure that tests are fair.

31   Today we are focussing on standardized admissions tests. These tests are familiar to many of us because we or our children have taken them for entrance to college, graduate or professional school. These tests have been developed by specialized testing organizations which adhere to professional standards of quality and fairness. The most recent and comprehensive testing standards were jointly developed by the American Psychological Association, the American Educational Research Association, and the National Council on Measurement in Education. ETS is committed to continuing to meet these and all other applicable standards.

32   In addition, ETS, under the leadership of our president, Gregory Anrig, has attempted to go beyond the standards of the profession as a whole and has created its own standards for the quality and fairness of the tests we

develop. These standards, which are set forth in this booklet, meet or exceed the general professional standards. Chairman Edwards, I request that a copy of these standards be inserted into the record of this hearing. In a further effort to address the dual goals of fairness and quality, ETS has established an accountability system of audits of all our testing programs. We have also invited numerous panels of distinguished educators and other specialists to critique our practices and to comment on them publicly.

33   We believe that our admissions tests are fair, as fair as anyone knows how to make them, and that they are fairer than alternatives such as interviews and letters of reference. Among the many steps taken to ensure the accuracy and quality of the tests we develop, two are especially important in ensuring racial and sex fairness: the "Sensitivity Review" and the "differential item functioning" process, which I would like to describe briefly.

34   First, every question in every test developed by ETS must undergo scrutiny by specially trained sensitivity reviewers who follow rigorous, documented criteria designed to identify questions that may be called biased because of inappropriate or offensive language or content. The reviewers also check to make sure that the test is appropriately balanced with respect to representation of people in different groups and in different roles. For example, we would consider it unacceptable to have a test of reading comprehension that showed women only in domestic roles. I would like to have a copy of an overview of our Sensitivity Review Guidelines included in the hearing record, Mr. Chairman.

35   Further, ETS has developed and is in the process of introducing operationally new statistical measures of potential bias, or "differential item functioning." The basic idea behind these statistics is that people who know approximately the same amount about the subject being tested by a question should have similar chances of answering it correctly, regardless of differences in their race, sex or ethnic background. The statistics therefore first match two groups of people in terms of their relevant knowledge and skill, then compare their performance on each test question. This gives us a measure of a test question's "differential difficulty." These statistics will thus help to identify differences in performance that may reflect potentially inappropriate characteristics of certain test questions. Such statistics will be used by all the major programs for which ETS develops tests. The combination of statistical analysis with thorough and detailed professional reviews of all questions provides a much stronger guarantee against potential bias than would either method used alone.

36   I should also mention that one of ETS's basic components in the test development process to ensure test validity is the use of committees of

educators to plan and develop tests. These committees are composed of subject matter experts, usually teachers or university professors. The committees include women and men and minority and majority group members from all parts of the country, all types of educational institutions, and all specialities within their disciplines. They bring a broad perspective to the material included in our tests and help ensure its accuracy. These committees work with an ETS test development staff made up of 86 women and 46 men.

37   ETS has a long history of contributing to research on test fairness and making the data we collect available to other researchers. Three current studies, funded by the College Board, are particularly relevant to today's topic. The first is a complete content history of all the SAT tests administered from 1960 to 1987, telling us exactly what was tested on the SAT and when. We can then examine over the years whether content variations did or did not coincide with group score changes. (As mentioned earlier, the changes in test content in the 1970's do not appear to have coincided with the dates of observed score changes.) Another study will use the "differential item difficulty" technique that I just described to examine SAT verbal questions to see whether content factors (such as science contexts) are responsible for score differences for men and women who are otherwise comparable in their overall verbal reasoning skills. A third study will expand our knowledge of the demographic characteristics of the women and men who take the SAT and the relationship of these characteristics to their SAT scores.

38   Fairness is also important in how tests are used. It is the job of testing companies to produce the best tests possible from a technical point of view, and to provide interpretive material and sound technical assistance to their clients and users as they decide how to use test scores. Admissions test results, obviously, are intended to enhance the equity and efficiency of the college selection process. Decisions about the use of test scores by colleges do not occur in a value-free context and are not under the direct control of ETS or any other agency.

39   Institutional and societal priorities are brought to bear on statistical data. A better geographical mix of students, for example, may be desired in the new first-year class at a small college in a Great Plains state. A larger number of ethnic minority students might be sought by an institution in the Pacific northwest; or a large, predominantly female first-year class may be sought by a formerly all-male private college in New England which has recently decided to admit women. Each of these colleges will and should make its own value judgments, according to its own priorities, as to how to use test scores equitably in the admission process. This was the view taken by the National Academy of Sciences' Committee on Ability Testing in 1977, which put it better than I can:

> *Even recognizing the inherent difficulties, we believe that admissions officers have to exercise judgment, case by case, as, in fact, many now do. The goal should be to effect a delicate balance among the principles of selecting applicants who are likely to succeed in the program, of recognizing excellence and of increasing the presence of identifiable underrepresented subpopulations. (p. 196)*

40　　Mr. Chairman, in closing I would like to summarize the major points I have made today:

- Carefully developed standardized tests are more fair than the available alternatives, which frequently rely on subjective personal judgments about groups and individuals;
- Without tests we would lack basic information about how well educational programs are working—information that is essential if we are to focus our resources on educational improvements at the state and national level that will be most beneficial;
- Score differences exist, but by themselves do not mean bias on tests; many factors contribute to such differences;
- ETS, a leader in research on testing and test bias, uses processes for developing standardized tests that are thorough, careful and designed to make our tests as fair as possible.

41　　I thank you for the opportunity to speak to you today about an issue that is near and dear to my heart. I will be glad to answer any questions you and the committee may have.

STUDY QUESTIONS

1. Do the following facts, taken together, suggest any possible explanation for the gender gap on the SAT's? (Source: Wolfe, Leslie R., and Phyllis Rosser, "The SAT Gender Gap," *Women and Language* 13:2, Winter 1990, 6.)

   - One research study has shown that in a science assessment test, girls thirteen to seventeen years old were more likely than boys to use an "I don't know" option.
   - On a math assessment test, when the "I don't know" option was removed, a gender difference appeared favoring females.
   - Although an "I don't know" option is not available on the SAT's, students taking the test are told at the time of administration that one-fourth point will be deducted for wrong answers but that blank answers will not be penalized.

2. In paragraph 17, Dwyer says, "If a college admissions staff's primary need is to predict as precisely as possible (without over- or under-prediction) the performance of a group of applicants' first year grades, they could use estimation procedures that will maximize that precision.") Apparently she is here referring to the College Board's advice to predict women's first year grades by an equation based on women's scores alone, because a College Board study showed that predictions based on the scores of the combined sexes underestimate women's grades by .04 grade points. Would critics who claim that the SAT is biased against women agree that this practice would solve the problem?
3. Dwyer uses the measurement of both height and weight as analogies for the measurements carried out by the SAT. Are these fair analogies?
4. Toward the end of her testimony, Dwyer, like other ETS spokespeople, stresses that a distinction must be made between the test as a technical instrument and the uses of the test by college or other elements of society. She says that the College Board cannot control uses of the test (beyond the dissemination of guidelines for its use) and is not responsible for uses of the test that are not equitable. Do you agree that the SAT is a value-free, technical instrument for measuring scholastic aptitude?
5. Dwyer explains the decline of women's average scores on the SAT relative to men's at least partly by the increased number of women from poorer backgrounds and weaker academic preparation who take the test. If it could be shown that the top 20 percent of women's scores had also declined relative to the top 20 percent of men's scores, would this explanation tend to be confirmed, rebutted, or unaffected?

PHYLLIS ROSSER

Testimony at the House Subcommittee Hearings on Sex and Race Differences on Standardized Tests April 23, 1987

Phyllis Rosser describes some of her background in the opening paragraphs of her testimony. She was also the principal author of a report entitled *Sex Bias in College Admissions Tests: Why Women Lose Out,* published by the National Center for Fair and Open Testing, Cambridge, Massachusetts, in the same month that she gave this testimony. Subsequently, she helped to compile *The SAT Gender Gap — Identifying the Causes* published in 1989 by the center for Women Policy Studies in Washington, D.C.

1   I have been a Contributing Editor to *Ms.* Magazine for the past fourteen years and I've had many articles on education and learning published in other magazines as well. I began researching sex bias in testing for *Ms.* in 1979, with an open mind. Tests had never kept me from anything I wanted to do. I don't even remember the SAT scores I received in 1951.

2   I examined the tests, read testing studies and interviewed the testing researchers who had written them. I wrote a report for *Ms.* in 1980 on Aptitude Tests that are used for college and graduate school admissions, Standardized Achievement Tests given from kindergarten through 12th grade, I.Q. tests administered by psychologists, and Interest Inventories used for Career Guidance in high school.

3   I am very pleased that Congress is interested in the effects standardized tests are having on females and sorry to report that the tests have not improved much since I began my research. In fact, on the college entrance examinations, the score gap between the sexes has widened.

4   What struck me first when I looked at these tests was the overwhelming number of males that populated them — all of whom were engaged in traditional occupations like doctor and lawyer while women were teachers, nurses and secretaries. According to recent research, there are still twice as many men as women on most tests and they are still shown in stereotyped roles, even though this doesn't represent the world of 1987 at all. Studies done by Educational Testing Service researchers as far back as 1979 ("Sex Differences and Sex Bias in Test Content" by Ekstrom, Lockheed, Donlon, *Educational Horizons*) show that "females tend to do better on items that have more female or neutral figures than on items in which there are male figures." This means that male-oriented content is not only offensive, it is also a source of bias.

5   But the tests where sex bias seems to have the greatest impact on girls' educational opportunities are the college entrance examinations. The Scholastic Aptitude Test (SAT) and the Preliminary Scholastic Aptitude Test/National Merit Qualifying Test (PSAT/NMQT) published by Educational Testing Service and the American College Testing Program's ACT Assessment (ACT) are systematically underpredicting the abilities of high school girls. Although females have higher grades in every subject in high school and higher college grades, they receive lower test scores on the SAT and the ACT.

6   The SAT is composed of two sections, Verbal and Math, each scored on a 200–800 point scale. The maximum possible score is 1600. Last year, women's average SAT scores were 61 points lower than men's — 50 points on the Math section and 11 points on the Verbal section — an area where girls excelled until 1972. Then boys began to outscore them verbally as well as mathematically (boys have always received higher math scores on this test), and the score gap has gradually widened.

7   This growing score gap is surprising since ETS says the main purpose of this test is to predict freshman year grades, but it's not doing that for girls. They make up 52% of the 1.5 million test takers so this means that scores are being underpredicted for approximately 800,000 females every year. If this test were accurately predicting freshman year grades, girls would score 20 points higher than boys rather than 61 points lower.

8   I'm sure, if boys were receiving higher grades and lower test scores, the tests would be rewritten.

9   Minority women are doubly penalized by the test. They all score lower than the men in their ethnic group, who, in turn, score lower than white men. In 1985, black women scored 43 points lower than black men and 264 points lower than white men.

10   A similar pattern of test bias can be found on ETS' Preliminary Scholastic Aptitude Test/National Merit Qualifying Test (PSAT/NMQT), taken by 1.1 million junior high school students last year (who were 54% female). ETS promotes this as a practice test for the SAT, but the National Merit Scholarship Corporation awards over $23 million in student scholarships to the highest scorers on this test.

11   Like the SAT, the PSAT/NMQT has two parts. Each is scored on a scale of 20–80. Testmakers claim an approximation of future SAT scores can be obtained by multiplying PSAT/NMQT scores by ten. In 1985–86, girls' score averages were 53 points lower, in SAT terms, than boys': 41 points in the Math, 12 points in the Verbal. To qualify for the National Merit Scholarship, verbal scores are doubled and the math is added — in order to give girls more of a chance. But their lower verbal scores, which are doubled, are now working against them.

12   An alternative college entrance exam to the SAT is the ACT Assessment, a survey achievement test taken annually by nearly a million

high school seniors (54% of whom are female), mainly in the Mid-West, Southwest and South. The ACT has four sections: English Usage, Mathematics Usage, Natural Science, and Social Studies. The test is scored on a scale that ranges from 1–36. In 1985–86, girls averaged 2.8 score units lower than boys in Math Usage, 2.5 units lower in Natural Science, and 1.7 units lower in Social Studies but slightly higher (1.0 units) in English Usage, averaging 6 units lower than boys on the test, overall.

13   Girls also receive lower scores on most of the Achievement Tests published by ETS which are required for admission to some colleges and universities. According to the College Board's *Profiles of College-Bound Seniors,* 1985, girls scored nine points higher on English Composition and Literature, one point higher on German but lower on all the other tests.

14   Sex bias on these tests is having a much greater impact on females than we realize. By underpredicting their academic performance, these tests affect girls' chances to gain entrance to colleges and universities that require SAT or ACT scores, or use them as cut-off scores for admission. They also markedly diminish their chances to obtain merit scholarships based on test scores, and to enter many special educational programs for gifted high school students that use SAT scores in their admissions criteria.

Test Scores Affect College Admission

15   Nearly all the 1500 accredited colleges and universities in the country require students to submit SAT or ACT scores for admission. Some use them as cutoff scores and others put them into an admissions formula. (See appendix I for a list of the colleges and universities requiring cutoff scores or using SAT scores as part of a numerical formula.) For example, the University of Texas at Austin requires out-of-state applicants to have minimum SAT scores of 1100. The University of California at Berkeley adds the SAT score, the scores on three ETS Achievement Tests (where girls also receive lower scores) and the Grade Point Average multiplied by 1000, to rank candidates for admission.

16   Although some colleges may not actually use scores in the selection process, they often publish the average SAT scores of their previous freshmen class to establish high academic credentials. As a result, women with lower SAT scores will lower their expectations and apply to less competitive schools than their grades suggest. Ernest Boyer recently reported in *College: The Undergraduate Experience in America* that 62% of the students questioned said they lowered their college expectations after receiving their SAT scores.

Low Test Scores Reduce Entry Into "Gifted" Programs

17   A large number of academic enrichment programs are offered to students with high SAT or PSAT scores. Fewer of these opportunities are offered to

females, due to their lower scores. This means they not only lose the opportunity to enhance or accelerate their high school program, but also have less impressive resumes of extracurricular academic activities to present on college applications.

18   In New Jersey, outstanding honors students in science and political science with high SAT scores are invited to attend the Governor's School, a summer enrichment program held on college campuses. 65% of the attendees at the science school this summer will be male, 35% will be female, from a pool of applicants that was 75% male. High PSAT scores and high grade point averages are also used to select one student from each high school in New Jersey to attend the New Jersey Scholars Program held at the Lawrenceville School each summer.

19   In Washington, D.C., students with high SAT Math scores are offered opportunities to take advanced math courses on college campuses during the summer. Additionally, high scoring students whose parents can afford summer school tuition have a smorgasbord of opportunities to develop their giftedness. Summer enrichment courses are offered by Ivy League and other competitive schools, and by well-known prep schools. This summer, the George School in Newton, Pennsylvania, and Blair Academy in Blairstown, New Jersey, will offer courses in advanced mathematics, college science, computer science, languages, literature, the arts and, ironically, PSAT and SAT coaching.

20   Johns Hopkins University's Center for the Advancement of Academically Talented Youth (CTY) invited 26,876 seventh grade boys and girls in 19 states to take the SAT, to determine if they were mathematically or verbally talented. Junior High School students qualify for this by scoring in the upper 3% on the mathematics section of a national standardized achievement test. Those who score 500 or more on the Verbal or Math section are invited to attend one of their five camps for "gifted and talented" students.

21   This summer, invitations to the Johns Hopkins program will be extended to over 2,500 boys but only 1,081 girls. Although an equal number of boys and girls take the test, girls' lower SAT scores keep them from qualifying for these high-powered summer programs. They may also suffer a blow to their self-esteem and lower their expectations about future SAT performance—before they even reach high school.

Low Test Scores Deny Merit Scholarship Money

22   Use of exam scores also means less merit scholarship money for female college students. Merit scholarships awarded by hundreds of corporations, foundations, government agencies, professional organizations and unions each year are partially based on ACT, SAT or PSAT scores. Most of these organizations refuse to provide a gender or racial breakdown of

scholarship recipients. However, the National Merit scholarship Corporation, which offers the most prestigious awards for academic excellence, publishes this data.

23   Over 23 million dollars, provided by 670 corporations, foundations, colleges and universities are given annually to students with the highest PSAT scores. Last year girls' qualifying scores averaged 65 points lower than boys' (in SAT terms) and they received only 36% of the 6,026 scholarships awarded while boys received 64%. This year the semi-finalist pool (based solely on PSAT scores) from which the winners will be chosen has 15,507 students. 34.7% are female and 61% are male (the sex of 4.3% is unknown).

24   Semi-finalist status is given to students whose PSAT scores (twice Verbal and Math score) rank them in the top half of 1% in each state. In order to obtain scholarship money, semi-finalists submit information about their academic records, extracurricular activities, leadership potential and intended college major, along with their principal's recommendation to the National Merit Corporation's selection committee. Students must also duplicate their high PSAT score with "an equivalent high Scholastic Aptitude Test performance," according to their Program Guide. This also works against lower-scoring females. In 1985–86, of the 13,777 Merit Finalists, 64.1% were male and 35.9% were female. 43.7% of the finalists actually receive Merit Scholarships.

25   An alarming trend for women is evident in the National Merit Corporation's Annual Reports. Although the total number of scholarships awarded annually has increased, the number and percentage of female recipients has decreased noticeably in the last three years. In 1983–84, National Merit Scholars were 40.2% female; in 1984–85, 37.9% were female; in 85–86, 36% were female.

26   It is impossible to calculate exactly how many millions of dollars girls lost in this uneven split because Merit Scholarships are awarded in three catagories. National Merit Corporation awards 1,800 of its own $2,000 scholarships annually. In addition, it administers the awarding of scholarships for 425 corporations and 2,800 colleges and universities in amounts ranging from $250 to $8,000 per year.

27   The National Merit Corporation also administers the awarding of 1,179 "Special" corporate scholarships worth $7.6 million. These scholarships are awarded to students with scores below the finalist level who are interested in a career the grantor wants to encourage, or who live in a community where the company has offices.

28   New York State's Merit Scholarships, worth over $40 million annually, are awarded to students who have the highest ACT or SAT scores in each of New York's counties. In 1986–87, 672 of the 1,000 Empire State Scholarships of Excellence awarded were to boys, while only 270 went to girls. The gender of 58 winners could not be determined by name.

29   Males also won more of New York State's 25,000 Regents College Scholarships, which are exclusively determined by SAT or ACT scores, and worth up to $1,250 each. Of the 109,266 students who competed for the scholarships, 47% were male and 53% were female. However, 57% of the 25,277 winners were male and 43% were female.

30   Once FairTest and NYPIRG made this discrepancy public, the New York State Board of Regents moved swiftly. Acknowledging that women's lower SAT scores kept them from receiving their fair share of merit scholarships, the Regents voted unanimously to ask the legislature for funds to develop a new, unbiased test.

31   Other states use a combination of grades and test scores for their merit programs with more equitable results. New Jersey requires students to have SAT scores of 1200 or more and also rank in the top 10% of their high school class to qualify for Garden State Distinguished Scholarships. Up to $4,000 is awarded annually to 800 students (at least 2 from each school) for a total of $3,200,000 to encourage them to attend colleges in New Jersey. Last year's Garden State Distinguished Scholars were 50% female and 50% male.

32   A computer printout from a typical northeastern high school guidance office lists 134 scholarships tied to test scores. These "merit" scholarships are given by unions, fraternal organizations, religious denominations, corporations (mainly sponsoring children of employees), professional organizations, and the military. Most of these scholarships are awarded to students with high test scores in combination with high grades, an interest in pursuing a particular course of study and/or financial need. Engineering societies predominate, giving more career-based merit scholarships than any other group.

33   In the escalating competition for top students, merit scholarships are being increasingly used for recruitment; according to a 1984 study, more than 85% of four-year private colleges and nearly 90% of public institutions offer no-need scholarships for academic excellence, and substantially more of these are being offered now than even five years ago. In private, four-year colleges, 44% of this no-need money is taken from tuition and fee income, raising important questions about the spiraling costs of college tuition.

34   Last year, one New Jersey student who received a $4,000 Garden State Distinguished Scholarship, found his mailbox full of additional scholarship offers. Thirteen New Jersey colleges offered him grants ranging from $2,000 to $12,000. Drew University in Madison, N.J., also told him that it offers $48,000 to students who score 1350 or better on the SAT and $32,000 to students with 1300 SAT's.

35   Two out-of-state colleges offered this student "honors" scholarships outright, ranging from $500 to $10,000. Sixteen other colleges and

universities told him he qualified for their merit scholarships, some of which covered full tuition. In addition, eight universities—including the Universities of Michigan, Indiana, and Delaware—offered him admission to their Honors Programs in which a small, select group of academically-talented students attend a smaller, select college within the university. They are given enriched academic programs, honors grants, and live together in a separate residence hall.

36   The final result of lower test scores is a real dollar loss for females in later life as they get less prestigious jobs, earn less money, and have fewer leadership opportunities. Of course, the life-long loss of self-confidence can't be measured in financial terms.

Why the Gender Gap?

37   It is impossible to tell which questions are biased by examining the tests. Only the test publishers know which questions females and minorities answer incorrectly and they have not made this information easily available. A bill is currently moving through the New York State Legislature which would require publishers to provide a gender and racial analysis of test questions for an entire year.

38   In the meantime, there are some theories about the gender gap, particularly on the SAT.

39   ETS President Gregory Anrig says that a larger pool of test takers will have lower scores. ETS also says that the larger pool of girls includes more girls from lower income families who have lower test scores, which in turn reduces the average female scores. However, the girls who took the SAT in 1985, according to the College Board's *Profiles of College-Bound Seniors*, had higher grades than the boys who took it, despite their larger pool and lower incomes.

40   Fred Marino, Assistant Director of Public Affairs for the College Board, says "girls take less math and science in high school than boys," to explain the 50-point gap on the math section. However, the College Board's *Profiles* for 1985 shows that girls who take the test are almost as likely as boys (50.5% vs. 57.6%) to have taken four years of math.

41   He also says that girls take easier courses in college. They are less likely to be taking science and engineering where grades are lower because the courses are harder. But the College Board's own validity studies show that women who major in engineering and math in college tend to receive higher grades than their SAT scores had predicted. Massachusetts Institute of Technology has been admitting women with lower SAT Math scores and finds they do just as well as men in freshman math classes.

42   ETS also says the tests reflect the bias against females in society. They suggest that girls are treated differently in the classroom, which may affect

the way they perform on standardized tests. Although the society is biased against females and the classroom reflects that, girls are able to overcome this handicap and earn better grades, even though they receive less classroom attention.

43   Most insidious of all are those who say girls' grades reflect good classroom behavior rather than high intelligence. As we all know, grades include much more than can be measured on a multiple-choice test, such as the ability to think complexly, solve problems, organize information and express oneself clearly. It is generally acknowledged that girls write better, and the writing tests even bear this out.

44   I have looked at SAT questions over the years and find them offensive in their consistent male orientation. I recently analyzed 24 reading comprehension passages that appeared on 4 SAT's given in the 1984–85 year. (There are six reading passages on each SAT.) I found references to 42 men and three women in the 24 passages. 34 of these men were famous and their work was cited. One woman, Margaret Mead, was famous and her work was criticized.

45   David White, a lawyer from California, has done considerable research on the graduate entrance exams published by ETS—the Law School Admissions Test (LSAT), the Graduate Record Examination (GRE) and the Graduate Management Admissions Test (GMAT) and found a number of questions that are emotionally loaded and offensive for women and blacks. For example, one question on the LSAT concludes that "children (should) be raised only by their mothers, and…not be farmed out to day-care centers and full-time babysitters." Certainly the mothers who are taking this test are going to be "farming out their children."

46   David White and I both feel this type of demeaning question slows down test takers *and* may even shake their confidence for a while on a test that requires the utmost in speed and risk-taking. At the very least, they cast doubt on ETS's Sensitivity Review.

47   ETS could change these tests to make them fairer for girls but has chosen not to do this. The widely-used Stanford-Binet I.Q. Test is written with the assumption that the sexes are equally intelligent. It is periodically revised to make sure the sexes score equally well.

48   I would like to ask ETS why it has decided that boys are smarter than girls? I would also like to know what the SAT is predicting, if it's not freshman grades? ETS receives $17,250,000 for this test every year that doesn't do what it's supposed to for over half the people taking it. I think that is consumer fraud.

49   I also think unfair college admissions tests may be the tip of the iceberg. Recent research indicates that other tests are also biased against girls, like the standardized achievement tests used for high school tracking

and the Armed Services Vocational Aptitude Battery (ASVAB), the most widely used aptitude test for career guidance in high schools.

50   I would like Congress to request that the Department of Education investigate tests that are having major impacts on students—to see if they predict what they are supposed to. In order to do this fairly and accurately, I think it is essential that the researchers who receive these contracts are not connected with the test publishers.

The statistics, charts and some of the information presented here were first published in the National Center for Fair and Open Testing Report on *Sex Bias in College Admissions Tests: Why Women Lose Out* by Phyllis Rosser with the Staff of National Center for Fair and Open Testing, April 1987.

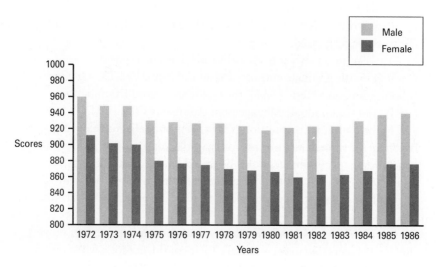

Figure 1. SAT score averages for college-bound seniors, 1972–86.

	Females	**Males**	**Diff.**
Asian-Pacific Americans	897	946	-49
Black	705	748	-43
Mexican-American	775	845	-70
Native Americans	790	855	-65
Puerto Rican	744	820	-76
White	912	969	-57
National Average	877	938	-61

Figure 2. Average SAT scores. (From *1985 Profiles, College Bound Seniors* by Leonard Ramist and Solomon Arbeiter, CEEB 1986.)

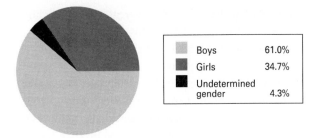

Figure 3. National Merit Scholarship semifinalists.

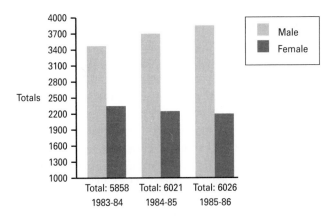

Figure 4. National Merit Scholarship winners, 1983–86, by gender.

STUDY QUESTIONS

1. Rosser's main point takes the form of a deductive argument:

   The only thing the SAT claims to do is to predict first-year college grades. Women achieve higher first-year college grades than men but score lower on the SAT than men.

   Therefore, the SAT fails in the only thing it claims to do.

   If you disagree with this argument, what aspect do you disagree with? one or more of the premises? the logic by which the conclusion is drawn from the premises?
2. Does Carol Anne Dwyer's testimony in the preceding selection engage Phyllis Rosser's basic argument as described in the first question above? If so, what does Dwyer say in response?
3. The College Board explains the fifty-point gap between boys and girls on the math SAT by the fact that boys take more high school math than girls. Rosser rejects this explanation on the grounds that "girls who take the test are almost

as likely as boys (50.5% vs. 57.7%) to have taken four years of high school math." How would you go about deciding whether this 7.2% differential is enough to explain the fifty-point gap in math SAT scores?

4. Near the end of her testimony, Rosser notes that the Stanford-Binet intelligence test is written on the assumption that both sexes are equally intelligent. That is, all questions considered for use in the test are first tried out in experimental administrations, and any items on which one sex does better than other are rejected. Given this fact, can the Stanford-Binet intelligence test be used to compare the relative intelligence of men and women as groups?

5. It has been suggested that the gender gap on the SAT is caused wholly or partly by the different ways in which the sexes are acculturated by their parents, by media stereotyping, and by the schools. Some of this difference in acculturation means that boys and girls may not be exposed equally to certain kinds of questions (e.g., figuring a sports team's won/lost percentage). Should the SAT be limited to questions to which the sexes have been equally exposed?

6. Besides these possible differences in acculturation regarding the subject matter and skills covered on the SAT, it is also possible that boys and girls are acculturated differently toward the very taking of such tests. Harvard's Carol Gilligan told Rosser in 1987, "This test is a moral issue for girls; they think it is an indication of their intelligence, so they must not cheat. But boys play it like a pinball game." (Wolfe, Leslie R., and Phyllis Rosser, "The SAT Gender Gap," *Women and Language* 13:2, Winter 1990, 6). If Gilligan's point is true, does it tend to strengthen or weaken Rosser's argument that the SAT is biased against women?

SUGGESTION FOR DISCUSSION AND WRITING

Return again to Rosser's point that the Stanford-Binet intelligence test is so designed that the average scores of women are always equal to those of men, and explore the ramifications of the principle that tests can be designed to yield a predetermined result at the group level. Do you think it would be possible to design an intelligence test that was free of such assumptions? If such a test were presented for a trial run and it turned out that women as a group did much better than men, could it be determined whether the test was picking up a genuine differential in intelligence or whether it was exhibiting a sexual bias?

Write an essay in which you review your basic thoughts on these issues, and then make recommendations about what the College Board should do about group differences on the SAT. Should the test be left as it is? Should it, like the Stanford-Binet, be adjusted to produce equal results for men and women at the group level? Should it be adjusted to produce equal results for groups defined by criteria other than gender, such as race or socioeconomic status?

DANIEL SELIGMAN

The Rich Are Different

Daniel Seligman is an editor of *Fortune.* Here he addresses empirical questions about the relationship between intelligence and wealth.

1   Are rich people smarter than poor people? Do rich kids get higher scores on aptitude tests than poor kids get? The answer to both questions, which is "yes, obviously," is perhaps less fascinating than the reactions you can get in certain quarters just by raising the question.

2   The question floated to the surface the other day on the Washington *Post* op-ed page, in a context that is by now somewhat familiar. Once again, the Naderites were onstage attacking the Educational Testing Service—the organization that develops and administers the scholastic aptitude tests. Once again, Nader and Allan Nairn (who is the main author of *The Reign of E.T.S.,* also known as "The Ralph Nader Report on the Educational Testing Service") were waxing wroth because someone had earlier said a kind word about E.T.S. As we recently pointed out in these columns (see the March 10 issue), the reason for the wax is that E.T.S. tests persist in showing some people to be smarter than others. And if some people *are* smarter than others, there might actually be some justification for an economic system in which some people have more money and authority than others.

3   There is no dispute about the fact that the S.A.T.'s show the high-income kids to be doing better. Nader and Nairn dwell heavily on this fact, and indeed quote gleefully from one E.T.S. document that states: "Every time you move from one income group to the next higher, the mean S.A.T. verbal and mathematical scores increase." Nader and Nairn are insistent on this point because they view it, not as evidence for a position that differs from their own, but as evidence that the tests have an obvious "class bias."

4   Writing in the *Post,* they heap scorn on the proposition that "working-class and low-income students…have less 'aptitude' generally than their upper-class counterparts." However, they have some trouble pointing to data that would support the scorn. They mention one study allegedly showing that freshman grades are uncorrelated with parental income, but this conclusion is actually not justified by the underlying data (aside from the well-known fact that freshman grades are not the same thing as aptitude). The data they're talking about lump together grades and income from many different colleges, instead of taking the results of one college at a time. When you lump them all together, the correlation between incomes and grades is inevitably smothered because the less selective colleges, with more low-income students, also tend to have more lenient grading policies.

5   In any case, numerous other studies show that aptitude and parental income are significantly correlated. The E.T.S. says that its own studies show a correlation coefficient of about 0.30 between S.A.T.'s and parental income. Looking at the relationship between intelligence tests and income, Christopher Jencks, the eminent Harvard sociologist (and socialist), concluded several years ago that "a family's economic status probably correlates about 0.35 with the children's test scores."

The really interesting question is not whether rich people are smarter, but why they are. Is it because of their superior environments or their superior genes? The answer—also attested to in endless studies—is "both, obviously."

STUDY QUESTIONS

1. Seligman says, "And if some people are smarter than others, there might actually be some justification for an economic system in which some people have more money and authority than others." Discuss the assumptions behind this statement. Do you agree with them?
2. An ETS document quoted in this article reports, "Every time you move from one income group to the next higher, the mean S.A.T. verbal and mathematical scores increase." How do Nader and Nairn interpret this, and how does Seligman interpret it? Can you think of any kind of experiment that might determine which side was right? If so, what kind of experiment?
3. Compare Seligman's views with those of David Owen earlier in this section.

JUDY GAHAGAN

Wisdom and Wealth: The Great Education Hoax

This selection served as the keynote article for an issue of the *New Internationalist* devoted to education and related issues. Judy Gahagan, who edited this number of the journal, is British, and while her essay is particularly applicable to the British educational system, it has general relevance to the way both education and educational testing are related to social values.

1   And on the first day they pile in through the door: noisy, shy, neat, untidy, polite, cheeky, dreamy, practical. The door is the school door; they the world's intellectuals. Who are the world's intellectuals? They are all people everywhere — but only on that first day. For humans have minds with power beyond the scope of any imaginable computer…to start with.

2   It's hard to stop them at the beginning. They will experiment and theorize, take things to pieces and reassemble them. They will invent, dream, tell jokes and stories, sing and cook and dance. They will help manage the classroom. They will help each other and look after the little ones. In short, they will use *all* of their brains. For these are still whole people.

3   And what will school do for them? If they are lucky, school will expand all that mind power in special ways. It will fill the gaps in their community's knowledge as snugly as a piece in a jigsaw. People can learn anywhere, but school will develop and focus their intelligence, will nurture all their talents. If they are lucky. But most of them won't be lucky. Whether they apparently succeed, or obviously fail, most of them will emerge more damaged than when they went in. The greater part of the world's brain power is unused, paralyzed or distorted.

4   But it's not the fault of schools or teachers. They, together with the potential they are supposed to nurture, are casualties in that monstrous power struggle we call civilization. School is used as a filter to identify and train the future holders of power. As for the rest, it is obvious that if they used *all* their minds and talents, they would be even harder to subjugate and exploit than they are at the moment. So school is a place that ensures that such a thing never happens. And even the teachers don't seem to know what's going on.

5   Do you remember those long-ago days of beans growing in jars? Of wall-charts about everything from earthworms to Aztecs? Do you remember the reading corners and spelling bees; the quiet hour for sums and writing, the songs and games? That was the beginning. You took your

whole mind to school and brought it home again, intact. But as time went on, some things you could do began to be much more important than other things you could do. You and your mind seemed to be being squeezed through a funnel that got narrower and narrower.

6   Maybe you'd been good at making complicated models of little cars. But later it was only geometry that was important. You liked geometry, but you liked making things as well. Or you'd loved making up fabulous stories. But later they only wanted you to compare and contrast other people's stories. You'd been especially good at helping the little ones, and stopping people bullying, and getting unpopular ones included. "Quite a knack," they'd always said. But later that didn't seem to be important at all.

7   And gradually it became clear that only a few people were really good at the things the teachers thought were important. Most people were not up to much. And some were hopeless. Yet at the beginning nobody had ever noticed whether people were better than each other at all. Because it hadn't seemed of any importance.

8   And then, one day, you noticed a huge gate just by the school exit. It was labelled Public Examination System. It was a special gate because, however hard you all pushed, it only opened wide enough to let a few through it. A notice on the gate said that if you did get through it you would have an important position and a lovely life. You noticed that teachers seemed to prefer people who looked like they'd get through the gate.

9   And one thing was very clear, it was impossible to get through the gate with all your skills and knowledge. They were far too bulky and couldn't be wrapped up tightly or neatly enough. So you had to get some pieces of paper on which you'd written the answers to some questions. The answers were supposed to represent all your skills and knowledge. And the questions were things like: what are the principles of x? or $X - a + b(x - yk) = ?$ or compare and contrast X with Y, or translate A into B. You had to write them very fast or they didn't count. Nor did the questions you would have liked to ask. Or the answers you would have liked to have given.

10   By this time you always studied on your own. You couldn't let anyone see your work in case they copied it and managed to squeeze through the gate ahead of you. You knew the fewer the people pushing at the gate, the better your chances of getting through. But by this time lots of people had stopped bothering about the gate altogether.

11   Many of them spent their time doing things that, at the beginning, had been important—like Childcare, or Drama, or Carpentry. But now they didn't seem to enjoy doing them much any more. Because there was a rumour going around that people who spent their time doing those things were thick. And some of them, annoyed by this rumour, spent their time fighting and smashing up the equipment and being rude to the teachers.

12   Nevertheless, everyone knew the system was fair. It was obvious. After all, the ones who were going to get through the gate were called Very Able Children. The ones who went on trying were called Average Ability. And the rest were called either Below Average, or Below Average With Behaviour Disorders, depending on whether they smashed the place up or not.

13   And, at last, school (and usually any other kind of study) was over and WORK began. The ones who'd managed to get through the gate were a mixed bunch. One or two of them were still as talented as they had been on that first day. And now they had multi-faceted *trained* minds. They still noticed the countryside and other people; they were always curious and never stopped learning.

14   But some of the others were weird. There were brilliant scientists who spent their lives working on germs and nerve gases to exterminate everybody. There were lots who worked 18 hours a day trying to keep ahead of each other. They never noticed the sunshine and they feared sudden death. There were others who worked in tiny labyrinths where nobody else ever went. They looked as if their bodies were full of sawdust and they never talked to you.

15   And the rest? Well they slotted in more or less where they could. A few of them, mostly women, even went on tending their minds, for *their* lives were filled with multi-dimensional and creative problems to be solved (though no-one called what they were doing "work"). Nevertheless for most, something had changed. They knew now that there were lots of things they were No Good At. So they left lots of questions and problems to Those In Charge (who had been Very Able Children), even though Those In Charge often seemed to be making a terrible cock-up of it.

16   But in fact it didn't really matter whether they used their minds or not—because they were living in a Modern Civilization, and they could never get bored. At the press of a button they got instant Fun. And if they felt creative they could go Shopping and choose things.

17   In the poor world (which was still Uncivilized) things were a bit different. A few people, hidden away in remote spots, had been rather like the children on the first day. Only they had no schools and they hadn't needed to invent the alphabet. But they were very inventive in other ways.

18   There were ocean dwellers who could navigate across thousands of miles of featureless water with no instruments beyond their own senses. There were forest dwellers who had observed minutely the medicinal properties of plants. There were islanders who could actually solve the biggest conundrum of all: how to resolve human conflict without destroying the earth while you resolve it. They were no fools! The funny thing about these people was that everybody in the community knew about and was able to do just about everything. There were no Great Men,

or Geniuses, or Professional Experts. But when Civilization came
pounding in, many of these people and their skills were obliterated.

19   The people who brought Civilization thought the poor could make
their resources much more *profitable*. So they decided to help them.
Because these civilized people were educated, they only noticed the things
the poor couldn't do, and not the things they could do. They thought that
education could help. They remembered their own schools back home,
especially The Big Gate; how it let just enough people through to organize
things (for they didn't want to have to stand over the poor while they
made themselves more profitable); and how school made the rest
employable (for the most part); and, best of all, how everyone knew The
Big Gate was fair, for the experts who had invented it had proved that
people do not have equal brain power, so naturally The Big Gate only let
the clever ones through.

20   So into forest and veldt and mountain and plain came a curious rash of
schools. At the start many of them were not much more than a corrugated
iron roof, in which children learned reading, how to cover their private
parts, and the Bible. But as things got off the ground, many poor countries
began to reap the benefits of advanced school systems: Latin mottos,
school hymns, uniforms, sports day and *esprit de corps*. And the ones who
had been selected to stand around making sure everything got more
profitable could incarcerate their children in boarding schools (at huge
expense) to be tormented and bullied and turned into rulers in their turn.

21   But unfortunately there were small pockets of discontent. In the rich
world some teachers were getting fed up with being blamed for producing
dead-eyed children who smashed the place up, and with having to compete
with Fun and Shopping for their pupils' attention. They began thinking up
ways of changing things. Some of them even suggested that pupils should
do whatever they liked, or even recommended the abolition of schools
altogether. But whatever they did, they never managed to get rid of The Big
Gate, although sometimes they tried painting it different colours or
covering it with camouflage. It was all very confusing.

22   But in the poor world it was clear as crystal. Most people there lived in
the countryside where, money being short, there were very few schools. So
they had to walk miles to the nearest ones. And often they weren't very
healthy, for they were nearly always hungry (because now, being profitable,
they had no land on which to grow food, nor money with which to buy it).
And, not having much Fun or Shopping to divert their attention, they saw
clearly that hardly anyone was getting through The Big Gate—even those
who lived in towns—and hardly anyone knew how to do the things that
their forebears had known. And although they were no longer part of The
Empires Where The Sun Never Set, it was clear that everything was being
controlled from elsewhere. And the skills of the first day, the ones that

their forebears had had, were the only ones which could make things any better. Not only that, it was clear that The Very Able Children could not be trusted to use their knowledge for everyone's benefit.

23   So just a few of them began to set up their own schools. And in those schools they learned everything they needed to get some purchase on their lives: from Fish Farming to Small Arms Handling, from Marxism to Childcare. Their Reading and Writing was not about Little Red Engine, but about How Things Work—and about Who's Really In Charge Around Here.

24   And a few teachers in the rich world saw this and realized how they and their pupils had been hoodwinked. And they wanted to bring back all the knowledge and skills of the first day. And make people see that Knowledge Is Power. And to realize that all the Fun and Shopping in the world cannot compensate for the atrophy of their marvellous brains, and their helplessness in the hands of the moguls. But they could only get a few people to listen.

STUDY QUESTIONS

1. At the end of the second paragraph, Gahagan says of children at the outset of their schooling, "For these are still whole people." What does she mean by this statement? What effect does she think their subsequent education has on their wholeness?

2. Gahagan likens school to a filtration system for selecting future holders of power. Those who are rejected by this system, she says, return to activities such as "Childcare, or Drama, or Carpentry," activities that had in early childhood seemed important, but that later lost their appeal. Why, in her view, have such occupations become devalued? Do you agree that the same process operates in your country?

3. What does the author mean by Fun and Shopping (both capitalized), and how are these relevant to education and the social structure as described in the essay?

4. In the last four paragraphs of the essay, what educational movement is being described in both the "poor world" and the "rich world"? What is the author's attitude toward this movement, how does it fit into society, and what are the prospects for its success?

SUGGESTION FOR WRITING

This essay is written from a British perspective. In some ways it describes most pointedly the British educational system, the British class structure, and the former territories of the British Empire. However, the essay is of general interest because it offers a view of the way education and educational testing are related to each other and to the social power structure in both developed nations and "the poor world." Write an essay exploring whether or to what degree these relationships, as described in the essay, apply to your own society.

LUIS ALBERT MACHADO

From *"The Right to be Intelligent"*

Dr. Luis Alberto Machado served as Venezuela's Minister for the Development of Intelligence for four years beginning in 1979. In this capacity he initiated the successful Venezuelan Intelligence Project whose mission was to raise the intelligence of Venezuelans of every age. His methods inspired a parenting program entitled *Day One: A Positive Beginning for Parents and Their Infants*, which is being widely used in the United States.

1   When a premise is accepted as true, all of the conclusions which derive from it must also be admitted.

2   If the theory is welcomed that intellectual differences among men have a genetic cause, it must be carried through to its ultimate consequences.

3   We solemnly affirm that all men are substantially equal.

4   In Constitutions, Fundamental Charters, and Declarations of Human Rights, equality among men is upheld, but at the same time, our point of departure is the basic notion that, in something as fundamental to the development of man as intelligence, we are by birth radically different.

5   One of the postulates of all ideological currents is the fight against inequality.

6   But if intelligence is found to be previously determined by factors of a natural order, there is no sense in speaking of equality among men.

7   Every fight for equality is irremissibly condemned to failure.

8   We are not equal and would never become equal....

9   Those who have in all ages tried to impose on the world the government of the best for the best, would have been right to do so.

10   Oligarchy would be the ideal system.

11   The one that would impose itself definitively, by means of its correspondence to one of the actual exigencies of genetic coding.

12   If human beings' inclinations are fixed from the very moment of conception in the maternal womb, what ground is there left to freedom?

13   Can a man be free whose vocation is previously determined?

14   If intelligence is a work of nature, can we really be masters of our own destiny?

15   If intelligence were innate, no man would be free.

16   If men were not equal, democracy as a system of government would lack a reason for being.

17   It would be a system which at length would have to succumb.

18   If by nature men are not equal, there is no logic in their having equal votes.

19   If equality is impossible, then democracy is impossible.

20   If intelligence is a hereditary gift, the democratic ideal is no more than a very beautiful dream, with no other final destiny than that of history's archive.

21   And a system based on that ideal, as any other, would be beneficial only to a group of privileged men.

22   Democracy without equality is a farce.

23   A new form of dictatorship.

24   …In the biological sciences it becomes more and more evident that there are no superior men.

25   Those who have concluded that races are not equal, start from the premise that their own race occupies a position of preeminence.

26   A scientific proof which demonstrates that one race is genetically more perfect than another has never been able to be adduced.

27   Step by step, biology has razed the elements which have been claimed as the basis for every type of racism.

28   Time and again racism has been condemned by science.

29   Yet time and again it comes back to raise its head.

30   In every man who believes himself superior to his fellows by nature, there exists a potential racist.

31   The belief that intelligence is determined by genetic reasons also contains a certain dose of racism.

32   If men's intelligence is already fixed from the moment of birth, can it be affirmed that there are no superior races?

33   If, for genetic reasons, there are men of superior intelligence, there must also be races of superior intelligence.

34   If this is true, then there is nothing censurable in seeking to assure the pre-eminence of one race over the other.

35   After all, that pre-eminence would correspond to a design by nature, that would eventually have to be carried out. It would be more than reasonable to accelerate the thorough execution of that design.

36   If intelligence has a genetic origin, the logical consequence is a humanity harmed by the reproduction of its less intelligent members.

37   With the multiplication of the better endowed, we could achieve a better humanity.

38   We ought to prepare ourselves now to combat a type of racism more dangerous than any previous one; a "social racism" which holds that social differences are of genetic origin.

39   In numerous statistics, the children of professional people show a higher degree of intelligence than the children of workers.

40   Can the reason for this difference be genetic?

41   If so, should not the conclusion be that social differences have a biological origin, transmissible by heredity?

42 According to the enslavers of all ages, it is nature that imposes all systems of slavery.

43 Slaves are inferior beings.

44 One has only to act accordingly.

45 Inferior…in what?

46 Not in brute strength.

47 Not in physical resistance.

48 Inferior…in what?

49 In Plato's version of a text of Homer, "Zeus removed half of the mind of the slaves."*

50 Many centuries have passed, but this text is still in force today.

51 Perhaps the most dangerous prejudice of all holds that intelligence is transmitted genetically.

52 "Innatism" is exceedingly difficult to eradicate from the mind of a man or a nation.…

53 Biologically, man has remained the same for more than forty thousand years.

54 No part of the human body had undergone, for hundreds of centuries, any modification that might even remotely explain the progress of humanity.

55 The human brain has not varied since the Upper Paleolithic Age.

56 With the same brain, the number and quality of creative men have been increasing constantly.

57 Who produces them?…chromosomes…or education?

58 Man's development has always been constant.

59 Growing.

60 Genetic factors have not produced it.

61 Man's brain is the same.

62 Man's life is radically different.

63 The reason for the change is not biological.

64 Education is the key.

65 What has changed and in turn caused change, is not the brain, it is education.

66 The brain and the body of man remain the same but man continues to evolve.

67 At the beginning of evolution all changes were biological.

68 But with the passage of time the proportion of those changes was to become progressively smaller.

69 While biological evolution maintains a more or less constant speed, the velocity of man's evolution becomes ever higher.

---

*Laws, vi; *Odyssey,* vii. 322–3

70   Now, evolution is not the work of nature, it is man's.

71   The present evolution of man is one that he learns.

72   At birth, the minds of children of forty thousand years ago were the same as the minds of today's children.

73   Their differences reside in what they manage to learn.

74   The mind of the cave man was already equipped to achieve the advances of the twentieth century.

75   And he would have achieved them, had he had an earlier generation to teach him.

76   It seems plausible to think that every child born to an advanced society of today carries with him through biological inheritance a sort of "cultural predisposition," the fruit evolved from the by-gone centuries in history. It would seem that every child born in the twentieth century is born a child of that century.

77   However, if a new-born from London were to be removed to one of the aboriginal tribes of Australia, to be raised and have his life unfold there, that child would grow up a primitive.

78   The normally healthy child of a Bushman who is incorporated into an atmosphere of western culture at birth, will prove capable of growing up as just another of its members.

79   In the few hours of a plane trip, he leaps over ten or twenty thousand years.

80   He becomes a twentieth century man on arrival in the twentieth century.

81   No one is born civilized or primitive.

82   The child of a civilized man and woman will never be a civilized being, if he does not acquire the necessary learning.

83   The child of a primitive man and woman will become civilized, if he is educated to be so.

84   The difference between a primitive man and a civilized one is not biological; it is educational.

85   It is not nature that explains the cultural diversity among peoples.

86   The diversity of behavior and custom is the fruit of learning.

87   Not one of the habits, attitudes, conventions or modes of conduct characteristic of human groups, races or nations is due to heredity.

88   The great social transformations of history have not obeyed genetic transformations in the peoples that produced them.

89   The changes undergone by man are due to an attribute that is exclusively his — education.

90   The determining reason for the difference between the stagnation of the animal species and man's progress is man's faculty for passing acquired knowledge from one generation to the next.

91   Cultural heritage distinguishes the human being and is the only causal explanation for the development of humanity.

92   Man owes his present situation to himself, not to nature.

93   The progress of man is the fruit of culture, not biology.

94   Culture is everything to man....

95   To believe that human attitudes have a genetic origin is a position that offers a multitude of social and personal advantages.

96   Initially, there is a tranquility produced by conformism and self-justification.

97   It is comfortable and easy to locate personal responsibility in the genes....

98   When something is preordained and beyond a man's control, what can he do?

99   We are accustomed to thinking of genius as an equally distributed gift of God, enjoyed only by a few.

100   And we are happy with that thought.

101   It does not disturb us because it asks nothing of us.

102   It is not merely that we are not obliged to try and attain genius.

103   It seems that even the attempt would be foolish.

104   First we build a God according to our criteria and then assign him the responsibility for everything we believe we cannot help and for much of what we do not want to do.

105   For some, God is an excuse to remain where they are.

106   For others, a rationalization for injustice.

107   Social life is not the result of a previously designed plan.

108   God is not a maker of privileges.

109   Privileges are made by man....

110   According to what is considered one of nature's own arrangements, women have been subjected to the greatest injustice ever perpetrated.

111   Schopenhauer's dictum "woman is a being with long hair and short ideas," corresponds to one of the basic blocks in society's foundation.

112   For centuries, men believed that women were programmed to feel and not to think, in the same way they were programed for pain because they bore their children in pain.

113   This fact—they thought—placed women beneath men in their capacity for intellectual development.

114   Historical facts seemed to bear this out totally: what woman can be compared with Aristotle or Kant, Copernicus or Einstein, Leonardo or Monet, Beethoven or Schoenberg?

115   Today we know children can be born without pain and that woman has demonstrated herself to be as unquestionably capable of excellence in any intellectual activity as is man.

116   Should the conclusion be that sometime in the last several decades nature has undergone a change of signals?

117   Social structure and the force of her own convictions have impeded woman's proportionate achievement of excellence in the fields of the human mind.

118   This has happened over generations.

119   There was no reason for it.

120   Woman's intelligence is not inferior.

121   It never was.

122   In the field of creativity, humanity has made its way with one leg hobbled until now.

123   For centuries woman has been sheared of the possibility of developing a basic element of her personality.

124   It is an enslaving myth that postulates talent as a work of nature.

125   No one is predestined in his or her mental capacity.

126   It is not only a few who are born with the option to be intelligent.

127   Privileges are not passed on by heredity.

128   They are repeated by social circumstance.

129   Consequently, a sort of caste of intelligence perpetuated through genetic factors is inadmissible.

130   ...Until now intelligence has been a privilege.

131   The last stronghold of privilege.

132   The most ill-distributed wealth on earth.

133   The cause and foundation of the remaining privileges.

134   Every oligarchy is in the last analysis an intellectual oligarchy.

135   Intelligence is a synonym of power.

136   Meditation on intelligence is meditation on power.

137   The power of intelligence constitutes the principal source of oppression in all of history.

138   The existence of social classes — and individual membership in one or another of them — is determined by a cultural factor — the degree of development of intelligence.

139   Castes, classes, social rank, every type of slavery and servitude have their origins in the domination of some intellects by others.

140   Today, as in the past, there are slaves to intelligence.

141   Social injustice is the result of a cultural injustice.

142   While talent is beneficial only for a minority, there cannot be any justice in the world.

143   For surviving life's hazards there is only one true superiority and that is intellectual superiority.

144   It is highly unlikely that an intelligent man will be used by anyone.

145   If a man does not make himself capable he will continue to be subject to those more capable than he.

146   The dullard would always be at the mercy of the intelligent.

147   But no one is born to be dominated.

148 …Intelligence is culture.

149 If it is not innate, it is a potentiality developed by life.

150 In fact, it has developed in us through some form of teaching and learning.

151 But without a method.

152 Or program.

153 Yet everything that can be learned in this way, can also be learned systematically.

154 Life as life cannot be systematized.

155 Nor can its individually considered facets be systematized.

156 It is certainly not even worth the effort to enumerate all of its facets.

157 Man cannot be defined as a function of his activities, because he is not unidimensional; he has as many dimensions as possibilities.

158 It is, however, possible to systematize all those processes which have developed anarchically.

159 Even spontaneity, systematized as such, can become more spontaneous.

160 Methods of teaching can be constructed concretely.

161 With a method, every learning process has to be more effective.

162 So, every normal human being, regardless of age, can become more intelligent with systematic teaching.

163 …Decades ago, if a child learned to read or master a musical instrument at three years of age, he was considered a genius. We see today, that any normal child is capable of the same.

164 The person whose intelligence is of a genius' caliber ought not be seen as a man endowed with extraordinary faculties.

165 A genius is not a superman.

166 He is a normal man.

167 The rest of us are infranormal.

168 We are called to reach the genius' level.

169 And in the future, to surpass it.

170 Today's exception will be tomorrow's rule.

171 Intelligence is only natural.

172 Stupidity requires explanation.

173 Every man is born with a live computer of limitless possibilities, but without the instruction manual.

174 The most important job of science today is to draw up that manual.

STUDY QUESTIONS

1. Machado says that if intellectual differences among people have a genetic cause, then oligarchy would be the ideal system of government. What is the missing premise (or premises) in this deduction?

2. In Machado's view, how does a belief in genetically determined intelligence produce racism?

3. What implications does Machado deduce from his premise that man's brain has undergone no biological changes for the last 40,000 years?

4. If "intelligence" or "talent" is not inborn, then what, in Machado's view, accounts for the apparent intellectual differences from person to person?

5. In Machado's view, is an individual's intelligence fixed or flexible throughout life?

SUGGESTION FOR WRITING

On a sheet of paper, construct a chart that looks like this:

	INTELLIGENCE	EDUCATION	SOCIAL POWER
Cutten			
Seligman			
Gahagan			
Rosser			
Machado			

Make some brief notes on the chart about each author's stated or implicit beliefs about each of the three topics. If you feel that the author gives no basis for an opinion, leave the space blank, but if you feel that you could make an educated guess about how the author might feel concerning that topic, write out what you think and be prepared to explain what in the author's statement led you to your speculative conclusion.

Now write an essay addressing the following question: "Do specific beliefs about the nature of human intelligence correspond with specific beliefs about education and the proper distribution of social power?" Cite examples from whichever of the authors on your chart serve your purpose, and feel free to discuss them within an explicit framework of your own beliefs and attitudes.

Appendix: More About Logic

Categorical Propositions: Rule, Case, and Attribute

Logic is nothing more than the codification of common sense. Our brains perform logical processes rapidly and often below the threshold of conscious awareness. When we study logic, we slow this process down, make all the steps explicit, and consider the principles of its operation.

We use logic in the most simple, ordinary situations. For example, assume that at a certain college, it is a bit of campus wisdom that students in Math 245 always carry calculators. You might hear this exchange:

> STUDENTS A, B, AND C: We're taking Math 245 this semester.
> STUDENT D: Oh, can I borrow a calculator from one of you?

Student D has run through a quick process of *inference*, a process in which we begin with propositions that are known to be true (or believed to be true, or for the moment assumed to be true) and conclude that on the basis of these propositions, some other proposition is or may be true. Student D has reasoned as follows:

> All students in Math 245 are students who carry calculators.
> These students are students in Math 245.
> _____
> Therefore these students are students who carry calculators.

The first two propositions, the ones on which Student D bases her inference, are called *premises*. The proposition that she derives is the *conclusion*. The sequence of two premises leading to a conclusion that follows logically from them is called a *syllogism*.

All three of the propositions that compose a syllogism describe relationships among categories. In each proposition, the grammatical subject names a category and the predicate states how it is related to another category. For instance, the first premise above states that the category composed of "students in   *495*

Math 245" is wholly included in the category of "students who carry calculators."
It leaves open the possibility that other students, not enrolled in this course, also
carry calculators. The verb "are" does not signify that the subject category and
predicate category are identical, but that the subject category is *included* in the
predicate category. The premises establish the conclusion by relating each of the
two categories of the conclusion ("These students" and "students who carry
calculators") to a common category, known as the *middle term* ("students in
Math 245"). Thus every term appears twice in the syllogism. The subject term and
predicate term of the conclusion each appear in the conclusion and one premise,
while the middle term appears in both premises but not in the conclusion.

The first premise above states a general *rule* about the subject term only. It
states that all students in Math 245 carry calculators, but it does not state a general rule about the predicate term, "students who carry calculators." Thus we say
that the subject term, "students in Math 245," is *distributed*, while the predicate
term, "students who carry calculators," is not distributed.

In the syllogism we are dealing with, the second premise, "These students
are students in Math 245," describes a *case* of the rule expressed in the first
premise. That is, the second premise states that Students A, B, and C are members
of the category that is distributed in the rule. *Whether a given proposition is a rule
or a case does not depend on its grammatical form, but on its relation to the other
propositions in the syllogism.* For instance, the proposition that served as the case
in the syllogism above can serve as the rule in a different argument.

> *Rule:* These students are students in Math 245.
> *Case:* Student B is one of these students.
> _____
> Therefore, Student B is a student in Math 245.

Let's return to the first syllogism we discussed, with particular attention to
the third proposition, which we may call an *attribute*[1] because it attributes a
quality to members of the category described in the case.

> *Rule:*   All students in Math 245 carry calculators.
> *Case:*   These students are students in Math 245.
> _____
> *Attribute:*   Therefore these students are students who carry calculators.

Grammatically the attribute resembles the case, but when we consider these two
propositions in relation to the rule, we see an important difference between
them: The *case* places students A, B, and C in the *distributed* term of the rule,
while the *attribute* places them in the *undistributed* term of the rule.

---

[1] The discussion of the three forms of inference presented in this appendix is adapted from the
logic of Charles Sanders Peirce. The term *attribute* to describe one type of proposition in an inference is my substitution for Peirce's term *result*, which makes perfect sense to describe the
conclusion of a deductive syllogism, but which might be misleading when used to describe a
premise in an inductive or abductive argument.

The Three Forms of Inference

1. Deduction

In the syllogism we have been considering, the premises consisted of a rule and a case; the conclusion was the attribute. Arguments in this form are called *deductive* arguments. A deductive argument has a quality that no other argument has. If the premises are true, then (provided it adheres to rules of deductive validity that we'll consider later) the conclusion is bound to be true. Thus if all students in Math 245 carry calculators, and Students A, B, and C are members of that class, they are necessarily students who carry calculators. Common sense tells us that whatever is true of all members of a category must be true of each individual member.

The conclusion of a syllogism does not add any new information to that contained in the premises. Consider the most ancient example of a categorical syllogism:

> *Rule:* All men are mortal.
> *Case:* Socrates is a man.
> _____
> *Attribute:* Therefore, Socrates is mortal.

Note that, if there had been any real doubt that Socrates was mortal, no one could have been sure that both the premises were simultaneously true. If it were accepted that all men were mortal but doubted whether Socrates were mortal, then it could not have been confidently asserted that Socrates was a man. Or, if it was certain that Socrates was a man but doubtful whether he was mortal, then it could not be determined that all men were mortal (because Socrates might have been the exception). In fact, it can never be known for certain that all men are mortal. It is in principle possible that you yourself may prove the exception, or that science may discover a cure for death. We can say with certainty that everyone born before 1550 was mortal, but from this fact we can never deduce that everyone living today will prove mortal.

If the conclusion of a deductive argument never gives us any information that was not already implicit in the premises, what is the use of deduction?

1 The most widespread use of deductive arguments is organizational, especially in arguments with one or more value premises. For instance, Peter Singer's "Animal Liberation" rests on two broad premises. The first, that any creature's claim to rights is based not on its intelligence but on its capacity for suffering, occupies several paragraphs near the opening. The second premise, that at least some animals suffer, occupies most of the rest of the argument. Every argument needs some way of showing how its major subarguments relate to each other. When the premises possess the deductive relationship of rule and case, and when each premise is adequately defended, the argument has enormous per-

suasive force. It is not even necessary that the syllogism be stated explicitly in one localized paragraph. If the deductive relationship is even implicitly present, its powerful logic will give strength to the conclusion.

2 The full implications of a set of premises may not be intuitively obvious.
Most people ignorant of geometry could not see without a demonstration that the Pythagorean theorem is fully implicit in the definitions,
postulates, and axioms of Euclidean geometry.

3 Some fallacious reasoning results from a failure to follow the rules of deductive reasoning. By understanding the common fallacies, we can be on
guard against them in our own reasoning and spot them more readily in
the arguments of others.

4 Most arguments in everyday life do not bother to articulate premises
that seem obvious. "Henry Kissinger can't be President; he wasn't born
in this country." (Hidden premise: No person born outside this country
can be President.) A knowledge of strictly logical form enables us to
supply such hidden premises.

5 Deductive reasoning plays an important structural role in science. By
deducing the observable consequences of their hypotheses, scientists discover what propositions need to be put to empirical tests. (See page 26
for a discussion of the hypothetico-deductive process.)

2. Induction

A second form of inference is called *induction,* in which a rule is inferred from a
case and an attribute. Suppose for a moment that you did not know the rule that
all students who take Math 245 carry calculators. Suppose that you were conducting a teacher-evaluation in that course and that, to compile your survey, you
stood outside the classroom door and asked students to fill out an evaluation
form. Suppose finally that although only about half of the 300 students in the
course exited by the door where you were standing, every student you saw, without exception, carried a calculator.

You would then arrive at two propositions that look much like the case and
attribute of our earlier syllogism:

> These students carry calculators.
> These students are students in Math 245.

Moreover, even though you were unable to observe everyone in the class, you
might feel fairly confident in reaching the inductive conclusion that all students
in Math 245 carried calculators. Thus you have one inversion of our earlier deductive syllogism:

> *Case:*   These students are students in Math 245.
> *Attribute:*   These students carry calculators.
> ———————————————————————————
> *Rule:*   All students in Math 245 carry calculators.

Common sense will tell you that this inductive argument differs from a deductive syllogism[2] in the level of confidence we can have in the conclusion. In the deductive syllogism, if the premises are true, the conclusion must be true; but in the inductive argument above, you can easily see that even though the premises are true, the conclusion might be false. Even though you have seen 150 students come out of Math 245 carrying a calculator, the next student may have forgotten hers or neglected to buy one or be such a prodigy as not to require one. Your conclusion gathers strength with every confirming observation you make, of course, but it also depends on your sample's being *representative.* For instance, if you make your observation in the late afternoon on the last day of class before a vacation, you may unwittingly have selected a day when only the most conscientious students have chosen to attend and so have observed an uncharacteristic sample.

In the inductive argument above, in keeping with the definitions of rule, case, and attribute, the case describes the distributed term of the rule while the attribute describes the undistributed term. But wait: When all you had was the two premises, how did you know which was the case and which was the attribute? And how did you know which should be the subject and which the predicate term of the rule? In other words, why couldn't your argument have taken this alternative form:

> *Case:* These students carry calculators.
> *Attribute:* These students are students in Math 245.
> _____
> *Rule:* All students who carry calculators are students in Math 245.

The answer lies in the way you came by your knowledge of the premises. You did not set out to sample students who carry calculators, but to sample students in Math 245. Thus the distributed term in your rule must be "students in Math 245"; they, rather than "students who carry calculators," are the group about whom your method of inquiry has entitled you to propose a general rule.

What method of inquiry might legitimately yield the alternative version of our argument? Suppose you ran a calculator repair shop on the college campus and made a point of asking all your customers what they used their calculators for; suppose they always answered that they were enrolled in Math 245. On this basis you might begin to conclude that no one on the campus used calculators unless they were in this course (or, in other words, that all students who used calculators were students in Math 245). In this hypothetical situation, however, you would have no basis for inferring that all students in Math 245 carried calculators.

Induction, then, is a form of inference whereby, having observed that individuals in a given category share a given characteristic, you conclude, perhaps only tentatively, that all members share that characteristic. (Or, if you observe

_____

[2] Properly speaking, the inductive sequence is not a syllogism. That term is reserved for deductive reasoning. For nondeductive reasoning, we shall use the terms *argument* or *inference*.

that a certain fraction of individuals share this characteristic, and if your sample were sufficiently large and representative, you might infer that the same proportion would hold for the category as a whole.)

3. Abduction

In the third form of inference, *abduction,* or *hypothesis,* one notices an anomalous fact and seeks to *explain* it. For instance, suppose you saw several students carrying calculators in some unusual setting—at the swimming pool, for example. You might search your store of general knowledge for one or more rules that might explain it, and in doing so you might recall that students in Math 245 always carry calculators. Thus you might construct an argument that is a second inversion of our original deductive argument, now with the case as the conclusion:

> *Attribute:* These students carry calculators.
> *Rule:* All students in Math 245 carry calculators.
>
> *Case:* (Perhaps) These students are students in Math 245.

Conclusions reached in this way must be considered extremely tentative. They are often merely wild guesses, but they can be strokes of genius. In fact, "conclusion" is a misnomer for the hypothesis that emerges from abductive premises, for it is really a speculation that initiates an inquiry into its truth. Every act of diagnosis, whether of human illness, mechanical breakdown, or social misfortune, involves abduction. Often the diagnostician, faced with an anomalous fact, will simultaneously entertain several mutually exclusive hypotheses and try to rule them out in turn until only one remains. For instance, if a patient telephones a doctor to complain of a rash, the doctor will ask a series of questions. The doctor might ask, "Have you ever had measles?" reasoning:

> My patient has the *attribute* of a rash
> It is a *rule* that patients with measles have a rash.
>
> Perhaps my patient represents a *case* of the measles.

If the patient has previously had measles, the doctor, knowing that the patient could not get the disease twice, will consider that hypothesis ruled out and go on to others: "Do you have any allergies? Have you, to your knowledge, been near poison ivy or poison oak?" etc. But even if the patient has never had measles, the doctor will still run through the other hypotheses to see which survive this initial test.

We have already considered the main uses of deductive reasoning in real-life arguments; you have perhaps already seen that induction and abduction tend to work hand in hand. It is commonly believed that empirical knowledge is gained chiefly by induction, but this is an oversimplification. Some years ago doctors recognized a previously unknown illness that they called AIDS. The early victims were homosexuals. All induction could have done with this information would have been to conclude the rule that all AIDS victims are homosexual. This conclusion, of course, would have been not only wrong, but unsatisfying. Until doctors had some explanation of the disease's mechanism, they could not have faith in the inductive conclusion. Abduction suggested that AIDS might be a case not of homosexuality per se, but of viral infection through an exchange of bodily fluids that could take such other forms as heterosexual intercourse, sharing of unsterile needles, or transfusions of infected blood. Induction could then be enlisted to confirm by multiple observations that this refined rule held true.

The Analysis of Deductive Arguments

The conclusions of abductive arguments are entirely speculative, and the conclusions of inductive arguments are only as reliable as the samples on which they are based, but the conclusions of deductive arguments are certain, provided that they are derived from the premises according to certain rules.

The Form of Categorical Propositions

Logical analysis of arguments demands that we understand how categories are related in individual propositions, but ordinary speech often obscures the categorical nature of the terms. "Everyone in Math 245 carries a calculator" does not sound at first as though it states that one category is included in another, and yet it can be translated, "All *students in Math 245* are included in the category of *students who carry calculators.*" When you are checking the logic of an argument, your own or someone else's, it helps to translate everyday phrasing into proper categorical form by observing the following rules:[3]

- The *terms* in the subjects and predicates are nouns or noun phrases, though often an adjective in the predicate is an unambiguous substitute for a noun phrase.
- The noun phrases may contain as many qualifiers as you wish, *provided that the whole qualifying phrase appears in identical form both times it is used.*

> All *persons who are retired and who neither earn over $1200 a year nor belong to a private insurance plan* are persons eligible for government benefits.
>
> I am a *person who is retired and who neither earns over $1200 a year nor belongs to a private insurance plan.*
> _____
>
> Therefore, I am a person eligible for government benefits.

---

[3] This is *not* to say that your writing will be improved if you apply these rules in your essays; in fact, to do so would be a stylistic disaster.

- Verbs are always a form of the verb "*to be.*"
- The subject terms of the premises and conclusions of a categorical syllogism carry a quantifier, which must be either "all," "some," or "no."

All electrons are negatively charged.
Some athletes are sprinters.
No triangles are quadrilaterals.

Exceptions

A proposition that has a proper noun or a pronoun as its subject (such as "Socrates is mortal" or "I am a baker") or that makes an unqualified statement about a subject in the form of a singular noun ("My car is blue"; "This disease is not contagious") does not carry a quantifier but is construed as a universal premise. A premise like "These students are students who carry calculators" means "*All* these students are students who carry calculators."

When the subject term is quantified by "all" or "no," it is a *universal* proposition; when it is quantified by "some," it is a *particular* proposition.

In ordinary speech, when we say that "some X's are Y's," we often mean that there are some X's that are not Y's as well, but when we encounter a "some are" statement in logic, we are not entitled to assume also that "some are not." (In our own arguments, if we wish to describe a situation in which "some are and some are not," we must use two different propositions to express this fact.)

- A proposition is negative either if the verb is modified by "not" or if the quantifier of the subject term is "no."

As these criteria imply, the premises and conclusions of categorical syllogisms may take four forms, as shown in the following table:

	AFFIRMATIVE	*NEGATIVE*
Universal	All X's are Y.	No X's are Y.
Particular	Some X's are Y.	Some X's are not Y.

EXERCISE

Put the following sentences into proper form for use in syllogisms, indicating whether your proposition is universal affirmative, universal negative, particular affirmative, or particular negative. Be careful about quantifiers. If you are in doubt about whether a subject term should be preceded by "some" or "all," choose the one that seems to you most likely to be true and be prepared to justify your decision.

1 No one can solve this problem.
2 A few lawyers in this city have proven to be dishonest.
3 Teenage drivers take too many risks.

4 All dogs are not friendly.
5 Most people who have had four years of math will have no difficulty with this program.
6 Hardly any of our products enter into harmful drug interactions.
7 Not all child-care centers are trustworthy.
8 In this town retired executives are available to serve as consultants to local businesses.

More about Distribution

As noted earlier, a term in a proposition is said to be *distributed* if it carries sure information about every member of the class that it represents. Reverting to the chart above, we can add information about when subject (S) and predicate (P) terms are distributed in each of the four kinds of propositions, as shown in the following table: (**Note:** It will help you to recall that the predicate terms of negative propositions are always distributed, while the predicate terms of affirmative propositions are never distributed.)

	Affirmative	*Negative*
Universal	S	Both S and P
Particular	Neither S nor P	P

EXERCISE

Determine whether the underlined terms in each of the following exercises are distributed or undistributed:

1 Some legal actions are unethical actions.
2 No nonprofit organizations are taxable organizations.
3 All chemistry majors are students eligible for the B.S. degree.
4 Some exercise programs are not beneficial to health.
5 Anthony Trollope was not a poet.

Rules of Deductive Validity

A syllogism is said to be *valid* if its conclusion is logically entailed by its premises. A conclusion may be valid without being true, as the following example demonstrates:

All mammals are warm-blooded.
All flounders are mammals.

Therefore, all flounders are warm-blooded.

The conclusion is valid because it follows from the premises; however, it is not true because the second premise is false. In order to be valid, a categorical syllogism must satisfy five conditions:

1 The middle term must be distributed at least once.
2 If either term is distributed in the conclusion, it must have been distributed in a premise.
3 At least one premise must be affirmative.
4 At least one premise must be particular if the conclusion is particular.
5 The conclusion must be negative if one of the premises is negative, affirmative if both premises are affirmative.

Common Errors in Using Categorical Syllogisms

1. Undistributed Middle

Of the five rules of syllogistic validity above, the one that is easiest to violate unwittingly is that which requires the middle term to be distributed at least once. Usually the violation occurs in arguments constructed like this:

> All rodents are mammals.
> This mouse is a mammal.
> _____
> Therefore, this mouse is a rodent.

This argument may look valid (particularly since both premises and the conclusion happen to be true), but it is not valid, as you can easily see for yourself by substituting the word "elephant" for "mouse." The fallacy of the undistributed middle has had a notorious role in witch-hunts of various sorts throughout history. For instance, arguments like the following are deductively fallacious:

> All children whose parents beat them show bruises.
> My neighbor's daughter shows bruises.
> _____
> Therefore, my neighbor's daughter is a child whose parents beat her.

The proper response to such an argument is, "Even if all abused children have bruises, that doesn't mean that all children with bruises have been beaten." This response is simply a way of pointing out that the middle term, "children who show bruises," is never distributed in this syllogism. (In both of its occurrences it is the predicate term of an affirmative proposition.) On the other hand, it must be pointed out that the pattern of argument here is an abduction. The only fallacy lies in believing that the conclusion is proven by the premises. If a neighboring child shows evidence of abuse, you might do as much of an injustice to the child by dismissing your hypothesis as illogical as you would do to the parents by treating your hypothesis as a logically proven finding. Here, as so often in logic, the secret is not so much in reaching "true" or "false" conclusions as in knowing what level of credence to give them and understanding what further steps of inquiry may be demanded.

Syllogisms with an undistributed middle may take different forms from the example above.

> Some products without preservatives are subject to spoilage.
> All of NatureFood's products are products without preservatives.
>
> Therefore, some of NatureFood's products are subject to spoilage.

To understand the weakness of this syllogism, assume that NatureFood sells only gin and whiskey, which are not subject to spoilage even though they have no added preservatives. In this case, the premises will both be true but the conclusion false, a sign of invalid reasoning.

2. Illicit Process

This fallacy involves violation of the rule that no term may be distributed in the conclusion that was not distributed in the premise. For example:

> All products made with milk are subject to spoilage.
> No ChemiFood products are made with milk.
>
> Therefore, no ChemiFood products are subject to spoilage.

This syllogism ignores the possibility that some products might be subject to spoilage even though they contain no milk. The term "subject to spoilage" is distributed in the conclusion because it is the predicate term of a negative proposition. It was not distributed in the first premise because it was the predicate term of an affirmative statement.

3. Faulty Quantifiers (or Hasty Generalization)

Obviously a syllogism will yield a false conclusion if a premise states that "all" of a term has a certain quality when the facts prove only that "some" possess that quality (or if a premise states that "none" of a term possesses a quality when the facts show only that "some" do not have that quality). More commonly, in normal discourse quantifiers are simply omitted but terms are treated as though the more inclusive quantifier applied.

> Someone with great physical strength will be best for this job.
> Men have greater physical strength than women.
>
> Therefore, a man will be best for this job.

Do *all* men have greater physical strength than any woman? If not, then the proper quantifier in the premise is "some" men, and the conclusion must also read, "Some men will be best for this job"…and some women. One common species of this fallacy occurs in arguments that justify retaliation against all members of a class because of acts committed by some minority or subclass within it. Would it be fair for your school to assess you a fee for breakage you didn't commit on the excuse that "It's students who cause the vandalism around here, so it's the students who should pay?")

4. Equivocation

The fallacy of equivocation occurs when a syllogism includes more than three terms.

> *The company directive sent out last fall said that sales representatives would receive a raise if they increased their sales by 15 percent. Since then, I have tried very hard to increase my sales. I have contacted 25 percent more clients than I did last year, and most of them, I am confident, will make substantial purchases over the next four years. Without pressuring them into immediate purchases, I have laid down a base of goodwill and awareness of our products. On this basis, I believe that my name should be added to the list of those scheduled for a raise.*

This argument from someone who has been passed over for a raise is roughly syllogistic in form.

All *sales representatives who improved their sales by 15 percent* are eligible
for a raise.
I am a *sales representative who tried hard to improve sales by 15 percent.*

Therefore I am eligible for a raise.

Here equivocation takes the form of a clear shift in the wording of one term. The first premise concerns those who have *actually* increased their sales, the second, someone who has *tried to* increase his sales.

Equivocation also occurs when a term retaining the same wording undergoes a shift of meaning.

> *All students are entitled to equal treatment in the assignment of grades. But while you gave me a D, the class average was B–, and my roommate even received an A. D is not equal to A or even to B–. Therefore you have not given me the equal treatment to which I am entitled.*

In this argument (which is seriously advanced more often than you might believe), the word "equal" has different meanings in the two premises. In the first, the equality to which students are entitled is an equality of the *standards* whose degree of fulfillment the grade represents. In the second, equality can logically refer only to the *grades themselves*. Notice that we can accept the truth of each premise so long as, in reading it, we assign the meaning of the equivocal term appropriate to that premise. We agree that students are entitled to equal treatment; we agree that D is not equal to B–. But if we now return to the first premise, giving the equivocal term "equal" the meaning it has in the second premise, we realize that it asserts a student's right to the same grades as everyone else in the class, and on this interpretation we would reject the premise.

Arguments resting on a shift of meaning in a crucial term are seductive precisely because we are able to accept the truth of the individual premises and because the invalidating introduction of a fourth term into the syllogism is not

reflected in an actual shift of wording. The danger of accepting this form of fallacious reasoning is all the greater when the arguments are not compressed into
three or four sentences, as they are above, but spread out over ten or twenty pages.

Equivocation is a particular danger in arguments including terms such as
"rights" and "responsibilities" that have both a legal and a moral sense, and terms
of literary and artistic criticism, such as "obscure," "grotesque," "colossal," and
"ambiguous" that have both a purely descriptive meaning and a pejorative or
honorific meaning.

Diagramming Syllogisms

Sometimes when you are evaluating the validity of a syllogism, it helps to visualize the relationships of the categories by creating a diagram. As examples, see
Figures 1–4.

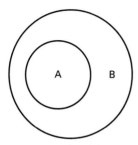

Figure 1. "All A are B." Here are the circles representing the two categories show that
all members of category A are also within category B.

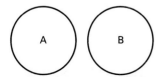

Figure 2. "No A are B." Here the circles representing categories A and B show that the
members of the two categories are entirely separate.

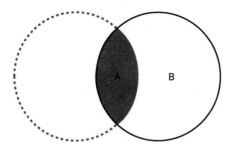

Figure 3. "Some A are B." Here the shaded part of the A circle shows that some members of A are also members of B, while the dotted line indicates that some members of
A *may* lie outside category B.

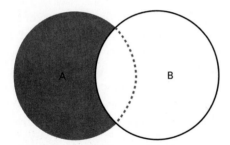

Figure 4. "Some A are not B." Here the shaded part of the A circle shows that some A exist that are not B, while the dotted part allows for the possibility that some A are B as well.

Now, let us see how we use these four diagrams to test the validity of a syllogism. For convenience, always let circle B represent the middle term; let circle A represent the other term of the first premise; and let circle C represent the other term of the second premise. Always diagram the first premise first. This diagram will always show the relationship of circles A and B. For example, suppose we are diagramming the syllogism,

> All local taxpayers are eligible to park free at the town beach.
> I am a local taxpayer.
> _____
> Therefore, I am eligible to park free at the town beach.

Since "local taxpayer" is the middle term of this syllogism, we shall let it be represented by circle B, and we shall use circle A to represent the other term of the first premise, people eligible to park free at the town beach. Our first premise, then, is diagrammed as in Figure 5:

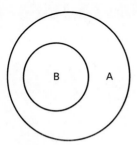

Figure 5.

Now proceed to the second premise. It will always tell you how to position circle C with respect to circle B. In our present example, "I am a local taxpayer," circle C must be placed wholly within circle B, as in Figure 6.

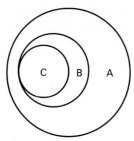

Figure 6.

Our diagram is now complete. We do not add anything to represent the conclusion. Instead we look at what we have drawn to represent the two premises and enquire whether the relationship between circle A and circle C is consistent with the relationship of the categories in the conclusion of the syllogism.

The conclusion of any categorical syllogism always expresses a relationship between terms A and C.

The conclusion we are checking affirms that "I am eligible to park free at the town beach." In diagrammatic terms, this would mean that circle C ("I") would be included in circle A ("those eligible to park free at the town beach"). Since our diagram indeed shows this, *and since our diagram is the only way of representing the two premises,* we know that the syllogism is valid.

Often, though, when we come to diagram the second premise, we face a choice of how circle C should relate to circle A. Consider the following syllogism:

> All physicians own a sphygmomanometer.
> All my uncles own sphygmomanometers.
>
> Therefore, all my uncles are physicians.

Letting A = physicians, B = owners of a sphygmomanometer, and C = my uncles, diagram the first premise:

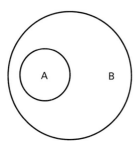

Figure 7. A diagram of the first premise (All physicians own a sphygmomanometer, or All A are B).

When we come to the second premise, "All my uncles own sphygmo-manometers," it is clear that circle C ("my uncles") will go inside circle B ("owners of sphygmomanometers"), but within circle B, how shall circle C be positioned with respect to circle A? Figures 8–10 illustrate three positions, all of which are compatible with the first two premises of the syllogism.

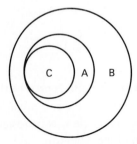

Figure 8. Within circle B, circle C may be totally included in circle A.

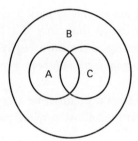

Figure 9. Within circle B, circle C may be partly included in circle A.

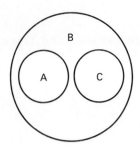

Figure 10. Within circle B, circle C may be totally excluded from circle A.

Figure 8 does reflect the situation expressed in the conclusion; Figures 9 and 10 do not. So is the conclusion valid? *No.* A syllogism is *not* valid just because a diagram reflecting the premises can be found that also reflects the conclusion. *A syllogism is only valid if all possible diagrams include the relationship between terms A and C that is specified in the conclusion of the syllogism.* This is the most difficult concept to grasp about diagramming syllogisms, but it need not pose problems for you if, in diagramming the second premise, you simply *try to position circle C so that it is consistent with the second premise but inconsistent with the conclusion.* If you can do so, the syllogism is invalid; if you cannot, it is valid.

It is possible for a syllogism to have more than one diagram and yet be valid. Consider the following pair of premises:

> Some Buddhists are altruists.
> No Christians are Buddhists.

In these premises, A = altruists; B = Buddhists; and C = Christians. The first premise is diagrammed in Figure 11:

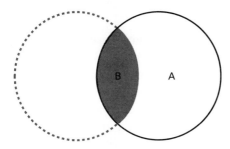

Figure 11. Some Buddhists are altruists, or some B are C.

When we add circle C, representing "Christians," we are required by the second premise to place it so that there is no overlap with circle B (Buddhists), but it may relate to circle A (altruists) in any of three ways, as shown in Figures 12–14.

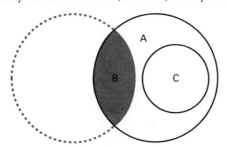

Figure 12. Circle C may be wholly within that part of A that is outside B.

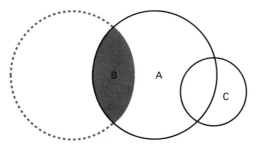

Figure 13. Circle C may be partly inside A and partly outside it.

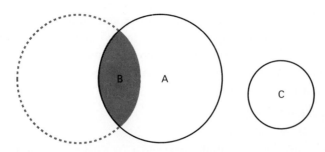

Figure 14. Circle C it may be wholly outside A.

What do these diagrams tell us about the possible valid conclusions to our syllogism? "Some Christians are not altruists" would *not* be a valid conclusion because one of the possible diagrams of the second premise places C wholly within A, signifying that, according to the premises, all Christians may be altruists. (Also, this conclusion would violate the rule that a term—in this case, "altruists"—may not be distributed in the conclusion if it was not distributed in a premise.) "Some altruists are not Christians" *would* be a valid conclusion, because in whichever of the three possible positions we place circle C, there will still be a part of circle A outside it (that part of circle A that is within circle B).

EXERCISE 1

In the following syllogisms, the terms have been reduced to letters to give you practice in dealing with the syllogistic forms without the distractions of meaning. Diagram each syllogism and tell whether the conclusion is valid or invalid. If the syllogism is invalid and there are several ways of diagramming it, you need provide only one diagram that is consistent with the premises but inconsistent with the conclusion. If the syllogism is invalid, which rule(s) have been violated?

1. All A are B.
   All B are C.
   _____
   Therefore, all A are C.

2. All A are B.
   All B are C.
   _____
   Therefore, all C are A.

3. Some A are B.
   No C are B.
   _____
   Therefore, some A are not C.

4. Some A are B.
   No C are B.
   _____
   Therefore, some C are not A.

5. Some A are B.
   Some B are C.
   _____
   Therefore, some A are C.

6. Some A are B.
   No B are C.
   _____
   Therefore, some A are not C.

7. Some A are not B.
   Some C are not B.
   _____
   Therefore, all A are C.

8. All A are B.
   All C are B.
   _____
   Therefore, all A are C.

9. No A are B.
   Some B are C.
   _____
   Therefore, some C are not A.

10. Some A are B.
    No B are C.
    _____
    Therefore, some C are not A.

11. All A are B
    Some B are C.
    _____
    Therefore, some A are C.

12. No B are A
    Some C are not B.
    _____
    Therefore, some C are A.

EXERCISE 2

Critique the following examples of syllogistic reasoning. Identify conclusions that you feel are either invalid or untrue or both. What causes the conclusions to be wrong? In addition to the formal fallacies, you may discover premises that are flawed by equivocation and faulty quantification. Be prepared to express each syllogism in proper form as described on pages 501–502.

1. Mr. Karpov has asbestosis.
   Only those exposed to asbestos fibers in excess contract asbestosis.
   _____
   Therefore, Mr. Karpov has been exposed to asbestos fibers in excess.

2. Mr. Karpov has been exposed by his employer to asbestos fibers in excess.
   Those whose employers have exposed them to asbestos fibers in excess are entitled to damages from their employers.
   ___
   Therefore, Mr. Karpov is entitled to damages from his employers.

3. Nazis are anti-Semitic.
   George Lincoln Rockwell was anti-Semitic.
   ___
   Therefore, George Lincoln Rockwell was a Nazi.

4. Alcoholic beverages are high in calories.
   This beverage contains no alcohol.
   ___
   Therefore, this beverage is not high in calories.

5. Male drivers under twenty-five are responsible for most traffic accidents.
   Alvin is a male driver under twenty-five.
   ___
   Therefore, Alvin is responsible for most traffic accidents.

6. Lies are untruths.
   What you told me yesterday was an untruth.
   ___
   Therefore, what you told me yesterday was a lie.

7. Actions that provoke others to violence are unlawful.
   The proposed Ku Klux Klan rally would provoke others to violence.
   ___
   Therefore, the proposed Ku Klux Klan rally is unlawful.

8. All pediatricians are physicians.
   Most physicians are well paid.
   ___
   Therefore, most pediatricians are well paid.

9. No students on provisional status are eligible for this course.
   Some students applying for the course are not on provisional status.
   ___
   Therefore, some students applying for the course are eligible for it.

Hypothetical Syllogisms

We have already been introduced to hypothetical syllogisms in our discussion of the hypothetico-deductive method in Chapter 2. Hypothetical syllogisms take two forms: *modus ponens* and *modus tollens*.

Modus ponens

If a is true, then b is true.
a is true.
___
Therefore, b is true.

Modus tollens
> If a is true, then b is true.
> B is not true.
> _____
> Therefore, a is not true.

In the first premise of a hypothetical syllogism, the "If" clause is called the *antecedent,* the "then" clause the *consequent.* The second premise is said to "affirm the antecedent" if it states that the antecedent of the first premise is true and to "deny the antecedent" if it states that it is false. Likewise, the second premise in other cases affirms or denies the consequent. Of these four possibilities, however, only affirming the antecedent (*modus ponens*) and denying the consequent (*modus tollens*) are valid argument forms; the other two are fallacies. To see why, consider the following illustrations.

First, suppose that you are writing a review of a first novel by a writer named Evelyn Smith. You aren't sure whether this writer is male or female, and you don't want to make a fool of yourself by using the wrong pronoun in your review. You have on hand an extremely reliable reference book entitled *A Guide to Contemporary Women Writers.* It occurs to you that if Evelyn Smith is listed in this book, then she is necessarily a woman. You check the book; her name appears; you conclude confidently that she is a woman on the basis of the following reasoning:

> If Evelyn Smith's name appears in the guide to women writers, she is a woman.
> This name does appear in the guide to women writers.
> _____
> Therefore Evelyn Smith is a woman.

This is a valid instance of *modus ponens.*

Now imagine that when we sought Evelyn Smith's name in the reference book we had not found it and had reasoned as follows:

> If Evelyn Smith's name appears in the guide to women writers, she is a woman.
> This name does not appear in the guide to women writers.
> _____
> Therefore Evelyn Smith is not a woman.

This reasoning is invalid because even if we accept the first premise, that if her name appears in the book she is a woman, we have no warrant to assume the converse, that if her name doesn't appear she is not a woman. We have committed the fallacy of "denying the antecedent," that is, by denying that the first clause is true, we have concluded that the second is not true either.

In the foregoing examples, we have imagined that in our second premise we discovered something about the antecedent of the first premise. Now imagine the two possible instances in which we discover something about the consequent. Suppose that before you can look up Evelyn Smith's name in the guide to women writers, you glance at the library's bulletin board and see a flyer advertising a lecture by the renowned Evelyn Smith. A picture and the use of personal pronouns clearly indicate the writer's sex.

First, assume that the flyer clearly indicates that Evelyn Smith is a man. You had already established the premise, "If Evelyn Smith's name appears in the guide to women writers, she is a woman." Now if you add a second premise denying the consequent, you can construct a valid argument:

> If Evelyn Smith's name appears in the guide to women writers, she is a woman.
> Evelyn Smith is not a woman.
> _____
> Therefore Evelyn Smith's name does not appear in the guide to women writers.

This is a valid example of *modus tollens.*

If on the other hand you had discovered from the flyer that Evelyn Smith was a woman, could you have reasoned as follows?

> If Evelyn Smith's name appears in the guide to women writers, she is a woman.
> Evelyn Smith is a woman.
> _____
> Therefore Evelyn Smith's name does appear in the guide to women writers.

This argument is not valid because the first premise had not guaranteed that if she were a woman writer, her name would necessarily appear in the guide. The way the first premise is stated leaves open the possibility that she is not a sufficiently established writer to appear in the guide.

Caution

When you use hypothetical syllogisms, it is easy to make the clause that should logically be the antecedent the consequent and vice versa. How did you know in the examples above that the first premise should read, "If Evelyn Smith's name appears in the guide to women writers, she is a woman," rather than, "If Evelyn Smith is a woman, her name appears in the guide to women writers"?

You knew simply because, assuming that the guide is very reliable, as we stipulated, it will contain only the names of women writers; but we are not warranted in assuming that it will contain the names of all women writers. (Ms. Smith may be too minor a writer for inclusion or too recently established.) Sometimes it doesn't matter which clause is the antecedent and which the consequent (e.g., "If this is a three-sided plane figure, then it is a triangle"), but you should give the matter careful thought before you commit yourself.

EXERCISE

Which of the following hypothetical syllogisms are valid? Identify the fallacies of the invalid syllogisms.

■ Assume that after a meal at a restaurant, your brother develops food poisoning. He had eaten Caesar salad and salmon with mayonnaise, and he suspects that the mayonnaise caused his illness. You decide to call your friend Louis who had joined your brother for dinner and had the same dishes. You reason that

If the mayonnaise was tainted, Louis will be sick too.

You call Louis and discover that

Louis feels fine.

You conclude that

Therefore, the mayonnaise was not tainted.

Is this hypothetical syllogism valid?

■ Imagine the same situation except that this time when you check with Louis, you learn that he has food poisoning too. You reason as follows:

> If the mayonnaise was tainted, Louis will be sick.
> Louis is sick.
> _____
> Therefore, the mayonnaise was tainted.

Is this hypothetical syllogism valid?

■ A friend asks you if her mother might be eligible for certain government benefits. You answer that if she is over 65, she is certainly eligible. Your friend says, "Oh, she is only 62, so I guess she is not eligible." Was your friend justified in reaching this conclusion from your response?

Disjunctive Syllogisms

Disjunctive syllogisms take the form,

> A and B cannot both be true.
> A is true.
> _____
> Therefore, B is not true.

Often the first premise is expressed, "Either A is true or B is true," But a proposition is disjunctive only in contexts where this means, "Either A is true or B is true, but not both." For example, one essay in this book, "Professional Responsibility of the Criminal Defense Lawyer" by Monroe H. Freedman, argues that in some circumstances "participating to some extent in the purposeful deception of the court" is ethical for the defense lawyer. This seems an unlikely proposition since, according to professional ethics, the office of attorney does not permit "any manner of fraud or chicane." But Freedman builds his argument on a disjunctive syllogism:

> In some cases, either lawyers must betray the confidence of their clients or they must participate in deceiving the court. (That is, they cannot both preserve the confidence of their clients and be entirely candid with the court.)
> It is essential that they preserve the confidences of their clients.
> ___
> Therefore, they must participate in deceiving the court.

Enthymemes

It is very rare to find fully developed syllogisms in ordinary argumentation. Most commonly, a conclusion is given supported by a single premise, and the reader is expected to supply the second premise that is logically required to validate the conclusion. If we convert into proper syllogistic form the sentence, "The porpoise isn't a fish; it breathes with lungs," the conclusion "No porpoise is a fish" is supported by a single premise, "All porpoises are animals that breathe with lungs." For the premise to give adequate justification for the conclusion, we must assume the hidden premise, "No animal that breathes with lungs is a fish." Only with this premise do we arrive at the valid syllogism:

> All porpoises are animals that breathe with lungs.
> No animal that breathes with lungs is a fish.
> ___
> Therefore, no porpoise is a fish.

Sometimes, though comparatively rarely, it is the conclusion that is omitted. "You are obviously a minor, and minors aren't allowed in here." (Implicit conclusion: "You aren't allowed in here.") We call a syllogistic argument with one of its three parts missing an "enthymeme."

EXERCISE

What is the hidden premise in each of the following arguments?
1. This cat must be female; it has three colors.
2. Modern apartment buildings are undemocratic; their managers put electronic surveillance equipment in the lobbies to exclude people.
3. This course cannot be taken for graduate credit because it is open to sophomores.
4. Apparently he is a very poor teacher. I understand that he never gives lectures, but only conducts class discussions.

5. Psychopathic murderers should be executed. They kill other people, don't they?
6. The United States was forced into war against Iraq in 1991 because economic sanctions had not worked.

Applications

The principles of deductive reasoning that we have been discussing are of no use in *constructing* arguments, but they are very useful in *testing* them (your own or someone else's). Though logic is only the codification of common sense, common sense succumbs to prejudice or wishful thinking often enough to require reinforcement by a systematic means of checking our reasoning. If your common sense tells you that a conclusion in something you are reading or writing is wrong, you should look for a flaw in the reasoning to account for the error. If you don't find one, you should consider changing your mind.

Testing the logic of normal discourse requires considerable practice at first and very careful attention and thought always. The conclusions and premises of arguments in most writing do not come neatly spelled out, labeled, and arranged. They may be expressed in highly abbreviated form. Concepts may be expressed in different terms at different points in the essay without any invalidating shift of meaning. Many premises will remain implicit. Much of the discourse may be irrelevant to the particular argument you are testing. Introspection might typically show you that you disagree with a crucial proposition on page 15 of a twenty-page essay. You might then find a premise for that conclusion back on page 6, and the other premise might very well not be expressed explicitly at all.

If you disagree with a writer's conclusion (or if a conclusion of your own seems suspect), you may find the problem fairly quickly and intuitively, but in stubborn cases the following procedure will provide you with a systematic approach:

1 **Identify the conclusion in question and express it in proper form.** Remember that the word "conclusion" here has its logical meaning: a proposition supported by at least one reason. It need not come at the end; it need not be the main conclusion of the discourse; it may be one of a great many conclusions in the argument. It may even be picked up as the premise of some other argument.

2 **Identify any explicit premises offered and express them in proper form.** Often, getting explicit premises (as opposed to hidden premises) into proper form demands that you supply quantifiers. If you are analysing someone else's argument, supply the quantifier that you feel is warranted by the facts. If you find that the facts warrant only a particular quantifier when the author's conclusion demands a universal, you have found an error in the reasoning.

3 **Identify any hidden premises required for deduction of the conclusion.** Express these premises in the form required for valid deduction (not the form that the facts warrant).

4 **Check the truth of the premises.** You may consider an explicit premise to be factually wrong or to express a value judgment with which you disagree. Or, more probably, you may find that a hidden premise required for the deduction is deficient in one of these ways.

5 **Check the syllogism for validity.** If you disagree with the conclusion of a syllogism, either you will disagree with a premise or the reasoning is invalid. It is logically impossible to derive a false conclusion from true premises by valid reasoning.

6 **Check for equivocation.** If the premises appear sound and the reasoning valid but the conclusion still seems wrong, check to see whether a term has undergone a shift in meaning between the two premises or between a premise and the conclusion.

Permissions

Acknowledgments

Philip Goldberg, "Are Women Prejudiced Against Women?" *Society,* vol. 5, pp. 28–30 © 1968. Used by permission of Transaction Publishers.

Martin Luther King, Jr., "Letter from Birmingham Jail." Reprinted from *Why We Can't Wait,* Harper & Row, 1963.

Charles Krauthammer, "Fetal Tissue Research: Hostage to Abortion Politics." Reprinted from the *Hartford Courant,* May 22, 1992.

Isaac Asimov, "Time and Tide." Reprinted from *From Earth to Heaven,* Avon Books, 1966.

Shannon Stern-Salb, "Recognize Sexuality Is a Political Issue." Reprinted from the *Connecticut Daily Campus,* Oct. 11, 1990.

Peter Singer, "Animal Liberation." *New York Review of Books,* 20, No. 5 (April 5, 1973), 17–21. © Peter Singer.

C. A. J. Coady, "Defending Human Chauvinism." Reprinted from *00: Report from the Center for Philosophy and Public Policy,* Fall 1986, 12–14.

Marian Dawkins, "Do Hens Suffer in Battery Cages?" Reprinted from *Animal Behaviour,* 25 (1977), 1034–46.

Timothy Noah, "Monkey Business." Reprinted by permission from *The New Republic,* 186, No. 22 (June 2, 1982), 20–23. © 1982 by The New Republic, Inc.

Michael E. DeBakey, "Holding Human Health Hostage." Reprinted from *Journal of Investigative Surgery,* 1 (1988).

Albert Carr, "Is Business Bluffing Ethical?" Reprinted from *Harvard Business Review,* 46, No. 1 (Jan.–Feb. 1968), 143–53.

Arthur Kelly, "Case Study—Italian Tax Mores," originally presented at Loyola University of Chicago at a Mellon Foundation symposium entitled "Foundations of Corporate Responsibility to Society," April 1977.

Leah Margulies, "Bottle Babies: Death and Business Get Their Market," *Business and Society Review,* 25 (Spring 1978), 43–49.

Editorials on U.S. opposition to the WHO code of ethics on the marketing of infant formula reprinted from the *Chicago Tribune,* May 27, 1981; the *Commercial Appeal,* May 24, 1981; the *Charleston Gazette,* May 20, 1981; the Baltimore *Sun,* May 14, 1981; the *St. Petersburg Times,* May 23, 1981; the *Des Moines Register,* May 22, 1981; the Vancouver *Sun,* May 22, 1981; the *Oklahoma City Times,* May 22, 1981; the *Charlotte Observer,* May 26, 1981; the Rochester *Democrat and Chronicle,* May 21, 1981; the Columbus *Dispatch,* May 20, 1981; the *Oregonian,* May 23, 1981; the *Hartford Courant,* May 21, 1981.

Joan Konner, from "Women in the Workplace." Reprinted from *Vital Speeches,* 56, No. 23 (Sept. 5, 1990), 726–28.

Katherine Fulton, From "Writing and Liberty in a Consumer Culture." Reprinted from *AWP Chronicle,* 24, May 1992, 12–14. © 1992. Used by permission of the author.

John Corry, "TV News and the Neutrality Principle." Reprinted by permission from *Commentary,* 91, No. 5 (May 1991), 24–27. All rights reserved.

Daniel Hallin, "TV's Clean Little War." Reprinted from *Bulletin of the Atomic Scientists,* 47 (May 1991), 24–27.

Morgan Strong, "Portions of the Gulf War Were Brought to You by…the Folks at Hill and Knowlton." Reprinted from *TV Guide,* 40, Feb. 22–28, 1992, 11–13.

Jack Tatum with Bill Kushner, "I Plead Guilty, but Only to Aggressive Play." Reprinted from *They Call Me Assassin,* Dodd Mead & Co., 1979.

Monroe Freedman, "Professional Responsibility of the Criminal Defense Lawyer: The Three Hardest Questions." Reprinted from *Michigan Law Review,* 64 (1966), 1469–82.

J. A. Koten, "Music Hath Charms to Soothe a Savage Breast, but Can It Put Bread on the Table?" Reprinted from *Vital Speeches,* 48, No. 24 (Oct. 1, 1982), 749–51.

Terry Eagleton, "What Is Literature?" Reprinted from *Literary Theory: An Introduction,* University of Minnesota Press, 1983.

Laura Bohannan, "Shakespeare in the Bush." Reprinted from *Natural History,* 75, No. 7, (Aug.–Sept. 1966), 28–33.

Eudora Welty, "A Worn Path." Reprinted from *A Curtain of Green,* Doubleday, 1943.

Neil D. Isaacs, "A Life for Phoenix." Reprinted from *Sewanee Review,* 71, No. 1, (1963), 75–81.

Roland Bartel, "Life and Death in Eudora Welty's 'A Worn Path.'" Reprinted from *Studies in Short Fiction,* 14, No. 3 (Summer 1977), 288–90. Copyright © 1977 by Newberry College.

Eudora Welty, "Is Phoenix Jackson's Grandson Really Dead?" Reprinted from *Critical Inquiry* 1, No. 1 (Sept. 1974), 219–21.

Robert Penn Warren, "Why Do We Read Fiction?" Reprinted from *New and Selected Essays,* Random House, 1989.

Index

Abduction: 23–25, 496n., 500–501
   definition of, 24, 500
   and induction, 23–24, 500–501
   vs. other types of reasoning, 23–24
   predictions from, 25
   premises in, 24, 496n.
   (*See also* Hypotheses)
ABI/INFORM index, 110
Abrams, Meyer, example of definition by, 14
Abstract, guidelines for writing of, 118
Accidental properties, 12
Aesthetic judgments, definition of, 38
Affirmative policy claims, 74, 75
"Against Interpretation," Susan Sontag,
      334–343
Agent, in policy arguments, 74, 78
AGRICOLA index, 110
Alternative Press Index, 110
Analogy, argument from, 53–55, 70
Analysis of arguments:
   critical thinking for, 3
   of evaluative argument, example of, 70–72
   of factual argument, example of, 33–34
   of policy arguments, 6–8, 78, 86
   writing of, guidelines for, 118–119
   (*See also* Deductive arguments, analysis of;
      Testing of arguments)
"Animal Liberation," Peter Singer:
   discussion of, 3, 497
   text of, 122–134
"Are Women Prejudiced Against Women?"
      Philip Goldberg:
   discussion of, 33–34
   text of, 28–32

Argumentative edge, 105
Arguments:
   contributions of, 104–105
   definition of, 1
   reading-reflecting-writing pattern in, 2
   scientific arguments, 5, 12, 498
   social context of, 1–2, 4–6, 104
   social functions of, 2, 3
   (*See also* Analysis of arguments; Deductive
      arguments, analysis of; Evaluative
      arguments; Factual arguments; Policy
      arguments; Writing of arguments)
"Arts Catch Up with a Society in Disarray,
      The," Richard Bernstein:
   discussion of, 119
   response to, 353–355
   text of, 344–350
Asimov, Isaac, "Time and Tide":
   discussion of, 92–100, 102, 106
   text of, 92–100
Assessment of writing, 104–108
Attributes, in inference, 496, 498, 499
Audience:
   for evaluative arguments, 41–42, 45
   guidelines for writing for, 90, 102,
      105–106
   for policy arguments, 76
   value systems of, 41–42, 45, 76

Ballarin, Oswaldo, "Prepared Statement to
   the United States Subcommittee on
   Health and Scientific Research,"
   212–215
Baltimore *Sun, The,* "Editorial on the U.S.   **525**

Vote against the WHO Code of Ethics for Companies Marketing Infant Foods," 219–220

Bartel, Roland, "Life and Death in Eudora Welty's 'A Worn Path:'"
discussion of, 119
text of, 325–327

Bernstein, Richard, "The Arts Catch Up with a Society in Disarray":
discussion of, 119
response to, 353–355
text of, 344–350

Bibliographies, for research, 109

Bohannan, Laura, "Shakespeare in the Bush," 303–312

Bono, Edward de, on lateral thinking, 107

Book Review Digest, 112

Book Review Index, 112

"Bottle Babies: Death and Business Get Their Market," Leah Margulies, 201–210

Carpenter, C.C.J., et al., "Public Statement by Eight Alabama Clergymen," 48–49, 106, 119

Carr, Albert Z., "Is Business Bluffing Ethical?"
discussion of, 54–55
text of, 183–195

"Case Study: Italian Tax Mores," Arthur Kelly, 197–199

Cases, in inference, 496, 498, 499

Catalogues, of subjects, 109–110

Categorical propositions, in deductive arguments, 495–496, 501–502

Categorizing and defining (*see under* Evaluative arguments; Factual arguments)

Causal claims, in factual arguments, 19

Causal factors, in factual arguments, 21
(*See also* Conditions, in causal reasoning)

Causal reasoning, in policy arguments, 8
(*See also* Factual arguments, causal reasoning in)

Cause, definition of 20–22

CD-ROM, research sources on, 110, 111

Change in status quo, 74–76, 78

Charlotte Gazette, The, "Editorial on the U.S. Vote against the WHO Code of Ethics for Companies Marketing Infant Foods," 218–219

Charlotte Observer, The, "Editorial on the U.S. Vote against the WHO Code of Ethics for Companies Marketing Infant Foods," 224–225

Chicago Tribune, "Editorial on the U.S. Vote against the WHO Code of Ethics for Companies Marketing Infant Foods," 216–217

Circular argument, definition of, 11

CIS Index, 110

Citation trails, 109, 111

Claims: (*see* Causal claims; Conclusions; Factual [empirical] claims; Policy claims)

Classification, in factual arguments (*see* Factual arguments, categorizing and defining in)

Cluster diagrams, 102–104

Coady, C. A. J., "Defending Human Chauvinism," 136–140

"Colonial Culture," Howardena Pindell:
discussion of, 119
text of, 353–355

Columbus *Dispatch, The,* "Editorial on the U.S. Vote against the WHO Code of Ethics for Companies Marketing Infant Foods," 226–227

Common cause, in factual arguments, 12–14

Conclusions:
in abduction, 500
in deduction, 49–51, 497, 502
in definition of argument, 1
identification of, for testing arguments, 519
in syllogisms, 495, 496, 502
(*See also* Causal claims, in factual arguments; Evaluative claims; Factual [empirical] claims)

Conditions, in causal reasoning:
controlled conditions, 27–28, 33–34
definition of, 20
function of, 20–22

Conflicting principles, in rebuttal, 53, 71

Connotations of terms (*see* Evaluative arguments, categorizing and defining in)

Constructive arguments by analogy, 53–55

Contested terms, avoiding, 15–16
(*See also* Semantic disputes)

Contributions of arguments, 104–105

Controlled conditions, 27–28, 33–34

Corry, John, "TV News and the Neutrality Principle," 238–244

Counterarguments:
  in evaluative arguments, 55
  in factual arguments, 35–37
  free writing of, 101
  in policy arguments, 74, 78
Counterexamples, in evaluative arguments, 52, 55, 71–72
Counterplans, in policy arguments, 75
Criteria:
  in factual arguments, 11–13
  for value judgments, 38
Critical analyses, guidelines for writing, 118–119
  (*See also* Analysis of arguments)
Critical thinking, definition of, 2–3
Critiques, guidelines for writing, 118–119
Cutten, George B., "The Reconstruction of Democracy," excerpt from, 398–402

Dawkins, Marian, "Do Hens Suffer in Battery Cages?" 142–161
DeBakey, Michael E., "Holding Human Health Hostage," 176–179
Debating principles, for policy arguments, 74–77
Deduction:
  categorical propositions in, 495–496, 501–502
  dangers of, 10
  definition of, 497
  empirical tests of, 9–10
  errors and fallacies in, 52, 498, 504–507
  in factual arguments: 9–10, 24, 26
  function of, 497–498
  history of, 9–10
  for testing arguments, 519–520
  (*See also* Deductive arguments, analysis of; Evaluative arguments, deduction in)
Deductive arguments, analysis of:
  diagramming syllogisms for, 507–513
  disjunctive syllogisms in, 517–518
  distribution in, 503
  enthymemes in, 518–519
  exercises on, 502–503, 512–514, 517–519
  form of categorical propositions in, 501–502
  hypothetical syllogisms in, 514–517
  recognizing common errors for, 504–507
  rules of validity in, 503–504
"Defending Human Chauvinism," C. A. J. Coady, 136–140

Definition of terms (see Equivocation; Evaluative arguments, categorizing and defining in; Factual arguments, categorizing and defining in; Semantic disputes)
Deliberative rhetoric, definition of, 73
  (*See also* Policy arguments)
Des Moines Register, The, "Editorial on the U.S. Vote against the WHO Code of Ethics for Companies Marketing Infant Foods," 221–222
Devil terms, 47, 119
Diagrams:
  for organizing writing, 100, 102–104
  of syllogisms, 507–513
Differentiae, 11–12
Direction, in writing (*see* Writing of arguments, direction in)
Disadvantages, in policy arguments, 7, 8, 77, 78
Discovered characteristics, 12
Distribution, of terms: 496, 503
"Do Hens Suffer in Battery Cages?" Marian Dawkins, 142–161
Documentation of sources, standards for, 117
Durick, Joseph A., et al., "Public Statement by Eight Alabama Clergymen," 48–49, 106, 119
Dwyer, Carol Anne, "Testimony at the House Subcommittee Hearings on Sex and Race Differences on Standardized Tests, April 23, 1987," 457–467

Eagleton, Terry, "What Is Literature?"
  discussion of, 45–46
  text of, 289–301
Editing, 117–118
"Editorials on the U.S. Vote against the WHO Code of Ethics for Companies Marketing Infant Foods," 216–230
Emotion in evaluative argument, 53
Empirical claims (*see* Factual [empirical] claims)
Empirical content of value terms, 44
Empirical reasoning:
  in defining factual issues, 4
  exercise on, 17–18
  testing deductions with, 9–10
Enthymemes, 50–51, 518–519
Equivocation, 506–507, 520

ERIC index, 110
Errors (*see* Fallacies)
Ethical judgments, definition of, 38
  (*See also* Value systems)
Evaluation, of policy arguments, 78
  (*See also* Analysis of arguments;
    Assessment of writing; Testing of
    arguments)
Evaluative arguments:
  analogies in, 53–55, 70
  analysis of, example of, 70–72
  audience for, 41–42, 45
  categorizing and defining in, 43–49, 70
    and audience's value system, 41–42, 45
    exercises on, 47–49
    in sample argument, 70
    ultimate terms in, 46–47
  deduction in, 5, 49–55, 497
    in argument by analogy, 53–55
    in counterarguments from specific
      judgments, 55
    from more general principles, 49–53
    organizational function of, 497
  definition of, 5
  emotion in, 53
  examples of, 48–49, 56–72
  exercises and study questions on, 47–49,
    72
  facts in, 39–41, 70, 71
  in policy arguments, 73
  purpose of, 5, 40, 42
  rebuttal to/testing of, 51–55, 70
  (*See also* Evaluative claims; Evaluative
    issues)
Evaluative claims:
  definition of, 38–40
  exercises on, 18
  vs. factual claims 38–40
  types of judgments in, 38
  (*See also* Evaluative arguments; Evaluative
    issues; Value systems)
Evaluative issues:
  definition of, 4–5
  opinion in, 4, 39
  in policy arguments, 5–8, 72–74
  (*See also* Evaluative arguments; Evaluative
    claims; Value systems)
Evidence:
  in definition of argument, 1
  for factual claims of existence, 18–19
  and hypothesis method of reasoning, 22, 27

  in writing factual arguments, 35–37
Examples:
  counterexamples, 52, 55, 71–72
  specific, in structure of value systems, 40,
    41
Existence, factual claims of, 18–19
Expanded Academic Index (Infotrac), 110
Expediency vs. justice, 42–43
Expository writing, definition of, 1

Factors, causal, 21
Facts, in evaluative arguments, 39–41, 70, 71
  (*See also* Factual issues)
Factual arguments:
  analysis of, example of, 33–34
  applications of, in writing arguments,
    34–37
  categorizing and defining in, 11–18
    applications of, for writing arguments,
      35–36
    contested terms in, avoiding, 15–16
    definition of, 11
    discovered characteristics in, 12
    by family relationships, 12–14
    and inadequate terms, 16–17
    by necessary and sufficient criteria,
      11–12
    operationally, 14–15
    semantic disputes in, 15–16
    stipulated characteristics in, 12
  causal reasoning in, 5, 20–33
    causes, conditions, and factors in,
      20–22
    errors and fallacies in, 21–22
    example using, 28–32
    exercises and study questions on,
      25–26, 32–33
    hypotheses in (see Hypotheses)
    hypothetico-deductive method in,
      26–27
    for specific types of claims, 18–20
  deduction in, 9–10, 24, 26
  definition of, 5
  evidence in writing of, 35–37
  example of, 28–32
  exercises and study questions on, 17–18,
    25–26, 32–33
  in policy arguments, 5–8, 73–74
  purpose of, 5
  (*See also* Factual [empirical] claims;

Factual issues)
Factual (empirical) claims:
  argument by analogy for, 54
  deductive vs. empirical support for, 9–10
  vs. evaluative claims, 38–40
  exercises on, 17–18
  of existence, 18–19
  refutability of, 10–11
  types of, 18–20
  verifiability of, 10, 11
  (*See also* Factual arguments; Factual
    issues)
Factual issues:
  definition of, 4–5, 18
  in expository writing, 1
  opinion in, 4
  in policy arguments, 5–8, 73–74
  and social context, 1
  (*See also* Factual arguments; Factual
    [empirical] claims)
Fallacies:
  in causal reasoning, 21–22
  in deduction, 52, 498, 504–507
  equivocation, 506–507, 520
  faulty quantifiers, 505
  hasty generalization, 505
  illicit process, 505
  post hoc fallacy, 22, 37
  "straw man" fallacy, 78, 120
  undistributed middle fallacy, 52, 504–505
Family relationships, in categorizing and
    defining, 12–14
Faulty quantifiers, 505
Feasibility, in policy arguments, 7–8, 76
"Fetal Tissue Research: Hostage to Abortion
    Politics," Charles Krauthammer, 87–88
Free writing, 101–103
Freedman, Monroe H., "Professional
    Responsibility of the Criminal Defense
    Lawyer: The Three Hardest Questions,"
    266–279
Fulton, Katherine, "Writing and Liberty in a
    Consumer Culture," excerpt from,
    234–237

Gablik, Suzi, "Toward an Ecological Self,"
    360–368
Gahagan, Judy, "Wisdom and Wealth: The
    Great Education Hoax," 481–485
Gardner, Howard, "What Is an Intelligence?"
    discussion of, 13–15

text of, 416–424
General claims, 19
General principles:
  deduction from, 49–53
  definition of, 40, 41
General Science Index, The, 110
Generalization, hasty, 505
Genus, 11
God terms, 47, 119
Goldberg, Philip, "Are Women Prejudiced
    Against Women?"
  discussion of, 33–34
  text of, 28–32
Gould, Stephen Jay, "The Hereditarian
    Theory of IQ," excerpt from, 372–397
Grafman, Milton L., et al., "Public Statement
    by Eight Alabama Clergymen," 48–49,
    106, 119

Hallin, Daniel, "TV's Clean Little War,"
    245–250
Hardin, Paul, et al., "Public Statement by
    Eight Alabama Clergymen," 48–49, 106,
    119
Harmon, Nolan B., et al., "Public Statement
    by Eight Alabama Clergymen," 48–49,
    106, 119
Hartford Courant, The, "Editorial on the U.S.
    Vote against the WHO Code of Ethics
    for Companies Marketing Infant
    Foods," 228–230
Hasty generalization, 505
"Hereditarian Theory of IQ, The," Stephen
    Jay Gould, excerpt from, 372–397
"Holding Human Health Hostage," Michael
    E. DeBakey, 176–179
Humanities Index, The, 110
Hypotheses, 22–28, 35, 105
  definition of, 24
  exercise on, 25–26
  forming of, 22–25
  in hypothetico-deductive method, 26–27
  testing of, 26–28
  writing arguments based on, 35
  writing of, guidelines for, 105
  (*See also* Abduction)
Hypothetical syllogisms, 26, 514–517
Hypothetico-deductive method, 26–27

"I Plead Guilty, But Only to Aggressive Play,"
    Jack Tatum with Bill Kushner, 254–264

Illicit process fallacy, 505

Inadequacy of terms, in factual argument, 16–17

Inclusion, in syllogisms, 496

Indexes, for research:
  of citations, 111–112
  of subjects, 109–111

Induction:
  and abduction, 23–24, 500–501
  definition of, 498
  premises in, 496n.

Inference, 495
  (*See also* Abduction; Deduction; Induction)

Infotrac indexes, 110

Inherency of need, 76

Interpretive claims, 19–20

"Is Business Bluffing Ethical?" Albert Z. Carr:
  discussion of, 54–55
  text of, 183–195

"Is Phoenix Jackson's Grandson Really Dead?" Eudora Welty, 328–330

Isaacs, Neil D., "Life for Phoenix":
  discussion of, 119
  text of, 320–324

Issues, definition of, 3–4
  (*See also* Factual issues; Evaluative issues; Stock issues)

Judgments:
  specific, in value systems, 40, 41
  types of, in evaluative claims, 38

Justice:
  argument by analogy for, 54
  vs. expediency, 42–43

Kelly, Arthur, "Case Study: Italian Tax Mores," 197–199

King, Martin Luther, Jr., "Letter from Birmingham Jail":
  discussion of, 56, 70–72, 105–106, 119
  exercise on, 72
  text of, 56–69

Konner, Joan, "Women in the Marketplace," excerpt from, 231–232

Koten, J. A., "Music Hath Charms to Soothe a Savage Breast but Can It Put Bread on the Table?"
  discussion of, 105, 106
  text of, 282–287

Krauthammer, Charles, "Fetal Tissue Research: Hostage to Abortion Politics," 87–88

Kushner, Bill, Jack Tatum with, "I Plead Guilty, But Only to Aggressive Play," 254–264

"Last Days of ETS, The," David Owen, 425–455

Lateral thinking, 107–108

Left Index, 110

Legal definitions, 12

"Letter from Birmingham Jail," Martin Luther King, Jr.:
  discussion of, 56, 70–72, 105–106, 119
  exercise on, 72
  text of, 56–69

Library of Congress Subject Headings, 110

"Life and Death in Eudora Welty's 'A Worn Path,'" Roland Bartel:
  discussion of, 119
  text of, 325–327

"Life for Phoenix," Neil D. Isaacs:
  discussion of, 119
  text of, 320–324

Lippmann, Walter, "Three Essays on Intelligence Tests":
  discussion of, 107
  texts of, 403–415

Logic:
  definition of, 495
  in policy arguments, 5
  (*See also* Abduction; Causal reasoning; Deduction; Fallacies; Induction; Syllogisms)

Machado, Luis Albert, "The Right to be Intelligent," excerpt from, 487–493

Margulies, Leah, "Bottle Babies: Death and Business Get Their Market," 201–210

Memphis *Commercial Appeal, The,* "Editorial on the U.S. Vote against the WHO Code of Ethics for Companies Marketing Infant Foods," 217–218

"Mental Age of Americans, The," Walter Lippmann, 403–406

Middle principles, 40, 41

Middle terms, in syllogisms, 496

MLA International Bibliography of Books and Articles on the Modern Languages and Literatures, 110

"Modest Proposal, A," Jonathan Swift:
  discussion of, 79, 86
  text of, 79–86
Modus ponens form of syllogism, 514, 515
Modus tollens form of syllogism, 515, 516
"Monkey Business," Timothy Noah, 163–169
Murray, George M., et al., "Public Statement
    by Eight Alabama Clergymen," 48–49,
    106, 119
"Music Hath Charms to Soothe a Savage
    Breast but Can It Put Bread on the
    Table?" J. A. Koten:
  discussion of, 105, 106
  text of, 282–287
"Mystery of the 'A' Men, The," Walter
    Lippmann, 407–411

National Newspaper Index (Infotrac), 110
Natural classes, 12–13
Necessary and sufficient criteria, 11–13
Need, in policy arguments, 7–8, 75–76, 78
Negative policy claims, 74–75
Noah, Timothy, "Monkey Business,"
    163–169

Observation, in hypothetico-deductive
    method, 26
Oklahoma City Times, "Editorial on the U.S.
    Vote against the WHO Code of Ethics
    for Companies Marketing Infant
    Foods," 223–224
Operational definitions, 14–15
Opinion:
  definition of, 4
  in evaluative issues, 4, 39
  in factual issues, 4
  in writing in response to writing, 120
Outlines:
  sentence outlines, 102, 113–114, 116, 117
  topic outlines, 102
Owen, David, "The Last Days of ETS,"
    425–455

Pacheco, Alex, "Testimony: House Hearings
    on the Use of Animals in Medical
    Research and Testing," 170–174
Paraphrase, guidelines for writing of, 118
Particular propositions, 502
Peirce, Charles Sanders, on induction, 23,
    496n.
Pindell, Howardena, "Colonial Culture:"

discussion of, 119
text of, 353–355
Plans, in policy arguments, 74, 76–78
Policy arguments:
  agents in, 74, 78
  analysis of, 6–8, 78, 86
  audience for, 76
  checklist for writing, 78
  counterarguments in, 74, 78
  debating principles for, 74–77
  disadvantage related issues in, 7, 8, 77, 78
  evaluation of, checklist for, 78
  evaluative and factual issues in, 5–8,
      72–74
  examples of, 79–86, 87–88
  exercises and study questions on, 87–89
  feasibility issues in, 7–8, 76
  need related issues in, 7–8, 75–76, 78
  plans in, 74, 76–78
  policy claims in, 73–75
  purposes of, 73
  stock issues in, 7–8, 75–77
  visualization in, 76
Policy claims, 73–75
Pollitt, Katha, "Why We Read," 356–358
Popper, Karl, on hypotheses, 27
"Portions of the Gulf War Were Brought to
    You by...the Folks at Hill and
    Knowlton," Morgan Strong, 251–253
Portland *Oregonian, The,* "Editorial on the
    U.S. Vote against the WHO Code of
    Ethics for Companies Marketing Infant
    Foods," 227–228
Post hoc fallacy, 22, 37
Precis, 118
Predictions:
  by abduction (hypothesis method), 25
  and causal conditions, 22
  defined as factual claims, 19–20
Premises:
  in abduction (hypothesis method), 24,
      496n.
  in deduction
    general discussion of, 10, 49–51, 497,
        498
    in syllogisms, 495–496, 502, 508–512,
        515–516
  in induction, 496n., 499
  in ordinary discourse, 50–51
  in testing of arguments, 519–520
"Prepared Statement to the United States

Subcommittee on Health and Scientific Research," Oswaldo Ballarin, 212–215
Principles:
  in rebuttal, 53, 71–72
  in structure of value systems, 40–41
  (*See also* General principles)
Priorities of issues, 8
"Professional Resonsibility of the Criminal Defense Lawyer: The Three Hardest Questions," Monroe H. Freedman, 266–279
Proposals (*see* Policy arguments; Propositions)
Propositions:
  in deduction, 502
  of policy, 74
  (*See also* Policy arguments)
PsychLIT index, 110
Public-policy arguments (*see* Policy arguments)
"Public Statement by Eight Alabama Clergymen:"
  discussion of, 106, 119
  text of, 48–49

Qualifying phrases, in categorical propositions, 501
Quantifiers, in categorical propositions, 502, 505
Quotation marks, in documenting sources, 117

Ramage, Edward V., et al., "Public Statement by Eight Alabama Clergymen," 48–49, 106, 119
Reader's Guide, The, 110
Rebuttals:
  to evaluative arguments, 51–55, 70
  guidelines for writing of, 119, 120
  writing responses to, 120
"Recognize Sexuality Is a Political Issue," Shannon Stern-Salb:
  discussion of, 114, 116–117
  text of, 114–116
"Reconstruction of Democracy, The," George B. Cutten, excerpt from, 398–402
Reductio ad absurdum strategy, 52
Reflection, in pattern of arguments, 2
  (*See also* Analysis of arguments)
Refutability, of factual claims, 10–11
Regulatory definitions, 12

"Reliability of Intelligence Tests, The," Walter Lippmann, 411–415
Representativeness, in induction, 499
Research, guidelines for, 100, 103, 108–112
Response to writing, guidelines for, 118–120
Results (attributes), in inference, 496, 498, 499
Revision, in writing arguments, 117–118
"Rich Are Different, The," Daniel Seligman, 479–480
"Right to be Intelligent, The," Luis Albert Machado, excerpt from, 487–493
Rochester *Democrat Chronicle,* "Editorial on the U.S. Vote against the WHO Code of Ethics for Companies Marketing Infant Foods," 225–226
Rosser, Phyllis, "Testimony at the House Subcommittee Hearings on Sex and Race Differences on Standardized Tests, April 23, 1987":
  discussion of, 39
  text of, 457–467
Rules, in inference, 496, 498, 499
  (*See also* General principles)

St. Petersburg Times, "Editorial on the U.S. Vote against the WHO Code of Ethics for Companies Marketing Infant Foods," 220–221
Scientific arguments, 5, 12, 498
Self-interest, and values, 42–43
Seligman, Daniel, "The Rich Are Different," 479–480
Semantic disputes:
  in evaluative arguments, 41–42
  in factual arguments 15–16
Sentence outlines, 102, 113–114, 116, 117
Sequence of issues, 8
"Shakespeare in the Bush," Laura Bohannan, 303–312
Singer, Peter, "Animal Liberation:"
  discussion of, 3, 497
  text of, 122–134
Social context of arguments, 1–2, 4–6, 104
Social Science Citation Index, 111
Social Sciences Index, The, 110
Sociofile index, 110
Sontag, Susan, "Against Interpretation," 334–343
Sources, standards for documentation of, 117

Specific judgments (specific examples):
counterarguments from, 55
in structure of value systems, 40, 41
Stalling, Earl, et al., "Public Statement by
Eight Alabama Clergymen," 48–49, 106,
119
Status quo, change in, 74–76, 78
Stern-Salb, Shannon, "Recognize Sexuality Is
a Political Issue":
discussion of, 114, 116–117
text of, 114–116
Stipulated characteristics, 12
Stock issues:
disadvantages in, 7, 8, 77
feasibility in, 7–8, 76
functions of, 7–8
need in, 7–8, 75–76
in preparing policy proposals, 75–77
"Straw man" fallacy, 78, 120
Strong, Morgan, "Portions of the Gulf War
Were Brought to You by...the Folks at
Hill and Knowlton," 251–253
Style, for documentation of sources, 117
Subject guides, for research, 109–111
Sufficient and necessary criteria, 11–13
Summaries, guidelines for writing of, 118, 119
Support for arguments, and social context,
1–2
(*See also* Abduction; Causal reasoning;
Deduction; Evidence; Induction)
Swift, Jonathan, "A Modest Proposal":
discussion of, 79, 86
text of, 79–86
Syllogisms:
basic structure of, 495–498
definition of, 495, 499n.
diagrams of, 507–513
disjunctive syllogisms, 517–518
enthymemes, 50–51, 518
exercises on, 502–503, 512–514, 517–519
hypothetical, 26, 514–517

Tatum, Jack, with Bill Kushner, "I Plead
Guilty, But Only to Aggressive Play,"
254–264
Terms, definition of (*see* Evaluative
arguments, categorizing and defining
in; Factual arguments, categorizing and
defining in; Semantic disputes)
Terms, in categorical propositions, 496, 501,
503–507

"Testimony: House Hearings on the Use of
Animals in Medical Research and
Testing," Alex Pacheco, 170–174
"Testimony at the House Subcommittee
Hearings on Sex and Race Differences
on Standardized Tests, April 23, 1987":
by Carol Anne Dwyer, 457–467
by Phyllis Rosser
discussion of, 39
text of, 468–478
Testing of arguments:
of evaluative argument, 51–55
steps for, through deduction, 519–520
(*See also* Analysis of arguments; Deductive
arguments, analysis of; Evaluation, of
policy arguments)
Thesis, writing of, 35
"Three Essays on Intelligence Tests," Walter
Lippmann:
discussion of, 107
text of, 403–415
"Time and Tide," Issac Asimov:
discussion of, 92–100, 102, 106
text of, 92–100
Topic outlines, 102
"Toward an Ecological Self," Suzi Gablik,
360–368
"TV News and the Neutrality Principle,"
John Corry, 238–244
"TV's Clean Little War," Daniel Hallin,
245–250

Ultimate (god and devil) terms, 46–47, 119
Undistributed middle fallacy, 52, 504–505
Unification of argument, 106–107
United States Congress, index of working
papers of, 110
Univeral propositions, 502
Utilitarian judgments, definition of, 38

Validity, rules of, 503–504, 520
See also (Deductive arguments, analysis of;
Fallacies; Testing of arguments)
Value-laden terms (*see* Evaluative
arguments, categorizing and defining
in)
Value systems:
of audience for argument, 41–42, 45, 76
justice vs. expediency (self-interest) in,
42–43
and social context, 1–2

structure of, 40–41
Values (*see* Evaluative arguments; Evaluative claims; Evaluative issues; Value systems)
Vancouver *Sun, The,* "Editorial on the U.S. Vote against the WHO Code of Ethics for Companies Marketing Infant Foods," 222–223
Verifiability, of factual claims, 10, 11
Vertical thinking, 107
Visualization, in policy arguments, 76

Warren, Robert Penn, "Why Do We Read Fiction," excerpt from, 332–333
Welty, Eudora:
  "A Worn Path"
    analyses of, 119, 320–330
    text of, 313–319
  "Is Phoenix Jackson's Grandson Really Dead?" 328–330
"What Is an Intelligence?" Howard Gardner:
  discussion of, 13–15
  text of, 416–424
"What Is Literature?" Terry Eagleton:
  discussion of, 45–46
  text of, 289–301
"Why Do We Read Fiction?" Robert Penn Warren, excerpt from, 332–333
"Why We Read," Katha Pollitt, 356–358
"Wisdom and Wealth: The Great Education Hoax," Judy Gahagan, 481–485

Wittgenstein, Ludwig, 13
"Women in the Marketplace," Joan Konner, excerpt from, 231–232
"Worn Path, A," Eudora Welty:
  analyses of, 119, 320–330
  text of, 313–319
"Writing and Liberty in a Consumer Culture," Katherine Fulton, excerpt from, 234–237
Writing of arguments:
  assessment of, 104–108
  beginning activities in, 100–104
  consideration of audience in, 90, 102, 105–106
  diagrams for, 100, 102–104
  direction in
    characteristics of, 90–91
    example of argument showing, 114–116
    exercises on, 91–100
  of factual arguments, 35–37
  first draft for, 113
  free writing, 101–103
  lateral vs. vertical thinking for, 107–108
  organizing for, 100, 102–104
  outlining for, 102, 113–114, 116, 117
  in pattern of arguments, 2
  research for, 100, 103, 108–112
  in response to other writing, 118–120
  revised draft for, 117–118
  unification in, 106–107